The Selected Works of Eugene V. Debs

THE SELECTED WORKS OF EUGENE V. DEBS

This groundbreaking project by Haymarket Books will republish more than 1,000 of the articles, speeches, press statements, interviews, and open letters of labor leader and socialist activist Eugene Victor Debs. More than 1.5 million words will be reproduced in six thick volumes—the vast majority of which seeing print for the first time since the date of their first publication.

Eugene Victor Debs (1855–1926) was a trade union official, magazine editor, political opinion writer, and public orator widely regarded as one of the most important figures in the history of American socialism. Five times a candidate for president of the United States and twice imprisoned for his role as a strike leader and antiwar agitator, Debs remains today an esteemed and iconic figure of twentieth-century political history.

The Selected Works of Eugene V. Debs

Volume IV: *Red Union, Red Paper, Red Train, 1905–1910*

edited by
Tim Davenport
and David Walters

Haymarket Books
Chicago, Illinois

Published in 2025 by
Haymarket Books
P.O. Box 180165
Chicago, IL 60618
773-583-7884
www.haymarketbooks.org

ISBNs: 978-1-64259-664-9 (hardcover)
978-1-64259-590-1 (paperback)

Distributed to the trade in the US through Consortium Book Sales and Distribution (www.cbsd.com) and internationally through Ingram Publisher Services International (www.ingramcontent.com).

This book was published with the generous support of Lannan Foundation, Wallace Action Fund, and the Marguerite Casey Foundation.

Special discounts are available for bulk purchases by organizations and institutions. Please email info@haymarketbooks.org for more information.

Cover and text design by Eric Kerl.
Cover photo by George Grantham Bain, ca. 1908, via Library of Congress.

Printed in Canada by union labor.

Library of Congress Cataloging-in-Publication data is available.
Library of Congress Control Number: 2024945819

10 9 8 7 6 5 4 3 2 1

Contents

1906

1907

1908

1909

1910

Appendix

Introduction

This is the fourth of a six-volume series gathering the most important speeches, writings, and unpublished communications of American socialist and trade union organizer Eugene Victor Debs (1855–1926). Although part of a chronological collection, this current installment follows three earlier volumes marked by more or less coherent themes.

In volume one, *Building Solidarity on the Tracks, 1877–1892,* we observed the youthful Gene Debs as an idealistic magazine editor and committed officer of a fledgling railway craft organization, the Brotherhood of Locomotive Firemen (B of LF). From a perspective initially limited to the essentially conservative doctrine of self-reliance and self-improvement, the young Debs gradually gained an appreciation in the efficacy and necessity of work stoppage to defend wage rates and working conditions of railway workers. The failure of a protracted strike by locomotive engineers and firemen against the Burlington Railroad in 1888–89 led Debs to pursue a mechanism for the united action of all railway crafts, an executive board known as the Supreme Council of the United Orders of Railway Employees. The comparatively well-paid and stolid associations of engineers and conductors refused to participate in this new body, however, and the Supreme Council came to grief in the summer of 1891 amidst a bitter jurisdictional dispute between two of its affiliated brotherhoods, the brakemen and the switchmen.

Volume two, *The Rise and Fall of the American Railway Union, 1892–1896,* saw Debs and his co-thinkers attempt to remedy the persistent problem of rivalry between railway crafts by establishing a new union to encompass all employees from the humble track maintenance worker to the most privileged veteran conductor under a single institutional umbrella. This new association, the American Railway Union, was born in the spring of 1893, just as the United States was plunged into a severe depression during which hundreds of thousands lost their jobs and wage rates of those fortunate enough to retain their jobs were strained. The issue of wage protection through collective action burned bright. A low annual dues rate allowed the new union to grow rapidly, albeit at the expense of the existing craft brotherhoods, which saw their membership and dues revenue cannibalized. The established railway brotherhoods would come to harbor a deep resentment toward Debs's upstart industrial union and would work to subvert it.

The American Railway Union won a quick victory in an April 1894 strike against the Great Northern system, owing to a favorable ruling through arbitration. Flush with this early success, the union walked into a buzzsaw just two months later when it endorsed an existing strike already being conducted by some of its members against Pullman's Palace Car Company. Arbitration was rejected by the company in no uncertain terms and a boycott of trains that included Pullman sleeper cars was called in an effort to bring the company to heel. Rail transportation was snarled from Chicago west by this ARU boycott, seriously inconveniencing shippers and the public alike. Joint action of railway managers to crush the new union would follow, aided in their task by a pliable and amenable court system, and President Grover Cleveland sent government troops to Chicago. In the ignominious aftermath, marked by gunfire and burning boxcars, Debs and seven other top ARU officials were sent to jail on contempt of court rulings. The six months Debs spent in jail broke the new union while fundamentally changing its president's outlook, shifting Debs's primary emphasis from trade unionism to political action.

Debs publicly proclaimed socialism as his new political creed with a statement to the press on January 1, 1897, an event which launches the third volume of the Debs works, *The Path to a Socialist Party, 1897–1904*. With an annual convention of the moribund American Railway Union already scheduled for Chicago in June, a deft turn was made and the gathering was promoted in the mainstream press as a major public event, the launch of a new national organization to be known as the Social Democracy of America (SDA). Debs would serve as president of this new organization. From its inception the SDA was neither fish nor fowl, its members fundamentally divided by questions of basic strategy. All could agree upon the ultimate objective, the birth of a cooperative commonwealth of brotherhood and harmonious economic collaboration. Some, however, sought to achieve this end through a network of cooperative rural communities in an unpopulated state in the West, which would grow by power of example, while others perceived of the question of change in the more conventional terms of electoral politics, arguing that fundamental economic change without the prior achievement of state power would be impossible. Debs seemed to agree with both positions.

An ineffectual year of activity following, in which money was raised and wasted with little progress to be shown. The first annual convention of the Social Democracy of America was captured by the procolonization faction, but their victory proved pyrrhic, ending in a bolt by Victor Berger and the pro-political action minority. Sick in bed at the moment of decisive action, an occurrence which would recur throughout his life, Debs ultimately joined Berger and the political actionists in establishing a new group, the Social Democratic Party of America (SDP). Gene's beloved brother and closest political confidant, Theodore Debs, would head this new organization as its national secretary while Gene would tour on its behalf while serving as a member of its governing National Executive Board.

The SDP was not established in a political vacuum. Its primary organizational rivals on the left were concentrated in the Socialist Labor Party of America (SLP), an explicitly Marxist organization established in 1876 that had gained national stature, if not mass membership, by the middle 1890s. In 1899 that organization split over the issues of trade union strategy and organizational centralization, with a dissident right wing headed by New York lawyers Henry Slobodin and Morris Hillquit and activists around the German-language *New Yorker Volkszeitung* trying and failing to depose the entrenched New York leadership group led by English-language party editor Daniel DeLeon. Two rival organizations, each presenting itself as the legitimate Socialist Labor Party and publishing dueling English-language weeklies called *The People,* briefly shared the field. The battle was ultimately decided in capitalist courts in favor of the party regulars. The dissidents moved to bolster their diminished forces through unification with the SDP in the spring of 1900. The two groups were quickly able to agree upon a joint ticket under the banner of the Social Democratic Party in the election of 1900, with the nationally recognized orator Gene Debs making his first run for president of the United States atop the unity ticket.

A cooperative campaign project was easy; true organizational amalgamation proved more difficult. A lengthy series of unity negotiations followed, with the Debs brothers, Berger, and other Social Democratic Party leaders of Chicago and Milwaukee becoming deeply distrustful of the ideology and motives of the Socialist Labor Party dissidents and using all means, fair and foul, to reverse growing support for unification among their own rank and file. Despite the SDP leadership's misgivings, local cooperation continued to blossom and the party began to atrophy. With membership and dues revenue in decline, the SDP leaders finally acceded to unity efforts early in 1901. In August of that year a convention was held in Indianapolis bringing the larger SLP dissident organization and smaller SDP together as a new political party, the Socialist Party of America. Eugene V. Debs remained aloof; he did not participate in the foundation of this new organization, and his brother Theodore made only a nominal contribution to the founding convention's work.

Although initially bitterly opposed to unification, the professional lecturer Debs soon accommodated himself to the new reality and began to advocate tirelessly on behalf of the new organization. He would remain in the party's ranks for the rest of his life, making the second of his five runs for president in 1904, this time under the banner of the Socialist Party.

This fourth volume, *Red Union, Red Paper, Red Train, 1905–1910,* focuses on three seminal events in the life of Debs, activities with which he would be associated forever. The first of these, the "red union," relates to the 1905 establishment of the Industrial Workers of the World (IWW), for which Debs played a brief role as the leading public face. The second event, his move to Girard, Kansas in 1907 to join the pugnacious staff of the "red paper," the mass circulation weekly *Appeal to Reason*, recast Debs as a rabble-rousing national journalist, further sponsoring hundreds of speeches on behalf of the paper. The third event, his legendary third campaign for president of the United States, required that he crisscross the country on a coast-to-coast whistle-stop tour aboard the "red train," the so-called "Red Special" chartered by the Socialist Party.

❧

Radical activists have long differed on trade union tactics and the relationship of the political party to the organized labor movement. Should the existing trade unions be won over to desired policies through a process of internal organization, debate, and persuasion—a tactic known as "boring from within?" Or should these imperfect but already established workplace organizations be scuttled as irredeemable and new and unsullied "dual unions" loyal to the party and its socialist mission be created in their stead?

The question in the United States is as old as socialist politics itself. The constitution of the first German-American international socialist organization, the Soziale Partei, declared in January 1868 that while new craft unions could continue to be established in accordance with the existing model, "new trade unions should be founded when existing unions decline to affiliate with the [party] organization."[1] These new dual union organizations—pledging loyalty to the party—were to be known as "Konkurrenz-Unions."[2] While the tiny and short-lived Soziale Partei's ideas about dual unionism in the late 1860s were limited to the theoretical plane, in only a few years the matter would attain practical significance. A parallel "progressive" union of cigar makers was established in the early 1870s to compete with the existing cigar makers' union, which was regarded as insufficiently militant. This trend was continued in 1884 when an effort was made in Chicago to establish a parallel progressive central labor organization for the city and was further amplified by the emergence of the multi-industrial Knights of Labors in an effort to supplant the network of "conservative" craft unions declaring loyalty to the American Federation of Labor.[3] Although these early efforts to establish radical dual unions proved failures, they marked the path for an even more ambitious attempt during the first years of the twentieth century—the establishment of the Industrial Workers of the World.

Late in the fall of 1904, a group of six socialist trade union functionaries gathered to organize a new radical labor entity. Taking seats at the conference table were Isaac Cowen, representative of the British Amalgamated Society of Engineers; Clarence Smith and Thomas J. Hagerty, respectively the national secretary and magazine editor of the American Labor Union (ALU), a de facto appendage of the Western Federation of Miners (WFM); Oregonian George Estes and his associate W. L. Hall, president and secretary-treasurer of the United Brotherhood of Railway Employees (UBRE), a short-lived attempt to achieve the dream of Debs of a potent industrial union encompassing all railway workers; and William E. Trautmann, editor of the *Brauer Zeitung*, official organ of the United Brewery Workers of America.[4] These six men determined to move forward with plans for a new general industrial union, an umbrella organization which would unite the American Labor Union's program for industry and the UBRE program for the railroad industry under one mighty red banner.

In light of the failures of the Knights of Labor and the American Railway Union to perfect enduring national industrial organizations before them, most impartial observers would have set long odds against success of the new project. Since its founding in 1902—cheered on by Debs—the American Labor Union had utterly failed to reach beyond its base of unionized hard rock miners in the western states to develop a national footprint. The fledgling UBRE had fared worse even worse, unable to establish even a single potent local organization.

Despite their previous documented shortcomings, these committed industrial unionists sought to leap once more into the breach. Late in November 1904 about 30 invitations were mailed to prospective supporters of the industrial union movement working as functionaries in the labor movement and its press. Debs was quick to lend his good name to the cause, signing the invitation letter despite never having personally attended an initial session of the group of six. Gaining Debs's signature did not gain his activity, however, as Debs begged off participating in the conference that he helped call, ostensibly for reasons of health, in a December 23 letter to Smith. This communication, technically a piece of literary output from 1904 but closely related to the unfolding story of the IWW, opens this volume.[5]

While Debs was sympathetic but absent, at least two of the 30 progressive labor activists invited to the January 2 organizing session took their leave due to antipathy to the project's mission. These opponents to a dual unionist assault on the American Federation of Labor included Debs's comrade from the leadership of the old Social Democratic Party, Milwaukee publisher Victor L. Berger, as well as Max S. Hayes, a typographical union activist and publisher of the weekly *Cleveland Citizen.* A total of 25 people did ultimately attend,[6] including two soon to become causes célèbres, top officials of the Western Federation of Miners Charles Moyer and William D. Haywood. Other leading figures attending the so-called "January Conference" included Charles O. Sherman, head of the dual United Metal Workers; Frank Bohn, organizer for the Socialist Trade & Labor Alliance (ST&LA), the trade union appendage of the Socialist Labor Party; and labor organizer "Mother" Mary Jones.

This organizing committee met for three days in Chicago, electing Bill Haywood permanent chairman of the conference and George Estes its permanent secretary. The body hammered out a manifesto which launched the Industrial Workers of the World, a document to which Debs would add his signature after the fact. This foundation document proclaimed that "separation of craft from craft renders industrial and financial solidarity impossible," leading to the scabbing of union workers upon their striking brethren and fostering mutual hatred among labor's ranks. The working class was thereby delivered "helpless and disintegrated into the hands of the capitalists." Craft division was blamed for a litany of ills, with extortionate initiation fees foisted upon their members and collaboration with price-gouging employers the subject of explicit rebuke. Moreover, craft division was said to hinder the achievement of class consciousness by organized workers, who instead were indoctrinated into believing in a commonality of interest between employers and workers. "Universal economic evils afflicting the working class can be eradicated only by a universal working class movement," the manifesto asserted. A foundation convention was called for Chicago, scheduled to begin June 27, 1905.[7]

Despite Debs's failure to attend either of the two organizing sessions preparing the ground for the IWW, his signature on the November 1904 invitation letter and the January 1905 manifesto were regarded as grave transgressions by Victor Berger and other advocates of the "boring from within" strategy for transforming the American Federation of Labor (AF of L). With sparks flying in April 1905, Berger requested a personal meeting with Debs to clarify the situation. Debs declined this request from Milwaukee, mincing no words in attacking Berger's ineffectual machinations against Gompers at the previous American Federation of Labor annual convention:

> Don't tell me about rescuing the AF of L from the gang of pirate capitalists that are now running it. They and their lieutenants who are the nominal leaders simply make laughing stock of you. You were in a pitiable role at San Francisco, you and your comrades, and it made my blood boil to see a man of your genius the sport and prey of a lot of five cent fakirs. Gompers has a better grip on the AF of L because of your opposition than if you had let him alone. He is strong in precisely the same way and for precisely the same reason that P. M. Arthur was strong with the engineers. I saw twenty years of efforts to dislodge the latter turn to nothing while at the last the opposition gave up and Arthur was triumphant by acclamation to the very last hour of his life.[8]

Though Debs was unwilling to click his heels and make a pilgrimage to Milwaukee for a dressing down by the self-sure Berger, a public lecture was hastily booked for Saturday, April 29 at the Belle City Opera House in Racine, Wisconsin, and plans laid for a face-to-face session of the two Socialist Party leaders afterward. Berger and his top lieutenant, *Social-Democratic Herald* editor Frederic Heath, hopped a train to Racine to see Debs address 600 paying auditors on the topic "Socialism and Economic Conditions of the Working Man" and to air their differences on socialist strategy toward the trade union movement. While the precise words exchanged at the Hotel Racine were never recounted by either party, the discussion was undoubtedly confrontational and brutally frank. A bitter personal break between Berger and Debs would result. The reprinted articles and speeches by Debs published in the *Herald* in virtually every issue were slashed at once, with only half a dozen Debs pieces seeing print for the rest of the spring and summer of 1905. This attenuated presence of Debs in the powerful Milwaukee press—which included English- and German-language publications with a national subscription list—became nearly complete after October 1905. Over the next five years only two 1908 Debs speeches and a tepid 39-word telegram of congratulations to Berger on his election to Congress in 1910 would be grudgingly printed in the *Herald* by Berger and Heath.

This severing of relations between Berger and Debs was not remarked upon in the socialist press, nor does it seem to have been fodder for widespread gossip. Both kept a stern public face, without public airing of grievances.

Understanding this break makes Berger's mysterious appearance and verbal sparring with Debs in a widely publicized 1908 interview by Lincoln Steffens in the mass circulation *Everybody's Magazine* particularly compelling, with Steffens coincidentally interviewing the Socialist presidential hopeful in Milwaukee during one of the only instances in which the two top leaders shared the same room in the half decade after their Racine blowup.[9] This complete interview appears in this volume.

Though polite communication would eventually be renewed, personal relations between Debs and Berger would never be the same.[10]

ᔓ

The founding convention of the Industrial Workers of the World met in Chicago at Brand's Hall on June 27, 1905. Over two hundred delegates were in attendance with the available space packed with additional spectators. Debs and Mother Jones joined Chairman Bill Haywood on the platform. Participants included a five-member delegation by the potent Western Federation of Miners, the largest and most potent labor organization to participate; representatives of the dual industrial unions representing metal and railway workers; and a substantial delegation from the Socialist Labor Party's Socialist Trade & Labor Alliance. This latter group would be retrospectively characterized by Haywood as "a sect which came to the convention not on account of its activity among the working class but because of having read and absorbed the manifesto which called the convention."[11] In addition, Lucy Parsons and a number of anarchists attended the convention; they saw in the prospective new union a chance at revitalizing the atrophied organized labor movement.

As had now become part of his established modus operandi with organizational gatherings, Debs did not participate in the nitty-gritty of convention committee work sessions at this founding convention. He instead limited himself to delivery of a keynote address, with his grey-bearded nemesis, Daniel DeLeon of the SLP, seated in the audience and paying close attention to every word passing the Hoosier orator's lips.[12]

"The American Federation of Labor has numbers, but the capitalist class do not fear the American Federation of Labor; quite the contrary," Debs declared:

> There are those who believe that this form of unionism can be changed from within. They are very greatly mistaken. We might as well have remained in the Republican and Democratic Parties and have expected to effect certain changes from within, instead of withdrawing from those parties and organizing a party that represented the exploited working

> class. There is but one way to effect this great change, and that is for the workingman to sever his relations with the American Federation and join the union that proposes upon the economic field to represent his class and we are here today for the purpose of organizing that union.[13]

Intimating to the Socialist Labor Party that one party of the working class would be the practical adjunct to the new unified industrial union, he offered DeLeon and his supporters a tip of the hat and vague intimation of a path toward possible organic unity of the two rival socialist organizations, conceding that the SLP's "theory is right, that their principles are sound," and that their members were "honest." Fault was found instead with the organization's "fanaticism," which was deemed as fatal to development of the working class movement as the "fakirism" of the established craft union bureaucracies.[14]

After Debs finished his address, DeLeon was called forward and delivered a 30-minute lecture of his own, followed by the orations of a succession of worthies. "The wild indiscriminate applause was the one discouraging feature of the day's session," Washington radical David Burgess noted, adding that "until the workers cease to worship men they can scarcely expect to possess self-confidence enough to emancipate themselves."[15]

On June 29 Debs delivered his sole speech to the delegates at the founding of the Industrial Workers of the World. He would speak not another recorded word from the convention floor. Debs did take time the following evening to tout the new organization at a mass meeting at Apollo Hall before boarding a train taking him out of the city. Debs would later claim his abrupt departure from the founding convention of the IWW was necessary for fulfillment of a Fourth of July speech scheduled months earlier in the tiny community of McKinney, North Dakota.[16] This one-off speech delivered to a crowd of 3,000 seems to have been no more than a convenient pretext for early departure from Chicago, however. Repeating a pattern shown at the formation of the Social Democratic Party and Socialist Party of America, Debs once again left to others the tedious and sometimes stressful set of negotiation and political machinations needed to organize and staff a new industrial union. Friday, July 7, found Debs in Streator, Illinois—just 80 miles southwest of Chicago—delivering a generic address on "Social Problems" in the early afternoon to a paid audience at the local Chautauqua assembly there.[17] Meanwhile, the foundation convention of the IWW in Chicago was on the eve of electing its national officers, effectively determining its future fate. He made no effort to participate in that process.

In short, although Debs was an early and passionate advocate of the Industrial Workers of the World and subsequently spoke at length and with eloquence in its behalf, it is a stretch to include Debs among the organization's true founders. As was the case throughout his life, Debs was distinctly averse to the mundane task of political organization. His personal appearances at political conventions, aside from cameo appearances to deliver a unifying keynote address from above the fray, may be counted on one hand without using a thumb or pinkie. Given the opportunity, Debs would always decline, beg off ostensibly for reasons of health, escape.

As we shall see in volume five, there was likely a mental or physiological explanation for this entirely predictable repeating pattern of behavior.

∽

Debs took to the road to speak in support of the fledgling Industrial Workers of the World during the fall of 1905, with four of these lectures transcribed by professional stenographers and published as pamphlets to promote the new industrial union. These included addresses at Aurora Hall, Chicago on November 23; Union Hall, South Chicago, November 24; Country Democracy Hall, Chicago, November 25; and Grand Central Palace, New York City, December 10. These "IWW lectures" featured greatly similar content and were assigned confusingly similar names as pamphlet literature, bearing the titles *Craft Unionism, Class Unionism, Revolutionary Unionism,* and *Industrial Unionism,* respectively. All four of these titles would remain in print without interruption for the next decade. Indeed, for the rest of the twentieth century this massive agglomeration of more than 35,000 words of repetitious content was repackaged and reprinted again and again as the core of compilations of Debs's writings, wrongly intimating to Debs an oratorical obsession with the Industrial Workers of the World and its industrial unionist mission.

Promotion of the IWW was, however, neither Debs's solitary or even his primary focus of discourse in 1905. In addition to a grand total of eight speeches under the official auspices of the IWW in that year must be added the other 50 or 75 or more presentations delivered by Debs for honoraria to general audiences in small towns and cities across America on such themes as "The Genius of Liberty," "The Issue of the 20th Century," "Twentieth Century Problems," and "Social Problems." While no organization paid stenographers to capture each syllable uttered by Debs at these more typical and mundane propaganda speeches, the fact remains that the number of hours Debs spoke on such topics outnumbered those committed to the IWW by a ratio of at least five to one. It is without apology or ulterior motive that this collection attempts to attenuate Debs's 1905 "IWW lectures" to a more representative percentage of total content of his work in the 1905–10 period.[18]

ᔓ

Debs spent most of 1906 on the road, opening the year in Michigan, hitting North Carolina at the end of January, visiting Minnesota and Iowa amidst the February snows. Debs's speaking tours generally ran for two or three weeks in this period, with the nightly lectures to paying audiences generally lasting about two hours. Downtime between these regional tours generally lasted a week or two. None of these speeches dealt with the Industrial Workers of the World, with representative titles including "Social Problems," "Social Revolution," "Socialism," "What Socialism Means," and "The Great Struggle."[19]

Truth be told, there was little reason for excitement about the new red union after the first excited flurry of activity in 1905, an upbeat moment when anything seemed possible, during which the Debs brothers had constituted themselves the resolutions committee of the IWW's "Terre Haute Local Union No. 9." The new industrial union was a feeble entity—tiny in stature, its bank account paltry and steadily attenuated by a president with a penchant for costly road trips and bloated expense accounts. The staggeringly large ambition of toppling the established craft union movement remained unfulfilled, with the new industrial union utterly incapacitated by factional squabbling. With its most effective captain, Bill Haywood, removed from action in Idaho, the rudderless ship appeared destined to be smashed on the rocks.

Internally the Industrial Workers of the World was divided between those favoring simultaneous political action to gain control of the state and those who scornfully dismissed electoral politics as a useless diversion from the main mission of industrial organization. Adding to the complexity of the situation, the political actionists were themselves divided between the disciplined adherents of the Socialist Labor Party, who sought to make that organization and its "scientific socialist" analysis the directing nexus of the labor movement, and the more eclectic supporters of the Socialist Party of America, who believed in the efficacy of victory at the ballot box under the banner of that organization as a necessary component of industrial unionist advance. In opposition to both of these factions, the "industrialists" styled themselves a new and different breed. Glorying in a self-image of proletarian purity and virtue, the industrialists had little patience for the lawyers, preachers, publicists, and newspaper editors that dominated the political action wing—even though such anti-intellectualism smacked of self-hatred on the part of many of these erstwhile "proletarians."

The already lightly populated fledgling union split into two even weaker parallel organizations at its second convention, which opened in Chicago on September 17, 1906. The war for control of the name and assets of the faltering organization resembled nothing so much as an intra-office squabble, pitting IWW President Charles O. Sherman and his associates against Secretary-Treasurer William Trautmann,[20] backed by éminence grise Daniel DeLeon. Hinting at the nexus of the dispute, Sherman made a pointed objection to the Socialist Labor Party in his report to the convention of September 24, declaring that "literature bearing on any complexion of a political nature should be barred from any economic industrial meeting" as he had often seen "men representing political organizations" distributing and selling political literature. In his report Sherman expressed a syndicalist perspective, calling for the IWW to be "kept clear of all political agitation," dismissing the ballot as "merely a paper-wad," and asserting that "the real weapon that will and must be used by the workers when organized is the cessation of work" through the general strike.[21]

Sherman's primary foe, former brewery workers' union editor William Trautmann, ironically, does not seem to have held political views greatly dissimilar from those of Sherman. He shared a belief in the primacy of the strike over the ballot box but was willing to make common cause with DeLeon and his acolytes to gain control of the organization. He was consequently more circumspect in expressing his views. Trautmann instead staked his case against the Sherman regime on the question of financial profligacy, charging that expenditure of scarce union funds on train fare, hotel rooms, and poorly documented "incidentals" was not commensurate with the organizing outcome produced.

The two factions spent a full week at the convention fighting among themselves over the naming of a credentials committee and battling over challenges of delegate credentials.[22] Ultimately, the Trautmann–DeLeon group outmaneuvered their opponents, unseating a number of delegates loyal to Sherman—as well as Sherman himself—in a narrow vote that decertified the union's metal and machinery department before going on to depose Sherman by striking the position of president from the constitution.

Refusing to recognize the legality of these Machiavellian parliamentary machinations, Sherman and his associates rushed to retain possession of the union's headquarters, back stock of printed literature, and official newspaper, with the Trautmann faction forced to rent a new office and launch a new official publication. Gene Debs, a staunch advocate of electoral politics as well as being temperamentally ill-disposed to factional warfare, had already removed himself from the equation, skipping the second convention and making no effort to lend support to either faction through public statement. He would never again write for the *Industrial Worker,* the monthly organ of the Sherman faction after July 1906. His only published contribution to *Industrial Union Bulletin,* organ of the Trautmann faction, was a reprint of an article originally written for a minor encyclopedia and editorially appropriated without Debs's initiative.

If Debs attempted to keep abreast of factional activities of the Industrial Workers of the World from 1906 to 1907—a period during which Daniel DeLeon was himself deposed in a second bitter factional split—there is no surviving record of the fact. The man who had proselytized so effusively for the IWW at the time of its foundation in 1905 had essentially walked away from the nearly moribund red union by the end of the summer of 1906.

ᔕ

At 6:45 p.m. in the evening of December 30, 1905, retired Governor Frank Steunenberg returned from downtown Caldwell, Idaho, to his modest two-story home at the edge of town. Reaching to open the front gate in the darkness, Steunenberg pulled a trip-wire attached to a stopper, spilling a vial of volatile sulfuric acid over blasting caps atop a dynamite bomb.[23] The force of the blast ripped away Steunenberg's right side, shattering both legs and nearly tearing off his right arm.[24] Neighbors ran to his aid and the governor's broken body was carried into the house; the bleeding was stopped to the extent possible. "Who shot me?" the governor queried before losing consciousness. Within 30 minutes he would be dead. Before the night was over, Idaho Governor Frank R. Gooding[25] would offer a $5,000 state reward for information leading to the arrest of the culprit in the assassination, with county and private reward funds quickly pushing the total toward the $20,000 mark.[26]

Steunenberg, ironically elected as a reform fusion candidate of the Democratic Party and the People's Party in 1896, had been responsible for a martial law declaration and the insertion of federal troops to quell a strike of the Western Federation of Miners against the Bunker Hill Mining Company, a bitter and violent dispute that had ended in the bombing of the company's mine at Wardner early in the spring of 1899. The military had rounded up striking miners and detained them in a concentration camp (a so-called "bullpen"), allowing the company to make use of non-union workers under a permit system.[27] The strike had been broken and the Western Federation of Miners effectively destroyed in the Coeur d'Alene district as a result, for which Steunenberg was blamed, providing what seemed ample motive for retaliatory assassination.

Law enforcement authorities raced into action, sealing the town and questioning all strangers. A stranger using the name Thomas Hogan, purporting to be a sheep buyer but who had purchased no sheep during his two-week stay in town, quickly came under suspicion. A visiting sheriff from Baker City, Oregon recognized this "Hogan" as a miner he knew by the name of Harry Orchard, prompting a search of Orchard's belongings which turned up copious physical evidence. Orchard was subject to house arrest on December 31 and formally arrested and charged with the Steunenberg murder on New Year's Day 1906.[28] He was locked up in the county jail at Caldwell.

After a week of investigation Governor Gooding brought in outside help, the chief of the Denver branch of the Pinkerton Detective Agency, James McParland. McParland was a former New York policeman turned detective who had infiltrated a secret miners' union known as the Molly Maguires. McParland's damning testimony about the group's alleged terroristic tactics had led to the conviction and execution of 19 Pennsylvania anthracite coal miners between 1877 and 1879. Within two days of arrival in Idaho, McParland was ready to claim he was "almost sure" that Orchard had been little more than the "tool" of the Western Federation of Miners leadership. McParland orchestrated the transfer of Orchard from the Caldwell jail to the more foreboding environs of the state penitentiary at Boise, where he was initially held in solitary confinement for 10 days. Having duly softened up the alleged bomber by brutal isolation, McParland met with Orchard for the first time on January 22, threatening him with the death penalty unless he turned state's witness. He met with Orchard again three days later, making it clear that it was the leadership of the Denver-based Western Federation of Miners whose heads he sought on a platter.[29]

Orchard was thereby persuaded to confess personal guilt for an amazing panoply of terroristic acts and to implicate the top leadership of the Western Federation of Miners in a 30-month reign of violence and destruction. Orchard admitted to helping light a fuse that blew up the Bunker Hill Mine (Idaho, 1899); destroying the Vindicator Mine by bomb (Colorado, 1903); murdering by gunfire alleged labor spy Lyte Gregory (Colorado, 1904); killing 13 strikebreakers and maiming six others in the bombing of the Independence train depot (Colorado, 1904); attempting to murder mine manager Fred Bradley by bombing his house (California, 1904); botching an attempt to bomb Judge Luther M. Goddard at his home (Colorado, 1905); accidentally killing an innocent man, Merrit Walley, in a failed attempt to bomb Colorado Chief Justice William H. Gabbert (Colorado, 1905); and plotting the murders of Colorado Governor James H. Peabody and Denver banker David Moffat. Orchard claimed that all these nefarious activities were directed by and paid for by an "inner circle" of top officials of the Western Federation of Miners, including specifically Secretary-Treasurer William D. Haywood, President Charles Moyer, general executive board member Jack Simkins, and a union bagman and technical adviser on terrorist matters, George Pettibone.[30] McParland sat with Orchard taking down this confession (or helping to fabricate the tale, as some would claim) for four full days at the end of January.[31]

Orchard's confession was in hand by February 1, 1906, but it was not until the night of the 17th that WFM officials Haywood, Moyer, and Pettibone were abruptly arrested. Moyer was detained at the train depot where he was waiting to catch a train to meet with Kansas smelter workers, Pettibone was detained at home, and Haywood taken into custody at 11:30 p.m. in his rooming house near the miners federation office. No arrest warrants were shown to those detained as none had been issued; the extradition of individuals who were not established to be fugitives from justice was a process that was both difficult and time consuming. State authorities, including two governors, sought to expedite matters by dismissing such legal niceties. This decision to circumvent the norms of conventional legality would prove controversial and go far to undermining the credibility of the entire case.

At about 5:00 a.m. the next morning the trio was hustled to the administrative office and driven away by carriage to the railway station, each prisoner in his own separate carriage under the watchful eyes of three armed guards. The prisoners were then rushed aboard a special train for Idaho, with the handcuffed union officials and their guards the sole occupants of a special car. The engine traveled at high speed, stopping at no large cities along the way, taking on the necessary coal and water at smaller towns along the route. It arrived at the depot in Boise the following morning.[32]

Seized without warrants and rushed across state lines for what seemed to be a speedy frame-up and execution straight out of the Molly Maguire playbook, the cases of Haywood, Moyer, and Pettibone would attract national infamy and drag through the court system for more than eighteen months. Gene Debs would perform yeoman's service raising public consciousness of the case and helping to keep the Idaho trials of the WFM leaders at the top of the agenda of the American labor movement. In his inflammatory March 1906 article "Arouse, Ye Slaves!" Debs declared he would stake his life on the "honor and integrity" of the Idaho defendants and urged his readers to prepare for armed revolt:

> We are not responsible for the issue. It is not of our seeking. It has been forced upon us; and for the very reason that we deprecate violence and abhor bloodshed we cannot desert our comrades and allow them to be put to death. If they can be murdered without cause so can we, and so will we be dealt with at the pleasure of these tyrants.
>
> They have driven us to the wall and now let us rally our forces and face them and fight.
>
> If they attempt to murder Moyer, Haywood, and their brothers, a million revolutionists, at least, will meet them with guns. * * *
>
> A special revolutionary convention of the proletariat at Chicago, or some other central point, would be in order, and, if extreme measures are required, a general strike could be ordered and industry paralyzed as a preliminary to a general uprising.
>
> If the plutocrats begin the program, we will end it.[33]

The fate of these comrades would eclipse all other issues for Debs during the years 1906 and 1907. Recalling his own incarceration in 1895, Debs would make their struggle his struggle and their victory his victory. Material related to these events makes up an important part of this book.

ᔓ

Gene Debs and his siblings were rocked by the loss of their beloved mother, Marguerite Marie Bettrich Debs, on April 29, 1906 after a protracted illness. Gene was in Superior, Wisconsin to deliver a lecture when he received the long-anticipated word of his mother's passing at the age of 77. He left for Terre Haute on a night train immediately after his lecture, rescheduling a Minneapolis appearance slated for the following night to the end of May. He would write a poem in his mother's honor, "Where Daisy Sleeps," publishing the simple but touching verse that summer.[34] Gene would tour the Midwest from June until August, booked solid for the month of July as a featured speaker on the lucrative Chautauqua circuit, a booming network of paid public gatherings combining adult education and entertainment which borrowed heavily from the protestant revival camp formula. Debs took time out of his Chautauqua lectures to make two explicitly partisan appearances that summer, including a speech to a massive Haywood–Moyer defense meeting in St. Louis on July 29 and an IWW-themed speech at a Labor Day picnic in New Castle, Pennsylvania, at which he shared the stage one final time with the group's Charles O. Sherman and Daniel DeLeon. These two major events were the exception rather than the rule; the hot months of 1906 were both extremely busy and intellectually unremarkable for the veteran socialist agitator.

As the days grew shorter, the 1906 general election drew nigh. Always an eager campaigner, Debs once again dove into the partisan fray, spending late October and early November in Colorado on behalf of jailed WFM leader Big Bill Haywood, controversial gubernatorial nominee of the Socialist Party of Colorado. Debs addressed overflow audiences for 13 nights over the two-week run, ending with a boisterous event in Denver judged to be the largest political meeting of the campaign. Haywood predictably ended the campaign a distant third.

With the 1906 election over, still locked out of writing for his previous home for written words, Victor Berger's *Social Democratic Herald,* Gene Debs found himself a true free-lance—a socialist propagandist in search of a new home and a new challenge.

ꟹ

The *Appeal to Reason,* which for a time in the early twentieth century was the largest circulation radical newspaper in the world, did not emerge fully formed. The paper is connected with the identity of its publisher, Julius Augustus Wayland, born on April 26, 1854 in Versailles, Indiana, a tiny community of about 400 souls located east of Bloomington.[35] His father and four siblings had died in a cholera epidemic four months after his birth, leaving his mother alone to fend for the baby and two surviving children. Poverty gripped the family, limiting Julius to just two years of formal education before being apprenticed as a young teenager to a local newspaper publisher. Serving as a printer's assistant, Wayland was gradually educated in the finer points of the English language while he learned the printer's trade, subsequently leaving the *Versailles Gazette* for a series of jobs in larger towns across southern Indiana. The young Wayland made his triumphant return to Versailles in 1872, buying out the publisher of the newspaper for whom he formerly worked.[36] He would eke out an existence as a small town publisher and printer for the next decade.

In 1882 the radical Republican Wayland and his bride of five years moved to the blossoming town of Pueblo, Colorado, where Wayland worked as a job printer, speculatively investing the proceeds of his business in various buildings around town. The town grew and so did his fortune, as Wayland energetically flipped real estate, buying low and selling high in a booming economy.

Wayland's politics had moved with the times during his Colorado interlude, with Laurence Gronlund's *The Cooperative Commonwealth* (1884) and Edward Bellamy's best-selling Utopian novel *Looking Backward, 2000–1887* (1888) regarded as particular landmarks on his ideological journey from egalitarian Republicanism to social democracy.[37]

Location, timing, and luck were all on Wayland's side. He fortuitously decided to cash out just ahead of the devastating economic panic of 1893, exchanging his small stack of property deeds for $80,000 in gold and government bonds.[38] Flush with the proceeds of this sale, the entrepreneurial Wayland headed home to southern Indiana, intent on doing his part for the cause with his next venture—a weekly socialist newspaper called *The Coming Nation.* Wayland selected the town of Greensburg, a community of about 4,000 located 22 miles up the road from his native Versailles, as his base of operations, making his start with a four-page edition dated Saturday, April 29, 1893.

Wayland, the self-proclaimed "One-Hoss Editor," nursed his paper through its early years, declining to run advertising and declining to offer credit, selling subscriptions and bundles of his paper on a strict cash-and-carry basis. At the end of six months he had managed to build a national subscriber base of 14,000 from the radical periphery of the People's Party movement, supplemented by a newsstand sale of approximately 3,000 copies per week, providing an income stream sufficient for survival. "As a careful and successful businessman, I see plainly that the future of the paper will return many thousand a year profit," Wayland presciently foretold. He sought to move beyond mere newspaper propaganda to "founding a village on economic equality that I may live and labor on an equality with my neighbors" and promised to launch such a colony as soon as his paper's circulation was expanded to 100,000—sufficient to clear about $23,000 a year, enabling the purchase of 3,000 or 4,000 acres of land.[39]

Wayland continued:

> Those who send in 200 subscribers or more or contribute as much, will be the charter members, who will proceed to organize the colony on such a basis of equality as in their judgment will produce justice. Each man and each woman shall have an equal voice no matter how much or little they have contributed. This land will be selected by this committee and the title vested in all. . . . All receipts of the paper will go to the common fund, and all the employees will draw their pay from the common fund. The store will be owned by the whole people and goods sold at wholesale prices, plus cost of storekeeper's salary. I can also influence several other factories to come on exactly the same terms.[40]

Wayland's newspaper rapidly achieved national prominence, growing to an average circulation of 60,000, deemed sufficient to launch his cooperative dream village. Making use of his deep pockets, Wayland purchased a tract of rocky land at Tennessee City, Tennessee, located just west of Nashville, and the colony was born, with 19 members each bearing one share of stock each incorporated as the Ruskin Cooperative Association on August 24, 1894. Wayland was named president with the other stockholders serving as a board of directors.

Wayland's communal experience proved to be short and unhappy. Hastily assembled shanties made of rough-sawn green timber were hurriedly constructed, but materials and workmanship were poor and the resulting dwellings uncomfortable. The soil was poor, making productive agriculture difficult. Work was disorganized; an inefficient time-slip system of payment was introduced while bureaucracy and loaferism blossomed. Bitter personal faction-fighting reared its head. Grandiose dreams of a "Ruskin College of the New Economy" were advanced as a primary mission of the colonists, but *The Coming Nation* remained the sole commercially viable industry of the collective, despite efforts to manufacture and sell suspenders and ersatz coffee made of chicory. By the summer of 1895, Wayland and his wife had reached the limit of their endurance. They cut their losses by selling their four shares of stock for $2,000—abandoning land, printing equipment, and the valuable *The Coming Nation* nameplate to the Tennessee colonists.[41]

ൟ

The 41-year-old Wayland, a true man of the Midwest, chose Kansas City, Missouri, as the nexus of his next venture—a new broadsheet socialist weekly called the *Appeal to Reason.* With issue number 1 hitting the mail on August 31, 1895, by the end of the year the entrepreneurial Wayland would already be touting a circulation of 15,000 atop the publication's front page. His prominent announcement of circulation growth week-by-week proved to be a clever bit of marketing, helping to build momentum by making the paper's fanatically loyal readers proud participants in a prominent campaign to expand of the *Appeal's* reach, and with it the cause of socialism. By 1901 the average circulation had expanded tenfold, reaching 150,000.[42]

Although remembered as a vehicle for publisher Wayland to provide idiosyncratic commentary on various issues of the day, from 1903 onward control of the *Appeal* was delegated to an energetic young journalist, Fred D. Warren,[43] publisher of a radical paper in Rich Hill, Missouri and drafted into service by

Wayland. The radical Warren would provide the energy, ideas, and direction necessary for the paper's continued growth.

The idea of reaching a mass audience via the written word appealed mightily to Debs, an evangelist of socialist ideas. No less attractive was the prospect of earning a decent living pursing a vocation less grueling than oratory. Relentless public speaking tours had now for more than a decade kept Debs on the road more nights than he ever spent at home. Constant sitting aboard jostling trains wore at Gene's back, contributing to chronic lumbago. Nightly addresses to large gatherings without amplification wore at his vocal cords. Moreover, as Debs moved into middle age he must have wondered about the efficacy of his career of public speaking—was it enough to win a nation to the socialist idea? There was no bigger soapbox than the *Appeal,* distributed coast to coast through bundle sales to the committed supporters self-identifying as the "Appeal Army." The paper's continued circulation growth hinted at the prospect of bigger and better possibilities.

Similarly, for the *Appeal,* always seeking to expand its circulation and influence, making common cause with the beloved Gene Debs as a member of its paid staff made sound business sense. Although unremarkable as a writer, Debs was a man of passionate opinions and the writer of readable prose. Moreover, he clearly did not seem to entirely sever himself from public speaking, but rather to limit the duration of tours and the associated strain upon body and voice. Terms were agreed upon, with Debs placed on a salary. He was to turn in regular columns for the *Appeal* at some times, to speak under the newspaper's auspices at others. The *Appeal* would henceforth take over booking his tours and promoting his appearances—with the reasonable ticket prices to a free 40-week subscription to the socialist newspaper. Promoters of Debs speeches—frequently locals of the Socialist Party—were induced to purchase subscription cards in advance, serving the dual purpose of covering Debs's honorarium and traveling expenses as well as boosting circulation of the weekly broadsheet.

The mutually beneficial union of Debs and the *Appeal* would be lasting, with Debs remaining at his desk in Girard until an ill-tempered break in 1913.

∽

One recurring theme in Debs's journalism of this period was his solidarity work on behalf of jailed Mexican revolutionaries in exile in the United States. Ricardo Flores Magón, founder of the radical newspaper *Regeneración* in 1900 and a harsh critic of Mexico's strongman president, Porfirio Díaz, was forced to emigrate to Texas in 1904. There he and his brother Enrique continued publication of his revolutionary newspaper, which was chased away from the border to St. Louis, Missouri in 1905.[44] Other political comrades, so-called Magónistas, made the trek from Mexico to St. Louis, where in 1906 they established a Mexican political party in exile, the Partido Liberal Mexicano (PLM).[45] This organization denounced the Mexican ruling regime and advanced a platform of land reform, higher wages for urban workers, and democratization of the political process, thereby drawing the ire of Díaz, who sought to neutralize this revolutionary opposition. This effort was soon to be rewarded.

The Díaz regime employed a private detective company to investigate and track leaders of the PLM in the United States, building evidence of violation of American foreign neutrality laws, which banned military expeditions against foreign powers from American soil. The US Department of Justice was pressured to act. During the afternoon of August 23, 1907, armed detectives encircled a residence in Los Angeles, California, where they arrested Ricardo Flores Magón and two of his leading associates, Librado Rivera and Antonio I. Villarreal. With these top leaders of the PLM behind bars, as well as their associate Manuel Sarabia, the Díaz government filed an extradition request to their American counterparts, seeking the three revolutionaries to be returned to Mexico to face trial for alleged violations of Mexican law. The three were denied bond and held in jail in Los Angeles pending trial, beginning a legal process over their fate that would stretch on for more than a year and a half.[46]

On December 28, 1907, a federal grand jury at Tombstone, Arizona returned an indictment against the four Liberal Party radicals, charging them with violation of the neutrality law by conspiring with others in St. Louis to begin a military expedition against Mexico. The prisoners were consequently moved to southern Arizona to face trial. Seeing "a striking similarity as to methods" with the government's attempt to decapitate the leadership of the Western Federation of Miners, the *Appeal to Reason* was quick to train its journalistic cannons on the prosecution, dispatching their ace correspondent George H. Shoaf to cover the trial.[47]

Having himself suffered as essentially a jailed political prisoner in the aftermath of the failed Pullman strike of 1894, Debs was stirred to the core by the plight of his Mexican comrades. He became active in the Magón defense effort early in 1909, writing on the prisoners' behalf to progressing US Senator Robert F. LaFollette in an attempt to start a congressional investigation of the case[48] and working together with editor Fred D. Warren sought to mobilize the readers of the influential *Appeal to Reason* on behalf of the Magónistas. A heavily promoted "Liberty Edition" of the *Appeal* was produced, edited by Debs himself, with the plight of the jailed Mexican revolutionaries effectively publicized through the special edition's massive print run of 2,225,000 copies.[49]

ɞ

The Socialist Party of America was exactly that—a political party which ran a slate of candidates in opposition the Republicans and Democrats in an effort to win control of the machinery of government through the electoral process. The two "old parties" were opposed with equal vehemence, the Socialists following their model of holding national conventions every four years to define a guiding national platform for the organization and to select nominees for president and vice-president of the United States. The party's ticket for 1908 was to be chosen at the third of these national gatherings, slated to begin in Chicago on Sunday, May 10, and expected to last one week.

Debs was always a reluctant candidate for high office, sidestepping an effort to draft him as the candidate of the People's Party in 1896, and only accepting with great reluctance the joint nomination of the two Social Democratic parties in 1900. While he donned the mantle of top Socialist nominee and sacrificial lamb willingly in 1904, as the election of 1908 approached Debs sought to escape the onerous chore of running for president of the United States for a third time. Some sentiment percolated among the rank and file for the nomination of radical trade unionist and party member Big Bill Haywood as the Socialist standard-bearer in 1908, but the Wobbly Haywood was already a controversial figure among party members with connections to the established trade union movement and had no taste for the nomination to boot. Debs indicated as much in a letter to a prominent New York party journalist, passing along that he had talked with Haywood about running for president and that he did not desire the nomination and "would only accept it from a sheer sense of duty to the party." Debs declared that should the public figure Haywood decline the Socialist nomination, "an entirely fresh candidate should be nominated" from among the party's ranks of well-known leaders. Debs observed that he had already been twice nominated and that there was thus "every reason why some other comrade should be chosen" in 1908, although he acknowledged that duty to the party overrode his personal preferences on the matter.[50]

There was strong demand for a third Debs campaign among the rank and file, with his running mate from 1904, New York journalist Ben Hanford, joining the chorus with a May 2 letter to Debs in which he begged:

> I do not know the state of your health, but if you are not in your grave clothes you must allow yourself to be the candidate this year. We must

> make no mistakes. We cannot take chances on dark horses. . . . I do not know the condition of your throat. I have heard all sorts of stories. But if you are not able you need make few speeches, and those only in halls. . . . If you are not able to speak, you can write, and the party can print and circulate. . . . To me it seems that I have no right to consider any other man unless you tell me you positively decline, and in the event that you do so you are in duty bound to give me your reasons, and I have a right to weigh them as well as yourself . . . Debs, you are the man, and it is your duty to let it be known that you can and will respond when called upon.[51]

Others were less convinced of the merits of the passionate Hoosier in 1908. Victor Berger, now a disgruntled personal antagonist, sought to take advantage of an apparently wide-open nomination by advancing the candidacy of Rev. Carl D. Thompson, a calm-tempered and moderate functionary hailing from the Wisconsin socialist organization. Efforts brewed elsewhere to name others to the head of the ticket.

However, by the time the May 1908 convention arrived, a consensus for a third Debs nomination had clearly emerged among elected delegates. Debs was immediately placed in nomination from the floor of the convention during the evening session of May 14, enthusiastically nominated by P. H. Callery of Missouri. Chicago attorney Seymour Stedman, a longtime Debs ally, did his best to accede to Debs's wishes to avoid the presidential nomination. Noting the deep physical exhaustion suffered by Debs during two previous presidential bids and particularly fearful of permanent incapacitation as an effective public speaker, a danger accentuated by recent throat surgery, Stedman pleaded for the reassignment of Debs to an auxiliary literary role in the campaign:

> If he cannot take the stump he must accomplish it through a literary campaign. If he can take the stump, his name will draw terrific audiences, [though], my friends, if you nominate another who by the prestige of your nomination can draw large audiences, do you not double the effectiveness of your campaign? For the greatest tribute you can ever pay to Eugene V. Debs would be to strike him from the possibilities of your coming election.[52]

Stedman read into the record a telegram received earlier that day from Debs reasserting his desire to stand aside from the nomination, to win plaudits for activity "as a private in the ranks and not by having my name associated with some public office or with what may seem to be the desire of some public office."[53]

Sentiment for Debs remained strong on the convention floor, however, and Stedman's health-based argument was immediately trumped by beloved New York journalist Ben Hanford, who in a speech seconding the Debs nomination read into the record a section of a letter written in reply to his May 2 letter in which Debs declared "as to my throat and general health, I have improved considerably since I have had a chance to lead something like a regular life and get a reasonable amount of rest." Debs had professed his general health to be "about all that could be desired" and his strength never better.[54]

Although the debate ran for two hours, Debs's May letter to Hanford removed any doubt in the final result, with Debs gathering 159 of the 198 votes cast in a four-way race. Ben Hanford was once again chosen by the delegates as the party's vice-presidential nominee. The 1904 ticket which had shown so well was restored for a second national campaign.[55]

ശ

Debs was shortly thrust into what would be the most physically demanding speaking tour of his life to date—more than two straight months aboard a chartered train delivering several short campaign speeches at railroad depots across the country during the day, followed each evening with a long hall speech to a paying audience. The idea for an official Socialist Party campaign train was first put forward by national secretary Mahlon Barnes, inspired by a similar effort by Democrat William Jennings Bryan during the 1896 race. Barnes first vetted the idea at a May 27 planning session at party headquarters in Chicago attended by Debs and a three-person subcommittee of the National Executive Committee (NEC) consisting of Victor Berger, A. M. Simons,[56] and Carl Thompson.[57] The tour of what Barnes dubbed the "Socialist Special" was tentatively slated to launch in Chicago on August 30, with an itinerary plotted all the way to the Pacific coast by the second week of September, before returning all the way across country to New York City and the industrial northeast two weeks later. Those booking evening hall meetings in association with this tour would be committed to remit a $25 guarantee to the Socialist campaign committee, plus half of the net proceeds generated by ticket sales. Any remaining balance was to be retained for use of the local organization.[58]

At the July monthly meeting of the NEC Barnes reported that $20,000 would be required to lease and operate a "Socialist Special" train. Barnes noted that $10,000 had already been raised and spent paying delegate expenses to the recently concluded nominating convention and that as the Socialist Party was "a big party now, capable of carrying through big undertakings," the amount needed to conduct a first-rate national campaign would be comparatively modest. Barnes noted:

> Comrade Debs can talk, with the ordinary arrangements, in the large cities only, at 60 night stands in 65 days, and that is the limit of your ordinary possibilities. Hundreds of locals and cities want to hear him and see our candidate . . . . Here is your opportunity: a Socialist Special, passing through thousands of towns and stopping at five hundred cities across the nation.
>
> The terms for a special car or for one man being the same as for a special train which will carry a number of passengers, I suggest that a call be issued for volunteer musicians to make up a band to accompany the train, sleeping accommodations and food to be provided by the committee for free. . . .
>
> Moreover, I contend that if we had $500,000 today and attempted to devise systematic advertising and spend that sum, the results would be less than secured by the continental trip of the Socialist Special train. It will command and force attention in thousands of publications.[59]

Barnes provided as a cost estimate the nonbinding bid of a Chicago tour company, which pegged the estimated maximum cost of an "engine, baggage car, first-class high-back passenger coach, and a strictly first-class Pullman hotel car, which is sleeping car and dining car combined" at $20,300—a sum which included car rental, operational mileage expenses, and sufficient food for twenty people for a period of sixty days. This proposal was formally accepted by the National Executive Committee.[60] The actual amount spent by the Socialist Party on the 1908 campaign would ultimately exceed this amount significantly.

Though it meant a torturous two-month speaking schedule for him, Debs was enthusiastic about the "bold and audacious" idea of chartering a special train in a July 31 statement to party members:

> The roar of it can already be heard in the distance and the eager crowds can be seen as they cheer the onrushing "red specter" with fiery enthusiasm in its flight across the continent on its mission of emancipation.
>
> In its wake the comrades will shout exultant and the track of the Red Special will be the path of the Revolution. Hundreds of thousands will be attracted who otherwise will be beyond our reach. Tons of literature will be distributed.
>
> The Special itself will be a thing of life and will throb with the spirit of revolution. Along its track the stray and scattered embers of revolt will be fanned into a sweeping conflagration.[61]

A massive itinerary of the Pacific coast leg of the trip was quickly released, detailing projected arrival times at multiple stops each day down to the minute. The campaign formally launched with a Chicago speech at Alton Park on August 30. At 9:15 a.m. the following day the Socialist Red Special departed from the city, with multiple speaking stops in Illinois and Iowa, en route to Kansas City, Omaha, and on to Denver. The West Coast was reached the evening of September 8, when the Red Special pulled into the station at San Bernardino, California for a speech in front of 2,500 paying supporters. After heading south to San Diego, the Debs campaign train made its way up the Pacific coast as far as the mill town of Everett, Washington, before making its way home through Idaho, Montana, South Dakota, and Minnesota. A special diversion was made to the Upper Peninsula of Michigan for an evening meeting in front of just 800 people in the town of Hancock—a hotbed of Finnish-American socialism. Proceeding south through Wisconsin, the 9,000 mile western leg was completed on September 25, when at 6:00 a.m. the special train, packed to the roof with literature and the instruments of the members of the 15-piece brass band who volunteered for the expedition, pulled into the station in Chicago. Debs and his compatriots had delivered 187 speeches over the course of 25 days, speaking at least once in every western state and territory.[62]

Unsurprisingly, these hundreds of hours speaking to large crowds without amplification took a toll on the Indiana orator's vocal cords. He would later complain that

> not even one day was allowed me before being rushed off to the East in a car so foul that it was not fit for an animal to be shipped in. From the start to the finish not a single day was allowed me to nurse my voice or to rest my body and at many of the places . . . three and four big meetings were arranged after a hard day's speaking along the road, and that I did not break down utterly, as most men would have done, is simply because of my love for the socialist movement and because I have [a] constitution of iron.[63]

Be that as it may, Debs's voice would periodically fail him entirely, leaving his traveling companions A. M. Simons, Terre Haute attorney Stephen Reynolds, and his brother Theodore to serve as pinch hitters. At some of the smaller towns along the route, Theo would serve as a substitute for Gene, with many among the crowd none the wiser that a switch of balding brothers had been made.[64] Accommodations on the road were trying, with Debs making a small state room inside the Pullman car his office on the road, bunking in the same tight quarters with his friend Reynolds and his typist brother, Theodore. Hundreds of letters were dictated aboard the train between speaking stops, with work proceeding at a frenetic pace. The state room was packed with luggage and literature and was so cramped, Theo Debs later recalled, that for one of the three roommates to have enough room to disrobe for the night, the other two had to either pile into their berths to make space.[65]

After a speech before a wildly demonstrative crowd at Tomlinson Hall in Indianapolis the evening of September 25, the train began its second leg, heading east without so much as a one-day respite in Terre Haute. From Indiana the Red Special proceeded to Detroit, then on across Northern Ohio and Pennsylvania before reaching Buffalo and several other enclaves of socialist support in upstate New York. The train pulled to the platform in New York City early in the afternoon of October 4, with a depleted Debs delivering a speech before a raucous crowd that packed the massive Hippodrome later that night.[66] From New York, Debs and his traveling partners, who included his brother, political confidant, and personal secretary Theo, proceeded to New England before moving south.

The middle-aged Debs was worn to a frazzle by the marathon of travel and speech, shortly afterward apologizing to Morris Hillquit for his performance:

> Some strange fatality has attended me at the New York meetings and my part in them was as insignificant as the meetings themselves were magnificent. It was there I wished to be strongest and was the weakest. Fortunately, the meetings did not need me and my strength was reserved for other places where it was needed. . . .
>
> The day I was on the East Side [October 13] I was little more than a portable corpse. I had an attack of grippe [influenza] which all but paralyzed me and it had to come at a time of course when I ought to have had all my powers. . . . The trouble is that I cannot speak worth a minute's listening if I do not speak with all the intensity of my nature. The result is that when I am through, I am drenched with perspiration and there is hardly a dry thread in my clothes. I then have to be more or less exposed to the drafts and the cold with the result that I am chilled through with the usual consequences.[67]

The 1908 campaign marathon came to a close on November 1 with a Sunday afternoon speech in front of a massive crowd of 5,000 people at the 7th Regiment Armory in Chicago. Debs was greeted with a demonstration by the exuberant throng which lasted 27 minutes, with men, women, and children cheering themselves hoarse. Debs attempted to speak above the din in a creaking voice with little initial success. Sharing the speakers' platform was William D. Haywood, who caused the auditorium to erupt anew when he waved a red handkerchief at the crowd in defiance of the Chicago chief of police, who had prohibited the flying of the red flag as a dangerous incitement to revolutionary violence. "Someone once said that if an Irishman were elected to the presidency he would paint the White House green," Haywood declared to the packed house. "If we carry the election, we will paint it red."[68]

There was little chance of any such a brightening of Pennsylvania Avenue that year. The Socialist Party entered the 1908 election with high expectations, anticipating a million votes or more. This projection proved to be fantastically optimistic. When the counting ended the team of Debs and Hanford garnered a mere 421,000 votes in 1908—barely exceeding the 403,000 votes cast by voters for the same ticket in 1904. The 2.83% share of total votes received by the Socialists in 1908 represented a decline from the 2.98% showing by the party four years earlier. By way of contrast, reformer William Jennings Bryan managed to add more than 1.3 million votes to the Democratic count in 1908 over the tally for his predecessor four years earlier, conservative judge Alton B. Parker. It was this change at the head of the Democratic ticket and its attractiveness to working class voters that had more than any other factor cannibalized the 1908 Socialist vote.

Although the costly Red Special campaign of 1908 was unquestionably a public relations boon that would eventually become the stuff of socialist legend, the effort failed in its final exam—performance at the ballot box.

∽

Eugene Victor Debs turned 53 years old two days after the 1908 election. He felt older than that, ground down by the rigors of two months on the road, confined in a train by day, passionately delivering extemporaneous speeches to large crowds each evening. His vocal cords were strained, his body ached from endless hours of sitting. He would spend much of the following year recovering from the ordeal. After the November finale of the Red Special campaign, Debs would not deliver a public speech again for months. He booked his first speaking appearance of the year for June 30, 1909 at a Chautauqua assembly in Fort Collins, Colorado, only to have his secretary, his beloved brother Theodore, cancel the appearance two weeks ahead of the date. In a published letter to the Chautauqua promoter, Theodore declared that "speaking engagements for the present are not possible" as his brother had been confined to bed for ten days in early June, causing a backlog of work to accumulate.[69] Gene would finally speak in public at a Socialist Party encampment at Elk City, Oklahoma on August 3—ten months and a day after his last public appearance at Terre Haute on election eve.

In 1904 the Socialist Party of Oklahoma borrowed a page from the Chautauqua movement and protestant religious revival encampments by launching an explicitly "socialist encampment" of its own, with the initial effort made over a long August weekend at a park six miles south of Oklahoma City.[70] The event was regarded as successful and saw emulation in Oklahoma and Texas during subsequent years. By 1909 the socialist camp-revival movement had become well entrenched, with the Oklahoma party organization dividing the state into 10 districts, with a series of five-day encampments featuring major speakers planned for each.[71] Unlike the for-profit model used by the Chautauqua, operating expenses for these gatherings were to be met by the party and admission made free, with voluntary donations toward the defrayal of expenses to be solicited from those in attendance. The gatherings featured debates with representatives of the Democratic and Republican parties as well as lectures by prominent Socialist orators, musical concerts, dramatic presentations, dancing, and amusements.[72]

Debs was drafted as a featured speaker for the ambitious 1909 Oklahoma propaganda blitz. He ended a public speaking hiatus of more than eight months in July, August, and September to appear at vast socialist encampments which gathered in small towns such as Waurika, Snyder, and Elk City. Sharing the platform with Debs at these popular events were the diminutive "Little Giant," Walter Thomas Mills, touted by organizers as the "greatest platform orator-debater in America," as well as folksy German-American humorist Oscar Ameringer and prominent Oklahoman stump-speaker Patrick S. Nagle. Encampment crowds were impressively large, with 15,000 materializing from every corner of the countryside to hear Debs and Mills on a Thursday afternoon in Waurika, while an estimated 5,000 were left disappointed when Debs telegrammed news that he was too ill to appear on August 13 at Aline.

These five-day events typically began with group singing at 9:30 a.m., followed by a Socialist Party organizing conference starting half an hour later which absorbed most of the morning. At 2:00 p.m. the "Ameringer brass quartet" played a 30-minute concert to draw a crowd, followed by a first speaker of the day, who would lecture for a good part of the afternoon. After dinner the process would be repeated, with the band taking stage at 8:00 p.m. for another half-hour concert, which once again gathered the campers and visitors in one place, with the evening keynote lecture beginning at 8:30 p.m. The final day was truncated with only one speaker in the afternoon, after which the encampment broke up, with the gear presumably transferred to another location. Debs only spoke one time per event and is believed to have spoken at no fewer than seven Oklahoma encampment dates in the summer of 1909.[73]

Debs took a break from his organizing work in Oklahoma during the second half of August 1909 to make appearances before crowds running into the thousands at Newark, New Jersey, and Revere, Massachusetts. Heading back to Oklahoma after his brief appearances, Debs routed through Pittsburgh, where he made a noontime address to strikers of the Pressed Steel Car Company at Indian Mound, McKees Rocks. An evening meeting in Pittsburgh to the local Socialist organization was lightly attended, possibly due to loss of the planned venue, the city's old city hall. His eastern sojourn was brief and before August was over, Debs was back in the Oklahoma heat, speaking on "Liberty" to encampments at Weleetka, Ardmore, and Hugo. The effort by Debs and the state party appears to have paid major organizational dividends, with the average monthly paid membership of the Socialist Party of Oklahoma rocketing from 1,858 members in 1909[74] to 5,842 in 1910[75]—fully 10 percent of the national membership of the Socialist Party in that year.[76]

ℭ

The Oklahoma organizing drive of 1909 was concluded with an appearance at Hugo in early September. With only a brief respite, Debs was enlisted into a new campaign—this time touring the nation proselytizing socialism and selling subscriptions to the *Appeal to Reason.* An eastern tour was launched on October 17, 1909, running to Indiana to Ohio, Pennsylvania, and Massachusetts, highlighted by a speech on November 1 in New York City, followed by a night in Philadelphia. Debs then returned to the Midwest and conducted a series of nightly lectures in Kansas and Missouri, keeping up the pace until the middle of December.

The intensive schedule booked by J. E. Snyder of the *Appeal* took a physical toll on the rapidly aging orator. Debs's health began to deteriorate. Recuperating in Terre Haute in preparation for the next leg of the *Appeal* speaking tour, slated to begin January 13 in Chicago and scheduled to run for six weeks, Debs was near physical collapse. His concerned kid brother, secretary, and personal assistant Theodore captured the moment in an anguished letter to *Appeal* editor Fred Warren:

> I have just left Gene and he is in bed and about used up, not having slept for three nights from nervous exhaustion. He wishes me to ask you to

> make no more dates as he feels that it will be necessary for him after he has filled the schedule in hand to resign from the *Appeal* and take a period of complete rest. This has got to be done if he is to avoid a complete collapse. . . . His present situation is such that no human being could stand it, and a horse would break down under the load . . .
>
> I want Gene to quit speaking, writing, and everything else and take a rest for a year at least, till he has gotten himself in shape again. All his life he has been in the thick of the fight, sacrificing his home, freezing in the winter and boiling in the summer, knocking around over the railroads and laying out at nights when he ought to be in bed. He has done his share of that sort of business and he is now at an age when it is telling on him, and if the warning is not heeded he will break down utterly and we are not going to allow that if we can help it.[77]

Gene was able to answer the bell and come out swinging, however, and he spoke almost nightly throughout Indiana, Iowa, Michigan, Ohio, and Pennsylvania, ending the run with a speech before 2,000 striking streetcar workers at Labor Lyceum Hall in Philadelphia on February 23. Though physically trying, Debs was upbeat about the trip, declaring it to be "in all regards the most successful in my experience" despite the illness which marred his opening performance in Chicago. Some 50,000 new subscribers were added to the *Appeal's* rolls, Debs indicated, with Socialist Party locals energized by the experience.[78]

ↄ

After breaking over the issue of industrial unionism in 1905, relations between Debs and his former ally in the Social Democratic Party, Milwaukee publisher Victor L. Berger, remained strained, the attitudes of both men bitter. The atrophy of the Industrial Workers of the World simultaneously with the steady growth in the size and influence of the American Federation of Labor-friendly Social Democratic Party of Wisconsin certain must have grated upon Debs, and the success of the electoral movement in Milwaukee figured precious little in Debs's speeches or journalism in this period. The first real watershed for the Milwaukee movement came in the spring of 1909 when Christian socialist Emil Seidel was elected to the Milwaukee city council in the April election. Seidel garnered more than 8,500 votes in a four-sided race, winning his seat with a healthy plurality of 1,000.[79] Victor Berger's wife Meta and *Social-Democratic Herald* editor Fred Heath were both elected to the city's five member school board at the same time, adding to the triumphant mood.[80]

Enthusiasm was rampant, with the Milwaukee Musicians Union assembling a band to salute Seidel outside his home, with local socialists joining the spontaneous party to sing along.[81]

The celebration grew even more frenzied in the Milwaukee city election held in April 1910, in a massive sweep that saw Seidel elected mayor by a large plurality, Daniel W. Hoan chosen as city attorney, and a resounding 21 of 35 seats on the city council filled by members of the Social Democratic Party of Wisconsin. Local party chief Victor Berger was enthusiastic:

> This is truly a historic moment, not only for the Social Democratic Party, but for America. It is the first time in the history of this country that the socialists have carried a large city.
>
> The Social Democrats of Milwaukee naturally feel proud of this. And anyone who witnessed the jubilee of the socialists at West Side Turner Hall and at the Freie Gemeinde [on April 5]—a night never to be forgotten by those that were there—must admit that the Social Democrats of Milwaukee were the happiest citizens in America.
>
> * * *
>
> Our party is by necessity a city party, first and foremost. We have to win our cities first before we can win in a state, and then in the country at large. I know of no American city where the socialist movement is so thoroughly enlightened and so class conscious as in Milwaukee. Years of continuous literature propaganda has made it so. Therefore, I am glad that this first victory came to Milwaukee, as I am sure we will take care of the situation to the credit of the city and the international movement.[82]

Debs seems to have been unmoved by the victory. He seems to have ignored the Milwaukee triumph of April 1910 entirely, spending not a word in print on the matter in his *Appeal to Reason* journalism; nor has any correspondence mentioning the Wisconsin win survived the subsequent century. What we do know with documented certainty is that Debs continued to hold newspaper publisher Victor Berger in low regard, writing in January 1910 to his friend Fred Warren that

> Berger is a coward. When he is attacked, promptly Elizabeth Thomas,[83] [Carl D.] Thompson,[84] and [Winfield] Gaylord[85] appear to tell what a big man he is. I can see it all from here. When [a hostile] *Appeal* article appeared Berger turned purple and green, sputtered like a coyote with the colic, and ordered Miss Thomas forthwith to get out the heavy artillery. Of course, the German movement is the only article. What is done in

> Germany is the only thing. So Berger's cabinet at once floods the socialist press with what has been done in Germany and how big a man Berger is. . . . No Berger, no socialist movement! That's the logic. The fact is that Berger needs and sorely needs the prestige of socialist office in his business. Without that he would cut a very small figure and well does he know it.[86]

The year 1910 was, in short, a resounding success for the electorally oriented socialists of Milwaukee, who had elected a mayor, a majority of the city's governing common council, and a representative to Congress. They would never repeat the feat again.[87] The victories marked a particular high water mark for Milwaukee party boss Victor L. Berger, but secretly cut Debs to the quick, inspiring him to write a biting criticism of electoral opportunism, "Trouble Ahead," the piece with which this volume closes. Written late in 1910 for Charles H. Kerr's glossy monthly, the *International Socialist Review,* the piece ultimately saw print in that magazine's January 1911 edition.

General Series Notes

The Selected Works of Eugene V. Debs will present his most important writings in six chronological volumes. Each book will include a brief introduction touching upon the major activities of Debs's life during the period of coverage and pointing toward key elements of his evolving thought. Archaic spelling, idiosyncratic punctuation, misspelled names, misquoted sources, and typographical errors appearing in the original published versions have not been treated as sacrosanct, but rather have been silently corrected and standardized for consistency and readability. A few words from defective source documents that had to be guessed from context are provided within square brackets, as are substantive clarifications provided by the editors. The inclusion of full articles rather than excerpts has been given high priority, although a few items have been shortened for reasons of space or clarity. These editorial alterations have been marked by ellipses (. . .) for very short deletions and asterisks (* * *) for longer content removals. Debs himself periodically used a question mark inside parentheses to denote irony about the apparent misapplication of a word or phrase. This editorial oddity has been retained.

Titles of articles and speeches as they appeared in the press varied greatly from publication to publication. Those appearing in *Locomotive Firemen's Magazine* were written by Debs himself and have been generally retained without change unless the same title was used multiple times, as Debs was wont to do. A few Debs-generated titles that are particularly nondescriptive of actual content have been revised. The titles of articles and speeches appearing in publications edited by others have been either kept or rewritten for clarity as deemed most appropriate; those appearing previously in reprints of Debs's works have generally been retained to avoid confusion. Whenever titles have changed, original names are also provided, along with other publication information.

Material has been chosen with a view to illustrating the evolution of Debs's thinking. Mundane contemporary affairs have been accorded low priority; matters touching on the events of the broader labor movement and society at large have been given closest attention. No material has been omitted or deleted for ideological reasons. We emphasize that Gene Debs was neither a saint nor a savant, but rather an evolving human being who was a product of his times, exhibiting at various times deficiencies of memory and a tendency toward self-glorification; ethnic, racial, and gender biases; and ideological inconsistencies. We have attempted to chronicle these foibles and flaws rather than hide them through tendentious selection of content.

Debs never wrote a full-length book in his lifetime, nor did he attempt to compile his memoirs. All of his literary output was of an oratorical or journalistic nature, with the great majority of this material published as newspaper or magazine articles or speeches reproduced in pamphlet form. The editors attempted to review at least cursorily every known article, speech, or pamphlet by Debs for the time period covered by this volume. This goal was more or less successfully realized in this instance, with no more than three or four of the approximately 510 Debs items cataloged for the time period of *Volume 4* escaping our grasp, none of which seeming to be imperative.

While the editors have received no financial support from any individual or institution in the preparation of this volume, they have nevertheless benefited immensely from the activity of others in the world of Debs scholarship, especially including those whose work is listed in the footnotes below. The editors also wish to thank Benjamin Kite of the Eugene V. Debs Foundation; historians Robert Bills, Paul Buhle, John Holmes, Micki Morahn, and Steve Rossignol; writer Cindy Ringer; archivist D. J. Alperovitz; and labor ephemera collectors Richard Grossman, Vince Keuter, and Wayne Standley for lending information and expertise.

Our good friend Marty Goodman of the Riazanov Digital Library Project has aided our investigation of certain rare publications. Additionally, the importance of radical booksellers to the cause of independent scholarship should constantly be reaffirmed, with John Durham and Alexander Akin of Bolerium Books in San Francisco and Lorne Bair of Lorne Bair Books of Winchester, Virginia, worthy of particular commendation. We also thank Nisha Bolsey, Amelia Ayrelan Iuvino, Rachel Cohen, Sam Smith, and Eric Kerl, who skillfully handled the manuscript and layout for Haymarket Books, as well as the entire Haymarket editorial board for their unflinching support of the Debs project.

The outstanding contribution to Debs scholarship was made by historian J. Robert Constantine and Tamiment Library archivist Gail Malmgreen, with their twenty-one-reel microfilm collection and printed guide, *The Papers of Eugene V. Debs, 1834–1945*. The editors note their debt to this pioneering effort to chronicle and collect the speeches, articles, and correspondence of Gene Debs. It is impossible to imagine the successful completion of this project without such an expert plowing of the field having previously been made. This material has already been harvested by Mr. Constantine for his outstanding three-volume collection, *Letters of Eugene V. Debs,* published by University of Illinois Press in 1990. The editors hope that these volumes edited by Mr. Constantine will occupy every shelf next to the volumes of the *Selected Works of Eugene V. Debs* and be viewed as integral parts of the same project.

It is a matter of regret that Bob Constantine, the dean of Debs studies, died in 2017 at the age of 93, before the editors were able to communicate news of this project to him. It is to his memory that this series is dedicated.

Notes

1. Hermann Schlütter, *Die Internationale in Amerika* (Chicago: German Federation of the Socialist Party, 1918), 88; cited in David Saposs, *Left Wing Unionism* (New York: International Publishers, 1926), 10.
2. Schlütter, *Die Internationale in Amerika*, 488, in Saposs, *Left Wing Unionism*, 10.
3. Saposs, *Left Wing Unionism*, 10–11.
4. Vincent St. John, *The IWW: Its History, Structure, and Methods* (Chicago: IWW Publishing Bureau, 1911), 3.
5. Debs, "Letter to Clarence Smith on the Forthcoming Meeting to Plan the Foundation of a New Industrial Union," December 23, 1904, this volume.
6. Frank Bohn, "Preliminary Explosion or Volcanic Rumblings Coming to a Head," *Weekly People*, vol. 14, no. 43 (January 21, 1905), 1.
7. For the complete text of the manifesto calling for the foundation of the Industrial Workers of the World, see William D. Haywood, *Bill Haywood's Book: The Autobiography of William D. Haywood* (New York: International Publishers, 1929), 75–8.
8. Debs, "I Can Imagine Nothing to Change My Mind: Letter to Victor L. Berger" (April 13, 1905), this volume.
9. See "What the Matter Is In America and What to Do About It: An Interview with Debs by Lincoln Steffens" (July 12, 1908), this volume, appendix.
10. Disrespect between Berger and Debs was deep and mutual. Around New Year's 1910, while en route to an important speech in New York City, Victor Berger wrote his wife Meta that "Debs has gone to pieces entirely—he has learned nothing in 15 years and is repeating parrotlike the same old speech." See Victor L. Berger to Meta Berger, circa January 1, 1910, in Michael E. Stevens, ed., *The Family Letters of Victor and Meta Berger, 1894–1929* (Madison: State Historical Society of Wisconsin, 1995), 103–4.

    For his part, Debs railed against the newly elected Socialist congressman in a November 1910 letter to Carl D. Thompson: "You are absolutely right when you say that at heart Berger is an aristocrat and not a socialist. He holds the common run in as much contempt as did Alexander Hamilton or as does Theodore Roosevelt or any other rank individualist. Berger really feels he is made of superior clay and that the tremendous responsibility of making the socialist movement rests upon his shoulders, and his egotism increases and his vanity inflates as he progresses in power. . . . To me there is something shockingly abhorrent about the boss in the socialist movement. He belongs to capitalism and its exploiting mechanism and rotten parties. There is no earthly place for him in the democratic party of the working class." See Eugene V. Debs to Carl D. Thompson, November 26, 1910, in J. Robert Constantine, ed., *Letters of Eugene V. Debs: Volume 1, 1874–1912* (Carbondale: University of Illinois Press, 1990), 393–4.
11. Haywood, *Bill Haywood's Book*, 182.
12. Haywood, *Bill Haywood's Book*, 183.
13. Debs, "Speech at the Founding Convention of the Industrial Workers of the World" (June 29, 1905), this volume.

14. Debs, "Speech at the Founding Convention of the Industrial Workers of the World" (June 29, 1905), this volume.
15. D. Burgess, "The Industrial Union Meets," *Montana News*, vol. 3, no. 42 (July 5, 1905), 1.
16. "State News," *Ward County Independent* [Minot, ND], vol. 4, no. 16 (July 12, 1905), 10.
17. "In Villa Park: News and Comment Pertaining to Chautauqua," *Streator Daily Free Press*, vol. 25, whole no. 7542 (July 6, 1905), 5.
18. Distortion caused by the surfeit of available material from Debs's IWW tour has been addressed by reprinting only the two best examples of these speeches and apportioning the approximately 6 percent of total pages thereby saved to other material. See "Craft Unionism: Address at Aurora Hall, Chicago" (November 23, 1905) and "Industrial Unionism: Address at Grand Central Palace, New York City" (December 10, 1905), this volume.
19. Tour dates and speech titles have been compiled from the local press, microfilm of which is being digitized and compiled into a massive searchable database accessible through Newspapers.com. As of August 1, 2025, there were 1.1 billion searchable newspaper pages available through this resource—a number which will continue to expand over time, making possible an even more precise reckoning of Debs's daily activities.
20. William E. Trautmann (1869–1940) was a German-American socialist activist and editor of the St. Louis *Brauer Zeitung* [Brewer's Newspaper], organ of the United Brewery Workers' Union. In 1905 Trautmann was one of the key organizers of the Industrial Workers of the World and co-author of the group's seminal "Industrial Union Manifesto." Trautmann was an early opponent of the administration of Industrial Workers of the World President Charles Sherman, allying himself with the opposition headed by syndicalist Vincent St. John. He worked as an organizer until 1912, when he broke with the IWW to join the rival Workers' International Industrial Union, the so-called "Detroit IWW." In later years he left radical politics altogether, living in California and writing several books espousing moderate labor reform.
21. Charles O. Sherman, "President's Report," in *Proceedings of the Second Annual Convention of the Industrial Workers of the World: Held at Chicago, Illinois, Sept. 17 to Oct. 3, 1906* (Chicago: Industrial Workers of the World [Sherman faction], 1906), 42–5.
22. The convention did not employ a stenographer during this first week of factional machinations, and the official report provides only unilluminating official minutes that hint at main events in the fight between the Sherman and Trautmann-DeLeon factions.
23. David H. Grover, *Debaters and Dynamiters: The Story of the Haywood Trial* (Corvallis: Oregon State University Press, 1964), 59.
24. "Ex-Gov. Steunenberg Killed," *Montpelier Examiner*, vol. 11, no. 47 (January 5, 1906), 1.
25. Frank R. Gooding (1859–1928) was an English-born Republican politician elected governor of Idaho in November 1904. He was complicit in plans to arrest and extradite Western Federation of Miners leaders Charles Moyer, William D. Haywood, and George Pettibone outside of normal legal processes in 1906. Gooding was elected to the first of two terms in the US Senate in 1920, dying while in office.

26. "A Cowardly Crime," *Caldwell Tribune*, vol. 24, no. 33 (January 6, 1906), 1.
27. Aaron Walton, "Wardner, Idaho," www.westernmininghistory.com/
28. Grover, Debaters and Dynamiters, 60–1.
29. Philip S. Foner, *History of the Labor Movement in the United States: Volume 4, The Industrial Workers of the World, 1905–1917* (New York: International Publishers, 1965), 41–2.
30. For Orchard's own story, see Harry Orchard, *The Confessions and Autobiography of Harry Orchard* (New York: McClure Co., 1907). This tale was revisited many years after the fact as Harry Orchard with LeRoy Edwin Froom, *Harry Orchard: The Man God Made Again* (Nashville, TN: Southern Publishing Association, 1952).
31. Foner, *History of the Labor Movement in the United States: Volume 4*, 45.
32. Haywood, *Bill Haywood's Book*, 192–3.
33. Debs, "Arouse, Ye Slaves!" (March 10, 1906), this volume.
34. See Debs, "Where Daisy Sleeps" (May 1906), this volume.
35. J. A. Wayland (1854–1912), a native of Versailles, Indiana, began work in the printing trade as a young boy, saving enough money to launch his own newspaper in 1873. He moved to Pueblo, Colorado in 1881, establishing a newspaper and print shop there, booming the growing town and engaging in real estate speculation. Wayland presciently cashed out his Colorado holdings for gold just ahead of the great economic crash of 1893. The economic collapse was pivotal, causing Wayland to take up the study of socialism. He returned to Indiana and established a socialist weekly there, *The Coming Nation*, and establishing a utopian socialist community in Tennessee, the Ruskin Commonwealth Association. The colony failed to produce in accordance with its promise and Wayland departed in disgust, leaving his paper behind. He founded a new publication, the *Appeal to Reason*, in the small southeastern Kansas town of Girard. Through relentless promotion and the effort of an "Appeal Army" of dedicated volunteers, the *Appeal* eventually grew to become the largest circulation socialist newspaper of its era. Wayland committed suicide in May 1912, despondent over the death of his wife in a car accident a year earlier and emotionally exhausted by relentless legal assaults against his publication.
36. John Graham, *"Yours for the Revolution": The Appeal to Reason, 1895–1922* (Lincoln: University of Nebraska Press, 1990), 1.
37. Graham, *"Yours for the Revolution,"* 3.
38. Graham, *"Yours for the Revolution,"* 2.
39. J. A. Wayland, "A Cooperative Village," *The Coming Nation*, whole no. 31 (December 2, 1893), 3.
40. Wayland, "A Cooperative Village," 3.
41. Isaac Broome, *The Last Days of the Ruskin Cooperative Association* (Chicago: Charles H. Kerr & Co., 1902), 11.
42. Graham, *"Yours for the Revolution,"* 8.
43. Fred D. Warren (1872–1959) was a midwesterner by birth and temperament, born in Arcola, Illinois and raised in the small mining town of Rich Hill, Missouri. Wayland learned the craft of printing as a young man and converted to socialism in the course of

his reading, launching a radical newspaper called the *Bates County Critic* in 1898. He and his paper gained the attention of Wayland; in 1901 he was made managing editor of the *Appeal to Reason*. Warren played the leading role in steering the paper's content and political line until his resignation in August 1914, ostensibly for reasons of health.

44. Robert C. Overfelt, "Mexican Revolution," Handbook of Texas, Texas State Historical Association, TSHAonline.org/
45. John W. Sherman, "Revolution on Trial: The 1909 Tombstone Proceedings Against Richardo Flores Magón, Antonio Villarreal, and Librado Rivera," *Journal of Arizona History*, vol. 32, no. 2 (Summer 1991), 173–4.
46. Sherman, "Revolution on Trial," 176–7.
47. George F. Shoaf, "Tragic Story of Mexican Revolution," *Appeal to Reason*, whole no. 684 (January 9, 1909), 1.
48. Eugene V. Debs to LaFollette, March 7, 1909, in Constantine (ed.), *Letters of Eugene V. Debs: Volume 1, 1874–1912,* 299–302.
49. The "Liberty Edition" edited by Debs was dated March 6, 1909, and also featured coverage of the ongoing legal cases of *Appeal* editor Fred D. Warren and American Federation of Labor officials Samuel Gompers, Frank Morrison, and John Mitchell, free on bail on a contempt of court proceeding related to a boycott of the Buck's Stove and Range Company.
50. Eugene V. Debs to Charles W. Ervin, March 14, 1908, in Constantine (ed.), *Letters of Eugene V. Debs: Volume 1, 1874–1912*, 257–8.
51. Ben Hanford to Eugene V. Debs, May 2, 1908, in Constantine (ed.), *Letters of Eugene V. Debs: Volume 1, 1874–1912*, 263–4.
52. Seymour Stedman, "Nomination of A. M. Simons," in *National Convention of the Socialist Party Held at Chicago, Illinois May 10 to 17, 1908*, 149.
53. Debs, "I Had Hoped That My Name Would Not Be Mentioned: Telegram to Seymour Stedman" (May 14, 1908), this volume.
54. Debs, "I Would Prefer to Give My Tongue a Rest: Letter to Ben Hanford in Chicago" (May 4, 1908), this volume.
55. For his formal acceptance of the nomination, see Debs, "Telegram Accepting the 1908 Nomination for President of the United States" (May 15, 1908), this volume.
56. Algie Martin Simons (1870–1950) was a college-educated speaker and writer who became an active socialist during the 1890s. Simons was an early writer on the topic of socialism and agriculture and served as the first editor of Charles H. Kerr's monthly, the *International Socialist Review*. Although Simons initially stood on the left wing of the Socialist Party of America, he became more conservative over time, leaving the Socialist Party and becoming a functionary in the Wisconsin Loyalty League during America's entry into World War I and coming to embrace Republican conservatism. In later years he worked as an economist for the American Medical Association.
57. This was likely the first time that Debs and Berger had met face to face since their acrimonious split over the trade union question at an April 29, 1905 meeting at the Hotel Racine in Racine, Wisconsin.
58. Report of the election subcommittee, May 27, 1908, in "Minutes of the National

Executive Committee, Socialist Party, Session June 11–12, '08," *Socialist Party Official Bulletin*, vol. 4, no. 10 (June 1908), 3.

59. "Minutes of the National Executive Committee, Socialist Party, Session July 10–11, 1908," *Socialist Party Official Bulletin*, vol. 4, no. 11 (July 1908), 1.
60. "Minutes of the National Executive Committee, 1.
61. Debs, "Comrade Debs' View of the Socialist Special" (July 31, 1908), *Socialist Party Official Bulletin*, vol. 4, no. 11 (July 1908), 1.
62. "The Socialist Party's Campaign," *The Public*, vol. 11 (October 2, 1908), 635. Cited in H. Wayne Morgan, "Red Special: Eugene V. Debs and the Campaign of 1908," *Indiana Magazine of History*, vol. 54, no. 3 (September 1958), 255.
63. Eugene V. Debs to J. Maylon Barnes, May 31, 1912, in Constantine, ed., *Letters of Eugene V. Debs: Volume 1, 1874–1912*, 476–7.
64. McAlister Coleman, *Eugene V. Debs: A Man Unafraid* (New York: Greenburg, 1930), 246.
65. Theodore Debs, *Sidelights: Incidents in the Life of Debs* (Terre Haute, IN: Marguerite Debs Cooper/Eugene V. Debs Foundation, 1973), 25–6.
66. See Debs, "The New Emancipation: Campaign Speech at the Hippodrome, New York City" (October 4, 1908), this volume.
67. Eugene V. Debs to Morris, October 15, 1908, in Constantine, ed., *Letters of Eugene V. Debs: Volume 1, 1874–1912*, 285.
68. "Debs Talks to Wild Throng," *Chicago Tribune*, vol. 67, no. 263 (November 2, 1908), 4.
69. "Eugene V. Debs Cannot Come to Fort Collins," *Weekly Courier* [Fort Collins], vol. 32, no. 3, whole no. 1615 (June 23, 1909), 9.
70. "Socialist Encampment," *Daily Oklahoman* (Oklahoma City), vol. 16, no. 100 (August 12, 1904), 5. This three-day event, taking place prior to Oklahoma statehood, was held under the joint auspices of the Socialist Party organizations of the Oklahoma and Indian territories.
71. "Debs Will Speak," *Waurika News* (Waurika, OK), vol. 7, no. 42 (June 25, 1909), 10.
72. For an ad promoting one of these events, see, for example "5 Days Socialist State Encampment," *Snyder Signal-Star* (Snyder, OK), vol. 7, no. 31 (July 16, 1909), 1.
73. For a daily schedule of one of these five-day Oklahoma state socialist encampments, see "Socialists Hold Sway, Great Crowd Attending," *Ardmore Morning Democrat*, vol. 4, no. 69 (September 1, 1909), 1.
74. *Socialist Party Official Bulletin* (Chicago), vol. 6, no. 8 (April 1910), 4.
75. *Socialist Party Official Bulletin*, vol. 7, no. 5 (January 1911), 3.
76. The Socialist Party of Oklahoma would remain one of the pillars of the Socialist Party of America during the decade of the 1910s before coming to grief during the nationalist hysteria associated with US entry into World War I.
77. Theodore Debs to Fred D. Warren, January11, 1910, in Constantine, ed., *Letters of Eugene V. Debs: Volume 1, 1874–1912*, 326–7.
78. See Debs, "First Speaking Tour of 1910: A Short Report" (February 24, 1910), this volume.
79. "Seidel Led by Nearly a Thousand Votes," *Social Democratic Herald*, vol. 11, no. 51, whole no. 559 (April 17, 1909), 4.

80. "Milwaukee Goes Social-Democratic," *Social Democratic Herald*, vol. 11, no. 50, whole no. 558 (April 10, 1909), 1.
81. "Seidel Serenaded!" *Social Democratic Herald*, vol. 11, no. 50, whole no. 558 (April 10, 1909), 4.
82. Victor L. Berger, "We Will Apply the Philosophy of International Socialism to a Local Situation," *Social Democratic Herald*, vol. 12, no. 50, whole no. 610 (April 9, 1910), 1.
83. Elizabeth H. Thomas was a leading activist in the Social Democratic Party with headquarters in Chicago from Haverhill, Massachusetts. A fierce partisan, Thomas came west to Chicago about 1900, where she worked closely with Executive Secretary Theodore Debs in an unsuccessful attempt to block merger with the rival Springfield organization. She was brought to Milwaukee by Victor Berger in January 1904 to work as business manager of Berger's two German-language weeklies, *Wahrheit* and *Vorwärts*. Thomas was elected state secretary of the Social Democratic Party of Wisconsin in 1904 and remained at that post until her resignation in April 1914. Thomas remained loyal to the Socialist Party through the wartime years, finally quitting to join the Social Democratic Federation in 1936.
84. Carl D. Thompson (1870–1949) was a graduate of the Chicago Theological Seminary who headed a Congregational parish in Elgin, Illinois until his January 1902 resignation. Thompson was state organizer of the Social Democratic Party of Wisconsin from 1898 to 1901 and was elected to the Wisconsin state legislature as a socialist in 1906. Thompson was a professional functionary for the Socialist Party in its Chicago office from 1914 to 1916, heading its information department and lecture bureau. He was defeated by Adolph Germer in a 1916 bid to become executive secretary of the Socialist Party of America. Thompson later served as national secretary of the Public Ownership League, continuing in that role into the 1930s.
85. Winfield Gaylord (1870–1943) was a Christian socialist who graduated from the Chicago Theological Academy in 1889 and served as a pastor for 13 years in Methodist and Congregationalist churches in the upper Midwest. In November 1908 Gaylord was elected the first socialist state senator in Wisconsin. He was close to Victor Berger, serving together with him on the 1914 Socialist Party National Committee. He was a delegate to the 1917 Socialist national convention, where he opposed the party's strong antimilitarist position against the war. In May 1917 he denounced the party to Senator Hustings, urging the prohibition of circulation of the St. Louis Resolution. He was expelled from the Socialist Party for party treason on May 23, 1917 by the Milwaukee county central committee in a vote of 63–3.
86. Eugene V. Debs to Fred D. Warren, January 10, 1910, in Constantine, ed., *Letters of Eugene V. Debs: Volume 1, 1874–1912*, 322.
87. Edward John Muzik, "Victor L. Berger: A Biography" (PhD diss., Northwestern University, 1960), 209.

Debs lent his name and speaking talents to the establishment of the Industrial Workers of the World, a radical industrial union aiming to unite all branches of industry in a single, coordinated body. This group photo gathers the delegates and friends of the Socialist Labor Party and its associated Socialist Trade & Labor Alliance at the founding convention of the IWW in 1905.

Back row: M. P. Haggerty, Philip Veal, Max Eisenburg, J. W. Johnson, Frank A. Wilke, Herman Richter, Gustave Harworth, T. Banks, John Kennoy (Kennedy). *Second row:* Theodore Bernne, Joseph Scheidler, Mark Postelwaite, Joseph Dillon, Boris Reinstein, Benjamin Frankford, Evan J. Dillon, J. T. H. Reinley, Daniel DeLeon, Walter Goss. *Third row:* Thomas H. Jackson, Kate Eisenburg, August Gillhaus, H. J. Brimble, Samuel J. French, Mrs. M. P. Haggerty, Thomas J. Powers. *Front row:* Duncan McEachren, Paul Dinger, Octave M. Held, Carl U. Starkenburg. *(Robert Bills, SLP)*

Debs's 1905 tour on behalf of the IWW was transcribed by professional stenographers for use as four pamphlets.

The biggest news story of Debs's journalistic career involved the 1906 prosecution of Western Federation of Miners officials George Pettibone, William D. Haywood, and Charles Moyer. The trio were arrested and deported to Idaho to face charges in the 1905 assassination of former governor Frank Steunenberg. Debs rushed to the scene and with a series of wrathful articles helped move public sentiment and win the freedom of the defendants. *(Myers / Library of Congress)*

The *Appeal to Reason,* edited by Fred D. Warren, was a very successful publishing operation in the early twentieth century, with a modern printing plant in Girard, Kansas. The building was destroyed by fire in 1978.

Gene Debs—who helped raise a nephew but never had his own children—poses with the offspring of other employees of the *Appeal to Reason*. This archival print provides substantial indentification of his "little Girard comrades." ***(Appeal to Reason / Labadie Collection, University of Michigan)***

Ten Cents a Copy One Dollar a Year

THE INTERNATIONAL SOCIALIST REVIEW

Volume IX OCTOBER, 1908 Number 4

Published by CHARLES H. KERR & COMPANY, (Co-operative) Chicago, U. S. A.

Copyright 1908 by Charles H. Kerr & Company.

Above: Debs bid adieu to his wife and his comfortable home in Terre Haute and took a room in Girard to work as a writer for the weekly *Appeal to Reason* in 1907. The paper handled logistics of his ceaseless speaking tours and he delivered hundreds of speeches on their behalf.

Right: The old locomotive fireman Debs posed with the engine crew of the "Red Special" campaign train of 1908 on the cover of *The International Socialist Review,* national voice of the left wing of the Socialist Party.

The True History

Of the Pullman Strike, the Great Northern Strike and other great battles between Labor and Capital, is graphically told in this work as only Eugene V. Debs can tell it.

DEBS:

HIS LIFE, WRITINGS and SPEECHES

No American Voter

And especially if he be a workingman, can afford to neglect this fascinating story of Unionism nd Socialism, by a Presidential Candidate. A valuable addition to any library.

With a Department of Appreciations. Over 500 Pages. Six inches wide by nine inches long. Illustrated.

DEBS—THE GREATEST LABOR LEADER OF MODERN TIMES

A complete BIOGRAPHY by Debs' life-long friend and co-worker in Socialism— Stephen Marion Reynolds. WRITINGS by Mr. Debs on "How I Became a Socialist," "The Federal Government and the Chicago Strike," and scores of other subjects of interest to the workingman; SPEECHES by Mr. Debs on "Liberty," "The Socialist Party and the Working Class," and other oratorical gems, as well as "THE PRESIDENTIAL ISSUE OF 1908." APPRECIATIONS by J. A. Wayland, Eugene Field, James Whitcomb Riley, Edwin Markham, Bartholdi and other world-renowned men.

WITHOUT GUILE.

"No man ever looked into the frank, blue eyes of Eugene V. Debs but felt the thrill of seeing the open soul of a man without guilt."— J. A. Wayland.

EUGENE V. DEBS

"This is one of the greatest names of the century. No one—not even a political enemy —has ever said that Debs is not sincere to the core of his heart." —Edwin Markham.

Prices: Fine Silk Cloth, Emblematic Design in Gold and White Leaf $2.00
Leather, Half Morocco, Design All Gold Leaf, Plain Edges 2.75

QUANTITY PRICES TO AGENTS AND DEALERS:

Five or more copies Cloth Edition at $1.25 per copy. 100 copies Cloth Edition, f. o. b. Girard or Chicago, $100.00.

Send All Orders to the APPEAL TO REASON, Girard, Kansas

The first collection of Debs's selected works—*Debs: His Life, Writings and Speeches*—was published by the *Appeal* in conjunction with the 1908 presidential campaign, with the book announced with an ad published in the September 19 issue. Later Debs compilations have all borrowed heavily from this work.

DEBS

Eugene V. Debs, Socialist Candidate For President Will Speak

IN WENATCHEE

Wednesday Morning Between 7 and 8

HE WILL BE THROUGH ON THE

"RED SPECIAL"

A Whole Train at His Service, With a Brass Band of 15 Pieces.

SPEAKING OPPOSITE GREAT NORTHERN HOTEL

EVERYBODY INVITED

The Socialist Party reprised its 1904 ticket of Debs and Ben Hanford in 1908. Hanford was ill with terminal cancer, leaving the bulk of the speechmaking to the orator Debs. The back of the "Red Special" made a fine makeshift platform, around which prospective voters could congregate, with a 15-piece brass band periodically providing entertainment. Formal hall speeches capped each day.

SOCIALIST SPECIAL TRAIN

Trans-Continental Campaign Tour

EASTERN TRIP

SPEECHES AND BAND CONCERTS

Time and Place of all stops of flyer sent out by the Working-Class in its record-breaking educational effort

EUGENE V. DEBS

CANDIDATE FOR PRESIDENT and OTHER SPEAKERS and the Famous Socialist Volunteer Band will be aboard

STOPS AND EXACT TIME

SEPT. 25—FRIDAY.

Chicago—Leave 10:00 a. m., I. C. R. R.
Kankakee—Arrive 11:30 a. m., I. C. R. R.; leave 12:00 noon.
Lafayette—Arrive 3:00 p. m., I. C. R. R.; leave 3:30 p. m.
Indianapolis—Arrive 5:30 p. m., Big Four. Evening meeting.

SEPT. 26—SATURDAY.

Indianapolis—Leave 8:00 a. m.
Kokomo—Arrive 9:40 a. m., P. F. & W.; leave 10:10 a. m.
Logansport—Arrive 11:10 a. m., P. C. C. & St. L.; leave 11:40 a. m.
South Bend—Arrive 2:15 p. m., Vandalia. Evening meeting.

SEPT. 27—SUNDAY.

South Bend—Leave 9:00 a. m.
Marcellus—Arrive 10:00 a. m., Grand Trunk; leave 10:30 a. m.
Battle Creek—Arrive 11:45 a. m., Grand Trunk; leave 12:15 p. m.
Albion—Arrive 1:25 p. m., M. C. R. R.; leave 1:55 p. m.
Jackson—Arrive 2:35 p. m., M. C. R. R.; leave 3:05 p. m.
Detroit—Arrive 5:00 p. m., M. C. R. R. Evening meeting.

SEPT. 28—MONDAY.

Detroit—Leave 9:30 a. m., M. C. R. R.
Wyandotte—Arrive 9:55 a. m., M. C. R. R.; leave 10:15 a. m.
Trenton—Arrive 10:35 a. m., M. C. R. R.; leave 11:25 a. m.
Monroe—Arrive 12:00 noon, M. C. R. R.; leave 12:30 p. m.
Toledo—Arrive 1:15 p. m., M. C. R. R. Evening meeting.

SEPT. 29—TUESDAY.

Toledo—Leave 8:00 a. m.
Bowling Green—Arrive 8:40 a. m., Ohio Central; leave 9:10 a. m.
Findlay—Arrive 10:30 a. m., Ohio Central; leave 11:00 a. m.
Fostoria—Arrive 11:30 a. m., L. E. & W. R. R.; leave 12:00 noon.
Fremont—Arrive 12:50 p. m., L. E. & W. R. R.; leave 1:00 p. m.
Sandusky—Arrive 1:40 p. m., L. E. & W. R. R.; leave 2:10 p. m.
Elyria—Arrive 3:00 p. m., L. S. & M. S. Go to Lorain by trolley.
Lorain—Arrive 3:45 p. m.; leave 4:15 p. m.
Elyria—Arrive 5:00 p. m.; leave 5:30 p. m.
Cleveland—Arrive 6:15 p. m., L. S. & M. S. Evening meeting.

SEPT. 30—WEDNESDAY.

Cleveland—Leave 9:45 a. m., L. S. & M. S.
Painesville—Arrive 10:00 a. m., L. S. & M. S.; leave 10:30 a. m.
Geneva—Arrive 10:50 a. m., L. S. & M. S.; leave 11:20 a. m.
Ashtabula—Arrive 11:45 a. m., L. S. & M. S.; leave 12:50 p. m.
Conneaut—Arrive 1:10 p. m., L. S. & M. S.; leave 1:40 p. m.
Girard—Arrive 1:55 p. m., L. S. & M. S.; leave 2:45 p. m.
Erie—Arrive 3:05 p. m., L. S. & M. S. Evening meeting.

OCT. 1—THURSDAY.

Erie—Leave 9:00 a. m., L. S. & M. S.
Westfield—Arrive 9:40 a. m., L. S. & M. S.; leave 10:30 a. m.
Dunkirk—Arrive 10:50 a. m., L. S. & M. S.; leave 1:30 p. m.
Silver Creek—Arrive 1:45 p. m., L. S. & M. S.; leave 2:20 p. m.
Buffalo—Arrive 3:20 p. m., L. S. & M. S. Evening meeting.

OCT. 2—FRIDAY.

Buffalo—Leave 9:30 a. m., N. Y. C. R. R.
Lockport—Arrive 10:35 a. m., N. Y. C. R. R.; leave 11:00 a. m.
Medina—Arrive 11:30 a. m., N. Y. C. R. R.; leave 11:50 a. m.
Albion—Arrive 12:10 p. m., N. Y. C. R. R.; leave 12:40 p. m.
Rochester—Arrive 1:40 p. m., N. Y. C. R. R. Evening meeting.

OCT. 3—SATURDAY.

Rochester—Leave 8:00 a. m., N. Y. C. R. R.
Geneva—Arrive 9:45 a. m., N. Y. C. R. R.; leave 10:00 a. m.
Waterloo—Arrive 10:45 a. m., N. Y. C. R. R.; leave 11:15 a. m.
Auburn—Arrive 12:00 noon, N. Y. C. R. R.; leave 1:30 p. m.
Syracuse—Arrive 2:20 p. m., N. Y. C. R. R. Evening meeting.

OCT. 4—SUNDAY.

Syracuse—Leave 5:00 a. m., N. Y. C. R. R.
Schenectady—Arrive 8:00 a. m., N. Y. C. R. R.; leave 8:30 a. m.
Poughkeepsie—Arrive 11:15 a. m., N. Y. C. R. R.; leave 12:00 noon.
New York—Arrive 2:00 p. m., N. Y. C. R. R. Afternoon meeting.

OCT. 5—MONDAY.

New York—Leave 6:00 a. m., N. Y. N. H. & H.
Danbury—Arrive 8:00 a. m., N. Y. N. H. & H.; leave 8:30 a. m.
Waterbury—Arrive 9:30 a. m., N. Y. N. H. & H.; leave 10:00 a. m.
Westfield—Arrive 11:40 a. m., N. Y. N. H. & H.; leave 12:10 p. m.
Springfield—Arrive 12:30 p. m., B. & A. Ry.; leave 2:10 p. m.
Worcester—Arrive 3:30 p. m., B. & A. Ry.; leave 4:20 p. m.
Natick—Arrive 5:05 p. m., B. & A. Ry.; leave 5:40 p. m.
Boston—Arrive 6:20 p. m., B. & A. Ry. Evening meeting.

OCT. 6—TUESDAY.

Boston—Leave 9:05 a. m., B. & M. Ry.
Lowell—Arrive 9:45 a. m., B. & M. Ry.; leave 10:25 a. m.
Nashua—Arrive 10:50 a. m., B. & M. Ry.; leave 11:25 a. m.
Manchester—Arrive 11:55 a. m., B. & M. Ry.; leave 1:55 p. m.
Concord—Arrive 2:25 p. m., B. & M. Ry. Evening meeting.

OCT. 7—WEDNESDAY.

Concord—Leave 9:00 a. m., B. & M. Ry.
Lawrence—Arrive 10:20 a. m., B. & M. Ry.; leave 11:02 a. m.
Haverhill—Arrive 11:45 a. m., B. & M. Ry.; leave 1:15 p. m.
Lowell—Arrive 1:50 p. m., B. & M. Ry.; leave 1:55 p. m.
Walpole, Mass.—Arrive 2:55 p. m., N. Y. N. H. & H.; leave 3:25 p. m.
Franklin—Arrive 3:45 p. m., N. Y. N. H. & H.; leave 4:05 p. m.
Providence—Arrive 5:05 p. m., N. Y. N. H. & H. Evening meeting.

OCT. 8—THURSDAY.

Providence—Leave 8:55 a. m., N. Y. N. H. & H.
Plainfield—Arrive 9:45 a. m., N. Y. N. H. & H.; leave 10:10 a. m.
Willimantic—Arrive 10:40 a. m., N. Y. N. H. & H.; leave 11:30 a. m.
Manchester—Arrive 11:55 a. m., N. Y. N. H. & H.; leave 12:30 p. m.
Hartford, Conn.—Arrive 1:00 p. m., N. Y. N. H. & H.; leave 2:30 p. m.
New Britain—Arrive 2:48 p. m., N. Y. N. H. & H.; leave 3:20 p. m.
Meriden—Arrive 3:38 p. m., N. Y. N. H. & H.; leave 4:08 p. m.
New Haven—Arrive 4:35 p. m., N. Y. N. H. & H. Evening meeting.

OCT. 9—FRIDAY.

New Haven—Leave 11:45 a. m., N. Y. N. H. & H.
Woodmont—Arrive 12:00 noon, N. Y. N. H. & H.; leave 12:30 p. m.
Milford—Arrive 12:40 p. m., N. Y. N. H. & H.; leave 1:10 p. m.
Stratford—Arrive 1:20 p. m., N. Y. N. H. & H.; leave 1:50 p. m.
Bridgeport—Arrive 2:00 p. m., N. Y. N. H. & H. Evening meeting.

OCT. 10—SATURDAY.

Bridgeport—Leave 8:00 a. m., N. Y. N. H. & H.
Stamford—Arrive 8:45 a. m., N. Y. N. H. & H.; leave 9:10 a. m.
Port Chester—Arrive 9:25 a. m., N. Y. N. H. & H.; leave 9:55 a. m.
New Rochelle—Arrive 10:10 a. m., N. Y. N. H. & H.; leave 10:40 a. m.
New York—Arrive 11:15 a. m., N. Y. N. H. & H.; leave 11:20 a. m.
Jersey City—Arrive 4:20 p. m., ferry; leave 4:25 p. m.
Trenton—Arrive 6:15 p. m., C. R. R. of N. J. Evening meeting.

OCT. 11—SUNDAY.

Trenton—Leave 10:00 a. m., P. & R. Ry.
Philadelphia—Arrive 12:00 noon, P. & R. Ry. Afternoon meeting. Evening meeting at Camden, N. J.

OCT. 12—MONDAY.

Philadelphia—Leave 8:00 a. m., P. & R. Ry.
Jenkintown—Arrive 8:30 a. m., P. & R. Ry.; leave 9:00 a. m.
Hopewell—Arrive 9:45 a. m., P. & R. Ry.; leave 10:15 a. m.
Boundbrook—Arrive 10:40 a. m., P. & R. Ry.; leave 11:20 a. m.
Plainfield—Arrive 11:35 a. m., C. R. R. of N. J.; leave 12:20 p. m.
Elizabeth—Arrive 12:35 p. m., C. R. R. of N. J.; leave 1:45 p. m.
Newark—Arrive 2:25 p. m., C. R. R. of N. J. Evening meeting.

OCT. 13—TUESDAY.

Newark, N. J.—Leave 1:00 p. m., C. R. R. of N. J.
Jersey City—Arrive 1:30 p. m., C. R. R. of N. J. Evening meeting, Brooklyn.

OCT. 14—WEDNESDAY.

Jersey City—Evening meeting.

OCT. 15—THURSDAY.

Jersey City—Leave 5:30 a. m., C. R. R. of N. J.
Bethlehem—Arrive 8:00 a. m., C. R. R. of N. J.; leave 8:30 a. m.
Catasauqua—Arrive 8:50 a. m., C. R. R. of N. J.; leave 9:20 a. m.
Mauch Chunk—Arrive 10:10 a. m., C. R. R. of N. J.; leave 10:50 a. m.
Lansford—Arrive 11:15 a. m., C. R. R. of N. J.; leave 11:45 a. m.
Tamaqua—Arrive 12:00 noon, C. R. R. of N. J.; leave 12:30 p. m.
Pottsville—Arrive 1:05 p. m., P. & R. Ry.; leave 1:45 p. m.
Schuylkill Haven—Arrive 1:55 p. m., P. & R. Ry.; leave 2:25 p. m.
Hamburg—Arrive 2:50 p. m., P. & R. Ry.; leave 3:20 p. m.
Reading—Arrive 3:50 p. m., P. & R. Ry. Evening meeting.

Stops of the "Red Special" were minutely timed, concluding each evening with a hall meeting.

16 Pages

THE SPOKESMAN-REVIEW

Land Scrip for sale. For further information consult the classified "want" ads in this paper.

20TH YEAR. NO. 93. WEDNESDAY MORNING. SEPTEMBER 16, 1908. SPOKANE, WASH.

HUGHES WINS ON FIRST BALLOT

Renominated for Governor by the Republicans of New York.

AMID WILD CHEERING

Choice Made Unanimous on Motion of His Leading Opponents.

SPECTACLE IS DRAMATIC

Intense Enthusiasm When the Votes of New York and Kings Counties Were Given to Hughes.

SARATOGA, N. Y., Sept. 15.—The republican state ticket:

For governor—Charles E. Hughes of New York (renominated).

For lieutenant governor—Horace White of Onondaga.

For secretary of state—Samuel S. Koenig of New York.

For attorney general—Edward R. ...

LAZY WORKMAN IS WANTED

One Who Can Do Nothing All Day and Not Get Tired.

PORTLAND, Ore., Sept. 15.—The North Bank railroad wants a workman who is lazy, the lazier the better. In choosing the man for the place laziness will be hired. A man is wanted who will sit in the sun all day and not get tired. A man is wanted to whom the day will not seem too long, no matter if he has nothing at all to do. The man is wanted to sit on the drawbridge of the Oregon slough span of the new Columbia river bridge and start the motor by pressing an electric button whenever boats want to pass the draw.

It is estimated that steamers will want to pass up the Oregon slough as often as perhaps twice a year. There is no traffic on the slough now and never has been any to speak of.

TAFT ON NEGRO QUESTION

DELIVERS FIRST CAMPAIGN SPEECH TO COLORED MEN.

Condemns Mob Violence and Praises Advance of Race Since the War.

CINCINNATI, O., Sept. 15.—Candidate William H. Taft delivered an address tonight to an audience of ministers comprising the Ohio conference of the African Methodist church, the first speech of his campaign to negroes. The address was not political, but gave a clear outline of the sympathetic understanding and feeling entertained for ...

LOOK OUT FOR YOUR COMBUSTIBLES.

HE JARRED CREAM ON MILK

Loafed on Carpet Beating Job and Wife Scolded.

BELLINGHAM, Wash., Sept. 15.—Maintaining that his wife has a mean disposition, in that she scolded him for disturbing the cream on the milk and that she grew indignant because he ceased beating a carpet during housecleaning time for a few minutes while he went to visit, John W. Godfrey, a schoolteacher, started suit in the superior court for divorce from Anna M. Godfrey. His wife today filed a demurrer to the complaint, alleging that it does not set forth sufficient facts to constitute a cause of action and asking temporary alimony.

CONNELL FLAME SWEPT

FIRE DESTROYS EAST SIDE OF NORTH MAIN STREET.

Big Mercantile Company and Bachelors' Club Among the Heavy Losers.

CONNELL, Wash., Sept. 15.—Fire originating in a restaurant in the rear of the Office saloon tonight about 9 o'clock, caused a $25,000 loss. From the Office saloon the fire spread north to the warehouse of the Campbell Mercantile company, which was full of farming machinery, thence north to the brick building used for hardware. South from the saloon the fire spread to the building occupied by the Bachelors' club then south to the Home Cafe building. All but brick buildings were completely burned and the brick were gutted. Most of the merchandise ...

"NO LONGER FEAR ME," SAYS BRYAN

Clerk and Tradesman, He Believes, Think He Is Harmless.

STIRS UP THE EAST

Arouses Great Enthusiasm of Crowds in New Jersey Cities.

CONTINUES FIRE ON TAFT

Republican Nominee, He Declares, Bids for Votes on the Recommendation of Roosevelt.

TRENTON, N. J., Sept. 15.—Pouring hot shot into Mr. Taft and the republican party at every point where he stopped, W. J. Bryan tonight, in this city, concluded a strenuous day of campaigning in New Jersey, following a few hours in Philadelphia, where, in front of a newspaper office and before an enthusiastic throng, he arraigned ...

GRAND MARAIS GIRDLED BY FIRE

KILLS DOG PAPER CARRIER

Wallace Trolo Crushes Faithful Cocker Spaniel.

ROBBER, TRAPPED, FELLS MAN, HIKES

NAIL WOUND MAY KILL TWO

THE SOCIALIST PARADE

During the 1908 presidential campaign, Debs's leadership of the 1894 American Railway Union strike was neither forgotten nor forgiven by the conservative press of the West. On September 16, with the "Red Special" traversing the Pacific Northwest, the Spokane *Spokesman-Review* went "page one above the fold" with a large anti-Debs political drawing.

That same day the Portland *Daily Oregonian*, a Republican paper, ran an anti-Debs cartoon of their own, featuring Debs in prison garb and French Liberty cap, bearing the flaming torch of revolution. In his right hand is held an inverted "full dinner pail," a common emblem of the Republican Party since 1896, emblazoned with sarcastic slogans denigrating the Socialist program.

Marguerite "Daisy" Debs
(1828–1906)

Victor L. Berger
(1860–1929)

Elizabeth H. Thomas
(18XX–19XX)

Theodore Debs
(1864–1945)

Julius A. Wayland
(1854–1912)

Fred D. Warren
(1872–1959)

Harry Orchard
(1866–1954)

Frank Steunenberg
(1861–1905)

William Jennings Bryan
(1860–1925)

A formal portrait from the 1908 presidential campaign. (*Wilshire's Magazine*)

1905

Letter to Clarence Smith on the Forthcoming Meeting to Plan a New Industrial Union†

December 23, 1904

Terre Haute, Ind., Dec. 23, 1904

Mr. Clarence Smith,[1]
Chicago, Ill.

My Dear Comrade:—

Your several favors have been received and noted. I have been unable to answer sooner on account of illness which has kept me confined to my room during the last several weeks and from which I am but slowly recovering. The doctor has just informed me that I shall probably have to go South before there shall be any appreciable recuperation of my strength.

I shall not be able to attend the meeting on the second [January 2, 1905].[2] I keenly regret this for I had counted on being with you and in giving such assistance as I could to the work of organizing that is to be undertaken along new and progressive lines. In spite of my best will this is now impossible.

For a good many years I have been working without regard to myself and in all my life I have never known what it is to have a rest. The last year's work was in many respects the hardest of my life. I spent myself too freely and have now reached the point when I must give up for a time as the doctor warned me that my nerves are worn down and that I am threatened with collapse.

There is nothing the matter with me except that I am compelled to let go for a time and so I have had to cancel all my engagements for the immediate future. How soon I may be able to resume I do not know, but I think I shall have to quit the public platform entirely, or almost so, for a year or such matter. There are too many demands constantly upon me and I shall have to turn them aside until I can get myself in physical condition to resume my activities.

† Published in William E. Trautmann (ed.), *Proceedings of the First Convention of the Industrial Workers of the World: Founded at Chicago, June 27–July 8, 1905* (New York: New York Labor News, 1905), 98–99. Not included in J. Robert Constantine (ed.), *Letters of Eugene V. Debs: Volume 1, 1874–1912* (Urbana: University of Illinois Press, 1990).

Under any other circumstances I should have considered it a privilege as well as a pleasure to attend your meeting.

Please find draft enclosed covering the amount you were kind enough to advance to me. Please accept my warm thanks for the favor.

Profoundly regretting my inability to be with you and hoping the meeting may be fruitful of all the good results anticipated, I remain

Yours faithfully,
E. V. Debs

Political Evolution and the Socialist Mission†

January 14, 1905

Political parties, like all other human institutions, are subject to the laws of evolution. The Republican Party of Theodore Roosevelt is vastly different from the Republican Party of Abraham Lincoln. The Democratic Party retains only the name given it by its founders. Once divided upon vital issues, these two parties are now so nearly akin to each other that the great trusts in control of the government are supremely indifferent as to whether the one or the other succeeds to power. In the next few years they will become one, or, at least, the dominant elements of both will unite in the same party. The evolution of capital and labor will make this inevitable.

Political parties express the material interests of those who compose them. Great economic issues divide the people politically and determine their party alignment. In the development of the present capitalist system, society has been mainly divided into capitalists and wage workers. Between these two economic classes there is a war. This conflict is the vital and paramount political issue of the day and upon this issue the people who have the intelligence to understand it are dividing according to their material interests.

† Originally written for the Hearst newspaper chain, which apparently did not run the piece. Published as "The Mission of Socialism" in *Social Democratic Herald* [Milwaukee, WI], vol. 7, no. 37, whole no. 337 (January 14, 1905), 1.

The late Senator Hanna[3] had the political foresight to discern the approaching party alignment on the basis of Labor vs. Capital and warned the Republican Party that its next great struggle would be with socialism.

The Socialist Party is the child of the class struggle. It was born of the necessity of the working class and is the party of that class as against the capitalist class.

The labor question is essentially a political question.

The capitalist class rule because they have control of government. The working class are preparing to profit by their example. Numerically they are overwhelmingly in the majority. They have simply to unite and act together politically as a class to put themselves in control of government and emancipate themselves from wage-slavery.

At the last election this working class party asserted its national power. Henceforward the working class are a distinct factor of increasing influence and portentous meaning in the politics of the nation.

Superficial observers express their surprise and conclude that it is but a flash on the political horizon and that the Socialist Party will soon go the way of all "reform" parties. Their delusion will soon be dispelled. As the contest proceeds they will note that the Socialist Party is a party of revolution, not of reform; that it stands for the revolutionary idea of collective ownership of the means of wealth production and the overthrow of the wage system and that no reform of the present order of society, however radical or sweeping it may be claimed to be, will satisfy its class-conscious supporters now counted by hundreds of thousands and soon to be numbered by millions.

Moreover, the Socialist Party is founded in the bedrock principles of scientific socialism. It understands the process of social evolution and philosophically prosecutes its propaganda and bides its time. It deludes itself with no promise of premature victory. It has no itching for office. Spoils have no temptation for it. This revolutionary party has but one mission and that is the political unity of the working class to wrest the government from the capitalistic class as the necessary means of abolishing the capitalist system and achieving industrial freedom and social justice.

This party knows no such word as fusion. The merest hint of compromise is rejected with scorn and indignation. No concessions that any capitalist party might offer would turn the Socialist Party the breadth of a hair from the clear-cut course through which it is hewing its way to ultimate victory.

The Social Democracy is composed of working men and women who have come into consciousness of their class interests. It is a party of thinkers and the only party in which the rank and file are supreme. This party has no use for a political Moses and can never be misled or sold out by ignorant or corrupt leaders.

The shibboleth of the movement is: "Workingmen of all countries unite; you have nothing to lose but your chains; you have a world to gain." Since these great words flashed from the lips of Karl Marx half a century ago, they have been caught up by the words of one nation after another, until the international socialist movement now girdles the globe and more than 8 million wage earners are keeping step to the pulse beats of their coming emancipation, which they know full well can be achieved only by themselves.

The present economic conditions are a denial of peace and order and if they had tongues would cry out in protest and hail the impending change. The extremest wealth and most abject poverty run riot side by side. Periodical industrial depression turns thousands of workers into loafers, vagabonds, tramps, outcasts, and criminals. Everything is done for profit. The very machine that labor invents to lighten its burden becomes in this system the means of throwing it into the street as a useless commodity, to find its way at last into the gulf of hell.

Private ownership of the means of life has reduced millions to hopeless poverty, ignorance, vice, and crime.

In the light of Colorado,[4] Fall River,[5] and the Packingtown[6] hells, what supreme hardihood to charge socialism with breaking up the home, disrupting the family, polluting the marriage relation, and destroying the religious life of the people! These things are being done at an appalling rate every hour in the day in the very system these false accusers are supporting and of which they are the pliant tools or the miserable mercenaries.

What is it that socialism proposes? Simply that the tools workingmen made and use and upon which their very lives depend shall be owned by themselves that they may fully produce the things that are required to keep themselves and their families in comfort and health. This is what socialism means, and when it comes to pass all the world will be the better for it.

Frances Willard,[7] great soul that she was, understood it all clearly when she declared that socialism and only socialism would put an end to intemperance and poverty. The trend of the evolution is toward socialism. The economic basis of society is shaping for the change. A new social order is dawning. The centralization of capital and the organization of labor are paving the way to the socialist republic. Capitalism and competition have had their day. Socialism and cooperation are next in order. This will mean society free from class rule and all the world at peace.

Very simple is the program of the Socialist Party: the organization of the working class for political conquest. When the working class succeeds to power, the rest will follow as a matter of course. The capital of the country will have been completely centralized, the middle class decimated, and competition practically eliminated, and at this point the people will be ready for the transfer of the means of production from private hands to the people in their collective capacity.

The sooner the trusts dispossess the people, the sooner will the people dispossess the trusts.

Then exploitation of class by class will cease—rent, interest, and profit will be no more. Wealth will be produced by social labor in such abundance as to satisfy all human wants. Then leisure, light, virtue, and joy instead of idleness, darkness, misery, and death.

A new era will dawn in the destiny of the race. In the words of Engels, "mankind will rise from the kingdom of necessity to the kingdom of freedom."[8]

Obstacles there will be, and many of them, but however formidable they may be, they will have to yield to the international revolutionary movement of the working class to abolish the last form of industrial servitude and dedicate the world to freedom and joy.

Women: To Get What Is Due, You Must Take It[†]

January 14, 1905

Dear Comrade[9]:—

Your favor of the 1st [January 1, 1905] has been read with special interest. There is but one thing for the women to do, and that is for them to come to the front and take hold without waiting for an invitation. If they get what is due them, they will have to take it. If they wait to be coaxed, they still have a dreary, weary siege before them.

† Published as "A Letter from Debs" in *Appeal to Reason* [Girard, KS], whole no. 476 (January 14, 1905), 1.

Many benighted women, like chattel slaves, resist all attempts to achieve their freedom. Socialist women ought to realize that their place is in the ranks, and that where socialist men are and have duties and responsibilities, there socialist women should be also, and any attempt at discrimination, whatever its motive or character, should be resented by the united voice of women.

If socialism does not mean equal rights, equal opportunities, and equal freedom of the sexes, it is a meaningless thing, and if I had any such conception of it I would reject it as a scorned and hateful thing.

It is unfortunately true that some socialists are still tainted with the barbaric doctrine that the brand of inferiority has been placed by the creative power upon the brow of womanhood. It is false and abhorrent to every sane and sensible being—entirely consonant with capitalist despotism, but totally at war with socialist philosophy.

You are right, and you have only to stand your ground and win.

Believe me, with best wishes,

Yours fraternally,
E. V. Debs

The Socialist Party and Woman's Freedom †

January 14, 1905

The Socialist Party is the party of the whole working class—men and women. It proposes that woman shall have every right that man enjoys. At present woman is not merely economically enslaved, but she is politically mute and dumb.

The Socialist Party proposes that woman shall be economically free. In the present society she must be provided for—must be supported. What does this mean? It means that she is a dependent, in economic servitude.

In a sane state of society, rationally organized, woman would be able to provide for herself. She would stand erect in the innate purity of her sex, and

† Untitled message written for a special women's issue of *Appeal to Reason,* whole no. 476 (January 14, 1905), 1.

she would not be compelled, if she happened to be the daughter of poverty, to exchange her womanhood for shelter. In marriage love would be the only consideration, and then we would not have 65,000 divorces in a single year in the United States.

The Earth for All†

January 14, 1905

The only worker who has an excuse to keep out of the social democratic movement is the unfortunate fellow who is ignorant and does not know better. He does not know what socialism is. That is his misfortune. But that is not all, nor the worst of it. He thinks he knows what it is.

In his ignorance he has taken the word of another for it, whose interest it is to keep him in darkness. So he continues to march with the Republican Party or shout with the Democratic Party, and he no more knows why he is a Republican or a Democrat than he knows why he is not a Socialist. It is impossible for a workingman to contemplate the situation and the outlook and have any intelligent conception of the trend and meaning of things without becoming a socialist.

Consider for a moment the beastly debasement to which womanhood is subject in capitalist society. She is simply the property of man to be governed by him as may suit his convenience. She does not vote, she has no voice and must bear silent witness to her legally ordained "inferiority." She has to compete with men in the factories and workshops and store and her inferiority is taken advantage of to make her work at still lower wages than the male slave gets who works at her side. As an economic dependent, she is compelled to sacrifice the innate refinement, the inherent purity and nobility of her sex, and for a pallet of straw she marries the man she does not love.

The debauching effect of the capitalist system upon womanhood is accurately registered in the divorce court and the house of shame. In socialism

† Published in *Labor,* January 14, 1905, unspecified page. Reprinted as "The Workers' Need and the Socialist Demand," in *The Worker* [New York], vol. 17, no. 22 (August 31, 1907), 6.

women would stand forth the equal of man—all the avenues would be open to her and she would naturally find her fitting place and rise from the low plane of menial servility to the dignity of ideal womanhood. Breathing the air of economic freedom amply to provide for herself in socialist society, we may be certain that the cruel injustice that is now perpetrated upon her sex and the degradations that result from it will disappear forever.

Consider again the barren prospect of the average boy who faces the world today. If he is the son of a workingman, his father is able to do little in the way of giving him a start. His father has no influence and can get no preferred employment for him at the expense of some other boy, so he thankfully accepts any kind of service that he may be allowed to perform.

How hard it is to find a place for that boy of ours!

"What shall we do with Johnnie and Nellie?" is the question of the anxious mother long before they are ripe for the labor market.

"The child is weak, you know," continues the nervous, loving little mother, "and can't do hard work; and I feel dreadfully worried about him."

What a picture! Yet so common that the multitude do not see it. This mother, numbered by the thousands many times over, instinctively understands the capitalist system, feels its cruelty, and dreads its approaching horrors which cast their shadows upon her tender, loving heart. Nothing can be sadder than to see the mother take the boy she bore by the hand and start to town with him to peddle him off as merchandise to someone who has use for a child-slave. To know just how that feels, one must have had precisely that experience.

The mother looks down so fondly and caressingly upon her boy; and he looks up into her eyes so timidly and appealingly as she explains his good points to the businessman or factory boss, who in turn inspects the lad and interrogates him to verify his mother's claim, and finally informs them that they may call again the following week, but that he does not think that he can use the boy.

Well, what finally becomes of the boy? He is now grown, his mother's worry is long since ended, as the grass grows green where she sleeps—and he, the boy? Why he's a factory hand—a hand, mind you, and he gets a dollar and a quarter a day when the factory is running.

He is an industrial life prisoner—no pardoning power for him in the capitalist system. No sweet home, no beautiful wife, no happy children, no books, no flowers, no comrades, no love, no joy for him.

Just a hand! A human factory hand! Think of a hand with a soul in it.

In the capitalist system the soul has no business. It cannot produce profit by any process of capitalist calculation. The working hand is what is needed for the capitalist's tool and so the human must be reduced to a hand.

No head, no heart, no soul—simply a hand. A thousand hands to one brain—the hands of the workingmen, the brain of the capitalist. A thousand dumb animals in human form, a thousand slaves in the fetters of ignorance, their heads having run to hands—all these owned and worked and fleeced by one stock-dealing, profit-mongering capitalist.

This is capitalism!

And this system is supported alternately by the Republican Party and the Democratic Party. These two capitalist parties relieve each other in support of the capitalist system, while the capitalist system relieves the working class of what they produce.

A thousand hands to one head is the abnormal development of the capitalist system. A thousand workingmen turned into hands to develop and gorge and decorate one capitalist paunch!

This brutal order of things must be overthrown. The human race was not born to degeneracy.

A thousand heads have grown for every thousand pairs of hands; a thousand hearts throb in testimony of the unity of heads and hands; and a thousand souls, though crushed and mangled, burn in protest and are pledged to redeem a thousand men.

Heads and hands, hearts and souls, are the heritage of all. Full opportunity for full development is the inalienable right of all.

He who denies it is a tyrant; he who does not demand it is a coward; he who is indifferent to it is a slave; he who does not desire it is dead.

The earth for all the people—that is the demand.

The collective ownership and control of industry and its democratic management in the interest of all the people—that is the demand.

The elimination of rent, interest, and profit and the production of wealth to satisfy the wants of all the people—that is the demand.

Cooperative industry in which all shall work together in harmony as the basis of a new social order, a higher civilization, a real republic—that is the demand.

The end of class struggles and class rule, of master and slave, of ignorance and vice, of poverty and shame, of cruelty and crime; the birth of freedom, the dawn of brotherhood, the beginning of man—that is the demand.

That is socialism!

The Russian Uprising†

January 26, 1905

The Russian uprising will have a marked tendency toward the solidarity of all the workers of the world.[10]

The uprising in Russia is not unexpected to those who have been watching the trend of events in that tsar-cursed country. The wretched condition of the working class in the industrial centers and among the peasantry has been exploited in the newspapers and magazines of all civilized countries during these many years, and all observant men have long since realized that the limits must finally be reached and that the inevitable crisis must come.

At last the oppressed and half-starved workers have risen in revolt and this revolt now presages revolution which may or may not be temporarily suppressed, but which, before it runs its course, will sweep the Russian monarchy out of existence. Emperor Nicholas might have given his reign a new and indefinite lease of power had he but received the petition from his meek and miserable subjects. But true to his instincts of royalty and of the ruling class of every age, the common people were not only spurned from the presence of the monarch, but were shot dead in their tracks like wild beasts by his army of heartless mercenaries.[11] It was these murderous volleys that transformed the lowly subjects into resolute and defiant men and lit the fires of the Russian revolution that now loom lurid and portentous on the horizon of the whole civilized world.

From the standpoint of organized labor, the revolution has special significance. It means that the working class of Russia, so long in the rear ranks of the international labor movement, are arousing from their lethargy and are at last resolved to break the political chains that fetter them and take their place where they properly belong in the bonds of international unionism. The uprising of the Russian toilers under such extraordinary conditions is watched with intense eagerness by the organized workers of all countries, who

† Shortened version published in *New York World,* approximately January 26, 1905. Reprinted as "Proletarian Cause" in *New Orleans Times-Democrat,* vol. 42, whole no. 17,395 (January 27, 1905), 2. Expanded and slightly restructured version published in *Social Democratic Herald,* vol. 7, no. 40, whole no. 340 (February 4, 1905), 1.

are profoundly in sympathy with their thrice enslaved Russian comrades and devoutly wish that they may triumph over the heartless[12] despots that have so long tyrannized over them.

There is no doubt that the Russian toilers have received some of their inspiration from their coworkers in the United States. The literature of labor is now international and the Russians are well advised of the progress that is being made by the working class of this country in organizing not only to resist injustice, but to emancipate the working class from wage-slavery and make it the ruling class of the world.

It is not probable that Count Tolstoy's[13] doctrine of nonresistance will meet with much favor among the outraged workingmen who have become full-fledged revolutionists. The doctrine of Father Gapon[14] will more likely become the shibboleth of the revolution. The Russian monarchy will rule with blood and iron until it is shot or blown out of existence.

Gorky,[15] the socialist leader, has the true spirit and his is in the veins of the revolution. He is the idol of the downtrodden millions of Russia and should he be put to death, the fate of the Russian Empire will be all the sooner settled.

The noteworthy feature of this revolt is the universal interest with which every move is followed. It is recognized to be a proletarian upheaval and the rulers of other foreign countries comprehend its significance and are gravely concerned about its results. Not only this, but the unanimity with which the Russian workers have stuck and the spontaneity with which the strike has spread from place to place suggests to the capitalist class of all countries, the United States included, that the time may be near when the workers of all lands, conscious of the wrongs they are suffering and the power they have to right them, will inaugurate a universal strike at the ballot box as well as in the factory, mill, and mine, and will not cease striking until the struggle is victorious and labor is free throughout the world.

I Can Imagine Nothing to Change My Mind: Letter to Victor L. Berger[†]

April 13, 1905

Terre Haute, Indiana, April 13th, 1905

My dear Victor:—

Your letter to Theodore was duly received by him and would have been acknowledged but for the fact that he expected my return and waited therefore to put it in my hands so that I could answer for myself. Theo wishes me to say for him that he appreciates very much the kind personal words your letter contains and that these are as warmly mutual as they always were in the old days.[16]

As to arranging for a personal meeting, I would be glad to see you as I always have been, and always expect to be, but I can see little prospect during the next few weeks unless you can travel a long distance to strike me at some point in my route.[17] I am just leaving for Illinois to fill some appointments. My dates are somewhat uncertain so I cannot advise you definitely, but barring Peoria I have no engagement in the northern part of the state.[18] It is possible that I may get into Chicago the latter part of this month or the early part of next, and in either case I will be glad to let you know so that we can have an hour together and a general talk over the situation. Of course, I shall be glad to have your views in regard to the new union, but I can imagine nothing you or anyone else could say to me that would change my mind that has been made up after long and careful deliberation.

You have already expressed yourself pretty freely in regard to the new union, perhaps too much for your good and the good of the party. I have had little to say aside from what has been necessary to state my position in response to inquiries, but I am as sure of my ground as you are of yours and I can conceive of no more dangerous position for a representative of our party than to be in the cesspools of pure and simple unionism with Belmont and his Christless gang in complete control. Don't tell me about rescuing the AF of L from the

† Typed letter-signed in *Victor L. Berger Papers, 1862–1980,* State Historical Society of Wisconsin, microfilm edition, reel 14, frames 34–35. Not published in Constantine (ed.), *Letters of Eugene V. Debs: Volume 1, 1874–1912.*

gang of pirate capitalists that are now running it. They and their lieutenants who are the nominal leaders simply make a laughing stock of you. You were in a pitiable role at San Francisco, you and your comrades, and it made my blood boil to see a man of your genius the sport and prey of a lot of five cent fakirs. Gompers has a better grip on the AF of L because of your opposition than if you had let him alone. He is strong in precisely the same way and for precisely the same reason that P. M. Arthur was strong with the engineers.[19] I saw twenty years of efforts to dislodge the latter turn to nothing while at the last the opposition gave up and Arthur was triumphant by acclamation to the very last hour of his life.

If the new movement starts right, that is to say, with the right people and on the right basis, I shall be with it and shall put all of my strength into it, totally regardless of consequences. I shall be guided solely by what I believe will be best for the labor movement in general.

I have some letters saying that you had declared I would have nothing to do with it; that you would see that I kept out of it. I cannot believe that you have said anything of the sort, for if you have it would imply that I had no will of my own and if that happens to be your estimate of me all I have to say is that you have still to know me. I have great respect for your judgment and there is no comrade to whose counsel I would rather listen, but when it comes to acting I act for myself.

Now, then, permit me to advise you a little along the same line that you advise me. Let the new movement alone until you know more about it than you do now. You have issued your "warning" and the *Herald* has done all that in its power lies to make it a stillborn affair, so you can afford to remain silent and let things take their course. You may commit yourself so far as to be embarrassing to you in the future. You little dream, seemingly, of the tremendous opposition to Gompers and Civic Federation rule. Thousands who are on the inside realize the hopelessness of escape from the constrictor grasp of the Belmont gang except through revolt, and I want to say to you that the revolt is brewing and that neither you nor any power can stay it and if the movement at Chicago starts right—and everything depends on that—it will tramp across the country with seven league boots and the best blood in the trade union movement will rush to its standard. The incident at New York, the subway strike, indicated clearly how fiercely the passion of revolt is already surging in the veins of the old movement. The rank and file are tired of their old leaders, have lost confidence in them, and not without good reason. These men ought to have had more encouragement from the socialist press than they received, our editors evidently fearing that they might give offense to their eminent highnesses, the pure and simple leaders and their pure and simple unions.

It would be a curious thing to see you and Gompers fighting side by side—perhaps as curious to see DeLeon and myself fighting together[20]—but in that sort of an alignment you will have to find yourself also fighting side by side with Belmont and Carnegie, the pirates, and Farley, the strikebreaker. That is the alignment to which your attitude will inevitably lead if you stick to it. I will find myself in no such dilemma. I may find myself pitted against some well-loved comrades, but whatever my position may impose upon me there will be no capitalist robbers and no labor fakirs and no professional strikebreakers fighting to sustain my side.

I will bear you in mind and the very first chance I have to get near enough for a personal interview I will let you know.[21] I am getting scores of letters from men who want to see me personally on the same matter, some to urge me to do one thing, and some another, but I will see but a few of them. You are one to whom, for reasons not necessary to state, I shall always owe the deference of a respectful hearing, and I shall never forget the obligation.

Theodore joins me as do our families in warmest regards and most affectionate greetings and good wishes to you and Mrs. Berger and the little folks.[22] Remember us also most kindly to Miss Thomas[23] and comrades at the office.

Yours always,
E. V. Debs

Revolt Against the AF of L Is Bound to Come: Letter to Frederic Heath[†]

April 22, 1905

Terre Haute, Indiana, April 22nd, 1905

My dear Heath:—

Yours of the 18th came in my absence.[24] You think that if I were to come out against the new movement Gompers would "gnash his teeth." You are exactly opposite the fact. He is "gnashing" now, and he will have occasion to do considerably more. In 1894 he did all in his official and personal power in opposition to the ARU and to defeat the Pullman strike. You know that as well as I, and notwithstanding this fact and a hundred others of equal import, reinforced by the fact that he is the incarnation of the false doctrine that the interests of labor and capital are identical, he flourishes like a green bay tree, and all efforts to dislodge him along the lines indicated by you will be as fruitless as they were in the case of P. M. Arthur. Nothing less than revolt will do this, and the outraged workers are ripe for that revolt and whether the new movement had been announced or not, that revolt is on the schedule of history and bound to come. In fact, it has already come. The western workers broke away long ago, and thousands and thousands of others are getting ready to follow out of the Civic Federation-cursed movement that has betrayed labor and led the workers into the shambles to be slaughtered by their capitalist keepers.

The charge of splitting the movement comes with devilish poor grace from those who have betrayed it. They are in fact the splitters and not those who have manhood enough to break away and loyally stand by working class principles. A united worker class will never come out of the AF of L. Mark that!

It does not matter to me that DeLeon sees an opening for himself in the new movement. He will not capture it, nor control it. Mark that!

When you tell me about the splendid progress that is being made within, I can hardly keep from concluding that you are joking. The San Francisco

† Typed letter, signed with handwritten postscript on personal letterhead in *Victor L. Berger Papers, 1862–1980,* State Historical Society of Wisconsin, microfilm edition, reel 14, frames 40–41. Not published in Constantine (ed.), *Letters of Eugene V. Debs: Volume 1, 1874–1912.*

convention was a pitiable exhibition of the farce. The few socialists that were there were made the laughingstock of the country—the footballs of fakirs. The really progressive rank and file understand, as a rule, that there is not hope and if the new movement starts right, as I believe it will, your eyes will be opened wide by the tremendous breaking away that will follow, and if you will take a word of friendly personal advice, you will let the new movement alone, for every word you say against it will one day come back to inspire vain regrets that it had been uttered. You need not worry unduly about DeLeon or Gompers or any other individual. The working class are going to unite and [neither] the AF of L, nor its leaders, nor any other person, influence, or element can prevail against this consummation.

Allow me to suggest that the personal journalism now running rampant in the *Herald* will do no good. It is in my opinion bad policy. Berger and Hagerty,[25] if they must fight, should attack each other's position and principles and let each other's persons alone. The charge of the *Herald*, in effect, that Hagerty is a grafter, is a great injustice to him. Whatever he may be, or not be, he is not that.

I have not forgotten that I promised you an article, but I have not yet had a chance to write it. Every day is full of exactions, but I shall get around to it soon.

I may be up your way in the not distant future and we will then have a chance to talk it over. I very much regret the Berger position in the judgeship matter. I think it is a great mistake to endorse a capitalist candidate, even by intimation, under any possible circumstances. It is a bad precedent and a dangerous tendency and I do not believe it can be successfully defended from any sound socialist point of view. Of course, I do not for a moment question Victor's integrity, nor his good intentions, nor do I allow these to be questioned in my hearing unchallenged, but I am bound to appeal from his judgment. These differences between us are natural enough, but as we know each other, even to the heart's core, these differences, however widely they may separate us for the time, will never affect our mutual confidence or mar our personal relations. I am wishing you and all of you well in all things and all places and all the time.

Yours always,
E. V. Debs

[PS:] Enclosed clipping is a little old, but is apropos and you may care to reproduce and comment.[26]

Splits Are Not Always Bad: Letter to Frederic Heath†

April 26, 1905

Terre Haute, Indiana, April 26th, 1905

My dear Heath:—

Your note is received. I will try to have the article for you for next issue as requested. The suggestion you make is a good one and I will be glad to write in accordance with it.[27]

Have just written Berger that I speak at Racine on Saturday night, asking him to, if possible, meet me there on Saturday afternoon. The same to yourself. I shall not be able to reach Milwaukee but perhaps you or Berger, or, better still, both of you may be able to run down to Racine.[28] The comrades, I am sure, would be delighted to see you besides the opportunity we would have of a heart to heart talk over the situation.

So Berger thinks, after his last meeting with the [National Executive Committee] that there is apt to be a party split on account of the trade union question. If that is true, then let it come. There was a time when I was seriously perturbed by a threatened split. Not so anymore. If the party can be split upon the trade union or any other question, then it ought to split and the quicker the better. I have learned that splits are not always bad. Corpses don't split. Of course, I would regret to separate from my comrades, but if the movement demands it, I will have to stand it. The movement is bigger than the party and bigger than the trade unions, and the movement may demand a shaking up of both party and unions to readjust itself to fundamental principles.[29] I belong to no labor union at present. There is none for me to join. There will be soon, I hope and believe.

There is as liable to be a split about Wisconsin as about anything I know. If it is true that Wisconsin has refused a charter from the national organization and if it is true that Wisconsin refuses to furnish the national office with a list of local unions, then there is going to be trouble and I would not be at all

† Typed letter on personal letterhead in *Victor L. Berger Papers, 1862–1980,* State Historical Society of Wisconsin, microfilm edition, reel 14, frames 45–46. Not published in Constantine (ed.), *Letters of Eugene V. Debs: Volume 1, 1874–1912.*

surprised to see Wisconsin compelled to conform to the national constitution or expelled from the national party.[30] I cannot understand why these things should be and yet they are and are being very warmly discussed all over the country. Besides, there is trouble brewing against the present order of things right in Wisconsin and even in Milwaukee. There are a good many of your members who are stirred up over your attitude in the judgeship matter which I am sure was a grave mistake and may yet have grave consequences, possibly amounting to a split, for which, should it come, the new trade union movement can hardly be charged with the responsibility.[31]

That was another great fizzle at Chicago the other day, proving the utter impotency of craft unionism in the presence of existing combinations of capital. The teamsters and tailors fell out with each other, the strike was lost, and now the teamsters, according to reports, are quarreling among themselves while the employers' association is after them red hot, has them on the run, and is determined to put them to rout. Thus will it always be with craft-divided unions up against a solid array of capitalist power. The industrial union is bound to come and the quicker it comes, the better it will be for the Socialist Party and if a temporary split is necessary it will serve a good purpose in the long run.

Then again, the mistake of the national convention of the Socialist Party in May last in taking an unnecessary slap at the ALU and the WF of M in the interest of Gompers and the AF of L is coming back for settlement.[32]

The June meeting in Chicago is going to be a big thing.[33] Many of the best trade unionists in the country and from every part of the country will be there, and I have faith in the outcome of the meeting.

Yours always,
E. V. Debs

Municipal Ownership, Capitalist and Socialist[†]

June 7, 1905

Just at present there is a widespread agitation in favor of municipal ownership of municipal utilities. This is important from a socialist point of view, because of its tendency rather than because of any actual achievement. Municipal ownership may have a socialist tendency, and then again, it may be reactionary and have the opposite effect. In the prevailing capitalist system, every experiment at municipal ownership and operation in a hostile environment is apt, if not to fail, to at least prove disappointing to those expecting great benefit from it, and to this extent may be used as an argument of convincing effect among the unthinking against the practicability of the socialist program.

Not only this, but municipal ownership of public utilities means little or nothing to the people so long as national government is in the control of the corporations and trusts, consisting of the larger capitalists who own the national resources and the means of production, and are therefore in a position to dominate all the powers of government and virtually control the destiny of people.

A concrete illustration may be in order. Suppose a city buys a street railway plant, paying half a million dollars therefor, issuing its bonds for that amount. The city comes into possession of the street railway, and the previous owners come into possession of the city's bonds. The capitalists are none the losers by the change. They now draw interest on bonds instead of dividends on stock, and the actual benefits that accrue to the people are in most cases very inconsiderable.

As a matter of course we socialists favor municipal ownership, but only as a part of the general program of collective ownership—municipal, state, and national—of all public utilities. Then again, in the socialist program every step that is taken in the conquest of the public powers by the ballot and in the enlargement of the circle of public ownership is used to its fullest extent in benefitting the condition of the workers, so that municipal ownership of a public utility under a socialist regime will mean its operation primarily in the interest

† Published as "The Real Difference" in Salem [OH] *Daily News,* probably June 8, 1905, unspecified page. Reprinted in *Appeal to Reason,* whole no. 500 (July 1, 1905), 3.

and for the benefit of the workers therein employed. Among these benefits are the shortening of the workday, the improvement of working conditions, and the application of all profits, over and above the cost of maintaining the plant in an advanced state of efficiency, to improving the conditions and advancing the material welfare of the workers.

There is no doubt that the present municipal ownership movement has received its greatest impetus from the appalling political corruption that scandalized our leading American cities during the past few years, and traceable, undeniably, to the private ownership of public utilities and their operation for private profit instead of their public ownership and their operation for the good of the people.

The same deplorable state of affairs has developed in every great metropolis of the nation, and from this has sprung the demand for public ownership. The socialists, seeing this tendency, the importance of which is conceded, call attention to the greater evil of the private ownership of the still greater utilities of the nation. If private ownership of municipal utilities is productive of municipal corruption, then it follows logically that private ownership of national utilities is productive of national corruption. It is a fact not to be gainsaid that every corruptor of the body politic is the owner or agent of some public utility. No one has ever heard of a workingman bribing a legislator or corrupting a court.

All these questions are now up for consideration, and while there is wide difference among the people, there is not the slightest doubt but that they will all be settled in good time in the interest of self-rule and a higher social order. The working class is being rapidly converted to socialism. They have everything to gain and nothing to lose by it. On the other hand, the capitalists are at war among themselves, the larger driving the smaller from the field, the trusts and syndicates eliminating competition and displacing the smaller competitors, all of which simply means that the capitalist system is running its historic course, and when its development is completed deterioration will set in, and in due time it will follow feudalism, from which it sprang, to the cemetery of the past, to make room for another social adjustment more compatible with the present and future needs of the race.

New Industrial Union to Be Organized†

June 22, 1905

The industrial union to be organized at Chicago the latter part of this month is looked forward to with increasing interest among workingmen, and attracting more general attention than any other event in the labor world. By many it is hailed with joy, and by others with scorn and derision, according to the point of view, but the fact remains that it will be largely attended by the most progressive union men of all trades and occupations, and that it will mark an epoch in the history of labor unionism.

The new union will be organized along industrial lines and will embrace all workers of whatever color or sex; it will not be a federation of unions, but a compact body of united workers, class-conscious and self-governing.

Will the new organization be a rival of the American Federation of Labor? Not at all. It will be a labor organization whose sole object will be to advance the material interests of the working class and ultimately to emancipate that class from wage-slavery.

The trade union, like every other organic thing, is subject to the laws of evolution. The trade unions of the past, good in their day, chiefly for what they have led to, are no longer adequate to the demands of the workers, and the evidence of this fact is so palpable that no intelligent workingman can fail to observe it.

Not only this, but the old union movement has become positively reactionary and is largely used in the interest of the capitalist class to the detriment of the workers who sustain it and whose interests are supposed to be conserved by it.

For a concrete illustration it is only necessary to point out the fact that the coal operators are the staunchest supporters of the miners' union, collect its dues, and keep a watchful eye upon its operations; and this for reasons so self-evident, when the principles and policy of the union are considered, that they readily suggest themselves.

According to the miners' union, the interests of the operators and miners are identical, and the object of the union is to promote these alleged mutual

† Published as "Industrial Unionism" in *Miners' Magazine* [Denver], June 22, 1905, unspecified volume number and page. Reprinted as "Principles of Industrial Unionism" in the *Chicago Socialist,* vol. 6, whole no. 330 (July 1, 1905), 2.

interests, and if this be the correct working class view, then it is highly commendable that the operators have such a friendly care for the miners' union and take pains to keep it in efficient working order. But it is not the correct view from the miners' standpoint, and a moment's reflection will prove it.

The economic interests of operators and miners are not only not identical, but diametrically opposite. The operators want as large a share of the product of the mines as they can get; the miners, on the other hand, want as large a share of the product as they can get. Here they stand, face to face, fighting over the division of the product and every joint conference proves that each side contests every inch of ground to the bitter end.

The operators need the miners to dig coal for them, and buy their labor-power as cheaply as they can. The economic interests of these two classes clash and we have in consequence the class struggle with its daily record of strikes, boycotts, lockouts, injunctions, riots, and bloodshed, and in the presence of these indisputable facts it is puerile and stupid, or designing and misleading, to talk about identity of interests between the exploiting operators and the exploited miners. As well talk of the identity of interests of a footpad and his victim.

If the interests of the operators and miners are identical, then the operators' association and the miners' union should merge into one and the same organization.

In the evolution of industry the various trades are more and more losing their separate identity and being interwoven and interlocked in harmonious cooperation, based on the subdivision and specialization of labor. The printer and the machinist used to represent distinct and widely different trades, and they then quite naturally had separate unions to represent their separate trades. Since the introduction of the typesetting machine, they have been brought into very close relation, practically merging in machine tenders, and their unions have clashed and will again and again in disputes over jurisdiction.

It is vain to attempt to maintain the old form of trade unionism, based upon a mode of production that has passed away. The trades are losing their identity, the lines that separated them are being obliterated, and, in spite of themselves, the workers of all kinds are being organized into great armies of cooperative labor, and the labor union must follow this industrial development and express the various stages of its progress or fail of its purpose and pass out of existence.

That the present trade union movement is sadly behind the times and palpably inefficient requires no argument to demonstrate; the conditions and tendencies speak for themselves.

The coal miners in Ohio and Indiana are allowed to work but an average of a day or two a week, and their condition is deplorable, as the deep mutterings of discontent among them abundantly proves; while the press dispatches report that the miners in the anthracite region have become discouraged and disgusted with the outlook and have deserted the union in droves.

The total collapse of the Fall River strike and the awful destitution and suffering incident to it were not mitigated by the comforting assurances of union leaders that it was not as bad as it might have been; nor will its lessons escape the thinking element of the defeated unions, thousands of whom recognize the inherent weakness of craft unionism in the presence of combined capital, and are reading in their bitter fate the mockery of a unionism that divides them and are hearkening to the stern command of sense and logic to close up the gaps which craft unions leave between them and unite in solid class-conscious array in the bonds of industrial unionism.

The utter route of the union employees in the subway strike in New York is another striking inefficiency of the old form of unionism. These workers had lost faith in their national organizations and confidence in their leaders, and went out on strike on their own account. The power house employees, organized in separate unions, remained at work while their brothers were being ruthlessly slaughtered. The national leaders upbraided the local leaders and the local leaders repudiated the national leaders, while the 6,000 or more union men were mowed down, figuratively speaking and otherwise, by an army of Cossack strikebreakers under the command of a trained guerrilla, and while Mr. Belmont, the American Vicar of Rothschild, smiled serenely upon the scene and drew inspiration for his subsequent speech to the National Civic Federation, in grand banquet assembled, proclaiming himself a union labor man and proving it to the evident satisfaction of the labor leaders in attendance.

That kind of labor unionism suits Mr. Belmont to his heart's fondest desire, and it suits every other labor exploiter in the land.

Does it suit the working class, who furnish the victims for these union shambles?

All the great strikes in the recent past have resulted in wretched compromise or flat failure. Scarcely an exception can be cited to relieve the gloomy monotony of disaster.

Such power of resistance as the union still possesses is waning and, to destroy even the last vestige of this, President Parry of the Citizens' Alliance and President Post of the Manufacturers' Association have organized their capitalist class and are making their onslaughts upon all legislative measures proposed by the unions and upon the unions themselves, especially in strikes, when all the capitalists combine to crush the workingmen involved, which they find it easy enough to accomplish with their united capitalist union against the craft-divided union, or rather, disunion, of the workers.

It should here be noted that these lessons of defeat are not without value. Parry and Post may crush the craft unions, but they will not crush the union spirit of the working class; on the contrary, they will fan that into a flame of industrial unionism, a unionism that combines and solidifies the workers on the basis of the class struggle and marshals these workers for the conflict upon the industrial field, the political field, and every other field until Parry and Post and their class are put to rout and the capitalist system is overthrown and wage-slavery wiped from the earth.

In plain words, the united capitalists will be confronted by the united workers.

The sympathetic strike will be of the past, and upon this point at least we will satisfy the yearning desire of the capitalist class.

One set of union men will not stand by and see the throats of their brethren cut, unable to help without violating the sanctity of some alleged contract.

Nor will the capitalists, through their labor lieutenants, be able to pit one union against another, engendering strife, promoting division, entailing defeat, and reducing all to impotency and contempt.

There will be but one union and that will embrace all the workers in the respective divisions of trade in which they are engaged, and when there is a grievance it will be that of the whole, and when there is a strike it will be that of all, and there will be no separate union jurisdictions to wrangle about, no neutrality to observe, no sympathetic strike to follow, no contract to violate, and no union leaders to be tampered with; and then the capitalists, through their "authorities," may appeal to their courts and march in their soldiers to operate their establishments.

The new union will express the now existing economic conditions. The machinery of production has become a vast mechanism, the trades have been merged, and the workers now constitute one great cooperative industrial army. Following this, the capitalist owners of this machinery are combining and presenting a solid phalanx to their exploited wage workers with the avowed purpose of keeping them in industrial slavery.

In the presence of this concentration of capital and combination of capitalists, is it not ignorant defiance of the evolution of industry and a foolish waste of time and substance to maintain trade isolation with nothing stronger than threads of expediency to bind the numberless unions in federation?

Can this properly be called unionism?

Is it not rather non-unionism?

The time has come for a new, up-to-date, all-embracing, and revolutionary economic movement of the working class, the form and functions of which must express the present stage of industrial development.

This union will repudiate all alleged identity of interests between capitalists and workers. It will be organized to combat and not to conciliate the exploiters of the working class.

Between capitalists and wage-slaves there can be no peace. The war of these classes is on and to the end.

The Industrial Union will recognize and express in economic terms the class struggle, which even President Roosevelt inferentially admits in his oft-repeated deprecation of class hatred.

That society has been divided into two hostile economic classes, and that they are at war with each other is inherent in the capitalist system itself, and not due to any mischievous agitation of the wanton demagogue, as the capitalist press would have deluded wage-slaves think. The capitalists are fighting for their lives. There can be no compromise that is more than temporary and no peace for the working class except at the price of slavery.

The National Civic Federation may for a time delude the workers; its thrifty promoters, including its plutocratic prelates, may staunch the wounds and salve the sores of the working class, but they cannot prevent other and more serious ones from being inflicted.

The capitalist press has already made haste to report that this industrial movement was initiated by the Socialist Party to disrupt the trade union movement. Nothing could be further from the truth. The Socialist Party, as a party, has absolutely nothing to do with it, and those of its members who are participants are so on their own individual account, and they, and they alone, are responsible, and quite willing to be, for their actions.

In the new union the workers in a great mill or other modern industry, whatever it may be, will not be parceled out among a hundred or more pigmy unions, with more or less rivalry, born of encroaching jurisdictions, and not infrequently controlled by petty politicians, the henchmen of the capitalists behind the scenes, and thus easily arrayed against each other in fratricidal conflict.

There has been enough, and more than enough of this kind of so-called unionism, and it is high time that the workers, so often defeated and scattered, blacklisted and persecuted, enjoined and imprisoned, exiled and starved, opened their eyes to the fact that they have been walking blindly into the traps set by their masters and their mercenaries, who have thwarted every design to efficiently unite the workers and who will now in concert warn the working class against the new union, seek to misrepresent its mission and discredit its promoters, but there is a vast body of class-conscious workers who will not be deceived and who will rally to the standard of the United Workers all the more resolutely because of the hostility, open and covert, of capitalist and alleged unionist, and of all the myriad foes of sound working class unionism.

With the workers united into one great economic body they can be trained and fitted to assume control of the respective industries in which they are engaged, so that when they are turned over to them, as they will be, with the conquest of the public powers through the political party of their class, they will be prepared to operate them free from capitalist domination and in accordance with the principles and program of industrial democracy and the Working Class Republic.

Berger and His Opponents: Letter to the Toledo *Socialist*†

June 24, 1905

To *The Socialist*

Toledo, O.

Comrades:—

That Victor L. Berger should be deposed from a position of trust in a party he helped to organize and for which he worked with all his strength of mind and body, seems to be the very irony of fate.[34]

What has been his crime? He advocated the support of a candidate of a capitalist party in a local election in which the Socialist Party had no candidate.

† Published in *The Socialist* [Toledo, OH], vol. 5, whole no. 248 (June 24, 1905), 2. Reprinted as "Debs' Letter on the Berger Case" in *Social Democratic Herald*, July 1, 1905.

Granted that he was wrong, are the peculiar circumstances surrounding the case to be ignored, and his many years of faithful service to the party to count for nothing in mitigation?

Victor L. Berger was wrong, flagrantly wrong, in my judgment; but in permitting the extremely exasperating indignities of a capitalist candidate upon the Socialist Party to sting him into preference for a rival capitalist candidate, his motive was pure and will not be impeached by any who know him or are familiar with the attending circumstances.

It is not my intention to defend Berger—to the extent that he erred in judgment he cannot be defended and to the extent that his motive was pure he does not need defense

To be as brief as possible, the Socialist Party in Milwaukee, for the very best of reasons, had no ticket in the field. Under such circumstances, Berger, for the moment absolved from the active support of his own party, saw, or thought he saw, an opening to rebuke a malodorously offensive tool of capitalism who had gone out of his way repeatedly to slur and discredit socialists; and seized by this impulse he struck the blow and by so doing violated the uncompromising ethics of the Socialist Party. For this he should have been called to account, but there was, and is, nothing in the case to warrant the extreme measures that have been taken against him and that, if carried into effect, would make of an unfortunate tactical blunder an act of foulest treason.

Victor L. Berger is human; intensely so. He is apt as any man I know to make a mistake, but his heart is right and as a socialist, there is no stain upon his honor.

The National Committee had the power to depose Berger and did depose him, but it did not humiliate him. In another year the National Committee may be given credit for having exalted him.

Not in the least do I question the motive of the National Committee, but I think they have erred by hasty action and undue severity, and that in due time they will realize it to their regret.

It is not that Berger was ignominiously beheaded, disproportionate as was this extreme penalty to his offense, that constitutes the gravest feature of the case, but the fact that *he was executed without a trial.* It will not do to plead that he admitted the substance of the accusation. Not a chicken thief or pickpocket is sentenced without a full hearing. Had Berger been duly charged with his offense, put upon trial and given full time and fair chance to make his defense, the verdict might have been the same, but it would not have been open to the serious objection now made to it and which may yet lead to its repudiation and to the rehabilitation of its victim.

A reasonable rebuke would have served a good purpose, while extreme harshness will react in favor of the accused and make his offense the means of praise instead of blame.

I yield to no comrade in any of the essentials to party integrity, but I am not scanning the party for flaws to vindicate my penetrating vision; nor am I ambitious to be first in crying treason when a comrade steps from the beaten path.

In dealing with Berger I am simply putting myself in his place; and knowing that I have made countless mistakes in the past and that I shall make as many more as time and opportunity will allow, I can well afford to counsel lenient judgment for my comrade, knowing not how soon my own turn may come to face the executioner.

Let us have done with the Berger case. He has been more than punished and the incident should now be closed. There is no danger of repetition of the offense. The Berger decapitation will stand as an awful warning; and as a deterrent will have greater effect than a constitutional inhibition.

The resolution of the National Committee that the state of Wisconsin investigate itself to see if it has been guilty of collusion is inoperative and would better be rescinded; and the further measures to expel Berger, which only his local has the power to do, and which it never will do, can serve no good purpose and ought to be abandoned.

A noteworthy feature of these extreme measures is that most of those who advocate them are comparatively new members, and it seems strange that these should pursue with relentless fury an old comrade who was battling for the cause of socialism when a socialist was regarded as an imp of hell and when they were yet in their mother's arms.

Let us preserve the party purity and vigilantly guard its uncompromising tactics, but let us not be too swift to condemn a mistake as a crime and an erring comrade as a vicious traitor.

For many years I have known Victor Berger and I have known him well. He needs no words of mine to shield or defend him. His record has been made and there it stands. For more than 20 years he has been a commanding figure on the battlefield. In the fiercest trials he never wavered, never lost courage, and never struck his colors to the enemy.

In every secret fiber of his being he is a socialist. Impulsive by nature, hot-blooded to fieriness, his judgment may at times go wrong, but never his ardent loyalty and passionate love for the socialist movement.

As to the Milwaukee local and Wisconsin state movements, they can and will take care of themselves. All that is required on their part is that they conform to the national constitution and party regulations as interpreted by the National Committee, and this they are undoubtedly willing to do. Beyond that it is not necessary to go, whether in the case of Wisconsin or any other state.

Having spent considerable time in Wisconsin, I know the comrades of that state and there are none anywhere who, as a whole, are clearer in their economics, more loyal to the party, or more active in pushing it to the front. They give their time and their substance freely to build up the party and if some of those who are finding fault with them would do the same, they would be farther advanced than they now are and there would soon be a Wisconsin movement in every state in the union.

The general outlook for the party is far better than at any previous time, and if we do not suffer ourselves to engage in hairsplitting and in factional feuds and internal dissensions over nonessentials, but rather close up the ranks and face and fight the enemy all along the line, the coming months will surpass all records in party achievement.

Speech at the Founding Convention of the Industrial Workers of the World†

June 29, 1905

Fellow Delegates and Comrades:—

As the preliminaries in organizing the convention have been disposed of, we will get down to the real work before this body. We are here to perform a task so great that it appeals to our best thought, our united energies, and will enlist our most loyal support; a task in the presence of which weak men might falter and despair, but from which it is impossible to shrink without betraying the working class. [*Applause.*]

† Published as "Speech of Eugene V. Debs" in *The Weekly People* [New York], vol. 15, no. 20 (August 12, 1905), 1. Reprinted in W. E. Trautmann (ed.), *Proceedings of the First Convention of the Industrial Workers of the World: Founded at Chicago, June 27 to July 8, 1905*, W. E. McDurmut, stenographer (New York: New York Labor News, 1905), 142–7.

I am much impressed by this proletarian gathering. I realize that I stand in the presence of those who in the past have fought, are fighting, and will continue to fight the battles of the working class economically and politically [*applause*], until the capitalist class is overthrown and the working class are emancipated from all of the degrading thralldom of the ages. [*Applause.*] In this great struggle the working class are often defeated, but never vanquished. Even the defeats, if we are wise enough to profit by them, but hasten the day of the final victory.

In taking a survey of the industrial field of today, we are at once impressed with the total inadequacy of working class organization, with the lack of solidarity, with the widespread demoralization we see, and we are bound to conclude that the old form of pure and simple unionism has long since outgrown its usefulness [*applause*]; that it is now not only in the way of progress, but that it has become positively reactionary, a thing that is but an auxiliary of the capitalist class. [*Applause.*]

They charge us with being assembled here for the purpose of disrupting the union movement. It is already disrupted, and if it were not disrupted we would not behold the spectacle here in the very city of a white policeman guarding a black scab, and a black policeman guarding a white scab [*applause*], while the trade unions stand by with their hands in their pockets wondering what is the matter with union labor in America. We are here today for the purpose of uniting the working class, for the purpose of eliminating that form of unionism which is responsible for the conditions as they exist today.

The trade union movement is today under the control of the capitalist class. It is preaching capitalist economics. It is serving capitalist purposes. Proof of it, positive and overwhelming, appears on every hand. All of the important strikes during the past two or three years have been lost. The great strike of the textile workers at Fall River, that proved so disastrous to those who engaged in it; the strike of the subway employees in the city of New York, where under the present form of organization the local leaders repudiated the national leaders and were in alliance with the capitalist class to crush their own followers; the strike of the stockyard's employees here in Chicago; the strike of the teamsters now in progress—all, all of them bear testimony to the fact that the pure and simple form of unionism has fulfilled its mission, whatever that may have been, and that the time has come for it to go. [*Great applause.*]

The American Federation of Labor has numbers, but the capitalist class do not fear the American Federation of Labor; quite the contrary. The capitalist papers here in this very city at this very time are championing the cause of pure and simple unionism. Since this convention met there has been nothing in these papers but a series of misrepresentations. [*Applause.*] If we had met instead in the interest of the American Federation of Labor these papers, these capitalist papers, would have had their columns filled with articles commending the work that is being done here. There is certainly something wrong with that form of unionism which has its chief support in the press that represents capitalism; something wrong in that form of unionism whose leaders are the lieutenants of capitalism; something wrong with that form of unionism that forms an alliance with such a capitalist combination as the Civic Federation,[35] whose sole purpose it is to chloroform the working class while the capitalist class go through their pockets. [*Applause.*]

There are those who believe that this form of unionism can be changed from within. They are very greatly mistaken. We might as well have remained in the Republican and Democratic parties and have expected to effect certain changes from within, instead of withdrawing from those parties and organizing a party that represented the exploiting working class. [*Applause.*] There is but one way to effect this great change, and that is for the workingman to sever his relations with the American Federation and join the union that proposes upon the economic field to represent his class [*applause*], and we are here today for the purpose of organizing that union. I believe that we are capable of profiting by the experiences of the past. I believe it is possible for the delegates here assembled to form a great, sound, economic organization of the working class based upon the class struggle, that shall be broad enough to embrace every honest worker, yet narrow enough to exclude every fakir. [*Applause.*]

Now, let me say to those delegates who are here representing the Socialist Trade & Labor Alliance, that I have not in the past agreed with their tactics.[36] I concede that their theory is right, that their principles are sound; I admit and cheerfully admit the honesty of their membership. [*Applause.*] But there must certainly be something wrong with their tactics or their methods of propaganda if in these years they have not developed a larger membership than they have to their credit.

Let me say in this connection, I am not of those who scorn you because of your small numbers. I have been taught by experience that numbers do not represent strength. [*Applause.*] I will concede that the capitalist class does not fear the American Federation of Labor because of their numbers. Let me add that the capitalist class do not fear your Socialist Trade & Labor Alliance. The one is too numerous and the other is not sufficiently numerous. The American Federation of Labor is not sound in its economics. The Socialist Trade & Labor

Alliance is sound in its economics, but in my judgment it does not appeal to the American working class in the right spirit. [*Applause.*] Upon my lips there has never been a sneer for the Socialist Trade & Labor Alliance on account of the smallness of its numbers. I have been quite capable of applauding the pluck, of admiring the courage of the members of the Socialist Trade & Labor Alliance, for though few in numbers, they stay by their colors. [*Applause.*]

I wish, if I can, to point out what I conceive to be the error in their method of propaganda. Speaking of the members as I have met them, it seems to me that they are too prone to look upon a man as a fakir who happens to disagree with them. [*Applause.*] Now, I think there is no delegate in this convention who is more set against the real fakir than I am. But I believe it is possible for a workingman who has been the victim of fakirism to become so alert, to so strain his vision looking for the fakir that he sees the fakir where the fakir is not. [*Applause*] I would have you understand that I am opposed to the fakir, and I am also opposed to the fanatic. [*Applause.*] And fanaticism is as fatal to the development of the working class movement as is fakirism. [*Applause.*] Admitting that the principle is sound, that the theory of your organization is right—and I concede both—what good avails it, what real purpose is accomplished if you cannot develop strength sufficient to carry out the declared purpose of your organization?

Now, I believe that there is a middle ground that can be occupied without the slightest concession of principle. I believe it is possible for such an organization as the Western Federation of Miners[37] to be brought into harmonious relation with the Socialist Trade & Labor Alliance. I believe it is possible that that element of the organizations represented here have the conviction, born of experience, observation, and study, that the time has come to organize a new union, and I believe it is possible for these elements to mingle, to combine here, and to at least begin the work of forming a great economic or revolutionary organization of the working class so sorely needed in the struggle for their emancipation. [*Applause.*] The supreme need of the hour, as the speaker who preceded me so clearly expressed it in his carefully and clearly thought address—the supreme need of the hour is a sound, revolutionary working-class organization.[38] [*Applause.*] And while I am not foolish enough to imagine that we can complete this great work in a single convention of a few days' duration, I do believe it is possible for us to initiate this work, to begin it in a way for the greatest promise, with the assurance that its work will be completed in a way that will appeal with increasing force to the working class of the country.

I am satisfied that the great body of the working class in this country are prepared for just such an organization. [*Applause.*] I know, their leaders know, that if this convention is successful their doom is sealed. [*Applause.*] They can already see the handwriting upon the wall, and so they are seeking by all of the power at their command to discredit this convention, and in alliance with the cohorts of capitalism they are doing what they can to defeat this convention. It may fail in its mission, for they may continue to misrepresent, deceive, and betray the working class and keep them in the clutches of their capitalist masters and exploiters. [*Applause.*]

They are hoping that we will fail to get together. They are hoping, as they have already expressed it, that this convention will consist of a prolonged wrangle; that such is our feeling and relations toward each other that it will be impossible for us to agree upon any vital proposition; that we will fight each other upon every point, and that when we have concluded our labors we will leave things in a worse condition than they were before. If we are true to ourselves we will undeceive those gentlemen. We will give them to understand that we are animated by motives too lofty for them in their baseness and sordidness to comprehend. [*Applause.*] We will give them to understand that the motive here is not to use unionism as a means of serving the capitalist class, but that the motive of the men and women assembled here is to serve the working class by so organizing that class as to make their organization the promise of the coming triumph upon the economic field and the political field and the ultimate emancipation of the working class. [*Applause.*]

Let me say that I agree with Comrade DeLeon upon one very vital point at least. [*Applause.*] We have not been the best of friends in the past [*laughter*], but the whirligig of time brings about some wonderful changes. I find myself breaking away from some men I have been in very close touch with, and getting in close touch with some men from whom I have been very widely separated. [*Applause.*] But no matter. I have long since made up my mind to pursue the straight line as I see it. A man is not worthy, in my judgment, to enlist in the services of the working class unless he has the moral stamina, if need be, to break asunder all personal relations to serve that class as he understands his duty to that class. [*Applause.*]

I have not the slightest feeling against those who in the past have seen fit to call me a fakir. [*Laughter.*] I can afford to wait. I have waited, and I now stand ready to take by the hand every man, every woman that comes here, totally regardless of past affiliations, whose purpose it is to organize the working class upon the economic field, to launch that economic organization that shall be the expression of the economic conditions as they exist today; that organization for which the working class are prepared; that organization which we shall at least begin before we have ended our labors, unless we shall prove false to the object for which we have assembled here.

Now, I am not going to take the time to undertake to outline the form of this organization. Nor should I undertake to test your patience by attempting to elaborate the plan of organization. But let me suggest, in a few words, that to accomplish its purpose this organization must not only be based upon the class struggle, but must express the economic condition of this time. We must have one organization that embraces the workers in every department of industrial activity. It must express the class struggle. It must recognize the class lines. It must of course be class-conscious. It must be totally uncompromising. [*Applause.*] It must be an organization of the rank and file. [*Applause.*] It must be so organized and so guided as to appeal to the intelligence of the workers of the country everywhere. And if we succeed, as I believe we will, in forming such an organization, its success is a foregone conclusion.

I have already said the working class are ready for it. There are multiplied thousands in readiness to join it, waiting only to see if the organization is rightly grounded and properly formed; and this done there will be no trouble about its development, and its development will take proper form and expand to its true proportions. If this work is properly begun, it will mean in time, and not a long time at that, a single union upon the economic field. It will mean more than that; it will mean a single party upon the political field [*applause*]; the one the economic expression, the other the political expression of the working class; the two halves that represent the organic whole of the labor movement.

Now, let me say in closing, comrades—and I have tried to condense, not wishing to tax your patience or to take the time of others, for I believe that in such conventions as this it is more important that we shall perform than that we shall make speeches—let me say in closing that you and I and all of us who are here to enlist in the service of the working class need to have faith in each other [*applause*], not the faith born of ignorance and stupidity, but the enlightened faith of self-interest. We are in precisely the same position; we depend absolutely upon each other. We must get close together and stand shoulder to shoulder. [*Applause.*] We know that without solidarity nothing is possible, that with it nothing is impossible.

And so we must dispel the petty prejudices that are born of the differences of the past, and I am of those who believe that, if we get together in the true working class spirit, most of these differences will disappear, and if those of us who have differed in the past are willing to accord to each other that degree of conciliation that we ourselves feel that we are entitled to, that we will forget these differences, we will approach all of the problems that confront us with our intelligence combined, acting together in concert, all animated by the same high resolve to form that great union, so necessary to the working class, without which their condition remains as it is, and with which, when made practical and vitalized and renewed, the working class is permeated with the conquering spirit of the class struggle, and as if by magic the entire movement is vitalized, and side by side and shoulder to shoulder in a class-conscious phalanx we move forward to certain and complete victory. [*Applause.*]

The Misrepresentation and Lies of the Capitalist Press†

Early July 1905

The delegates who assembled in Chicago last month in response to the call for the industrial convention were as representative a proletarian gathering as ever met in this or any other country. The task that awaited them was as difficult, all things considered, as any that ever confronted a body of workers, but they were equal to it and as a result of their deliberations and actions there is now a sound economic working class organization in the field; and although its progress will be beset with difficulties, it will sturdily face and successfully overcome them all and fulfill the great mission for which it has been organized.

From the very first the capitalist papers misrepresented and in fact deliberately lied about the convention. I have it upon good authority that all the Chicago dailies united in instructing their reporters to "knock" the convention wherever possible and in other respects to ignore it. They did even worse than this, in that they resorted to downright mendacity to accomplish their purpose of defeating a body of men who by their records had proved that they were above the corrupting influences of capitalist bribery and whose object it was to unite the working class for their liberation from wage-slavery.

† Published as "The Industrial Convention" in *International Socialist Review* [Chicago], vol. 6, no. 1 (July 1905), 85–6.

The capitalist organs are all very loyal to the American Federation of Labor for reasons that readily suggest themselves.

To show how the capitalist press treated us, it is only necessary to say that at their own solicitation I furnished a statement in regard to the convention and its objects. All the Chicago papers were supplied with a copy of it and *all of them suppressed it.* Not a single line appeared, although the statement was furnished at their own solicitation. Next, they sent reporters accompanied by shorthand writers to interview me in regard to the convention and the work it was expected to accomplish. I took the time to dictate an extended and detailed statement. *Not a single line appeared.* Then again, when I was obliged to leave the convention before adjournment to fill some speaking engagements, these same papers reported that I had left in disgust, which was an unqualified falsehood.

The work of the convention, on the whole, was and is entirely satisfactory to me. It was in point of fact, in many respects, the greatest labor convention I ever attended.

The delegates differed widely in matters of detail, which was to be expected, but upon the great vital principle of uniting the working class upon the economic field in a revolutionary organization recognizing and expressing the class struggle they were one, and the record they made for themselves and their class was in every respect creditable to both their head and their hearts and will bear the severest tests of time.

Of course, there is no disposition on our part to avoid criticism. We expect it and are prepared to meet it. We have taken our stand, and all the capitalist class and their cohorts of whatever name cannot dislodge us.

The predictions so freely made before the convention that Debs was seeking an office and that DeLeon would show his fine Italian hand were all designed to discredit the convention, and the fact that neither the one nor the other of these "self-seekers" holds office in the new organization forces these critics to find other reasons for opposing industrial organization in the interest of the working class.

DeLeon did not "capture" the organization and Debs is not "disgusted" with it. Such silly and stupid falsehoods will have no effect on the body of men and women who met in Chicago on June 27th and who performed their task with such ability and such fidelity to the working class that the organization formed by them, so much needed at this time, will at once appeal to the workers of the land and they will rally to its standard in ever-increasing numbers until it becomes the dominant power on the economic field in the working class struggle for emancipation.

Municipal Ownership versus Social Revolution†

July 8, 1905

The socialist has no longer to stand alone in the United States, the target for every ribald jest of every ignorant and vulgar lackey of the prevailing system. According to the latest count he now numbers half a million, and this in itself is a long stride toward sanity and respectability.

The trouble now is not to convert the people to socialism, but to prevent socialism from being converted to the people. Every hint at public ownership is now called socialism, without reference to the fact that there can be no socialism, and that public ownership means practically nothing, so long as the capitalist class are in control of the national government.

Just at this moment the air is filled with the cry of municipal ownership, and many thousands of misguided people are led to expect great things if the city, now virtually a capitalist corporation, takes over certain public utilities, such as street railways and lighting plants, and operates them instead of the lesser corporations that now own and control them. These people are doomed to disappointment. Municipal ownership in the capitalist system will not change economic conditions in any appreciable degree. The city of Glasgow is known the world over for its municipal ownership of public utilities, but there is the same proportionate poverty and misery in Glasgow that there is in any other great city in the civilized world.

Municipal ownership has done little or nothing for the working class in Glasgow, and it will do little or nothing for them here. Government ownership of public utilities means nothing for labor under the capitalist ownership of government.

In the evolution of the present system society has been divided mainly into two classes, and these are at war with each other—war to the death. In the presence of this fact it is vain and foolish to talk about "the public." There is no "public"—there are classes, capitalists and wage workers, and these are locked in a worldwide class struggle that will grow more and more intense as the working class come into consciousness of their overmastering power—a struggle that

† Published as "The Social Revolution" in *Appeal to Reason,* whole no. 501 (July 8, 1905), 2.

will end only with the complete overthrow of the capitalist class and the substitution of the Working Class Republic for the existing capitalist bureaucracy.

This means a social revolution, and we are now in the midst of it.

We socialists are wasting no time over municipal ownership in the capitalist system. We are not appealing to the "public." We know that the "public," as at present constituted, consists wholly of the capitalist class, and that the 25 million wage-slaves are not in it. We know that this is the "public" that now controls the government, absolutely—municipal, state, and national—the press, the pulpit, and the school, and we know that this class that masquerades as the "public" have exploited and debauched the nation and hold its toilers in subjection, and that this class must be driven from power before relief can come to the people.

To accomplish this is the historic mission of the working class revolution of the twentieth century. We would rather open the eyes of a single workingman to the class struggle than convert ten thousand to the hallucinations of public ownership in a privately owned and privately controlled municipality.

In a recent editorial in the *New York World,* under the caption of "Triple State Socialism versus Democracy," the country is warned that William Jennings Bryan[39] is in conspiracy with others to forge the triple chains of municipal, state, and national socialism for the American people. This awful calamity is denominated "Triple State Socialism"—a compound fracture of terms.

To any who have read even a primer on socialism, the article is hilariously ridiculous.

In the first place, Mr. Bryan is not only not a socialist, but the very extremest of individualists.

In the next place, what the *World* writer has on the brain is not state socialism—there is no such thing—but state capitalism. That is what Liebknecht called it when Bismarck cunningly conceded capitalist government ownership of certain things to the working class to head off the socialist movement, and that is precisely what it is.

But it failed in Germany, and so it will here.

The thing the *New York World* calls socialism bears about as much relation to socialism as a lobster does to a man. The next time the *World* has to attack socialism, it should engage a writer who has at least a glimmer of an idea as to what socialism really is, and not allow its horse editor to create such havoc in its editorial columns.

There are many millions of wage workers in the United States. Their economic interests as such are absolutely identical. Day by day this great army is being hammered into revolutionary solidarity. They have the power to conquer the earth—they need only light. This light is now breaking. The horizon is already aglow with the dawn.

From the blazing eyes of the aroused and arousing working class there flashes athwart the pathway of progress the doom of capitalist misrule and wage-slavery.

The working class made all our marvelous machinery, do all our work, and produce all our wealth; and since the working class could and can perform all these miracles they can also make themselves the masters of this machinery and use it freely to produce wealth in abundance for themselves.

Nothing is more simple, more sane, more inevitable.

The working class do not need the Rockefellers,[40] the Morgans,[41] the Vanderbilts,[42] and the Goulds,[43] and in due time these industrial despots will be given their certificates of dismissal as rulers and the working class will rule themselves.

The parasite lords of capitalist society are no more necessary and no more ornamental than were the feudal lords of the middle ages or the slaveholders of the last century. While the workers are under a thousand disadvantages in this world-struggle, they have the votes, and they are being trained and drilled every hour of the day and night to aim at the capitalist system and vote straight.

The capitalist politicians may exploit municipal ownership to their heart's content. They will not fool the socialists. The working class know what they want and how to get it.

On with the Social Revolution!

Now for Action[†]

July 27, 1905

The convention has done its work and the new organization is in the field.

All hail to the "Industrial Workers of the World."

Now for action!

† Published in *Miners' Magazine,* July 27, 1905, unspecified page. Copy preserved in *Papers of Eugene V. Debs microfilm edition*, reel 7, frame 224.

Every progressive unionist, and every other honest worker, should rally to the standard of the new union.

Let no lying press reports deceive or mislead you. The convention was a splendid success and the results will make working class history.

The Chicago daily papers were uniformly loyal to the American Federation of Labor and its affiliated bodies, and uniformly hostile to the Industrial Workers. When capitalist papers become the mouthpieces of labor unions, it is high time for the members of those unions to open their eyes, for there is surely something rotten in Denmark.

A few days before the industrial convention met, all the Chicago dailies were publishing columns and columns of reports showing that the local labor leaders had accepted thousands of dollars of bribes, that the labor unions were honeycombed with corruption, and the grand jury, then in session, was urged to probe the foul disclosures to their depths without fear or favor, but presto! As if by magic, the investigation ceases, the grand jury is paralyzed, and the Chicago dailies are dumb.

Not another word. Not one.

The batteries are now turned upon the industrial convention which promises a clean labor movement which the Chicago press had been clamoring for.

Every lie that malignity could conceive was told about the convention, while the same capitalist press appealed to union men to beware of the industrial organization and to remain loyal to the good old "conservative" unions which a few days before they had been denouncing for their corruption and their crimes.

Do the Chicago papers, the organs of the capitalist class, and run for the profit of that class, want a clean labor movement?

Does not a clean labor movement mean death to the capitalist system and to the robbery of the working class?

Does not the salvation of the capitalist class depend upon a weak, perverted, and corrupt labor movement?

It can be set down as a rule that a labor organization that is sanctioned by the capitalist press has betrayed the working class and ought to be deserted by that class as an unclean thing to be shunned by honest men.

I shall always be proud of having been a delegate to the industrial convention. There was more class-consciousness there to the square inch than I have ever before seen in a labor convention. If there was a self-seeker in the whole delegation, I failed to see him. Not one wanted office; not one sought any personal favor, but all were seriously concerned about uniting the whole working class to fight the battles of the working class on the economic field, and it was this great object that absorbed the attention of the delegates and consumed the time of the convention.

The general officers of the industrial union are commanding types of the proletarian—honest, efficient, courageous, and unswervingly true to their class—while the rank and file are the stuff with which to build a revolutionary organization.

In May next another convention will be held to complete the work so auspiciously begun, and I want to make the prediction that it will be the greatest labor convention ever assembled in this country.

Let a local union be organized at once at every available point and let every member everywhere do his whole duty, and, in spite of all the opposition that can be brought against it, the Industrial Workers will hew out its pathway to victory.

The Industrial Workers of the World Convention and Its Work†

(July 29, 1905)

A few words in regard to the new industrial union recently organized in Chicago may be of interest to the readers of *The Socialist,* especially since the capitalist press reports designedly played fast and loose with the convention and made special efforts to have it appear ridiculous and contemptible.

It is worthy of remark that the Chicago dailies rallied about the American Federation of Labor as loyally as if they had been its own official organs, and in the name of "organized labor" these capitalist mouthpieces poured their venom upon the industrial convention, misrepresented its mission, and lied outright about its personnel and proceedings. I state this fact not merely because of its obvious significance, but because these organs, during the Teamsters' strike, howled

† Published as "The Industrial Workers: Eugene V. Debs Writes of the Convention and Its Work" in *The Socialist* [Toledo, OH], vol. 5, whole no. 253 (July 29, 1905), 2.

incessantly about the corruption of organized labor, the depravity of its leaders, and the barbarity of its methods, as if these talking tools of the capitalists wanted a clean labor movement. On occasion, when it suits their interest, they decry pure and simple trade unionism, but let there be an honest effort to unite the workers in a clean movement, and presto! these same organs rally round these same old unions and scrupulously guard them as their own precious charge, well knowing that a clean labor movement means death to the capitalist system and that the salvation of the capitalist class depends literally upon a rotten labor movement.

This preliminary statement will account for the uniform hostility of the capitalist dailies to the industrial convention and for the instructions that were issued to the reporters to "knock" it from start to finish.

In the 30 years I have been connected with organized labor, I have never attended a more representative gathering of the working class. It was in the true sense a proletarian parliament, class-consciousness being the distinguishing characteristic of the body.

In all the convention there was not, so far as could be observed, a single delegate who sought office, or any personal favor whatsoever. If there was a self-seeker in the delegation, I failed to see him.

The proceedings were marked with all the severities of debate, but at no time were the bounds of propriety exceeded; and although the delegates were intensely in earnest, they accorded each other the fullest privilege of being respectfully heard from the opening to the close of the proceedings.[44]

It is quite true that the results of the convention are subject to criticism; that the objects of the meeting were not fully and perfectly carried out; but there is reason for this and it can be easily explained. The delegates who composed the convention did not meet upon the same uniform footing as is the case with other conventions; some represented organizations with full power to act, some with limited powers, some with instructions to report back, while others represented themselves only, and under such circumstances it was not to be expected that the work of organizing a full-fledged industrial union could be carried out according to the general plan and in detail, and the most that could be reasonably expected was that a provisional plan of united action could be adopted and a clean beginning made in the right direction, and this much was accomplished beyond all doubt, and in May next another convention will be held, more largely attended to complete the work and furnish the new organization its full equipment for its great mission.

The need for a great, sound economic organization of the working class, industrial in form and expressing the class struggle, is urgently felt in this country. The political movement depends largely upon it and I cannot conceive that the political movement could ever develop great strength without it. This, I think, is pretty generally conceded, but there is considerable difference of opinion as to whether our comrades should stick to the old unions and "reform" them, or join the new organization. Needless to say that I take the latter view. The comrades who still support the old unions are honest, no doubt, but they are mistaken in supposing that they can convert the old unions into new agencies in the interest of the working class. The capitalists have gotten hold of the old unions and will never relax their grasp on them. The comrades who imagine they can change these unions from within had just as well remain in the Populist, or Democratic, or Republican parties, expecting to change them from within, instead of pulling out and organizing a new party to accomplish a new mission.

Some of the criticisms upon the comrades who have joined the new organization prompt me to put it upon record that the Socialist Party is not in any way, directly or indirectly, committed to the American Federation of Labor; and there is nothing compared in the party resolutions which prevents a member from joining any trade union which he may see fit; so that certain comrades have as good a right, from the standpoint of the Socialist Party, to join the Industrial Workers as certain others have to be in the American Federation of Labor.

With these differences the party, as a party, has nothing to do, and if they are brought into the party to the detriment of the party, it will be simply because certain comrades are officiously intent upon controlling the trade union action of certain other comrades.

To me it seems not only impossible but absurd to expect the American Federation of Labor, under its capitalistic Civic Federation supervision, to turn itself inside out, as certain of our comrades expect it will do in the course of a few years or centuries, but I do not in the least question their right to stick to the old unions. If the old unions suit them, well and good; they don't suit me, and what I claim is that I have as good a right to join a trade union that suits me as they have to join one that suits them.

When it comes to the charge of "splitting" the trade union movement, there is something so silly and stupid about it in the light of existing facts that it seems nothing less than idiotic. The Teamsters' strike in Chicago has just collapsed as the result of a "split" in the pure and simple movement, which is made up of "splits" and could not exist if the workers were really united, as they ought to be, and as they will be in spite of those who are dividing them while charging those who are seeking actually to unite them as splitters of the union labor movement.

Look at Chicago today. The American Federation of Labor has had almost complete jurisdiction and what does it consist of but a mass of snarling "autonomists" and slugging factions?

Under the old regime every handful of men that are ground through the hopper of industrial evolution must have a separate union, separate jurisdiction, and above all, and most important of all, a separate set of "grand" or "supreme" officers, of whom there is an army and to whose personal interest it is to keep the workers divided into innumerable petty factions, looking to and depending upon their "leaders" to keep the wolf from the fold.

An old backwoods preacher, in a moment of perfect candor, said to his flock: "I am your shepherd and ye are my mutton."

The working class are going to unite, economically and politically, for their emancipation. A united, class-conscious working class on the economic field has long been needed—needed by the workers, needed by the Socialist Party, and needed, above all, as an essential part of the labor movement; and the Industrial Workers is now in the field and progressive unionists are rallying to its standard, and with the splendid start that has been made and the thousands of tried and true class-conscious workers already enrolled, there is not the least doubt but that the late convention will prove an historic one and that the new organization, with all the opposition that can be marshaled against it, will march steadily to the front and hew out its way to success.

The New Working Class Union†

August 5, 1905

The new working class union, the Industrial Workers of the World, recently organized in Chicago, starts out under the most cheering auspices, notwithstanding the false and malicious reports of the capitalist press.

† Published as "Working Class Unionism" in *Appeal to Reason,* whole no. 505 (August 5, 1905), 4.

In all the 30 years of my experience in organized labor, I never attended a more typical convention of class-conscious workers. The usual candidates for office and self-seekers were conspicuous by their absence.

It would have been interesting if members of Congress and of the Senate of the United States could have been lookers-on. They would have heard more solid truth about the labor question than they ever have or ever will in the museum for congressional fossils at the national capital.

The debates were carried forward on a high plane, and although at times the fire flashed, there was no unfair advantages taken, and one object uppermost in every mind was the unification of all workers in a great class-conscious industrial organization to fight the battles of workers in the struggle for better conditions and for their ultimate emancipation from wage-slavery.

And this was accomplished. The new organization is now in the field, and progressive unionists and many who have hitherto held aloof from unions are flocking to its standard.

Charles O. Sherman, the general president, is a thoroughly seasoned fighter for the working class. He was a loyal member of the American Railway Union, made an honorable record in the Pullman strike, and through all these years has been at the front as the fearless and uncompromising champion of organized labor. Upon his record as a workingman, as a unionist, and as a man there is not a blemish. Sherman—and I have seen him in the fire of battle and know him well—is honest in every hair of his head and every drop of his blood. He is mentally wide-awake, class-conscious, and has patience, courage, and energy, and if duty demands it, he has the heroism and self-forgetfulness to walk straight into the jaws of hell.

As chairman of the executive board, Charles H. Moyer of Colorado is the very man for the place, and his name is of itself sufficient guarantee of loyalty to the working class. The rest of the officers are typical unionists, and each has a record of fidelity to the cause of labor which will bear the closest inspection.

The rank and file of the membership consists of the most progressive trade unionists in the country. Several national organizations are already included and several others are on the way. From every section of the country come applications for membership and for charters for local unions. The printed matter is now in course of preparation and in a few days organizers will be in the field and the work of organizing will begin in earnest. The most aggressive measures will be taken to prosecute the propaganda and to build up the organization.

Every worker everywhere should join this great new industrial organization. The old union movement is in control of the capitalist class and used as a bulwark to the capitalist system.

The Industrial Workers, the new union, is organized to wage relentless warfare upon the exploiting class, and to use all its powers in the interest of the wealth-producers of the nation. There will be no Civic Federation attachment to the industrial union and the term compromise will be unknown in its lexicon.

Those who are interested in the new organization and desire information in regard to it should address W. E. Trautmann, general secretary, 148 W Madison Street, Chicago, Illinois.

Labor Is the Great Power: Chautauqua Lecture in Dixon, Illinois [excerpt]†

August 8, 1905

Through all the centuries past, the few have ruled while the many have served; the few have worn the purple and wielded the scepter while the many have borne the burdens, lived in poverty, and died in despair. The primary being was a brute. He lived in a cave. His wants were few and he depended upon his brute force and his low cunning to obtain them. It has required thousands of years to lift man from that low plane and raise him to his present exalted place—but he is not yet a free and independent being. In this discussion I do not wish to appeal to your prejudices or to excite your passions; I will simply address myself to your reason.

Labor the Great Power

Labor is the great power that made the world what it is. Labor it is that fashions the ore of the hills into blade and tool; labor it is that gathers the fleeces and

† Published as "Eugene V. Debs Lectured Upon Social Problems" in *Dixon [IL] Evening Telegraph,* vol. 22, no. 184 (August 9, 1905), 1, 5.

transforms them into myriad of fabrics; labor it is that bids the forest to fall and in its place builds the home and factory. Everywhere labor has been responsible for the advancement of mankind in every direction. Shall it then not come into its own? Is it not time that labor should receive its just reward?

A century and a quarter ago the inhabitants of this country were subjects. They obeyed the laws of the crown, whatever those might be. But there were a few who were in advance of their time, a few who were pioneers in progress, a few who dared to say that man had the capacity to govern himself. And so these few began an agitation.

Thomas Jefferson was one of these and he was denounced by the Tory press as a rebel. Patrick Henry, who delivered that immortal oration, was another, but he was condemned as one who would overthrow the existing institutions of government and was therefore an enemy of the people. It is a fact that when our forefathers began their struggle for freedom, the majority of the people believed they were in the wrong. They did not see how it would be possible for a nation to exist without a king. But in spite of the protest of the majority, these men continued to agitate until the American revolution broke forth, and as a result, for the first time in history man stood forth a coronated sovereign.

Then the people applauded. Then the minority became the majority.

Causes of Inequality

But though the American revolution made us political equals it did not make us economic equals, and if men deserve to be political equals, do they not also deserve to be economic and social equals? When they are such then caste and class will disappear.

The history of the development of man is largely the history of the development of the tool he uses to develop the land. In the early history of our country there was a reasonably fair distribution of wealth. There were no multi-millionaires and comparatively few paupers. Today there are thousands on the one side and millions on the other side, and both are a menace to society. In the early days the employee owned the tools with which he earned his living; today the tool is owned by the employer.

Today the capitalist buys labor as cheap as he can buy it and the employee sells it as dearly as he can sell it. Society has been divided into two classes as a result of this and we are living today under the capitalist system. Under this system labor produces, not for its own benefit, but for the benefit of its employer. It has employment only so long as the employer can find a profitable market for the manufactured goods. The result is that when the capitalist has manufactured so many of his goods that there is no longer a profitable market in which to dispose of them, he closes down his shops and his mills and laboring men are left, often to suffer or starve in the very shadow of the wealth that his labor has created.

It makes no difference whether the tariff be high or low, the money standard be of gold or silver—overproduction is bound to result from the present capitalistic system and the outcome is in every case a panic. The first of these panics occurred in 1873. The men then left idle started roaming about looking for work with which to support their wives and children. The work could not be found. When 400 or 500 miles away from their own homes, these men, finding no employment anywhere and tormented by the thought that at home their families were suffering from want and privation, grew despondent; their self-respect deserted them, their ambition was killed in their breasts, and they fell to the level of a tramp. But he did not remain a mere tramp. Enforced idleness made him degenerate and he became a criminal.

A Change Must Come

This is one of the results of the capitalist system. Every society has its period of growth, its maturity, and then its death. This is true of the present social system. It has fulfilled its mission and it will soon be put an end to.

In the feudal ages, man worked five days for his master and one day for himself. The lords claimed an alliance with God and that they were the natural masters of the common man. They believed their system would prevail forever. But their age came and went and in the place of the lords came the tradesmen, who have since developed into the capitalists.

The capitalist system has run its race and a change is in sight. When your great-grandfather made a pair of boots, they were his. He received the full value of his toil in making them. Today you may make a thousand pairs of boots and you won't own a single pair of them. The capitalist owns the tool and you can use it only for his benefit. He operates his factory while there is a profit in it for him and then he closes it up, leaving the employees to suffer.

Andrew Carnegie is a capitalist. He owns the tool by which great quantities of steel are made. Carnegie didn't make that tool. He just owns it, and he appropriates all the profits accrued from its use to himself. When he has made more steel than he can dispose of profitably, he closes the mills. He does not consult the men about it, for the capitalist system says that he can't take the men into account. It doesn't matter how much suffering may result from the closing of the mills, for under the capitalist system labor is the cheapest commodity in the world. Carnegie is a parasite, a profit-taker. If this body of men whom the capitalist employs has the brains to make and use this machinery, they ought to have intelligence enough to get some of the profit out of it.

The income of John D. Rockefeller is $33,000 an hour. Just think of it. As much as a man working for $1.50 a day could make in 74 long years. Thus it is possible for the capitalist to exploit the laboring man.

The middle class, once called the bulwark of the nation, is fast disappearing. The department store is crushing the small dealer; the bonanza farmer is outstripping the common farmer. It is said that the time is not far distant when ten men will control all there is of value in this country.

Deplorable Conditions

It is impossible to impress upon the people of small western cities the truth of what I have said about the sufferings of the laboring people. In Dixon, for instance, you have no multimillionaires, but go to any large city and you will see the deplorable conditions of which I have spoken. Every large city has a slum and efforts are being continually made to wipe them out or to at least confine them to certain districts. From what are the slums recruited? From the cities. The big mercantile and industrial establishments that wear out the lives of innumerable girls and children, paying them from $2 to $3 a week, furnish the majority of the recruits to this undesirable feature of city life. Subject to temptations on every hand and able to earn only a miserable pittance, they soon yield to the tempter and fall.

Why is it that the young are seized and destroyed by the hand of Mammon? Not because capital has no feeling, but because the present competitive system requires the capitalist to hire the cheapest possible help. He must buy labor as cheap as possible. The man is displaced and a woman employed at a cheaper scale. The woman is displaced in order that a child may be hired at a still cheaper wage.

Socialism

Socialism would establish cooperation instead of competition. Socialism is opposed today by the capitalist and the small merchant who has hopes of being someday himself a capitalist. They who oppose socialism believe that it would take from those who have and give to those who have not. Nothing is more untrue. We do not want your small capital, Mr. Merchant; we want the earth. We will simply leave you to the capitalist and when he gets through with you, you will come to us of your own accord. There are thousands of socialists today who were opposed to the system yesterday.

Socialism is not anarchy; it is diametrically opposed to anarchy. Anarchy proposes the overthrow of government; socialism proposes the perfection of government. Socialism believes in all for all, not all for a few.

The socialist believes instead of enslaving his fellows he should consecrate himself to his fellows' service. Under the capitalist system men must fight each other for bread; under that condition men cannot love each other. Our economic conditions must always determine our conduct toward each other. Slavery was legal while it was considered an economic necessity; when it was no longer a necessity it was made illegal. Under the present system a man can't walk up to you on the street and rob or kill you, but he can rob and exploit you by more subtle means. Ruskin[45] says it is just as bad to rob a man with a long head as with a long arm.

Socialism finds no fault with the individual but rather with the system. The earth is or should be an equal heritage for all that inhabit it. A man ought not to be dependent on any other man for work and a livelihood. Socialism now has 8 million adherents, men and women in every part of the globe who are working for economic equality. Political liberty is of no great benefit without economic freedom, and so the workers of the world are organizing themselves for the overthrow of capitalism.

In 25 years there will be no capitalists, for we are on the eve of a great change. Workingmen should follow the example of the capitalist. The capitalist does not want competition, he wants cooperation with other capitalists, and hence we have the trusts. What is a trust? It is the 1905 machine. We talk about smashing trusts. We could no more destroy the trusts than we could force the rivers back from the ocean. The evil of a trust is not in the trust itself but in its operation for the benefit of a few. No man on the inside of a trust says it is a bad thing. It is only the fellow on the outside, who has failed to get on the inside, that is against it. We are not going to destroy the trust. We are going to take possession of it.

There is a single great question before us today. It is the question of capital and labor. The workers are separating from the party of the trusts and are organizing one of their own. Socialism favors the collective ownership of everything. It is the true friend of humanity. It wants to put an end to strife and bloodshed and war, for war is only the result of commercial conquest. I wish I could get just one appropriation from Congress and that would be for enough money to sink every fighting vessel in the navy.

Socialism will put an end to child labor. There are men enough to do all the work there is to be done in the country. Under socialism we will produce to use, not to sell, and labor will get all the profit to which it is entitled.

The Chautauqua Platform and Its Opportunities[†]

August 26, 1905

The rapid development of the Chautauqua[46] as a means of popular education and entertainment in the summer season suggests the increasing possibilities thus afforded of reaching the masses with the propaganda of socialism.[47]

Until recently the line has been drawn on socialism, and no advocate of socialist doctrine has been allowed a place on a Chautauqua platform—but it is different now, as the pressure has become too great and the bars have been lowered, and now the voice of the socialist is heard from the Chautauqua rostrum.

The Chautauqua, according to my experience, is usually under the management of liberal-minded men who, while perhaps opposing socialism, are yet willing that it shall have a full and fair hearing, and this, coupled with the fact that there is always a large and increasing demand among all sorts and conditions of people for light upon this vital subject, makes it possible, with a little effort, to get more and more socialist speakers upon the programs of the Chautauqua assemblies, which are increasing rapidly in number and spreading to all the states of the Union.

Some of the advantages of getting our comrades on the Chautauqua platform may be stated as follows:

First—The Chautauqua is a great popular outdoor school, usually in a fine grove, where a day's or a week's outing and entertainment may be enjoyed at very small expense.

---

† Published in *Appeal to Reason,* whole no. 508 (August 26, 1905), 4.

Second—The people of the surrounding country camp on the grounds and are there until the close of the season, so that, rain or shine, a great crowd, running into thousands, is almost invariably assured.

Third—The Chautauqua furnishes a perfectly free and untrammeled platform, and the speaker on its program is given the fullest opportunity to deliver his message in all its integrity and without the least restraint.

Fourth—Thousands of persons attend the Chautauqua gatherings who do not go to socialist meetings.

Fifth—Exceptional opportunities are afforded for reaching the farm workers, who take advantage of the Chautauqua to give themselves and families the benefit of the outing and its program of education and recreation.

Sixth—No better place could be found for the distribution of socialist papers and pamphlets, and our literature could thus be sent to thousands of homes that are ready for it and would eagerly receive and read it.

Seventh—There is a high average intelligence at Chautauqua gatherings, those attending being reading and thinking people, and nowhere is the message of socialism given a more attentive hearing or hearty reception.

Eighth—At the close of the lecture, the people always gather about the speaker, ask about literature, papers, party matters, etc., and the very best chance is given to start these people on the right road.

It is interesting to note that while thousands of those who attend the Chautauqua meetings were once Populists, they are no longer so; they want no populist discussion, but they do want to know about socialism, and are ready at almost every point to join in the demand to put a socialist speaker on the program.

We have scores of comrades who are in every way qualified to speak for socialism on the Chautauqua platform, and they can and should be put there. The program for the season is usually made up in the fall preceding, and wherever a Chautauqua is located—and there are now hundreds scattered over the country—our comrades, however few they may be, should be united in requesting the committee to place a socialist speaker on the list, and it surely will be done in many cases.

Although we have had but a limited hearing thus far, Socialist Day at the Chautauqua has already proved to be one of the biggest days and often the most largely attended day of the session.

Here is a great and growing opportunity if we but take advantage of it, and I hope soon to see every available comrade on the Chautauqua platform.

Working Class Unity†

September 9, 1905

The burning question of the hour is that of unity, and by this I mean the unity of all workers for the overthrow of capitalism. The country is full of object lessons demonstrating its imperative necessity.

The attempts to unite the working class in the past have all failed, in the main, and at the same time it must be admitted that all have succeeded to some extent.

The philosophical insight of Karl Marx enabled him to foresee the absolute necessity of the unification of all workers of all countries, and the evolution of industry has made it so clear that only the mentally blind now fail to see it. The interests of the working class are so self-evidently identical that their unity would seem to follow as a matter of course, but it is just here that the ingenuity and satanic cruelty of capitalism is taxed to prevent the workers from uniting and acting together to throw off the yoke of wage-slavery, which keeps them in a state of brutal servility and submissiveness scarce a degree above the beasts of the field.

The trade union movement is filled with spies, spotters,[48] and sneaks, whose craven natures fit them for their damnable treachery in secretly betraying their brethren while wearing the union badge and pretending to be loyal to its principles.

The Socialist Party has not yet developed sufficient power to be an actual menace to the capitalist system, but even now there are those in its ranks who will bear watching, and when the point is reached where the party becomes a contesting factor in the political field, the same spies and traitors will infest its councils and attempt to thwart the honest efforts of the loyal comrades to unite the workers and keep them united in the struggle for emancipation.

But despite these dangers and difficulties through which the labor movement will be required to pass, and which are in fact necessary to its development, working class unity will be achieved, for only by this means can the impending revolution be accomplished; and when the time comes, all obstacles to unity that may be thrown in the way by the hirelings of the capitalist class will be swept aside by the resistless march of the workers to the goal of freedom.

† Published in the *Chicago Socialist,* vol. 6, whole no. 340 (September 9, 1905), 1.

The central theme for Labor Day should be the unity, industrial and political, of the working class. Without this, failure is a foregone conclusion; with it, success is inevitable.

The last two years are replete with valuable experience for workers, organized and unorganized. Practically every strike of consequence has been defeated; scores of unions have been disrupted; courts have encroached steadily upon labor unions until they are so hedged about that even if they had the power for successful resistance, they would be helpless to exercise it in any way that would benefit the rank and file.

Besides this, the capitalists, manufacturers, and employers generally have organized for economic and political action in the interest of their class, and they are so conscious of their class interests and so responsive to them in every hour of trial that when there is a battle on they move with the precision of a well-drilled army and not the slightest friction prevents complete unity of action; and this is why they are uniformly successful in sweeping the field and leaving their adversaries, the poorly organized and class-unconscious workers, a routed and demoralized mob, with their best fighters stark and dead where they fell in their tracks.

There can be no true and lasting working class unity that is not based upon sound principles and that does not express sound working class economics.

The American Federation of Labor and its affiliated unions, denying the class struggle and attempting to anchor the exploited workers to their exploiting masters on a mutually satisfactory basis of exploitation, will never effectually unite the workingmen of the United States. Its daily record bears testimony to its increasing impotency. It has numbers enough, but lacks solidarity. Numbers alone count for little and not even that little long.

Ten thousand class-conscious workers have far greater dynamic power than a hundred thousand whose only conception of unionism is to fawn at the feet of their masters and boast loudly of a great victory when the miserable wage pittance has been increased 15 cents a week, or the defeated members allowed to wear their union buttons on the patched seat of their trousers.

There are certain so-called labor leaders who court the smiles and wiles of the capitalist class in the vain hope of effecting permanently harmonious relations between them and their fleeced and miserable victims. The working class will never be united on that basis or under that leadership.

In the first place, true working class unity must be of the working class itself. It must be class-conscious and if it is this, it will also be self-reliant, self-disciplined, determined, and in the end victorious. A thousand defeats may fall to its lot and each of them will but leave it stronger than before.

Next, there can be no perfect unity, no real solidarity, except that which has both economic and political foundations. The class-conscious trade union is absolutely essential to the class-conscious political party, and both are indispensable to the labor movement if that movement is to mean unity and unity is to mean unconquerable determination to abolish wage-slavery and emancipate the working class.

Next, the form of the union must express the state of industry. The pure and simple union of 25 years ago is as completely out of date as are the tools that were in use at that time. That form of unionism is based upon tools that have long since been discarded and, upon consideration, that no longer exist. The concentration of industry and the combination of capitalists necessitates concentration in unionism unless unionism is to become as obsolete and useless as the trades from which it sprang. The hundreds of old unions, more or less in conflict with each other and striving vainly to maintain their independent jurisdictions to the benefit only of the staff of salaried officers they support, and such walking delegates[49] and agents as traffic in unionism to line their own pockets, bear sufficient testimony to their inefficiency, and it is but a question of time until they must entirely disappear in that capacity.

The Industrial Workers recently organized at Chicago expresses clearly and logically the industrial demands of the working class up to date. This new industrial organization declares in favor of political action in waging the class struggle. It actually unites all workers so that any given industry is under the sole jurisdiction of a single union and the workers in any given department are assured of the united support of all their coworkers in the event of a strike or other exigency that requires the united action of all.

This is the only kind of unionism that will prevail against the capitalistic combinations of the present day. The working class must be organized as never before, must be united as never before, and above all, must be class-conscious, economically and politically, as never before.

A single union on the industrial field and a single party on the political field, each the counterpart of the other and supplementing and strengthening the other; each supreme in its respective sphere, the union recognizing the need for political action and the party recognizing the need for industrial action, and both in harmonious cooperation with each other, is the great and imperative demand of this time and to bring this about every worker should bend all his energies and put forth all the ability at his command.

What Socialism Proposes†

September 23, 1905

In the United States, as in other countries, international socialism is making tremendous strides and its millions of supporters, spread over all the belts and zones of the globe, and the most active propagandists ever known, will in the next few years be multiplied into controlling majorities in all lands which have modern industry as the basis of their civilization, socialism being wholly a question of economic development. This will mean the end of the present capitalist competitive system and the introduction of its successor, the cooperative commonwealth.

The movement is international because it was born of and follows the development of the capitalist system, which, in its operation, is confined to no country, but by the stimulus of modern agencies of production, exchange, communication, and transportation, has overleaped all boundary lines and made the world the theater of its activities. By this process all the nations of the earth must finally be drawn into relations of industrial and commercial cooperation, as the economic basis of human brotherhood.

This is the goal of modern socialism, and it is this that inspires its disciples with the zeal and ardor of crusaders.

What is socialism? To answer in a single sentence, it means the collective ownership by all the people of all the means of wealth production and distribution. It is purely an economic question; the evolution of industry has developed socialism. Man can only work, produce wealth, with tools. The mere hand tools of former times have become ponderous and costly machines. These machines, socialists contend, represent progressive social conceptions. These and the factories, mills, and shops in which they housed, as well as the lands and mines from which the raw materials are drawn, are used in common by the workers, and in their very nature are marked for common ownership and control. Socialism does not propose the collective ownership of property, but of capital; that is to say, the instruments of wealth production, which, in the form of private property, enable a few capitalists to exploit vast numbers of

† Published in *The Metal Worker,* unspecified issue. Reprinted as "What Socialism Proposes!" in *Social Democratic Herald,* vol. 8, no. 21, whole no. 373 (September 23, 1905), 1.

workers, thus creating millionaires and mendicants and inaugurating class rule and all its odious and undemocratic distinctions.

Socialism proposes equal rights and opportunities for all without reference to sex, color, or other conditions. Equality is the vital principle of socialism. Its mission is to abolish class rule by making all equal proprietors of the means upon which all depend for employment, and without which there can be no "life, liberty, and the pursuit of happiness." This insures economic freedom for every human being. As no one would have private property in that upon which another depended for employment, industrial mastery and slavery would disappear together and competition for profit would give way to cooperation for use.

The rapidly changing economic conditions are paving the way for the transition from competitive capitalism to cooperative socialism. Socialists are simply indicating the trend of evolution, and seeking to prepare the way for its orderly reception. The coming of socialism is with them not a debatable question. That is not a matter of debate or conjecture, but of scientific socialism.

The evolution of the social organization is a fact in nature. In the ceaseless process one state of society follows another in the sequence of succession. Capitalism, the present system, was warmed into life in the womb of feudalism and sprang from the medieval system. Within the span of two centuries this system has practically reached the climax of its development, and the marvelous material progress of that period exceeds the achievements of all the centuries since the slaves of Pharaoh built the pyramids.

The rapid centralization of capital and the extensive cooperation of labor mark the high state of economic development. Individual initiative and competitive efforts are becoming less and less possible. The day of small production has passed, never to return. Notwithstanding all outcry, trust and department stores, these great modern agencies increase in number and power. They are the inevitable outgrowth of the competitive system. The efforts of the small capitalists to destroy trusts will prove as fruitless as the efforts of the workingman to destroy labor-saving machines when first introduced in the last century.

Socialists take the ground that the trust in itself is not an evil, that the evil lies wholly in the private ownership, and they propose to transfer all such agencies from private hands to the collectivity, to be managed and operated for the good of all.

In the last century, millions of workers were exploited of the fruit of their labor under the institution of chattel slavery. Work, being done by hand, ownership of the slave was a condition necessary to his exploitation. But chattel slavery disappeared before the march of industrial evolution, and today would be an economic impossibility. It is no longer necessary to own the body of the workingman in order to appropriate the fruit of his labor; it is only necessary to own the tool with which he works, and without which he is helpless. This tool in its modern form is a vast machine which the worker cannot afford to buy, and against which he cannot compete with his bare hands, and in the very nature of the situation he is at the mercy of the owner of the machine, his employment is precarious, and his very life is suspended by a thread.

Then, again, the factory and mine are operated for profit only and the owner can, and often does, close it down at will, throwing hundreds, perhaps thousands, out of employment who, with their families, are as helpless as if in the desert wastes of Sahara.

The few who own the machines do not use them. The many who use them do not own them. The few who own them are enabled to exploit the many who use them; hence a few millionaires and many mendicants, extreme opulence and abject poverty, princely palaces and hideous huts, riotous extravagance and haggard want, constituting social scenes sickening to contemplate, and in the presence of which the master hand of Hugo or Dickens is palsied and has no mission.

The Socialist Party is organizing in every village and hamlet, every town and city of every state and territory of the Union. It is appealing to the people. It will neither fuse nor compromise. It proposes to press forward, step by step, until it conquers the political power and secures control of government.

This will mark the end of the capitalist system. The factories and mills and mines, the railroads and telegraph and telephone, and all other means of production and distribution will be transferred to the people in their collective capacity, industry will be operated cooperatively, and every human being will have the "inalienable right" to work and to enjoy the fruit of his labor. The hours of labor will be reduced according to the progress of invention. Rent, interest, and profit will be no more. The sordid spirit of commercial conquest will be dead. War and its ravages will pass into history. Economic equality will have triumphed, labor will stand forth emancipated, and the sons and daughters of men will glorify the triumphs of social democracy.

Discourse on Liberty: Excerpt from a Speech at Leavenworth, Kansas†

October 12, 1905

It does not matter that the Creator has sown with stars the fields of ether and decked the earth with countless beauties for man's enjoyment.

It does not matter that air and ocean teem with the wonders of innumerable forms of life to challenge man's admiration and investigation.

It does not matter that nature spreads forth all her scenes of beauty and gladness and pours forth the melodies of her myriad-tongued voices for man's delectation.

If liberty is ostracized and exiled, man is a slave, and the world rolls in space and whirls around the sun a gilded prison, a doomed dungeon, and though painted in all the enchanting hues that infinite art could command, it must still stand forth a blotch amidst the shining spheres of the sidereal heavens, and those who cull from the vocabularies of nations, living or dead, their flashing phrases with which to apostrophize liberty, are engaged in perpetuating the most stupendous delusion the ages have known.

Strike down liberty, no matter by what subtle art the deed is done, and the spinal cord of humanity is sundered and the world is paralyzed by the indescribable crime.

Strike the fetters from the slave, give him liberty, and he becomes an inhabitant of the world. He looks abroad and beholds life and joy in all things around him. His soul expands beyond all boundaries. Emancipated by the genius of liberty, he aspires to communion with all that is noble and beautiful, and feels himself allied to all the higher order of intelligences, and walks abroad, redeemed from animalism, ignorance, and superstition, a new being throbbing with glorious life.

† Published as part of the article "Eugene V. Debs on Socialism" in *Leavenworth Post*, vol. 1, no. 47 (October 13, 1905), 1.

The Coming Labor Union†

October 26, 1905

The opponents of the Industrial Workers, numerous, varied, and powerful though they be, will find themselves baffled in every attempt they make to stem the tide of the new organization.

These opponents, strange as it may seem, embrace, besides the capitalist class and their "labor lieutenants," socialists who profess to favor industrial unionism and trade unionists who profess to be class-conscious workingmen!

An anomalous situation indeed!

The only national labor union that recognizes the class struggle, the Industrial Workers of the World, is opposed, and the American Federation of Labor, whose leaders deny the class struggle, is supported by men who call themselves socialists and class-conscious workingmen.

But in spite of all this, the Industrial Workers is the coming labor union in the United States, and all the powers of capitalism and all the resources of its emissaries cannot prevent it. The conditions are mature for it and the working class will embrace it and stand by it as rapidly as they learn to comprehend meaning and grasp its mission.

Three years ago when the Western Federation of Miners and the American Labor Union, in national convention assembled, in Denver, struck the new trail of class-consciousness and declared in favor of independent political action along working class lines, the very thing socialists had been clamoring for, the press of the Socialist Party, almost solidly, instead of cheering the new departure and encouraging and supporting the movement, treated the matter coldly, or damned it with faint praise.

These papers felt themselves committed to the American Federation of Labor and feared to offend that anti-socialist organization. Under no other ground is such opposition to socialist action by socialist papers conceivable.

When the Industrial Workers of the World was recently organized at Chicago, the same socialist papers fought the movement openly, or, what revealed the same antagonistic attitude, remained silent.

† Published in *Miners' Magazine,* October 26, 1905, unspecified page. Reprinted in *The Weekly People,* vol. 15, no. 32 (November 4, 1905), 3 after running in *The Daily People* earlier that week.

These socialist papers, smiling patronizingly upon the American Federation of Labor, which repudiates and despises them, and frowning scornfully upon the Industrial Workers, a truly working class organization, have committed a grave mistake and appearances indicate that they are beginning to realize it. The open opposition has died out and silence has taken its place. They have evidently heard from the rank and file. In any event it will be well for them to know that DeLeon's *Weekly People* is getting a harvest of new subscribers, including many members of our party, because of his espousal of the Industrial Workers.

That socialists can still find it consistent to remain in the American Federation of Labor in light of its fixed pro-capitalist policy is, I confess, incomprehensible to me. Why do they not apply their peculiar logic to the political situation? The Republican and Democratic parties both consist mainly of workingmen. Why not turn them into working class parties? The workingmen have a majority of both—why organize a Socialist Party?

The workingman who reasons in that way and attends Republican or Democratic conventions as delegates is by socialists set down as an ignoramus or fakir, and yet that is precisely the attitude of certain socialists with reference to the old anti-labor Federation and the new working class union.

The American Federation of Labor, which is simply an attempt to harmonize pure and simple trade unions that were built up on tools long since discarded and on principles long ago out of date, is the enemy of working class solidarity. It is in control of the capitalist class. The Civic Federation and its personnel is sufficient proof of this fact.

It leers at the class struggle.

Professing to oppose independent political action by the working class and even forbidding the discussion of political questions, it connives with the political hucksters of the capitalist parties in consideration of beggarly "handouts" for its henchmen. This aggregation of one-time labor organizations has veered about and is now thoroughly reactionary, and every inch of genuine working class progress from this time forward will have to be made in spite of them.

Would but socialists remain away from the national convention of this alleged federation, the jurisdictional lightnings would then have full play and soon strike and sever the flimsy bonds that hold the antiquated old unions together. The few socialists serve the federation leaders in the valuable role of lightning rods to attract and divert the bolts of disintegration.

These socialist comrades are on a cold trail. Their misguided zeal is worthy of a better cause. There was a time when their efforts bore fruit, but that day is passed. They might as well spend their time, as Thomas Paine put it, "administering medicine to a corpse." The role they are now in at a federation convention is almost pathetic. Even the applause in the gallery is dying out. They are sadly out of place. They are in truth laughingstock—the footballs of two by four labor fakirs that serve the capitalist press for their stereotyped dispatch reporting the annual kicking out of socialism by the American Federation of Labor.

When the moon turns into green cheese will these socialists succeed in converting the American Federation of Labor, honeycombed with capitalistic influences, into a revolutionary working class organization. But in the meantime they are extremely valuable to the Federation leaders, who would undoubtedly seriously regret to be deprived of their services.

The opposition to the Industrial Workers, inspired by personal hatred for Daniel DeLeon and the Socialist Trade & Labor Alliance, is puerile, to say the least. With all that has been said about the latter, it has never been charged with being a capitalist annex and as for DeLeon personally, he is not an issue to be considered when choosing between a bona fide labor union organized for the benefit of the working class and a bogus labor organization defended by every capitalist paper and supported by every capitalist politician in the land.

DeLeon is sound on the question of trade unionism and to that extent, whether I like him or not personally, I am with him. My personal likes and dislikes are secondary to my allegiance to the working class.

The choice is between the AF of L and capitalism on one side and the Industrial Workers and socialism on the other. The AF of L is for the wage system; the Industrial Workers for its abolition. How can a socialist hesitate in his choice an instant?

The AF of L keeps the working class divided into trades which have ceased to exist; the Industrial Workers unites them into one compact militant body. Which of these truly expresses the present industrial situation and which actually stands for working class solidarity?

As a member of both the Industrial Workers[50] and the Socialist Party, I want to see one class-conscious labor union on the industrial field and one class-conscious labor party on the political field, each the counterpart of the other, and both working together in harmonious cooperation to overthrow the capitalist system and emancipate the workers from wage-slavery.

The Industrial Workers has made a sound beginning and at its next convention the work will be rounded out and the organization fairly started on its mission of proletarian emancipation.

The time has come to strike out boldly and cut loose from all associations that are not with and for the revolutionary program of the working class. Any professed labor organization that does not recognize the class struggle and stand squarely on the right side of it forfeits all claim to the respect of intelligent workingmen; and to remain with it is not to help the union get right, but to risk personal contamination.

The way to serve the working class through the AF of L is to get out of it and leave the capitalist class and their henchmen in undisputed control.

The paramount question is the labor movement and working class victory. All other things—parties and unions included—are secondary.

Therefore, organization, economic and political, along class lines. Any organization that attempts to obscure these lines damns itself.

The Industrial Workers is right. It has come at the right time and it will fight its way to the front! It is asking no favors of capitalism and granting none; it is pandering to no organization and no man or set of men to curry favors; it stands squarely on the class struggle, defiantly challenging the capitalist class, relying only upon the awakening working class to rally to its standard and carry it to victory.

Craft Unionism: Address at Aurora Hall, Chicago†

November 23, 1905

We have met under the auspices and in the interests of the Industrial Workers of the World. Organized here in Chicago less than five months ago, the Industrial Workers already number almost, if not quite, a hundred thousand workingmen and women, enrolled as dues-paying members in a revolutionary economic organization of the working class.[51]

† Published as the pamphlet *Craft Unionism: Speech by Eugene V. Debs, at Chicago, November 23, 1905* (Chicago: Industrial Workers of the World, n.d. [1905]). Reissued by Charles H. Kerr & Co. in 1909, ostensibly as a revised edition but actually virtually unchanged.

Why has this new organization been instituted? Why will not the old trade unions that already occupy the field serve the purpose? Why a new organization? These are questions that are up for consideration; that address themselves to all the workers of the country, whether they favor or oppose the new organization.

For many years I have been connected with one and another of the old trade unions. Indeed, since February 1875, when I first joined the Brotherhood of Locomotive Firemen, I have been an active member of a trade union; and during that time I have had some experience by virtue of which I trust I have profited sufficiently to enable me to determine whether a trade union is organized for the purpose of serving the working class or not.

At the very threshold of this discussion I aver that the old form of trade unionism no longer meets the demands of the working class. I aver that the old trade union has not only fulfilled its mission and outlived its usefulness, but that it is now positively reactionary and is maintained, not in the interests of the workers who support it, but in the interests of the capitalist class who exploit the workers who support it.

Let me cite an instance or two for illustration. The Brotherhood of Locomotive Engineers has been organized about 40 years. It professes to be a trade union, an organization of and for the working class. This organization has the favor and support of practically every railroad corporation in the United States. The late P. M. Arthur was its grand chief for many years. In the beginning of his official career he was true to the working class. As the organization developed in numbers and in power, and became a menace to the corporations, they realized the necessity of securing control of that organization. And how did they go about it? By making certain nominal concessions to that so-called brotherhood, by flattering its grand chief, by declaring that they had no objection to a labor organization such as this brotherhood, especially while under the supervision of so conservative a leader as Mr. Arthur. Every time the corporations made a concession to the engineers, it was at the expense of poorly paid employees in other departments who were unorganized; and when the men in these departments protested and when finally they went out on strike, the engineers have invariably been used by the corporation to defeat their fellow workers, who were in revolt against degrading economic conditions.

Mr. Arthur was, therefore, a prime favorite with the railroad corporations. They granted him annual passes over their lines; and when the Brotherhood of Locomotive Engineers met in convention, their delegates were provided with special trains to transport them to and from the convention, free of charge, as evidence that the corporation appreciated the value of the Brotherhood of Locomotive Engineers.

Since the engineers were organized, the firemen, conductors, brakemen, switchmen, telegraphers, and trackmen have also been organized, and several other departments have been partially organized, and they all have practically the same form of organization. They are all conservative. They all operate within the bounds set and approved by the railroad corporations. Are they, can they be true to the men who pay the dues, to the workingmen who support them? I answer that they cannot. Not only are they not true to the wage workers who support them, but they are pressed into service, politically and otherwise, when occasion demands it, in the interest of these corporations, and to the detriment of their own.

Only the other day, since this much-discussed matter of rate legislation has been pending, the grand chiefs of these various brotherhoods have been convened. By whom? By the railroad corporations. For what purpose? This will appear as I proceed.

Just after the grand chiefs of these labor unions met with the railroad officials, another meeting took place. Of whom? Of the representatives of the principal of these several organizations, who, acting under the advice of their grand officers, proceeded to the city of Washington, held a conference with President Roosevelt, and protested that the labor unions they represented, consisting of the railway workers of the country, were opposed to any sort of legislation that would have a tendency to reduce railroad rates in the United States. The announcement also went forth at the same time that these brotherhoods would make their political power felt in the interests of the railroad corporations; that is to say, against the common people, the toiling millions of the land.

What a picture, indeed!

One glance proves beyond the shadow of a doubt that these unions are exceedingly useful to the corporations; and to the extent that they serve the economic and political purposes of the corporations, they are the foes—and not the friends—of the working class.

The United Mine Workers, in point of numbers a powerful labor organization, embraces a large majority of the coal miners of the country. Is this organization of any real benefit to coal miners? What has it actually done for them during the last few years? What have the miners, who have paid millions of dollars from their scant earnings in support of the organization, what have they to show in return?

These miners are well organized. They have the numbers. They ought to have real economic power. But they lack it. And why? For the simple reason that they are not organized upon the basis of the class struggle. Their union principles are not right; and it is for this reason that their organization has the hearty support of the coal operators of the country, who, by the way, are in session in Chicago at this very time, for the purpose of uniting, for the purpose of dealing with the miners, not through the rank and file of their union, but, as they themselves declare, *through their national board.*

And this is a very important point for the union miners to take into consideration. These operators, these exploiters, who are conscious of their class interests, propose to deal, not with the union at large, not with the great body of the miners, not with the rank and file, not with the common herd, not with the black beasts of burden, but with their National Executive Board. They will fix things that are out of joint and settle matters generally. They will arrive at mutually satisfactory conclusions. They will harmonize beautifully. And when they do harmonize, it will be in the interests, not of the miners who do the work, who dig the coal, who produce the wealth, but in the interests of the operators who own the mines and exploit the slaves of the pits.

Why, the most zealous supporter of the United Mine Workers is the coal operator himself. The simple fact that the coal operator collects the union dues, and discharges the miner who refuses to pay his dues, is sufficient evidence of this fact.

The coal operator does not collect the dues from the man who happens to belong to the Industrial Workers. He knows enough to know what is good for him; and he knows that the miners, organized as they are at present, can do him little harm, but can do him great good. And this is why he wants the miners organized in the pure and simple old-fashioned way. He knows that if they were totally unorganized, they would spontaneously go out on strike. But they cannot strike as they are now organized without securing the sanction of their national, district and local officers; and so the operator keeps a friendly eye upon the union which fortifies and facilitates the exploitation of the coal diggers in his mines.

At stated periods the operators and representatives of the miners meet; and sometimes the sessions are very spirited, the miners insisting upon an increase, and the operators upon a decrease of wages, as was the case at the last interstate conference, when the union officials declared that under no circumstances would they accept a reduction, and the delegates voted by practically a unanimous vote not to accept any reduction, and for a while there was every indication of a strike. But the national officers met with the operators, and a reduction of wages was agreed to, and then the union officers went out among the rank and file and told them that if they were foolish enough to go out on strike, they would certainly be defeated, and that the best thing they could do was to accept the reduction. So these union officials, backed by the operators, virtually forced the reduction upon the miners.

The operator can well afford to support that kind of a labor union.

The United Mine Workers, under its present policy, denies and seeks to obscure the class struggle. President Mitchell[52] used to be quoted as saying that the interests of the miners and the operators were identical. He made an address the other day in which he claimed that he had been misquoted; he had not said that their interests were identical, but that they were reciprocal. I would like to have Mr. Mitchell show in what way the operator who fleeces the miner, reciprocates to that miner. The simple fact is that the operator—and I don't know why he is called that, he doesn't operate anything—the operator takes from the miner what the miner produces. He serves him in that capacity, and no other.

The miners' union denies, in effect, the class struggle, and vainly seeks to harmonize the economic interests of these two antagonistic classes—the exploiting masters and the exploited wage-slaves, the robbers and the robbed. It cannot be done; not permanently at least; and if it be done even temporarily, it is always at the expense of the wage-slaves. Such an organization as that cannot truly serve the best interests of the working class. It is impossible.

There are many who concur in these views, yet insist that the organization must be changed from the inside; that it can only be brought to its proper position by "boring from within." I deny it. It is historically impossible. This organization has practically run its course. It has fulfilled its mission as a labor union, whatever that has been. It is now practically in charge of the mine owners; and the only way the miners can get away from that situation is to sever their relations with that capitalist-controlled union and join and build up one of their own upon the basis of the class struggle; and then they will be in a position to fight the capitalist class with some chance of success.

The most important fact in all the world for workingmen to take cognizance of is the class struggle. The Industrial Workers expresses economically the interests of the working class in that struggle. The Industrial Workers declare that there can be nothing in common between the exploiting capitalist and the exploited wage worker; that there is inevitably a struggle between them, and that this struggle cannot end until the capitalist class is overthrown and the wage-system wiped out. Then and then only can there be an end to class rule.

Now, if you are a workingman and if you believe that you have an economic interest in common with that of the capitalist who employs you, remain in the old trade union. That is where you belong. If that is your conviction, we do not want you to join the Industrial Workers. You do not properly belong to us. You do belong to the American Federation of Labor and its affiliated organizations. But, if you believe as I believe, that the working class have economic interests of their own, separate and apart from and in conflict with, the economic interests of the capitalist class, then you should, and sooner or later will have to, sever your relation with the old trade union, and join the Industrial Workers, the only union organized upon the basis of the class struggle.

And now, let me ask, have we a class struggle? The answer comes of itself. This struggle finds expression daily, hourly, in strikes, in boycotts, in lockouts, injunctions, riots, assaults, and bloodshed. It is not an unmixed evil, however, for in this great worldwide class struggle, that is shaking the foundations of civilized society everywhere, there are being wrought out the most important problems of our modern civilization.

The working class are in an overwhelming majority. They have the numbers. They ought to have the power. And they would have the power, if only they were conscious of their interests, *as a class.* Every effort is put forth by the exploiting capitalist to prevent workingmen from seeing the class struggle. The capitalist insists that there is no such struggle. The editor in the employ of the capitalist echoes "no class struggle." The teacher, professor, and the minister, all of them dependent upon the capitalist for the chance to make a living, agree that there are no classes and no class struggle. In unison they declaim against class agitation and seek to obscure class rule that it may be perpetuated indefinitely.

We insist that there is a class struggle; that the working class must recognize it; that they must organize economically and politically upon the basis of that struggle; and that when they do so organize, they will then have the power to free themselves and put an end to that struggle forever.

Now, have not the workers, especially here in Chicago, had sufficient experience during the last few years? Have they not been defeated often enough to demonstrate the inherent weakness of the old trade union movement? Haven't they been enjoined by the courts often enough? Clubbed by the police and flung into jail often enough? Haven't they had experience of this kind enough to open their eyes to the fact that there is a mighty class struggle in progress, and that there will never be any material change in their condition until they unite their class in every department of industrial activity?

Speaking for myself, I was made to realize long ago that the old trade union was utterly incompetent to deal successfully with the exploiting corporations in this struggle. I was made to see that in craft unionism the capitalist class have it in their power to keep the workers divided, to use one part of them with which to conquer and crush another part of them. Indeed, I was made to see that the old form of unionism separates the workers and keeps them helpless at the mercy of their masters.

Object lessons are presented to you every day in the week. You have hundreds of thousands of workers organized in Chicago, in every conceivable kind of a union, and under the direction of an infinite variety of leaders. I will not say that these leaders are all incompetent or corrupt. That would not be true. But many of them are corrupt, and in that capacity have it in their power to betray and sell out the workers who trust them. In this position the workers will remain—where there is no hope for them—so long as they cling to the outgrown old trade union and its inefficient methods. We have had the proof of this over and over again. Take all the great strikes that have occurred in Chicago during the last few years. Have any of them been successful? Have they not uniformly failed?

The capitalists have not entirely stamped out the defeated unions, that is true. They have had the power to do this in the hour of the workers' defeat, but they have refrained from doing it, because they are shrewd enough to know that if they destroyed those unions, another and better one would take their places. Is it not a fact that they had the butcher workmen absolutely at their mercy, and could have compelled the members to entirely withdraw from the unions before giving them employment? They did not crush the unions out. When they had conquered they were satisfied. They had driven the unionists back to their reservations and they were perfectly satisfied that they should build up again along the same old lines.

The Employers' Association had the striking teamsters completely at their mercy, and could, had they seen fit, have utterly crushed out their union. They did not do it. In the closing part of the negotiations the settlement hinged upon the alleged privilege of the teamsters wearing their union badges, and this the Employers' Association finally conceded; and then the claim was put forth that the striking teamsters had come out victorious. The truth is that they lost everything; but the employer was not anxious to crush out their organization. He knew very well that if he did a stronger one would spring from the ruins; that a crushed union at least teaches workingmen to see its inherent defects.

The employer is shrewd enough to know that when you totally crush out organizations you drive the workers into solidarity.

The teamsters were entirely defeated, nothing left; and yet their leaders boasted that they had saved their organization. It reminded me of the dispatch once sent from a field of battle by a general who had been completely routed: "There is nothing left but honor, and damn little of that!"

It is true that there are some employers who are supposed to be entirely opposed to unionism, even the old form of trade unionism. But the great majority of capitalists, especially the shrewder, far-seeing ones, unqualifiedly approve the pure and simple labor union. And now let me show that between these two sections of the capitalist class there is, after all, no vital difference with regard to the trade union movement.

C. W. Post,[53] president of the Citizens' Industrial Association, and David M. Parry,[54] president of the Manufacturers' Association, who are opposing the American Federation of Labor, have repeatedly said that they are not opposed to trade unionism if it will confine itself to its "legitimate" functions. In other words, they are not opposed to trade unionism if it does not antagonize the capitalist class. That is their position. Now, what is the position of the great body of capitalists who avow their friendship for the trade union movement? Precisely the same. They are in favor of the trade union as long as it does not menace or attack the capitalist class; that is, as long as it doesn't do anything. And in its present shape it is not doing anything; and that is why the capitalists are not opposed to it. Let these trade unions unite tomorrow; let them declare in favor of waging this fight along the lines of the class struggle, and they will soon find out whether these capitalists are in favor of trade unionism or not.

The very fact that the great majority of capitalists favor trade unionism proves that it is doing little or nothing for its members. Were it really doing something for them, it would be antagonizing the capitalist class, and that class would fight it. But the capitalists are not fighting the pure old brand of unionism; they have, in fact, formed an alliance with it and the union is the silent partner in the firm.

You have all doubtless heard of the Civic Federation. This federation is supposed to be fair and impartial. It is organized for the one purpose of dovetailing the interests of labor and capital, and every member of this body insists that these interests can be harmonized; that there is no necessary conflict between them. That is what Mr. Gompers says; that is what Mr. Mitchell says; that is what Archbishop Ireland[55] and Bishop Potter[56] say, and that is what they all say—that there is no necessary conflict between capitalists and wage workers. If there be no necessary conflict between them, it follows that all the fighting that is going on must be unnecessary. I suppose then that that ought to be very easily eliminated.

A gentleman named August Belmont presides over this harmonizing body. Not long ago, in an address, he claimed that there was no better trade unionist in the country than he, and he proved it during the Interborough strike in the city of New York, when several thousand union employees of that corporation, of which he is president, went out on strike because they were driven to that extremity by his pernicious policy. He proved that he was a loyal trade unionist when he employed James Farley, the notorious professional strikebreaker and his army of Hessians[57] to take the places of his former employees. Just a little while after Mr. Belmont had thus defeated his employees and disrupted their unions, he met at the hospitable banqueting board of the Civic Federation with the national officers of the American Federation of Labor, and its allied unions, and there made good his claim that he was a true trade unionist of the old school.

Do you think that a labor leader who is absolutely true to the working class could sit at such a banqueting board with such a capitalist as Belmont? Do you think he would be the guest of such an organization as the Civic Federation, whose only purpose is by subtle schemes to reduce the trade union movement to harmless impotency?

It is for this and this alone that the Civic Federation has been organized. This is its real mission. The American Federation of Labor has fallen within the fatal influence of this emasculating alliance, and has thus proven that it is not organized to advance the true interests of the working class.

The American Federation of Labor is now holding its annual convention in the city of Pittsburgh. What are its delegates doing there? Simply passing the same old resolutions. Once more they are going to petition Congress to enact an eight-hour law. They have done that over and over again, and their petition has been as repeatedly pigeonholed. They have also resolved to petition Congress to restrict the powers of capitalist courts in dealing with labor. They have done that time and again, and what have they gained by it? Absolutely nothing. No attention has been paid to these servile supplications. They have been disregarded, thrown aside, treated with contempt; but the delegates solemnly meet in convention once more to pass the same hoary resolutions, to introduce the same stale petitions, with the same inevitable results. Now, is not this a perfectly stupid procedure? Are these men incapable of profiting by experience? Do they not by this time understand the nature and essential functions of capitalist-class government? Can they not see that we have a capitalist-class Congress, and capitalist-class legislatures, elected in every instance by an ignorant working class, kept ignorant, designedly, in the name of unionism, and with the aid of the labor lieutenants of the capitalist class? And that it is the very height of folly and depth of humiliation for a committee of the working class to beg the representatives of the capitalist class to legislate in the interests of the working class?

They were elected to serve the masters. And they are serving them. And we have no right to find fault with them—at least, those of us who are responsible for their being where they are.

Now, we who have organized the Industrial Workers have had enough of this kind of experience. We have quit the old unions. We have organized the Industrial Workers for the purpose of uniting the working class; the whole working class. Not only the skilled workers, not only those who are favored, but the working class, skilled and unskilled, male and female, in every department of activity, are united upon the principle of industrial unionism.

The old unions were built up on tools that have been discarded and upon trades that have ceased to exist.

Half a century ago the trade union was right; it was adapted to the then existing industrial conditions. For illustration, a cooper shop was a cooper shop. It contained coopers and coopers only, and the Coopers' Union was organized. That embraced the coopers who were employed at their trade in the shop. Since then there has been half a century of industrial evolution. Compare the great cooperage establishments of today with the cooper shop of 50 years ago, in which the old hand tools were used, in which the apprentice learned his trade, and having mastered this, could seize the small tools with which work was done and virtually employ himself. There has been a marvelous change since that time. A modern cooperage establishment is the result of industrial evolution; and if you will visit one of them you will find that scores of different kinds of labor are performed there. Indeed, you will find almost any kind of worker there except a cooper!

Now, we hold that the form of the union must correspond to the mode of industry. In other words, the union, like the trade, is subject to the inexorable laws of evolution. We want a union today that expresses all the various subdivisions of labor that are now engaged in a cooperage establishment. Suppose there are 500 such employees in a plant. We organize them all, and they are assigned to their various departments; and if one of them has a grievance it becomes the concern of every worker in that establishment.

How is it now? Certain departments are organized in craft unions, meet with the officials and make an agreement or contract. They do not care what becomes of the rest, if only they can get what they are after for themselves. After they are thus tied up, the employees in some other department present a grievance and are turned down and out. They go out on strike. Those tied fast in an agreement say: "We would like to help you, we are in sympathy with you, but you see we have an agreement, and that agreement is sacred; it must be preserved inviolate; and while we are in sympathy with you, and while we hate to see you defeated and lose your jobs, we cannot go back on our agreement." And in this way one union is used to crush another, labor is defeated and scabs are made by thousands.

It is a fact that nearly all scabs and strikebreakers are ex-unionists. Go among them and interrogate them and you will find that they will tell you in almost every case that at heart they are in favor of union labor, but that they were beaten by it and found this the only way of getting even. I know of hundreds of instanccs, of my own knowledge, of men who have been made scabs in precisely this way. Now, the trade unions feel very bitter toward scabs, and pursue them relentlessly until the unfortunates seek escape in suicide. And yet, while they so bitterly oppose the scab, they support the union that makes the scab.

What we want today, above all things, is united economic and political action, and we can never have that while the working class are parceled out among hundreds, aye, thousands, of separate unions, that keep them divided for reasons many of which very readily suggest themselves.

Who is it that is so violently opposed to the Industrial Workers? It is not the rank and file of the trade unions. It is their officers. And why are they so fiercely opposed to the Industrial Workers? For the reason that when the working class are really united a great many labor leaders will be out of jobs.

There are at present thousands of unions. Some of them have a few members and others have a great many; and every time, in the evolution of industry, there is a new subdivision of labor, however minute, a new union must be launched, clear down to the Grand International Brotherhood of Peanut Peelers, Polishers, and Packers, or whatever it may be. And they elect a staff of their own grand international officers, and their names are put upon the payroll; and let me say to you that their interests are primarily in keeping themselves there.

Why should the railroad employees be parceled out among a score of different organizations? They are all employed in the same service. Their interests are mutual. They ought to be able to act together as one. But they divide according to craft and calling, and if you were to propose today to unite them that they might actually do something to advance their collective and individual interests as workers, you would be opposed by every grand officer of these organizations. The payroll and expense account of the officers of the railroad brotherhoods alone amount to more than a quarter of a million dollars a year.

There is an army of men who serve as officers who are on the salary list who get a good living keeping the working class divided. They start out with good intentions, as a rule. They really want to do something to serve their fellows. They leave the shops or the mines as common workingmen. They are elected officers of a labor organization and they change their clothes. They now wear a white shirt and a standing collar. They change their habits and their methods. They have been used to cheap clothes, coarse fare, and to associating with their fellow workers. After they have been elevated to official position, as if by magic they are recognized by those who previously scorned them and held them in contempt. They find that some of the doors that were previously barred against them now swing inwards, and they can actually put their feet under the mahogany of a capitalist.

Our common workingman is now a labor leader. The great capitalist pats him on the back and tells him that he knew long ago that he was a coming man, that it was a fortunate thing for the workers of the world that he had been born, that in fact they had been long waiting for just such a wise and conservative leader. And this has a certain effect upon our new-made leader, and unconsciously, perhaps, he begins to change—just as John Mitchell did, when Mark Hanna patted him on the shoulder and said, "John, it is a good thing you are at the head of the miners. You are the very man. You have the greatest opportunity a labor leader ever had on this earth. You can immortalize yourself. Now is your time." Then John Mitchell admitted that this capitalist, who had been pictured to him as a monster, was not half as bad as he had thought he was; that, in fact, he was a genial and companionable gentleman. He repeats his visit the next day, or the next week, and is introduced to some other distinguished person he had read about, but never dreamed of meeting, and thus goes on the transformation. All his dislikes disappear and all feeling of antagonism vanishes. He concludes that they are really most excellent people and, now that he has seen and knows them, he agrees with them that there is no necessary conflict between workers and capitalists. And he proceeds to carry out this pet capitalist theory and he can only do it by betraying the class that trusted him and lifted him as high above themselves as they could reach.

It is true that such a leader is in favor with the capitalists; that their newspapers write editorials about him and crown him a great and wise leader; and that ministers of the gospel make his name the text for their sermons, and emphasize the vital point that if all labor leaders were such as he, there would be no objection to labor organizations. And the leader feels himself flattered. And when he is charged with having deserted the class he was supposed to serve, he cries out that the indictment is brought by a discredited labor leader. And that is probably true. The person who brings the charge is very likely discredited. By whom? By the capitalist class, of course; and its press and pulpit and "public" opinion. And in the present state of the working class, when he is discredited by the capitalists, he is at once repudiated by their wage-slaves.

The labor leader who is not discredited by the capitalist class is not true to the working class. If he be unswervingly loyal to the working class, he will not be on friendly terms with the capitalist class. He cannot serve both. When he really serves one, he serves that one against the other.

The labor leader who is in high favor with the exploiters is pronounced safe, conservative, wise, and honest, and the workers are appealed to look to him for advice, for guidance and leadership. The unthinking accept the advice with enthusiasm. And so the labor leader who serves the capitalist class instead of the working class is hailed as deliverer and basks in the public favor.

But let me say to you that in spite of all this, the honest and discredited leaders will be lovingly remembered long after the popular ones of today are forgotten.

Now, in these matters, I am not asking you to take my advice. I am not asking you to follow me. I simply want you to think over these things for yourselves. The very first need is that you open your eyes and see for yourselves. Take nothing for granted.

So many of you are satisfied to blindly follow where others lead; and so you are deceived and betrayed; you have to pay all the penalties.

It is high time you were ceasing to depend upon someone to "lead" you; that you were opening your eyes; that you were doing your own thinking. And that is all I am asking you to do.

I have already told you that I have had some experience and that I hope I have in some measure profited by it. I have been involved in strikes enough to satisfy me. I have so often been saddened by the outcome of such strikes.

I have seen men by scores and hundreds and thousands, after striking for weeks and months, lose their jobs. I have seen the poor wretches blacklisted and I have seen them persecuted until they were in rags, and their families were upon the streets, and I have said there must be another and a better way. I have seen enough of this to satisfy me. There is a better way. But you will never find it by pursuing the old lines. You have got to unite the whole working class, and this can be done. It is not an impossible task. Every worker, however limited his mentality, ought to be able to see that there is little or nothing to be accomplished along the old lines; that, in fact, there is no hope; that you are engaged in an unequal struggle, and that the ultimate outcome is certain to be defeat, despair, and death.

The capitalists have at present ten thousand advantages over us. They own and control all the sources and means of wealth production. They are the masters of the tools; they act together. They control all the powers of government. They can at their own sweet will shut down their mills and factories and mines, and they can wait patiently weeks and months and even years, until the impoverished workers become hungry and are glad to be taken back at any terms. The capitalists have all these advantages, and they never hesitate to do anything, everything, that may be required to keep the working class in subjection. And they can and will keep them there just as long as they are divided.

There is but one hope, and that is in the economic and political solidarity of the working class: one revolutionary union and one revolutionary party. It is for this reason that the Industrial Workers, an economic organization, has been launched and now makes its appeal to you as wage-slaves aspiring to be free. You cannot be satisfied to live and die as beasts of burden; to toil unceasingly to enrich masters who hold you in contempt; to be dependent upon these masters for your jobs and crawl like sycophants at their feet. You may not be satisfied, even though you have sufficient food and clothing and shelter. You are a human, not a hog; a man, not a mere animal. You have a manhood to sustain; you have freedom to achieve, and you have an intellect to develop; and these questions will appeal to you with ever-increasing force and compel an accounting at last, if you have the pith and purpose of a typical, self-respecting workingman.

In the capitalist system you workers are simply merchandise; your master can at his own will sentence you to idleness, your wife to want and your child, perhaps, to a brothel. You cannot be satisfied with such a slavish lot, and now is the time to make up your mind to change it. In your heart you will feel the thrill of a newborn joy. You will join the Industrial Workers, the one international labor union that proposes to unite all workers, that all of them may act together in harmonious cooperation for the good of all; a union that recognizes no aristocracy, but the whole working class; that insists that each member shall have all the rights that are accorded every other; a union built upon the class struggle, appealing to all workers to get together on the right side of that struggle and achieve the revolutionary solidarity[58] of their class.

It is true that this is a stupendous task; that there are great opposing forces; that every falsehood that malignity can devise will be put in circulation to defeat the object of this industrial organization, but nevertheless, those of us who have quitted the old unions and organized the Industrial Workers have done so with the determination that no matter what opposing forces may be set in operation, we will stand together side by side in the true spirit of class-conscious solidarity; we will move forward, step by step, in one solid body; we will speak the truth as we see the truth, and defy all opposition that may be brought to bear against the Industrial Workers by all the capitalist class and all its vassals and emissaries.

This organization has a mission as high and as noble as ever prompted workingmen, or any other men, to action in this world.

The primal need of the working class is education. By education I mean revolutionary education; the kind that enables them to see that the 20-odd millions of wage workers in the United States are wage-slaves; that the economic interests of these many millions of human beings who do all the useful work and produce all the wealth are absolutely identical; that they must unite; that they must act together; that they must assert their collective power. When they reach this point they will cease to be slaves and become the masters of the situation; they will wipe out the wage system and walk the earth free men.

They can do this, and only *they* can do it.

I cannot do this for you, and I want to be frank enough to say that I would not if I could. For if I could do it for you, somebody else could undo it for you. But when you do it for yourself it will remain done forever. And until you do it, you have got to pay the penalty of your ignorance, indifference, and neglect. You have got to pay it to the last farthing. Nobody on earth or in heaven can relieve you of the consequences of your inaction. As long as you workers remain divided and at cross purposes, instead of closing up the ranks and acting together you will have to pay the penalty of defeat and humiliation and slavery and all their attendant brood of festering evils.

But day by day you are increasing the sum of your revolutionary knowledge. You are becoming wiser by experience. The Industrial Workers would not have been possible a few years ago. It is an outgrowth of the very conditions I have described. It has become an imperative necessity. The workers everywhere are beginning to recognize it, and that is why they are flocking to its standard. That is why they are subscribing to its principles; why they are working for it day and night with a zeal that has never been known in the history of the organized working-class movement; and why it is rapidly spreading over the whole country and increasing grandly in numbers and in power. Let me say to you that no matter what formidable or subtle opposition may be marshaled against it by the capitalist class, the ultimate triumph of its principles is as certain as that tonight I stand in your presence.

There are a great many workers who insist that the old unions are good enough; and as long as they are of that opinion that is where they belong. So far as I am concerned, I gave the old unions a fair trial. I am sure I had no prejudice against them. I am equally certain I did all I possibly could to build them up. For 15 years I traveled almost continuously over this country organizing railroad men, and all kinds of workingmen, under the mistaken conviction that if we could only get them into the several unions of their trades and occupations we could in some way lift them out of their slavery. My mind was disabused. We had the railroad men, especially in this part of the country, pretty thoroughly organized. We had the numbers and to some extent the power, but we didn't know about the class struggle. We had that to learn. Then came the great conflict with the combined railroad corporations. We defeated them; and then we learned that the corporations control the powers of government. We got our first vital lesson in the class struggle. All the corporations had to do was to press the judicial button in their private office and the judges acted promptly in obedience to the command of their capitalist masters; the police and militia and regular troops followed in regular order; the press and pulpit and deputy marshals did the rest—and that was enough.

I never knew exactly how it happened until I understood the meaning of economic determinism and the class struggle, and then it was perfectly clear to me. And from that time I realized the imperative necessity for a different kind of organization. I then said, we have got to organize, not only the railroad employees, but the whole body of workers for concerted economic and political action; organize them all, so that all of them shall act together and assert the full measure of their power in the interests of all. As soon as a beginning was attempted the railroad corporations said, "This vicious thing must be stamped out of existence," and so, for two years, I scarcely traveled a foot without being shadowed by detectives of the railroad corporation. No matter where I went, the detectives were there. When I would reach the end of a certain line, the detectives who had followed me would go back where they came from and others would take their places. I remember when I got to Providence, Rhode Island, one night, I was conscious that detectives were watching me very closely. I learned that the railroad officials in New England had announced that the American Railway Union should never get a foothold there. There were two or three loyal men there I knew I could trust; I sent them word not to come to the hotel and not to hold a meeting, but to come to my room at midnight, and come one at a time. And they did come to my room one at a time and I organized them in my room at midnight. I left the city early next morning, and when I got to the next point I received a telegram reporting that they were all discharged, every one of them.

Notwithstanding our secrecy, the corporations knew who had entered my room and for what purpose; and the men were summarily discharged. Why was it that the railroad corporations would not allow the American Railway Union to organize? For the simple reason that the American Railway Union proposed to line up all the railroad employees as the beginning of a thorough reorganization of the working class in general, and the railroads did not propose to tolerate that kind of an organization.

They were and are entirely satisfied with the old brotherhoods, supplying their officers with annual passes and their delegates with special trains to take them to and from their conventions. To such an extent is this partiality carried on some railroads, that if a member of one of the brotherhoods refuses to pay his dues and is expelled by the brotherhood, he is promptly discharged by the corporation. The corporation favors the organizations that divide but is implacably hostile to the one that unites the workers.

For the same reason the capitalist newspapers have so ferociously denounced the Industrial Workers.

They have warned workingmen that the Industrial Workers consists of anarchists, socialists, revolutionists, and chronic fault-finders and peace-disturbers, who have been kicked out of other reputable labor organizations; of discredited leaders who do not lead, in whom the workers have no confidence and for whom they can have no respect.

The capitalist press is a unit in denouncing the Industrial Workers, and practically a unit in commending the American Federation of Labor.

If you workers think that the capitalist press is a safe guide in such a matter, you properly belong with the American Federation of Labor. But if you believe, as I believe, and as every intelligent workingman must believe, that the kind of labor organization that the capitalists endorse is not the kind that is for your good—that the organization the capitalist press condemns is the one that has working class virtue and efficiency —then you will do as we have done; you will join the Industrial Workers of the World.

Think it over for yourself!

Take a backward look over the last three or four years; satisfy yourself by your own observation that there has been little but defeat for the workers in the struggle during all that period; that they have gained substantially nothing; that they are divided and disrupted and not organized in any true sense at all. The time has come for a real economic organization of the workers, and that organization is now in the field and makes its appeal to all workers, and its principles and purposes deserve the encouragement, the support and the loyalty of every workingman who has intelligence enough to understand his best interests and manhood enough to assert and stand by them.

I shall occupy your time no longer. I think that no great argument is required in support of our position. The preamble to the constitution states clearly and in few words the object of the Industrial Workers. You will find it written there that the workers and capitalists have nothing in common; that there are a few who have all the good things of life, while millions writhe in poverty and cry out in despair; that those who do nothing and produce nothing are rich, while those who do everything and produce everything are poor; that these two classes consist of capitalists who own tools they do not use, and of workers who use tools that they do not own; that the capitalists who own the tools have it in their power to take and do take from the workers what they produce, and that the workers must organize both their economic and political power to take and hold that which they produce by their labor.

This is brief and to the point, and every workingman is capable of understanding it.

As the chairman has stated, the Industrial Workers has no object in concealing any part of its mission, and while it proposes to ameliorate the condition of the workers in every way in its power as far as that is possible in capitalist society, its ultimate object is to entirely abolish the capitalist system, by making the workers themselves the masters of their tools, that they may work freely, unrestrained and unexploited; that they may secure to themselves and enjoy all the fruit of their own labors.

This is the object of the Industrial Workers, and if it has your approval, join it and help it to fulfill its mission, and thus hasten the emancipation of the working class, and the brighter, happier day for all humanity.

Questions

Q. ***In the Industrial Workers are you going to separate the different trades, or has a man who joins the privilege of going where he chooses?***

Mr. Debs: He joins the department that represents his particular trade or occupation. The Industrial Workers is organized in separate departments, so that the autonomy of the trade is preserved within the organization. Take the men of a certain trade; they belong to a certain department of the organization; they have jurisdiction over their own trade affairs. They are subject, however, to the supervision of the general organization. Take the machinists, for instance; they have a grievance; it will be adjusted, primarily, if possible, within their own department. If that is not possible then it becomes the grievance of the general organization—the concern of all. Instead of merely the machinists going out on strike as now, all their fellow workers lay down their tools and support them to a finish.

Q. ***Is it true that the Industrial Workers was organized because the workers cannot gain anything by political action?***

Mr. Debs: No, that is not true. The workers have never yet tried to get anything by united political action. They will some time, I do not doubt. The Industrial Workers was organized because under the old form of organization they could get little or nothing by economic action. If they had secured satisfactory concessions under the old forms there would be no Industrial Workers. It has been organized because of the failure of the old unions on the economic field. Now, if it can be shown that they have succeeded, or even measurably succeeded, then there is no necessity for the Industrial Workers. But if, on the other hand, it can be shown that they have repeatedly and wretchedly failed, then there is an unanswerable argument in favor of the Industrial Workers.

Q. ***What is a tradesman or a skilled worker? Why should there be any distinction between a tradesman and any other worker in a shop?***

Mr. Debs: That is not a very easy question to answer. There used to be a great many skilled mechanics who are now common workers. In proportion as machinery is improved the skill of the trade is transferred from the worker to the machine; and the skilled labor of one day becomes the common labor of the next. The locomotive engineer has always regarded himself as a skilled worker, and he has refused to affiliate with what is called the common laborer. Within the next few years the locomotive engineer will probably become a motorman and he will then come off the perch. The work will be so simple that almost any worker can perform it. I have already referred to the coopers. In the town where I live there used to be a number of cooper shops in which there were skilled men; and they had a large and strong Coopers' Union. All the coopers that worked there belonged to it. And these coopers didn't have anything to do with common labor. They flocked by themselves upon the theory that they were skilled men and could not afford to put their skill on the same level with the common labor of unskilled workers. During the last few years that trade has undergone a complete change. The skilled coopers have practically disappeared and but a shadow of the old union remains.

Now, if you will ask that old cooper, who was a skilled man and belonged to a union that represented skilled labor a few years ago—if you will ask him who the skilled man is, I think he can give you a satisfactory answer to your question. The skill of the trade is being gradually eliminated, and we are taking cognizance of this fact. We Industrial Workers recognize no aristocracy of skill. If any partiality were to be shown, however, I would give the unskilled man the benefit of it, because he needs it most. But there is no such discrimination in the Industrial Workers. The workingman, skilled or unskilled, is a worker; a man; and, whatever his occupation, has all of the wants and aspirations and is entitled to all the rights and opportunities of a human being for self-development. The machine is rapidly reducing workers to a common industrial equality, making the unskilled man the productive equal of the skilled man. The machine is the skilled man, and when he gets through, that question will have answered itself.

Q. ***Does the Industrial Workers make any provision for a wage scale?***

Mr. Debs: Yes; it is going to get all the wages for its members that it possibly can, while the wage-system lasts.

Q. ***How are you going to prevent the leaders from being as bad as those of the trade unions are today?***

Mr. Debs: In the first place, there will be but a single organization. There will not be a hundred different and conflicting organizations and as many different sets of officers.

Q. ***Then they will have only one to buy; it won't cost so much.***

Mr. Debs: All the chances will be reduced to the minimum. Take the railroad brotherhoods, for instance. If every locomotive engineer running into Chicago voted tomorrow to go out on strike, they could not go out without the official sanction of the grand chief of the Brotherhood of Locomotive Engineers, and he alone could prevent the strike. That is, they might vote unanimously to strike, but the power of one single grand officer would outweigh that of the entire organization. With us it is the rank and file that decides and is the supreme power. It is not likely they will sell themselves out. Besides, the Industrial Workers is made up of a body of class-conscious industrial revolutionists, who will not be sold out. They are wide-awake workers who think for themselves, and act for themselves, and that is why they are in the Industrial Workers. The old trade unions are mainly run by the officers. Didn't you notice in the papers this morning that the coal operators who were here in session declared that they proposed to deal, not with the rank and file, the common herd, but with the national officers of the union? They will settle things, and that is how they are generally settled in the old unions; but that is not the way they will be settled in the Industrial Workers.

This is an important point. Take a plant such as a brewery, for instance; a score of different kinds of labor represented by as many different organizations, and as many different sets of officers. Here are temptation and opportunity multiplied by twenty. Here we have wide-open chances and incentive to bribery, corruption, and treachery. Suppose now, that the same plant is organized in the Industrial Workers. Instead of being parceled out among twenty different unions they are all embraced in one. The men in one department have a grievance. That plant has a general committee; and if the grievance fails of adjustment in the department in which it arises, it is referred to the general committee that has supervision of the plant, and if they fail to satisfactorily adjust it, the matter goes to all the employees, as Industrial Workers, for action. They vote to go out on strike and that settles it. In the Industrial Workers no national officer and no set of national officers have power to override the action of the rank and file. And when they vote to go out, they go out and stay out, until they vote to go back.

Industrial Unionism: Address at Grand Central Palace, New York City[†]

December 10, 1905

There is an inspiration in your greeting and my heart opens wide to receive it. I have come a thousand miles to join with you in fanning the flames of the proletarian revolution. [*Applause*]

Your presence here makes this a vitalizing atmosphere for a labor agitator. I can feel my stature increasing, and this means that you are growing, for all my strength is drawn from you, and without you I am nothing.

In capitalist society you are the lower class; the capitalists are the upper class—because they are on your backs; if they were not on your backs, they could not be above you. [*Applause and laughter.*]

Standing in your presence, I can see in your gleaming eyes and in your glowing faces the vanguard; I can hear the tramp, I can feel the thrill of the social revolution. The working class are waking up. [*A voice: "You bet."*] They are beginning to understand that their economic interests are identical, that they must unite and act together economically and politically, and in every other way; that only by united action can they overthrow the capitalist system and emancipate themselves from wage-slavery. [*Applause.*]

I have said that in the capitalist society, the working class are the lower class; they have always been the lower class. In the ancient world for thousands of years they were abject slaves; in the Middle Ages, serfs; in modern times, wage workers; to become free men in socialism, the next inevitable phase of advancing civilization. [*Applause.*] The working class have struggled through all the various phases of their development, and they are today engaged in the last stage of the animal struggle for existence; and when the present revolution has run its course, the working class will stand forth the sovereigns of this earth.

In capitalist society the working man is not, in fact, a man at all; as a wage worker, he is simply merchandise; he is bought in the open market the same as hair, hides, salt, or any other form of merchandise. The very terminology of the capitalist system proves that he is not a man in any sense of that term.

† Stenographic report by Waldo Typewriting Co., New York, published in *The People* [New York], vol. 15, no. 40 (January 20, 1906), 1–2. Published as a pamphlet by the IWW, 1906. Reprinted by New York Labor News Co., 1906.

When the capitalist needs you as a workingman to operate his machine, he does not advertise, he does not call for men, but for "hands"; and when you see a placard posted, "Fifty hands wanted," you stop on the instant; you know that that means *you,* and you make a beeline for the bureau of employment to offer yourself in evidence of the fact that you are a "hand." When the capitalist advertises for hands, that is what he wants. He would be insulted if you were to call him a "hand." He has his capitalist politician tell you, when your vote is wanted, that you ought to be very proud of your hands because they are horny; and if that is true, he ought to be ashamed of his. [*Laughter and applause.*]

What is your status in society today? You are a human being, a wage worker. Here you stand just as you were created, and you have two hands that represent your labor-power; but you do not work, and why not? For this simple reason, that you have no tools with which to work. You cannot compete against the machinery of the capitalist with your bare hands, you cannot work unless you have access to it, and you can only secure access to it by selling your labor-power, that is to say, your energy, your vitality, your life itself, to the capitalist who owns the tool with which you work, and without which you are idle and suffer all of the ills that idleness entails.

In the evolution of capitalism, society has been divided mainly into two economic classes: a relatively small class of capitalists who own tools in the form of great machines they did not make and cannot use, and a great body of many millions of workers who did make these tools and who do use them, and whose very lives depend upon them, yet who do not own them; and these millions of wage workers, producers of wealth, are forced into the labor market, in competition with each other, disposing of their labor-power to the capitalist class, in consideration of just enough of what they produce to keep them in working order. They are exploited of the greater share of what their labor produces, so that while, upon the one hand, they can produce in great abundance, upon the other they can consume but that share of the product that their meager wage will buy; and every now and then it follows that they have produced more than can be consumed in the present system, and then they are displaced by the very products of their own labor. The mills and shops and mines and quarries in which they are employed close down, the tools are locked up and they are locked out, and they find themselves idle and helpless in the shadow of the very abundance their labor has created.

There is no hope for them in this system. They are beginning to realize this fact, and so they are beginning to organize; they are no longer relying upon someone else, but they are making up their minds to depend upon themselves and to organize for their own emancipation.

Too long have the workers of the world waited for some Moses to lead them out of bondage. He has not come; he never will come. I would not lead you out if I could; for if you could be led out, you could be led back again. [*Applause.*] I would have you make up your minds that there is nothing that you cannot do for yourselves.

You do not need the capitalist. He could not exist an instant without you. You would just begin to live without him. [*Laughter and prolonged applause.*] You do everything and he has everything; and some of you imagine that if it were not for him you would have no work. As a matter of fact, he does not employ you at all; you employ him to take from you what you produce, and he faithfully sticks to his task. If you can stand it, he can; and if you don't change this relation, I am sure he won't. You make the automobile, he rides in it. If it were not for you, he would walk; and if it were not for him, you would ride.

The capitalist politician tells you on occasion that you are the salt of the earth; and if you are, you had better begin by salting down the capitalist class.

The revolutionary movement of the working class will date from the year 1905, from the organization of the Industrial Workers of the World. [*Prolonged applause.*] Economic solidarity is today the supreme need of the working class. The old form of unionism has long since fulfilled its mission and outlived its usefulness, and the hour has struck for a change.

The old unionism is organized upon the basis of the identity of interests of the capitalist and working classes. It spends its time and energy trying to conciliate these two essentially antagonistic classes; and so this unionism has at its head a harmonizing board called the Civic Federation. This federation consists of three parts: a part representing the capitalist class; a part supposed to represent the working class, and still another part that is said to represent the "public." The capitalists are represented by that great union labor champion, August Belmont. [*Laughter and hisses.*] The working class by Samuel Gompers, the president of the American Federation of Labor [*hisses and cries: "sic him!"*], and the public, by Grover Cleveland. [*Laughter.*]

Can you imagine a fox and goose peace congress? Just fancy such a meeting, the goose lifting its wings in benediction, and the fox whispering, "Let us prey."

The Civic Federation has been organized for the one purpose of prolonging the age-long sleep of the working class. Their supreme purpose is to keep you from waking up. [*A voice: "They can't do it."*]

The Industrial Workers has been organized for an opposite purpose, and its representatives come in your presence to tell you that there can be no peace between you, the working class, and the capitalist class who exploit you of what you produce; that as workers you have economic interests apart from and opposed to their interests, and that you must organize by and for yourselves; and that if you are intelligent enough to understand these interests, you will sever your relations with the old unions in which you are divided and subdivided, and join the Industrial Workers, in which all are organized and united upon the basis of the class struggle. [*Applause.*]

The Industrial Workers is organized, not to conciliate, but to fight the capitalist class. We have no object in concealing any part of our mission; we would have it perfectly understood. We deny that there is anything in common between workingmen and capitalists. We insist that workingmen must organize to get rid of capitalists and make themselves the masters of the tools with which they work, freely employ themselves, secure to themselves all they produce, and enjoy to the full the fruit of their labors. [*Applause.*]

The old union movement is not only organized upon the basis of the identity of interests of the exploited and exploiting classes, but it divides instead of uniting the workers, and there are thousands of unions, more or less in conflict, used against one another; and so long as these countless unions occupy the field, there will be no substantial unity of the working class. [*Applause.*]

And here let me say that the most zealous supporter of the old union is the capitalist himself. August Belmont, president of the Civic Federation, takes special pride in declaring himself a "union man" [*laughter*]; but he does not mean by that that he is an Industrial Worker; that is not the kind of a union he means. He means the impotent old union that Mr. Gompers and Mr. Mitchell lead, the kind that keeps the working class divided so that the capitalist system may be perpetuated indefinitely.

For 30 years I have been connected with the organized labor movement. I have long since been made to realize that the pure and simple union can do nothing for the working class; I have had some experience and know whereof I speak. The craft union seeks to establish its own petty supremacy. Craft division is fatal to class unity. To organize along craft lines means to divide the working class and make it the prey of the capitalist class. The working class can only be unionized efficiently along class lines; and so the Industrial Workers has been organized, not to isolate the crafts but to unite the whole working class. [*Applause.*]

The working class has had considerable experience during the past few years. In almost every conflict between labor and capital, labor has been defeated. Take the leading strikes in their order, and you will find that, without a single exception, the organized workers have been defeated, and thousands upon thousands of them have lost their jobs, and many of them have become "scabs." Is there not something wrong with a unionism in which the workers are always worsted? Let me review hurriedly some of this history of the past few years.

I have seen the conductors on the Chicago, Burlington & Quincy Railroad, organized in a craft union, take the place of the striking union locomotive engineers on the same system.

I have seen the employees of the Missouri, Kansas & Texas Railway, organized in their several craft unions, stand by the corporation as a unit, totally wiping out the union telegraphers, thirteen hundred of them losing their jobs.

I have seen these same craft unions, just a little while ago, on the Northern Pacific and Great Northern systems—I have seen them unite with the corporation to crush out the telegraphers' union, and defeat the strikers, their own co-unionists and fellow employees.

Just a few weeks ago, in the city of Chicago, the switchmen on the grand trunk went out on strike. All their fellow unionists remained at work and faithfully served the corporation until the switchmen were defeated, and now those union switchmen are scattered about looking for jobs.

The machinists were recently on strike in Chicago. They went out in a body under the direction of their craft union. Their fellow unionists all remained at work until the machinists were completely defeated, and now their organization in that city is on the verge of collapse.

There has been a ceaseless repetition of this form of scabbing of one craft union upon another until the working man, if his eyes are open, is bound to see that this kind of unionism is a curse and not a benefit to the working class.

The American Federation of Labor does not learn by experience. They recently held their annual convention, and they passed the same old stereotyped resolutions; they are going to petition Congress to restrict the power of the courts; that is to say, they are going to once more petition a capitalist Congress to restrict the power of capitalist courts. That is as if a flock of sheep were to petition a pack of wolves to extract their own fangs. They have passed these resolutions over and over again. They have been totally fruitless and will continue to be.

What good came to the working class from this convention? Put your finger upon a single thing they did that will be of any real benefit to the workers of the country!

You have had some experience here in New York. You have plenty of unionism here, such as it is, yet there is not a city in the country in which the workers are less organized than they are here. It was in March last that you had here an exhibition of pure and simple unionism. You saw about six thousand craft union men go out on strike, and you saw their fellow unionists remain at work loyally until all the strikers were defeated and sacrificed. Here you have an object lesson that is well calculated to set you thinking, and this is all I can hope to do by coming here, set you thinking, and for yourselves; for when you begin to think, you will soon begin to act for yourselves. You will then sever your relations with capitalist unions and capitalist parties [*applause*], and you will begin the real work of organizing your class, and that is what we of the Industrial Workers have engaged to do. We have a new mission. That mission is not merely the amelioration of the condition of the working class, but the complete emancipation of that class from slavery. [*Applause.*]

The Industrial Workers is going to do all for the working class that can be done in the capitalist system, but while it is engaged in doing that, its revolutionary eye will be fixed upon the goal; and there will be a great difference between a strike of revolutionary workers and a strike of ignorant trade unionists who but vaguely understand what they want and do not know how to get that. [*Applause.*]

The Industrial Workers is less than six months old, and already has around a hundred thousand dues-paying members. [*Applause.*] This splendid achievement has no parallel in the annals of organized labor. From every direction come the applications for charters and for organizers, and when the delegates of this revolutionary economic organization meet in the city of Chicago, next year, it will be the greatest convention that ever met in the United States in the interest of the working class. [*Applause.*]

This organization has a worldwide mission; it makes its appeal directly to the working class. It asks no favors from capitalists.

No organization of working men has ever been so flagrantly misrepresented by the capitalist press as has been the Industrial Workers of the World. Every delegate to the Chicago convention will bear testimony to this fact, and this is as it should be—the capitalist press is the mouthpiece of the capitalist class, and the very fact that the capitalist press is the organ, virtually, of the

American Federation of Labor, is in itself sufficient to open the eyes of the working class.

If the American Federation of Labor were not in alliance with the capitalist class, the capitalist press would not pour its fulsome eulogy upon it.

This press has not one friendly word for the Industrial Workers, not one, and we do not expect it to have. These papers of the plutocrats know us and we know them [*applause*]; between us there is no misunderstanding.

The workers of the country—the intelligent ones at least—readily see the difference between revolutionary and reactionary unionism, and that is why they are deserting the old and joining the new; that is why the Industrial Workers is building up so rapidly; that is why there is such a widespread demand for organizers and for literature and for all other means of building up this class-conscious economic organization. [*Applause.*]

As I have said, the Industrial Workers begin by declaring that there is nothing in common between capitalists and wage workers. The capitalists own the tools they do not use, and the workers use the tools they do not own. The capitalists, who own the tools that the working class use, appropriate to themselves what the working class produce, and this accounts for the fact that a few capitalists become fabulously rich while the toiling millions remain in poverty, ignorance, and dependence.

Let me make this point perfectly clear for the benefit of those who have not thought it out for themselves. Andrew Carnegie is a type of the capitalist class. He owns the tools with which steel is produced. These tools are used by many thousands of working men. Andrew Carnegie, who owns these tools, has absolutely nothing to do with the production of steel. He may be in Scotland, or where he will, the production of steel goes forward just the same. His mills at Pittsburgh, Duquesne, and Homestead, where these tools are located, are thronged with thousands of toolless wage workers, who work day and night, in winter's cold and summer's heat, who endure all the privations and make all the sacrifices of health and limb and life, producing thousands upon thousands of tons of steel, yet not having an interest, even the slightest, in the product. Carnegie, who owns the tools, appropriates the product, and the workers, in exchange for their labor-power, receive a wage that serves to keep them in producing order; and the more industrious they are, and the more they produce, the worse they are off; for the sooner they have produced more than Carnegie can get rid of in the markets, the tool houses are shut down and the workers are locked out in the cold.

This is a beautiful arrangement—for Mr. Carnegie. He does not want a change, and so he is in favor of the Civic Federation, and a leading member of it; and he is doing what he can to induce you to think that this ideal relation ought to be maintained forever.

Now, what is true of steel production is true of every other department of industrial activity. You belong to the millions who have no tools, who cannot work without selling your labor-power, and when you sell that, you have got to deliver it in person; you cannot send it to the mill, you have got to carry it there; you are inseparable from your labor-power. You have got to go to the mill at 7:00 in the morning and work until 6:00 in the evening, producing, not for yourself, but for the capitalist who owns the tools you made and use, and without which you are almost as helpless as if you had no arms.

This fundamental fact in modern industry you must recognize, and you must organize upon the basis of this fact; you must appeal to your class to join the union that is the true expression of your economic interests, and this union must be large enough to embrace you all, and such is the Industrial Workers of the World.

Every man and every woman who works for wages is eligible to membership. Organized into various departments, when you join you become a member of the department that represents your craft, or occupation, whatever it may be; and when you have a grievance, your department has supervision of it; and if you fail to adjust it in that department, you are not limited to your craft alone for support, but, if necessary, all the workers in all other departments will unite solidly in your defense to the very last. [*Applause.*]

Take a plant in modern industry. The workers, under the old form of unionism, are parceled out to a score or more of unions. Craft division incites craft jealousy and so they are more or less in conflict with each other, and the employer constructively takes advantage of this fact, and that is why he favors pure and simple unionism.

It were better for the workers who wear craft fetters if they were not organized at all, for then they could and would spontaneously go out on strike together; but they cannot do this in craft unionism, for certain crafts bind themselves up in craft agreements, and after they have done this, they are at the mercy of the capitalist; and when their fellow unionists call upon them for aid, they make the very convenient excuse that they cannot help them, that they must preserve the sanctity of the contract they have made with the employer. This so-called contract is regarded as of vastly more importance than the jobs, aye, the very lives of the workingmen themselves.

We do not intend that certain departments shall so attach themselves to the capitalist employers. We propose that the workers shall all be organized, and if there is any agreement, it will embrace them all; and if there is any violation of the agreement, in the case of a single employee, it at once becomes the concern of all. [*Applause.*] That is unionism, industrial unionism, in which all of the workers, totally regardless of occupation, are united compactly within the one organization, so that at all times they can act together in the interests of all. It is upon this basis that the Industrial Workers of the World is organized. It is in this spirit and with this object in view that it makes its appeal to the working class.

Then, again, the revolutionary economic organization has a new and important function which has never once been thought of in the old union, for the simple reason that the old union intends that the wage system shall endure forever.

The Industrial Workers declares that the workers must make themselves the masters of the tools with which they work; and so a very important function of this new union is to teach the workers, or, rather, have them teach themselves, the necessity of fitting themselves to take charge of the industries in which they are employed when they are wrested, as they will be, from their capitalist masters. [*Applause.*]

So when you join the Industrial Workers you feel the thrill of a new aspiration; you are no longer a blind, dumb wage-slave. You begin to understand your true and vital relation to your fellow workers. In the Industrial Workers you are correlated to all other workers in the plant, and thus you develop the embryonic structure of the cooperative commonwealth. [*Applause.*]

The old unionism would have you contented. We Industrial Workers are doing what we can to increase your discontent. We would have you rise in revolt against wage-slavery. The working man who is contented today is truly a pitiable object. [*Applause.*]

Victor Hugo once said: "Think of a smile in chains"—that is, a working man who, under the influence of the Civic Federation, is satisfied with his lot. He is glad he has a master, someone to serve, for, in his ignorance, he imagines that he is dependent upon the master.

The Industrial Workers is appealing to the working class to develop their latent powers and above all, their capacity for clear thinking. You are a working man and you have a brain and if you do not use it in your own interests, you are guilty of treason to your manhood. [*Applause.*]

It is for the very reason that you do not use your brain in your interests that you are compelled to deform your body in the interests of your master.

I have already said that the capitalist is on your back; he furnishes the mouth, you the hands; he consumes, you produce. That is why he runs largely to stomach and you to hands. [*Laughter.*]

I would not be a capitalist; I would be a man. You cannot be both at the same time. [*Applause.*]

The capitalist exists by exploitation, lives out of the labor, that is to say the life, of the working man; consumes him, and his code of morals and standard of ethics justify it and this proves that capitalism is cannibalism. [*Applause.*]

A man, honest, just, high-minded, would scorn to live out of the sweat and sorrow of his fellow man—by preying upon his weaker brother.

We propose to destroy the capitalist and save the man. [*Applause.*] We want a system in which the worker shall get what he produces and the capitalist shall produce what he gets. [*Applause.*] That is a square deal.

The prevailing lack of unity implies the lack of class consciousness. The workers do not yet understand that they are engaged in a class struggle, that they must unite their class and get on the right side of that struggle economically, politically, and in every other way. [*Applause.*] Strike together, vote together, and, if necessary, fight together. [*Prolonged applause.*]

The capitalist and the leader of the pure and simple union do what they can to wipe out the class lines. They do not want you to recognize the class struggle. They contrive to keep you divided, and as long as you are divided, you will remain where you are, robbed and helpless. When you unite and act together, the world is yours. [*Prolonged applause.*]

The fabled Samson, shorn of his locks, the secret of his power, was the sport and prey of the pygmies that tormented him. The modern working class, shorn of their tools, the secret of their power, are at the mercy of a small class who exploit them of what they produce and then hold them in contempt because of their slavery.

No master ever had the slightest respect for his slave, and no slave ever had the least real love for his master. Between these two classes there is an irrepressible conflict, and we Industrial Workers are pointing it out that you may see it, that you may get on the right side of it, that you may get together and emancipate yourselves from every form of servitude.

It can be done in no other way; but a bit of sober reasoning will convince you workers of this fact.

It is so simple that a child can see it. Why can't you? You can if you will think for yourselves and see for yourselves. But you will not do this if you were taught in the old union school; you will still look to someone else to lead that you may follow; for you are trained to follow the blind leaders of the blind. You have been betrayed over and over again, and there will be no change until you make up your minds to think and see and act for yourselves.

I would not have you blindly walk into the Industrial Workers; if I had sufficient influence or power to draw you into it, I would not do it. I would have you stay where you are until you can see your way clear to join it of your own accord. It is your organization; it is composed of your class; it is committed to the interests of your class; it is going to fight for your class, for your whole class, and continue the fight until your class is emancipated. [*Applause.*]

There is a great deal of opposition to this organization. The whole capitalist class and all their labor lieutenants are against it [*applause*]; and there is an army of them, and all their names are on the payroll and expense account. They all hold salaried positions, and are looking out for themselves. When the working class unite, there will be a lot of jobless labor leaders. [*Applause.*]

In many of these craft unions they have it so arranged that the rank and file do not count for any more than if they were so many sheep. In the railroad organizations, for instance, if the whole membership vote to go out on strike, they cannot budge without the official sanction of the "Grand Chief." His word outweighs that of the entire membership. In the light of this extraordinary fact, is it strange that the workers are often betrayed? Is it strange that they continue at the mercy of their exploiters?

Haven't they had quite enough of this? Isn't it time for them to take an inventory of their own resources?

If you are a working man, suppose you look yourself over, just once; take an invoice of your mental stock and see what you have. Do not accept my word; do not depend upon anybody but yourself. Think it out for yourself; and if you do, I am quite certain that you will join the organization that represents your class [*applause*]; the organization that has room for all your class; the organization that appeals to you to develop your own brain, to rely upon yourself and be a man among men. And that is what the working class have to do, cultivate self-reliance and think and act for themselves; and that is what they are stimulated to do in the Industrial Workers.

We have great hope and abiding faith, for we know that each day will bring us increasing numbers, influence, and power; and this notwithstanding all the opposition that can be arrayed against us.

We know that the principles of the Industrial Workers are right and that its ultimate triumph is assured beyond the question of a doubt; and if you believe in its conquering mission, then we ask you to be true enough to yourselves and your class to join it; and when you join it you will have a duty to perform and that duty will be to go out among the unorganized and bring them into the ranks and help in this great work of education and organization, without which the working class is doomed to continued ignorance and slavery.

Karl Marx, the profound economic philosopher, who will be known in the future as the great emancipator, uttered the inspiring shibboleth a half century ago: "Workingmen of all countries unite; you have nothing to lose but your chains; you have a world to gain."

You workers are the only class essential to society; all others can be spared, but without you society would perish. You produce the wealth, you support government, you create and conserve civilization. You ought to be, can be and will be the masters of the earth. [*Great applause.*]

Why should you be dependent upon a capitalist? Why should this capitalist own a tool he cannot use? And why should not you own the tool you have to use?

Every cog in every wheel that revolves everywhere has been made by the working class, and is set and kept in operation by the working class; and if the working class can make and operate this marvelous wealth-producing machinery, they can also develop the intelligence to make themselves the masters of this machinery [*applause*], and operate it not to turn out millionaires, but to produce wealth in abundance for themselves.

You cannot afford to be contented with your lot; you have a brain to develop and a manhood to sustain. You ought to have some aspiration to be free.

Suppose you do have a job, and that you can get enough to eat and clothes enough to cover your body, and a place to sleep; you but exist upon the animal plane; your very life is suspended by a slender thread; you don't know what hour a machine may be invented to displace you, or you may offend your economic master, and your job is gone. You go to work early in the morning and you work all day; you go to your lodging at night, tired; you throw your exhausted body upon a bed of straw to recuperate enough to go back to the factory and repeat the same dull operation the next day, and the next, and so on and on to the dreary end; and in some respects you are not so well off as was the chattel slave.

He had no fear of losing his job; he was not blacklisted; he had food and clothing and shelter; and now and then, seized with a desire for freedom, he tried to run away from his master. You do not try to run away from yours. He doesn't have to hire a policeman to keep an eye on you. When you run, it is in the opposite direction, when the bell rings or the whistle blows.

You are as much subject to the command of the capitalist as if you were his property under the law. You have got to go to his factory because you have got to work; he is the master of your job, and you cannot work without his consent, and he only gives this on condition that you surrender to him all you produce except what is necessary to keep you in running order.

The machine you work with has to be oiled; you have to be fed; the wage is your lubricant, it keeps you in working order, and so you toil and sweat and groan and reproduce yourself in the form of labor-power, and then you pass away like a silk worm that spins its task and dies.

That is your lot in the capitalist system and you have no right to aspire to rise above the dead level of wage-slavery.

It is true that one in ten thousand may escape from his class and become a millionaire; he is the rare exception that proves the rule. The wage workers remain in the working class, and they never can become anything else in the capitalist system. They produce and perish, and their exploited bones mingle with the dust.

Every few years there is a panic, industrial paralysis, and hundreds of thousands of workers are flung into the streets; no work, no wages; and so they throng the highways in search of employment that cannot be found; they become vagrants, tramps, outcasts, criminals. It is in this way that the human being degenerates, and that crime graduates in the capitalist system, all the way from petty larceny to homicide.

The working millions who produce the wealth have little or nothing to show for it. There is widespread ignorance among them; industrial and social conditions prevail that defy all language properly to describe. The working class consist of a mass of human beings, men, women, and children, in enforced competition with one another, in all of the circling hours of the day and night, for the sale of their labor-power, and in the severity of the competition the wage sinks gradually until it touches the point of subsistence.

In this struggle more than 5 million women are engaged and about 2 million children, and the number of child laborers is steadily increasing, for in this system profit is important, while life has no value. It is not a question of male labor, or female labor, or child labor; it is simply a question of cheap labor without reference to the effect upon the working class. The woman is employed in preference to the man and the child in preference to the woman; and so we have millions of children, who, in their early, tender years, are seized in the iron clutch of capitalism, when they ought to be upon the playground, or at school; when they ought to be in the sunlight, when they ought to have wholesome food and enjoy the fresh atmosphere they are forced into the industrial dungeons and there they are riveted to the machines; they feed the insatiate monsters and become as living cogs in the revolving wheels. They are literally fed to industry to produce profits. They are dwarfed and deformed, mentally, morally, and physically; they have no chance in life; they are the victims of the industrial system that the Industrial Workers is organized to abolish in the interest, not only of the working class, but in the higher interest of all humanity. [*Applause.*]

If there is a crime that should bring to the callous cheek of capitalist society the crimson of shame, it is the unspeakable crime of child slavery; the millions of babes that fester in the sweatshops, are the slaves of the wheel, and cry out in their agony, but are not heard in the din and roar of our industrial infernalism.

Take that great army of workers, called coal miners, organized in a craft union that does nothing for them; that seeks to make them contented with their lot. These miners are at the very foundation of industry and without their labor every wheel would cease to revolve as if by the decree of some industrial Jehovah. [*Applause.*] There are 600,000 of these slaves whose labor makes possible the firesides of the world, while their own loved ones shiver in the cold. I know something of the conditions under which they toil and despair and perish. I have taken time enough to descend to the depths of these pits, that Dante never saw, or he might have improved upon his masterpiece. I have stood over these slaves and I have heard the echo of their picks, which sounded to me like muffled drums throbbing funeral marches to the grave, and I have said to myself, in the capitalist system, these wretches are simply following their own hearses to the potter's field.

In all of the horizon of the future there is no star that sheds a ray of hope for them.

Then I have followed them from the depth of these black holes, over to the edge of the camp, not to the home, they have no home; but to a hut that is owned by the corporation that owns them, and here I have seen the wife—Victor Hugo once said that the wife of a slave is not a wife at all; she is simply a female that gives birth to young—I have seen this wife standing in the doorway, after trying all day long to make a 10-cent piece do the service of a half-dollar, and she was ill-humored; this could not be otherwise, for love and abject poverty do not dwell beneath the same roof. Here there is no paper upon the wall and no carpet upon the floor; there is not a picture to appeal to the eye; there is no statue to challenge the soul, no strain of inspiring music to touch and quicken what Lincoln called the better angels of human nature. Here there is haggard poverty and want. And in this atmosphere the children of the future are being reared, many thousands of them, under conditions that make it morally certain that they will become paupers, or criminals, or both.

Man is the product, the expression of his environment. Show me a majestic tree that towers aloft, that challenges the admiration of man, or a beautiful rosebud that, under the influence of sunshine and shower, bursts into bloom and fills the common air with its fragrance; these are possible only because the soil and climate are adapted to the growth and culture. Transfer this flower from the sunlight and the atmosphere to a cellar filled with noxious gases, and it withers and dies. The same law applies to human beings; the industrial soil and the social climate must be adapted to the development of men and women, and then society will cease producing [*cry of "Down with capitalism!"*] the multiplied thousands of deformities that today are a rebuke to our much vaunted civilization, and, above all, an impeachment of the capitalist system. [*Applause.*]

What is true of the miners is true in a greater or less degree of all workers in all other departments of industrial activity. This system has about fulfilled its historic mission.

Upon every hand there are the unerring signs of change, and the time has come for the education and organization of the working class for the social revolution [*applause*] that is to lift the workers from the depths of slavery and elevate them to an exalted plane of equality and fraternity. [*Applause.*]

At the beginning of industrial society men worked with hand tools. A boy could learn a trade, make himself the master of the simple tools with which he worked, and employ himself and enjoy what he produced; but that simple tool of a century ago has become a mammoth social instrument; in a word, that tool has been socialized. Not only this, but production has been socialized. As small a commodity as a pin or a pen or a match involves for its production all of the social labor of the land, but this evolution is not yet complete: the tool has been socialized, production has been socialized, and now ownership must also be socialized. In other words, those great social instruments that are used in modern industry for the production of wealth, those great social agencies that are socially made and socially used, must also be socially owned. [*Applause.*]

The Industrial Workers is the only economic organization that makes this declaration, that states this fact and is organized upon this foundation, that the workers must own their tools and employ themselves. This involves a revolution, and this means the end of the capitalist system, and the rearing of a working class republic [*prolonged applause*], the first real republic the world has ever known; and it is coming just as certainly as I stand in your presence. You can hasten it, or you can retard it, but you cannot prevent it.

This the working class can achieve, and if you are in that class and you do not believe it, it is because of your ignorance; it is because you got your education in the school of pure and simple unionism, or in a capitalist political party. This the working class can achieve and all that is required is that the working class shall be educated, that they shall unite, that they shall act together.

The capitalist politician and the labor lieutenant have always contrived to keep the working class divided, upon the economic field and upon the political field; and the workers have made no progress, and never will until they desert those false leaders and unite beneath the revolutionary standard of the Industrial Workers of the World. [*Applause.*]

The capitalists have the mills and the tools and the dollars, but you are an overwhelming majority; you have the men, you have the votes. There are not enough of them to continue this system an instant; it can only be continued by your consent and with your approval, and to the extent that you give it you are responsible for your slavery; and if you have your eyes opened, if you understand where you properly belong, it is still a fortunate thing that you cannot do anything for yourself until you have opened the eyes of those that are yet in darkness. [*Applause.*]

Now, there are many workers who have had their eyes opened and they are giving their time and energy to the revolutionary education of the working class [*applause*], and every day sees our minority increasing, and it is but a question of time until this minority will be converted into the triumphant majority [*applause*]; and so we wait and watch and work in all of the circling hours of the day and night.

We have just begun here in New York, and with a vim and an energy unknown in the circles of unionism. In six months from this night you will find that there is a very formidable organization of Industrial Workers in New York [*applause*]; and if you are a working man and you have convictions of your own, it is your duty to join this union and take your place where you belong.

Don't hesitate because somebody else is falling back. Don't wait because somebody else is not yet ready. Act and act now and for yourself; and if you happen to be the only Industrial Worker in your shop, or in your immediate vicinity, you are simply monumental of the ignorance of your fellow workers, and you have got to begin to educate them. For a little while they may point you out with the finger of contempt, but you can stand this; you can bear it with patience; if they persecute you, because you are true to yourself, your latent powers will be developed, you will become stronger than you now dream, and then you will do the deeds that live, and you will write your name where it will stay.

Never mind what others may say, or think, or do. Stand erect in the majesty of your own manhood.

Listen for just once to the throbbing of your own heart, and you will hear that it is beating quick-step marches to Camp Freedom.

Stand erect! Lift your bowed form from the earth! The dust has long enough borne the impress of your knees.

Stand up and see how long a shadow you cast in the sunlight! [*Applause.*] Hold up your head and avow your convictions, and then accept, as becomes a man, the consequences of your acts!

We need you and you need us. We have got to have the workers united, and you have got to help us in the work. And so we make our appeal to you tonight, and we know that you will not fail. You can arrive at no other conclusion; you are bound to join the Industrial Workers, and become a missionary in the field of industrial unionism. You will then feel the ecstasy of a new-born aspiration. You will do your very best. You will wear the badge of the Industrial Workers, and you will wear it with pride and joy.

The very contempt that it invites will be a compliment to you; in truth, a tribute to your manhood.

We will wrest what we can, step by step, from the capitalists, but with our eye fixed upon the goal; we will press forward, keeping step together with the inspiring music of the new emancipation; and when we have enough of this kind of organization, as Brother DeLeon[59] said so happily the other day [*applause*], when we are lined up in battle array, and the capitalists try to lock us out, we will turn the tables on the gentlemen and lock them out. [*Applause.*]

We can run the mills without them but they cannot run them without us. [*Applause.*]

It is a very important thing to develop the economic power, to have a sound economic organization. This has been the inherent weakness in the labor movement of the United States. We need, and sorely need, a revolutionary economic organization. We must develop this kind of strength; it is the kind that we will have occasion to use in due time, and it is the kind that will not fail us when the crisis comes. So we shall organize and continue to organize the political field; and I am of those who believe that the day is near at hand when we shall have one great revolutionary economic organization, and one great revolutionary political party of the working class. [*Cheers and prolonged applause.*] Then will proceed with increased impetus the work of education and organization that will culminate in emancipation.

This great body will sweep into power and seize the reins of government; take possession of industry in the name of the working class, and it can be easily done. All that will be required will be to transfer the title deeds from the parasites to the producers; and then the working class, in control of industry, will operate it for the benefit of all. The work day will be reduced in proportion to the progress of invention. Every man will work, or at least have a chance to work, and get the full equivalent of what he produces. He will work, not as a slave, but as a free man, and he will express himself in his work and work with joy. Then the badge of labor will be the only badge of aristocracy. The industrial dungeon will become a temple of science. The working class will be free, and all humanity disenthralled.

The workers are the saviors of society [*applause*]; the redeemers of the race; and when they have fulfilled their great historic mission, men and women can walk the highlands and enjoy the vision of a land without masters and without slaves, a land regenerated and resplendent in the triumph of Freedom and Civilization. [*Long, continued applause.*]

Progressive Unionism: Letter to the *Chicago Socialist*†

December 23, 1905

Editor, *Chicago Socialist*[60]
Dear Comrade:—

As many of your readers in Illinois and elsewhere are members of the Industrial Workers, and many others are interested in industrial unionism, a few words in regard to the progress of the organization may not be out of place.

† Published as "Progressive Unionism" in *Chicago Socialist,* vol. 6, whole no. 355 (December 23, 1905), 2.

The writer has just returned from New York, where a series of extraordinary meetings has been held under the auspices of the Industrial Workers. President [Charles O.] Sherman has temporarily made his headquarters there, and so numerous and urgent have the demands been upon him that from sheer exhaustion he was obligated to leave for home to recuperate his vital forces.

After the holidays a branch headquarters will be established in New York, with President Sherman in personal charge, until the office and its connections are in good working order. The lack of organizers in the eastern field has seriously handicapped the general officers, and as these will be provided for under the new arrangement, the work of organizing New York and vicinity will be prosecuted in a methodical manner and with renewed vigor and determination.

Five great mass meetings were held in New York, Brooklyn, and Paterson [New Jersey] while I was there. All of them were crowded and most of them overflowing. There could have been 15 meetings held instead of five, and all of them packed full, if we could have made arrangements and provided speakers for them. At the last of the meetings I attended, 80 new members joined, nearly all of them old trade unionists.

The philosophy of industrial unionism is irresistible. The rank and file of the working class grasp it with vigor and enthusiasm. No labor union ever organized has met with such intelligent and decided approval.

From three to five local unions are being organized in New York City alone each week. This number will be doubled under the new regime to be established on President Sherman's return to the East after his recuperation.

It is impossible to conceive of the rottenness of trade unionism in New York without being upon the ground and hearing the stories at first hand. It is not craft unionism that is inadequate there, but graft unionism that has gotten in its foul work until the very term is a stench in the nostrils of honest men.

It would be too sweeping an indictment to charge all the leaders with being corrupt, but it will not be denied that very many of them are not only dishonest, but criminally guilty of collusion with the bosses; and in that infamous capacity are sucking the very hearts' blood of their organized, betrayed, and helpless followers.

It is even worse than Chicago, and this is hardly imaginable.

In both of these cities craft unionism has gone to seed, and from it has spouted graft unionism of the most vulgar and debasing character. The local leaders, whose name is legion, have in many instances secret arrangements with the bosses, under which the leader gets his graft for wheedling his union dupes into a state of helpless and hopeless servitude to their capitalist masters. These are the labor-leading Judases who, for a few dirty dollars, lead their pure and simple followers into the slaughter pens of capitalism; and the unions of which they are the leaders are the corrals of wage-slaves, rounded up to have their own throats cut, and to be the means of cutting the throats of others in the struggle of the working class to free themselves from the piracy and brutality of capitalism.

Such rotten barracks as these, miscalled trade unions, and very properly denominated "bulwarks against socialism" by the *Wall Street Journal*, must be battered down and blown up to clear the way for industrial unionism, the real and complete unity of the working class, for the overthrow of capitalism and freedom from wage-slavery.

To talk about reforming these rotten, graft-infested unions, which are dominated absolutely by the labor boss, as is Tammany by the political boss, is as vain and wasteful of time as to spray a cesspool with attar of roses. The cesspool must be cleaned out and so must the rotten union, and that is the only rational way to deal with them.

Comrade [Victor] Berger expresses intense disgust with the American Federation of Labor, and well he may after the final drubbing administered to him at the Fakirs' Festival,[61] but he proposes to cling to the old hulk; and with ardor that would be amusing if were not so pathetic, cries aloud to save the old graft-eaten derelict and turn it into a first class battleship.

It is far easier to construct a new man-of-war, and the Industrial Workers is well under way. Victor declares that the Industrial Workers will not do, because it has been "planned" and has no "connections." To this it is only necessary to say that the new unionism has sprung from the old, just as socialism is springing from capitalism.

Let me ask our old Comrade Berger what is the matter with such an organization as the Western Federation of Miners, with its almost 40,000 militant members, the terror of the capitalist class, and the only union that class actually fears?

This union is affiliated with the Industrial Workers. What is the matter with its connections? Comrade Berger is all awry on the trade union question and he will realize it before the bluebirds come again.

There will be a regular landslide from the old unionism to the new in the near future, and Comrade Berger will be rapping for admission to the Industrial Workers before he knows it. He will not long ride the waves alone after his hulk has gone down.

The cry has gone up in New York that the Industrial Workers is organizing scabs. The charge, needless to say, is absolutely false. It is the croak of the grafter, or nest of grafters, that have been uncovered. It is the last appeal to their dupes. The grafting little leaders who make this cry do not dare to meet the officers of the Industrial Workers before the rank and file of the working class. The simple truth is that the disgusted unionists are deserting their old craft concerns, in which they have been repeatedly betrayed, and through which their leaders, in collusion with their bosses, have a mortgage on their bodies and souls—and are joining the Industrial Workers, and the moment they do this, by the peculiar process of reasoning of the grafter, who sees his booty vanishing, they become scabs. The fact is that they are the best of unionists, and this is proven in their determination to turn their backs upon unions that betray the working class, and their faces toward a revolutionary economic organization that has been organized to fight fakirs of all descriptions and emancipate the toilers of the nation from the hell of industrial slavery.

The Industrial Workers is making grand progress in every part of the country, and its coming convention, in May next, will be the greatest revolutionary gathering of the working class ever held in America.

A sound and united economic movement is the supreme need of the working class. As long as the workers are economically divided, as they are in the craft unions, they will be politically divided, and the strong trade union centers will continue to be, as they are now, with but one or two exceptions, the weak spots in the socialist movement.

Economic solidarity cannot but express political solidarity. Without the former, the latter is impossible. With a sound economic basis to build on, we shall soon have a united working class party and the time is ripe for it.

Thousands have been driven from the socialist movement in disgust by the factional quarrels among socialists themselves, and this, more than any one thing, is the cause of the slough in the vote in places where all the conditions are favorable for a good showing.

The Industrial Workers, as a necessary part of its mission, proposes that the workers shall be trained and fitted in their economic organization to assume control of every branch of industry and operate it successfully when the working class take possession.

This means, not only economic solidarity, but the embryonic structure of the cooperative commonwealth.

Notes

1. Clarence Smith was the general secretary and treasurer of the American Labor Union and one of the primary organizers of the Industrial Workers of the World.
2. The January 5, 1905 meeting in Chicago, to which some three dozen prominent labor leaders and radical journalists were invited, adopted a document retrospectively known as the Industrial Union Manifesto, which called for the founding convention of the Industrial Workers of the World.
3. Marcus A. "Mark" Hanna (1837–1904) was an Ohio Republican Party boss who was elected to the first of two terms in the United States Senate in 1896, a position which he held until his death. A conservative but a pragmatist, Hanna was the first president of the National Civic Federation, established in 1900.
4. Several hard rock mining towns in Colorado were the scene of bitter strikes and brutal repression during the first years of the twentieth century.
5. Fall River, Massachusetts was the site of a July 1904 strike of textile workers.
6. Packingtown is the name of the Chicago meat-packing district, location of a great strike in 1904.
7. Frances Willard (1839–1898) was the college educated co-founder of the Woman's Christian Temperance Union, the leading prohibition organization in the United States. She served as president of that organization from 1879 until the time of her death. Willard turned to Christian socialism during the last decade of her life.
8. Frederick Engels, *Anti-Dühring* [1878] in *Marx–Engels Collected Works: Volume 25* (Moscow: Progress Publishers, 1987), 270.
9. This was apparently a letter to Josephine Conger-Kaneko (1874–1934), women's editor of the *Appeal to Reason* and future editor of *The Socialist Woman.*
10. A wartime strike movement beginning in December 1904 in St. Petersburg culminated in mass protests and revolt against the regime of Tsar Nikolai II in January. Faced with possible overthrow of the autocracy, certain modest concessions were made with respect to press censorship and democratic governance. The regime was able to definitively reassert hegemonic control of the political establishment and daily life in 1907. This period of revolt and ephemeral reform is remembered as the Revolution of 1905.
11. The reference is to Bloody Sunday, January 22, 1905 (NS), during which a procession of more than 50,000 people marched to the Winter Palace to present a supplicating petition to the tsar calling for freedom of speech, free public education, adoption of a progressive income tax in lieu of indirect taxation, abolition of land redemption payments, termination of the Russo-Japanese War, establishment of the eight-hour day and overtime, freedom of workers to unionize, and other reforms. The singing demonstrators were met by mass gunfire from troops defending the palace, with an official death toll—perhaps understated—of 130 killed and 299 seriously wounded. See Abraham Asher, *The Revolution of 1905: Russia in Disarray* (Stanford, CA: Stanford University Press, 1988), chapter 3.
12. The *New York World* version has "soulless."
13. Lev Tolstoy (1828–1910) was a Russian novelist and social thinker who espoused

a vision of pacifism, nonviolence, and quasi-anarchist rural cooperation based on collective ownership of land.

14. Georgii Gapon (1870–1906) was a Russian Orthodox priest who became involved in missionary work among the nation's poor. At the behest of the tsarist secret police, he was persuaded to act as a moderating force; he channeled discontent away from politics and toward simple economic ends. He established an organization called the Assembly of Russian Workers of St. Petersburg in 1904 as a conduit for this activity. Amidst the popular discontent of that year, the organization developed a volition of its own, pushing Gapon to action. Gapon authored a petition for the tsar calling for a set of ameliorative reforms and led a labor procession to the Winter Palace for its presentation on January 22, 1905, which was shot down, triggering the Revolution of 1905. After the massacre, Gapon emigrated to Switzerland, returning after the October Manifesto of the tsar providing minimal democratic reforms. In cooperation with the new administration of Sergei Witte, Gapon advocated support of the regime instead of further pursuit of the revolution to overthrow autocracy. Gapon was hung as a collaborator by a four-member hit squad of the Party of Socialist-Revolutionaries on March 26, 1906.
15. Maxim Gorky (born Alexei Maximovich Peshkov, 1868–1936) was a leading Russian literary figure of the late nineteenth and early twentieth century. Gorky made use of a social realist style, breaking with convention to highlight the daily struggles of common people in many of his novels and short stories. A socialist activist, Gorky supported the revolutionary movement but came to oppose the brutality and stifling of dissent by the Bolshevik regime during the civil war period. He emigrated to the West in 1921, eventually settling in Italy. The rise of fascism in Italy prompted Gorky to accommodate himself to the Stalin regime. He returned to the Soviet Union in 1931, thereafter dutifully writing in support of the government and serving as president of the Union of Soviet Writers. Gorky died of natural causes in 1936; the top two Soviet leaders, Joseph Stalin and V. M. Molotov, led the procession at his widely publicized funeral as pallbearers.
16. This letter marks the growing estrangement between the Debs brothers and Victor Berger over the formation of the Industrial Workers of the World. Theodore Debs had previously served as executive secretary of the Social Democratic Party, with both Berger and his brother Gene members of that organization's five-member National Executive Board. As a newspaper publisher and local political leader, Berger was a strong advocate for the existing craft unions of Milwaukee, organizations that incidentally supported his papers with advertising and which after years of careful cultivation had come to lend their political support to the socialist cause. The new Industrial Workers of the World was seen as a rival dual union and an existential threat by these actually existing craft organizations. The strong-willed Berger was additionally scornful of the ideological and tactical incoherence of the new radical industrial union.
17. Despite this intimation, Debs does not seem to have been booked on a lengthy tour to distant places at this juncture.

18. While this statement may well be entirely accurate, no details of such speaking engagements have surfaced as of this writing. It is known that Debs filled various Illinois dates during the second half of May.
19. Peter M. Arthur (1831–1903), née Peter McArthur, was the Scottish-born head of the Brotherhood of Locomotive Engineers from 1874 until his death. A conservative, Arthur was an opponent of acting in concert with other railway brotherhoods and was an opponent of strikes and an advocate of mediation for the resolution of wage disputes.
20. The former Populist and ethical socialist Debs was long the bitter opponent of Socialist Labor Party leader Daniel DeLeon (1852–1914), a doctrinaire and unsentimental orthodox Marxist.
21. Debs seems to have hastily booked a one-off appearance at the Belle City Opera House in Racine, Wisconsin for Saturday, April 29, where he delivered a lecture to a crowd of about 600 titled "Socialism and Economic Conditions of the Workingman." Afterwards he met with Victor Berger and his right-hand man, *Social Democratic Herald* editor Fred Heath, at the Hotel Racine, where they discussed the trade union issue that divided them. Debs does not seem to have departed on an extended lecture tour again until the second week of May.
22. Victor and Meta Berger had two daughters—Doris (b. 1898) and Elsa (b. 1900).
23. Elizabeth H. Thomas managed the office of the *Social Democratic Herald* and was for many years the state secretary of the Social Democratic Party of Wisconsin. A political power player behind the scenes, Thomas was a veteran of the Social Democratic Party with headquarters in Chicago and had previously worked closely with Theodore Debs and the National Executive Board during the unification controversy of 1900–1901.
24. The April 18, 1905, letter from Heath to Debs has not survived.
25. Victor Berger and radical labor priest turned union organizer Thomas Hagerty represented polar opposites on the question of political action, with the first fixated upon building an electoral organization and the latter dismissing political action as an ineffectual shadow of the labor movement.
26. The clipping has not been preserved. Heath was editor of the *Social Democratic Herald.*
27. Reference is apparently to the Debs article "Growth of the Injunction," revisiting the December 1893 injunction by retiring federal judge James Graham Jenkins (1834–1931) barring Northern Pacific workers from striking for higher wages issued. See *Social Democratic Herald,* vol. 8, no. 1, whole no. 353 (May 6, 1905), 1. This would be the penultimate original article of the decade written by Debs for the *Herald.*
28. Both Heath and Berger were able to make the 30-mile trip to Racine, located directly south of Milwaukee, where they met with Debs following his evening speech.
29. Victor Berger had been engaging in polemics with William Trautmann and Thomas Hagerty of the embryonic Industrial Workers of the World over the matter of a minimum program in the Wisconsin state and national Socialist platforms. Berger charged the pair with attempting to transform the Socialist Party into a "little sect" and ersatz Socialist Labor Party by eliminating attainable practical planks from the party platform. "There is no room in our party for Trautmann,

Hagerty & Co.," Berger vigorously declared in a front page editorial in his English language Milwaukee weekly. "Let us recognize facts and not be deceived in regard to fundamental differences by smooth phrases and scheming phrasemongers." See Berger, "The Fight Against Sectarianism," *Social Democratic Herald,* April 8, 1905, 1.

30. As a pointed means of reinforcing the doctrine of state autonomy, the Wisconsin State Committee of the Social Democratic Party long refused to accept a charter from the national office of the Socialist Party of America, even though it continued to pay dues for support of the national organization.
31. In a tangent to the 1905 union debate, Missouri socialist and future secretary of the Industrial Workers of the World William Trautmann preferred charges against National Executive Committee member Victor Berger and the Milwaukee party organization for their tacit endorsement of a progressive over a reactionary old party judge in a November 1904 race in which the Social Democratic Party declined to field a candidate. This action of Berger and the Milwaukee organization was regarded as an act of "political fusion"—a serious violation of party law.
32. Under pressure from delegates from Milwaukee and St. Louis, the 1904 national convention of the Socialist Party failed to offer an endorsement of the American Labor Union, instead passing a resolution that stated "neither political or other differences of opinion justify the divisions of the forces of labor in the industrial movement."
33. Debs refers to the June 27 convocation of the Industrial Union Congress, the gathering which founded the Industrial Workers of the World.
34. For endorsing a progressive judicial candidate over a reactionary opponent in a local election in which the Social Democratic Party of Wisconsin had declined to field a candidate, Victor L. Berger was removed from the National Executive Committee by action of the National Committee early in 1905.
35. The National Civic Federation was a nongovernmental organization founded in New York City in 1900 to ameliorate labor conflict by bringing together leaders of industry, organized labor, and representatives of consumers to foster discussion and negotiated settlement of differences. The group was the brainchild of Ralph M. Easley (1856–1939) of New York City, who served as head of the organization's executive council from its founding until the time of his death. The National Civic Federation was earnestly supported by American Federation of Labor President Samuel Gompers but fell from favor with organized labor after his death in 1924.
36. The Socialist Trade and Labor Alliance was a dual industrial union sponsored by the Socialist Labor Party in 1895 as a successor to the Knights of Labor. Largely an adjunct of the political party, the ST&LA never had more than 15,000 members until it was subsumed in the Industrial Workers of the World in 1905.
37. The Western Federation of Miners was a trade union of hard rock miners established in May 1893. The organization was an umbrella organization of largely autonomous local unions and played a pivotal role in a series of major strikes in Colorado, Idaho, and Montana beginning in 1894. Socialist in orientation and hostile to the conservative approach of the American Federation of Labor, the Western Federation of Miners was the chief sponsor of the rival American Labor Union in 1902 and the

Industrial Workers of the World in 1905. The federation left the Industrial Workers of the World to resume an autonomous existence shortly after its formation due to the latter group's ineffectual nature, surviving as the International Union of Mine, Mill, and Smelter Workers until its dissolution in 1967.

38. Debs was preceded at the lectern by a journeyman paperhanger named Duncan McEachren.
39. William Jennings Bryan (1860–1925), a Nebraska lawyer and newspaper publisher, was the three-time nominee of the Democratic Party for president of the United States. An advocate of loosening the money supply, Bryan was regarded as the leader of the labor-friendly reform wing of the Democratic Party. Bryan was named Secretary of State by Woodrow Wilson in 1913, ultimately resigning that position in protest of the Wilson administration's steady drift toward war with Germany.
40. John D. Rockefeller, Sr. (1839–1937) was the organizer of the Standard Oil Trust, ruthlessly crushing competitors and generating sufficient monopoly profits in the oil, mining, and railroad industries to make him the richest person in the world.
41. J. Pierpont Morgan (1837–1913) was the leading financier and banker of America's so-called Gilded Age. Morgan was instrumental as an underwriter of a number of powerful industrial corporations that dominated the American economy in this era, including US Steel, International Harvester, American Telephone & Telegraph, and General Electric.
42. Cornelius Vanderbilt (1797–1877) was a massively wealthy investor who dominated the American steamship and railway industry during the mid-nineteenth century.
43. Jason "Jay" Gould (1836–1892) was a leading railroad financier of the nineteenth century. Forced out of the lucrative eastern market by competition with Cornelius Vanderbilt, Gould emerged as a dominant figure in the development of railways in the western states.
44. An editorial note in *The Socialist,* probably by editor William Mailly, states: "We must disagree with Comrade Debs's statement that the delegates to the recent convention 'accorded each other the fullest privilege of being respectfully heard from the opening to the close of the proceedings.' As Comrade Debs was absent from the convention part of the time, he may not have been aware of the disgraceful treatment accorded [A. M.] Simons and [James] Murtaugh when they attempted to express their views, although in all justice it must also be said that those mostly responsible for this were the delegates who clustered around Mr. DeLeon. These gentry showed that they had not been chastened by the cleansing fire of industrial unity through which they had just passed."
45. John Ruskin (1819–1900) was an English artist and social critic. He was an opponent of orthodox laissez-faire economics, arguing that division of labor had led to the alienation of workers from their output, diminished pride of craftsmanship, and contributed to general dissatisfaction. A prolific author on a myriad of topics, Ruskin's published collected works ran to 39 volumes.
46. The Chautauqua movement was an adult educational school campaign which borrowed pages from church revival meetings and vaudeville. Prominent public

speakers and musicians were brought to well-prepared and comfortable rural surroundings to entertain and enlighten large audiences seeking to escape the summer heat. The movement was begun in 1874 by a Methodist clergyman and took its name from the original encampment, located near Chautauqua Lake, New York. Speakers such as Debs were routed from one Chautauqua assembly to the next so that several events could be promoted simultaneously, with standardized, high-quality content and travel expenses kept to a minimum. The ventures were commercial and speakers were compensated.

47. This article, written for the *Appeal to Reason,* was accompanied by a cover letter from Debs in which he noted: "Have just returned from the West. I addressed some tremendous crowds under Chautauqua and the thought occurred to me that we out [sic] to get as many of our comrades on the Chautauqua platform as possible, and so I prepared the enclosed which I will thank you to print at your earliest convenience. At every Chautauqua I addressed in Missouri, Kansas, and Illinois, there were scores of *Appeal* readers and workers in attendance."
48. A spotter was an undercover company employee, generally in the railroad industry, who pretended to be an ordinary passenger so as to covertly observe acts of corruption or violations of company rules.
49. A walking delegate is a union employee who travels from workplace to workplace making sure that contractual agreements were being observed.
50. Debs would allow his membership in the Industrial Workers of the World to silently lapse in 1908.
51. In his October 1909 revision, published by Charles H. Kerr, Debs drops the words "of the working class."
52. John Mitchell (1870–1919) was president of the United Mine Workers of America from 1898 until 1907. Mitchell was close to American Federation of Labor chief Samuel Gompers and an active advocate and participant in the National Civic Federation.
53. Charles William "C. W." Post (1854–1914) was an innovator and manufacturer of breakfast cereals, becoming wealthy through the marketing of such products as Postum, Grape-Nuts, and Post Toasties. The opinionated Post was one of the most extreme conservatives of his day and a fanatical public opponent of the trade union movement.
54. David M. Parry (1852–1915) was a former newspaper reporter and regionally successful midwestern businessman who was elected president of the National Association of Manufacturers in October 1903. Parry was a force in Republican politics for nearly three decades. He was a bitter and outspoken opponent of the trade union movement and the author of a dystopian anti-socialist novel, *The Scarlet Empire.*
55. John Ireland (1838–1918) was Catholic archbishop of St. Paul, Minnesota, from 1888 until his death. He was active in the National Civic Federation.
56. Henry C. Potter (1834–1908) was bishop of the Episcopal Diocese of New York. He was active in the National Civic Federation from its establishment in 1900 until the time of his death.

57. James Farley (1874–1913) was a Brooklyn detective who became a professional strikebreaker in 1895, when he helped scuttle transportation strikes in Brooklyn and Philadelphia. His agency was the first to employ mass numbers of professional thugs and scabs, who were shipped in from outside to replace striking workers. Farley was instrumental in busting dozens of urban transit strikes over the next decade, including a 1905 New York City strike, during which he housed 2,000 strikebreakers on a large docked ship. Farley became a millionaire from his efforts before dying of tuberculosis in 1913 at the age of 39. Hessians were German mercenaries who fought with the British against the colonists in the American Revolutionary War.
58. Subsequent versions have "emancipation" in lieu of "revolutionary solidarity."
59. Note that Debs uses the title of the trade union movement, "Brother," rather than the title of the socialist political movement, "Comrade."
60. A. M. Simons was the editor of the *Chicago Socialist.*
61. That is, the most recent annual convention of the American Federation of Labor.

1906

Industrial Revolutionists†

January 1906

Such are the Industrial Workers—industrial revolutionists. They stand against the present system of enslaved wage-labor and for the coming system of free cooperative labor.

The Industrial Workers is, therefore, a revolutionary economic organization. It has a stupendous mission. It has come at the right time, and is catching on amazingly.

The very unanimity and concord of bitter opposition of the capitalist class and its press; the politicians and professors and preachers; and, of course, its "labor leaders" has been duly marked by the thinking element among organized workers and has inspired their confidence from the beginning; and their daily accretions to the revolutionary movement are creating consternation and dismay in the ranks of the conservative reactionaries.

The Pittsburgh convention of the American Federation of Labor[1] incidentally heard of the Industrial Workers, and the principal representatives, although refusing to "dignify" it by mentioning its name, paid homage to it in the only compliments they have to bestow.

Wait another year and then watch the performance when the name is mentioned!

The capitalist press of the land, with substantial unanimity, approves and supports the American Federation of Labor—and condemns and opposes the Industrial Workers. This indisputable fact is of immense significance. The capitalist press is the property, and therefore, the representative and defender of the capitalist class—and the capitalist class lives by exploitation of the working class.

With this fact clearly blazoned, how stands the case with the American Federation of Labor, greeted with the "God bless you"—and with the Industrial Workers, spurned with the "God damn you"—of the capitalist press?

Which of these two labor organizations antagonizes the capitalist class and serves the working class? And vice versa?

Every thinking unionist will answer these questions for himself by joining the Industrial Workers. That is what he is doing today.

---

† Published in *The Industrial Worker* [Joliet, IL], vol. 1, no. 1 (January 1906), 1.

And that is why the Industrial Workers, the lusty little giant six months of age, already numbers almost, if not quite, 100,000 dues-paying members.

And why the most seasoned trade unionists are everywhere at the head of the advancing columns.

And why applications for charters, for organizers and speakers are pouring in at national headquarters in a continuous stream from every corner of the continent.

There is no parallel to this in all the annals of the working class. It simply means that the workers are arousing from their lethargy; that they have had enough of "leaders" who keep them divided and at war with each other, to display their "leadership," and, incidentally, keep their names on the salary list and expense account.

Trade autonomy, in the name of which the reactionary unionist makes his case, is insignificantly contemptible compared to the industrial unity, the organized oneness of the working class. The former divides the workers into crafts and groups, more or less weak and isolated, and these foster jealousies, one of the other, each vainly seeking its own petty supremacy, while the capitalist, shrewdly playing them against each other, diligently fleeces them all.

And this accounts, in a nutshell, for the partiality and exceeding deference of the fleecing class and its parasites for the pure and simple trade unionism, or trade union simpletonism, which keeps the army of workers divided into a thousand jealous and impotent squads, an easy prey to their designing and brutal exploiters.

The workers of the world must unite!

A trite saying, it is true, but one that cannot too often be repeated. And though it be worn threadbare, it must be repeated again and again, ten million times ten million times, until at last the cry comes echoing back around the world:

The workers are united.

And this is the mission of the Industrial Workers—to unite the workers of the world for their own emancipation.

And to accomplish this great work of organization the principle means is education—revolutionary education.

The workers must be taught, or, rather, teach themselves, that their industrial interests are one and the same; that unorganized and ignorant, they are a mass of helpless and despised menials; that united and class-conscious, they are the mightiest power on this planet, and can, with a single breath, extinguish their oppressors and despoilers.

The first thing workers have to do is to teach themselves to think; to think clearly, and then teach others to do the same. Clear thinking is as fatal to ignorance, to superstition and slavery, as the sunlight is to darkness.

The working class must think!

And then the working class will act!

When the working class begin to think they will unite with the Industrial Workers; they will be bound together as with sinews of steel; they will strike together, when required to strike, all of them, not by regiments and detachments, but as a grand army; and on election day they will vote together in the same united fashion and the very earth will then resound with the triumphant tramp of the hosts of Industrial Emancipation.

The workers are an overwhelming majority and have but to act together to conquer the earth and free themselves from every species of servitude.

For a million years the workers have been on the march. Painfully slow, but certain as gravity, they have been pushing toward the heights; toward freedom and the light. The last great battle is drawing near and thc Industrial Workers is marshaling the hosts of labor for that historic conflict of the ages which cannot fail.

All greetings to *The Industrial Worker*—tongue of the Industrial Workers of the World—whose clarion appeal rings out today, a new voice which, trumpet-toned, will arouse sleeping labor, bid it to lift its bowed form from the dust and take possession of the earth and the fullness thereof in the name of Emancipated Humanity.

The 1905 Mayoral Election in New York City†

January 6, 1906

The recent campaign in New York, upon which you desire an expression of views, was in some respects the most unique municipal contest in the annals of American politics. The main issues, while purely local, sprang from conditions which at bottom are national and international, and the complications which ensued and multiplied with the progress of the campaign, involving the disregard of party lines and the disruption of old affiliations, indicated widespread dissatisfaction and the breaking up of party subservience, the unfailing precursors and symptoms of organic change.

The municipal administration of New York had been honeycombed with jobbery and corruption. Great corporations secured franchises worth millions for the asking. So openly and brazenly was the continuous performance of "Graft and Boodle" carried on that the people looked on with speechless amazement, if not admiration.

Railroads, subways, public works, franchises, building contracts—in short everything in New York, including labor unions—have been permeated with the spirit of graft, the vital principle of capitalism, called business, and not only in New York, but the whole country is rampant with the madness it has engendered, and which now rages with all the fury of an epidemic.

With the coming of the election in Greater New York, the spell of the people was broken, and there was a stampede, as there usually is, for what is vaguely called "reform." The situation would have been interesting and complicated enough if the field had been left to the old parties, but with William Randolph Hearst tossed to the surface by the roaring billows of "reform," the roof of the old wigwam fell in, the wild animals roared and snorted in fury, and the free for all circus was open and in full blast.

In such a violent upheaval it is not strange that every pinfeather that was not copper riveted was torn from the Socialist goose. Add to this the fact that the plutocracy vomited a deluge of corruption funds, and it can

† Written for the *New York Zeitgeist* at their request and published there in Yiddish translation, unspecified issue. Reprinted in English as "The New York Campaign" in *Chicago Socialist*, vol. 6, whole no. 357 (January 6, 1906), 1.

be readily understood why the Socialist vote was reduced to its stark-naked minimum.

The introduction, not of Hearst, but of Hearstism, into the campaign is an interesting and immensely suggestive phenomenon from the socialist point of view. In the New York local campaign, Hearst was the political crater though which the volcano of ignorant discontent discharged its fury.[2] Mr. Hearst was not elected, nor desired to be, and more's the pity he was not, that his reform administration might have proved, as it must inevitably have done, an impotent failure and crushing disappointment.

There will be little "reform" in New York or elsewhere this side of the social revolution, but only the failure of reform remedies, after actual trial, will convince the benighted and unthinking millions of that fact.

The flat failure of the reform administration of Judge Dunne[3]—political classmate of Hearst—in Chicago has been an eye-opener to many and there have been corresponding accretions to the socialist movement; and even better than this, no reform wave will ever reach high enough to sweep them back whence they came, and the Socialist Party of Chicago is now fortified and secure, and the winds of reform, howl as they may, will never break it from its moorings, nor blow the shingles from its revolutionary roof.

The defeat of Hearst—or, rather, his failure to be counted in (and this incident is another point of special value to socialists) —was as fortunate for him as it was unfortunate for socialists; for, had he succeeded, his administration in New York would have been as barren as that of Dunne in Chicago, and there would have been a fresh crop of socialists spawned in Gotham.

However, the "reformers" must have their inning and the sooner the better. Disgusted reformers are very often embryonic revolutionists.

Since the elections in New York, Pennsylvania, and Ohio, "reform" has been on the rising tide and anti-graft has been the battle cry of the populace. Little do these millions who are shrieking against graft and for reform realize that the stenches that offend their nostrils and sicken their stomachs rise from the rottenness of the capitalist system; and while trying to expel the stenches, they protest vehemently against the removal of the system.

Socialists are digging the grave in which to bury from sight and smell the putrescent anatomy of this pestilential system.

But for the present, the "reformers" of capitalism, the one-step-at-a-timers have the floor, and socialists must patiently bide their time, meanwhile keeping up the work of agitation, education, and organization with unrelaxing energy and determination.

The people are breaking camp and are on the move, and although having no definite line of march mapped out, they are in a peculiarly receptive state of mind and ripe for socialist propaganda.

Mr. Hearst, having been counted out in New York, after a most extraordinary contest, is now the idol of the people and is being borne swiftly upon the popular current toward the presidential nomination in 1908; and if he is made the standard-bearer of the Democratic Party on a platform declaring against trusts and for government ownership of railroads, telegraphs, and coal mines, there will be a repetition of the New York municipal campaign on a national scale, and the socialist movement will, for the time, be out of the running, and the vote will sink to the lowest reducible point.

We can in some measure prepare for this by shaping our propaganda, program, and platform to suit the exigencies of the situation, without the least sacrifice of principle or modification of revolutionary demand, and may thus turn some of the drift into socialist channels to the advantage of the party and for the general good of the movement, but in any event, the winds that now and again beat upon the party, as in New York, are not ill winds, as they but sweep from us the chaff, leaving only what can't be blown away, and while we are reduced in size, we are in fact sounder and stronger than before.

But after all that may be said in mitigation of the Socialist campaign in New York, the fact remains that some of the responsibility for the small showing lodged with the Socialists themselves. It is in no spirit of captious criticism that I say this, but only that possible good may come by obviating in future campaigns the errors of the one now closed.

Our candidates in the New York campaign did all they could have done in their places; our active comrades gave them loyal support and the campaign was conducted with ability, pluck, and vigor, but yet there was something essentially lacking, a realizing sense of weakness, and consequent failure to marshal the forces and strike decisive blows in the critical hours of the struggle.

Without attempting to elaborate, it is my conviction that this weakness in the campaign was traceable to two principal sources:

First—The everlasting factional quarreling among socialists themselves, the rancor and vituperation, the interruption of socialist speakers by other socialists, and the vulgar rows at socialist meetings incited by other socialists, have served to repel and turn back thousands of honest inquirers and searchers after truth, and drive hundreds of socialists from the party organizations in disgust. The time has come for a united Socialist Party in New York and elsewhere;[4] the rank and file are ready for it and when we have such a party, and enthusiasm takes the place of disgust, strength will follow weakness and we will have a movement as impervious to Hearstism as granite is to zephyrs.

Second—Our New York comrades have made the mistake to pander to the corrupt and disintegrating pure and simple trade unions, and when the test came, were thrown down in the mud by them. The Socialist Party had been trying to win the pure and simple favors of union corruptionists, and compromised character and principle to do it, and was punished for it with desertion and humiliation.

The pure and simple unionism of New York—foul as carrion and for sale to the highest bidder—smiled like a prostitute upon the Socialist Party until the horn of Hearst was blown and sounded the campaign slogan of "Graft and Boodle," and then the whole mercenary gang who want "no politics in the union" rushed to the Hearst camp and there remained steadfast and true while there was a dollar in sight or a pocket to pick. The old strumpet, true to her depraved nature, peddled her wares in other markets for ready cash, and now she may return to smile once more upon the credulous and confiding socialists she deserted and betrayed.

The Chicago Socialists used to bow and scrape to the moribund and mortgaged old unions, and while they did, they were weak, factious, and contemptible; but they do so no more. They now stand squarely on their own character and hew straight to the revolutionary line, and they have today a united, militant party, and if they maintain that attitude for a year they will have the leading local movement in America.

The socialists of New York may profit by their recent experience. They have everything to lose, including self-respect—and that means moral death—and nothing to gain, by concession to, connection with, or any sort of relation but antagonism to the capitalist-owned, stench-breeding sewers of perverted old trade unionism.

Proletarian integrity, economic and political, is essential to proletarian emancipation.

Is Man Immortal?
A Contribution to a Symposium†

January 13, 1906

Your communication was received during my absence from the city. The question you ask is a large and serious one, and it is doubtful if in the hurry of the moment I can make myself intelligible to yourself and readers. I am so busy with the affairs of this life, so much concerned with the wrongs that exist here, with the suffering that prevails now, and so profoundly impressed with the sense of duty I owe myself and my fellow man, here and now, that I have but little time to think of what lies beyond the grave; and but for the earnestness and anxiety so apparent in your letter, I should feel obliged to decline the attempt to answer such a question which at best must still remain unanswered.

The most scientific minds have thus far failed to demonstrate the immortality of human life, and yet the normal being, the wide world over, be he learned or ignorant, wise or foolish, good or evil, longs for, yearns for, hungers and hopes for, if he does not actually believe in, life everlasting; and this seems to be to present the strongest proof that immortality is a fact in nature.

There are many truths that are not demonstrable to the ordinary senses and yet they are so obvious and self-evident that it would be folly to attempt to deny or contradict them.

Coming more directly to your question, as to whether I, my personal, identical, conscious self, shall continue to live after my body goes back to dust, I confess I do not know, nor do I know of any means of knowing; but as I, in that narrow capacity, am infinitesimally insignificant, it is a question which does not greatly concern me. I believe firmly, however, in the immortal life of humanity as a whole, and as my little life merges in and becomes an elementary part of that infinitely larger life, I may, and in fact do, feel secure in the faith and belief in immortality.

Men are small, but *man* is tall as God himself.

The universal life is eternal and will bloom with perennial glory after all the planets wheel dead in space.

---

† Published in *Chicago Socialist,* vol. 6, whole no. 358 (January 13, 1906), 2.

Socialist Papers and the Labor Unions: Letter to the *Chicago Socialist*[†]

January 18, 1906

Editor, *Chicago Socialist*:—

Some comrade, I suppose, signing himself "Socialist," asks me to explain through the *Chicago Socialist* why "the press of the Socialist Party is so friendly to the Gompers unions that are opposed to socialism, and so bitterly opposed to the Industrial Workers of the World that is in favor of socialism."

I would rather that "Socialist" had signed his or her name. Socialists, as a rule, are open and above board and little given to anonymous letter writing. Still, the writer may have good reason for remaining unknown, and so I answer as requested.

Strictly speaking, the Socialist Party has no press.[5] The papers published in the interest of the Socialist Party are owned by party members, but not by the party; and they are not necessarily the exponents of party policy, nor is the party in any way responsible for their attitude.

Therefore, the socialist papers that oppose the Industrial Workers do so purely on their own account as personal publications, and not in any sense as the party press, any more than the socialist papers that favor the Industrial Workers do so as party papers.

The party, as a party, has no press, and the party, as a party, is no more committed to the American Federation of Labor than it is to the Industrial Workers.

The Socialist Party, in general terms, commends trade unionism, but expresses no partiality to any particular organization. Its policy is that of strict neutrality. A member may, therefore, with equal consistency, belong to the IWW, the AF of L, or to no union at all, as he may elect, so far as the party is concerned.

That is the present attitude of the party, and it cannot be twisted in favor of any particular organization, and any attempt to do so is very apt to result in trouble.

---

† Published in *Chicago Socialist,* vol. 6, whole no. 361 (February 3, 1906), 4.

As to the reason for certain socialist papers opposing the Industrial Workers, that is their own personal affair. I may question their consistency, but not their right to pursue any policy that to them seems proper. If they were party-owned papers, it would be different.

"Socialist" must have heard of the law of economic determinism. The law was discovered by socialists, but socialists are no more exempt from it than was Newton from the law of gravitation. The papers in question oppose the Industrial Workers because a majority of their union labor subscribers belong to the American Federation of Labor. In due course of time they will all be supporting the Industrial Workers of the World.

Yours fraternally,
Eugene V. Debs

Evolution of the Anthracite Miner† [excerpt]

February 1906

The particular part of the address delivered by President [John] Mitchell of the United Mine Workers, at the tri-district convention of the anthracite miners, held at Shamokin, Pennsylvania, on December 14th [1905], that pleased the "public" and inspired lavish comment was as follows:

> I have watched during the time I have been associated with you the evolution of the miner, the development of his manhood, the gradual uplifting of the great masses of the people who for generations have been oppressed and crushed. I do not know whether you fully realize what a wonderful transformation has taken place among the anthracite mines. Everywhere are evidences of increased intelligence, of a better manhood, of a nobler womanhood, of a better and more cheerful childhood.

† Published as "Evolution of the Miner" in *The Industrial Worker,* vol. 1, no. 2 (February 1906), 2.

It is not probable that many are gifted with optimistic vision sufficient to see this "wonderful transformation." Quite natural, therefore, that Mr. Mitchell should express his doubt as to whether others besides himself are conscious of it.

It is more likely that Mr. Mitchell is the victim of an optical illusion than that all the rest of us who have been in the anthracite regions are afflicted with defective visual organs; or, as seems more probable still, the "wonderful transformation" has taken place in Mr. Mitchell himself, instead of the miners, and he no longer sees them as he did when as an Illinois coal digger, fresh from the mines, manly and wholesome, his heart was filled with the suffering and his whole being throbbed with the aspiration of his class.

Mr. Mitchell, since that time, like many other leaders of labor, has inhaled the poison fumes of plutocracy; has been patronized and pampered by its saints and has feasted at its banquets, and may himself be blissfully unconscious that he no longer sees through proletarian eyes the class from which he sprang and without which his name would never have been known.

The close and cordial relation Mr. Mitchell maintains with the exploiters and oppressors of his class makes it necessary that he shall see a "wonderful transformation" in the slaves of the mines, and every predatory plutocrat of the pits will bear eager testimony to the truth of the transformation.

If but the miners can be impressed with the miracle of the "transformation" they will hug their chains in calm content and continue to pay the salaries of the transformationists and diligently dig coal for their masters.

Oh, no, there has been no transformation in the anthracite, wonderful or otherwise, and only a civic federationized vision can conjure up a consummation so devoutly to be wished.

I would like to travel over the anthracite wastes with Mr. Mitchell and have him point it out to me, that I might rejoice with him over the "wonderful transformation."

The naked fact is that the miners in the anthracite are in an infinitely worse condition than they were 35 years ago. I have met in the Rocky Mountains and in the far West many of the old-time anthracite miners, sturdy specimens of the working class, filled with the spirit of manly independence, and have heard them tell of the early days in the anthracite when work was steady, wages high, and they were both respected and feared by the mine owners.

It is far different today. The poor devils of all nationalities, half starved, many of them suspicious from repeated betrayal of even one another, in fear and trembling obey the behests of the brutal masters.

For these wretched slaves there is no "transformation" in capitalism; and the "increased intelligence," "better manhood," "nobler womanhood," and "more cheerful childhood" Mr. Mitchell thinks he sees are illusions born of his own pathetic transformation.

It is true that there is "increased intelligence" in the anthracite, but it is not the kind that Mr. Mitchell sees, nor is it due to his efforts, or those of his lieutenants, but to the revolutionary agitators who are firing the spirit of the slaves and molding the mass into solidarity to overthrow the monstrous system that brutalizes them; and when they are at last triumphant there will be a transformation, but Mr. Mitchell and his conservative associates in the support of capitalism and wage-slavery will be entitled to no credit for it.

A few weeks ago the air was filled with reports of a great impending strike in the coal fields at the expiration of the present contract. This has quieted down and little is now heard except that there is not likely to be a strike. Probably not. The thing will no doubt be "amicably arranged" in due time and peace and slavery will have another lease in the anthracite.

But there is now another factor to be reckoned with. Revolutionary socialism is in the field, and it is no respecter of peaceable relations based on slavery.

The anthracite regions are the chosen field for action and in good time will be reclaimed by the proletarian revolution.

You Railway Men![†]

February 3, 1906

This article is addressed particularly to railway employees, among whom I began my career as a wage worker, with whom I spent 27 consecutive years—the complete span of my young manhood—as co-employee, labor organizer, and union official, and for whom I shall have an affectionate regard of peculiar tenderness that will end only with my days.

---

† First published as "Railway Employees and the Class Struggle" in *Appeal to Reason*, whole no. 530 (January 27, 1906), 2, and whole no. 531 (February 3, 1906), 3. Reprinted in pamphlet form as *You Railroad Men*! (Chicago: Charles H. Kerr, n.d. [1906]).

The very relation I bear to them inspires me with the liveliest sense of obligation to that great body of brave and brawny men whose hands, as hard as their hearts are soft, first grasped my own in welcome as a recruit to the army of toil; whose honest faces, beaming with approval, first warmed my heart and stirred my blood, and whose applause, the first I ever knew, fired my boyhood years with high resolves. In every dark and trying hour these comrades of my early years stood staunch and true and pushed me on and raised me up that others might see my face and know my name, while they remained unnoticed, unapplauded; the soldiers of obscurity—the rank and file, the lower class, the common herd, who made and move this world and should be, and will yet be, its ruling aristocracy.

I believe it can be said with truth, as I am sure it can without vanity, that I personally know and am personally known to more railroad employees than any other man in the country; and with equal truth, I believe, that the great majority who know me—better than this, the whole body of them, with few exceptions—feel kindly toward me and may be claimed my personal friends.

In all my travels—and I have been touring almost continuously these 12 years past, over all the railways of the continent, especially since the railway corporations forcibly divorced me from their employees—in all my travels I never made a trip, nor ever expect to, without feeling many times the touch of kindness, oft in stealth, of my old comrades of railroad days.

It is not, therefore, because of any lessening of our mutual regard that I am no longer in active touch with them, but because of the stern decree of fate which commanded me to go where they might not yet follow for a while, but where they will be found in good time, united with their class, and battling manfully for freedom.

I could yet be the "grand" officer of a railway brotherhood, have a comfortable office, large salary, plenty of friends, including railway and public officials, and read my praises as an "ideal labor leader" in capitalist newspapers, but my convictions would not allow it, and so I had to resign, and having no choice about it, I am entitled to no credit for quitting a "good" position and plunging recklessly into "a career of folly, failure, and disgrace."

It was not easy to resign and I had to insist upon it in a way that hurt me as much as it did the loyal comrades from whom I had to tear myself apart; and it has been the first and almost the only case of voluntary resignation from a similar position.

I had been with the Brotherhood of Locomotive Firemen almost from its birth; had organized the Brotherhood of Railroad Brakemen, now the

Brotherhood of Railway Trainmen, had helped to organize the Switchmen's Mutual Aid Association, the Brotherhood of Railway Carmen, the Order of Railway Telegraphers, and other labor unions, and was now to organize, with half a dozen others, the American Railway Union, to embrace all railway workers, so that the engine wiper and section man might come in for their share of consideration as well as the engineer and conductor.

There is where I broke with the railway officials. They were perfectly willing that we should have a firemen's union, but they were not willing for us to have a union that would unite all employees in the service in the equal interest of all.

This much by way of introduction. Now a word as to the purpose of this writing. I have something to say to the railway employees of America. It may not be considered as amounting to much, but I think it of importance enough to ask the railway workers into whose hands, many of them for the first time, this paper will fall, to follow me through with patience and think over what I have to say at their own leisure.

You railroad men are told that I am too radical, that I am dangerous, that as a "leader" I am a failure, and a good many other things, but the time will come when you will know that from first to last I have been true to you, and that because of that very fact the corporations you work for warn you against me; and you will furthermore know that for the opposite reason most of your present leaders are not true to your best interests, that they are "popular" with the public, and your railway officials sing their praises on every occasion and tell you over and again how wise and good these "leaders" are and how lucky you are and how proud you should be to command their valuable services.

Time will tell and I can wait. I am not courting your flattery or evading your blame. I am seeking no office; aspiring to no honors; have no personal axe to grind. But I have something to say to you and shall look straight into your eyes while saying it. I shall speak the truth—as I see it—no more and no less, in kindness and without malice or resentment.

I should tell you what I think you ought to know, though all of you turned against me and despised me forever.

I am not wiser than you, but have had more experience with capitalists and more chance to study their system of fleecing and fooling labor than most of you. I am not better than you—not so good, in fact—for there is no better man on earth than an honest workingman. So I shall not preach to you, nor moralize you, nor even venture to advise you, but I shall put a few facts before you that may temporarily disturb your digestion, but if you will stick to them and assimilate them you will feel yourself growing stronger and you will thank me for having changed your mental bill of fare.

❧

Taken in the aggregate, there is no division of the working class more clannish and provincial, more isolated from other divisions of labor's countless army, than railway employees, the workers engaged, directly and indirectly, in steam railway transportation. Nor is there a group or department in the entire working class that, outside of its own sphere of industrial activity, is more ignorant of the true essentials of the labor question or more oblivious of the class struggle and the fundamental principles and objects of the labor movement.

To verify this statement it is not necessary to refer to the unorganized, unskilled, and poorly paid employees; on the contrary, let a dozen engineers and the same number of conductors, picked at random, be put upon the stand and catechized from a primer on economics, and see what percentage of them can give even a definition of the term. They know how to run engines and trains and, as a rule, that is practically the limit of their knowledge. That is all the corporations want them to know and, from their point of view, all they are fit to know.

It is true that they read journals published by their unions in which a five-column account is given of a reception to some "noble grand chief" and as many columns more about babies born and brothers buried, but which may be searched in vain for a line of revolutionary economics to nourish the brain, open the eyes, give cheer to the heart or aspiration to the soul of a corporation slave.

The several unions of railway employees, considered in any militant sense, are not labor unions at all. Warren S. Stone, grand chief of the Brotherhood of Locomotive Engineers, worthy successor of the late P. M. Arthur, is on record as having pledged his word to a well-known railway manager that the Brotherhood of Locomotive Engineers should never go out on strike while he was its executive head. The same grand chief is on record as threatening John J. Hannahan,[6] grand master of the Brotherhood of Locomotive Firemen, with keeping his engineers at work on the Northern Pacific system, virtually scabbing the firemen, if the latter went out on strike.

If the Brotherhood of Locomotive Engineers was a bona fide labor union instead of the fossilized tool of railway corporations, its grand chief would be peremptorily impeached for treason to the working class.

The *Civic Federation Review* loves to print the portrait of Mr. Stone and idealize him as a "leader of labor" worthy to sit at the feast with, and at the feet of, August Belmont, Andrew Carnegie, Archbishop Ireland, and other millionaire labor exploiters who regard workingmen as sheep to be sheared and skinned and slaughtered, and asses to be harnessed and worked and whipped, and, from that point of view, the engineers and the rest of the railway unions are to be congratulated upon their astute leadership.

It is not that Mr. Stone is personally dishonest or corrupt; he may be, and I think he is, perfectly conscientious in what he says and does, and the same is doubtless true of the grand officers of the other railway unions, but that is not the question.

If workingmen are betrayed and defeated and made to suffer, it makes little difference if their misfortunes are due to dishonest or ignorant or competent leadership.

The question is not, are these leaders honest? Let that be conceded. The question is, are they true to the working class? If their official attitude does not square with the working class as a whole, then they are not in line with the true interests of their own union and not, in fact, the friends, but the enemies of labor; not serving, but betraying those who trust and follow them.

In saying this and making the further statement that the existing railway brotherhoods are of far more actual benefit to the railway corporations than they are to the employees who support them and that, in some essential respects, they are a positive detriment to their members in teaching them to venerate a "grand" officer, subjecting themselves, bound and gagged, to his "official sanction," and keeping them in economic ignorance—in saying these things it is probable that Grand Chief Stone of the engineers and other grand officials will take issue, and here let me say that nothing would suit me better than the chance to meet Mr. Stone before his engineers or any other grand official before his followers, at any time, or in any public place, to make good every assertion herein made, and more, too; and I shall not object if the grand officers invite their friends, the railway officials, to occupy their accustomed seats on the platform, but I will not guarantee that the menu will be as agreeable to their corporation palates as that served at the recent Chicago banquet of the Order of Railway Conductors, or at the average brotherhood convention.

Now to another branch of the question. According to the report of the Interstate Commerce Commission there were, for the year ending June 30, 1904, a total of 1,296,121 employees on the railways of the United States, as against 1,017,653 in 1900—an increase in four years of 278,468. How many thousands of unemployed there are, ready to take jobs when they are offered, in event of a strike, or otherwise, the reports do not say. Since 1904 there has been a great increase in railroad activities and it is probable that the total has since reached 1,400,000. In 1894 the number was 779,608. That was during the last period of "hard times." In the ten years since, from 1894 to 1904, from "panic" to "prosperity," the number of railway employees has been almost doubled, the actual increase being 620,392, an average of over 60,000 a year. Fully 500,000 new railroad men have been made in that time and they have swelled the brotherhoods to unprecedented limits.

Now keep your eye peeled for the signal for the return trip from "prosperity" to "panic."

That is not a matter of guess, but of arithmetic.

It may not come next month or next year, but it will come, and the longer it is coming the longer will be the backward trip.

Railway employees, as a rule, do not know why there are alternating periods of "panic" and "prosperity," panic that paralyzes but prosperity that does not prosper, except for the plutocrats, and the reason they do not know is that they are ignorant of working class economics, which are not discussed by their leaders, nor in their journals, and this accounts for the further fact that nearly all of them vote these sufferings upon themselves, as nonpolitical labor unionists uniformly do, while their unions, vaccinated by the corporation doctor against politics, become parties to "grand balls," such as the Brotherhood of Locomotive Firemen has given in Chicago, and the "grand banquet" just held by the Order of Railway Conductors in the same city, where the "grand march" is led by the capitalist mayor and a "grand" officer and "grand" officials of the railroads beam approvingly, while the "grand" corporation politicians disport themselves in huge diamonds and swallow tails and "grand" speeches are spouted about the "brotherhood of capital and labor"—the choicest lobster on the bill—the whole "green goods" affair being concocted by a tool of the corporations who belongs to the union and who, as a smooth politician, is on the payroll at the city hall, or the state house, or capitol. Such nauseating exhibitions—planned by sycophants and patronized by plutocrats—are given to hoodwink the common herd and keep them forever in the capitalist corrals of wage-slavery.

Political conspiracy is the term to apply to these doings of the henchmen of capital, masquerading in the garb of labor, who are so fearful that their dupes will wake up and go into politics.

But to return for a moment. Keep your eye open for that signal! When Wall Street says the word you'll see the signal, but it will not prevent you and your little union from going into the ditch. The signal and slump will come together.

Several hundred thousand of you will be left high and dry—no jobs, but plenty of time to tramp and think. What next? Sweeping reductions of wages. Next—strikes? Probably! And then? Defeat and disaster!

That's the history of all the "panics" of the last 30 years. They have all been ushered in with widespread railroad strikes and when the crash has come the brotherhoods have burst like bubbles and been crushed like eggshells, utterly powerless to give their members the least particle of protection. This is what has uniformly come to the unions that waste their time at such child's play as "exemplification of secret work" and studying signs and passwords, as if every union did not have a corporation reporter to inform them of every move worth knowing.

And so it will be again. Mark it! Make a note of it! Ask your grand officer about it and make a note of his answer. Don't allow him to dodge by calling me a calamity howler. He will help you after the lightning has struck your job by certifying that you are entitled to another, but you will have to hunt it alone, and in the meantime the "brotherhood of capital and labor" will have suspended and cannot save your wife from eviction nor your child from starvation.

Think it out. Don't let go till you do. Don't take my word: rely on yourself. I can't help you railway slaves. You can only help yourselves. No one else can. If you don't even know that you are slaves in the existing capitalist system, the gods have mercy on you, for your blindness is complete; your condition is pitiable and there is no hope for you but death.

The most pathetic object to me is a corporation slave with a dazzling diamond or a constellation of brass buttons to decorate his deformity and hide the hollows in his grey matter. He swells like a toad as he talks about the good wages "we" are paying; he is a part of the corporation, just as a pimple is part of a plutocrat. He has hinges in his knees. He fawns like a spaniel at the feet of an official, but snarls like a cur at the car inspector or track man. He believes in the "brotherhood of capital and labor;" he is "conservative;" is opposed to politics in the union or the journal; talks about his masters as "our superiors;" is proud of his pusillanimity; does with alacrity what he is ordered to do and asks no questions; is a scab at heart, if not in fact; has no trace of manhood, no self-respect, no honor—craven-hearted and stony-souled—and when he dies Judas Iscariot will have another recruit for his army of the damned.

ᔕ

In his address to the joint committee of the several brotherhoods of railway employees that called at the White House on November 14, 1905, to plead on behalf of the railway corporations, President Roosevelt, among other things, said: "I would be false to your interest if I failed to do justice to the capitalist as much as to the wage worker."

The President was much impressed by the delegation and the delegation by him. The president was really addressing his own brethren, for, like themselves, he was a brotherhood man, and had the grip, sign, and passwords, all up to date; and they were all agreed that no injustice must be done to the poor capitalists. The latter were not in evidence. Their President and their brotherhoods would see that no harm came to them.

In his message to the banquet of the Order of Railway Conductors, given at Chicago on December 31, 1905, on behalf of the railroad corporations, and presided over by Major (?) B. B. Ray, paymaster USA, in recognition of his faithful services in lining up railway employees in support of the corporation ticket on election day—and as smooth a politician as ever came down the avenue—in his communication to this corporation auxiliary, regretting his inability to mingle with the railway presidents and managers who were in attendance to point around at the conductors as evidence that the working class in general, and the railway slaves in particular, were opposed to rate legislation—in his telegram of regret Vice President Fairbanks, once himself a railroad attorney and now a magnate, said:

> The Order of Railway Conductors . . . recognizes in full degree the right of both employer and employee and understands full well that in a large sense the interests of one are the interests of the other, and that the interests of neither can be disregarded without harm to both.

Precisely! "Our interests are one," exclaimed the fox, after devouring the goose. "Same here," answered the hawk, with the feathers of the dove still clinging to his beak. "I'm with you," said the shark; and "I congratulate you upon your wise political economy," was the amen of the lion as the lamb's tail disappeared down the red lane.

Toastmaster Ray, the mortgaged major of the railroads, read another telegram of regret from President "Jim" Hill, of the Great Northern, and then President Delano, of the Wabash, was introduced and proceeded to orate on "Opposition to Railroad Rate Legislation." The dummies are reported to have nodded in hearty approval every time he looked at them. President Delano might have stayed at home and used a string to operate his puppets.

Upon this important point of "identity of interests" between lion and mutton, President Roosevelt, Vice President Fairbanks, and all the railroad presidents, corporations, and brotherhoods are a unit.

The railroads furnish the lion and the brotherhoods the mutton.

It is upon this false basis, this vicious assumption, this fundamental lie, that the railroad brotherhoods are organized, and in that capacity they are of incalculable value to the railroads, the very bulwarks of their defense, and the sure means of keeping the great body of railway employees in economic ignorance, and, therefore, unorganized, divided, and helpless.

Such unionism means organized strength for the railroads and organized weakness for the employees. And the latter foot the bill. No wonder their grand officers get annual passes and their delegates free trains. The stupid employees pay for them all a hundredfold.

And to what base purpose the railroad magnates put these brotherhoods to still further entrench their power and perpetuate their reign of robbery!

At this very moment they are using them as political pokers to stir up the fire of public sentiment against rate legislation. And the poor dupes that pay the dues don't even know that their unions are in politics, corporation politics, the dirtiest kind of politics.

On their own account the unions are forbidden to have anything to do with politics—that would fracture their delicate diaphragm—but when the corporations need them as political tools—ah, that's different; that's what they are for!

Cannot you hoodwinked railway slaves begin to see something?

In all the history of organized labor, from the earliest times to the present day, no body of union workingmen ever served in a more humiliating and debasing role than that in which the railway unions appear at this very hour before the American people and the world.

It is a spectacle for the gods, and future generations will marvel that such an exhibition of servility was possible in the twentieth century: union workingmen, rallying round the robbers of the working class and defending them against their own people!

It is true that there is nothing in rate legislation for the workingman, but the incident loses none of its significance on that account.

The free use of the brotherhoods by and for the corporations at election time, when the legislature meets, when Congress is in session, whenever and wherever required—that is the point.

How smoothly this emergency appliance works!

The corporations sniff danger; they send for their officials—the officials for the "grand chiefs" of the brotherhoods—the "grand chiefs" for their decoy ducks, and presto! a joint committee—and it is a "joint" committee—serves notice on the President and the country that the million and more railway employees want no interference with the divine right of the railroad robbers to hold up the people.

Then another set of political tools of the same robbers take their cue and bound to their feet in the capitalist congress and in a serio-comic burst of paid-for passion, exclaim: "Don't you see, gentlemen, that organized labor, the horny-handed nobility of the land, the muscle and sinew, the very backbone of the nation, recognizes this measure as a menace to its 'full dinner pail' and interposes its righteous indignation? Gentlemen, we dare not make such an assault upon the dignity, the sacred rights, aye, the very life of honest toil!"

That settles it! The trick is done. The Goulds and Vanderbilts and Harrimans[7] on top, their slaves at the bottom, and their "identity of interests" once more triumphantly vindicated.

I propose now to deal briefly with that ghastly lie itself.

In what way, Mr. Railroad Slave, is your interest identical with that of Jim Hill,[8] your master?

He owns the railway system that you workingmen built and now operate.

He pulls every dollar of profit out of it for himself he can and leaves you not one dollar more than he must.

If you don't suit him he discharges you, and you then have to pull up stakes and hunt another master. He gets the lion's share; you get what's left, and in the aggregate that is fixed by what is required to fill your dinner pail, cover you with overalls, and maintain a habitation where you can raise more wage-slaves to take your place when you are worn out and go to the scrap heap.

The Jim Hills live out of your labor—out of your ignorance—for if you were not densely stupid you would not be their dumb-driven cattle.

Now they and their politicians and preachers and "labor leaders" tell you how bright and smart you are to flatter your ignorance, and keep you from opening your eyes to your slavish condition, and, above all, to the wage system, that is, the cause of your poverty and degradation.

Your interests as wage-slaves are not only not identical with, but are directly opposed to, the interests of the Jim Hills and the railroad corporations, and I challenge any of your "grand chiefs" to deny it in my presence on any public platform in the country.

You have got to get rid of the capitalist leeches that suck your hearts' blood through the quill of "identity of interests."

They are in the capitalist class; you are in the working class. They gouge out profits; what's left you get for wages. They perform no useful work; you deform your bodies with slavery. They are millionaires; you are paupers. They have everything; you do everything. They live in palaces; you in shanties. They have abundance of leisure and mountains of money; you have neither. Finally, they are few; you are legion!

Poor, dumb giant, you could in a breath extinguish your pigmy exploiter were you only conscious of your overmastering power!

The workers made and operate all the railroads; the capitalists had and have nothing to do with either. They pocket the proceeds on a basis of watered stock and other "stock," in the form of employees, and then issue fraudulent reports to show on what a small margin of profit they are actually doing business.

In this connection it should be said that the railroads pad their "operating expenses" outrageously to deceive their employees and the general public, and their reports can be shown to be full of duplicity and fraud. They are not required to itemize their "operating expenses" in their reports to the Interstate Commerce Commission; this they only do in the reports of the directors to the stockholders, and an examination of these will disclose the swindle and show how much reliance can be placed in the public reports of private grafters.

Mr. Railway Slave, to resume our interview, you are not in the same class with the Jim Hills of the railroads. You don't visit at their homes, nor they at yours. You don't ride in their private cars and yachts and automobiles. Your wives don't wear the same kind of clothes and jewelry and move in the same circle with theirs. You don't join them in their luxuriant travels to Europe when they are received by the crowned heads of other parasites and given a private audience by the pope. You stay at home and sweat and suffer to foot all the bills; they do all the rest.

To sum up: They are in the capitalist class; you in the working class. They are masters; you slaves. They fleece and pluck; you furnish the wool and feathers.

That is the basis of the class struggle.

Upon that basis you have got to organize and fight before you can move an inch toward freedom.

You have got to unite in the same labor union and in the same political party and strike and vote together, and the hour you do that the world is yours.

The railroads will oppose this; they want to keep you divided and at their mercy. Your grand officers will oppose it; they want to keep you divided and draw their salaries.

When you have a little time figure out the amount annually paid to the grand officers of the railway unions in salaries and expenses and you will be amazed; you will also understand why railroad employees will never get together as long as their grand officers can prevent it.

By the way, why do you persist in calling your officers "Grand Chiefs" and "Grand Masters?" Are they "grand" because you are petty?

The working class, the rank and file, are grander than all the labor leaders, good and bad, that have ever lived.

A "Master" implies slaves. It is bad enough to be slaves without glorying in it. A "Master" is bad enough; a "Grand Master" is the limit, especially if the title is voluntarily conferred by the slaves.

There was a time when I did not realize this and many other things I do now. The difference is that I have learned to think and can now see these things as they are.

The capitalist class! The working class! The class struggle! These are the supreme economic and political facts of this day and the precise terms that express them.

These are the grim realities in the existing capitalist system, and the sooner you drop your brotherhood toys and deal with the labor question, to which most of you are strangers, the better will it be for you.

What is the labor question?

It is the question of the working class organizing to overthrow the capitalist class, emancipating itself from wage-slavery and making itself the ruling class of the world.

Can this be done?

Anything can be done by the working class.

Labor has but to awaken to its power. Then the earth and all its fullness will be for labor. Now the exploiters of labor have it; and they must be put out of that business and into useful service.

First of all, you railroad workers, you million and almost a half of slaves, must wake up; realize that you are a part of the working class and that the whole working class must unite, close up the ranks, and present a solid front, every day in the year—election day, especially, included.

As individual wage-slaves you are helpless and your condition hopeless.

As a class, you are the greatest power between the earth and the stars. As a class, your chains turn to spider webs and in your presence capitalists shrivel up and blow away.

The individual wage-slave must recognize the power of class unity and do all he can to bring it about.

That is what is called class-consciousness, in the light of which may be seen the class struggle in startling vividness.

The class-conscious worker recognizes the necessity of organization, economic and political, and using every weapon at his command—the strike, the boycott, the ballot, and every other—to achieve his emancipation.

He, therefore, joins the union of his class and the party of his class and gives his time and energy to the work of educating and lining up his class for the struggle of his class.

You railroad men may think you are doing this now, but you are not. You are wasting most of your time and money for that which will bring no returns.

Let me tell you a few of the things the railroad corporations and your leaders, between whom there is an "identity of interests," are having you do to occupy your time and keep you chained to the kennels of your masters.

First: They have you divided into petty groups, each trying to be it, and not one having any real power for working class good.

Second: They have you quarreling about jurisdiction and about an "open door," and the corporations smile serenely while you play with these toys.

Your jurisdiction squabbles never will be settled, but grow worse. At places the B of LE [Brotherhood of Locomotive Engineers] and B of LF [Brotherhood of Locomotive Firemen] are at swords' points, and the ORC [Order of Railway Conductors] and BRT [Brotherhood of Railroad Trainmen] are ready to fly at each others' throats; and so intense is the petty craft jealousy that they are ready to scab on one another.

And if they ever go out on strike, particularly the B of LE, their own former members, victimized by them, will rise up to smite them.

The other day I met a man who had an official position that paid him $5,000 a year. Said he to me: "I will quit this job but for one thing, and that will be to take an engine when the B of LE go out on strike." He used to belong to it.

There are any number of men scattered over the country, most of them its own former members, waiting for the B of LE to strike. The day is not distant when the B of LE will reap the crop it has sown.

Third: You are kept apart from other workers, for it would be dangerous if you affiliated with them and got an idea above the roundhouse or caboose or cab you work in. Besides, you might get class-conscious and that would endanger your slavery.

Fourth: You spend hours in the lodge room "riding the goat," getting the secret work "down fine," giving "passwords" and "signs," and unpacking job-lots of "secret work" that any railroad official in the country can have any day he wants it.

These are bibs and rattles for mental babies, and the more time you amuse yourselves with them, the less danger there is of your thinking about anything that will break your chains and set you free.

These are a few of the things; I have not space for more. The hundreds of columns of stale stuff rehashed for years in your journals that might be called goose gossip would, perhaps, be excusable in the official organ of some feeble-minded institution, but it is woefully out of place in a working class publication.

Now let me say a few more things—and space will allow only a few of the many that might be put down—that you may think about at your leisure.

The Brotherhood of Locomotive Engineers is 42 years old and has never won a railway strike of any consequence in all its career.

It is called a success because the corporations make some concessions to it so as to use it as a battering ram against other employees in the service; and this is substantially true of all the brotherhoods.

Then, again, the brotherhoods are used against each other.

The union switchmen on the Denver & Rio Grand, at Pittsburgh and other places; the engineers on the CB&Q;[9] the telegraph operators on the A&P,[10] MK&T,[11] Great Northern, and Northern Pacific; and the machinists on the Santa Fe are but a few of the long list of the "dog-eat-dog" method of unionism, a quarter of a century behind the times.

But the grand officers of the several unions attend one another's conventions and join in solemn chorus in telling the delegates of each other's unions what wise grand officers they have, how kind the corporations are to them, and how proud they ought to be of their noble brotherhoods.

In the next few years locomotive engineers will become motormen and firemen will disappear. It is safe to say that in another 20 years locomotive firemen will be practically of the past. They can then cling to their last straw—the insurance policy—and that is the main thing that holds them together today. But for that they would soon cave in, and that is true of them all. They are then, primarily, coffin clubs and not labor unions. They care for the sick and bury the dead—a good thing, incidentally, for the corporations. To get the full benefits it is necessary to be maimed or killed.

It is well to bury the dead, but the living are infinitely more important.

One effective blow to break the chains of wage-slavery is better than a century of attention to dead bodies.

Class-consciousness is better than corpse consciousness.

ꕥ

A great deal more that should be said must be omitted for the want of time and space.

It is my hope that the facts here presented will lead the railroad workers to study the real labor question. A few of them only know what socialism is and they are socialists. The rest are opposed to it because the little they know about it is not true. No honest workingman understands socialism without embracing it.

The railroad workers, if they want their eyes opened, must read class struggle literature. The paper in which they are reading these articles, the *Appeal to Reason*, with a circulation of almost 300,000 copies, can be obtained for a trifle—50 cents for a whole year—and if they can't afford that, they can send 10 cents for a trial subscription. They cannot afford to remain in ignorance of the class struggle, or of what socialism really means.

A mighty social revolution is impending—it is shaking the earth from center to circumference and only the dead may be deaf to its rumblings. Revolutionary education and organization is the vital need of the working class.

Let every railroad employee who is alive enough to want to know how the working class can emancipate the working class and walk the earth free, and enjoy all its manifold blessings, subscribe for a revolutionary paper and read it for a year; and he will then find himself with the rest of us, in class-conscious array in the struggle for freedom.

The *Appeal to Reason*, already suggested, will make an excellent beginning. There is a long list of other papers and magazines that can be read with profit.

Drop a postal card to W. E. Trautmann, National Secretary of the Industrial Workers of the World, 148 West Madison Street, Chicago, and ask him to send you printed matter explaining this great and growing industrial union; ask him also to send you a copy of *The Industrial Worker*, its official paper, which every workingman should have.

Drop another card to J. Mahlon Barnes, National Secretary, Socialist Party, 269 Dearborn Street, Chicago, asking him to send you printed matter in regard to this working class party, and also to send you a list of socialist papers and magazines, and a catalog of working class books and pamphlets.

Great is the privilege we enjoy in being permitted to take part in this mighty historic struggle. The base and cowardly will sneer and sneak to the rear, but the brave and true, though Hell itself gap, will do battle with all the blood that flows in their veins, and write their names on the shining scroll of Labor's Emancipation.

A Diabolical Plot: The Arrest of Charles H. Moyer and William D. Haywood†

February 22, 1906

The secret arrest of President Charles H. Moyer and Secretary William D. Haywood, of the Western Federation of Miners, and the secret extradition from their homes in Denver by means of a special train to Boise City, Idaho, and their incarceration there upon the alleged charge of complicity in the assassination of Governor Steunenberg, of Idaho, is the latest of a long series of outrages perpetrated upon these leaders by the western mine owners and their Standard Oil allies in their desperate determination to crush out the Western Federation of Miners, the only thing that stands in the way of their absolute and despotic sway in the mountain states. Governors of states are their tools, judges their vassals, editors their special pleaders, and preachers their apologists and defenders. The police departments of the cities are their personal watchmen and the state militia their private armies.

But one thing they could not get in their clutches. The rigid integrity, unfaltering loyalty, intrepid courage, and unceasing vigilance of the leaders of the Western Federation baffled every attempt they made to corrupt and crush organized labor. For once they were dealing with men whose honor was absolutely proof to the jingle of gold.

These men must be put out of the way. Fair (?) means had failed. Foul ones are now in order. Pirates have no scruples. Murder will succeed where gold fails.

That is why this whole infamous outrage was concocted and perpetrated in secret instead of the requisitions being issued and the arrests and extraditions made in the usual way and under the forms of law.

Every detail was prearranged in this dark and devilish conspiracy, this foul and damnable plot, hatched out in the festering brains of the mine owners and eagerly and sympathetically entered into and carried into execution by their political hirelings, the governors of Colorado and Idaho, and clinched by the railroad corporations—to ambush, kidnap, and destroy the officials of a labor union they had not gold enough to debauch, cunning enough to outwit, or power enough to frighten or intimidate.

† Published as "Diabolical Plot of Capitalists" in *The Industrial Worker*, vol. 1, no. 3 (March 1906), 1–2. The piece is emphatically signed "Washington's Birthday, 1906."

In all the history of the country there is no parallel to this monstrous outrage. It is as black and infamous as any crime of the Inquisition committed in the Middle Ages.

The charges are preferred in the dark by unknown persons, the tools of corporations who do anything they are paid to do, from arson to assassination; the governors of two alleged sovereign states, both the venal vassals of the same corporations, pool their powers to pounce upon the unsuspecting victims, and the railroad corporations have the special train all ready to tear these men, free citizens of the republic, from their families and ace them over a cleared track to separate cells in a foreign penitentiary to await their doom.

Language fails utterly to do justice to the cold-blooded brutality of these hyenas in human form; and I cannot but wonder if the railroad men who handled that train knew what a crime they were committing against their brethren in toil, and if they did, what kind of union hearts they carried in their bodies.

Moyer, Haywood, Pettibone, St. John[12], and their associates had no more to do with the assassination of Steunenberg than babes unborn. I know them thoroughly well, and they are brave and honorable men to the last drop in their veins. Cowardly assassination does not lurk in their honest, fearless natures.

To every decent man the very thought of assassination is shocking and abhorrent, but is it strange that Frank Steunenberg came to his death by that ignominious means? Is there not in the tragedy the element of retributive justice? Ask the hundreds of innocent miners brutally bullpenned by him in the Coeur d'Alene! Ask the defenseless wives and daughters of these same bullpenned victims who were insulted and violated by the black hirelings in uniform who were doing Steunenberg's bidding! No defense of assassination is attempted in saying that when ex-Governor Steunenberg was blown into eternity, he but reaped what he himself had sown, for even the dogs cannot stand between men and the consequences of their acts.

What, then, is the object of these swift and summary proceedings against Moyer, Haywood, and their co-workers? The slimy "sleuth" who "worked up" the case tells us bluntly that it is to murder them, to get them out of the way. Brutally horrible as is this confession, now that the victims are safely within the walls of a plutocratic bastille, it is to be commended as the only straightforward feature of the whole criminal conspiracy.

And now that we understand the program of the plutocrats, what are we going to do about it? Fold our hands supinely and see our comrades murdered to glut the vengeance of our enemies for having been true to us? Are we, the workingmen of the land, whom they have so loyally and fearlessly served at such a terrible price to themselves, to desert them in the hour of their direct need? No! By the gods we will have the manhood to stand by them, and if they hand these innocent victims, these incorruptible men, we will make them hang or shoot us also, for it is infinitely better to die like men than to live in the damning disgrace of our own craven cowardice.

Moyer and Haywood and their associates could have had millions of dollars if they had been corruptible. They have had rare opportunities to line their pockets by betraying labor, but they have spurned the dirty gold of the bribe-givers and have stood faithfully at their posts, and now they must die, for the Standard Oil brigands have decreed it and their command is the supreme law of the land.

The miserable pretext that more confessions have been made, that incriminating testimony has been "unearthed," that the lives of other political and judicial hirelings have been "threatened," that certain unexploded bombs have been "dug up," will not deceive men who have had experience with these corporate criminals and know, as the writer knows by his own personal experience, that they are totally destitute of scruples and will stop at nothing to put out of the way any who refuse to do their bidding.

If ever the working class had true leaders, Moyer, Haywood, and their colleagues are those leaders. They have fought the good fight; they have stood staunch and true, and that is their crime and their only crime—loyal devotion to the working class—and this is the crime of crimes against the Standard Oil bandits that rule the nation, crush and rob the people, and riot in the bloody booty.

If Moyer and Haywood are criminals, so are all workingmen who know their rights and dare maintain them. If they ought to be hanged, so ought we, and there is but one course for us to pursue, and that is to call upon all who are read to do their duty to come to the front and see that fair play is done their comrades, or fight to the last ditch and, if need be, die there. Patrick Henry said, "We must fight." It looks very much as if that point has again been reached. A hundred thousand courageous men can strike terror to the hearts of the craven criminals who have throttled the republic. Even a few thousand who have the right spirit can turn the tide.

Appeal to the courts, does someone suggest? What courts? The courts that belong to the criminals that are murdering us? The late Judge Lyman Trumbull and the late Judge John Reagan, great jurists and honest judges, both declared that the courts were controlled by the plutocracy, and more recently Judge Steele, of the supreme court of Colorado, declared that civil liberty had been stabbed to death by the supreme court of that state, while District Attorney

Jerome, of New York, charged that the supreme court of that state was the creature of a saloon-keeping boss of corporate capital.

The plutocrats control Congress, the courts, the army and navy, and we have but ourselves to rely on, and the sooner we realize this fact and act accordingly, the better it will be for the working class and the country at large.

Moyer, Haywood, Pettibone, St. John, and their comrades are not only innocent of crime, but they are the manliest of men. They have been tried by fire and proved true. That is at once their virtue and their crime. Their honor is unsullied, their character stainless. They have fought for labor and bear the scars of battle upon their bodies. They are our comrades. We know them and we love them, and by the eternal we are not going to dishonor them and disgrace our cause by abandoning them to their enemies.

The working class of the United States are about ready for action. Thousands upon thousands will scorn to act like whipped spaniels when their leaders are ambushed by the hirelings of their exploiters.

The cooked-up testimony of sneaks and assassins in the service of capital shall not hang the honest men in the service of labor. Upon this issue all the organized workers of the land will unite and a million others will join with them. From Massachusetts and New York to California and Washington, and from Minnesota to the Gulf, the working class will arise and their tramp will be heard in the land, and the plutocracy, by God, would better think twice before they attempt to carry their murderous program into execution.

Prepare for Action![†]

February 26, 1906

[Boone, Iowa],[13] February 26, 1906

What I have to say about the latest and boldest stroke of the plutocracy will require but little space. It is not talk that is wanted, but action.

The issue is clear. There can be no mistake about it.

† Published in *The Socialist* [Toledo, OH], vol. 6, whole no. 284 (March 3, 1906), 1.

The labor leaders that cannot be bribed or bullied must be ambushed and murdered. That is the situation in a nutshell. How shall we meet it? In just one way: *We have got to fight.*

Another Haymarket attempt will precipitate a revolution.

If murder must be committed, it is not the working class alone that will furnish the victims this time.

Moyer, Haywood, and their colleagues are absolutely innocent. The writer knows them to the heart's core and will stake his all on them.

The only crime they are guilty of is that they have been unswervingly true to the working class, and the working class can do no less than to stand by them to a finish.

A million men at the least will meet the issue with guns.

All workingmen and all other men who have red blood in their veins will rise up against this murderous plot of the plutocracy.

They have stolen our country, debauched our politics, defiled our judiciary, and ridden over us roughshod, and now they propose to murder those who will not abjectly surrender to their brutal domination.

Totally regardless of all other differences, organized labor from the Atlantic to the Pacific and from Canada to the Gulf can unite in one solid phalanx against plutocratic tyranny and crime.

We have no courts to appeal to. They belong to the plutocracy. We have tried them for years, and for one I am opposed to squandering our means going up against a brace game[14] judiciary.

We are men and we have got to prove it. This fight is not of our seeking. It has been forced upon us and we can only evade it by showing the white feather of cowardice.

If we stand by supinely and see our loyal leaders murdered in cold blood, we deserve a similar fate and shall not escape it.

Let mass meetings be held all around the country and the workers aroused.

If they put our leaders in the penitentiary without trial, we will pull them down as they did the Bastille in France a hundred years ago.

The governors of Colorado and Idaho are but executing the mandates of their masters, the plutocracy.

The issue is the Workers versus the Plutocracy.

If they strike the first violent blow, we will strike the last.

In Full Swing: Excerpt from a Speech in Waterloo, Iowa†

(February 27, 1906)

To have lived to see the modern social revolution in full swing is to have achieved a measure of success. To see it, I say, for, alas, there are many millions of blind beings unable or unwilling to see it, and the sun of their lives, if any there be, must set in failure and gloom.

They who see the social revolution in full sweep, who have conscious comprehension of its cosmic scope and significance, are living life at its fullest tide and their souls are attuned to, and their hearts are keeping time with, the symphonies of the universe.

In full swing is the latest and greatest revolution in history, and each passing day speeds it along the highway of destiny.

A thousand times have all of us already been paid for all we have done to pave the way for the revolution and keep it on the main track.

A moment's survey of the present and an imaginative one of the future is sufficient compensation for all that has been and all that may yet have to be done to strike the age-old fetters from the children of toil and emancipate the race.

Thirty-one years ago this day I joined the Brotherhood of Locomotive Firemen and was swept into the current of agitation.[15] It all comes back to me like a dream. Every incident of the day is revived and passes in review. The years are gone—have rushed by on wings of lightning—and here I am on the summit, looking toward the west.

Only the other day I was a boy!

But all is well, for I am still a boy and shall remain one. The wrinkles are in my features only; they can never reach my soul, for I am a socialist, and can see the revolution in full swing.

Thirty-one years have passed like a flash—the rest will soon follow, but not before the revolution has swung around the planet, and shoulder to shoulder with my comrades we march triumphantly into the Socialist Republic.

† Published as "In Full Swing" in *Appeal to Reason*, whole no. 560 (August 25, 1906), 2.

Your Only Prerogative Is to Think: Speech in Davenport, Iowa [excerpt]†

March 2, 1906

This is a wonderful age in which we live—an age of scientific miracle, wonderful advancement in everything that goes to make civilization, and yet an age of widespread unrest. The material achievements of this age far outstrip those of any other but pave the way to the nobler triumphs of the spirit.

To know today, we must know the past. History is the record of class struggles. Through all time we find that the many have lived in poverty and died in despair. Primitive man was a brute, satisfying his brute instincts by brute force. But he had in himself the possibilities of advancement, and he has developed these through thousands of years, until today he is civilized man.

But he is not quite civilized yet, nor yet quite free. He finds his last and greatest problem, which must be solved before he shall become really civilized and free in modern industry. In the inequalities and injustices of our industrial system he finds his greatest obstacle to further progress.

Labor creates and conserves all civilization, and yet the working class bears upon its bow the mark of inferiority and subjection. This problem must be solved before man is really civilized and free.

Problems Omnipresent

During the history of the world the working class has always been in subjection. In the ancient world, there were two classes, the masters and their slaves. In the Middle Ages, the feudal system superseded the early slavery and, while the worker was not owned by the master, the latter possessed the land and practically controlled the lives of those who did the work of which he reaped the benefits. For a thousand years Europe was a great feudal despotism.

† Published as "Debs Lectures at the Grand" in *The Daily Times* [Davenport, IA], vol. 20, no. 66 (March 3, 1906), 4. Merged with material from "Eugene V. Debs at the Grand," published in the *Davenport Democrat and Leader*, vol. 51, no. 121 (March 4, 1906), 20.

Then in the eighteenth century came shock after shock of wonderful inventions, marvelous discoveries, the rise of the trading class, and with the dawning of this wonderful century the problem shifts again. The death knell of feudalism has sounded and capitalism reigned supreme. And now today, after a century and a quarter of wage-slavery, we again see upon every hand the unerring signs of change. Let us look closely at today and its possibilities.

The economic dependence of man began with the taking away of the tool with which he labored. Before the modern industrial system had developed, industry was upon a small scale. Each man manufactured mainly for his own family, and exchanged with like small producers for what he needed and could not himself produce.

He owned the tool with which he worked. There is the key to the situation. He owned the tool with which he worked, and was free. But with invention and discovery, the tool came gradually to be large and complex, more and more so every year. And so the tool became inaccessible to every producer, but remained in the hands of one man. It was necessary for the others to work, in order to live, and to do so they must get permission from the owner of the tool. They got this permission on condition of giving up the greater part of the product created by their labor and his machine, and so drifted into economic bondage.

Since man is a tool-using animal, the working class became as completely subject to the will of the capitalistic class as though they were in actual slavery. Without the tools, the workers began to compete against each other, beating down wages, and as the machine became more perfect, the struggle became more intense and wages went down. The larger and more complex the machine, the more intense the struggle and the lower the wage.

The machine has brought about an increase in the productive power of man and in the wealth produced. But the worker did not reap the benefit. The capitalist became richer and, with his increased riches, more powerful. The question that now confronts us is how to bring about a just distribution of that wealth.

And so today, with 26 million workers in the United States, man stands forth toolless and helpless. With increasing wealth on the one hand and increasing poverty on the other, the great problem of today becomes plain. We must find some way to distribute wealth justly among those who produce it. And in the light of economic progress, the answer is also plain. The tool, used collectively, has remained in private hands. Ownership must keep pace with production, and the tool become collective property of those who use it.

Use the Tool Collectively

Why should the capitalist own the tool that he does not use? Why should not the workers own the tool they do use? There is but one thing that keeps them from solving the problem, one thing that stands between them and freedom, and that is ignorance. [The worker] has not used his mind but has worked with his hand for the benefit of another, who took away from him all he produced except just so much as was necessary to keep him in running order, the same as any other machine.

The hour the working class become united it becomes the greatest power between the earth and sky. To make the workers conscious of their power is the work of socialism.

Socialism is a political as well as an industrial question since without a change in government there can be no change in system. He who owns the wealth will control the government. The Supreme Court in this country is composed of trained corporation lawyers.

The same evolutionary forces are now at work to bring about socialism that caused the growth of the present capitalistic system out of the feudal system. The small producer and little capitalist are being forced into the ranks of the socialists and, while the capitalists are centralizing, we are organizing. Finally, they will have the money but we will have the people. Then we will transfer the possession of the means of production by legal means from the capitalists to the people.

There is nothing to the argument that human nature will not warrant socialism. The industrial system does not depend upon human nature, but human nature depends upon the system. Change the economic conditions and human nature will change.

If the workers have intelligence enough to make the machine, and intelligence enough to use it, they have intelligence enough to own it. They must be the masters of the tools with which they live, and that is just what socialism proposes to make them.

The tool your great-grandfather used is today a curiosity. The modern tool is not individually used, it is a great social instrument. It is so great that the owner of it becomes the absolute master of those who use it. Evolution is not yet complete. As collective ownership of the individual tool was once an absurdity, today the individual ownership of the collective tool is not only an absurdity, but a crime.

The lesson will be learned by the workers in the next few years, and then the machine will be, not a means of oppression, but an instrument of industrial emancipation and social exaltation.

The slave driver of yesterday is gone. The feudal lord is gone. And the capitalist must soon follow. He has written an important chapter in economic progress, but he has done his work, and he lingers, an anachronism. Social ownership takes the place of individual ownership, as social production took the place of individual production, and the cooperative commonwealth rises upon the ruins of the competitive system.

On Child Slavery

The first thing socialists will do when they get in power is abolish child labor. If there is a crime that should bring to the cheek of society the tinge of shame, it is child slavery. I never see a child-slave but my heart stands still; and I determine to work with renewed energy for the abolition of the system that makes child slavery possible and necessary.

There is only one period in the life of man that is entirely free and that is childhood. It should be made as long as possible. When girls are sent into the factories in early life, they are unfit for motherhood when they arrive at the age of maturity. Child labor is a great evil which must be stamped out.

Socialism will not destroy the home but found it stronger than ever. We will make women economically free and then marriage will be founded on love and love alone.

It is all well enough to say that if the working man would stop drinking he would be all right. Or save his money, or go to Sunday school, or something else. But we know that the great mass of working people are deformed, physically, mentally, and morally. All this is the inevitable result of the economic system under which we live. The economic basis of life must be right before those parts of human nature that lead to nobility and altruism can have full play and encouragement.

It is not necessary to root out selfishness to found socialism. Altruism is enlightened selfishness. We will reward the able according to their ability and they will gain more through service of the people than in a struggle for dirty dollars.

Finally, there will be no war. War is murder in uniform and the production of instruments of death is the prostitution of genius. War is caused by international competition and is carried on for monetary profits.

An economic system founded upon injustice must produce the effects that we see about us every day—degradation, misery, and despair. And in the face of these facts it is blindness and foolishness to try to find the remedy in the reform of some effect. We must go to the root of the matter. Once all men stand in a just relation to each other economically, the other things will follow. The other problems must be worked out for themselves, it is true, but the economic problem must be solved first.

You have the opportunity in the coming municipal election to vote for these conquering principles, and hasten the dawn of that brighter day of socialism. You have one prerogative—to think. I only ask you to do that.

Arouse, Ye Slaves!†

March 10, 1906

The latest and boldest stroke of the plutocracy, but for the blindness of the people, would have startled the nation.

Murder has been plotted and is about to be executed in the name and under the forms of law.

Men who will not yield to corruption and browbeating must be ambushed, spirited away, and murdered.

That is the edict of the Mine Owners' Association of the western states and their Standard Oil backers and pals in Wall Street, New York.

These gory-beaked vultures are to pluck out the heart of resistance to their tyranny and robbery, that labor may be left stark naked at their mercy.

Charles Moyer and William D. Haywood, of the Western Federation of Miners, and their official colleagues—men, all of them, and every inch of them—are charged with the assassination of ex-Governor Frank Steunenberg, of Idaho, who simply reaped what he had sown, as a mere subterfuge to pounce upon them in secret, rush them out of the state by special train, under heavy guard, clap them into the penitentiary, convict them upon the purchased perjured testimony of villains, and strangle them to death with the hangman's noose.

† Published in *Appeal to Reason*, whole no. 536 (March 10, 1906), 1.

It is a foul plot; a damnable conspiracy; a hellish outrage.

The governors of Idaho and Colorado say they have the proof to convict. They are brazen falsifiers and venal villains, the miserable tools of the mine owners who, themselves, if anybody, deserve the gibbet.

Moyer, Haywood, and their comrades had no more to do with the assassination of Steunenberg than I had; the charge is a ghastly lie, a criminal calumny, and is only an excuse to murder men who are too rigidly honest to betray their trust and too courageous to succumb to threat and intimidation.

Labor leaders that cringe before the plutocracy and do its bidding are apotheosized; those that refuse must be foully murdered.

Personally and intimately do I know Moyer, Haywood, Pettibone, St. John, and their official co-workers, and I will stake my life on their honor and integrity; and that is precisely the crime for which, according to the words of the slimy "sleuth" who "worked up the case" against them, "they shall never leave Idaho alive."

Well, by the gods, if they don't, the governors of Idaho and Colorado and their masters from Wall Street, New York, to the Rocky Mountains had better prepare to follow them.

Nearly 20 years ago the capitalist tyrants put some innocent men to death for standing up for labor.

They are now going to try it again. Let them dare!

There have been 20 years of revolutionary education, agitation, and organization since the Haymarket tragedy, and if an attempt is made to repeat it, there will be a revolution and I will do all in my power to precipitate it.

The crisis has come and we have got to meet it. Upon the issue involved the whole body of organized labor can unite and every enemy of plutocracy will join us. From the farms, the factories and stores will pour the workers to meet the red-handed destroyers of freedom, the murderers of innocent men and the archenemies of the people.

Moyer and Haywood are our comrades, staunch and true, and if we do not stand by them to the shedding of the last drop of blood in our veins, we are disgraced forever and deserve the fate of cringing cowards.

We are not responsible for the issue. It is not of our seeking. It has been forced upon us; and for the very reason that we deprecate violence and abhor bloodshed, we cannot desert our comrades and allow them to be put to death. If they can be murdered without cause so can we, and so will we be dealt with at the pleasure of these tyrants.

They have driven us to the wall and now let us rally our forces and face them and fight.

If they attempt to murder Moyer, Haywood, and their brothers, a million revolutionists, at least, will meet them with guns.

They have done their best and their worst to crush and enslave us. Their politicians have betrayed us, their courts have thrown us into jail without trial, and their soldiers have shot our comrades dead in their tracks.

The worm turns at last, and so does the worker.

Let them dare to execute their devilish plot and every state in this Union will resound with the tramp of revolution.

Get ready, comrades, for action! No other course is left to the working class. Their courts are closed to us except to pronounce our doom. To enter their courts is simply to be mulcted of our meager means and bound hand and foot; to have our eyes plucked out by the vultures that fatten upon our misery.

Capitalist courts never have done, and never will do, anything for the working class.

Whatever is done we must do ourselves, and if we stand up like men from the Atlantic to the Pacific and from Canada to the Gulf, we will strike terror to their cowardly hearts and they will be but too eager to relax their grip upon our throats and beat a swift retreat.

We will watch every move they make and in the meantime prepare for action.

A special revolutionary convention of the proletariat at Chicago, or some other central point, would be in order, and, if extreme measures are required, a general strike could be ordered and industry paralyzed as a preliminary to a general uprising.

If the plutocrats begin the program, we will end it.

Labor's Awakening†

April 7, 1906

Nothing that has ever occurred in the history of the country has been so deeply, widely, and instantaneously felt as the dastardly assault upon our leaders in the western states. The effect has been marvelous, and for the first time the solidarity of labor becomes something more than a meaningless phrase. The reason for this is that labor now has something of a press and can now reach its millions with the truth as they have hitherto been reached only by the falsehoods of the enemy.

Hundreds of mass meetings are being held, or on the calendar, and hundreds more are on the way.

The governor of Idaho has hastened to explain that no wrong is intended, but that Moyer and Haywood shall have a "fair trial," and that was the intention from the beginning.

He lies. Every step in the conspiracy, from the time it was concocted in his office, proves that the intention was to rush these men—infinitely his moral superiors—to the penitentiary and scaffold.

The sworn officers of the state struck down every law that stood between them and their victims and stole them bodily and bore them away like thieves in the night, and yet they have the hardihood to claim that they propose to do justice to these men.

When Governor Gooding proclaimed these men's guilt in advance of trial—he who above all others should have preserved the dignity of silence until they had an opportunity to be heard—he not only disgraced his office and merited impeachment, but he inadvertently, in his eagerness and haste, revealed the whole foul conspiracy and in the coming trial, his "confession," for such it is, must be put in evidence, and no stronger proof of the damnable plot to murder innocent men could be adduced.

The fact that the governor has begun to "explain" to organized labor is in itself significant. We now know the governor, and before we get through he will know us.

---

† Published in *The Socialist* [Toledo, OH], vol. 6, whole no. 289 (April 7, 1906), 1. Many italics in original, almost certainly editorially created, have been removed for readability.

He and his papers would have it appear that we are thirsting for violence and bloodshed. The exact opposite is true. He and his gang are the ones who have taken the law, their own capitalist law, into their own hands—and by what right do these outlaws now talk to us about law and order?

We of the working class, who have been clubbed and jailed repeatedly in defiance of law and without trial, know precisely by what means the two western outlaw governors and their allies will try to have it appear that we are the criminals when, as a matter of fact, their whole career is one of plunder and brazen disregard of law.

Governor Gooding, who has flagrantly violated law to get our comrades into his clutches, need not take the pains to assure us that they will have a fair trial. Several million American workingmen will see to that.

So sure are we that our comrades are totally innocent that from the very start we would have courted trial if we had not been convinced beyond all doubt that a conspiracy had been hatched to cold-deck these victims without a ghost of a chance to defend themselves. Every step thus far taken proves it, but now that the people are being aroused to the gravity of the situation all over the county, the conspirators are beginning to relent and show some sign of giving the prisoners a show for their lives.

Labor has just begun to awaken and stretch itself. From now on there will be something doing.

Must Have Fair Trial

Moyer, Haywood, St. John, and Pettibone must have a fair trial. This is matter of supreme importance to labor and the whole people.

They will get a fair trial only if the toiling masses see to it and that is now our special business.

All differences that temporarily divide us must for the time be forgotten. We must put ourselves in the places of our comrades and our families in the places of their suffering wives and children.

These loyal leaders of labor are innocent and their lives must be saved. Their death would be the deep disgrace and foul damnation of the working class.

Let the indignation meetings be held in every corner and crevice of the country and let the reports and resolutions pour upon the head of Governor Gooding in a roaring torrent.

John Mitchell proclaimed his faith in the innocence of these men and advocated the appropriation of $5,000 for their defense from the treasury of the

United Mine Workers, in convention assembled, and it was allowed amidst demonstrations of heartiest approval. This was the finest act in John Mitchell's life and he is entitled to full credit for it. It is also an act on the part of the United Mine Workers which shows that, notwithstanding all differences, the hearts of workers, East and West, throb in unison when an attack is made upon their class.

The Illinois members of the United Mine Workers voted $5,000 and the Indiana members $500, acts of generous and fraternal significance, not without pathos when the scant wages of these hard-worked and sorely oppressed diggers of coal, themselves on the verge of a strike, are taken in account.

These incidents and scores of others of a like nature are immensely suggestive, and it is not strange that the Idaho governor has begun with his assurances of a fair trial and a square deal to labor. *But for the spontaneous uprising of the workers no such polite palaver would have been dished out, but the marked comrades of the mine owners' hostility would have been expeditiously put out of the way in accordance with the original program.*

At first but little interest was shown in this extraordinary conspiracy. But when the great mass of labor began to move, everything else followed, and in the last few days there has been a veritable transformation.

Labor first sensed the crime and scented the conspirators. Labor first had its correspondents upon the scene. This was a revelation. As labor's startling reports of the true inwardness of affairs blazed forth and aroused the workers, other things began to move and one after another, labor unions—even the most conservative—public men, and newspapers fell into line and now nearly the whole country is awake to the plot of the plutocracy.

The Hearst papers were silent for a full month, but have now burst forth in scathing denunciation and have a special correspondent on the ground.

Provide a Labor Representative

The thing now in order is to provide for a regular representative of the working class to be at the trial and to daily report the testimony to the labor and socialist papers of the country. The real jury will consist of the more than 20 million wage workers of the United States. The attack is upon them and they must and will meet it.

We do not propose that labor's brave leaders shall be legally murdered; that self-confessed assassins shall swear away their lives; that bloodthirsty Pinkertons with no more conscience than cobras shall be allowed to consummate their dastardly plot to hang honest men that they may riot in the proceeds of their own infamy.

Neither shall a packed jury, following in the footsteps of a packed grand jury, at the behest of a packed governor, pronounce murder instead of rendering an honest verdict.

Let Governor Gooding understand right now that labor has an eye on him and his man-catching machinery and that every move will be scrutinized and that labor reserves to itself the right to decide if the trial is fair or not, and if there is any attempt at crookedness, some other buttons will be pressed and the governor will witness some further developments to impress him with the majesty of an aroused working class in the United States.

[Socialist publisher Hermon] Titus[16] is doing great work. He has shown himself to be the man for the mission. He must now give us character sketches of all the principals in the great drama. We want to know exactly who Governor Gooding is, what he is, his antecedents and connections. Every material fact about him must be dug up and every relevant fact of his life must be laid bare. The searchlight must be turned upon this man so that the workers of the land may see him exactly as he is.

Judge Smith[17] and other judges must also be dissected to the very marrow of their judicial bones. We have a good idea as to who they are, but we want accurate, life-sized, inside and outside views of them, and then we can better judge as to their acts in the great conspiracy.

Then, too, we must have, when the jury is empaneled, a searching analysis of each member. We must know his character, his politics, his financial obligations and to whom, and all other things that will enable us to judge them truly, for they are very important factors in what Governor Gooding promises shall be (and what the millions of workers in the United States will make it their special business to see that it is)—a fair trial.

We must arrange to have at least 12 representatives of organized labor to sit at the trial from the opening day. Each national labor union should delegate a representative for this purpose. With 12 men sitting close to the regular jury, 12 honest representatives of the organized millions of labor, 12 good men and true to keep their eyes on the jury and on the witnesses and the proceedings, and the millions waiting day by day for their report, there will be a fair trial and consequent acquittal; and to do this will require but a few thousand dollars and we can easily raise it.

The central labor body of every large city can easily afford to send one such representative. A great mass meeting in each such city can raise the necessary funds at a single collection.

If gentlemen of the capitalist class wonder about these things, it is only necessary to say: Gentlemen, we know you and we know your courts and your methods. We know that as an exploiting class you have no scruples and we know, by bitter experience, that in every trial, when labor and capital are involved, the courts do your bidding. You and your public officials do not hesitate, when it suits your purpose, to take the law into your own hands and of this there is abundant proof, beginning with the infamous legislature of Colorado, purchased by you as if they had been so many swine, and utterly refusing to carry out the expressed and lawful will of the people; and if we, the workers of the country, take things into our hands, in a crisis such as this, you gentlemen have set us the example and you can give yourselves full credit for having pushed us to the wall and driven us to whatever extremities may follow.

Workers of all trades and occupations, awaken!

Workers of no trade and without jobs, arise!

The crisis is upon us, our leaders have been seized and we must go to their rescue!

Keep your eyes and ears open for reports from the Rockies—the scene of the arch-conspiracy!

A Few Words, Mr. President: Open Letter to Theodore Roosevelt†

April 15, 1906

Dear Mr. President:—

The address delivered by you yesterday at the cornerstone ceremony at Washington[18] has been carefully read and among other things I observe the following.

† Published as "A Few Words, Mr. President" in *The Socialist* [Toledo, OH], vol. 6, whole no. 291 (April 21, 1906), 1.

We can no more and no less afford to condone evil in a man of capital than evil in a man of no capital. The wealthy man who exults because there is a failure of justice in the effort to bring some trust magnate to an account for his misdeeds is as bad, and no worse than, the so-called labor leader who clamorously strives to excite a foul class feeling on behalf of some other labor leader who is implicated in murder.

Obviously you have reference in this paragraph to the leaders of labor in Colorado who were recently seized without warrant of law, forcibly taken from the state of which they are citizens, and incarcerated in the penitentiary of another state in which only convicted criminals are confined. I know of no other labor leaders to whom these remarks could apply, and it seems equally plain that I am one of the "so-called" leaders, if not the particular one, who is "striving to excite a foul class feeling on their behalf."[19]

Permit me to ask you, Mr. President, how you know that these men are implicated in murder? Have they been tried and found guilty by due process of law?

Since when, Mr. President, are men charged with crime presumed and pronounced guilty until they are found innocent?

It is true that you do not name these men, but convict them by innuendo. Is this fair? Is it just? A square deal? Is it not, in fact, Mr. President, cowardly to take such an advantage of your high office to pronounce the guilt of three of your fellow citizens, who have as yet not been tried and against whom nothing has been proved?

These men, Mr. President, are workingmen; do you know of any capitalists who have ever been treated in the same way?

Suppose a lot of thugs were to seize a number of capitalists at the hour of midnight, put them in irons, hustle them aboard a special train, rush them into another state, and throw them into the penitentiary. Would you take the same view of the case, coolly pronounce their guilt and proceed to deliver your homily upon good citizenship, the "square deal," and law and order?

If instead of Moyer, Haywood, and Pettibone it had been Depew,[20] Platt, and Paul Morton—that is to say, if instead of innocent workingmen they had been criminal capitalists—would you have treated them in precisely the same manner?

You have told us over and over again, Mr. President, that rich and poor should be treated alike; that all are entitled to the equal protection of the law. That is what you say in substance in the paragraph above quoted. You have repeated this so often that it has become a stale platitude. You have also repeatedly stated that profession without practice is dishonest and hypocritical.

Very well, Mr. President, we will take you at your word; we will judge you by your acts.

I shall not now address myself to you as a "so-called" labor leader, but as your fellow citizen of the United States.

You, Mr. President, are the chief executive of the nation. You are the conservator of the constitution of the United States and you have publicly sworn to support it.

Three citizens have been forcibly seized and deported from the state of their residence into another state in flagrant violation of the constitution of the United States. These men now languish in prison cells.

Let me repeat the charge, Mr. President, without detail. Three citizens of the republic have been deprived of the protection vouchsafed to them under the constitution of the United States. This fact is known of all men; denied by none, not even their accusers. There is not a shadow of doubt about it. It is a clear-cut case. All the country knows it. You, Mr. President, know it. Now, then what are you going to do about it?

Will you make your acts square with your words; your practice with your profession?

It is up to you, Mr. President! You are reputed to have great moral courage and you certainly have great power. Under the constitution, the one that has been violated, the one you have sworn to support, you have the power to redress the wrong that has been done. Will you do it?

All that I am asking is that you shall perform your sworn duty; you are not expected to do more, and you cannot do less without violating your oath of office and betraying your official trust.

If you do not believe, Mr. President, that the constitution has been violated, or, if you have the least doubt about it, please call upon me to prove it.

I am not now handling a "muck-rake;" not looking down, but up—up to you and awaiting your answer.

You are perhaps aware, Mr. President, that some of us are accused of advocating violence. It is not true. As a matter of fact we are resisting violence. In your address yesterday you quoted the commandment, "Thou shalt not steal!"[21] Let me quote another, "Thou shalt not kill."[22] This is precisely what we are trying to prevent, not lawful punishment, but coldblooded murder.

In treating with Moyer, Haywood, and Pettibone, our comrades, every law and all decency have been trampled under foot. The state in which these men have been stripped of their legal rights and treated as felons is notoriously in control of corporations whose absolute sway has been questioned by these leaders of the working class; and this, and this alone, constitutes their crime, and for this they have been marked for corporate vengeance.

These men, Mr. President, are our comrades, our brothers, and we propose to stand by them and see that justice is done them.

A fair trial will free and vindicate them as certain as the sun shines.

Knowing them as we do to be men of pure character, of absolute integrity and all other things of good report among men, we know that they are wholly incapable of committing the crime with which they have been charged.

It is not pretended that they were in the same state at the time the crime was committed. Not a shadow of crime rests upon them other than the alleged confession of a self-confessed criminal.

These are facts, Mr. President, and in view of these facts we would be craven indeed if we allowed our brothers to be made the victims of such an infamous conspiracy without doing all in our power to save them.

Every step thus far taken against these men has been in violation of law, and the purpose of the whole proceeding is so apparent that any man with eyes can see it.

In this connection, Mr. President, when the question of law and order is raised, I beg of you to remember that we are dealing with corporations that have usurped the powers of state governments; that defy the legally expressed will of the people, as in Colorado, where a majority of 46,000 votes was overridden and treated with contempt; corporations whose crime-inciting shibboleths are: "To hell with the constitution;" "To hell with habeas corpus."

These corporations rule the states and we have had evidence enough to know how they treat law when it interferes with their predatory program.

We are not in favor of violence, but seeking to avoid it. The facts prove it.

We are not objecting to a fair trial, but to a packed jury and a corporation court and the consummation of a criminal conspiracy.

"Thou shalt not kill!" This applies to capitalists as well as workingmen.

If Moyer, Haywood, and Pettibone were capitalists instead of workingmen we should still do our utmost to see that they were given a "square deal."

Murder in any form is abhorrent, but most terribly so when committed under the forms and in the names of law and justice.

Wendell Phillips[23] said that John Brown would have had twice as good a right to hang Governor Wise[24] as Governor Wise had to hang John Brown.

All we are asking and insisting upon is that our accused brothers shall have the protection of the law, a fair hearing and just verdict, and upon that issue we are prepared to go before the American people.

Respectfully yours,
E. V. Debs

To the Rescue![†]

April 28, 1906

There is no power without justice.

—Napoleon Bonaparte

It seems to me that in such a land there must be, not this question of slavery, sluggards to be awakened, as well as doubters to be convinced. Many more, we verily believe, of the first than the last. There are far more hearts to be quickened, than confused intellects to be cleared up—more dumb dogs to be made to speak, than doubting consciences to be enlightened. We have use, then, sometimes, for something beside argument.

—Wendell Phillips

I am aware that many object to the severity of my language; but is there not cause for severity? I will be as harsh as truth, and as uncompromising as justice. I am in earnest—I will not equivocate, I will not excuse, I will not retreat an inch—and I will be heard.

—William Lloyd Garrison

† Published in *Appeal to Reason*, whole no. 543 (April 28, 1906), 1.

There is not a scintilla of creditable evidence against the leaders of the Western Federation of Miners who are now locked up in the prison pens of Idaho.

The kidnaping of these men is prima facie evidence of their innocence. It is not a case, not of lawful prosecution, but of diabolical conspiracy and premeditated murder.

Governor Gooding, the central figure in the atrocious plot, has already declared guilt and pronounced judgment.

The simple question is, Shall it be carried into execution?

The answer, NO, NEVER! swells from a million hearts and the thunder of their righteous indignation reverberates from shore to shore.

There is no spark of justice, and, therefore, no shadow of real power in their wicked, heartless conspiracy.

The very isolation of the scene projects these midnight assassins into bold relief, while the finger of retributive justice points them out as they flit from cover to cover in their gumshoe maneuverings to wind and twist the deadly coils about their innocent victims.

Compared to such hyenas, ordinary highwaymen become reputable citizens.

The whole infamous plot will collapse like a soap bubble and every conspirator will flee for his miserable life the very moment the light is turned on and an aroused working class and an outraged people close in on the gang of dark-lantern guerillas.

Caught in a trap of their own setting, and buried in the pit of their own digging, will be the final verdict of the higher court in which inexorable Justice is meted out to all.

With one mailed clutch upon the throats of his victims and the other brandishing the dagger of assassination, the so-called governor of Idaho presents a spectacle for men and angels to contemplate.

He has no particle of evidence, and knows it, else he would have proceeded by lawful means instead of waylaying his unsuspecting victims and bludgeoning them in midnight darkness. That such a malefactor has the grim audacity, after striking down all law, to invoke its protection is the very climax of criminal conspiracy.

He may surround himself—this Standard Oil candidate for the United States Senate—with his state militia and armed Hessians, but he will never escape the consequences of his brutal acts.

It is not the fair trial that we are protesting against, as they would have it believed, but the foul conspiracy to murder innocent men that cries to heaven.

It must not, shall not, be consummated.

The doors of the prison cells can be made to swing wide open and our comrades walk forth free men without a single violent blow.

To the rescue, ye toiling millions!

Your leaders have been ambushed by the enemy and their cry should arouse you like a trumpet blast upon the field of war.

Awaken, ye hosts of Labor! For you and your loved ones, these faithful sentinels on the watchtowers have been put to torture; and must they now seal their fidelity and devotion with their lives?

To suffer these men to perish as the bloody consummation of a satanic conspiracy to destroy organized labor that the Standard Oil brigands and their murderous minions may have unbridled sway would cover the working class with obloquy, outrage civilization, and make the twentieth century infamous to the last stroke of recorded time.

It is not Moyer, Haywood, Pettibone, and St. John alone who are in the balance. It is the working class of the United States and of the world.

It is, in fact, an acute stage in the class war.

That is precisely what it is! The attack of the mine-owning capitalists upon the mine working wage-slaves!

The "sovereign" states of Colorado and Utah, with all their civil, political, and military machinery, belong to, and do the bidding of, the Standard Oil Company. John D. Rockefeller and Henry H. Rogers are the real governors. The dummies strut and swagger but do the bidding of the syndicate of sharks that list them in their assets.

And what is the shibboleth of this gang of pirates who have swooped down upon these states and extinguished civil government?

"To Hell with the Constitution!"—"To Hell with Habeas Corpus!"

Choice specimens, these, to pose as law-abiding citizens and moralize the people about peace and order!

A majority of 46,000 votes in Colorado is received with a volley of tobacco juice from the legislative and judicial hirelings of the mine and mill-owning brigands who are the state.

In such a state citizens are good or bad, safe or dangerous, as they serve or refuse to serve the brigands. Moyer, Haywood, Pettibone, and St. John would not crook the knee and bow prostrate to the tyrants. That was treason to the State of Rockefeller.

Swiftly followed the intrigue of the brigands, the conspiracy of the governors, the midnight ambush, the kidnaping, iron handcuffs, special train, secret deportation, sneaking "sleuths," and solitary penitentiary cells.

Thus endeth chapter one. Now for the next!

Sound the Alarm!

Far and wide let the cry resound, *"To the Rescue!"*

Arouse, ye sleeping Hosts of Labor!

The working class must write the second chapter, and it shall not end in tragedy. The issue is clear as the light of day at noontide. The life of the labor movement is in peril. The blow has been foully dealt from the dark and aimed at the heart.

Awaken, you workers, from Maine to Mexico! Close up the ranks and lift high your banners!

To allow your loyal leaders to be wantonly massacred would brand you all with everlasting shame and bring disgrace upon your children and your children yet to be. We must meet this issue of life and death with becoming courage and determination. We should scorn to desert our comrades; we must be true to them as they have been to us.

Whatever cowards may say or traitors may do; whatever mercenary retainers may write or preach or charge or threaten, we shall stand loyally by our comrades to the very end, be that what it may.

The four names of our brothers in chains shall constitute our battle-cry: Moyer, Haywood, Pettibone, and St. John!

Let them proceed with their hellish plot and we will make it the political issue of the nation and dare them to face us before an outraged working class.

Let the mass meetings be renewed and all join in them, regardless of past differences.

Let no man dare divide the forces at this critical hour, lest he be looked upon as an emissary of the enemy.

Let one meeting be followed by another, and still another, increasing in numbers, intensifying in determination, and swelling the volume of protest and indignation until its roar is heard across the continent.

New York and California! Minnesota and Texas!

When you workers shake hands you shake the nation.

You need not assault Gooding's jail in which our heroes are captives. You have but to open your eyes, great Samson that you are, and fix your gaze upon the culprits and they will shrivel and crawl in the dust at your feet.

Let the warning notes be sounded and repeated! Let the workers be aroused as if by alarm bells at midnight.

Come forth ye toiling masses, from mill and mine, from shop and store, from farm and factory, from land and lake! Come forth ye organized and unorganized! Come forth ye men and women and children who are oppressed and heavy laden! Come forth ye people all who honor good men and true, and who love the right and dare defend it!

Crowd all the halls and streets and commons everywhere! You are the people!

Parade the streets and bear aloft your flags and banners! Let unnumbered voices rise and ring in warning protest! The cause is just; it must prevail.

Let woman's voice be also heard and woman's influence felt. The wives of our imprisoned comrades have suffered more than we shall ever know, and their children cry to us to save their fathers.

Be not deceived by any seeming lull in the plutocratic program. The tide of protest must rise higher day by day. The burning resolutions must be made to pour in a blazing torrent upon the heads of the conspirators.

Every dollar that can be raised at every meeting must be gathered in for the defense. A million dollars may be needed to trail the serpent, unearth the reptile, and lay bare the vile conspiracy.

Duly authorized representatives of organized labor must attend the trial from the opening hour, a dozen at least, to hear the evidence and keep an eye on the proceedings. Every national union should send a delegate; every large city a representative. The cost would be but a trifle; the effect incalculable.

Such a representation could absolutely bar chicanery, compel a fair trial, and thus win vindication. Through such a medium, in case of emergency, the whole nation could be aroused.

Labor now has its own press that reaches the millions, and the results are already cheeringly apparent.

Labor has its own correspondents on the scene and their work has had a telling effect on the public mind.

In this connection, the work of the *Appeal* and of [George H.] Shoaf, its special representative, cannot be too highly commended. It has had a really magical influence, and in this crisis every nerve should be strained to increase its circulation to a million copies.

The fight is on. It has been forced upon us. We are not responsible for it.

We are not favoring violence, but resisting it.

We are seeking, not to commit, but to prevent murder.

"Thou shalt not kill!"

Hear that, Gooding and McDonald!

Beware! A promised senatorial toga may yet turn into prison stripes.

Beware the wrath of an avenging people!

Where Daisy Sleeps†

May 1906 [25]

(To Mother! Sweetest to us of all the earth. We call her "Daisy.")[26]

The grass grows green
Where Daisy sleeps;
The mulberry tree its vigil keeps
Where Daisy sleeps.

The wind blows soft
Where Daisy sleeps;
The modest, blue-eyed violet peeps
Where Daisy sleeps.

The birds sing sweet
Where Daisy sleeps;
The mournful willow bends and weeps
Where Daisy sleeps.

The sun shines bright
Where Daisy sleeps;
Each changing season sows and reaps
Where Daisy sleeps.

The flowers bloom fair
Where Daisy sleeps;
The evening shadow softly creeps
Where Daisy sleeps.

Our hearts beat true
Where Daisy sleeps;
And love its watch forever keeps
Where Daisy sleeps.

---

† Published in *Appeal to Reason*, whole no. 560 (August 25, 1906), 8.

On Farm Workers and Small Farmers: Letter to J. E. Snyder†

May 4, 1906

Terre Haute, Indiana, May 4, 1906

Mr. J. E. Snyder[27]
Oklahoma City, Oklahoma

Dear Comrade:—

I know of no reason why farm workers and small farmers who accept our principles and are imbued with the revolutionary spirit should not be organized into locals of the Socialist Party. The fact is, we need this very element and should organize them to the fullest extent compatible with the uncompromising principles and tactics of the socialist movement.

I have met many of the farmers down your way who were revolutionary to the heart's core, and furnished the very best material for the party movement.

With best wishes to yourself and comrades, I remain

Yours fraternally,
Eugene V. Debs

---

† Published in *Oklahoma Bulletin*, April–May 1906, unspecified page. Reprinted in *Appeal to Reason*, whole no. 548 (June 2, 1906), 3. Not included in Constantine (ed.), *Letters of Eugene V. Debs: Volume 1, 1874–1912*.

Moses Harman's Mission†

May 10, 1906

Not as a writer nor as an author will Moses Harman be remembered in history, although he has won enviable fame as both; but as a liberator will he be known to future generations.

In his prison cell at Joliet he is today the most powerful advocate of sexual purity and the freedom of the press.[28] His enemies are doing infinitely more for his cause than he could possibly do without their opposition.

Such men as Harman, born to serve, must go to jail, to the rack and the scaffold. This has always been so and always will, as long as a large majority of mankind are subject to the will of a small minority—as long as the world is ruled by ignorance and superstition.

To shed light has always been a crime, for the simple reason that light is a menace to the rule of darkness. If Moses Harman had shed as much blood as he has light he would be honored as some great conqueror, and instead of lying in a prison pen in the sunset of his life he would be feted as a popular idol and his statue would adorn the parks of the cities. Better a thousand times this pure man in stripes of a felon than an apostate in purple and fine linen.

It is the very irony of fate that this apostle of purity should be punished for alleged impurity; that the gross and sensual in our sex life and social relations, so abhorrent to his refined and sensitive nature, and against which he has waged unceasing war, should have sufficient power to so distort his features as to have him appear the author of their being. The vulgar, ignorant censors of Moses Harman have no conception of his real mission; he is as great as they are small, and is destined to live as nobly as they are doomed to perish ignominiously.

From Jesus Christ to Moses Harman the fate of all true men has been the same; from Calvary to Joliet not one has escaped.

Not lightly are men considered who essay to serve humanity. The severest tests are applied to them and the extremest penalties imposed upon them, but the Moses Harmans no more shrink from the one or the other than if they were approaching their crowning festival.

† Published in *Lucifer* [Valley Falls, KS], whole no. 1065 (May 10, 1906), 5.

In his prison garb today, our elder brother is a powerful instrumentality in setting the dead hearts of the people to beating and opening their eyes to what is going on in the world. Every hour of his sentence will hasten by a year the end of mental and moral despotism.

Such freaks as Anthony Comstock[29] are the products of a perverted social order and an abnormal civilization. Freedom will finally be achieved in spite of all the insects that light upon the chariot wheels of progress.

The capitalist system, based upon the private ownership by the few of the earth and the fulness thereof, is the prolific parent of ignorance and all the ills that ignorance entails, and when this is overthrown, as it certainly will be, such monstrous crimes as Moses Harman is now the victim of will be unknown.

Political Action[†]

June 30, 1906

The tardy acknowledgment now comes from President Gompers of the American Federation of Labor that a labor lobby at a capitalist Congress is a failure, and that organized labor must betake itself to the field of political action. In arriving at this conclusion, Mr. Gompers, the leading leader of labor, is about a quarter of a century behind his more intelligent followers. The hundreds of thousands of dollars spent by organized labor in maintaining lobbies at the seats of capitalist legislative bodies, elected by the votes of labor, have been wasted in a vain and hopeless cause.

The Republican and Democratic parties are capitalist parties, committed to capitalist principles and policies, and to expect them to legislate in the interest of the working class upon whose fleecings depend their power and prestige is about as reasonable as to expect a tropical sun to convert sour milk into ice cream.

In his address before the convention of the International Steel and Copper Plate Printers' Union a few days ago, President Gompers is reported to have said that he was "tired of seeing the laboring man made a plaything of by the

† Published in *Chicago Socialist*, vol. 6, whole no. 382 (June 30, 1906), 1.

politician."[30] Indeed! Since when? Has President Gompers just made this discovery since he and his cabinet were turned down cold and flat by President Roosevelt, Vice President Fairbanks,[31] and Speaker Cannon?[32]

And why should not the president of the United States treat with contempt the presumptuous obtrusion of the officials of the American Federation of Labor? They don't represent anything nor anybody, but themselves, in any political sense, and well does the capitalist Roosevelt administration know it. When you approach a capitalist politician you must have money or political power to back you up; otherwise you are turned down and out.

Continuing his address to the Copper Plate Printers, Mr. Gompers said: "What we have a right to do is to take the hand of the oppressor from our throats and his foot from our breasts by the exercise of our sovereign political rights."

Isn't Mr. Gompers getting a little rash? Why not convene the Civic Federation in extraordinary session? The language of Mr. Gompers would seem to indicate that he is in desperate straits and laboring under great excitement; that the stranglehold on his throat is getting the better of him, and that the foot on his breastbone is getting in its deadly work, and yet I never knew Mr. Gompers to risk his throat or breastbone in the lead of any great strike or within range of any injunction or gatling gun.

If at long range Mr. Gompers so keenly feels the hand on his throat and the foot on his breast, how would he feel if his leadership had been fearless enough to put him where Moyer and Haywood are?

The truth is that the heated rhetoric of Mr. Gompers is nothing but a foolish bluff. It means nothing and the politicians will pay no more attention to it than would an alligator to a flea bite.

Mr. Gompers and his official colleagues have been literally driven to the verge of socialism and are now making their last stand against working class political action. When they talk about the "exercise of political rights" they don't mean that the working class shall vote as a unit, the only possible way that anything can be accomplished; they mean that in the future, as in the past, the labor vote shall be divided between the Republican and Democratic parties, provided only that men "friendly to labor" shall be elected.

A candidate "friendly to labor" on a capitalist ticket and on a capitalist platform! Of all the bunko deals that have ever victimized labor, this is the favorite of the ward heeler and labor fakir—and the worst in the whole bunch.

At the late meeting of the executive council of the American Federation of Labor, Mr. Hearst, invited by Mr. Gompers to give the council the benefit of his advice in the matter of political action, said, among other things: "I would not have the workingmen go into politics as partisans." Precisely! Mr. Hearst would not have wage-slaves go into politics *as a class*. He does not say that, but that is what he means, and he doubtless received a hearty amen from the Gompers cabinet.

Political action, to be of any value to labor, must be by the working class for the working class, and this is socialism, and anything less may hurt but will not help in any appreciable degree the exploited slaves of capitalism.

More and more the demand for economic and political unity is being pressed by the rank and file. Industrial unionism instead of trade division—solidarity instead of segregation! The evolutionary process has decreed it and it is bound to come.

The next few months will be vital ones for the labor movement. The time is opportune for our most vigorous propaganda. Subscriptions to socialist papers should now be increased to their maximum, and in this very necessary work every comrade and sympathizer should lend hand and heart, as also in the spread of other literature, and this should be kept up with increasing activity until the close of the campaign.

Our good comrades are still in the prison pens of the plutocracy, but their skies are brightening, and in good time they will join their loved ones again. The mine-owning brigands dare not try them and will not release them. The trial has now been postponed until after the election. This appeals clarion-tongued to the workers of the nation for political action.

Sever your relations, ye workers—as clean and complete as if with the keen edge of the sword of wrath—with the Republican and Democratic parties who are responsible for the infamous outrages perpetrated upon our comrades, Moyer, Haywood, St. John, and Pettibone, and for numberless other crimes suffered by the children of toil. Join the Socialist Party and register at once your protest and your high resolve by casting your vote for *the Emancipation of Labor and the Socialist Republic.*

Duties of the Hour†

July 1906

These are days that test the fighting fiber of men; the weak and spineless go down, while those who have the true stuff in them grow strong and resolute and rise to commanding positions on the industrial battlefield.

What greater than to face the world and fight for the right without fear! What nobler than to scorn discouragement, defy adversity, and remain unconquerable, though alone, to the end!

Clear-headed, calm-pulsed, and brave-hearted need to be the men and women who make up the Industrial Workers of the World. This proletarian organization has carved out for itself a stupendous work such as cowards and weaklings would not dare to undertake. Never was an organization more timely, or better adapted to the pressing needs of the times.

The American Federation of Labor and its allied organizations have for years demonstrated little else except their utter incapacity to serve the working class. The few nominal concessions which may be claimed by some of the unions are completely swamped by the flood of failures which has drenched the industrial field.

The recent abject surrender of the organized anthracite mine workers is a case in point. The arrogant, brutal mine owners cracked their lash over the heads of their organized slaves and dared them to make a move. The humble petition they had ventured to present was rejected with contempt. Not a single concession, no matter how trivial, was made. Not one! It was a cold and brutal victory for the capitalist brigands, and a humiliating defeat and surrender for the organized vassals of the mines.

And yet some of the officials of the routed wage-slaves had the hardihood to claim a victory. *The union had been recognized.* The kicks it had received, the scars it bears, the mutilation inflicted upon it prove it.

Yes, *the union was recognized*, and upon that plea the officials may, for a while longer, hold their jobs—but it will not be recognized in the anthracite fields in a few months from now, for there will not be enough left of it to recognize.

---

† Published in *The Industrial Worker*, vol. 1, no. 7 (July 1906), 1–2.

A few letters received from various parts of the anthracite region since the "victory" satisfy me that the mine workers have all they want of civic federation unionism, and that at an early day they will be ready to adopt the revolutionary program and transfer their allegiance to the Industrial Workers of the World.

Let us suppose for a moment that when the anthracite mine workers met the cold-blooded and defiant mine owners, they were members of the Industrial Workers; that the railroad employees and other workers in Pennsylvania were also organized in the same revolutionary union, ready to back the miners to a finish, . . . serving notice that not an ounce of scab-mined coal should be hauled an inch. Is it probable that, facing such a battery of class-conscious unionism, the Baer bandits would have issued their swaggering demand for unconditional surrender? Is it not more likely that they would have slid down from their high horse with alacrity and made at least some concessions to avoid collision with the proletarian battleship?

The capitalists, whatever else may be said about them, are no fools. In dealing with organized labor they know, as a rule, what they are up against, and have to meet it, and when they stand face to face with a labor union, they carefully sound it and satisfy themselves as to what it is, what it amounts to, and how to deal with it, and then they proceed accordingly, and if they do not attack and smash the union, it is for one of two reasons: either they are afraid of it, or they see a chance to make an ally of it and convert it to their own base use.

The labor union that the capitalists approve is branded with treason in living letters. The capitalists can no more endorse a bona fide labor union than the powder trust can endorse Hades as a powder house.

Not long ago a prominent mine owner at Terre Haute, in conversation with a businessman of the same place, said: "The truth is we can't afford to break with the union, for it's the only thing that stands between us and socialism."

∽

And now, what are some of the pressing duties of the hour? Manifestly, to take advantage of the increasing opportunities to open the eyes of the workers to the true causes of their grievances, their defeats, and their humiliation, and this can best be done by having our papers penetrate their ranks and our literature placed in the hands of the rank and file. To this end, each member should do his utmost to secure subscribers for *The Industrial Worker*. A little effort on the part of all would soon double the subscription list and quadruple the awakening power of this excellent proletarian publication.

Next, each local union, and, in fact, each member should carry a supply of party pamphlets, leaflets, and circulars and make systematic distribution of them. In places where there is no union, one should be organized without unnecessary delay, care being taken to admit those only who are qualified by character and conduct to serve the organization.

There should be no time for bickering, for chronic fault-finding, nor for mere personalities. The organization is too great and its mission too important to be jeopardized by personal imbroglio or internecine strife. Let us reserve all our vigor, all our resources, and all our equipment for the enemy, for unless I mistake the signs, we shall require our full capacity to weather the storm and safely reach our destined port.

Another duty, and of the first importance, is unflinching loyalty to our western comrades. Not for one moment dare we forget or neglect Moyer, Haywood, St. John, and Pettibone. They are the bravest boys we have, and whatever fate may have in store for them, we shall loyally share it.

The recent postponement [of the Moyer-Haywood trial] is doubly significant. The spontaneous uprising of the working class has paralyzed the capitalist arm of murder. But the intended victims are not yet safe, nor will they be until they are free. Let the agitation, therefore, continue, and let the protests rise and burn from coast to coast. Let it be remembered, too, that the long postponement until December is due mainly to political reasons, that this is a congressional year, and that every worker in the land will have a chance this fall to carry his protest to the ballot box, and if he would be true to his imprisoned comrades and drive the nail in the coffin of capitalism, let him cast a straight vote for *socialism and freedom.*

Collapse of the Conspiracy†

July 7, 1906

Still another postponement has been forced by the prosecution in the capitalist conspiracy against Moyer, Haywood, and Pettibone, this time until December.[33]

† Published in *Appeal to Reason*, whole no. 533 (July 7, 1906), 1.

The contention that this action has been taken pending the decision of the United States Supreme Court is the shallowest subterfuge.[34]

What regard have these criminals, official and otherwise, shown for courts and constitutions and laws in the prosecution of this infamous conspiracy from the time it was hatched into life in their festering brains?

The truth is that this stay of proceedings is due to the uprising of the working class and the threatening wrath of an aroused people. But for this the trial (?) would have been of a piece with the crimes that preceded it; promptly held and speedily terminated, and then—"guilty" and the gallows. That was the program—cut-and-dried—of Gooding and McParland, and we have their word for it.

With the extremest caution and minutest attention to details was the murderous kidnaping conspiracy concocted. Everything was perfectly ready before the trap was sprung. Nothing was overlooked. But one thing Gooding and McParland, in their whispered consultations over the plans and specifications, failed to take into account: the socialist and labor press!

This proved their sunken road of Ohain on their field of Waterloo.[35]

They were not to blame for overlooking this powerful battery. It is new and has never before been in action when capitalist conspiracies to murder labor have been evolved and executed.

When this battery, led by the *Appeal to Reason*, unlimbered and sent its shells crashing into the camp of the kidnappers and then trained its guns on the whole capitalist class and their venal and iniquitous system, consternation seized the conspirators, the capitalists of the whole nation were startled and alarmed, and many of their own papers began to denounce the crime against our comrades and demand for them a fair trial.

This and this alone thwarted the cruel and craven conspirators, and paralyzed the black hand of legal assassination.

A fine spectacle the vassal executives of Idaho and Colorado present today! They should be photographed with their pals and accessories, James McParland and Harry Orchard, that future generations might have a picture of the foul degeneracy that masqueraded in the Rocky Mountains as twentieth century civilization.

It is but just to Harry Orchard to make generous allowance for his deficient and perverted moral sense. He is undoubtedly a born degenerate, and with all the crimes there may be upon his head he still is entitled to the profoundest pity. He has been the tool of others, and as such has been used for criminal purposes; and now that his usefulness is ended, he has been coached for his final role by McParland, his tutor, the mercenary creature of the mine owners.

The best citizens of Parsons, Kansas, where McParland had his criminal rendezvous some 20 years ago, when robbery and murder ran riot there, recently held a mass meeting to expose and denounce McParland, whom they well remember as the notorious consort of the most vicious and criminal elements that infested that early community. Among other things these people, his former neighbors and townsmen, say of him in a burning series of denunciatory resolutions: "There is not today in the United States outside prison walls a more conscienceless and desperate criminal than McParland."

Let me call on every reader of the *Appeal* to cut out that paragraph and post it for public inspection and pass it from mouth to mouth until our innocent comrades now in prison cells, the victims of this heartless fiend, are given their liberty.

Harry Orchard and James McParland—degenerate and criminal—are to furnish the sole testimony upon which brave and honest men are to be sent to the gallows.

Think of it! And if you have a single drop of red blood in your veins, it will leap and burn with indignation.

In postponing the trial until December, the persecution was influenced by another factor of prime importance—one the capitalists never lose sight of—and that is the political one.

This is the year of our state and congressional elections, and October and November are the months in which they are to be held. The trial has been postponed until after the elections with the hope and expectation that the working class will subside and popular interest in the case die out.

They are again reckoning without our hair-trigger revolutionary press, and we will continue to camp on their trail day and night, year in and year out, until our comrades are rescued and restored to their homes and their loved ones.

They dare not go to trial and they know it. Their conspiracy has collapsed and they are hunting holes, like rats in a trap, through which to make their exit.

Yet we dare take no chances in dealing with these legal desperadoes. They know not what a conscientious scruple is. Only the fear of an outraged and avenging people will prevent such dastards from committing the hideous crime of judicial assassination.

Let all comrades and all friends bear these facts in mind, keep up the agitation, renew and enlarge the indignation meetings, and continue to raise all possible funds until the cell doors are made to swing open and our brothers shall walk forth free men, without a stain upon their honor.

They are innocent and no honest man who knows them has ever doubted it.

Now for another point that must not be obscured: They postponed the trial until December to **get the case out of politics**.

Recollect it! Don't forget it!

If, in the face of these facts, you vote the Republican or Democratic ticket, or any part of them, *you vote to hang Moyer, Haywood, Pettibone, and St. John.*

The capitalists don't want this case to be a political issue; we do!

They started it; we will end it.

In the persons of our imprisoned comrades the whole working class is on trial.

Election day is the day of the trial.

If you want to save our comrades and secure their freedom beyond all doubt; if you want to strike terror to the craven hearts of capitalist conspirators and their murderous minions, go to the polls like a man and *vote the straight Socialist ticket on election day.*

Remember Moyer, Haywood, Pettibone, and St. John, and roll up a million votes for *socialism and a square deal.*

Now is the time to spread working class literature broadcast over the land, and every comrade should have a hand in the work.

Now also is the time to increase the circulation of the socialist press to the maximum point. The circulation of every socialist paper in the country can and should be doubled this year. *The Appeal should go to 300,000 before the campaign closes, and every nerve and fiber should be strained to do it.*

Industrial unionism and socialism! The Industrial Workers and the Socialist Party!!

On and on and ever on, until the class struggles of the centuries are crowned with victory and *labor is free.*

The Congressional Campaign†

July 7, 1906

It should not be necessary to remind any Socialist of the importance of the congressional campaign this fall. The election being a national one, the party will have the opportunity to poll its full vote and this should show a decided increase over any national vote hitherto polled. Whether it does or not will depend largely upon the manner in which the campaign is conducted.

Since the last national campaign a vast amount of literature has been distributed, hundreds of locals have been organized, and thousands of speeches made; deep-seated prejudices have been uprooted, false impressions corrected, and now, on the eve of the election, this sentiment should be properly guided and directed so as to crystalize it into straight Socialist votes.

In this connection the most important thing is method. A large amount of work may be done and yet, in the absence of method, prove barren of results. Each state committee should plan its campaign months in advance and every move that is made should be in concert with every vote and all in accord with the general plan of campaign.

Planless, disconnected, isolated effort should be supplanted by organized, systematic, comprehensive action.

Every available congressional district in the land should place a candidate in the field and every such candidate should, in my opinion, challenge his Republican and Democratic competitors to joint debate. Most of them will be wise enough not to accept, some can scarcely dodge the issue and will have to accept, but in any event, our candidates, evincing the aggressive spirit of revolutionary socialism, will appeal to the working class and to the whole people and thus become not only a nominal but an actual factor in the campaign.

As for campaign material for the stump, there has never been such variety and abundance that could be used with such crushing effect. The record of the Congress near closing emits more stenches than Coleridge discovered in Cologne.

† Published in *The Worker*, vol. 16, no. 14 (July 7, 1906), 1.

The Republicans and Democrats are alike venal and vulnerable and the merest Socialist novice, discussing the main issue and current developments, can drive the foxiest old party politician from any hustings in the land.

We ought, in fact, to elect our first congressman this fall. It is high time that the Socialist Party had its representative in the national congress to break the doleful monotony of capitalist special pleading by the old fossils and put life, real life, the palpitating proletarian current into the proceedings.

All other nations in which there is a socialist movement have already their quota of representatives in their national deliberative bodies, and we should make our start in the congressional elections this fall.

It may be suggested that this is an opportune time to enlarge the circulation of socialist papers, and special efforts should be made to that end. If only half the readers of *The Worker* will determine to double the circulation, it can easily be done. Let each reader whose eye falls upon these lines start forth *at once* and capture just one yearly, semiannual, or quarterly subscriber and the trick is done.

Another suggestion I venture to make is that no campaign speech be made by any Socialist this fall without special reference to the Moyer-Haywood affair. The incident expresses and illustrates the class struggle more clearly and vividly than could the most powerful speech. Here we have the real issue of the campaign in living, concrete form.

The late postponement of the trial of our comrades was due mainly to political considerations. Such a trial on the eve of election would not do at all. As an object lesson it would be extremely embarrassing to both Republican and Democratic politicians, and so the curtain must be rung down on the scene until after the election.

Every crime perpetrated upon these loyal comrades has been perpetrated upon organized labor and upon the working class as a whole, and every protest that has been made against these crimes should be carried to the ballot box this fall.

If you want Moyer, Haywood, Pettibone, and St. John—true men, loyal leaders, staunch comrades—to live, and the cause for which they have suffered untold agony to triumph, go to the ballot box like a man and cast a clean vote for *socialism and emancipation.*

The Socialist Party and the Trade Unions†

July 28, 1906

The very limited time at my command makes it impossible for me to write an article on industrial unionism that will satisfactorily serve the purpose of the symposium of *The Worker* and under the circumstances I can but hope to meet the general requirements of the discussion, and even this may be but imperfectly accomplished.[36]

Industrial unionism, as I understand it, is an outgrowth of modern industrial development; it means, primarily, the unification of all the industrial workers within one comprehensive organization, divided and subdivided into departments corresponding to their various industries, each supreme within its own jurisdiction, yet limited by, and subject to, the constitution and other enactments of the general organization, the purpose being prompt and efficient action and mobility of power in every movement, offensive and defensive, of the organized workers, in part or as a whole, in all matters pertaining to their industrial interests.

Under this form of organization all the workers of a given employer, or in a given industry, however varied their trades or occupations, are compactly organized in the same body, while at the same time distributed among the various departments representing their several trades and occupations.

The superiority of this form of organization over the antiquated and impossible autonomic plan in this day of concentration is so apparent that argument would weaken rather than strengthen the proposition.

Next, industrial unionism is class-conscious in character and revolutionary in aim, its mission being not only to mitigate the ills of the workers, but to abolish the wage system and achieve complete emancipation. Without this character and ultimate end in view, the mere solidarity of the trade amounts to nothing more than "pure and simpledom," and cannot properly be called industrial unionism. This does not mean that each member must be class-conscious and revolutionary, but that the organization must be so as a whole and so declare, as the Industrial Workers has done, in its organic law.

† Published in *The Worker*, vol. 16, no. 17 (July 28, 1906), 5.

With this general understanding of what industrial unionism is—to which, I do not doubt, exception will be taken—the Industrial Workers of the World is the only American labor union of a general character organized upon the principle of industrial unionism.

The Industrial Workers has no "patent" on this "scheme" as some of its critics have facetiously charged, but it is so far the only union organized upon the industrial basis, with its militant character stamped upon it and its revolutionary aim boldly avowed and clearly stated in its fundamental law.

Up to this point I apprehend that there is but little difference of opinion among socialists, in or out of the Industrial Workers or the Socialist Party.

The trouble begins with the revolt of the progressive element of its membership against the American Federation of Labor. Curiously enough, the most violent critics of this industrial secession from the AF of L in 1897 (beginning with the withdrawal of the Western Federation of Miners themselves), two years later, in 1899, organized the political secession from the Socialist Labor Party.

They persist in asking us why we did not remain in the AF of L and "bore from within," and we ask them why they did not remain in the Socialist Labor Party and do likewise, instead of bolting and setting up a rival party.[37]

They criticize and condemn us unsparingly for "dividing" the workers industrially and organizing "dual" unions. Then why did they divide the workers politically and organize dual locals? Is revolt against a labor party a virtue and revolt against a labor union a crime? Upon what principle of reasoning and by what rule of logic is one commended and the other condemned?

The revolt against our secession from the American Federation was not only timely and wisely ordered, but simply inevitable, and in due time will be vindicated as a historic necessity. Upon this point I feel strongly tempted to digress sufficiently to make clear my reason for justifying the break with the AF of L and the necessary argument in support thereof, which I am presumptuous enough to believe is conclusive and unanswerable, but neither time nor space will allow at this writing.

The Industrial Workers is on the bedrock and occupies the correct industrial attitude of the labor movement, while the American Federation of Labor and its allied bodies are on the shifting sands and will be compelled to seek quarter in industrial unionism or go the way of the Knights of Labor and its defunct predecessors.

Compare these two organizations for but a moment. The IWW is revolutionary; the AF of L reactionary. The IWW is committed to the overthrow of the wage system; the AF of L is its main support. The IWW recognizes the class struggle; the AF of L denies it and has its Civic Federation to gloss it over and reconcile the wage-slave to his exploiting master.

How is it possible for a socialist to choose the AF of L, which violently opposes everything he stands for, and attack the IWW, which loyally supports his principles and program? Such a socialist embraces the enemy who has repeatedly treated him with contempt and, figuratively, spat in his face, while hurling his anathema at the friend who would dissolve such an unclean relation that a true union of industrial and political force might be consummated.

It has been claimed that the IWW does not favor political action. To silence controversy upon this point, all that is required is the reading of its preamble. What a few individual members may think of the ballot is beside the point, the fact being, not only that the organization declares in favor of political action, but that a vast majority of its members are socialists, if not party members.

For obvious reasons the organization had to declare against affiliation with any particular party. To have done otherwise would have entirely defeated the movement at its inception. When once there is but one working class party, the IWW will, without a doubt, assume the proper attitude toward it, but in the meantime it is not only vain and silly, but untrue that the Socialist Labor Party is "dead," and the writer who makes that assertion does himself no credit by it. Quite sufficient proof that it is not dead is the attention given it by those who call it so, but if they really believe what they say, it is hard to understand what satisfaction they find in kicking a corpse.

And now in the matter of recognizing and declaring in favor of the IWW, let me say that from the Socialist Party, as a party, the IWW neither asks nor expects anything of the kind, and personally I am opposed to any such party action. It can result in no good to either and may, and probably will, cause harm to both.

This does not mean that I approve our party attitude toward the union movement. There is a mischievous interpolation in our declaration aimed at the American Labor Union and negatively endorsing the AF of L, and sooner or later, the sooner the better, that clause, which never should have been inserted, will have to be stricken out.[38] What right has the party to meddle with the union and decide for the union whether or not its members may revolt against the capitalist misrule of its affairs? The same right that the union would have to dictate to the party in a similar manner.

Suppose the IWW were to resolve that the members of the Socialist Party have no right to break away from their party under any circumstances—would not our party members, the very ones who don't support the same measure with reference to trade unions, resent it as mischievous, intermeddling, and uncalled for impertinence?

The members of the IWW are, as a rule, seasoned old unionists; they did not drop from the skies, nor come up out of the seas; they are not interlopers or new beginners, but they are of the vey heart and marrow of the labor movement, and I think their records as fighters and builders in point of time and character of service will compare favorably with those of their reactionary critics; and when credit is claimed for what has been done in the past let it be remembered that the members of the IWW figured in it all and are entitled to their full share of it.

In leaving the AF of L, after being long identified with it, we had good reason, and if time and space were not limited nothing would give me more pleasure than to go into detail upon this important point. A thousand evidences of the decadent state of pure and simple unionism appear on every hand, not the least of which is its abnormal growth under capitalistic patronage.

The United Mine Workers is dominated by the capitalist mine owners. The latter constitutes the financial agent of the former, collecting its dues and assessments, and if a member protests against this pure and simple arrangement he is expelled from the union and discharged by the mine owner.

A beautiful relation this is for a socialist to sanction and the Socialist Party to endorse.

The grip of the mine owners upon the organized mine workers will never be broken; only revolt will accomplish that end and revolt it will be in spite of the interposition of reactionists.

The railway unions specifically declare that their interests and those of the corporations are identical and only a few weeks ago their grand officers and committees were before the president and Congress protesting against private legislation on the ground that "an injury to the corporation is an injury to the employees."

The railway unions are the auxiliaries of the corporations and implicitly do their bidding, and this relation is fixed and will never be altered or broken except by revolt. The same is true to a greater or less extent of all the unions affiliated with the AF of L and they who support that body in its present attitude, honest though they be, are opposing and not advancing the true interests of the working class.

The Civic Federation is another excrescence in evidence of the rank growth of the AF of L in capitalist favor, and of its alignment with capitalist interests, and this state of affairs is possible only at the price of treason to the working class.

The scores of separate national and international unions, the thousands of locals, the great army of big and little "labor lieutenants," ward heelers, and petty grafters, the conflicting jurisdictions and interminable wranglings, the monotonous round of defeated strikes and depleted treasuries, all bear testimony to the moribund state of the AF of L, and all of this vast array of office-holders, walking delegates, and local "leaders" who fastened upon the union and feeding upon its body are opposed to any change, and the mere mention of the IWW is sufficient to fan their hostility into a mad frenzy.

The workers, at least, are getting wise and "onto" the game, and if there are not some serious breaks and radical departures in the coming twelvemonth I shall certainly miss my prediction.

Our opponents have no right to charge us with "dividing" the working class. We are guilty of no such offense against unionism. To divide the workers implies preceding unity, and this never existed. Instead of dividing them, we are arousing them from their slaving submission to capitalist domination under the form and in the name of unionism.

Better a thousand times that labor is divided fighting for freedom than united in the bonds of slavery.

I have been following with interest the interchange between Comrade Boudin[39] and Comrade Untermann.[40] Comrade Boudin is insistent upon proof, which is quite proper in a controversy, but some things are axiomatic and self-evident, and time spent in furnishing proof is simply wasted. It seems to me that the essential points in Untermann's contention for industrial unionism are self-evident. It is true, as Boudin says, that Untermann's statements are mere assertion, but they are assertions of fact that cannot be successfully controverted.

I think it was Emerson who said that assertion is the highest form of agreement. If I say the sun shines, that is a mere assertion and at the same time a palpable fact. A man may be blind or shut his eyes and say: "Prove your assertion that the sun shines," but that it would have no appreciable effect upon the obvious fact.

Ben Hanford comes in for his turn at the IWW, but makes no attempt at argument and his effort hardly rises to the level of ridicule. Ben is usually clever and original and always interesting, but his last column and a half of nonpareil must have been a keen disappointment to his friends. Of course Ben had to remind us that DeLeon is a "liar" and a "blackguard," but this added little, if anything, to the tone or force of his weak and ill-tempered diatribe.

It is not infrequent that we hear complaint from our members of DeLeon's so-called blackguardism, but I observe that these same members are ceaselessly fulminating against DeLeon, and the language some of them use hardly qualifies them to take exceptions to billingsgate.[41] The fact is that most of the violent opposition of Socialist Party members to the IWW is centered upon the head of DeLeon and has a purely personal animus, and this attitude is so clearly wrong and so flagrantly at war with justice and common sense as to be not only weak, but pusillanimous and utterly indefensible. DeLeon is not the IWW, although I must give him credit for being, since its inception, one of its most vigorous and active supporters.

It may be that DeLeon has designs upon the Socialist Party and expects to use the IWW as a means of disrupting it in the interests of the Socialist Labor Party, and if he succeeds it will be because his enemies in the Socialist Party, in their bitter personal hostility to him, are led to oppose and denounce the revolutionary IWW and support the reactionary AF of L, thereby playing directly into his hands, and if the Socialist Party is disrupted in this class of trade unions, it will be the result of their own deliberate acts and they will have to bear the responsibility for it.

I know there are members of the Socialist Labor Party who are using the IWW as a weapon to strike the Socialist Party, but they will make little progress along that line unless our attitude is vulnerable and imparts to their blows the destructive force that of themselves are lacking. I know, too, that there are members of the Socialist Party who would scruple at nothing to destroy the Socialist Labor Party, but we must be carried away by neither of these extremes.

Let us pursue the straight course and stick without wavering to the clear-cut revolutionary movement, and hew to the line of industrial and political unity for the overthrow of wage-slavery.

As for myself, I expect to remain, as I always have been, a loyal member of the Socialist Party, but I shall continue to do what little I am able to unite all workers within one industrial union and one political party for the achievement of their emancipation.

Idaho Election Should Prove Historic†

July 28, 1906

The eyes of the country, particularly of the working class, will be turned toward Idaho in the battle of ballots this fall. A situation not only unique, but unprecedented in American politics, is presented in that Mountain state, and in consequence of that situation, the political contest this year, which would ordinarily attract little attention beyond the boundaries of the state, promises to prove of such historic interest as to be memorable in the annals of a nation.

This being a congressional year, the campaign throughout the country will be a national one and most of the states, including Idaho, also have their state elections, and in the case of Idaho, for reasons every workingman in the land well understands, the state election will completely overshadow the national election in the importance of its outcome.

In the state campaign in Idaho this year, there will be involved not only a national, but an international issue. In the persons of Moyer, Haywood, and Pettibone, the whole working class of the nation is in jail in Idaho, the whole working class is on trial in Idaho, and the whole working class must prepare for its defense in Idaho.

When the criminal governor of Idaho conspired with the criminal governor of Colorado to kidnap our loyal and devoted leaders in defiance of national and state constitutions, and in brutal contempt of the common decencies shown even to convicted felons, they not only committed rape upon the law and outrage upon humanity, but they committed an assault upon the working class of the nation and the world.

That is the political issue in Idaho this year AD 1906.

The criminal governor of Idaho will deny this, but his word is of no value. A high official of the state who tramples under foot the law he has sworn to uphold to curry favor with plundering corporations is not to be believed, even under oath. Governor Gooding has forfeited all claim to veracity as well as official integrity upon the principle that an evil-doer will naturally lie to cover up his crime.

† Published as "Whole Working Class of the Nation in Jail" in *The Socialist* [Caldwell, ID], whole no. 301 (July 28, 1906), 1.

The kidnapping governor, his kidnapping pals, and kidnapping administration are on trial this year, and the case will be called in the court of the people on election day.

Governor Gooding snatched our brothers in the dead of night and ran with them to his mountain cave to do them to death; he stole them as any other robber steals from and perhaps slays his innocent victims, and he resorted to this monstrous crime because he knew that he had no case against his intended victims and that he could never get them in his cruel claws by any fair or lawful means.

In this arch-conspiracy, which will bear the name of Gooding to eternal infamy, the governor's accomplice and accessory was one James McParland, whose red-handed and black-hearted career has been laid bare to the nation.

The citizens of Parsons, Kansas, where McParland had his rendezvous at a deadfall in which many a wayfarer met his doom during the early days when the Bender family lay in ambush for their victims,[42] held a mass meeting recently, attended by public officials, merchants, clergymen, lawyers, doctors, and the people in general, and passed resolutions branding McParland, the kidnapping pal of Governor Gooding, as the most hardened and conscienceless criminal out of the penitentiary.

At the same time the citizens of Winnemucca, Nevada, where William D. Haywood, the imprisoned victim of the Gooding-McParland combine lived, met and unanimously bore written testimony to his clean character, his unimpeachable integrity, and his upright and blameless life.

It is not that Haywood, Moyer, and Pettibone are bad men and have committed crime that merits punishment, but that they are good men and absolutely innocent that now worries the governor, for he dares not allow them to go to trial before an aroused nation whose keen eyes are fixed upon him and his gang, and beneath whose keen and penetrating flashes he quails and cowers like a midnight assassin caught red-handed in the act.

In the conspiracy against labor, for such it is, the sole object is to fasten infamous crime upon its leaders by the use of perjured testimony and sensational "confessions," and Governor Gooding and his sodden henchmen are the political tools of the Standard Oil trust and its allied parties in crime in this dastardly attempt to crush out all opposition to corporation plunder and trust rule.

That is the Idaho case in a nutshell, and if Governor Gooding and his accessories carry out the conspiracy and deliver the goods, there will be smooth sailing to a seat in the United States Senate and to other desirable sinecures in which these political apostates may enjoy blood-bought luxuries as the reward of their revolting crimes.[43]

Upon this issue—and there is no other in Idaho this year—the Republican Party stands for Governor Gooding, James McParland, Harry Orchard, Prosecutor Borah, Standard Oil and its official organ, the *Boise Statesman*, the Federal Mining Co., Amalgamated Copper Co., Colorado Fuel and Iron Co., and other brigands, kidnappers, and cracksmen; and upon that issue the working class represented by the Socialist Party and all their friends and sympathizers and all who love justice and abhor crime, especially when committed in the name of law—upon that issue the Socialist Party will meet the Republican Party face to face in battle array in the approaching campaign, and no quarter will be asked or given.

In this fight between lawless corporate power and the working class there will be no compromise. The issue must be squarely met, and no subterfuges will be tolerated.

Where the Republican candidate speaks, no matter in what out-of-the-way camp or digging, his "hurrah-for-the-flag" harangue must be punctured with the interrogatory, "How about Moyer, Haywood, and Pettibone?"

Let that cry be heard at every Republican meeting, and don't allow a single Columbian orator to dodge it.

In this connection the Democratic Party is ignored as it has no place in the fight. It is neither on one side or on the other. It just wants to break into office, and so it sympathizes with both sides, and opposes both by turns, hoping to sneak into the political pie factory while the fight is going on.

William Jennings Bryan, the Democratic chieftain and peerless champion of the "common people," has not opened his mouth to say a single word of protest since Moyer, Haywood, and Pettibone were ambushed in the interest of his friends, the silver mine owners of the West, and his silence in the presence of such an atrocious crime against the working class is more eloquent than speech in fixing his true status as the "friend of labor."

There are about 60,000 votes in Idaho and of these about 8 percent, or 5,000, have been cast for socialism. The field is, therefore, an inviting one from the socialist point of view, and becomes fascinatingly so in contemplating the life and death issue involved in the present campaign.[44]

Now, comrades, let the socialists and the workers and their friends of all the nation roll up their sleeves and itch in to win the fight for Idaho. The fight can be won and the state redeemed and our innocent brothers set free and vindicated, and the kidnappers wiped out and relegated to eternal oblivion.

Let every available socialist speaker turn toward Idaho, so that the state can be thoroughly canvassed and the people aroused. All the people require is that falsehood shall be exposed, facts stated, and the truth made known.

They will take care of the rest.

Every nook and corner of the state must be sought out and its voters aroused to the enormity of the crimes about to blacken the escutcheon of the state. Let no county, no township, no ward, no precinct, no schoolhouse or crossroads be overlooked.

Next in order is the spread of socialist literature. The state ought to be sown knee-deep in it. Every socialist paper should be circulated as widely as possible, and chiefly in Idaho, *The Socialist*, published at Caldwell by Comrade [Hermon] Titus,[45] who, from the very start, has shown the most commendable interest and activity in this case, and who, for the very prompt, thorough, efficient, and courageous service rendered by him, deserves the recognition, confidence, gratitude, and support of every workingman in the land.

The Socialist will be published on the field of battle, in the very center of the contest. It will be in position to give the latest and most reliable news, impart the soundest counsel and advice, expose the machinations of the malefactors, and hurl its shot and shells at the blowholes in the armor of the enemy.

It therefore becomes the duty of every comrade to constitute himself a special agent to swell the circulation of *The Socialist* during this campaign that it may reach the people and fulfill its extremely important mission in this crucial contest.

To Governor Gooding and his pirate crew all we have to say is:

Lay on, MacDuff,
And damned be him that first cries, "Hold, enough!"[46]

Man and Mule†

August 4, 1906

Have you ever looked searchingly into the large, lustrous, knowing eye of a mule while he looked into yours? If so, you cannot fail to have observed a twinkle with an intimation in it that he knows you and has his opinion about you, although he may not be able to express it in language you understand.

The fact is, as I suspect, that the mule knows man better than man knows the mule, and I have often wished I might have the transcript of a mule's mind, or understand his tongue, that I might know just what the mule thinks of his human master.

That the opinion would not be a flattering one I am quite convinced, for the mule has not one single reason to look upon man as his superior. Quite the contrary; there is not a crime known to the catalog that man has not perpetrated upon the mule.

Of all the domestic animals that serve man, it is doubtful if there is one, not even excepting the horse, that has been of greater usefulness than the mule, nor is there one that has been more patient and submissive under the harsh treatment inflicted upon him in return for his useful and laborious services.

I have been led to these reflections by the masterful book of Professor J. Howard Moore, *The Universal Kinship*,[47] which should be read by every seeker after truth and light; and today, as I saw a brutal human lash a starved and worn-out mule, I said to myself, if that mule were not as far above that man in heart and soul, in sense and conscience, as popular human ignorance supposes him to be below him, he would have but murder in his heart and hooves, and kick his brutal tormenter into kingdom come.

The mule is not only the most serviceable, but he is also the wisest of animals, and the fact that man regards him as dull and stupid is due to man's ignorance of the mule's wisdom, and when the average man who is called a mule resents the epithet, he again reveals his stupidity, for if he were but wiser he would know that he had been flattered and not insulted.

That the mule is "mulish," that is to say, stubborn and slow-going, apparently lazy, is eminently to his credit, and these qualities, properly understood,

† Published in the *Chicago Socialist*, vol. 6, whole no. 387 (August 4, 1906), 2.

show the mule to be possessed of the highest virtues which adorn the nature and character of our four-legged comrade.

Who would not be stubborn and lazy who had man for a master? Look at the wage-slaver, and if there is any difference between him and the mule it is all in the mule's favor.

The mule serves man in and out of season, for but his provender, and when at last his usefulness is impaired by age he is cast adrift to starve on the highway with but the scars of his master's lash to show for man's humanity to the mule.

What must be the mule's reflections when he stalks blind and halts toward his pathetic doom as the vultures circle lower to end the tragedy of his life?

What must he think of man when at twilight he surveys the field of battle and sees the mingled and mangled flesh and blood of man and mule scattered as far as eye can see?

Would this dumb, patient brute, had he the choice by ballot, vote over and over again to have himself hitched and harnessed by another brute, overworked and underfed, exposed to heat and cold, whipped and lacerated and finally turned adrift to perish from neglect in the winter of old age, or torn to shreds by shrieking shell on field of horror in the name of Christian civilization?

The mule is meek, it must be said, but meekness with the mule is not without its limitation, and when that is reached a kick is registered that may snuff out the human light.

The main trouble with the mule is that he does not kick often enough, and with man that he does not kick at all.

The kick of the mule is nature's means of defense, and if the mule but used it freely he would soon inspire man's respect and admiration, whereas his meekness but provokes the malice of his master.

To paraphrase another, the better I know man the fonder I am of mules.

Organization for Emancipation†

September 1906

If there had been any lingering doubt in the minds of those who organized the Industrial Workers as to the wisdom of their course, subsequent developments would certainly have removed it, as each passing day has served to vindicate the timeliness and emphasize the demand for the revolutionary economic organization of the working class.

That there are those, especially among socialists, who are opposed to the Industrial Workers, either because of their fealty to the American Federation of Labor or their fear that economic unionism may absorb some of the means and energy which should be devoted to political propaganda, seems strange enough, and in either case we shall have to ascribe their hostile attitude to superficial reasoning or improper conceptions of economic unionism in its relation to the labor movement and the historic mission of the working class.

It is difficult to understand why so many socialists treat contemptuously, or with indifference, the whole question of labor unionism, in view of the fact that the Socialist Party movement sprang from the trade union movement and the further obvious fact that if the political organization of the working class is to develop its full power and fulfill its mission, it will be only as the necessary outgrowth and result of the revolutionary economic solidarity of that class.

In their everyday lives the workers have to fight for their economic existence, and their fundamental need in this economic warfare is an economic weapon, and this weapon is the labor union, and without this the workers would be left naked and defenseless at the mercy of their enemy, and all attempts to interest them in the political aspects of the labor question and to build up a political movement would end in dismal failure.

The principal leaders of the socialist movement have all recognized the prime necessity of organizing the workers along economic lines, and conspicuously among these are Marx, Engels, Liebknecht,[48] Bebel,[49] Vandevelde,[50] and others.

Marx, while urging the necessity of trade unionism, pointed out its inherent defects and shortcomings in the following words:

† Published in *The Industrial Worker*, vol. 1, no. 9 (September 1909), 1.

> Trade unions work well as centers of resistance against the encroachments of capital. They fail partly from an injudicious use of their power. They fail generally from limiting themselves to a guerrilla war against the effects of the existing system, instead of simultaneously trying to change it; instead of using their organized forces as a lever for the final emancipation of the working class, that is to say, the ultimate abolition of the wage system.

Here we have precisely stated the essential difference between pure and simple trade unionism of the old school and modern unionism of the revolutionary type represented by the Industrial Workers of the World.

While the old unions under the jurisdiction of the American Federation of Labor are "limiting themselves to a guerrilla war against the effects of the existing system," the Industrial Workers has as its declared fundamental object "the ultimate abolition of the wage system."

While proclaiming its economic mission in plain terms, the Industrial Workers as an organization also recognizes the need and importance of united political action and the necessary organization to secure it, and there is not a doubt that the economic solidarity and the class-conscious teaching of the raw recruits admitted to the Industrial Workers will be followed as a natural sequence by their political solidarity and a united working class vote on election day.

It is not claimed that the form of the Industrial Workers has been fully developed, or that its constitution is free from defects or immune against reasonable criticism. On the contrary, it is freely admitted that the work of organizing the Industrial Workers, undertaken under great and peculiar difficulties, was but fairly initiated at the first convention,[51] that what was actually accomplished was the embryonic structural work in outline, the features of secondary importance to be added and the necessary details worked out at subsequent conventions and in the natural course of the growth and development of the organization.

What has been and is claimed with increasing emphasis is that the fundamental principles and general plan of organization of the Industrial Workers are sound and logical and will bear the light of development and the test of events.

Upon this proposition the advocates and supporters of the Industrial Workers challenge the most searching scrutiny and are prepared to meet all comers.

Time and space forbid me to consider the approaching convention.[52] A great work awaits the delegates and I have complete faith in their fidelity and ability to perform their allotted task and speed the Industrial Workers on its second year of *organization for emancipation.*

Crumbling Capitalism†

September 1, 1906

The highest point in the development of capitalism has about been reached and symptoms of decline, the forerunners of collapse, are now setting in.

The daily happenings all about us foreshadow the impending organic change in society. The average capitalist daily is almost exclusively a chronicle of crime. The fully developed capitalist metropolis is a seething madhouse. The countless schemes of reformation that have been and are being tried are at best so many drops of laudanum administered to soothe the patients with no possible hope of returning sanity.

The man who can calmly survey the situation in capitalist society and see its hell of horrors and remain unmoved is himself a victim of its debasing influence, and upon examination will be found to have a heart turned to adamant, a condition peculiar to those who write and preach about the wonderful prosperity of the country.

The numerous and increasing ills with which the body social is afflicted are all traceable to the capitalist system, in which the dollar is the ruling deity, and man, especially the working man who makes the dollar, is its most abject victim.

Strange, indeed, to a reasoning being that the easier it becomes to produce wealth, the more uncertain is the portion and the more precarious the position of those who produce it.

Socialism, and socialism alone, explains this and the many other contradictions in capitalist society. The abolition of the capitalist system and the wage-slavery upon which it is based will put an end to the misery of the millions, and nothing else can do it.

The socialist movement has this end for its supreme aim and, keeping pace with the economic development, is increasing and will continue to increase in power until the fateful hour strikes and the working class triumphant rear the superstructure of the socialist republic upon the foundations laid for it in the capitalist system.

† Published in *Socialist Review* [West Hoboken, NJ], September 1, 1906, unspecified page. Copy preserved in *Papers of Eugene V. Debs* microfilm edition, reel 7.

The millions of workers—wage-slaves, male and female, the immediate victims of the capitalist system, its breathing, suffering, and despairing merchandise—must be aroused to consciousness of their class interests and their class power, industrial and political. Great as the task is, it must be accomplished, and mainly by the working class itself. Little help will come from without. All hope and all of the latent powers necessary to realize it lie within it.

The slumbering hosts must be wakened, the apathetic and indifferent must be aroused, the ignorant must be educated, the contented must be stirred to discontent, and all must have their eyes opened and be made to see and feel and realize the pressing need of a united working class for the overthrow of the present exploiting and brutalizing system, which makes the producers of wealth the despised victims of the parasites who absorb it.

Industrial and political unity of the workers will accomplish this great historic end and solve the problem of the ages.

This is a year of great opportunity for socialists and all should strive with all their might to make the most of it. The spreading of sound literature is of great importance and in this every comrade should take an active part. The quiet single-handed work of the rank and file is the most important of all in building up the movement and this should be pressed to the limit by every socialist and every class-conscious worker in the land—in factory, mill, and shop; in quarry, mine, and railway yard; in depot, store, and marketplace; in short, everywhere, day and night, each worker—should do his best to sow the seed and spread the light, and if all, or even half of all will make up their minds to engage in the propaganda to the fullest extent of their ability and opportunity, the Socialist vote in the United States this fall will be heard around the world.

Wage-Slavery the Only Issue: Election Speech at Brand's Park, Chicago[53] [excerpt][†]

October 7, 1906

There is but one issue involved in this campaign so far as the working class is concerned. That issue is capitalism and the wage-slavery upon which capitalism is built. There are several parties in the field. They have nominated their candidates and adopted their platforms. Read the platforms for yourselves. They are plainly written; they can be easily understood. Read them for yourselves, and if you do you will find that so far as the workers are concerned, there is not the slightest difference between the Republican and Democratic parties. They are precisely alike. Both are committed to the capitalist system, both to wage-slavery, and whether one or the other wins, it is certain that you will lose.

There are not enough of the capitalists to elect their candidates. They rely upon you to do that for them, and you are stupid enough to do it. After you have done it, then you further stultify yourselves by standing like mendicants at the door of the capitalist. You ought to be ashamed of yourselves, begging for the crumbs and the crusts; begging when you ought boldly to command and when you servants ought to be in duty bound to execute your orders.

Why are there two capitalist parties? For the simple reason that there are two sizes of capitalists, big ones and little ones—but they are all capitalists. The big ones are trying to swallow the little ones, and the little ones object to being swallowed, and so they divide and fight each other.

Hearst and Bryan have it not in their power to reverse the forces of evolution that are paving the way to the new social order which is steadily evolving from the present competitive chaos.

The Republican Party

The Republican Party is the party of the capitalist class; that is, the dominant element of the capitalist class. It has been in almost uninterrupted power for

† Published as part of "Socialists Open Campaign" in *Chicago Socialist*, vol. 6, whole no. 397 (October 13, 1906), 1.

nearly half a century. What has this party done for the working class? Ask yourselves the question. Answer it at your own leisure. This party during all of the half century that it has had power and controlled the administration has been the subservient political tool of the capitalist class, and in all of the list of those who have faithfully served it, no one is entitled to a greater share of credit from the capitalist standpoint than the present incumbent of the White House.[54]

There are a great many working men who talk about our "square deal" president—the one president, they tell us, who is in favor of a square deal for the capitalist and also a square deal for the wage worker. The wage worker always get his square deal in a round place. You ought to know where that is. Stop and ask yourselves the question: How can a man be for a robber and his victim and give them both a square deal?

The capitalist gets what you produce. He produces nothing and gets everything; you produce everything and get nothing. You do everything and he has everything. And if you can stand this, I think he by strict economy can manage to get along. And if you don't change this, it is not at all probable that he will.

No living man can be for [both] the capitalist and the wage worker. If he is for the one, he is against the other, and no living man can take and hold a halfway ground—the man who tries it fails.

Roosevelt Servant of Capitalists

Theodore Roosevelt is the president of the capitalist class, and the faithful servant of that class. True, on every conceivable occasion he takes time enough to tell the workingmen what fine fellows they are, how friendly he feels toward them, to what extent he is interested in their well-being, and so on. He came to Chicago not a great while ago, and he actually received a committee representing the working class. He gave that committee 14 minutes of his precious time, and then he spent 14 hours with the plutocrats of the city. In that 14 minutes he took occasion to rebuke the working class: they must be law-abiding.

At that very time he had in his cabinet Paul Morton, a notorious violator of law, a criminal under the statutes. You workingmen here in Chicago ought to remember him well. I do, for I was here in 1888 when Paul Morton won his spurs as the strikebreaker of the Burlington system of railways. You remember that an investigation was instituted. Certain lawyers were employed, but they suddenly withdrew when they found that if they conducted their investigation and made their report the prosecution against him would result in his landing in the penitentiary, and that prosecution was then abandoned and it became necessary for Morton to retire from the cabinet. Before he did so, President Roosevelt gave him a bill of moral health as long as the moral law, telling all of his virtues, what a splendid specimen of integrity he was, and this recommendation of the president landed him at the head of the Equitable Assurance Company, where he is now drawing $80,000 a year.

The same President Roosevelt has in his cabinet as Secretary of War William Howard Taft, who issued the very first injunction that ever paralyzed a railroad organization in the United States.

Organized Appetite

During all this time the Democratic Party, based upon a decaying middle class, has been trying to break into power. It has been well said that the party is simply an organized appetite, hungering for the spoils, ready to declare in favor of anything or against anything. Read its platform. It is a blessed thing that you don't have to understand it. What does the Democratic Party stand for—under Tammany, under Bryan, under Hearst, or any other leadership? Reform, we are told. Reform of what? Reform of the capitalist system.

But let me tell you that the capitalist system cannot be reformed. It has fulfilled its historic mission. It is now in a state of decline and decay, and the quicker it is totally abolished the better for the working class and all humanity.

Only Room for Two Parties

There is just room for two parties. Let the capitalists have their Republican Party. We have our Socialist Party. Then we will meet the exploiters face to face. We outnumber them overwhelmingly. While they have the capital we have the votes. The trouble is that we do not yet know how to use them. But fortunately the Socialist propaganda is organized in all of the states of the Union, making its appeal to the workers, opening their eyes so that they can see for themselves, and to the extent that they are developing intelligence enough to understand their material interests, they are severing their relations with the Republican and the Democratic parties and joining the revolutionary working class party that is marching steadily to victory.

It is true that just at this moment industry is at high tide. It may be that you have a job, but it is suspended by a slender thread. You do not know how long you are going to have it. You do not know how soon that thread may be severed. You do not know how soon you are to be out of work.

Life and Work

Now, you are told that you have an inalienable right to work, for you can only live by work. But under capitalism you have no inalienable right to work. You have no tools of your own with which to work. You cannot work unless you have a job. Between you and your job there stands the man or the agent of the man who owns the tool with which you work, and before you are allowed to use the tool, before you are allowed to accept the job, it is on condition that you will surrender to him most of what you produce.

What is the result? You get a wage in exchange for your labor-power. You are compelled to sell that labor-power. You do not sell yourself bodily under the law, but you sell your energy, the expression of your lives, 10 hours a day, for a wage of perhaps $2 a day. You go to work at 7:00 a.m. and you work two hours, and with the aid of modern machinery you produce the equivalent of the exchange value of your wage. After you have produced that, you proceed to produce surplus value for the idle capitalist who lives in the Far East or has a palace on the boulevard. You don't know him; he never saw you and never expects to. The truth is that you would not know your master if you saw him. . . .

He has no more to do with the operation of the factory, mill, mine, or shop in which you are employed than if he lived on the moon. He does not employ you, as a matter of fact. You employ him to take from you what you produce. And he sticks to his job. Now, what you want to do is to discharge him. Give him a square deal by setting him to work. He has no job now—give him one, and then he will produce what he gets and you will get what you produce. That is the Socialist square deal.

Now, there will never be any material change in your condition as workers unless you have tools of your own, unless you can freely employ yourselves without consulting any human on earth.

Conflict of Interests

Your interests as wage workers are opposed to their interests as capitalists. They own the tools; you use them. They buy labor-power as cheaply as they can; you sell it as dearly as you can. Between you there is an irrepressible conflict for a division of what is produced. Why should there be any division at all? Why should not the workers get all they produce? Why should they work to produce multimillionaires and themselves remain in poverty?

Social Progress

Every social state has its periods of birth and development and maturity. It fulfills its mission, outlives its usefulness, and then it passes away to make room for one more in harmony with the forces of progress and the onward march of civilization. Capitalism evolved from feudalism. Socialism is now evolving from capitalism.

Socialism is a theory of society based upon the line of evolution in which the workers are to own the social means of production and in which the workers will use them, not to produce multimillionaires, but to fill the land with wealth, so that poverty such as we now understand it may be abolished; that the workers may have not only work and wealth, but may have leisure, that they may cultivate their mines and give their hearts a chance.

Gompers in Politics

Do not deceive yourselves with the belief that you will improve your condition in the least by choosing between the two old capitalist parties. The cry of reform is raised in every instance to deceive you, and as long as you are deceived conditions will remain substantially the same. It is gratifying to note the fact that upon an ever-increasing scale, the workers are going into politics. Even Sam Gompers, after 20 years or more of declaration that union men had no business in politics, has been forced to declare in favor of political action. But as usual he is on the wrong side.

The kind of political action he favors is the division of the workers. He says that wherever you find a man who is in favor of labor, support him. If you find that there are none friendly to labor, why, then make a nomination of your own, but don't nominate a working man if you can possibly help it. He still has the old idea that the working man is fit for nothing but to dig and delve and grub; that he has intelligence enough to use his hands, but not his brains.

You have a brain—use that; and if you do, you won't have to depend on your hands and thus make a very wretched living.

* * *

Working Class Awakening

Within the last few years there has been a marvelous awakening. The future is rich with promise. The working class, so long in darkness, are steadily finding their way to the light, increasing in numbers, in clearness of vision, in mental and moral grasp. They have undertaken a great work. They do not underestimate its magnitude. They understand that all kinds of obstacles will be thrown in their way; that all the opposition that the capitalists can devise is to be used; that the workers are to be deceived and misled; that the workers are to be kept in darkness.

First of all, make up your mind where you properly belong. It will require but an instant of serious thought to satisfy you. The issue is so clear that it can be easily understood. When you have made up your mind that your place is in the Socialist Party, then take a beeline for the post of duty, and stand there as becomes a man.

The Socialist Party is organized in all of the states and territories in this Union. Its members are working with the enthusiasm born of the throb and thrill of the worldwide social revolution. The working class, nourished by its misery, vitalized by its aspirations, is raising the revolutionary standard of international socialism, and in due course of time the hour will again strike for an organic change, and the socialist movement, the greatest in all history, will spring into power, emancipate the working class, and proclaim freedom to all mankind.

The Labor Question and Humanity†

October 15, 1906

The labor question, broadly stated and understood, is the question of *humanity*. On it depends the welfare of *all* the people. The capitalist system, which springs from feudal times, has divided society into two classes—capitalists and the workers—and these classes are pitted against each other in *worldwide struggle*. Unfortunately for the workingmen, the capitalists own the tools, which in these days consist of machinery. A different state of affairs existed a hundred years ago, when men worked by hand. Then there were no millionaires and no tramps. Today we have one thousand of the former and approximately one million of the latter.

† Syndicated newspaper article, as published in *Muncie [IN] Evening Press*, vol. 4, no. 8 (October 15, 1906), 4.

There are 26 million working people in the United States at the present time. Five million are women and 2 million are children. Having no tools of their own, they are forced to enter the labor market, competing with each other for a livelihood. They do not sell themselves bodily, but they sell 10 and 12 hours of their time each day for a stipend. With the wealth their labor produces, men and women of the capitalist class make merry in New York and Newport.

The capitalist class is unnecessary to society. Its members do absolutely nothing that is useful. Their function is to spend what the working class produces.

Let me use Andrew Carnegie as an illustration. He is a fully developed capitalist and therefore a fully developed parasite. Carnegie owns or practically owns a great modern steel plant, in which 70,000 men toil for a living. These 70,000 men do the work and produce Carnegie's wealth. Carnegie spends most of his time in Scotland and has no more to do with the direction of the steel industry in Pittsburgh than if he were on another planet. The same is true of the capitalist class generally.

Politicians employed by capitalists endeavor to keep the workingmen of America divided on *alleged issues* in which the laboring classes have no interest whatsoever. As long as they succeed in doing this, the capitalists will hold the reins of power.

Both the Republican and Democratic parties are capitalist parties. The Republican Party protects the interests of the Carnegies, the Rockefellers, the Morgans, the Hills, and all of the great trusts and corporations. The Democratic Party represents the small capitalists and the middle classes. If either party wins, the laboring man loses, because both enact laws to protect capital.

Workingmen of all classes will secure justice only when they control the social machinery, of which they are the greatest part.

The middle class is rapidly disappearing, owing to the encroachments of capital, and it is only a matter of time before all men of the so-called middle class will be socialists.

Notes

1. The 25th Annual Convention of the American Federation of Labor was held at Old City Hall, Pittsburgh, November 13–25, 1905.
2. William Randolph Hearst, Sr. (1863–1951) was one of the leading newspaper publishers of his day, beginning his career with the *San Francisco Examiner* before making the *New York Journal* the flagship of his burgeoning newspaper empire in 1895. By the 1920s Hearst owned newspapers in a large number of metropolitan centers, including Boston, Washington, Chicago, Baltimore, Atlanta, Pittsburgh, Omaha, Los Angeles, and Seattle. As a young man Hearst was close to the progressive movement, winning two terms in Congress as a Democrat beginning in 1902. In 1905 Hearst made the first of two bids to become mayor of New York City. In the 1930s Hearst flipped and emerged as a reactionary Republican.
3. Edward Fitzsimmons Dunne (1853–1937) was mayor of Chicago from 1905 to 1907. He previously served for 13 years as a Chicago circuit court judge before resigning to run for mayor. A member of the Democratic Party, Dunne was an advocate of municipal ownership of utilities. After defeat in his 1907 bid for reelection, Dunne returned to private legal practice. He staged a political comeback and was elected to a single term as governor of Illinois in 1912.
4. Reference is to a merger of the Socialist Party with the Socialist Labor Party. Negotiations to this end were begun by the Socialist Party of New Jersey, which appointed a 12-member negotiating committee. This was matched by a committee of identical size and geographical distribution by the New Jersey sections of the Socialist Labor Party. A series of six meetings took place from December 17, 1905 to March 4, 1906. These ultimately arrived at a basis for unity of the two parties on the controversial and decisive questions of relationship of the party to the trade union movement, ownership and control of the party press, and degree of party discipline. Despite consensus between the two negotiating committees, no unity would be forthcoming, however, as the radicals of the Socialist Party of New Jersey could not win over a majority support of the Industrial Workers of the World over the American Federation of Labor, the elimination of the privately owned socialist press in favor of a centrally controlled party-owned press, and adoption of a policy of strict party discipline. See James M. Reilly and John Hossack, eds., *Proceedings of New Jersey Socialist Unity Conference* (n.c.: n.p., [1906]).
5. Debs oversimplifies here. The 1904 National Convention voted to initiate a monthly newspaper dedicated to party affairs, the *Socialist Party Official Bulletin.* The first issue of this paper was published in September of that same year for mass distribution to the entire party membership via meetings of locals and branches. It continued through March 1913. The national office also published a mimeographed *Weekly Bulletin* for members of the National Committee and National Executive Committee, state secretaries, and representatives of the privately owned socialist press.
6. John J. Hannahan (1856–1925), an Indiana native, was a career functionary in the Brotherhood of Locomotive Firemen. He was elected vice grand master at the convention of 1885 and succeeded Frank P. Sargent as grand master—top elected

official of the brotherhood—in 1902. He retired from the brotherhood around 1910 to become a vice president of the Westinghouse Locomotive Stoker Company.

7. Edward Henry Harriman (1848–1909) of New York was an American railroad financier. He was the top figure in the Union Pacific Railroad from 1898 and president of the Southern Pacific Railroad from 1901 until his death. His son W. Averell Harriman (1891–1986) was a governor of New York and a diplomat.
8. James J. Hill (1838–1916) was a Canadian-born railway financier who headed the Great Northern Railway, a line that was dominant in the upper Midwest and Great Plains. Hill and his railway were embroiled in a strike conducted by the American Railway Union in 1894, a battle won by Debs and the union through arbitration.
9. That is, the Chicago, Burlington & Quincy Railroad—the so-called Burlington line. The failure of the so-called Great Strike of the Burlington in 1888–89 was a seminal event in the process of Debs's radicalization. See the *Selected Works of Eugene V. Debs: Volume 1, Building Solidarity on the Tracks, 1877–1892*, 239–319 and *passim*.
10. The Atlantic & Pacific Railroad, a railroad running segments between St. Louis and Tulsa, Oklahoma, and another between Albuquerque and Southern California.
11. The Missouri, Kansas & Texas Railroad, today part of the Union Pacific line.
12. Vincent St. John (1876–1929) was a Kentucky-born miner who became president of the Western Federation of Miners affiliate at Telluride, Colorado, in 1900. He was the leader of a successful 1901 strike in that camp, which earned him the enmity of mine owners of the region. St. John was active in the Industrial Workers of the World from its inception and worked for the union as an organizer. He was president of the local miners' union at Burke, Idaho, and was arrested in February 1906 for alleged complicity in the assassination of Idaho Governor Steunenberg, the incident to which Debs alludes here. St. John shortly emerged as the chief spokesman of the Industrial Workers of the World's anti-political syndicalist faction and was elected general secretary of the union in 1908. He remained in that position until 1914, when he retired to work a copper claim in Colorado. Although no longer a leading figure in the IWW, St. John was swept up in the 1918 mass dragnet of Wobbly leaders and sentenced to a term in the federal penitentiary at Leavenworth. He was freed by a pardon from President Warren G. Harding in 1923. He spent his final years in California, dying after a protracted illness.
13. Debs spoke at Sioux City, Iowa the afternoon of Sunday, May 25, 1906, and at Boone, located about 150 miles away, the evening of May 26, the published date of this article.
14. A corrupt gambling game organized for planned swindle.
15. Debs previously marked February 27, 1875, as the date he joined the Brotherhood of Locomotive Firemen in the article "Reminiscent," *Locomotive Firemen's Magazine*, vol. 18, no. 7 (July 1894), 681.
16. Hermon F. Titus (1852–1931) was a Baptist minister turned medical doctor from Massachusetts who relocated to Seattle, Washington, in 1893. There Titus became involved in socialist politics and launched a newspaper, *The Socialist*, in 1900, originally as a means of supporting the Debs presidential campaign. Titus moved the paper to Toledo, Ohio, in 1905, bringing former Socialist Party national secretary

William Mailly as editor. Closely associated with the left wing of the Socialist Party, Titus's paper provided intense scrutiny of the brazen attempt to decapitate the Western Federation of Miners in the Moyer–Haywood trial. Titus returned to Seattle with his newspaper in July 1906 where it played an important part in the ongoing free speech struggle in the Pacific Northwest and as a tool for organizing the radical wing of the Socialist Party of Washington. In July 1909 Titus led a left-wing bolt from the Socialist Party of Washington to found a short-lived party known as the Wage Workers Party—a sect that incidentally included among its members future communist leader William Z. Foster. Titus attempted to rebrand his periodical as *The Workingman's Paper* in connection with this new organization, but the paper folded in 1910. Titus later returned to medicine in New York, dying there in obscurity in 1931.

17. Frank J. Smith (1865–1912) of Caldwell, Idaho, was the state district court judge who presided over the arraignment of Charles Moyer, Bill Haywood, and George Pettibone on March 20, 1906. The venue of the trial was subsequently moved from Canyon County to Boise, located in Ada County, and Smith therefore did not preside.
18. Roosevelt spoke in the plaza between the Library of Congress and the US Capitol on April 14, 1906, at a ceremony held for the laying of the foundation stone of a new office building for the House of Representatives. This was the speech in which Roosevelt quoted from *Pilgrim's Progress* by John Bunyan (1628–1688) in reference to the "man with the muck-rake." This widely reported reference effectively attached the term "muckrakers" to the progressive journalists of his era.
19. Reference by Roosevelt is apparently to Debs's sensational "Arouse, Ye Slaves!" article of the previous month—a piece that caused the *Appeal to Reason* to be banned from the mail in Canada.
20. Chauncey M. Depew (1834–1928), the staunchly anti-union president of the New York Central Railroad, was an arch-nemesis of Debs during his railroad union years. The Republican Depew was tapped by the New York legislature for the first of two terms in the US Senate in 1898.
21. Exodus 20:15; Deuteronomy 5:19.
22. Exodus 20:13; Deuteronomy 5:17.
23. Wendell Phillips (1811–1884) was an 1833 graduate of Harvard Law School who was converted to the abolitionist cause in 1836. Phillips was a renowned public orator and one of the most effective anti-slavery advocates of his day.
24. Henry A. Wise (1806–1876), a lawyer from Richmond, was the governor of Virginia who signed the death warrant for abolitionist revolutionary John Brown in 1859. During the Civil War, Wise was a brigadier general in the army of the Confederate States of America.
25. According to Debs biographer David Karsner, this poem was written in May 1906, shortly after his mother's death. It was first published in August of that year. See David Karsner, *Debs: His Authorized Life and Letters* (New York: Boni and Liveright, 1919), 113–14.
26. Marguerite Bettrich "Daisy" Debs (1828–1906) died in Terre Haute on April 29, 1906 after a long illness. She was survived by her husband, four daughters, and two sons.

27. At the time of this letter, J. E. Snyder was the state secretary of the Socialist Party of Oklahoma. A socialist from his days at Wichita College, Snyder studied at the party-affiliated Rand School of Social Science in New York City in 1907. Upon completion of the program there, he returned to the Midwest, making his home in Girard, Kansas, where he worked for the *Appeal to Reason*. Snyder was elected state secretary of the Socialist Party of Kansas in December 1907. Snyder later moved to the San Francisco Bay Area, where he was editor of the *Oakland World* from 1917 to 1919. He was a founding member of the Communist Labor Party in 1919, for which he was arrested and unsuccessfully prosecuted under the state's criminal syndicalism law. In 1921 he briefly edited the *Western Worker* until it was absorbed by the official organ of the Workers Party of America. He would remain a Communist Party functionary through the 1930s.
28. At the age of 75, Moses Harman—publisher of the rationalist magazine *Lucifer* and author of the book *Motherhood in Freedom*—was sentenced to one year of hard labor in the Illinois state penitentiary at Joliet. Seven issues of his publication had been declared unmailable under the Comstock Law in the summer of 1905, ostensibly for advertising for sale publications on the topic of sex.
29. Anthony Comstock (1844–1915) was a conservative activist in the Young Men's Christian Association movement. In 1873 he founded the New York Society for the Suppression of Vice, an organization which successfully lobbied Congress later that year for passage of the so-called "Comstock Law" prohibiting the mailing of "obscene, lewd, or lascivious" publications—a broad category that included medical publications on gynecology, birth control, abortion, venereal disease, and basic sex education. Comstock was subsequently made a special agent of the United States Postal Service, which enabled him to escalate his moralistic crusade—a campaign that resulted in thousands of arrests, self-censorship, and the destruction of tons of printed publications. Although portions of the Comstock Law were ruled unconstitutional over the years, it was not until 1957 that the law was finally stricken from the books.
30. Gompers made his remarks on June 21, 1906 in a speech in Washington, DC, to open the 14th annual convention of the International Steel and Copper Plate Printers' Union. One version quotes Gompers as saying: "We are tired of being the plaything and football of politicians. . . . I don't look for the millennium though the ballot box. It comes through a man's own heart. What we want to accomplish in politics is to take the hand of the oppressor of organized labor from our throats." See *Houston Post,* June 22, 1906, 1.
31. Charles W. Fairbanks (1852–1918), a conservative Republican senator from Indiana, was elected vice president of the United States in 1904. He was also the party's nominee for the same position in 1916 as part of a losing ticket headed by Charles Evans Hughes.
32. Joseph G. Cannon (1836–1926), a conservative Republican from Illinois, was the powerful speaker of the House of Representatives from 1904 to 1912. He was a member of Congress for a total of 46 years and the namesake of the first congressional office building, completed in 1908.

33. The trial would be postponed yet again, with Haywood finally being brought to trial as a sole defendant in a test case in June 1907. Jury selection was completed on June 3, with the prosecution's opening statement delivered at the Ada County courthouse in Boise the next day. Haywood was unanimously acquitted on July 28. George A. Pettibone, a lesser figure in the Western Federation of Miners' firmament, was brought to trial later and was himself acquitted in January 1908. Western Federation of Miners President Charles Moyer was released on $25,000 bail at the time of the Haywood verdict and was never tried.
34. The legality of the warrantless arrest and deportation of Moyer and Haywood was appealed all the way to the Supreme Court, which professed sympathy with the argument of the defendants but claimed that no legal remedy existed.
35. The Chemin d'Ohain was a deeply sunken lane that bisected the battlefield at Waterloo, which enabled Field Marshal Arthur Wellesley, the Duke of Wellington, to conceal his forces and entrap and defeat the advancing French army of Napoleon Bonaparte on June 18, 1815.
36. This was the eleventh installment of a symposium in which the New York *Worker* asked prominent socialists to answer four questions about the relationship of the Socialist Party of America to the trade union movement. Writers were asked to provide their definition of industrial unionism, to expound upon the defects in existing unions, and to answer whether the tactic of supporting a new union or attempting to transform existing unions should be pursued.
37. *The Worker*, it should be noted, was originally the official organ of the Socialist Labor Party dissidents of 1899 (the so-called "Kangaroos"). This party split revolved in large measure around the trade union issue and the emphasis of Daniel DeLeon and the party leadership on building the Socialist Trade & Labor Alliance (ST&LA) in competition with the American Federation of Labor. The Socialist Labor Party dissidents favored attempting to radicalize the American Federation of Labor from within. The Industrial Workers of the World was established on the same basic strategic premise as had been the Socialist Trade & Labor Alliance half a decade earlier; Debs's endorsement was effectively the reopening of an old wound among many of *The Worker's* longtime readers.
38. Debs seems to refer to a rather innocuous-sounding line in the labor resolution of 1904 Socialist Party national convention: "The trades and labor union movement . . . is a weapon to protect the interests of labor under the capitalistic system. However, this industrial struggle can only lessen the exploitation, not abolish it. * * * *Neither political or other differences of opinion can justify the divisions of the forces of labor in the industrial movement . . . .*" (emphasis added)
39. Louis B. Boudin (1874–1952) was a Russian-born Jew who emigrated to the United States with his family in 1891. After working briefly in the garment industry, he entered college, eventually gaining a master's degree from New York University and being accepted into the New York State bar association in 1898. Boudin was active in the Socialist Labor Party, exiting with fellow New York attorneys Morris Hillquit and Henry Slobodin in that organization's bitter 1899 split and finding his way

into the Socialist Party of America at its founding in 1901. He was a seven-time candidate of the Socialist Party of America for various judicial offices during the decade of the 1910s. A founding editor of *The Class Struggle,* a theoretical magazine of the Socialist Party's proto-communist left wing. Despite his revolutionary socialist proclivities, Boudin ended his participation in organized party politics at the time of the 1919 Socialist–Communist split. He nevertheless continued to write for radical publications and to occasionally conduct classes in the Communist Party's New York Workers' School in the 1920s and 1930s. He renounced the Communist Party in 1940, remaining a committed civil libertarian and contributor to academic publications in later years.

40. Ernest Untermann (1864–1956) was a German-born American who worked for a decade sailing aboard merchant ships. He is best remembered as the translator of *Das Kapital* by Karl Marx for Charles H. Kerr & Co., work which kept him occupied from 1905 to 1909. Untermann sat on the governing National Executive Committee of the Socialist Party of America from 1908 to 1910. At the party's 1910 "national congress," Untermann was a chief author of a resolution supporting racist exclusion policies targeting immigrants from Asia. He worked on the staff of Victor L. Berger's daily *Milwaukee Leader* from 1921, abandoning radical politics later in that decade. In later years he gained a degree of fame as a painter of landscapes and prehistoric natural themes
41. Foul and abusive language.
42. John Bender was the patriarch of a murderous family who operated in rural Labette County, located 13 miles west of Parsons, Kansas. He, his wife, and two children—nicknamed "the Bloody Benders" in the contemporary press—befriended passing travelers, inviting them into their home only to rob and murder them. At least a dozen people were killed in this manner before the family's deeds were discovered in the summer of 1873. Before they could be apprehended, the family fled the area and vanished. Multiple theories about the fate of the family were bandied in the press over the next decade.
43. This piece silently incorporates a handwritten correction preserved in the Debs scrapbooks of a typographical error.
44. Republican Governor Frank R. Gooding was re-elected to a second two-year term of office in the November general election by a majority of about 10,000 votes.
45. Radical newspaper publisher Hermon Titus briefly moved his weekly, *The Socialist,* from Toledo, Ohio to Caldwell, Idaho to better cover the Moyer-Haywood affair. He subsequently would return with the paper in 1907 to its original home, Seattle, Washington.
46. From William Shakespeare, *The Tragedy of MacBeth* (1603), Act 5, Scene 8.
47. J. Howard Moore, *The Universal Kinship* (Chicago: Charles H. Kerr & Co., 1906).
48. Wilhelm Liebknecht (1826–1900) was a primary founder of the Social Democratic Workers Party of Germany, a forerunner of the Social Democratic Party of Germany. A contemporary of Marx and Engels, Liebknecht was imprisoned numerous times for his political activities throughout his life. He was editor-in-chief of the party's official

organ, *Vorwärts,* from 1891. Liebknecht 's son Karl (1871–1919) was a founder of the German communist movement.

49. August Bebel (1840–1913) was originally a worker from the bench who was won over to socialism in 1865 though the influence of Wilhelm Liebknecht. An effective orator and journalist, he was elected to the Reichstag in 1871, where he was an outspoken supporter of the Paris Commune. Together with Liebknecht, Bebel was tried for treason in 1872, ostensibly for morally aiding the French cause in the war against Germany. The pair were found guilty and served two years in the fortress, with Bebel given an additional nine months of ordinary imprisonment. Bebel was a chief organizer of the unity convention that established the united Social Democratic Party of Germany in 1890.
50. Emile Vandevelde (1866–1938) was a Belgian socialist politician who as Minister of State supported Belgian resistance to Germany's invasion in 1914. Vandervelde was president of the Second International from 1900 to 1918 and of the Labour and Socialist International from its founding in 1923 until the time of his death.
51. The founding convention of the Industrial Workers of the World was held in Chicago from June 27 to July 8, 1905.
52. The second convention of the Industrial Workers of the World was held in Chicago from September 17 to October 3, 1906.
53. Debs was the keynote speaker at a Socialist campaign festival held on Sunday afternoon, October 7, 1906, at Brand's Park in Chicago. The gathering was preceded by a socialist parade for several miles along Belmont and Elston Avenues with marchers four abreast stretching three blocks long in the procession behind a brass band playing "La Marseillaise." An estimated 3,000 people gathered at the park for socializing and dancing; two socialist vocal choruses performed. Following a short introduction, Debs's appearance was greeted by a massive ovation.
54. That is, Theodore Roosevelt.

1907

A Personal Word†

January 5, 1907

To the many comrades and others who have written and have expected to hear from me, there is due a few words of personal explanation. During the past few months, beginning with the death of my mother,[1] afflictions of all kinds have come to our family. Only a few days ago my father was laid to rest,[2] the third death in rapid succession, besides the illness of other members, myself included—an affliction of the throat and an attack of sciatica,[3] due to exposure, tending to incapacitate me for a considerable time from following my usual duties. The result has been the accumulation of heaps of letters, papers, and other documents, the interruption of correspondence, and the neglect of many other urgent matters for which the indulgence of comrades and friends is requested.

During the past year or more my work, especially in the field, has been carried forward under great difficulties, and very much of it has been wholly unsatisfactory to myself, and probably equally so to others. This word of explanation is all I have to offer along this line.

I wish to thank, on behalf of all our family, the many comrades, friends, and sympathizers, some of whom are strangers to us in name, for their beautiful letters filled with the touching tokens of their sympathy in our bereavement. When death enters the home and takes from us those dear to us, there is no comfort equal to a loyal comrade's sympathy and love.

I am now endeavoring to clear up the accumulation, get things in their usual order, and resume my work.

These are pregnant times and we all have work to do and must do it with all our strength and ability. The cause we serve is entitled to our first and last consideration. All other things are secondary.

Eugene V. Debs

† Published as "A Personal Word from Debs" in *Appeal to Reason,* whole no. 579 (January 5, 1907), 4.

Show Your Hand†

January 5, 1907

The Supreme Court decision in the Moyer-Haywood-Pettibone case marks a historic epoch and makes this the most important issue before the nation.[4]

This decision constitutes the blackest chapter in the annals of that tribunal. It not only legalizes kidnapping, but means that the workingman has no right the capitalist is bound to respect.

We shall see!

The working class of the nation must, shall, and will again be aroused. The former demonstrations were tame compared to those which this infamous decision will now convoke from sea to sea.

The working class must save these men.

The president of the United States, the miserable mountebank, has shown his hand, pronouncing our comrades guilty without a trial and sending his fat Man Friday to Idaho to pave the way for the execution of his sentence.[5]

We pronounce our comrades innocent and we shall now proceed to show our hand, and before they get through with their program of kidnapping and murder, they will wish they had never begun it.

In an early issue of the *Appeal* I shall have more to say upon this subject. Meantime, it is suggested that a series of meetings be promptly arranged for by all labor and socialist organizations, culminating in a monster international demonstration to be held on the anniversary of the outrage upon our comrades. In this connection it is suggested that all labor and socialist papers issue a special edition, to be known as the *kidnapping anniversary edition*, with which to flood the land and make known to every man, woman, and child this hideous crime against the working class, pointing out in red letters the precise politicians, beginning with the president, who are responsible for it.[6]

† Published in *Appeal to Reason*, whole no. 579 (January 5, 1907), 1.

The Center of the Fight: Letter to the *Appeal to Reason*[7†]

circa January 17, 1907

* * *

I am getting over my rheumatic attack[8] and I leave for Cincinnati Monday, where a specialist will treat my throat. I expect to be out in a few days. As soon as I get through with this and am in physical shape, I will come to Girard and stay until the kidnapping edition is made up and take a hand at helping you on the *Appeal*.[9] I would like a chance to edit the *Appeal* for a couple of weeks, or help you edit it, or help in any way to do the thing that this supreme hour tells me must be done.

Now is the time to strike!

A few weeks more and it will be too late. I have a rush of ideas and want to fuse them with yours and I believe that in combination we can raise hell with the capitalist plans, so far as Moyer, Haywood, and Pettibone are concerned. I believe, furthermore, that we can do work in three or four weeks' time that will give you a hundred thousand more subscribers and after the trial begins send it up to half a million and climbing toward a million. I say I believe this can be done and I would like a chance to try it.

Should the trial be announced while I am in Girard, I could go from there straight to Caldwell,[10] *for I propose to be in the center of the fight.*

To do the kind of work I have in mind, and to make it blaze and flash, awaken and inspire, I would have to be on the ground. I feel burning within me the fire of righteous indignation, lightened by the Supreme Court decision and fanned into crackly flame by Roosevelt's infamous action and attitude as set forth in Gooding's message to the Idaho legislature.[11] Besides the regular articles I have in mind, there is a variety of short stuff that can be used to great advantage, and, included in the plan, the central part of it, in fact, is the attempt to raise the *Appeal* circulation to the highest possible pinnacle. This will be the sure way, and, in fact, the only way to save our Idaho comrades. If we cannot arouse the people sufficiently to threaten revolt on a large scale,

---

† Published as part of "Debs on Deck" in *Appeal to Reason*, whole no. 581, Extra edition (January 19, 1907), 1. Not included in Constantine (ed.), *Letters of Eugene V. Debs: Volume 1, 1874–1912.*

they are gone. Nothing else can save them. The case in outline is already fully developed and its tragic culmination inevitable. To prevent the catastrophe we have got to reach out in all directions and in every state, township, and county and take hold of and shake the people into action. If we let this chance go by unimproved, the good Lord help us, for we will need it.

The thing must be a tremendous victory or a tragic failure. If we grasp this opportunity in all its offers and use our brains in unison and our energies in harmony, to their full capacity, steadfastly following the dictates of our consciences and fearlessly faithful to our own souls, we shall achieve a glorious victory for our fellow workers, ourselves, and humanity. *The great clock is striking an epoch!*

Yours always,
Eugene V. Debs

My Case Is Obstinate: Letter to Fred Warren of the *Appeal to Reason*†

January 22, 1907

Cincinnati, Oh., Jan. 22 [1907]

My Dear Warren:—

Have yours of the 18th.[12] My case is obstinate, yields slowly, account of long neglect. It is painful and trying, but I am hopeful of outcome and shall leave here on earliest train. The doctor thinks I may leave in a day or two, but he himself cannot tell from day to day the effect of the operation.[13]

Note all we say about the Feb. 7th limit and not a minute shall be lost on my account.

E. V. Debs

† Published as "A Note from Comrade Debs" in *Appeal to Reason*, whole no. 583 (February 2, 1907), 1. Not included in Constantine (ed.), *Letters of Eugene V. Debs: Volume 1, 1874–1912.*

We Must Fight![†]

January 26, 1907

The Supreme Court and the president of the United States have left us no other alternative. We have got to stand up like men or crawl on our bellies like cravens. There is no compromise.

The class struggle is as clearly reflected in the Supreme Court decision and the president's action as if traced in the skies in letters of fire. All the powers of capitalism, from Standard Oil down, are combined against Moyer, Haywood, and Pettibone, and find expression along the political line all the way from Ruzvlt[14] to McParland and along the judicial line all the way from the Supreme Court of the United States to a police magistrate in Idaho.

It is not a case of punishing crime that law may be vindicated, but the violation of law that crime may be committed.

The case against our comrades is notorious in court annals for the utter defiance of all law—state and national, statutory and constitutional—that has marked its proceedings from its inception. Indeed, the case, to be properly understood, must be traced back at least as far as the purchase by the mine owners and smelter trust of the legislature of Colorado, at the current Colorado rates per head, thereby defeating the eight-hour amendment which the people of that Guggenheim state[15] by a clear majority of nearly 50,000 votes had commanded these political perverts to enact into law. This was followed by the military despotism of the infamous Peabody and his sodden satraps, who emblazoned the escutcheon of his murderous administration with the immortal shibboleths: "To hell with the constitution," "To hell with habeas corpus," and "To hell with any court that decides against us." These are some of the foundation stones of the fabric of law and order which Ruzvlt sent Taft out to Idaho to commend to the people of that state.

This law-and-order cry issues from the brazen throats of political hirelings, the tools of capitalism, to conceal its own crimes.

When such monsters as Peabody and Gooding and such misshapen degenerates as McParland talk about law and order in the lurid light of their own crimes, and President Ruzvlt sends his fat special emissary to the scene of these

† Published in *Appeal to Reason,* whole no. 582 (January 26, 1907), 1.

crimes to give them the backing of the national administration, all in the name of law and order, and this in the very shadow of the dungeon in which innocent kidnapped American citizens are guarded by criminal body-snatchers—when it comes to this, then, indeed, has Justice fled to brutish beasts, all law is miserable mockery, and even Hypocrisy, used as she is to sickening saturnalia, is nauseated and deserts the scene.

That our comrades have been kidnapped and are unlawfully held by legalized brute force is admitted; there is no question about it, not even by the Supreme Court. That the preconceived purpose is to do them to death, regardless of their innocence, has been apparent from the start.

It is not as individuals that these workingmen are to be murdered, but as the incarnation of class-conscious organized labor that they must be annihilated.

That makes the issue my issue and their cause my cause.

These brothers of mine have served and suffered for me. Their enemy is my enemy and their fate must be my fate. To abandon them in this extremity would be to desert and dishonor myself and despise myself forever. I prefer to be a man, and, as such, to assert myself and the cause of my class.

How shall it be with you millions of workers, of whom I am but one? You and I and all of us are in the same boat and we go to port or to the bottom together.

The situation is clear—where do you stand? Are you a man or a microbe? Have you a spine to keep you straight and nerve enough to hold up your head?

The question confronts you; you cannot evade it, and if you attempt to sneak away it will follow you and denounce you even in your dreams.

For myself, I am going to Idaho, or wherever I may be needed; and I am going to do whatever duty may demand. The cause being absolutely righteous and my duty clear, I am going to act as conscience dictates regardless of consequences to myself.

Now, what can we do? A thousand things! We can think and act, and the first thing to think about is that we must act without delay. We are on the eve of battle; the lines are drawn and the forces are gathering.

Our first appeal is to the working class, the whole of it, from sea to sea, old and young, male and female.

Our next appeal is to every human being who loves justice, abominates crime, and abhors murder.

The most monstrous crimes in all history are those committed in the sacred name of justice. Legal murder is the crime of crimes and its perpetrator the fiend of fiends.

Our comrades are already the victims of a thousand legal crimes, and the sufferings they and their loved ones have endured no mortal being can ever describe. From their prison cell, dark as a cave, here issues a cry to the working class and to all humanity and *the voice of God is in that cry.*

Let the working class respond like the waves of the sea when the storm god touches the organ keys and the motionless surface is transformed into surging billows, and then that gloomy cell in Idaho will become all radiant with light.

Let me summarize a few of the things that may be done at once to arouse the working class:

First—Arrange public protest meetings in every city, town, village, hamlet, schoolhouse, and crossroads. These meetings should be held under joint auspices and for the time all differences laid aside, so that all may join in one protesting mass against the judicial sanction of kidnapping and assassination. The life of labor is involved in this issue.

Second—Tell your neighbors, friends, fellow workers, and everybody you meet about the crime, put literature in their hands bearing the proof and seek to arouse them to a realization of the impending catastrophe.

Third—Ten million copies of Justice McKenna's dissenting opinion should be run off as swiftly as possible and distributed broadcast over the land.[16] The capitalist press, Republican and Democratic, has discreetly ignored it. We must use our million hands in placing it before the people. The decision of the Supreme Court is a monstrous perversion of justice and an eternity of damnation will follow the fossils who pronounced it.

Fourth—Every indignation meeting that is held should have a copy of its protest mailed to the president and vice president of the United States, each member of the United States Senate and each member of the House of Representatives. This will involve a little work, but it is necessary and should be done.

Fifth—In every congressional district a petition should be circulated and signed as largely as possible, demanding a congressional investigation of the kidnapping conspiracy, and this should be forwarded to the member of Congress in that district, with a copy of Justice McKenna's opinion attached, coupled with the request that the petition be read in Congress and that said member of Congress introduce in that body a resolution calling for the investigation. Let the millions unite in this demand and move upon Congress with indignant protest and resolute determination. The politicians will listen to an aroused people.

Sixth—Wherever a state legislature is in session, the matter should be introduced by petition or resolution and made the subject of discussion, inquiry, and investigation. It can be forced into every legislature and these bodies set in motion. Wherever the issue can be raised and discussion precipitated it should be done. Agitation will result in action and every particle of both will help us. We have to fear only the dead calm of ignorance and indifference. The enemy want the country lulled to sleep while the murder is being committed. We must wake up the people, stimulate thought, provoke controversy, and incite action. In a word, we must wake up and turn the light on the conspirators and criminals.

Seventh—We must have a jury of twelve representatives of the working class at the trial to hear and weigh the evidence and render a verdict. It is clear as the noonday sun that a packed jury to convict is on the calendar of the criminals in control of the political machinery. A straight jury would not fit a crooked court. The case is Capital vs. Labor, Standard Oil vs. The Working Class, Millions of Money vs. Millions of Men. They will have their own jury picked by themselves. We must have our jury picked by ourselves. We know the kidnapping gang and what to expect. Their asseveration about a fair trial is pure gammon.[17] Kidnappers are criminals and criminals will pack juries to convict innocent men. We must have our own jury and by this means alone will justice be secured. A crooked jury facing a jury of honest men will be up against it. There can be no miscarriage, no trumped-up charges, no cooked-up testimony, no made-to-order "confession" in such a trial without instantaneous detection and prompt exposure.

Eighth—The Supreme Court of the United States, the final tribunal in the service of the capitalist class versus the working class, has placed its judicial seal upon kidnapping; and kidnapping now is no longer a crime, but a constitutional prerogative, a legal right and a personal privilege. Kidnapping being a legitimate practice, we all have a perfect right to engage in it. Let us take advantage of the opening. For every workingman kidnapped, a capitalist must be seized and held for ransom. Let us put the law laid down by the Supreme Court into practice. It is infamous, to be sure, and should be repealed, and the certain way to repeal it is to make it work both ways. The kidnapping of the first capitalist will convulse the nation and reverse the Supreme Court.

Finally—Let us use our brains and our energies; let us have self-respect and courage and face without flinching the issue that has been forced upon us by criminal conspirators masquerading as conservators of civilization.

I Have Come to Girard: Open Letter to Readers of the *Appeal to Reason*†

February 1, 1907

Girard, Kansas, Feb. 1, 1907

Comrades and Friends:—

The approaching trial of Moyer, Haywood, and Pettibone, involving not only the lives of these worthy fellow workers, but other issues of the gravest concern, is of deep and vital moment to every man, woman, and child, and its outcome may determine the destiny of a nation.

It is impossible to exaggerate the importance of this case and the effect of its outcome, and so deeply does it affect me as a comrade of the accused and as a fellow worker in the ranks of labor—so certain am I that their innocence of crime is as absolute as their loyalty to labor, and that in fact this is their only crime—that the conviction has been forced upon me that it is my duty, a duty I dare not shirk, to go to the aid of my comrades and stand by them unflinchingly, and thus prove my fealty to the cause. To do less than this would be to desert my comrades and prove a wretched recreant to the whole working class.

In pursuance of this line of duty, I have cancelled all other engagements that I might devote my whole time to this case and give it precedence over all other matters.

Through the kindness and cooperative spirt of Comrades Wayland and Warren, the columns of the *Appeal to Reason* have been placed at my disposal, and I have come to Girard to make the best possible use of its extensive circulation in reaching and awakening the people to a realization of the historic drama being enacted before their eyes.

Knowing well how loyally the supporters of the *Appeal* have always responded to its calls, I feel no hesitancy in addressing upon a subject so vital as the conspiracy which menaces the cause they love and serve so well.

† Published as "A Personal Word to *Appeal* Readers" in *Appeal to Reason*, whole no. 584 (February 9, 1907), 1. Not included in Constantine (ed.), *Letters of Eugene V. Debs: Volume 1, 1874–1912.*

The socialist and labor press is the most powerful agency of the working class, and in this crisis a duty so great and a responsibility so grave rests upon it that no words can give it adequate expression.

The *Appeal*, having by far the leading circulation, is in the forefront and must set an example that will be an inspiration to the rest and swell the volume of protest into an irresistible torrent that shall sweep midnight conspirators into oblivion and bear our comrades in triumph to freedom and their loved ones at home.

Comrades and fellow workers, the *Appeal* must be made to talk to the whole nation. The crisis demands it. Our cause is on trial and the lives of our comrades are at stake. The millions must be reached with the awakening and inspiring message the *Appeal* has for them.

In 30 days the trial begins. Every day, every hour, every minute between now and then must count. The circulation of the *Appeal* must be raised, and at once to the highest possible point.

Let each of us take hold—each of us—right now. There is not one of us but can help—not one but can get at least one subscriber.

Let every comrade, every friend, every man, woman, and child, unite in one supreme effort to add another hundred thousand to our circulation in the next 30 days.

I see, in fancy, the workers at their task, and I have no fear of disappointment.

Eugene V. Debs

First Anniversary of the Kidnapping of Moyer, Haywood, and Pettibone in the Capitalist Conspiracy to Russianize the United States†

February 16, 1907

A gruesome anniversary we are commemorating today!

The legally authorized commission of a monstrous crime.

The kidnapping in the dead of night by two governors and a pack of Pinkerton bloodhounds of three honest, unoffending workingmen, their secret and swift abduction a thousand miles from home, and their incarceration in the separate, solitary cells of a state penitentiary.

All without a whisper of warning.

Without a hint of what it was for;

Or a ghost of a chance to protest,

Or to ask a question, or consult a lawyer, or make a defense, or even send word, a farewell word, to wife and child.

Not a sound! Not a sign!

Swift and violent deportation by an armed private mob—dazed and alone in the black solitude of a penitentiary cell.

That is the introduction to the story of the crime committed at Denver, Colorado, February 17th, 1906, one year ago—a crime that will mark distinctly the beginning of the end of wage-slavery as certainly as October 16th, 1859, at Harper's Ferry, marked the beginning of the end of chattel slavery.

~

Who were the two governors to commit this dastardly assault?

Frank Gooding, of Idaho, and Jesse McDonald, of Colorado.

The political tools of the Mine and Smelter Trust—that is to say, the Standard Oil octopus.

Who were the victims of this midnight ambuscade of Pinkerton mercenaries, led by Gum-Shoe Gooding and Dark-Lantern McDonald at the behest of their Standard Oil masters?

---

† Published in *Appeal to Reason*, "Kidnapping Edition," whole no. 585 (February 16, 1907), 1, 4.

Charles H. Moyer, William D. Haywood, and George A. Pettibone, president, secretary, and ex-board member, respectively, of the Western Federation of Miners.

What was their offense?

They had organized workingmen and had refused to betray them.

They could be neither bought, bribed, nor browbeaten.

Their incorruptibility marked them for murder.

In a state where mine and smelter brigands buy boldly and bodily the legislature, Supreme Court, and United States senatorship, *loyalty to labor is a crime against capital, punishable by death.*

Standard Oil has decreed it.

Two governors have approved it.

The United States Supreme Court has confirmed it and

The president of the United States has proclaimed it.

ꕥ

The power of organized labor in the Rocky Mountains is centered in its tried and trusted leaders; this power must be destroyed. Everything else had succumbed, and so must this, to the iron rule and despotic sway of the looters. From governor to constable, the mine owners ran the whole gamut of public power. Officeholders were but the keyboard in the instrument of exploitation upon which they played at will.

They had bought or bullied everybody and everything—except one.

They had millions of easy money which they had filched from labor, and these millions had made them the executive, legislative, judicial, and military masters of the state.

But there was one thing these pirates still lacked, just one, and they were quick to realize it.

They lacked control of the magnificent labor organization known as the Western Federation of Miners.

This was the only wall between them and their Eden of unbridled power and plunder.

And this wall must be undermined by corruption, pierced by intimidation, or battered to the earth by brutal force.

But for once money failed of its magic power. The leaders were proof against temptation. They could not be debauched. They were above price.

And neither could they be frightened from their posts. They stood immovable as granite.

This sealed their fate.

They must now be removed by stealth or crushed by force.

The kidnapping of February 17th is the sequel.

❧

What excuse was made by the kidnapping governors for pouncing upon the leaders of the Western Federation and rushing them out of the state by special train?

A man had been killed in Idaho.

Who? Frank Steunenberg, once governor of that state and member of a labor union.

The leaders of the Western Federation did not know him and had never seen him.

But Governor Gooding said that a Pinkerton detective had said that another detective had told him that Moyer, Haywood, and Pettibone, who did not know and had not seen Steunenberg, and could have no possible interest in or connection with him, were in some way connected with his death.

Not that they had killed him. That could not be charged because they were a thousand miles away when it happened. But they had guilty knowledge of his death.

Who said so?

Just one person!

One!

Who?

Harry Orchard.

Who is he?

A murderer.

To whom did he tell it?

To James McParland, alias "Jim McKenna."

Who is he?

Another murderer.

And both these murderers, Orchard and McParland, detectives, spies, and secret agents in the employ, and on the payroll, of the Mine Owners' Association!

This is the foundation, and all there is of it, for the kidnapping and proposed judicial massacre of the Federation leaders.

"They shall never leave Idaho alive."

The governor has said it,

And he is the state!

Their epitaph follows:

Kidnapped, Killed! —Gooding, Governor.

To sum up: Orchard told McParland, McParland told Gooding, and Gooding told McDonald.

The first two are the secret detectives and the last two are the political tools of the Mine Owners' Association.

These are the facts.

Black as ravens' wings.

Would you know more about Orchard, the poor degenerate?

He, himself, says he has committed 26 murders.

If this be true or false, his word, though supported by a thousand oaths, is worthless.

Utterly and everlastingly worthless.

Governor Gooding knows this and would not prosecute a stray dog on such information.

And yet he embraces purchased perjury as eagerly as a drowning man does a straw. It has the ring of gospel truth to ears attuned to his master's voice and is all sufficient to destroy the reputation of honest men, who have never known the taint of crime, and swing them from the gallows' tree with the expectation that their dislocated necks will mean death to the organized body of which they have been the official heads.

Would you know more about McParland?

Go to the anthracite coal fields of Pennsylvania, where stalk the ghosts of the victims his perfidy sent to the gibbet.

He joined the Molly Maguires to betray them.

For pay!

For 30 pieces.

The meanest Molly Maguire that ever lived was infinitely his moral superior.

Ask the reputable people of Pottsville, Shenandoah, and that region who James McParland, alias "Jim McKenna" is, and you will get his reputation at first hand.

The first man I asked about him, an old and respected citizen, answered: "Jim McKenna? The blackest-hearted villain that ever cut a throat, and if you ever see him, tell him I said so."

Go to Parsons, Kansas, where McParland made his rendezvous and where he and his pals had their deadfall a quarter of a century ago, and you will be told that his record there, every line of it, is written in the blackest infamy.

Upon the unsupported word of these two wretches, the constitutions of Colorado and Idaho and of the United States have been disemboweled by the very chief executives who had sworn to obey and support them.

And these outrageous violations of the organic law of the land, they tell us, as if they expected any sane human being to believe it, is to establish the supremacy of law and preserve the peace and order of society.

They have admitted the violation of the constitution, they have admitted the kidnapping, they have boasted like bullies that they are going to kill our comrades, and with the brutal insolence of villainy triumphant they have sneeringly asked: "What are you going to do about it?"

Time will show what we shall do about it.

∽

Let me ask every reader of the *Appeal* to read carefully every line of the story of this crime written by George H. Shoaf and printed on another page and then to pass the paper to some other person and to as many others as can be reached.

Shoaf was on the ground when the Independence platform was blown up, resulting in thirteen deaths, and was an eyewitness to the military maneuvers and strike scenes in the Cripple Creek district.[18] He has personally gone over all the territory in Colorado and Idaho covered by the fierce struggle which reigned there during the past few years and interviewed all the leading figures on both sides, including governors, judges, military officers, detectives, labor leaders, strikers, and other interested persons. The knowledge of Shoaf is, therefore, at first hand, and absolutely reliable. He has been an eyewitness to much and a careful follower and close student of all, and his story of the historic struggle in the Rocky Mountains, culminating in the kidnapping and intended murder of the labor leaders, in the name of outraged law and order, should be familiar to every person not wholly dead to every sentiment of liberty and humanity.

∽

December 30, 1905 is the date of the assassination of ex-Governor Steunenberg. February 17, 1906, the date of the arrest of Moyer, Haywood, and Pettibone, and March 5, 1907, the date of trial last set by the prosecution.

From the hour of their arrest, trial was promptly demanded and denied; demanded and denied ever since. Repeated postponements have taken place, all due to the prosecution and to reasons that come very nearly revealing themselves.

Why this long and inexcusable delay? These repeated postponements? Refusal of bail?

Is it the intention to let these men rot in prison since the American people have shown an unmistakable determination to see to it that they are not legally murdered?

If the trial is called March 5, the prisoners will then have been in jail almost 13 months, saying nothing of their previous bullpen experience under Peabody military law.

What redress is there for this unspeakable outrage of the kidnappers, the suffering our brothers have endured, the torment and agony inflicted upon their loved ones?

In the eye of the law, as well as in fact, our comrades are absolutely innocent, and yet they have already been sentenced to more than a year of imprisonment and torture.

Let it not be imagined that this will be overlooked in the final reckoning.

Conspiracy, like murder, will out. Sooner or later the truth will be known. That crime has been committed is only too true, but the criminals are not in the Ada County jail. The finger of guilt points in another direction, and as steadily as the needle to the pole.

The men now under indictment were workingmen, plain, honest, and straightforward, who from their earliest youth have had to battle for a livelihood, and their affectionate devotion to their wives, their little children, and aged parents bears touching testimony to their blameless lives. Trained in the rugged school of honest labor, and graduated in all its privations and hardships, they have had neither time nor taste for the cultivation of criminal tendencies. Guile and duplicity had no part in forming their habits or tainting their lives. These are the graces and accomplishments of the idle class, who live out of the sweat and misery of honest toil.

Chicanery and fraud, corruption and crime, are the very essence of exploitation.

Moyer, Haywood, and Pettibone had no hand in the buying or selling of the Colorado legislature, the corruption of the Supreme Court, or the cashing in of the United States senatorship.

Oh, no, these are the exclusive functions of the "upper class," the graduates in "frenzied finance" and stock-jobbing statesmanship; the sinless saints of modern society, whose cant about law and order is the sum of all hypocrisy and a stench in the nostrils of honest men.

The moral lepers who rob the body economic and debauch the body politic are the instigators of the crimes that have cursed Colorado.

The miscreants who are responsible for the assassination charged against Moyer, Haywood, and Pettibone are not workingmen.

The buyers of legislatures are the patrons of kidnappers and the purveyors of assassination.

These crimes spring from the same source; they are closely related and go hand in hand.

The scene in Idaho will be shifted in due time. Millions of eyes are steadfastly fixed upon the actors. The puppets are now playing their parts. The strings are in the hands of persons behind the scenes and these unseen persons are the real villains in the performance.

The working class of the world are the lookers-on, and they will never suffer their innocent fellow workers to expiate the crimes of the guilty conspirators.

The Kidnapping Case in Congress†

March 2, 1907

Washington, DC, March 2 [1907]

At the opening of Congress this morning, the Moyer, Haywood, and Pettibone case was introduced, together with petitions for investigation and the dissenting opinion of Justice McKenna, of the Supreme Court. Senator Carmack,[19] of Tennessee, presented the case on the floor of the United States Senate, with the request that it be admitted to the records, and this was consented to.

The introduction of the conspiracy was a great surprise to most of the senators, but when the statement was made that the demand for an investigation was backed by 2 million organized workers, the unanimous consent which was necessary, and without which it would have failed, was given by the Senate, excepting that Heyburn,[20] of Idaho requested that the decision of the Supreme Court be included with the dissenting opinion of Justice McKenna, to which no objection was made on our side.

† Published as "Kidnapping Case in Congress: *Appeal* Succeeds in Placing Facts of Moyer-Haywood Case on Record in Washington" over byline of "Eugene V. Debs, Staff Correspondent" in *Appeal to Reason*, whole no. 588 (March 9, 1907), 1.

The foundation is now laid for a congressional investigation and both senators and congressmen agree that in obedience to the demands of organized labor, this will certainly be authorized by the next session of Congress. Senator Carmack has been particularly helpful in this matter and Senator LaFollette,[21] of Wisconsin, has also treated me with great courtesy.

With this impending congressional investigation, which will develop all the facts in the conspiracy and reveal the whole horrible truth to the people, it is now perfectly safe to predict that Moyer, Haywood, and Pettibone will soon have been rescued from the clutches of their kidnappers and would-be murderers and walk forth free men without a blemish upon their honor.

Quick Work in Short Time

When I first arrived and called on Senator Carmack, of Tennessee, whom I had previously met and knew to be a man of fair mind and friendly to organized labor and to the working class in general, he advised that I at once procure as many petitions in the form of protests and demands for investigation on behalf of organized labor as were obtainable. The time being short, I used the telegraph freely in making the requests and within 24 hours the petitions, protests, and demands began to roll in in an amazing volume and within a week I had demands for investigation representing upwards of 2 million organized workers.

These came from officers of international and local unions, central bodies, and other organizations without number, most of them being duly authenticated with official seals and signatures. These made an enormous heap and have been filed with the dissenting opinion of Justice McKenna in the United States Senate by Senator Carmack.

In this connection it should be stated that I was officially commissioned by the Western Federation of Miners through their general officers to represent the organization before the Congress in the demand for an investigation of the Moyer and Haywood affair. I was thus in position to act as the special representative of organized labor in its petition to Congress, and Senator Carmack was able to say in the petition that the investigation was demanded by 2 million organized wage workers. Nothing less than the expiration of Congress could have prevented the measure from going through. As it is, the matter is now of record and by this means will be brought to the attention of great numbers of people who otherwise would never have seen it; and it will especially be the means of getting into wide circulation Justice McKenna's dissenting opinion.

Then, again, the foundation has been laid for future action in the way of congressional investigation, this being contingent, of course, upon the continuance of the prosecution of our comrades in Idaho. It can be safely predicted that unless the case is abandoned, there will be an investigation by Congress and there will be such developments as will make the mine owners wish they had never resorted to the crime of kidnapping to further their infamous ends.

It should also be said that although there is not a socialist in Congress, there are quite a number of men in both branches who speak out boldly in condemnation of the kidnapping of our comrades. While they do not pretend to decide the question of guilt or innocence, they insist that, whatever the circumstances may have been, there could have been no possible justification for the crime of kidnapping on the part of the state authorities, who were sworn to execute the law and not to trample it underfoot.

The Democratic members of Congress declare that if it comes up again, they will take hold of the case and make it a political issue. They insist that every man prominently connected with the kidnapping, without a single exception, is a Republican, and that the responsibility for it therefore rests with the Republican Party, and its leaders must show cause why organized labor should not fix the responsibility accordingly. They go further and say that they will make kidnapping a political issue in the national campaign next year, and that they will make the leaders of the Republican Party explain how it is that their party, that professes to be friendly to the working classes, is in league with the mine owners, and not only this, but in conspiracy with them to destroy the labor movement, they profess to patronize by kidnapping and conspiring to murder its official leaders.

Appeal Known in Washington

It is quite sure that it is here at Washington that we must converge our efforts if we expect to save our comrades by peaceable means. On the kidnapping proposition we have a large number of outspoken friends in both branches of Congress, and if the trial has not been abandoned by the time Congress meets again, an investigation is sure to be made; and, in connection with it, there is apt to be a test fight on the floors of Congress greater than any seen in many a day. You would be surprised to see how many there are here who know of the *Appeal*, and especially among the men who are high in public life.

They have all heard of it, most of them have read it, and not a few are subscribers. I am not much surprised at this, for I know that special efforts have been made since the *Appeal* has taken hold of the kidnapping cases to have them brought to the attention of men prominent in politics and other affairs. Every senator and every member of the house has been lately reading the *Appeal*, and those I have talked to have read of the Moyer and Haywood case, and are well informed in regard to it. It is this special propaganda of the *Appeal* here in Washington during the last 30 days that has prepared the way for congressional action. President Ruzvlt and his cabinet, the Supreme Court, members of Congress, and other high officials have been getting the *Appeal* regularly, and are all more or less familiar with the contents, especially with respect to what it is doing on the part of the working class with reference to the rescue of our Idaho comrades.

The personal suffering of our comrades is a thing which we all regret, but it is certain that no incident in all the history of organized labor has been fraught with greater benefit to the labor propaganda or contributed more to the solidarity of the working class. The kidnappers have unwittingly aroused the workers of the whole nation and have hastened by many days the cause of emancipation.

Worker Solidarity and Mouth Revolutionists†

March 16, 1907

The case of our kidnapped comrades is now in the United States Senate, admitted by the unanimous consent of that body and supported by signed and sealed petitions and resolutions representing more than 2 million organized workers spread over all the states and territories of the Union.

For one strongly opposed, as is the writer, to going before a capitalist legislative body to ask anything in the interest of the working class, this may seem strange and inconsistent; and so it is in a sense, and there must be some extraordinary feature of the case to justify it.

† Published as "Investigation by Congress of the Kidnapping of Moyer, Haywood, and Pettibone Is on the Calendar and Next in Order" over the byline "Eugene V. Debs, Staff Correspondent" in *Appeal to Reason*, whole no. 589 (March 16, 1907), 1.

As a matter of fact, the kidnapping of our comrades by conspiracy of the governors of two states adds this extraordinary element to the case, and makes of it a special cause no less than a great emergency in which the lives of loyal comrades are at stake; and, under such circumstances, it is not strange that there should be departure from our usual tactics in dealing with the enemy.

Taking another view of the matter, kidnapping is not necessarily a feature of the class struggle, nor is it binding upon us to confine ourselves to class struggle tactics in dealing with that crime.

Assistance Without Compensation

There are thousands upon thousands of capitalists and supporters of capitalist institutions who are avowedly opposed to the crime of kidnapping, as perpetrated upon our comrades, and are ready to join in any effort to redress the wrong done and punish those responsible for it; and not a few of these are in the Congress of the United States.

A man does not have to be a workingman, or a socialist, to be opposed to the crime of kidnapping, especially when it is compounded into murder by the chief magistrates of the people.

Proceeding on the theory that all that was needed to defeat the conspiracy and set our comrades free was the light of publicity, we came to Washington with the hope and expectation of having the plot laid bare and facts made known in the supreme councils of the nation. In this we have succeeded, and to the fullest extent hoped for.

While the time was too short for the passage of any measure, the case was introduced and admitted to the congressional records and the foundation thus laid for further action at the next session.

One of the most remarkable elements in the proceedings at Washington was the marvelously swift response of the organized hosts of the nation. Within 10 days signed and sealed documents, speaking for more than 2 million workingmen, were rushed into the national capital. It is certain that in 30 days more, the number of workers and others petitioning and protesting could have been increased to 5 million. All this preliminary work was done quietly to prevent the enemy from wholly excluding the matter from consideration and barring it from the records, as could have been done under the rules by a single objection in the closing days of the short session of Congress just adjourned.

New York Conference

In this connection, while giving general credit to the organized workers all over the country for their gratifying activity in this emergency, special mention must be made of the invaluable aid rendered by our New York comrades under the auspices of the Moyer and Haywood Conference. This provisional organization spreads over a large territory, and its constituent elements are under such control that quick action can be secured in such an emergency as this, and when the call reached them from Washington, within 24 hours the petitions and resolutions were rolling in by scores from all over the New England and Eastern states.

In all my experience in the labor movement I have never had such a gratifying surprise. When I presented that case to Senator Carmack, of Tennessee, and we were planning for its introduction in the Senate, he suggested that we could make but little progress, and probably none at all, unless we had petitions from a large number of organized workingmen. The time being very short, I used the telegraph and immediate delivery service in reaching our most active workers as far west as the Rocky Mountains, and in less than 10 days, as already stated, the mails brought demands for an investigation representing more than 2 million of the organized labor forces.

It was truly a marvel to me, this perfect flood of communications, denoting a condition of activity and of solidarity on the part of the workers without a parallel in the history of the movement.

Mouth Revolutionists

There are a few, and fortunately only a few, who are inclined to sneer at these efforts to save our comrades. They are of that small element who profess to be completely enlisted in the cause and contemptuously wave aside all claims of individual consideration. Some of these have been frank enough to say that Moyer, Haywood, and Pettibone ought to be allowed to go to the gallows rather than compromise our revolutionary propaganda.

These gentlemen are what may be called *mouth revolutionists*.

They never do anything to get their own necks in the noose.

When the battle is on, they are never up against the guns, but always in the rear telling how it ought to be done and pronouncing judgment upon those who are at the front doing the fighting. They are very brave in their willingness to sacrifice the lives of others, but they never jeopardize their own. If but for 15 minutes these so-called revolutionists were in the shoes of Moyer, Haywood, and Pettibone, looking into the nooses dangling before their eyes, they would make the most abject pleas to save their necks by any possible means.

The writer is one who believes in sacrificing all for the cause, but absolutely nothing unnecessarily. The spirit of mock heroics and revolutionary bravado should not prevent us from saving the life of a single comrade by any conceivable means within our power, and in such a fight as we are now waging against a gang of desperate kidnappers and murderers, any form of strategy is allowable, and it is not only our right but our duty to use any weapon with which we can deal an effective blow to the enemy.

Taking this view of the situation, it appears quite certain that the most telling work yet done in the interest of our imprisoned comrades has been done here in Washington through the power of organized labor during the past two weeks.

Protest Jarred Statesmen

Never before has such a petition been filed with the Congress of the United States. The members of the conservative old Senate were never more surprised.

Within five minutes after it was read, everybody about the capital was talking about it, and there was an air of suppressed excitement over it. The Washington papers have given a full and fair account of it, incorporating the salient points in our petition. The Associated Press has also sent the matter over the wires, thus placing the protest of labor and its demand for an investigation before practically the whole population of the country.

The impending investigation by Congress will undoubtedly have an immediate effect upon the cases against our comrades. The conspirators and kidnappers know that such an investigation will bring to light all the hidden horrors which up to this time they have been able to conceal; and they know furthermore that it will also reveal a state of industrial and political facts which will put all the capitalist powers on the defensive and give the socialist movement such an impetus as it has never known.

Unless the prosecution is abandoned, the next Congress will surely order an investigation. Scores of senators and congressmen openly declare themselves in favor of it, and insist that it shall be done.

For the first time since their arrest, I now feel that our comrades are safe. But we know the enemy and are taking no chances.

We shall press the fight more vigorously than ever and keep it up all along the line *until Moyer, Haywood, and Pettibone are free.*

Hold Your Nerve†

March 23, 1907

To join the socialist movement implies a declaration of war—war on the capitalist system and all its profit-fed institutions!

To issue such a declaration requires some measure of moral courage; to make it good requires a vast deal more.

Many a convert joins with enthusiasm to be extinguished a few months later in ignominy. He lacks the nerve to stand his ground.

Many another joins the movement and grows stronger from the hour the battle begins; the more he is resisted the stauncher he becomes; the more he is persecuted the more resolute he becomes, and in the storm of battle all the heroic fiber within him becomes steel and he rises to the stature of a full-grown man who has the strength to stand alone though all the world turn against him.

He has the nerve!

This is the secret of real heroism.

In writing this brief article on the subject of nerve, we have in mind a large number of socialists and semi-socialists who are more or less anxious to serve the movement, but who are so easily deflected from their purpose. They happen to hear of an uncomplimentary remark directed against them, and it strikes at the very heart of their allegiance to the cause. They hear of some temporary defeat of the party, or of some friction within the ranks, and they are at once discouraged.

The trouble is with their nerve. It is this that should have their immediate attention. The comrade lacking nerve, or having but a weak support of himself, will be kept in very hot water in the socialist movement.

As previously stated, the man who joins the socialist movement declares war against the capitalist system and capitalist society, and war of this kind is not a May festival. Ferdinand Lassalle, the brilliant social revolutionist, once said that the war against capitalism was not a rosewater affair. He was right. It is rather of the storm and tempest order. All kinds of attacks must be expected, and all kinds of wounds will be inflicted. The new comrade of tender

† Published in *Appeal to Reason*, whole no. 590 (March 23, 1907), 1.

sensibilities will soon get used to having his feelings torn and lacerated if he remains in the movement.

Many honest and well-meaning persons have been completely driven out of the movement because they could not stand the metaphorical shot and shell that was crashing about their heads. Their hearts were right, but they lacked the nerve.

A fatal defect!

No matter what other good qualities a convert to socialism may have, he must have the nerve to stick, the nerve to stay, if he is to be of any value to the movement. He must make up his mind that all the trials to which mortal man is subject will fall to his lot one after the other, and that if he lacks the nerve the weak spot in him will sooner or later be put to the test and he will go down and out, never to rise again.

But it is this very trial that serves a most beneficent purpose for both the individual and the movement; it eliminates the weak and unfit, and tempers those qualified for the higher service to which they are to be called, because they have the nerve and can stand the test.

It is therefore very essential that he whose conviction it is that socialism is right, and whose sense of duty impels him to do battle for it, shall make sure that his nerve is equal to the test when it comes, for come it will, not once, but with frequent and increasing severity to every man and woman in the movement.

It is well for a member to be sensitive about his honor, but he must not permit his lack of nerve, coupled with his super-sensitiveness, to drive him out of the movement when he learns from others that he has joined it to promote his own individual or selfish ends.

He or she who declares war on capitalism by joining the Socialist Party must make up his or her mind to tramp as thorny a pathway as led to Calvary, provided, of course, every duty such a course imposes is fearlessly met and every obligation faithfully discharged. Every socialist who has proved his right to a place in the ranks can verify this fact by his own personal experience.

When you part company, so to speak, with capitalist society, when the war actually begins, the war of the revolution in which there can be no compromise, you will be driven back in humiliation and defeat unless you have the nerve to bear all the wounds that are sure to be inflicted.

You will be told that you joined the movement to seek notoriety, or because you have always been a failure, or a mischievous agitator; that you want to make money out of socialism; that you are not sound, that you are only half-baked, and a hundred other things. You will be assailed within and without, spat upon by the very ones you are doing your best to serve, at certain crucial moments will find yourself isolated, absolutely alone, as if to compel your surrender, but in those very moments, if you have the nerve, you become supreme, and instead of abjectly capitulating, you felt within yourself the thrill of new-born powers of which you never dreamed, and you realize for the first time the ecstasy of man's greatest victory—the victory over self.

Nerve is necessary to such an enviable achievement. Some men are dowered with the quality, others lack it, but the weakest may cultivate it. So highly can this quality be developed that the human being may become absolutely impervious to dread and fear, to the weaknesses of the flesh, and walk among men almost as if he were a god.

The war we are waging, be it ever remembered, is not for brutal conquest, not for empty glory, but for the peace and happiness and civilization of the whole human race.

It is the grandest war in all the annals of mankind.

It will require the bravest warriors that ever gave up their lives upon the field of battle. And they will be known as the greatest heroes and rest in the blessings of a thousand generations yet unborn.

The Date Fixed![†]

April 6, 1907

Are you with us?

May 9th, at Boise, Idaho?

∽

Now must every loyal man hoist his colors; show the stuff of which he's made.

Moyer, Haywood, and Pettibone are about to be led forth, as was the Man of Galilee, for crucifixion by the priests of Mammon.

The date is fixed for the trial before Pilate.

---

† Published in *Appeal to Reason*, whole no. 592–Extra (April 6, 1907), 1. This article replaced a piece by Debs called "Before the Battle" which ran in the same spot in *Appeal* regular edition no. 592, also dated April 6.

Judas McParland has the evidence, according to agreement with the mine and smelter kings.

Now summon the people!

ᔕ

Comrades, you have worked without weariness or complaint but only the beginning has been made.

The supreme hour of your lives is striking now.

May 9th appeals to you for superhuman service.

The fate of your brothers is in your hands; you dare not deliver them up to the bloody executioner.

Now, even now, thirty thousand Paul Reveres are leaping into their saddles to carry the news and arouse the people.

ᔕ

Fellow workers: Thirty days remain for action. Each of these must count. A hundred thousand people more must read the *Appeal* the day our comrades step into the dock.

Go out among your people, and go now. You never have and never can do holier work.

Cast but a glance into the darkened homes of your faithful brothers. The aged parents, the loving wives, the sweet and tender children look to you, entreat you, trust to you.

Shall you deny them?

Woe to you, if you be without soul, for your perfidy shall seek you out and your turn shall be next!

ᔕ

We shall be at the front to blast the intrigues; to tear the mask of virtue from the leer of villainy; to lay bare the cold-blooded plot, the satanic conspiracy to *break the neck of organized labor,* and make a bullpen of the Rocky Mountains.

That will be our duty, the duty of the *Appeal*; yours to *spread the truth among the people.*

Every loyal comrade will do his duty, and we shall do ours.

ᔕ

May 9th shall find us at the front, and if men are needed to die in this fight to save innocent men from judicial murder, we shall be first in line for that privilege.

Haywood at the Bar[†]

April 13, 1907

Thursday, May 9th is the day set for the trial of William D. Haywood at Boise, Idaho. The trial of George A. Pettibone follows next, and that of Charles H. Moyer last. Thus far Gooding has had his way in every particular. The regular trial judge has stepped aside, the change of venue asked for has been denied, and Gooding's assurance that the men would be tried by a judge and at a time and place suitable to him has been verified.

Haywood is to be tried first, and it is well understood that, being the strong central character, the moving spirit of the Federation, he is the one man McParland has been engaged to send to the gallows. For the rest, the mine owners are satisfied that Pettibone shall serve a sentence in the penitentiary and that Moyer shall go free.

That is the *Appeal's* forecast of the frame-up of the conspirators. So long as they get Haywood, the keystone in the arch of the hated Federation, they will be satisfied, and the modified sentences of Moyer and Pettibone will give the proceedings all the outward appearance of fair trials, while settling all doubt as to Haywood's guilt and justifying, in his case, the extreme penalty of the law.

There is quite sufficient evidence that Haywood has been marked as the victim. The original design was to hang them all, but there has been such a howl about it that there had to be some modifications, and these are fully expected to quiet the clamor and appease the mob.

What, now, is to be our attitude, since it appears quite clear that Haywood is marked for sacrificial slaughter? There can be but one answer. We must stand by him to a man and to a finish.

Gooding and his backers have boasted that they have the state militia, that the regular troops are on the ground, and that the latter have been reinforced and equipped with riot guns. It is also stated that Boise will be filled with thugs and gunmen, and it has been freely given out that the first move made by the friends of the defendants would be followed by a massacre.

Admitting all this to be true, what of it? We have no concern in regard to it, not the slightest. Were Boise surrounded by federal forts instead of having

† Published as "Haywood at Bar" in *Appeal to Reason*, whole no. 593 (April 13, 1907), 1.

but one, our duty would remain the same. The show of force on the part of the kidnappers simply betrays their cowardice and their guilt, their weakness and their fear, while it does not daunt us to the slightest degree.

Having absolute faith in the innocence of our comrades and in the justice of our cause, we are unafraid and shall stand up like men, at all hazards, in the performance of our duty.

The jury of the working class, the representatives of the organized American hosts, will be in the courtroom when the case is called, and no blood-bought McParland brand of made-to-order evidence shall be allowed to serve the infamous ends of judicial murder.

In the meantime, the working class of the United States must be on the alert for developments and ready to act as emergency may require.

The *Appeal* will be fully installed at Boise when the case is called. The staff will embrace editors, reporters, and cartoonists, and every incident of the trial will be served with all the promptness and efficiency the *Appeal* can command.

The month of May looms large on the horizon, and if ever there was a time to stand staunch and true, that time has now come to the working class of America.

Roosevelt and His Regime†

April 15, 1907

The only time in my life have I ever seen Theodore Roosevelt was years before he became president of the United States. I was aboard a train in the far West, where Roosevelt was then said to be following ranch life, and as he and several companions in cowboy costume entered the car at a station stop, he was pointed out to me. I did not like him. The years since have not altered that feeling of aversion except to accentuate it.

---

† Published in *Appeal to Reason*, whole no. 594 (April 20, 1907), 1. Released to the press pre-publication by the "Appeal to Reason Bureau"; see, for example, the excerpt published as "Debs Stretches Teddy's Hide to the Side of the Barn Door to Tan" in *Chicago Daily Socialist*, vol. 1, no. 147 (April 15, 1907), 1–2. Alternate excerpt distributed by wire service; see, for example, "President Subject of Vicious Attack by Eugene Debs," *The Evening Star* [Independence, KS], vol. 7, no. 279 (April 15, 1907), 2.

I have since seen the nation mad with hero worship over this man Roosevelt, but I have not been impressed by it. Very "great" men sometimes shrivel into very small ones and finally vanish into oblivion in the short space of a single generation.

The American people are more idolatrous than any "heathen" nation on earth. They worship their popular "heroes," while they last, with passionate frenzy, and with equal madness do they hunt down the sane "fools" who vainly try to teach them sense. Theodore Roosevelt and George Dewey[22] as "heroes" and Wendell Phillips and John Brown as "fools" are notable illustrations. American history is filled with them.

But my personal dislike of the cowboy in imitation who has since become president, however justifiable, would scarcely warrant a public attack upon his official character, and this review, being of such a nature, is inspired, as will appear, by entirely different motives.

There are those, and they constitute a great majority of the American people, who stand in awe of their president, supposedly their servant, but in fact their master; they speak of him with a kind of reverential adulation as a lordly personage, a superior being to be looked up to and worshipped rather than a fellow man to be respected and loved. There are others who betray equal ignorance in a more vulgar fashion by coarse tirades for which there is often as little excuse as extreme adulation.

Regarding the president of the United States, as I do, simply as a citizen and fellow man, the same as any other, I shall speak of him and his acts free alike from awe and malice, and if I place him in the public pillory, where he has placed so many others, to be seen and despised of men, it will be from a sense that his official acts, so often in flat denial of his professions, merit the execration of honest men.

In arraigning President Roosevelt and his administration I have no private spite nor personal grudge to satisfy, but an obligation to redeem and a principle to vindicate. I shall go about it as I would any other moral duty, asking no favors and prepared to accept all consequences.

In the first place, I charge President Roosevelt with being a hypocrite, the most consummate that ever occupied the executive seat of the nation. His profession of pure politics is false, his boasted moral courage the bluff of a bully, and his "square deal" a delusion and a sham.

Theodore Roosevelt is mainly for Theodore Roosevelt and incidentally for such others as are also for the same distinguished gentleman—first, last, and all the time. He is a smooth and slippery politician, swollen purple with self-conceit; he is shrewd enough to gauge the stupidity of the masses and unscrupulous enough to turn it into hero worship. This constitutes the demagogue, and he is that in superlative degree.

Only a few days ago he appeared in a characteristic role. Rushing into the limelight, as necessary to him as breath, he shrieked that he and "Root,"[23] were "horrified" because of certain scandalous and revolting charges made by one of his own former political chums. Of course, he and "Root," of Tweed fame,[24] the foxiest "fixer" of them all, were "horrified" because of the shock to their political virtue, but it so happened that the horror took effect only when they found themselves uncovered. The taking of Harriman's[25] boodle for corruptly electing him president and the use of the stolen insurance funds for the same criminal purpose did not "horrify" the president and "Root," nor would they be "horrified" yet if they had not been caught red-handed in the act with the booty upon their persons.

The cry of the exposed malefactor and all his pack of yelpers that he is the victim of a "plot" by his own friends and supporters, the very gentlemen (sic.) who furnished him with free special trains, paid his campaign expenses, and in fact bought the presidency for him, is so palpably false as to be absolutely ridiculous and only brings into bolder relief the hypocrisy and fraud it was designed to conceal.

This much is preliminary to the extraordinary official conduct of the president, which has "horrified" not only its victims but millions of others, and now prompts this review and protest.

Something over a year ago, Charles Moyer, William Haywood, and George Pettibone, of Colorado, leading officials of the Western Federation of Miners, were overpowered and kidnapped by a gang of thugs and torn from their families at night by conspiracy of two degenerate governors and another notorious criminal acting for the Mine and Smelter Trust, one of the most stupendous aggregations of force and plunder in all America.

Every decent man and woman was "horrified" by this infamy and the whole working class of the nation cried out against it.

Was Roosevelt also "horrified?"

Yes!

Because the Mine and Smelter Trust had kidnapped three citizens of the republic?

Oh, no!

The three citizens were only working cattle and he never had any other conception of them.

He was "horrified" because the Mine and Smelter Trust, unclean birds that feather their nests, especially in Colorado, with legislatures and United States senatorships, had not killed instead of kidnapped their victims.

Then and there, Theodore Roosevelt disgraced himself and his high office, and his cruel and cowardly act will load his name with odium as long as it is remembered.

The Mine and Smelter Trust had put up the funds and used its vast machinery for Roosevelt, and now Roosevelt must serve it even to the extent of upholding criminals, approving kidnapping, and murdering its helpless victims.

When Roosevelt stepped out of the White House and called Moyer, Haywood, and Pettibone "murderers," men he had never seen and did not know; men who had never been tried, never convicted, and whom every law of the land presumed innocent until proven guilty, he fell a million miles beneath where Lincoln stood, and there he grovels today with his political crimes, one after another, finding him out and pointing at him their accusing fingers.

No president of the United States has ever descended to such depths as has Roosevelt to serve his law-defying and crime-inciting masters. The act is simply scandalous and without a parallel in American history.

What right has Theodore Roosevelt to prejudge American citizens, pronounce their guilt, and hand them over to the hangman? In a pettifogging lawyer, such an act would be infamous; in the president of the nation it becomes monstrous and staggers belief.

All that Roosevelt knows about Moyer, Haywood, and Pettibone he knows from his friends, their kidnappers. The millions of working men and women, embracing practically every labor union in America, count nothing for him. He is not now standing for their votes. He is fulfilling his obligation to the gentlemen (!) who put up the coin that elected him; paying off the mortgage they hold upon his administration.

Theodore Roosevelt is swift to brand other men who even venture to disagree with him as liars. He, according to himself, is immaculate and infallible. The greatest liar is he who sees only liars in others.

When Theodore Roosevelt, president of the United States, denounced Charles Moyer, William Haywood, and George Pettibone as murderers, he uttered a lie as black and damnable, a calumny as foul and atrocious as ever issued from a human throat. The men he thus traduced and vilified, sitting in their prison cells for having dutifully served their fellow workers and having spurned the bribes of their masters, transcend immeasurably the man in the White House, who, with the cruel malevolence of a barbarian, has pronounce their doom.

A thousand times rather would I be one of those men in Ada County jail than Theodore Roosevelt in the White House at Washington.

Had these men accepted, with but a shadow of the eagerness Roosevelt displayed, the debauching funds of the trust pirates, they would not now languish in felons' cells. The same brazen robbers of the people and corrupters of the body politic who put Moyer, Haywood, and Pettibone in jail also put Theodore Roosevelt in the White House. This accounts for his prostituting the high office Lincoln honored and resorting to methods that would shame a Bowery ward-heeler.

Moyer, Haywood, and Pettibone are not murderers; it is a ghastly lie, and I denounce it in the name of law and in the name of justice. I know these men, these sons of toil; I know their hearts, their guileless nature, and their rugged honesty. I love and honor them and shall fight for them while there is breath in my body.

Here and now I challenge Theodore Roosevelt. He is guilty of high crimes and deserves impeachment.

Let him do his worst. I denounce him and defy him.

During my recent visit to Washington I learned from those who know him what they think of Roosevelt. Among newspaper men he is literally despised. Their true feeling is not apparent in what they write, for they know that the slightest offense to the president is *lèse-majesté* and means instantaneous decapitation.

For the second time, Theodore Roosevelt, president of the United States, has now publicly convicted Moyer, Haywood, and Pettibone. He has not pronounced condemnation upon Harry Thaw[26] or any rich man charged with murder. He has, however, made a postmaster of a man at Chicago charged by the *Chicago Tribune* with having shot another man in a midnight brawl over disreputable women, and then used his influence to make the same man mayor of that city.[27]

Moyer, Haywood, and Pettibone, the three workingmen kidnapped by the Mine and Smelter Trust, have now been in jail 14 months; they have not been tried, but twice condemned by President Roosevelt, the last time but a few days ago in connection with Harriman, his former political pal and financial backer. These men are in prison cells, their bodies in manacles and their lips sealed. They cannot speak for themselves. They are voiceless and at the mercy of calumny. No matter how grossly outraged, they must submit.

For a man clothed with the almost absolute power of a president to strike down men gagged and bound, as these men are, he must have an unspeakably brutal and cowardly nature, just such a nature as the governor of an Empire state must have to turn a deaf ear to the agonizing entreaties of a shrieking, shuddering woman and see her dragged into the horrors of electrocution.[28]

The true character of this man is becoming gradually revealed to the American people. He has never been anything but an enemy of working people. His writings, before he became a politician, show how he held them in contempt. When he entered political life he soon learned how to shake hands with a fireman for the camera and have his press agent do the rest, and it was this species of demagoguery, the very basest conceivable, that idolized him with the ignorant mass and gave him the votes of millions he in his heart despised as an inferior race.

In his book *Ranch Life and the Hunting-Trail*, page 10, written long before he entered politics, Roosevelt reveals his opinion of the toilers. After describing cowboys when "drunk on the villainous whiskey of the frontier towns," he closes with the comparison, which needs no comment: "They are much better fellows and pleasanter companions than small farmers or agricultural laborers; nor are the mechanics and workingmen of a great city to be mentioned in the same breath."[29]

The pretended friendship for the great body of workingmen who are not to be compared to drunken cowboys has served its demagogical purpose, but the final chapter is not yet written. There will be an awakening, and every official act of Theodore Roosevelt will be subjected to its searching scrutiny. He has always been on the side of capital wholly, while pretending the impossible feat of serving both capital and labor with equal fidelity, and only the deplorable ignorance of his dupes has applauded him in that hypocritical role.

The anthracite miners, or their children at least, will someday know that it was President Theodore Roosevelt who handed them over to the coal trust with a gold brick for a souvenir, labeled "Arbitration."

Theodore Roosevelt is an aristocrat and an autocrat. His affected democracy is spurious and easily detected. He belongs to the "upper crust" and at the very best he can conceive of the workers as only contented slaves. And no one knows better than he how easily these slaves are duped and how madly they will cheer and follow a cheap and showy "hero."

The simple fact is that Theodore Roosevelt was made president by the industrial captains and the robbers in general of the working class. They picked him for a winner and he has not failed them. Elected by the trusts and surrounded by trust attorneys as cabinet advisers, Roosevelt is essentially the monarch of a trust administration.

If this be denied, Roosevelt is challenged to answer if it was not the railroad trust that furnished him gratuitously with the special trains that bore him in royal splendor over all the railways of the nation. He is challenged to publish the list of contributors to his political sewer funds, amounting to millions of dollars, and freely used to buy the votes that made him president.

Did, or did not, the men known as trust magnates put up this boodle? Boodle drawn from the veins of labor?

Will Mr. Roosevelt deny it?

Did he not know at the time that his man Cortelyou[30] was holding up the trusts for all they would "cough up" for his election?

Will he dare plead ignorance to intelligent persons as to who put up the money that debauched the voters of the nation?

It is true that a spasm of virtuous indignation seized him when he found that the trusts had slipped the lucre into his slush funds when he was not looking, but this was only after he saw the people looking behind the curtain. Then he bounded to the footlights and denounced Alton B. Parker as a liar for charging that the trusts were furnishing the boodle to make him president, but no man not feebleminded was deceived as to who was the liar.

Read the Washington press dispatch in the *Kansas City Journal* of April 4th: "It was declared in banking circles that light could be shed on the question of campaign contributions in 1904 if the books of the National Republican Committee were thrown open."

The books will not be thrown open. Roosevelt will not allow it; he knows they contain the damning evidence of his guilt.

The case is clearly stated in the platform of the Democratic State Convention of Missouri, adopted in 1906, which reads as follows:

> We believe Theodore Roosevelt insincere. Pretending to inveigh against the crimes of trusts and corporations, he openly defended Paul Morton when, as manager of the Santa Fe Railroad, he was compelled to confess enormous rebates to the Colorado Fuel and Iron Company. It was Roosevelt who advanced the pernicious doctrine that you must punish the corporation, not its officials who cause it to commit crime. It was Roosevelt who denounced large campaign contributions, while his secretary of commerce and labor was fleecing the corporations out of one of the biggest slush funds ever known in the history of American politics.

President Roosevelt may shout "liar" until he turns as black in the face as are the cracksmen at heart who burglarized the safes of the New York insurance companies to land him in the White House, while he was toying with the names of "Jimmy" Hyde[31] and Chauncey Depew as pawns in the corrupt game, but the "damned spot" will not out until the whole truth is known and the whole crime expiated.

The publication of the Roosevelt-Harriman correspondence places the president in his true colors before the American people. It explains his hot haste in condemning Moyer, Haywood, and Pettibone to the gallows and sending Taft to Idaho to assure the smelter trust and warn the protesting people that the kidnapping of the workingmen had the sanction of the White House and would have the support of the national administration.

A more shameful perversion of public power never blackened the pages of history.

This national scandal shows up the president's two-faced character so clearly and convincingly that it leaves not so much as a pinhole for escape. It is a damning indictment of not only the president, but the whole brood of plutocrats, promoters, and grafting politicians who have been looting this nation for years.

There is one among these illuminating epistles which I want to burn into the minds of the working class dupes who have been bowing in the dust before this blustering bully of the White House:

Personal. October 1, 1904.

My Dear Mr. Harriman:—

A suggestion had come to me in a roundabout way that you do not think it wise to come to see me in the closing weeks of the campaign, but that you are reluctant to refuse, inasmuch as I have asked you. Now, my dear sir, you and I are practical men, and you are on the ground and know the condition better than I do.

If you think there is any danger of your visit to me causing trouble, or if you think there is nothing special I should be informed about, or any matter in which I could give aid, why, of course, give up the visit for the time being, and then, a few weeks hence, before I write my message,[32] I shall get you to come down to discuss certain government matters not connected with the campaign. With great regards,

Sincerely yours,
Theodore Roosevelt

Does not this brand the president with the duplicity of a Tweed and the cunning of a Quay[33]? Would a president who is honest with the people clandestinely consort with the villain he characterizes as a liar and all that is vicious?

The disclosures made in the secret correspondence strip the president of the last shred of deception with which to cloak his perfidy. The mask is lifted and the exposure is complete. It is in the president's own handwriting in a letter to Harriman that would never have seen the light in a thousand years had not circumstances forced it upon the attention of a betrayed people. It is adroitly phrased, but its meaning is not in doubt. He knew Harriman then as he knows him now; wanted his boodle and insinuatingly coaxed him to sneak to the White House when no one was looking, and only after he was discovered did he denounce Harriman as a liar and fall into his usual fit of moral epilepsy.

From now on there will be a sharp decline in the stock of Theodore Roosevelt. The capitalist papers may continue to boom him as the only savior, and his corps of press agents at the White House may continue to grind out three-column stories about the awful conspiracy of his "trusty" friends to ruin him, but his bubble is pricked and the cheap glory in which he reveled is departing forever.

The people have been sadly deceived for a time, but the march of events is opening their eyes. Only the very ignorant or the very foolish believe that a president who has surrounded himself with Wall Street pets as cabinet ministers has any serious designs on the trusts.

The Roosevelt, Ryan, and Root combination is ideal. It speaks for itself, and with such shining lights as Taft, Cortelyou, Knox, and Paul Morton surrounding it, all lingering doubt is removed and the fools' paradise is in the full blaze of its glory.

Space will not permit a review of the personnel of the president's official family, at least two of whom, had the law been enforced, would not be in penitentiary.

The story of President Roosevelt and Paul Morton, if truthfully told, would make a luminous chapter in the story of railroad rascality and political jobbery. It was to this notorious strikebreaker and self-confessed criminal that Roosevelt issued a bill of moral rectitude as long as the Pope's essay that landed him into the $80,000 a year insurance graft he now holds down. There is in this "promotion" the very climax of the irony of "boodle."

Paul Morton, who began as a strikebreaker on the CB&Q road and reared a monument to theft at Hutchinson, Kansas, and left his trail of crime all the way from the Mississippi to the Pacific, is fit, indeed, to be the cabinet associate and confidential chum of a president who puts him at the head of the company whose funds were stolen to buy his election.

William H. Taft is another of the elect, and it is easy to understand why Roosevelt has decided to make this illustrious son his successor as president of the United States and is now grooming him with the patronage of the federal administration. Taft is a man after Roosevelt's own heart. Among his early acts as a judge, he fined the bricklayers of Cincinnati $2,000 for going on a strike; he was next whirled to Toledo by special train and ordered by the Toledo, Ann Arbor & North Michigan Railroad to issue an injunction binding and gagging its striking engineers and firemen and locking their leader up in jail, and he complied with alacrity. From that time on it has been smooth sailing for the accommodating judge, and there is not a plutocrat in the country who would not hail with joy the election of William Taft as president—he would be almost as acceptable as Roosevelt himself.

The manner in which President Roosevelt manipulates the Supreme Court by bestowing lucrative offices upon the sons and other relatives and friends of its dignitaries can only be hinted at here, but will receive due attention later on. The case of ex-Senator J. R. Burton of Kansas is an example of Rooseveltian tactics. Other senators had taken thousands in similar cases to Burton's paltry few hundred dollars, but Burton was marked by Roosevelt for refusing to crook the knee to the sugar trust and pursued with merciless ferocity until he was lodged behind prison bars. The president did not have a call to "go after" his old friends, Chauncey Depew and Thomas Platt, with the same virtuous passion to see crime punished and criminals jailed.

When Roosevelt was making his continental campaign in the palatial special trains furnished free by the railroads, he stopped at Abilene, Kansas, the home of the then Senator Burton, and opened his speech there in these words:

> I am glad to be at the home of the senior senator from Kansas and am delighted to meet and greet his neighbors and friends. I want to say that no man in this world has done more, and I had almost said, as much, to place me where I am now, than your distinguished senator.

Fine way the president had of expressing his gratitude. Burton should have known better and taken warning. Whenever Roosevelt gets that close to a man, something is going to happen. "My dear" is then to be metamorphosed with startling suddenness into an "atrocious liar."

Roosevelt can brook no rivalry. He is the self-appointed central luminary in the solar system. All others must be contented with being fireflies. He must violate all traditions and smash all precedents. He is spectacular beyond the wildest dreams. He must have the center of the stage and hold the undivided attention of the audience. Any stunt will do when the interest lags. A familiar turn with a prizefighter or a "gunman" is always good for an encore. Nothing is overlooked. A dash to Panama with a fleet of battleships and a battery of cameras and a squad of artists and reporters is good for thousands of columns about the marvelous virility and fertility of the greatest president since Washington. He is followed in minute detail as he darts from the cellar to the roof, wears a solemn expression, throws a shovelful of coal into a furnace, snatches a bite from a workman's pail, shakes hands with a section man, and is off like a flash to look after some other section of the planet, that it may not drop out of its orbit.

Mighty savior of the human race!

Such is Theodore Roosevelt, the president who condemns workingmen as murderers when they are objectionable to the trusts that control his administration.

Archbishop Ireland, the plutocratic prelate, will cheerfully certify Roosevelt as the anointed of the Lord. And this will make another interesting chapter for a later review; a chapter that will deal with Ireland as the political as well as spiritual advisor of "Jim" Hill and the Great Northern, and of court decisions awarding him thousands of acres of land and making of the alleged follower of the Tramp of Galilee a multimillionaire; a chapter that will tell of a high priest sounding the political keynote to his benighted followers in exchange for a promised voucher for a red hat to be worn in a land of freedom in which the state and church are absolutely divorced.

Only a few of the facts about Roosevelt and his regime have been here stated, but enough to satisfy all honest men that *Theodore Roosevelt is the Friend of the Enemies and the Enemy of the Friends of this Republic.*

Calumny and Mendacity: Telegraphic Letter to the *St. Louis Post-Dispatch*†

April 24, 1907

Girard, Kansas, April 24 [1907]

To the Editor of the *Post-Dispatch*:—

After many days President Roosevelt concluded to revise his publicly announced determination to treat the communications of organized labor with silent contempt. He changed his mind only when he saw the representatives of the working class preparing to move on the White House. In the voluble and vague explanation just issued, the president is guilty of a most extraordinary lapse of memory or a deliberate falsehood. In defense of his unenviable position he now claims that he never said anything concerning the guilt of Moyer and Haywood. I answer by quoting the exact words he used in his speech on the occasion of the laying of the cornerstone of the office building of the House of Representatives, April 14, 1906, as follows:

> The wealthy man who exults because there is a failure of justice in the effort to bring some trust magnate to an account for his misdeeds is just as bad and no worse than the so-called labor leader who clamorously strives to excite a foul class feeling on behalf of some other labor leader who is implicated in murder.

Moyer and Haywood had been arrested and I had made what was called a sensational appeal on their behalf but a short time before this speech was delivered.[34] Roosevelt's words were clearly meant for Moyer, Haywood, and myself. They could by no possibility apply to anyone else. The press so understood it, and the whole country knew who it was that the president was condemning. There was not the least room for doubt.

Upon reading this extraordinary speech in the public press I at once wrote an open letter to the president protesting against his condemnation of untried men, which he ignored.[35] Fred D. Warren, editor of the *Appeal to Reason*,

† Published as "Roosevelt's Memory at Fault or He Prevaricates, Debs Says" in *St. Louis Post-Dispatch*, vol. 59, no. 247 (April 25, 1907), 13. Published simultaneously as "Debs Challenges Roosevelt to Say Whom He Did Mean" in *New York World*, April 25, 1907.

wrote to the White House at the time, refusing to believe that the president was correctly quoted in his reference to Moyer, Haywood, and Pettibone as being guilty of complicity in murder, and the answer of Secretary Loeb[36] admitting that the president had been correctly quoted is now before me.

The president made no attempt to shift his position at that time. He had denounced these labor leaders as murderers and proposed to stand by it. That was his attitude a year ago. There is not a shadow of a doubt in regard to it.

Bear in mind that the president did not say that Moyer and Haywood were alleged to be implicated in murder, but he made the charge direct and emphatic that they were so implicated, thus pronouncing their guilt in unmistakable words.

I now challenge President Roosevelt to deny that he meant Moyer and Haywood in this charge of murder a year ago. If he did not mean them, whom did he mean? If he did not mean them, why did he not deny it at the time?

I challenge President Roosevelt to name any persons, except Moyer, Haywood, and myself, to whom his words could by any stretch of possibility apply. If he will name them, I agree to tender him a public apology. If he will not name them he must stand branded from his own mouth with calumny and mendacity.

A year ago it was that President Roosevelt charged Moyer and Haywood with murder, in a public speech that went broadcast to the country. He now claims never to have said anything concerning their guilt. He thus stands pilloried before the American people. If he attempts to deny the charge, I shall convict him with the proof.

As between himself and those of us he has denounced as "undesirable citizens," the people shall decide when they have heard both sides.

The reference of President Roosevelt to debauched legislatures comes with poor grace from a president who is cheek by jowl with the mine and smelter owners of Colorado, who have repeatedly bought the legislature of that state and have now seated their chief as a representative in the Senate of the United States.

In the nearly twelve hundred words of his reply, President Roosevelt found no room for even a hint as to what he thought of the kidnapping of working men at midnight and rushing them by special train into another state. That, being the work of "desirable" citizens, has, doubtless, the hearty sanction of the alleged square-deal president.

The "explanation" of President Roosevelt is the first decisive victory for organized labor in the kidnapping battle of the class war of the United States.

Eugene V. Debs

A Short History of the *Appeal to Reason*†

April 27, 1907

We hold in our hands a bound file of *The Coming Nation* for the year 1893–94. The first number is dated April 29, 1893. This was the birth of *The Coming Nation* and Greensburg, Decatur County, Indiana, was the town in which it first saw the light.

J. A. Wayland, now of the *Appeal to Reason*, was the founder, editor, and publisher of *The Coming Nation*, and this child of his heart and brain was born to a tempestuous career.

This was the first venture of the "One-Hoss" Philosopher[37] to spread the new gospel that had struck root and was seething in his soul. Little did he realize what he was undertaking, nor what vicissitudes lay in wait for him, but if he had, it would not have daunted him, for with the revolution of ideas that had come to him there had also come to him the spirit of determination to go forth and do battle for them with all his might without regard to personal consequences.

This spirit has ever since been his guide and marked his course, and were it not for his characteristic modesty, his utter aversion to personal notoriety, and his abhorrence of obtruding his personality upon the propaganda, some very interesting facts relating to this anniversary might be here written down, but as it is, the friends and readers of the *Appeal*, the many thousands who have followed its career through tempest and sunshine, over the hilltops and down through the valleys, must wait until the "One-Hoss" Philosopher moves on and beyond this scene of strife to read the real story of his struggle, his services, and his achievements, and when this is written it will have a permanent place in the new thought library as one of the most interesting, vital, and dramatic biographies in socialist literature.

Curiously enough, Davis H. Waite,[38] the grand old warrior of Colorado—as grand a man, in the governor's chair or in his private walks, as his successors have been degenerate—was the very first subscriber of *The Coming Nation*, and his name heads the list of 98 original subscribers with which the paper began

† Published as "Fourteenth Anniversary of the Birth of *The Coming Nation* at Greensburg, Decatur County, Indiana, April 1893" in *Appeal to Reason*, whole no. 595 (April 27, 1907), 1. Reprinted as a leaflet.

and whose names are printed in the initial issue. Other names in the list are Eugene Engley,[39] B. Hirsch, and others who have made honorable history in the struggle since that time. To show that even then the new thought was fairly clear, though hazily expressed, we quote the following paragraphs from the first issue:

> If all labor was directed into proper channels, all the wealth now produced could be created in three hours a day, giving work to all and an equitable division of the products. * * *
>
> The trusts and combines are dividing up the millions of wealth they have taken from the producers under the system of capitalism. * * *
>
> The millionaire today lives in a palace, surrounded by menials, and the people who feed, clothe, and supply his wants live in tenements and cellars. Read up, see the truth, and you will be free. * * *
>
> Man plows and produces for idlers—monkeys don't. * * *
>
> In this country the working people have the suffrage which they use to furnish the rich the laws, officers, and courts to keep them in servitude.

Soon after the first issue appeared, the subscriptions began to roll in by scores and hundreds, showing that the people were ready for the new economic and social doctrine which since has spread so rapidly over the civilized globe. The name of *The Coming Nation* was soon spread broadcast, and its enthusiastic devotees vied with each other in giving it the full measure of their unwavering and unwearying support.

Then followed the exodus from Greensburg, Indiana to Ruskin, Tennessee, where the Ruskin colony was established.[40] In bidding farewell to the old Hoosier state, the cradle of its birth, *The Coming Nation* was not without regrets, but the future seemed to loom so brightly on the horizon that all misgivings were dismissed, and with joyous hearts the modern crusaders, for such they were in spirit and in purpose, set their faces toward the Sunny South, the land of cane and cotton, of magnolias, mockingbirds, and dreams.

Alas! The glimpses of Utopia were fleeting as they were fascinating. This vision of a beauty spot in the primeval forests, like a mirage that lures to deceive, had to be dispelled. The colonists, animated by the purest of motives, had to learn by bitter experience that there is no royal road to the socialist commonwealth; that there is no escape from capitalism for any favored few; that a miniature socialist republic is as impossible as a miniature tidal wave or sunrise, and that instead of attempting the impossible feat of abolishing capitalism by fleeing from it to the wilderness, it was their duty to organize and extend the revolutionary socialist propaganda in its very strongholds, and from its center to its circumference for its complete overthrow and the emancipation of all from its cruel and debasing thralldoms.

The colonists were bought to realize that, after all, it is a fortunate fact in social evolution that the few cannot desert the old ship and paddle away in their little canoes to escape the tempests.[41]

The lesson was dearly bought, but no regrets remain to mar the memories of the voyage to Altruria.[42] Most of those who shared the fortunes and misfortunes of Ruskin life are now active propagandists in the wider field,[43] and if the colony experiment did not more for them, it at least clarified their vision, dispelled their delusions, and opened the way to their proper places in the greater movement.

The Coming Nation was not intended to die with the colony. Its spirit lived and it must have a new incarnation. The trials and privations in the wilderness might sap the physical vitality of the little community, but they could not quench its revolutionary spirit and aspirations. Freedom's battle had begun, the bridges behind were all down, and the only course lay forward.

This indomitable spirit found expression in the *Appeal to Reason* in 1895, first at Kansas City and later at Girard [Kansas], where its sturdy growth and expanding vigor and usefulness have excited the consternation and dismay of capitalist exploiters, and evoked the surprise and delight of the working class.

The trials, the sufferings, the heart-burnings, the disappointments of Wayland, the founder of this great enterprise, need not be recited here. Few, indeed, have heard of them, and not at all, so far as the writer knows, from the lips of the man himself.

It was exceedingly fortunate for J. A. Wayland that Fred D. Warren joined him at what seems to have been a critical and psychological moment in the *Appeal's* career. The *Appeal* had grown too great a burden for its publisher, and as if the very man to bring relief had been in waiting, Warren stepped into the harness, and since that day these men have worked together in such efficient harmony that the spirit of their unity has permeated all the working force, and as a result the *Appeal to Reason* is a monument of cooperative achievement, and promises complete fulfillment of its great mission in the international propaganda of the socialist movement.

Let not the impression be conveyed that the *Appeal* is, or pretends to be, a socialist establishment, or operated upon socialist principles. That, as every socialist knows, would be an impossibility in the existing order. The *Appeal to Reason* is established, maintained, and operated to advance the interests of the socialist movement, and this it does by methods its own experience has taught it to be most efficient and practicable in that great work.

From the 98 subscribers with which *The Coming Nation* began, the *Appeal to Reason* has built its pyramid of over 300,000 supporters, and there never was a time in the 14 years since the paper was born when the interest in it was as keen, the activity as great, and the support as unwavering as it is today.

The *Appeal* has set its mark at *one million subscribers* in the next three years, and those who know the men and women who are committed to that proposition do not in the least doubt its literal realization.

The *Appeal* has undertaken to secure more subscribers, that is to say, develop more power for the propaganda, two to one, in the next three years than it has in the last 14 years.

This means nerve and will, energy and execution, and the *Appeal* has them all. The "Old Guard" at Girard and the Army of Veterans[44] spread all over the land are all keeping step to the heartthrobs of the revolution, whose spirit flashes from their eyes and vanquishes obstacles to victory as the rising sun disperses the mists of the morning.

But little has been said in this rapid sketch of the personal life of its central character. For obvious reasons no panegyric has been here attempted. Socialists are not given to fulsome adulation, no matter how meritorious the services rendered. They hold that a socialist does his duty merely when he serves the cause, and that no special need of praise is due on that account.

Nevertheless, a few words from one who has known Wayland long and under varying circumstances will hardly seem amiss on this anniversary occasion, so fruitful of reminiscences of other days, especially in the light of the many wrongs he has suffered at the hands of men who do not know him, or, knowing him, have done him great injustice.

It is true that he has been financially successful in spite of all his costly experiences and narrow escapes from disaster. He has always known how to make money, but has hated and denounced the methods of its making in the capitalist system. Had these methods been unobjectionable and he had remained in the commercial game, he would today be a millionaire. He has yielded to the rule and sway of exploitation from necessity, while fighting the system with all the proceeds it has brought him.

Unlike many scores of others, he has not considered it wise policy nor sound tactics to be conscientiously starved into submission, frozen out of the movement, or driven into apostasy, and the future surely will vindicate his course.

All money is tainted in capitalism, one dollar as much as another, for in the last analysis it is all wrung from labor, and the founder of the *Appeal to Reason* believes it better to make money, contaminated though it be, and plenty of it, if possible, and fight capitalism with it than to let the capitalists capture all the dollars and use them to keep the workers in ignorance and perpetuate their brutal domination over the working class.

J. A. Wayland has to his credit 14 years of service in the socialist cause, the value of which will be known only after "One-Hoss" has ceased to feel the shafts of personal detraction; long after he has fallen into his last sleep and rests in the shade and fragrance of the flowers.[45]

He is human, Wayland is, intensely so. He has made mistakes, many of them, and no one has acknowledged them more freely than himself, but his whole heart is in the cause; every selfish thought is subordinated to the good of the movement, and when its victory has been at last achieved and its history fairly written, J. A. Wayland's name will appear in immortal letters upon its pages.

The Crimson Standard[†]

April 27, 1907

A vast amount of ignorant prejudice prevails against the red flag. It is easily accounted for. The ruling class the wide world over hates it, and its sycophants, therefore, must decry it.

Strange that the red flag should produce the same effect upon a tyrant that it does upon a bull.

The bull is enraged at the very sight of the red flag, his huge frame quivers, his eyes become balls of fire, and he paws the dirt and snorts with fury.

The reason of this peculiar effect of a bit of red coloring upon the bovine species we are not particularly interested in at this moment, but why does it happen to excite the same rage in the tsar, the emperor, and the king; the autocrat, the aristocrat, and the plutocrat?

† Published unsigned as "The Red Flag" in *Appeal to Reason*, whole no. 595 (April 27, 1907), 1. Reprinted with minor amendment as "The Crimson Standard" in *Debs: His Life, Writings, and Speeches* (Girard, KS: Appeal to Reason, 1908), 245–6.

Ah, that is simple enough.

The red flag, since time immemorial, has symbolized the dis- content of the downtrodden, the revolt of the rabble.

That is its sinister significance to the tyrant and the reason of his mingled fear and frenzy when the "red rag," as he characterizes it, insults his vision.

It is not that he is opposed to red as a color, or even as an emblem, for he has it in his own flags and banners, and it never inflames his passion when it is blended with other colors; but red alone, unmixed and unadulterated, the pure red that symbolizes the common blood of the human family, the equality of mankind, the brotherhood of the race, is repulsive and abhorrent to him because it is at once an impeachment of his title, a denial of his superiority, and a menace to his power.

Precisely for the reason that the plutocrat raves at the red flag, the proletarian should revere it.

To the plutocrat it is a peril; to the proletarian a promise.

The red flag is an omen of ill, a sign of terror to every tyrant, every robber, and every vampire that sucks the life of labor and mocks at its misery.

It is an emblem of hope, a bow of promise to all the oppressed and downtrodden of the earth.

The red flag is the only race flag; it is the flag of revolt against robbery; the flag of the working class, the flag of hope and high resolve—the flag of Universal Freedom.

Revolution: Written for May Day 1907†

April 27, 1907

This is the first and only International Labor Day. It belongs to the working class and is dedicated to the Revolution.

† Published as "Revolution" in *The Worker*, vol. 17, no. 4 (April 27, 1907), 4. Reprinted in two parts as "Revolution" and "Vive la Revolution!" in *Debs: His Life, Writings, and Speeches* (Girard, KS: Appeal to Reason, 1908), 305–7.

Today the slaves of all the world are taking a fresh breath in the long and weary march; pausing a moment to clear their lungs and shout for joy; celebrating in festal fellowship their coming freedom.

All hail the Labor Day of May!

The day of the proletarian protest;

The day of stern resolve;

The day of noble aspiration.

Raise high this day the blood-red standard of the Revolution!

The banner of the workingman;

The flag, the only flag, of Freedom.

ᔕ

Slavery, even the most abject—dumb and despairing as it may seem—has yet its inspiration. Crushed it may be, but extinguished never. Chain the slave as you will, O Masters, brutalize him as you may, yet in his soul, though dead, he yearns for freedom still.

ᔕ

The great discovery the modern slaves have made is that they themselves their freedom must achieve. This is the secret of their solidarity; the heart of their hope; the inspiration that nerves them all with sinews of steel.

They are still in bondage, but no longer cower;

No longer grovel in the dust,

But stand erect like men.

Conscious of their growing power the future holds out to them her outstretched hands.

ᔕ

As the slavery of the working class is international, so the movement for its emancipation.

The salutation of slave to slave this day is repeated in every human tongue as it goes ringing round the world.

The many millions are at last awakening. For countless ages they have suffered; drained to the dregs the bitter cup of misery and woe.

At last, at last the historic limitation has been reached, and soon a new sun will light the world.

ᔕ

Red is the life-tide of our common humanity and red our symbol of universal kinship.

Tyrants deny it; fear it; tremble with rage and terror when they behold it.

We reaffirm it and on this day pledge anew our fidelity—come life or death—to the blood-red banner of the Revolution.

ೞ

Socialist greetings this day to all our fellow workers! To the God-like souls in Russia marching grimly, sublimely into the jaws of hell with the song of the revolution in their death-rattle; to the Orient, the Occident, and all the Isles of the Sea!

Viva la Revolution!

ೞ

The most heroic word in all languages is *revolution*.

It thrills and vibrates; cheers and inspires. Tyrants and time-servers fear it, but the oppressed hail it with joy.

The throne trembles when this throbbing word is lisped, but to the hovel it is food for the famishing and hope for the victims of despair.

Let us glorify today the revolutions of the past and hail the greater revolution yet to come before Emancipation shall make all the days of the year May Days of peace and plenty for the sons and daughters of toil.

It was with revolution as his theme that Mark Twain's soul drank deep from the fount of inspiration. His immortality will rest at last upon this royal tribute to the French Revolution:

> The ever-memorable and blessed revolution, which swept a thousand years of such villainy away in one swift tidal-wave of blood—one: a settlement of that hoary debt in the proportion of half a drop of blood for each hogshead of it that had been pressed by slow tortures out of that people in the weary stretch of ten centuries of wrong and shame and misery the like of which was not to be mated but in hell. There were two "Reigns of Terror," if we would but remember it and consider it; the one wrought murder in hot passion, the other in heartless cold blood; the one lasted mere months, the other lasted a thousand years; the one inflicted death on ten thousand persons, the other upon a hundred millions; but our shudders are all for the horrors of the minor Terror, the momentary Terror, so to speak; whereas, what is the horror of swift death by the axe, compared with life-long death from hunger, cold, insult, cruelty, and heartbreak? What is swift death by lightning compared with death by slow fire at the

stake? A city cemetery could contain the coffins filled by that brief Terror, which we have all been so diligently taught to shiver at and mourn over; but all France could hardly contain the coffins filled by that older and real Terror—that unspeakably bitter and awful Terror which none of us has been taught to see in its vastness or pity as it deserves.[46]

I Shall Soon Be Off for Idaho: Letter to Stephen M. Reynolds in Terre Haute[†]

April 27, 1907

Girard, Kansas, April 27, 1907

My dear Stephen:—

I have your very beautiful letter and am moved by what you say, especially touching your dear daughter Jean. What you say of her is of very deep interest to me, for you know I love her almost as you do yourself.[47]

I have but a moment or two to write as I am extremely busy with a great variety of matters on all sides. I shall soon be off for Idaho. Possibly you may join me there. Who knows? I know you will be there in the spirit and so truly that I shall almost feel and see you in the flesh. It is a great comfort to have such a comrade as you, always loyal, always devoted, always sweet, and always wholly forgetful of self. There may be others like you. I do not happen to know them.

When you write to Chicago I wish you always to send my love and good wishes to Mrs. Reynolds and the little folks. I am always

Your loving comrade,
E. V. Debs

† Included in *The Papers of Eugene V. Debs*, microfilm edition, reel 1, frame 512. Not published in Constantine (ed.), *Letters of Eugene V. Debs: Volume 1, 1874–1912.*

"Bat" Masterson a Fiction Writer: Letter to the Editor of the *New York Telegraph*†

circa May 10, 1907

Editor, *Telegraph*
New York

Dear Sir:—

In your issue of the 5th Inst. there appears an article by B. W. B. "Bat" Masterson[48] on Moyer and Haywood, the union officials now being tried in Idaho, which has been widely copied. Let me call your attention to the fact that you failed to label this article fiction. I never read such a tissue of false statements and misinformation, and it seems unbelievable that a great metropolitan daily such as the *Telegraph* would deliberately circulate such rot as sober truth. I shall not ask for space enough to expose all these glaring untruths, but only one or two of them to show the character of the article. I could easily dispose of all the rest in the same way.

The article begins with the Coeur d'Alene riots and says that the careers of Moyer and Haywood begin with these riots.[49] As a matter of fact, neither Moyer nor Haywood was in these riots or had anything to do with them. Neither one of them was near there at the time. Ed Boyce was at that time president, and James Maher secretary, of the Western Federation of Miners. Moyer and Haywood had no official connection with the union, and had never been heard of at that time, nor for many years afterwards.

Next, the article describes the strike in Colorado and the fight on Bull Hill under the administration of Governor Waite[50] and says:

> Moyer and Haywood were the first to make their escape. They ran like scared coyotes at the first crack of a gun and allowed about 20 of their men to be tried and convicted and sent to the penitentiary for long terms without so much as raising their hands to help them.

† Published in *New York Telegraph*, circa May 10, 1907, undetermined page. Reprinted as part of "Debs Arraigns the Editors of the *Times* and the *Telegraph* of New York" in *Miners' Magazine*, May 23, 1907, undetermined page.

This is pure fiction. There is not a word of truth in it. As a matter of fact, Moyer and Haywood were not at Bull Hill, nor had any part in this strike, nor were in the state of Colorado at all at that time, nor for several years afterwards. These facts can be easily verified. As to the Coeur d'Alene statement, call on Governor Gooding of Idaho; and as to the Bull Hill statement, on Governor Buchtel of Colorado. Both are deadly enemies of Moyer and Haywood but they know the facts as I have stated them and as your article has misstated them.

The rest of the article is made up mainly of the same kind of stuff, and it is this that is palmed off on the people as showing the character of Moyer and Haywood. To thus lie about men who are on trial for their lives is in itself a crime that certainly no respectable paper, even the *Telegraph*, should be guilty of.

The capitalist papers are now flooding the country with whole pages of such malicious falsehoods, made to order to influence public sentiment by their hireling scribes. Their purpose is clear. Moyer and Haywood must be hanged because they could not be corrupted to betray and deliver the working class; and, to justify this monstrous crime, the capitalist press engages in the conspiracy to make the American people believe in advance of the trial that they are murderers, and that no mercy must be shown them.

Of course there have been crimes committed in the Rocky Mountains during the past 15 years. No one disputes that. In the war between capital and labor it is only too true that blood has been shed, but the assumption is monstrously false that capital is wholly innocent and that labor is wholly responsible for this bloodshed. I need not say to you that capital rules today and is equal to any crime that may be necessary to perpetuate its sway. You know that. Everybody knows it. Men who will not bow to its imperious rule must be murdered. That fits the Moyer and Haywood case precisely.

Fortunately you can no longer deceive the working class and the people, as you once did by such criminal mendacity. The working class now has a press of its own and this letter will be read by 10 million people whether you publish it or not.

Eugene V. Debs

Monstrous Falsification: Letter to the Editor of the *New York Times*†

May 16, 1907

Girard, Kansas, May 16, 1907

Editor, Times
New York

Dear Sir:—

The *Kansas City Journal* of May 11th and other papers in the West have copied an editorial from a recent issue of your paper entitled "Undesirable Citizens."[51] Allow me to say that this editorial consists of a maze of outright falsehoods, half-truths, and whole perversions of statement. For instance, I quote as follows: "It is the organization which procured the dropping of a cage containing fifteen non-union workmen down a shaft 1400 feet deep, whereby all fifteen died."

It is befitting this falsehood that after stating that the men fell 1400 feet the startling announcement should be made that they died! As a matter of fact, no such thing ever occurred at any time or anywhere. It is a cut-to-order falsehood, a part of the warp and woof of the conspiracy of the capitalist press to blacken the character of honest men who would not betray and deliver their fellow workers and must therefore be put to death. I challenge you to show where and when this alleged calamity which you charge upon the Western Federation of Miners occurred. Read the report of Carroll D. Wright, national labor commissioner, who investigated the affair and you will find the fact you so viciously falsify honestly stated, but you will not find even a hint that the Western Federation of Miners had anything to do with this appalling calamity. It was a mine accident due to capitalist cupidity in not providing proper safety appliances, and no one connected with the affair ever dreamed of charging it to any other cause.

What do you think of a great, powerful metropolitan daily that resorts to such monstrous falsification to prejudice the public mind and send three workingmen without taint of wrong upon them to the gallows?

† Rejected by the *New York Times*, having been received about two weeks after the editorial's publication. Published as part of "Debs Arraigns the Editors of the *Times* and the *Telegraph* of New York" in *Miners' Magazine*, May 23, 1907, undetermined pages.

Quite true it is that in the fearful war between capital and labor in the Rocky Mountains crime has been committed, but our cool assumption that capital is spotless as a saint and that labor is the monster of iniquity will no longer deceive the thinking American people.

Men's lives are hanging in the balance here, and the farmers of Boise valley entertain a proper appreciation of the gravity of the situation. It is almost 18 months since Governor Steunenberg was blown to destruction, and passion and prejudice have been largely supplanted by sober sense and reason.

The one break during an otherwise monotonous week occurred yesterday, when Judge Wood, taking judicial cognizance of the published interviews with Harry Orchard, and some comments by Governor Gooding touching upon Orchard's relations to the state, referred the matter for investigation to Prosecuting Attorney Koelsch. Judge Wood made it plain to the state's attorneys that he would not tolerate any interference, by the governor or anybody else, with the course of the trial, and this position of the court lost none of its effect even though the report of Koelsch filed at adjournment today dismissed the incident with a finding that neither the governor nor the newspaper men was actuated by improper motives in the premises.

While it is early to speculate upon the relative advantages gained by either side, it is accepted that the defense scored a point in bringing to the attention of the entire venire the questionable character of evidence such as Orchard is expected to give. One talisman acknowledged that he would be unable to give credence to anything that Orchard might testify to. Following his declaration, at short intervals, two other prospective jurors expressed themselves in similar terms. The state's attorneys were visibly disturbed at the turn, and the fact that they have had continual encounters with jurymen who advance conscientious scruples against accepting circumstantial evidence in capital cases adds to their annoyance.

There was a time when your capitalist press had the power to send honest men to the gallows whose only crime was their refusal to stain their souls in the service of Mammon, but that power is broken forever. You remember John Swinton.[52] He once did honorable service on the *Times*. I had the honor to count this grand man as my personal friend to the day of his death. It was he who coined the phrase, "The Satanic Press." He knew the press as few others did and he told the truth about it as no other could.

Just at this time the capitalist press is flooding the country with pages of illustrated calumnies upon Moyer and Haywood to poison the public mind against these men that they may be sent to the gallows as felons to expiate the crime of having been true to their fellow workers and having spurned with contempt the bribes of corporate power.

The mine and smelter trust, the lumber trust that has been stealing the timber lands of the western states, and other thieving combinations, backed by the Standard Oil Company, have complete sway in Idaho and Colorado except for the Western Federation of Miners, and being unable to corrupt its leaders, as it has done the politicians of both parties, it kidnaps them and decrees that they shall pay the penalty with their lives. That is the program and every honest man who knows the facts is up in arms against it and if it should be carried to a successful issue and these workingmen "never leave Idaho alive," as Governor Gooding, the degenerate tool of the Mine Owners' Association and the lumber trust, has declared, it will be the saddest day that ever dawned for the capitalist class of the United States.

Eugene V. Debs

Roosevelt's Labor Letters†

May 18, 1907

The letter of President Roosevelt to the Moyer and Haywood conference of New York is in strange contrast with the one previously addressed by him to the Chicago conference on the same subject. The two letters are so entirely dissimilar in spirit and temper that they seem to have been written by different persons. In the first the president bristles with defiance, in the last he is the pink of politeness. The first letter utterly failed of its purpose.[53] Organized labor did not lie down and be still at the command of the president. On the contrary, it growled more fiercely than before; in fact, showed its teeth of the president who has become so used to exhibiting his own. And lo—what a change! The president receives a labor committee, talks over matters for an hour, and then addresses a letter to the conference through the chairman, beginning "My Dear Mr. Henry," explaining that he is ready to perform his duty if only the conference will point it out to him, and putting the whole blame on "Debs and the

---

† Published in *Appeal to Reason*, whole no. 598 (May 18, 1907), 4.

socialists," whom he charges with using "treasonous and murderous language," but not a word of explanation does he vouchsafe in regard to his denunciation of Moyer and Haywood, the real and in fact the only point at issue.[54]

Again has the president vindicated his reputation as one of the smoothest of politicians and one of the most artful and designing of demagogues.

We hope the lesson here taught as to what workingmen can accomplish by the power of united effort is not lost upon the working class. The first letter of the president was an insult to labor and had labor submitted, the president's contempt for it would have been intensified by its cravenness.

The second letter was a virtual apology and nothing less than the firm attitude of labor extorted it.

The president's position, however, is not less enviable than before. Since he seeks escape from castigation for his outrageous attack upon Moyer and Haywood upon the ground that Debs had used "treasonable and murderous language" and that it was his duty as president to denounce it, a few questions will be in order, and when the president has answered these we have a few more to which answers are also desired.

Did the president ever hear of one Sherman Bell?[55]

Is it not a fact that said Sherman Bell is a personal friend of the president and that in a letter written in the president's own hand he commends said Sherman Bell in the most exalted terms?

Has the president ever heard of the expression, "To hell with habeas corpus; we'll give 'em post mortems," commended as "patriotic" by the capitalist press at the time it was made?

Does not the president know that it was his highly esteemed personal friend, Sherman Bell, who coined this phrase?

Is it "treasonable and murderous"?

Did the president condemn it?

Will he do so now?

Would he have done so if it had been Debs instead of Bell?

Why does he "conceive it to be his duty" to condemn Debs and not Bell?

Because Bell stands for capital and Debs for labor?

Has Debs ever said anything that, with reference to treason and murder, can be compared to this expression of his boon companion, Sherman Bell?

Will the president please answer?

Again, has the president ever heard of one Lieut. T. E. McClelland?

And of the expression, "To hell with the constitution," made by said McClelland?

Is this treasonable language?

Did the president condemn it?

Or is it patriotic language when used in defense of capital and treasonable only when used in defense of labor?

Does the president know one Adjutant General Bulkley Wells,[56] the "officer of the law" who forcibly seized Moyer, Haywood, and Pettibone and "special-trained" them to Idaho?

Does he know that his labor commissioner, Carroll D. Wright, condemns said Bulkley Wells as a "mob leader" in his official report of the Colorado troubles?

Does the president approve of mobs?

And consort with mob leaders?

While denouncing mobs?

Has he denounced Bulkley Wells?

Will he do so?

Is the president aware that the Mine and Smelter Trust behind the persecution of Moyer, Haywood, and Pettibone bought the legislature of Colorado outright, thereby defeating an eight-hour measure which a popular majority of more than 46,000 votes had commanded said legislature to enact into law?

And that those mine and smelter owners are among his personal friends?

Is there any treason in this?

Has the president condemned it?

Dare he do so?

Is this his idea of "exact justice?"

A "square deal?"

Again, is kidnapping according to "law and order?"

If the kidnapped are workingmen?

And charged with their kidnappers with being murderers?

And by the president as "undesirable citizens?"

Would the president have taken the same view if workingmen had kidnapped capitalists instead of capitalists kidnapping workingmen?

If it had been Ryan, Root, and Paul Morton, instead of Moyer, Haywood, and Pettibone?

Will the president kindly answer?

Has the president ever heard the expression, "they shall never leave Idaho alive?"

Is this "murderous" language?

Except when used by "officers of the law?"

Has the president condemned it?

Does he approve it?

Has the president heard of one W. E. Borah, senator-elect, indicted for theft?

Visiting at the White House and coming out "smiling and confident"?

Is he innocent and desirable in spite of his indictment and Haywood guilty and undesirable in spite of the lawful presumption to the contrary?

Has the president ever heard of one Theodore Roosevelt?

Charged by the *New York Tribune* and other leading capitalist papers in 1896 with threatening to lead an armed force to Washington to prevent the inauguration of a lawfully elected president of the United States?

Is there any "treason" or "murder" in this?

Does the president remember one John Altgeld?

And one Theodore Roosevelt who in the same year of 1896 said that said Altgeld and one Debs should be lined up against a dead wall and shot?

Which said Roosevelt never denied until four years later when he became candidate for vice-president?

Is this the "temperate" language of a perfectly "desirable" citizen?

Does the president remember one Governor Roosevelt, of New York, who ordered his militia to Croton Dam to shoot some of the workingmen who elected him for venturing to ask the enforcement of the eight-hour law of the state?

And to protect the contractors who were violating the law?

Is this more of the president's "exact justice for all"?

Will the president kindly explain what he regards as inexact justice?

Or exact injustice?

Or injustice of any kind?

Or if his "exact justice for all" is not buncombe served in stilted style?

Can the president say or do anything wrong?

Would he admit it if he did?

Has he ever done so?

When the president rebuked the labor unions for attempting to "influence the course of justice," did he not know it was violent kidnapping they were protesting against?

That they were seeking to influence the course, not of justice, but of injustice?

Resisting, not law, but mob violence cloaked as law?

At the time the president administered this rebuke had he not himself read his letter condemning Moyer and Haywood to members of the Supreme Court when their case was pending in said court?

Was this not an attempt to "influence the course of justice"?

Will the president publicly rebuke it?

When Moyer, Haywood, and Pettibone, three workingmen, rugged as Patrick Henry, honest as Abraham Lincoln, and brave as John Brown, were brutally kidnapped and told that they would be killed by the outlaws who kidnapped them; when two conspiring governors were the instigators of the kidnapping and all legal rights denied; when the special train lay in wait to rush them to their doom while their wives listened in vain all night long for their returning footsteps; when all law was cloven down, all justice denied, all decency defied, and all humanity trampled beneath the brutal hooves of might, a monstrous crime was committed, not against Moyer, Haywood, and Pettibone merely, but against the working class, against the human race, and, by the eternal, that crime, even by the grace of Theodore Roosevelt, shall not go unwhipped of justice.

"Undesirable citizens" they are to the Christless perverts who exploit labor to degeneracy and mock its misery; turn the cradle into a coffin and call it philanthropy, and debauch the nation's politics and morals in the name of civilization.

"Undesirable citizens" though they are, these are the loyal leaders of the men who have toiled in the mines and who have been subjected to every conceivable outrage; "who have had their homes broken into and who have been beaten, bound, robbed, insulted, and imprisoned;" who have been chained to posts in the public highway, deported from their families under penalty of death, and bullpenned while their wives and daughters were outraged. In the light of all these crimes perpetrated upon these men in violation of every law by brutal mobs led by the president's own personal friends, as the official reports of his own labor commissioner will show, without a word of protest from him, it requires sublime audacity, to put it mildly, for the president to affirm that he stands for "exact justice to all" and that he "conceives it to be his duty" to denounce "treasonable and murderous language."

If the miners of Colorado had been less patient than beasts of burden, they would have risen in revolt against the outrages perpetrated upon them by their heartless corporate masters.

Were a mob of workingmen to seize Theodore Roosevelt and chain him to a post on a public street in Washington in broad daylight, as a mob of his capitalist friends seized and chained a workingman in Colorado; or throw him into a foul bullpen, without cause or provocation, prod him with bayonets, and outrage his defenseless family while he was a prisoner, as was done in scores of well-authenticated cases in both Colorado and Idaho, would he then be in the mood to listen complacently to hypocritical homilies upon the "temperate" use of language, the sanctity of "law and order," and the beauty of "exact justice for all?"

And if he heard of some man who had sufficient decency to denounce the outrages he and his family had suffered, would he then "conceive it to be his duty," as he tells us, to condemn the language of such a man as "treasonable and murderous" and the man himself as "inciting bloodshed" and therefore an "undesirable citizen?"

The Coming Climax in the Irrepressible Struggle for Emancipation[†]

May 18, 1907

There's a divinity that shapes our ends, rough hew them how we will.

—**Shakespeare,** *The Tragedy of Hamlet, Prince of Denmark*

The prosecution in the pending trial is doing its utmost to have it appear that it is simply the trial of three men charged with killing another—an ordinary case of murder. It insists that there is no other issue involved, and flouts the idea that the case has anything to do with the struggle between labor and capital.

The capitalist press has uniformly taken the same position, declaring that an "atrocious murder" has been committed and that no question of a class struggle should be raised in connection with the prosecution of those charged with the crime.

How many people seriously believe that Moyer, Haywood, and Pettibone would be on trial today if they had not been leaders of labor in battles between labor and capital in the Rocky Mountains during the last 15 years?

Ignorance or Design?

How many believe that there would be any such trial at all but for this war of the classes?

† Published in *Appeal to Reason*, whole no. 598 (May 18, 1907), 1.

To speak of the trial, therefore, as an "ordinary murder case" betrays either deplorable ignorance or sinister design.

What is the object of this extreme concern in having a case that has aroused the whole nation and achieved international notoriety regarded as a "simple murder trial"? The answer is ready. The prosecution and the capitalist "interests" behind it fear that the working class, the "dumb-driven cattle,"[57] may comprehend its true significance and awaken to their economic class interests, and this would mean the speedy end of capitalist exploitation and wage-slavery.

Capitalist class rule is based upon working class fools. Ignorance is the title deed of the capitalist to his wage-slaves.

Hence the prosecution in this case with the aid and collusion of the capitalist newspapers and magazines must allay any suspicion of the working class that its loyal leaders are to be put to death for faithfully serving it, but that instead they are common criminals, guilty of ordinary murder, and that the wage-slaves will be all the better off for being rid of such vicious reprobates.

"Law and Order"

But fortunately this is not their first experience with corporate capital in the virtuous role of "punishing crime for the protection of society." A few of them have observed that the so-called criminal is always a workingman and that the self-appointed guardians of society are themselves the plotters of crime and the enemies of the people. They have observed, moreover, that it is the very ones who declaim so unceasingly about "law and order" who are themselves the corrupters of the nation's morals, the buyers of its legislatures, the polluters of its courts, the defilers of its electorate, the stealers of its public domain, and the heartless vampires that suck the lifeblood of the people.

A few of them having made these observations are now seeking to impress them upon the whole working class, and it has been the agitation incident to this process that has invested the Moyer-Haywood-Pettibone prosecution with worldwide interest in spite of the persistent contention of the capitalist press that it is "only a case of ordinary murder."

In the course of history and the sweep of events, great crises develop on the eve of great social changes and in every such crisis great characters, born of the revolution and expressing its spirit, appear upon the stage of action, take the heroic parts assigned to them, and write their names in imperishable deeds in the history of humanity.

Such men are Haywood, Moyer, and Pettibone.

In the impending industrial crisis these men, developed in the travail of society, have been called to play important parts.

Patrick Henry, Sam Adams, and John Hancock served in similar roles a century and a half ago and Elijah Lovejoy, Wendell Phillips, and John Brown a century later. These men were all loathed, hated, denounced, and persecuted in the name of "law and order" and "the peace of society," of which they were supposed to be the relentless enemies.

Haywood and Moyer and Pettibone are not more reviled today than were their revolutionary and anti-slavery prototypes of the last two centuries.

Patrick Henry was denounced by King George[58] and William Haywood by President Theodore. Both Henry and Haywood incarnated the subject class, exposed its cause, voiced its protest, and defied the ruling class, and this has always been denounced as "treason," and never more fiercely than today.

But Haywood is charged with murder. So was John Brown; and he never denied it. John Brown was the sworn enemy of the slaveholders. He spat upon their "morals" and held their laws in contempt. He not only advocated violence and incited bloodshed, but led in both, and yet many of the best men and women living today regard this "monster of depravity" as the greatest man, the loftiest soul, the sublimest hero that ever walked the earth.

At Harper's Ferry

Think of John Brown in the engine house at Harper's Ferry, his cocked rifle in one hand and the pulse of his wounded and dying boy in the other—the grizzled old warrior facing death in the holy cause of freedom with God-like serenity. Think of that sublime spectacle in the presence of which the spirit rises to exaltation and then recall the hideous shrieks of "treason" from the throat of slavery in the name of "law and order" to mock the solemn majesty of that supreme hour!

Treason to despotism is devotion to freedom. "Law and order" is a phrase mouthed by hypocrites to command the obedience of cowards.

The capitalist class buys law, as it does labor, using the one to fleece the other, and what it means by "law and order" is cringing submission to slavery.

"Law and order is the wand of the imposter, the mask of the robber. Beware of him who ceaselessly gabbles about the sanctity of the law.

Every ward-heeling politician, grafter, boodler, vote-buyer, labor exploiter, ballot box stuffer, franchise robber, timber thief, jury-briber, thimble-rigger, and kidnapper is the vaunted patron of "law and order." Every one of them. That is their chief stock in trade.

Buchtel, the savage, now governor of Colorado by the grace of the Mine and Smelter trust and other thieves; Buchtel, the flint-faced, heartless priest who is going about telling the people [that] Moyer, Haywood, and Pettibone are guilty of countless crimes for fear they will not be murdered; Buchtel, for whom the red-light districts turned out en masse on election day at the behest of the corporation "bosses;" Buchtel, the chancellor who has changed offices and functions with the hangman, is a shining specimen of the capitalist apostle of "law and order."[59]

Peace Based on Justice

Let no capitalist hireling charge that we favor violence and bloodshed. It is false and malicious. We are not opposed to law and order. We are opposed to the shams and hypocrisies, the frauds and crimes that resist threatened exposure as an attack upon "law and order."

"Law and order" based upon industrial robbery and social crime have an insecure foundation, and all the armed forces of the world cannot prevent such a foul fabric from going down.

There are not three men in America who by nature and habit are more peaceable and order-loving than William Haywood, Charles Moyer, and George Pettibone; not three men anywhere less inclined to incite strife or more responsive to the harmony and goodwill of human fellowship. They are all men of family, with loved and loving wives, devoted children, and pure, ideal homes. There is not a blemish upon the character of one of them as citizen or man.

Had you visited their homes before they were despoiled, as I have done, you would have been charmed by these types of splendid manhood, graced by the affections of their loved ones as great oaks are caressed by tender vines. Had you asked their neighbors you would have been told that they were sober, honest, manly men, who walked upright before their fellows, and even the children would have eagerly added their testimony of affectionate regard.

There is not a man who knows "Bill" Haywood who does not believe him square as a die; truthful, honest, generous to a fault. In his massive frame he carries the tender, loving heart of a child. He does not know what guile is; and to duplicity he is a total stranger. I would freely stake my life on his unsupported word. There is no scar upon his integrity; no shadow upon his honor.

Aroused, this Rocky Mountain miner has the strength of a giant and the courage of a Spartan. But no man I have ever known is calmer, serener, or has more perfect self-control. This is real strength, true courage, perfect manhood. It was this that extorted from the lips of Wendell Phillips as he stood beside the cold and pulseless form of John Brown, the soul-inspired exclamation: "Marvelous old man!"

History Again Culminating

History is again approaching its culmination. Industrial freedom is today the shibboleth of the working class. No conceivable artifice, no possible sophistication can more than temporarily retard the movement toward emancipation.

The settlement of one grievance of the working class becomes the basis for the next; one concession begets another, while the defeated strike and the harrowing blacklist are the recruiting agencies of the proletarian army of revolt.

The working millions were never as class-conscious, active, and determined as they are today. Hundreds of publications devoted to their interests are springing up, thousands of speakers and agitators are leaping from their own ranks to arouse the masses, and millions of tracts, leaflets, and pamphlets proclaiming the new gospel of industrial freedom are being scattered broadcast among the people.

The working class is ceasing to blindly follow the political tools of its exploiting masters; taking counsel of its own sad experience and developing a solidarity—industrial and political—that is already shaking the foundations of capitalist society over all the civilized world.

Bitter Lessons

Many bitter lessons have workingmen been compelled to learn, but not one has been in vain. The very misery ignorance has inflicted upon them has been the means of their education, and thousands who have suffered together in the depths are now keeping in step together toward the heights.

But the one supreme lesson the working class in part has already mastered—the lesson taught it by the duplicity and deceit of its rulers—is that the working class must rely upon itself, develop its own inherent powers, and instead of whining in impotency, help itself freely to all the earth affords in the satisfaction of all its physical, intellectual, and spiritual desires, and in the realization of all its cherished ideals and aspirations.

Here in the United States the last 150 years have wrought some wondrous changes, but the working class is still in fetters. the forces of nature have been harnessed, but the children of toil have not yet been released. The struggle was begun long ago, but the victory has not yet been achieved. King George ruled then "by grace of God"; King John rules now by the grace of capital.[60]

War of the Revolution

The war of the revolution settled forever the "divine right" fraud and imposture. The king and his throne, his crown and his scepter went down never to rise again. We read with pride and joy of the battles fought and victories gained until at last the stars and stripes waved in triumph over the emancipated colonies.

It was in the crisis of that struggle that Paine, who would have been executed for treason if the British government could have gotten hold of him wrote: "These are the times that try men's souls." Old Ben Franklin, fired by the spirt of the revolution, said, "We've got to hang together or we will singly." He was a rebel and gloried in it. Nathan Hale, the fire flashing from his eyes, exclaimed, "I regret that I have but one life to lose for my country." Another rebel, and he paid the penalty like a hero. Fitting words these, and the sentiments they express, to Patrick Henry's immortal outburst: "Give me liberty or give me death!"

The pulse is quickened and the blood leaps in our veins as these rebels pass in imaginary review. They dared the king and pledged "their lives, their fortunes, and their sacred honor" to the revolution.

These men were the Moyers, Haywoods, and Pettibones of their day and it is a noteworthy fact that the great grandsire of one of these industrial patriots signed the Declaration of Independence and fought bravely on the fields of the American Revolution.

Rebels and Patriots

The "rebels" and "ragged continentals" the Tories hated and King George would hang for treason are revered today as patriots and heroes.

Nearly a century later history again culminated in a bloody revolution. The aristocracy of chattel slavery ruled the land. Its word was law; its power supreme. To question its authority was treason; to dispute its power was death.

Again, the rebels appear upon the scene; the "black abolitionists" take their places. All of them are "the scum of society," the fomenters of strife, the inciters of violence, the "enemies of law and order." They were in league with the devil and infamous enough to attack "the sacred rights of property." Elijah Lovejoy, one of the pioneers, was murdered in cold blood. Garrison narrowly escaped lynching; Wendell Phillips was repeatedly threatened with assassination.

How vividly I remember the evening 30 years ago I spent with Phillips and how he fired my boyish imagination by his recital of the thrilling scenes of the abolition conflict. An agitator was Wendell Phillips, every inch of him; an apostle of freedom, one of the grandest souls that ever glorified this planet and yet the foul minions of the slave owners hunted him as relentlessly as the Pinkerton detectives of the mine owners are hunting Haywood, Moyer, and Pettibone today.

John Brown, another of the elect of God, was a fiend incarnate in the eyes of men who trafficked in human souls in the name of "law and order." Victor Hugo hailed him deliverer, but the American people, degraded by the brutal domination of the slave lash, murdered him by law to vindicate its sordid supremacy.

"Monster of iniquity" was the verdict of the slave owner and his "civilization," but the verdict of one age becomes the mockery of the next. The mills of the gods grind on. John Brown has ceased to be a monster. His name has been rescued from the cruel aspersions of the slaveholder long ago. The slaveholder himself is now forgotten, but his despised victim is lovingly remembered by all the race.

John Brown, were he living today and saw the slaves in the pits and mills and their babes in the sweatshops, would again don the panoply of battle and swear death to wage-slavery. Were he living today he would be hated and persecuted as fiercely as he was by the chattel slave aristocracy half a century ago. But he is dead. And the ruling class against which he rebelled, the ruling class which put him to death and which he cannot now resist, seizes him as one of its own heroes and insults his memory by enrolling his name in its calendar of saints.

It is only because he is dead that the capitalist class pays tribute to Brown. He needs no ruling class laurels to keep his memory green. He belongs to the agitators and the liberators and not the enslavers of humanity.

Nearly 50 years ago John Brown was hanged as a felon for being a man, while the felons who took his life were honored as men. Today the vice-president of the United States journeys to Osawatomie[61] in pomp and circumstance to do honor to his memory while a grand monument is erected where he trampled on the "law" and incited violence and bloodshed in the cause of human freedom.

Wage-slavery and Proletarian Patriots

Chattel slavery has disappeared. Wage-slavery has yet to be conquered. The struggle has already begun. There can be no compromise and no retreat. Again are the leaders stepping from the ranks and taking their places at the heads of the advancing columns. Defiance is on their lips and the spirit of the revolution in their souls. Like their prototypes of the past they are marked for ostracism, hated, contumely—some of them for death. But they falter not, they are the royal sons of destiny. Upon their eager faces falls the dawning of the coming day.

The voice of Freedom has called them to her standard and when they have sealed their devotion to her cause, their names will shine in living letters on the scroll of the immortals.

William Haywood, Charles Moyer, and George Pettibone have fought the good fight. They have never betrayed their cause, nor ever sounded a retreat.

For serving the working class with matchless valor and unwavering devotion, these proletarian patriots have been seized by the enemy, and it now becomes the solemn duty of the working class of all the nation to rally to their rescue.

They are men, not murderers. Were they less than men they would not now be on trial for their lives. The aristocracy of capital that rules today does not object to murder. Thousands of the children of toil are murdered every day whose lives could and would be saved if they were of greater value than the material means required to save them.

The capitalist power rules by corruption. Where that fails it employs persecution and death.

The disclosures made in the recent exposé of the Pinkerton Detective Agency show clearly by what villainous methods labor unions are invaded by those assassins and how crime is instigated and committed by them to discredit the unions. The bills for all such treacherous services are paid by the mine owners and other capitalists who profit by the disruption of organized labor in the unrestrained exploitation of its product.

The war that has been raging in the Rocky Mountains these many years is a class war. Upon the one side are the mine owners and upon the other the mine workers. Between these two classes there can be no peace. The clash of material interests forbids it. The idle owners, by the mere fact of ownership, get most of what the miners produce. The workers have submitted to this exploitation long and patiently, but the limit has about been reached. Why should they have to deliver up to others the wealth they produce? Why not themselves enjoy the fruit of their own labor?

These are the questions being asked by more and more workingmen and with steadily increasing emphasis.

The wage system has only slavery for the working class and oft-times even that is denied them. It has served its time and purpose and must soon be abolished. The workers do not need masters; they can and must be their own.

Class Organization

To abolish wage-slavery requires the organization of the working class, both economic and political, and this work is now under way as never before. The economic organization of the workers on a revolutionary basis enables them to act together aggressively and effectively in the protection and promotion of their common interests.

Political organization has already been carried forward to such an extent that many thousands of workers now understand that their economic interests as a class are opposed to the economic interests of the class that exploits them, and that these opposing interests must express themselves in opposing parties and that, therefore, the working class must have a political party of its own and that this party, to be true to its historic mission, must demand the overthrow of the capitalist system that the cooperative commonwealth may be established and industrial freedom proclaimed.

The Socialist Party has already taken its place as the party of the working class. It is based upon the class struggle and demands the unconditional abolition of the capitalist system. All the workers of the land and all their sympathizers may here united upon revolutionary political ground.

Approaching the Crisis

The trials now in progress in Idaho are culminating scenes of fierce engagements in the class struggle. They are of vital and far-reaching interest to the whole working class. The lives of trusted leaders and issues of supreme importance are at stake. All the resources of the working class should be freely available in this crisis.

What the outcome of the trials may be no one knows, but of one thing we feel absolutely certain, and that is, if the trials are fairly conducted and the verdicts honestly rendered, Moyer, Haywood, and Pettibone will walk forth free men.

But regardless of the outcome of the trials, the issue involving the life and freedom of the whole working class has to be fought out. There can be no retreat, nor even a cessation of the struggle.

The kidnapping of Moyer, Haywood, and Pettibone, the representatives of the working class, and their heartless persecution in the name of "law and order," has opened the eyes of many thousands to the real issue involved, and they are now ready to join their class in the political battlefield.

Should the courts of Idaho fail to do our comrades justice, we will appeal their cases to the working class of the nation.

Next year, 1908, is a presidential year. The kidnapping trial in Idaho is a fitting prelude to the national campaign. We welcome the issue and the contest. Working class sentiment is rapidly crystalizing and in another year the hosts of labor will be ready for the greatest political campaign since 1860. The issue then was chattel slavery; today it is wage-slavery.

Again the bugle blasts of the "irrepressible conflict"[62] are heard in the land and the toiling millions are rallying to the standard of their class.

The Idaho trial is the signal for the revolutionary alignment on both the industrial and political fields and for the opening of the national campaign in which that stalwart champion of labor, William D. Haywood, now persecuted by the capitalist class, shall be the candidate of the working class for president of the United States.

The capitalist class has flung down the gauntlet in the name of the Standard Oil Company, the Mine and Smelter Trust, and other combines of brigandage and boodle, and we pick it up in the name of all the millions in the fetters of wage-slavery.

With William D. Haywood as the standard bearer and industrial freedom as the shibboleth, the campaign of 1908 will shake the nation from its center to its circumference.

Our Candidate

No words of eulogy are required in presenting William D. Haywood to the working class of America. He is a sturdy type of the twentieth century wage-slave. His strength of mind and body are of the lower class from which he sprang. Brave, resolute, and incorruptible, he has fought the battles of his enslaved fellow men. The character of his friends and his enemies are equally eloquent of the purity and strength of his own.

The highest ambition of this proletarian leader is to serve the class that shares his fetters in honest toil. For that class he has stood as staunchly as any general ever stood on a field of battle and freely sacrificed all he had except his sacred honor.

For 15 months William D. Haywood, in the Ada County jail, ready to die for the working class, has proved himself worthy to live for his class in the White House of the Republic.

The Trial and Its Meaning†

June 8, 1907

Perhaps the most unfortunate thing about the trial now in progress in Idaho from the working-class point of view is that so few understand its true meaning, its real significance, its full import. It is one of the strange freaks of history that its makers are not to be understood by their contemporaries, but that they, especially the greatest among them, must die ignominiously and wait for succeeding generations to interpret their works and do them justice.

When John Brown was put upon trial in Charlestown, Virginia, 48 years ago, few people, extremely few, understood its meaning. Although half a century has passed and the fiercest civil war in history, of which that trial was but the prelude, has been fought, the great mass of the people has not yet awakened to its significance. Another century or more will be required before the strike at Harper's Ferry and the trial at Charlestown will be understood in their larger meaning, as written in subsequent events, by the American people and the world.

Ralph Waldo Emerson[63] was one of the few who understood that historic trial of half a century ago, the trial of a despised agitator and hated insurrectionist. His prophetic eye pierced the future as he said: "John Brown will make the gallows as glorious as Jesus Christ make the cross."[64] The coming centuries will vindicate the prescience of the Sage of Concord and the gallows upon which John Brown, the liberator, perished will be kept green with wreaths of immortelles[65] by the countless children of freedom.

The outcome of the pending trail is awaited with equal concern by the tsar of Russia and the president of the United States. They at least understand in some measure the vital issue that is involved and the widespread influence the outcome will have upon their respective countries.

When the tsar of Russia expressed his imperial approval of President Roosevelt's characterization of Moyer and Haywood as "undesirable citizens," he not only added his testimony to the worldwide interest in the trial, but unwittingly recognized the international class struggle of which the trial in itself is but the merest incident.[66]

† Published in *Appeal to Reason*, whole no. 601 (June 8, 1907), 1.

It is this very fact—a fact of the supremest importance—that the capitalist powers are striving by all conceivable means to conceal from the working class; upon their success in so doing depends the consummation of the conspiracy to destroy organized labor and rule the wage-slaves of the western mines and smelters with a rod of iron for years to come.

The trial now going on, viewed from any comprehensive standpoint, is anything but a murder trial. In the war between labor and capital in the Rocky Mountains during the last 30 years—sometimes in pitched battles and again in guerrilla fashion—hundreds have been slaughtered, but not all of them combined have created a tithe of the furor aroused by the taking off of Frank Steunenberg, the particular murder which lies at the foundation of this prosecution and which must be understood in at least its essential features to account for the worldwide interest it has awakened.

Hundreds of miners have been killed under circumstances quite as cruel as the assassination of Steunenberg, but who can pronounce the name of even one of them?

Why was no great reward offered for their slayers? Why did not the legislature of Idaho appropriate $100,000 for the conviction of the murderers of these miners?[67] And why did the governor of that state not lay snares to kidnap the supposed instigators of these crimes? Or the president of the United States pronounce them "undesirable citizens?"

Ah, that is the point! Why were the hundreds of workingmen slain so inconsequential and easily forgotten, while the killing of Steunenberg has aroused the whole universe?

The answer comes of itself. Frank Steunenberg belonged to the ruling class. As governor of Idaho he had served that class with particular fidelity. As a retired capitalist he was identified with that class. Had he been killed while still a union printer under precisely the same circumstances scarcely anyone outside of Idaho would have ever heard of it and by them it would soon have been forgotten.

With Frank Steunenberg it was different. He was dear to the hearts of the Mine and Smelter Trust and the lumber trust and the Standard Oil trust. He had served them loyally in a grave crisis and under peculiarly trying circumstances. Elected as a union man and supported solidly by the Western Federation of Miners upon the express understanding that he was and would continue to be a true friend to organized labor, no governor of any state ever served the master class with more abject servility than did Frank Steunenberg, the supposed union man, as every old miner in Idaho knows to his sorrow. It is not now necessary to dwell upon this feature of the case. The record is there and will speak for itself now and for years to come. The Mine and Smelter Trust and its organs declare it a record of honor, but it must be remembered that their testimonials are based upon services received and it would be strange indeed if even an octopus without conscious failed to vouch for those who conserve its interests.

It is not that these sharks had any particular love for Steunenberg. Not at all. They have no love for anybody, for the reason that they are incapable of love. They devour; they do not love. And when they are not devouring the working class, they turn on each other. But Steunenberg had become one of them and the attack upon him was an attack upon the capitalist ruling class and could be made the excuse for a formidable assault by the whole capitalist administration, state and national, upon the strongholds of labor unionism, the only menace to the undisputed sway of the corporate brigands.

Steunenberg amounted to something—he was not a workingman. He was a capitalist and had been the governor of Idaho for the capitalist class. Having so basely betrayed the union workingmen who elected him, rewarding them with bullpens and bullets, the presumption was natural that they had a hand in his death, but why they should have waited seven years to avenge their grievances has not yet been explained.

We are not now interested in any theory or motive relating to the assassination, but only in showing that this case is not a murder case at all; that at bottom it is a secret plot to destroy organized labor and that it is this, and this alone, that gives it national and international character and significance.

Had Davis H. Waite, the grand old governor of Colorado, been assassinated, as he was often threatened, would the Mine and Smelter Trust have turned heaven and earth and two governors turned kidnappers to punish his suspected slayer?

Had John Altgeld, the greatest governor in all the Union, been murdered by his enemies, as they swore he should be, would the Standard Oil Company have set all its vast machinery in operation and President Grover Cleveland, a twin Roosevelt, applied all his administrative powers to apprehend the culprit and bring him to justice?

Had it been William D. Haywood instead of Frank Steunenberg, what capitalist governor would have been the least concerned? What legislature would have changed the organic laws of the state to punish his alleged assassin? What capitalist daily papers would turn black in the face denouncing editorially the atrocity of the crime?

Everything connected with this case, from the perjured affidavit in which it had its legal (?) inception, the gubernatorial conspiracy, the secret arrest, the midnight kidnapping, the special train, the Pinkerton "confessions," the special acts of the legislatures, the denial of habeas corpus, the princely treatment of Orchard, the Taft invasion, the support of the national administration, the concerted cry of the capitalist press from New York to California for revenge—everything from the infernal beginning to the empaneling of a jury without a workingman upon it proves conclusively, in detail and on the whole, that all the powers of capitalism are behind the prosecution and that it is folly to expect justice when all the machinery of government has been primed for the one specific purpose of pronouncing death upon the leadership of organized labor and carrying the sentence into execution.

Nevertheless, there is plenty of room for hope. The capitalist powers may commit crime without compunction, but they are not fools. They are wise enough to know how far they can go and when to call a halt.

They did not dream of the uprising of the working class that has swept across the country like a tidal wave. They cannot yet realize that 100,000 indignant and protesting workingmen and women thronged Boston Common and made the welkin ring; that 50,000 marched through the streets of New York and 30,000 through the streets of Chicago proclaiming their fealty to the heroic leaders on trial in Idaho.

This it is that is making itself felt in the trial and will continue to be an increasing factor until the final outcome. So far as the alleged "fair trial" is concerned, when the ruling powers make up their minds to commit murder they scruple at nothing, and since they control the legislative and administrative machinery it is an easy matter for them to commit their crimes "legally," according to the "forms of law," and thus satisfy the feeble-minded, who are quite prepared to see even their best friends hanged by the necks until they are dead, provided the ropes are of the legal length and the proceedings bear the "legal" trademark of the capitalist regime.

So much for the scruples of the ruling class.

But as already stated, they have sense, if not scruples. They have their fingers upon the social pulse and know precisely how it is beating.

Will it pay? is the only question with them.

Will it pay to convict innocent men? What will be the consequences? That is what they are asking themselves from Rockefeller down. They hate Bill Haywood as the devil hates a white soul, and for the same reason.

Bill Haywood has been bravely fighting for his class. They know it. He is not a murderer. They know that. He is loved and honored by millions of his fellow workers. They know that, also. To hang him would make him a martyr and a hero, precipitate a conflict, and a million aroused workingmen would spring from the soil fertilized by his noble blood to avenge his cruel death.

The working class of the United States may not comprehend the full meaning of this historic trial, but they are sufficiently awake to its significance that they will watch it eagle-eyed from day to day and from hour to hour, no matter how far it may be prolonged, until the end, and their vigilance and determination will not relax until justice has been done, and in that hour their fellow workers will walk forth free men.

The Drift of Our Times: Chautauqua Lecture at Appleton, Wisconsin[68] [Excerpt][†]

July 7, 1907

When called upon to respond to such a generous and touching reception as that which you tendered to me a year ago and repeat on this occasion, words, no matter how fitly chosen and how feelingly expressed, seem but cold, formal, and meaningless. I am deeply sensible of your kind consideration, the more so because I am aware that most of you differ with me upon some of the great questions of the day. My appreciation, though not expressed in words, is no less genuine and shall find its expression in deeper devotion and consecration of the cause of our common humanity.

* * *

Underlying society are great forces constantly in operation, and these are

† Published as "Eugene V. Debs on Socialism: Brilliant Man Speaks to Big Chautauqua Audience: The Drift of Our Times" in *Appleton Evening Crescent*, vol. 17, no. 219 (July 8, 1907), 1, 8. Integrated with "Says Socialism the Final Goal," in *Appleton Weekly Post*, vol. 51, no. 27 (July 11, 1907), 1.

making for a new social order based upon cooperative industry. There is a hue and cry against concentration of capital, but it is in vain. This concentration in our modern industrial life can no more be effectually checked than can the law of gravitation be suspended. Concentration and combination, based upon cooperation, are the new forces born of our industrial development, which are transforming capitalist society into a socialist commonwealth.

The spirit of the present system is selfish, that of the survival of the fittest, only except in few cases, the fittest do not survive. John D. Rockefeller is not the fittest. I bear no malice toward Rockefeller and I am sure no man envies him. Individual capitalists such as Mr. Rockefeller are the mere product of the prevailing system. Mr. Bryan is quoted as saying that Mr. Rockefeller ought to be put in the penitentiary. I don't agree with him. If this is true of Mr. Rockefeller, it is true of every other capitalist, large or small, in the country. The reason so many small capitalists hate Rockefeller is not because of a difference of principle or purpose between them, but simply because of a difference of capacity. Rockefeller has succeeded and they have failed at precisely the same game. They are all Rockefellers in principle and desire, and only differ as to size and capacity.

I would not imprison Rockefeller or punish him in any manner; I would simply abolish the system that produces him. Senator LaFollette, Mr. Bryan, and a number of other political reformers propose to curb the greed of corporate capital and reform existing abuses in our politics and industrial life. They propose, for example, that the national government should regulate our railroads. They are wasting their time and energy in a vain and hopeless cause. The fact is that the railroads and allied corporate interests are the government. In the existing system it is not the government that regulates the railroads, but it is the railroads that regulate the government.

Politics is simply the reflex of economics. The economic master is always and everywhere, has always been in every age and always will be, the political ruler. In other words, the owners of things are the rulers of men. This seems strange, but it is nevertheless a fact of history and of economic science.

To verify this fact, it is only necessary to occupy a seat, as I did for two weeks, in the United States Senate and the House of Representatives and there see the agents and attorneys of all the varied corporate interests do the political bidding of their masters.

The railroads, for illustration, control one million votes because they have that number of men who depend upon them for themselves and their families. The results that flow from this state of economic dependence of the great masses of people express themselves daily in municipal, state, and national political corruption and administration. This state of affairs never can be remedied so long as the sources and means of life upon which the great masses of the people depend are the private property of the few and are operated upon the basis that millions of dollars in their hands are of more consequence than the property happiness of the people.

These facts in combination ensure the coming of socialism. It is inevitable. The concentration will go on until the masses are propertyless and they will then make common cause against the few surviving economic monarchs, sweep them from power, take possession of the government, and make themselves, the collective people, the masters of industry, the sovereigns of the nation.

This will mean industrial democracy, a real republic, the triumph of the people, and will express itself in a higher and nobler civilization than mankind has ever known.

Under this system each one is forever pitted against each other one. I want a system in which we can live side by side like brothers. I want an era of love, when the standard of greatness will be service to others; when we will not have to spend all of life to earn bread, but will have time for the moral and intellectual life. When art, literature, and music will be for all the people, to brighten all lives and make for a better civilization. I am converging all my energy to bring about the abolishment of the system which makes this impossible and to bring the system which will [enable] all men and women to walk erect and free in the full majesty of their glorious manhood and womanhood.

The people are not ready for the change. They are never ready for a change. It has been thus with man's first upward step, from a brute to a savage, from a savage to a barbarian, from barbarian to serf, from serf to wage-earner, and thus it is with his march into the full orbed day of true civilization and perfect freedom which will come with the change.

For myself, I am glad the change is coming. I stand here a socialist, even if I stand alone. You can retard or hasten the change, but you cannot prevent it, no more than you can prevent the rivers from finding their way to the sea. Capitalization can no more be stifled under the present system than the law of gravitation can be overcome. It is only a question of time when a few will control all. Then the people will see, then all will join, we will form the great socialistic party, sweep into power, and reorganize society on a social basis. The Rockefellers will have appropriated all. We will lawfully expropriate the appropriators.

Socialism is not anarchy. They are direct opposites. The one would abolish all government, the other perfect government. Under socialism we would have a real democracy, a real republic, the first in the world; all would have equal opportunities, all would work for all. Socialism does not mean equal pay to all. Under socialism Rockefeller, with his great brain, his marvelous executive ability, would give his service to the people and would be loved and amply rewarded. He would not have his millions, but would be the happier for it.

All I ask is that you be true to yourselves, that you have the moral courage to think and act for yourselves and accept the consequences. This is what we need today. The drift of our times is toward socialism. When the few have all, you will come to see that this is true, if not before.

I am not a pessimist. I realize that in the long last, right will prevail.

The Haywood Verdict: Statement to the Press†

July 28, 1907

The verdict of acquittal is a gratifying surprise to Haywood's friends. Few were sanguine enough to expect it. Tried in a hostile community and by a jury of his political enemies, the best that was generally expected was a mistrial, based upon disagreement of the jury. The instructions of Judge Wood indicated a sharp turn in the trial in favor of the defendant. I am at a loss to understand it unless the pressure of powerful influences was brought to bear at this juncture in favor of acquittal.

My own opinion is that the mine owners and capitalists generally concluded they could not afford to risk conviction, for the reason that the public in general and the working classes in particular would not have stood for it. The original design of the Mine Owners' Association was the summary execution of Moyer, Haywood, and Pettibone. The utterly unexpected and unprecedented demonstration of protest on the part of organized labor thwarted the conspiracy and defeated its malign purpose.

† Wire report, published as "Eugene V. Debs Comments on Haywood's Trial and Talks Strongly in Doing So" in *Daily News-Democrat* [Paducah, Kentucky], vol. 40, no. 226 (July 29, 1907), 2.

The verdict not only vindicates the defendants, but it places President Roosevelt in an awkward position, which can only be relieved by an apology to the innocent men he condemned.

The fact that we are approaching a presidential election was fortunate for the defendant. The powerful interests back of the prosecution realized that a conviction would have a far-reaching effect upon the working class. Some time ago I suggested the nomination of Haywood as the candidate for the Socialist Party for president,[69] and now believe his nomination will be an acclamation, and that the working classes of the nation will rally to his support.

Statement to the *Appeal to Reason* on the Haywood Verdict†

July 29, 1907

Terre Haute, Indiana, July 29 [1907]

The acquittal of Haywood, as announced by the press dispatches, is a distinct triumph of the organized workers of the nation—the greatest, I think, in all the history of the labor movement. The report came as a great and gratifying surprise to me, as it did, I am sure, to us all. I expected a mistrial based upon a disagreement of the jury, and I do not know of anyone who was sanguine enough to predict an absolute acquittal. It is not that any of us had the slightest doubt as to Haywood's innocence, but there was every reason, until Judge Wood delivered his instructions to the jury, to regard the proceedings with suspicion and to be prepared for a verdict that would correspond to the kidnapping.

The turn in the trial came with the instructions of the judge, which were in striking contrast to his holdings and decisions during the entire trial. The judge virtually instructed the jury to find in favor of the defendant. There is something mysterious about this, and I confess myself unable to fathom it. Of one thing, however, I am sure, and that is that the ruling element of the capitalist

† Published as "Cheering Words from Debs" in *Appeal to Reason*, whole no. 609 (August 8, 1907), 3.

class concluded that it could not afford the conviction of Haywood, and I am satisfied that pressure was brought to bear on the court by some powerful interests to secure his acquittal.

It is this that constitutes the victory of the working class, and it is great enough to cause universal rejoicing. The lawyers for the defense, notably [Clarence S.] Darrow, [E. F.] Richardson, and [John] Murphy, served the defendant loyally and with exceptional ability and fidelity. But of itself their magnificent defense would have availed no more than the innocence of the defendant.

Guilty or not guilty, defense or no defense, the conspiracy of the mine owners and smelter trust, with the connivance of Standard Oil, backed by President Roosevelt and approved by the United States Supreme Court, had for its purpose the execution of Moyer, Haywood, and Pettibone. There was to be a repetition of the judicial massacre at Chicago 19 years ago.[70] As to that there is not the slightest doubt. McParland boldly announced the plot. Gooding confirmed it, and the capitalist press echoed and re-echoed it from shore to shore.

Then came the unexpected. The alarm was sounded by the labor press and the workers of the nation arose as if by magic and issued a cry of protest that startled the nation. It was this, and this alone, that thwarted the infamous conspiracy. But for this our three comrades would long since have sealed their fidelity to labor with their martyrdom.

The verdict of acquittal has put a quietus on this entire prosecution. It completely vindicates our comrades, and they stand before the world without a blemish. It is also a triumphant vindication of the labor press and the labor movement, and both will be vitalized and strengthened by it beyond measure.

This historic verdict not only vindicates our comrades, but impeaches their detractors, especially Theodore Roosevelt, president of the United States, and if he has so much as a spark of humane manhood he will tender Moyer and Haywood the most humble apology for the cruel outrage he perpetrated in using the prestige of his high official position to prejudice their cause and consummate the conspiracy of the mine owners to send them, though innocent, to the gallows. The Supreme Court is also scathingly rebuked by this verdict, with the single exception of Justice McKenna. Every one of its subservient members should hand his head in shame.

The whole organized working class, with but a few wretched exceptions, which need not be named here, will rejoice in this glorious victory. It has demonstrated the power of the labor movement and is exclusively the victory of that movement. Let us all unite in love and congratulations to our three comrades who have passed through the ordeal of fire and in joyous acclaim of the new era which now dawns to the working class. The trial and the verdict both emphasize the necessity for industrial unionism and for socialism, and from this time forward the movement along these lines will be accelerated with such force as to bear down all opposition. The blow the capitalist conspirators aimed at the labor movement has recoiled upon themselves.

The revolutionary movement of the working class has received an impetus that nothing else could have given it, and all over the land the organized workers have caught the new spirit, are falling into line and joining in the demand for the overthrow of capitalist despotism and the establishment of the socialist commonwealth.

The trial is over, comrades, and the victory won, but this is only the beginning. We have been imbued with fresh courage, greater strength, and stronger determination, and now we must unite our class as never before and move on to the next conflict and the next until final victory is achieved and the working class proclaims its emancipation to the world.

Eugene V. Debs

Industrial Unionism Defined†

November 2, 1907

The term "industrial unionism" is used to express a modern form of labor organization whose jurisdiction is not confined to any particular trade or craft, but is coextensive with the industrial development, and embraces the entire working class. Industrial unionism is the outgrowth of trade unionism and expresses the highest form of industrial organization the working class has yet attained. As its name implies, this form of unionism contemplates the organization of industries in their entirety, uniting all employees within the same economic body, subdivided into a number of departments equal to and corresponding with the several trades or general occupations in which they are engaged.

† Written for *Editors' American Encyclopedia*, possibly not published. Published as "Industrial Unionism" in *Industrial Union Bulletin* [Chicago], vol. 1, no. 36 (November 2, 1907), 5.

In organizing the workers along the lines of their general industrial interests rather than their particular craft interests, it is claimed that the friction due to overlapping craft jurisdictions is obviated, and that a higher degree of solidarity and efficiency is thus secured in the interest of all.

The industrial union in its present form came but recently into existence, the trade union having preceded it, the latter dating back to a time near the beginning of industrial life in Great Britain, about the middle of the eighteenth century.

The earlier unions were confined principally to the skilled trades, and hence were called trade unions. These unions were built up on the basis of the skilled use of the tools used in the several trades during the period of handicraft in industry, and later on were loosely joined together in a federation of trades, without, however, abridging their autonomy or invading their separate jurisdictions.

Organized upon this basis, each craft was left free to negotiate its own wage scale, and enter into agreement with the employer upon terms most advantageous to itself, regardless of other crafts that might be employed in the same industry. The results that followed in the way of disastrous strikes resorted to by one or more crafts because of having failed to obtain a satisfactory agreement, while others employed in the same industry, perhaps in the identical factory, remained at their tasks, in cooperation with the non-union element which had displaced their own fellow workers, paved the way for industrial organization.

The trade union rose with the modern trade and flourished with it, the foundation of both being the skilled use of certain tools in the making of certain commodities for market use. This stage of industrial development prevailed for many years, but has now been largely superseded and is rapidly declining before the march of industrial evolution, made manifest in the concentration of capital, the displacement of the small shop by the great factory, the handicraft tools by steam-driven machinery, the segregated trade by associated industry, and competitive effort by cooperative labor. Along the same line the trade union of the past is now expressing itself more and more in industrial unionism.

Industrial unionism, having evolved from the lower primal forms of trade unionism through the successive stages of the industrial development, and adapting itself to present industrial conditions and their tendencies, has encountered serious opposition on the part of trade unionists as well as the employing class, the former tenaciously adhering to the craft form of organization and resisting all attempts to materially change it, and the latter opposing it on account of its aggressive and revolutionary character; but, notwithstanding this, the new unionism has made rapid advance during the past two or three years, and its principles have now come to be generally recognized by the progressive elements of the labor movement.[71]

Greatly as the industrial union differs from the trade union structurally, the difference in their tendencies and ultimate objects is still more radical and far reaching. Whereas the trade union occupied itself mainly with establishing and maintaining satisfactory wage scales, hours of labor, and working class conditions, industrial unionism, based upon the mutual economic interests of all workers and the solidarity arising therefrom, aims not only at the amelioration of the industrial conditions of the workers, but at the ultimate abolition of the existing productive system, and the total extinction of wage servitude.

It is in this fundamental principle that industrial unionism is most radical and revolutionary in contrast with the earlier trade union forms of industrial organization.

The concentration of capital and the highly complex productive mode of the present day, grouping in vast industrial establishments thousands of workers engaged in scores of different trades, and forcing them into closer and closer cooperation, based upon the minutest division of labor, have tended to obscure, or perhaps totally obliterate, the lines that once so sharply defined the skilled trades, and in this interweaving of the trades the jurisdictions of the several unions based upon them have overlapped each other, and this has been the prolific source of the increasing friction between many of the larger unions which have approximately reached their maximum of growth and are jealous of maintaining the prestige of an expanding membership regardless of the effect upon a rival union which may lay claim to jurisdiction over the same craft or division thereof. Following the lines of least resistance, the tendency of these unions, so far as external forms are concerned, is toward industrial unionism, and this is undoubtedly the form that will ultimately supersede the trade union of the present and past.

Not only in the matter of organic form and fundamental aim does industrial unionism differ from trade unionism, but also in the matter of tactics and methods. Quite as revolutionary as the ultimate end of industrial unionism are the tactics its adherents have adopted for its realization.

The trade unions of the present and past have with rare exceptions eschewed political action in any independent capacity as an organized body; have accepted, in the aggregate, the prevailing industrial system as a finality, subject only to such modification as might be effected through the power of organized effort in the amelioration of conditions, and have uniformly affirmed, in express terms and by clear implication, an identity of economic interests between the employing and employed classes.

In contradistinction to this conciliatory and nonpolitical attitude of the trade unions toward the existing wage system and the capitalist class, it is the declared principle of industrial unionism that the wage workers have no interests in common with capitalists; that, in fact, their material interests are in conflict, and it is its declared purpose to abolish the wage system and supplant it by a system of industrial cooperation in which the workers themselves shall have full control for their own benefit, and to this end they recognize the necessity of organizing the political as well as the economic power of the working class, and of the harmonious exercise of both by such means as will make industrial unionism the medium of attaining industrial democracy.

Looking Backward: Thirty Years of Struggle for Labor Emancipation†

November 11, 1907

Before me lies a copy of the *Philadelphia Evening Herald*, bearing the date of June 21, 1877. On that day the "Mollie Maguires"[72] were executed, six of them—Boyle, McGeehan, Munley, Roarity, Carroll, and Duffy—at Pottsville; four of them—Campbell, Doyle, Kelly, and Donahue—at Mauch Chunk, and one—Lanahan—at Wilkes Barre. They all protested their innocence and all died game. Not one of them betrayed the slightest evidence of fear or weakening. The issue of the *Herald* referred to contains a full account of the executions, with portraits of the hapless victims.

Not long ago in the jail at Pottsville I stood on the spot where the six "Mollies" met their doom, and I uncovered in memory of their martyrdom.

Not one of them was a murderer at heart. All were ignorant, rough and uncouth, born of poverty, and buffeted by the merciless tides of fate and chance.

To resist the wrongs of which they and their fellow-workers were the victims and to protect themselves against the brutality of their bosses, according

† Published as "Looking Backward" in *Appeal to Reason*, whole no. 625 (November 23, 1907), 1, 3.

to their own crude notions, was the prime object of the organization of the "Mollie Maguires." Nothing could have been farther from their intention than murder or crime. It is true that their methods were drastic, but it must be remembered that their lot was hard and brutalizing; that they were the neglected children of poverty, the products of a wretched environment.

At the scenes of the execution the tragedy is today, 30 years later, still spoken of in whispers. A vague dread of reviving the fearful past seems to silence the tongue of the resident when the subject is introduced. But bit by bit the truth has slowly and painfully filtered through the dungeon doors of false history, and the world is beginning to understand the true inwardness of the "Mollie Maguire" organization and its real relation to the labor movement.

These unfortunate victims of the basest betrayal since the days of Judas had no possible means of defense or justification. The corporate press howled like fiends incarnate for their blood. They had dared to assert themselves against a powerful and piratical corporation, and this was sufficient warrant for their extermination. Spies, informers, and assassins wormed their slimy way into their councils. Bloody crimes were instigated and committed; the innocent and ignorant "Mollies" walked into the traps set for them.

The powers of the law now fell upon them with crushing effect. Their organization was annihilated. No friendly voice pleaded in extenuation of the crimes charged upon the leaders.

The labor movement was in its infancy; it had no press and no standing; no influence and no power. There was but one side to the tragedy and that was, of course, the capitalist side. The poor, dumb victims, bound and gagged, had but to await their bloody fate. At the grates of their cells the hounds of hell snarled and growled with savage ferocity to lap their blood. No helping hand was extended, and scarce a whisper of kindness was ventured on their behalf.

On June 21, 1877, the curtain fell upon the last mournful act in this tragedy of toil. The executioner did his bidding and the gallows-tree claimed its victims.

On that day history turned harlot and the fair face of truth was covered with the hideous mask of falsehood.

For 30 years the press of corporate power has been lying grossly and outrageously about the "Mollie Maguires" and their organization. But the truth will out at last, and the time is near when the history of the Pennsylvania tragedy, as now written, will be radically revised and the names of these martyrs rescued from the cruel calumny with which they have been loaded.

The "Mollie Maguire" episode was incidental to the organization of the working class; a link in the chain of the labor movement.

The men who perished upon the scaffold as felons were labor leaders, the first martyrs to the class struggle in the United States.

It is profoundly significant that Franklin B. Gowen,[73] president of the Philadelphia & Reading Railroad, and chief prosecutor and persecutor of the "Mollie Maguires," sought in suicide a refuge from the avenging Nemesis that pursued him.

In the year 1876 the Workingmen's Party was organized, and in the following year, 1877, after the execution of the "Molly Maguires," it became the Socialist Labor Party.

This same year the great railroad strikes swept like a tidal wave from the eastern to the western states.

Eight years later, in 1885, the Knights of Labor came into national prominence, and the great strikes on the Gould Southwest system in that year and the year following were inaugurated.

On May 1, 1886, hundreds of thousands of workers in various parts of the country went on strike to enforce the eight-hour work day, the agitation incident to the movement culminating in the Haymarket tragedy of May 4.

On November 11 of the following year, 1887—twenty years ago today—occurred the infamous execution of the anarchists at Chicago. This judicial massacre constitutes the blackest page in American history. When Parsons, Spies, Fischer, and Engel were launched into eternity to "vindicate the majesty of the law," a crime was committed of such enormity, that even at this late day the sober senses reel in its awful contemplation.

These fellow workers and their four comrades—Lingg, Fielden, Schwab, and Neebe—the first of whom died by violence in his cell, and the last three of whom were sentenced to the penitentiary and subsequently pardoned by the immortal Altgeld—were martyrs to the labor movement in the noblest sense of that term. They had fearlessly espoused the cause of labor and consecrated themselves body and soul to the working class. They had the true revolutionary spirit, were animated by the loftiest motives, and were utterly void of selfish ambitions.

The sordid capitalism which preys upon the life-blood of labor, whose ethics are expressed in beastly gluttony and insatiable greed, and whose track of conquest is strewn with the bones of its countless victims, pounced upon these men with the cruel malignity of fiends and strangled them to death.

A more cruel and heartless crime, a more flagrant outrage of justice, was never committed. Twenty years have passed since these leaders of labor paid the penalty of their loyalty, and marvelous have been the changes in public sentiment since that day. They would not now be executed under the same circumstances. The workers today are too far advanced, too well organized and too conscious of their class interests and duties to submit to such a monstrous outrage.

The recent trial and acquittal of William D. Haywood proves it. Had labor been no farther advanced than it was 20 years ago, Moyer, Haywood, Pettibone, and Adams would long since have shared the fate of Parsons, Spies, Fischer, and Engel.

Since that fateful period of two decades ago, events have pressed each other closely in the world of labor. Three months after the execution of the Haymarket victims, the CB&Q strike broke out in Chicago, and the issue was hotly contested for almost a year before the employees finally succumbed to defeat.[74] From that time forward strikes, boycotts, and lockouts were numerous, a long series of industrial battles marking the path of the class struggle and the progress of the labor movement.

Homestead, Buffalo,[75] Chicago,[76] Latimer, Virden, Pana, Leadville, Coeur d'Alene, Telluride, and Cripple Creek followed in swift succession, each the scene of a bloody battle in the historic struggle for emancipation.

The battle of the American Railway Union with the allied railroad corporations in 1894 developed extraordinary activity on the part of our capitalist government. The strikers were completely victorious at every point when the government openly took sides with the railroads and employed all its vast repressive machinery to defeat the strike and crush out the union.

The lessons of this strike were among the most valuable ever learned by the working class, and many thousands date their class-consciousness from that memorable conflict.

The more recent strikes in Colorado, Utah, and other western states, culminating in the kidnapping conspiracy of the mine owners and the bold attempt to repeat the Haymarket and "Mollie Maguire" massacres, are still fresh in the memory of the people, especially the rugged miners who, under the banner of the Western Federation, fought with all the energy and bravery of desperation against the plots and wiles of the organized mine owners, as unscrupulous and heartless an aggregation of exploiters as ever robbed and murdered their fellow beings.

Looking backward over the last 30 years, the progress of the labor movement can be clearly traced, and its contemplation is fruitful of inexpressible satisfaction. Looking forward, the skies are bright and all the tongues of the future proclaim the glad tidings of the coming Emancipation.

John Brown, History's Greatest Hero†

November 23, 1907

The most picturesque character, the bravest man and most self-sacrificing soul in American history, was hanged at Charlestown, Virginia, December 2, 1859.

On that day Thoreau said:

> Some eighteen hundred years ago Christ was crucified. This morning, perchance, Captain Brown was hung. These are the two ends of a chain which is not without its links. He is not "Old Brown" any longer; he is an Angel of Light. * * *
>
> I foresee the time when the painter will paint that scene, no longer going to Rome for a subject; the poet will sing it, the historian record it, and with the landing of the Pilgrims and the Declaration of Independence it will be the ornament of some future national gallery, when at least the present form of slavery shall be no more here. We shall then be at liberty to weep for Captain Brown.[77]

Few people dared on that fateful day to breathe a sympathetic word for the grizzled old agitator. For years he had carried on his warfare against chattel slavery. He had only a handful of fanatical followers to support him. But to his mind his duty was clear, and that was enough. He would fight it out to the end, and if need be alone.

Old John Brown set an example of moral courage and of single-hearted devotion to an ideal for all men and for all ages.

With every drop of his honest blood he hated slavery, and in his early manhood he resolved to lay his life on Freedom's alter in wiping out that insufferable affliction. He never faltered. So God-like was his unconquerable soul that he dared to face the world alone. How perfectly sublime!

He did not reckon the overwhelming numbers against him, nor the paltry few that were on his side. This grosser aspect of the issue found no lodgment in his mind or heart. He was right and Jehovah was with him. His was not to reckon consequences, but to strike the immortal blow and step from the gallows to the throne of God.

† Published in *Appeal to Reason*, whole no. 625 (November 23, 1907), 1.

Not for earthly glory did John Brown wage his holy warfare; not for any recognition or reward the people had it in their power to bestow. His great heart was set upon a higher goal, animated by a loftier ambition. His grand soul was illumined by a sublimer ideal. A race of human beings, lowly and despised, were in chains, and this festering crime was eating out the heart of civilization.

In the presence of this awful plague logic was silent, reason dumb, pity dead.

The wrath of retributive justice, long asleep, awakened at last and hurled its lurid bolt. Old John Brown struck the blow and the storm broke. That hour chattel slavery was dead.

In the first frightful convulsion the slave power seized the grand old liberator by the throat, put him in irons and threw him into a dungeon to await execution.

Alas! it was too late. His work was done. All Virginia could do was to furnish the crown for his martyrdom.

Victor Hugo exclaimed in a burst of reverential passion: "John Brown is grander than George Washington!"[78]

History may be searched in vain for an example of noble heroism and sublime self-sacrifice equal to that of Old John Brown. From the beginning of his career to its close, he had but one idea and one ideal, and that was to destroy chattel slavery; and in that cause he sealed his devotion with his noble blood. Realizing that his work was done, he passed serenely, almost with joy, from the scenes of men.

His calmness upon the gallows was awe-inspiring; his exaltation supreme.

Old John Brown is not dead. His soul still marches on, and each passing year weaves new garlands for his brow and adds fresh luster to his deathless glory.

Who shall be the John Brown of wage-slavery?

Childhood[†]

December 21, 1907

What emotions the recollection of childhood inspires and how priceless its treasured memories in our advancing and declining years!

Laughing eyes and curly hair, little brown hands and bare feet, innocent and carefree, trusting and loving, tender and pure—what an elevating and satisfying influence these little gods have upon our maturer years!

Childhood! What a holy theme! Flowers they are, with souls in them, and if on this earth man has a sacred charge, a solemn obligation, it is to these buds and blossoms of humanity.

Yet how many of them are prematurely plucked, fade and die, and are trampled in the mire. Many millions of them have been snatched from the cradle and stolen from their play to be fed to the forces that turn a workingman's blood into a capitalist's gold, and many millions of others have been crushed and perverted into filth for the slums and food for the potter's field.

Childhood is at the parting of the ways which lead to success or failure, honor or disgrace, life or death. Society is, or ought to be, profoundly concerned in the nature of the environment that is to mold the character and determine the career of its children, and any remissness in such duty is rebuked by the most painful of penalties and these are inflicted with increasing severity upon the people of the United States.

Childhood is the most precious charge of the family and the community, but our capitalist civilization sacrifices it ruthlessly to gratify its brutal lust for pelf and power, and the march of its conquest is stained with the blood of infants and paved with the puny bones of children.

What shall the harvest be?

The millions of children crushed and slain in the conquest of capitalism have not died in vain. From their little graves all over this fair land they are springing up, as it were, against the system that murdered them and pronounce upon it, in the name of God and humanity, the condemnation of death.

† Published in *Appeal to Reason*, whole no. 629 (December 21, 1907), 4.

Panic Philosophy†

December 28, 1907

The average man understands in a vague way there is a panic, so-called, and he is more or less concerned about it according as it affects his business or his employment. But he has never studied economics and knows nothing at all about the laws governing social development. The panic distresses him, it is true, but he is not philosophic enough to inquire into its cause; he simply wants to get rid of the plague.

And so the average man falls easy prey to the political quack in the service of the industrial baron, who glibly rings the changes on "financial stringency," "elastic currency," "lack of confidence," "tariff revision," "trust regulation," and like meaningless twaddle.

It is a fact to be deplored that the average man is a mental child; reads little and that mostly vapid nonsense; thinks less, and reasons not at all. He has to have a "leader" in politics, a "boss" in industry, and a "shepherd" in religion, and they all have a hand in fleecing him to a respectable standstill.

When this average nonentity who is potentially a man hears of a panic, he thinks of it as a screw loose in a machine which a turn or two of the magical monkey-wrench of "confidence" will tighten up, when all will be well again.

That a panic, i.e., industrial congestion and social paralysis, accompanied by widespread poverty, misery, and despair, is the logical effect of an antecedent cause, the poisoned fruit of a corrupt and decaying system, does not occur to his inchoate mentality. This point, the simplest and yet most fundamental in the philosophy of panics, must be driven home to his simple mind.

The business "panic" follows in the wake of its corollary, "business prosperity," as inevitably as the tides rise and fall in obedience to the laws governing their motion.

In a word, the "panic" and its attendant suffering and distress are the corrupt fruit of the corrupt system of capitalism, whose foundations are laid in the broken lives of a quivering mass of wage-slaves.

Abolish the capitalist system and the "panic" will scourge the people no more.

† Published in *Appeal to Reason*, whole no. 630 (December 28, 1907), 2.

Notes

1. Marguerite Marie Bettrich Debs (b. 1828) died on April 29, 1906.
2. Jean Daniel Debs (b. 1820) died on November 27, 1906 and was buried shortly thereafter at Highland Lawn Cemetery in Terre Haute.
3. Chronic pain in the lower back and legs, generally caused by compression of vertebrae impinging on the sciatic nerve.
4. The case of *Pettibone v. Nichols*, a case which began with a writ of habeas corpus challenging the legality of the arrest and transfer of George Pettibone, was argued before the Supreme Court on October 10–11, 1906. Writing for the majority on December 3, Justice John Marshall Harlan wrote that while Pettibone may not have met the legal requirements of a fugitive from justice in Idaho, nevertheless the fact that he had "no reasonable opportunity to present these facts" to a court "before being taken from Colorado constitutes no legal reason why he should be discharged from the custody of the Idaho authorities."
5. Portly Secretary of War William Howard Taft made a last-minute 1906 campaign appearance in Boise in support of the re-election effort of Republican Idaho Governor Frank R. Gooding. Speaking before a packed auditorium of 4,000 supporters on November 3, Taft declared that if Gooding was defeated, "the people of the state would serve notice on the world that criminals or men charged with crime . . . can bring down condemnation upon the officers of law having the courage to bring them to trial."
6. February 17, 1907 was recognized by the labor and socialist movement as "Kidnapping Day," with the *Appeal to Reason* issuing a special edition with a print run of 3 million copies—said to have been the largest edition of any newspaper in the world up to that date.
7. This press-stopping special delivery missive was probably addressed to *Appeal to Reason* editor Fred D. Warren.
8. In his earlier letter to the *Appeal* published January 5, Debs characterized his ailment as "sciatica"—pain of the lower back or legs caused by a pinched nerve. See Debs, "A Personal Word," this volume.
9. The special "Kidnapping Edition" of the *Appeal* was published February 17, 1907.
10. Caldwell, Idaho was the location of the trial of William D. Haywood.
11. Frank R. Gooding took the oath for a second term of office at noon, January 7, 1907 and sent a message to the state legislature immediately afterward. In it, Gooding called for the state of Idaho to assume the cost of trying the Steunenberg case from Canyon County and declared "this is a murder case, and as such it should be tried, regardless of the position the accused men have occupied, or may now occupy in labor organizations . . . . The confession of Harry Orchard, which is corroborated in large part by the late confession of Steve Adams, tells a tale so full of horror as to be almost unbelievable. The proceedings . . . were matters of strict inquiry by the president of the United States, who, acting through his personal representative, the first assistant attorney general of the United States, visited Idaho and made a careful and painstaking investigation of the matter. He reported to the president, and Mr.

Roosevelt has since that time, by word and action, expressed himself heartily in accord with the state in prosecuting the case." See: *Lewiston Evening Teller*, vol. 31, no. 7 (January 9, 1907), 7

12. This letter has not survived. This was probably an answer written to the published letter reprinted here as "The Center of the Fight," this volume.
13. Debs underwent throat surgery by a Cincinnati specialist, a procedure probably made necessary by his occupation as a public orator.
14. Roosevelt.
15. Reference is to Meyer Guggenheim (1828–1905), an industrialist behind a mining and smelting empire spanning the United States and Mexico. Guggenheim was a leading investor in Colorado silver mining and smelting centered in the Leadville region, helping him to build one of the largest family fortunes of the Gilded Age. Guggenheim's son Solomon (1861–1949) was a dedicated modern art collector and is the namesake of the famed museum in New York City.
16. Joseph McKenna (1843–1926) was attorney general under William McKinley and thereafter appointed to the Supreme Court in January 1898 when the seat previously held by Stephen Field became vacant. In his dissent in the case of *Pettibone v. Nichols*, McKenna wrote: "Kidnapping is a crime, pure and simple. . . . But how is it when the law becomes the kidnapper, when the officers of the law, using its forms and exerting its power, become abductors? . . . The foundation of extradition between the states is that the accused should be a fugitive from justice from the demanding state, and he may challenge the fact by habeas corpus immediately upon his arrest. If he refute the fact he cannot be removed. * * * The accused, as soon as he could have done so, submitted his rights to the consideration of the courts. . . . He should not have been dismissed from court, and the action of the Circuit Court in so doing should be reversed." See: *Fredonia [KS] Daily Herald*, vol. 3, no. 266 (February 18, 1907), 1.
17. Humbug.
18. During the evening of June 6, 1904, a railway platform in Independence, Colorado, occupied by strikebreaking miners from the Deadwood mine awaiting a train to return them to home in Victor was destroyed by a bomb, killing 13 and wounding nine others, at least one of whom subsequently died. The bomb, which was estimated to contain between 150 and 300 pounds of black powder, was detonated by the report of a revolver attached to the powder, the trigger of which was pulled by a long wire. Historians and popular writers continue to dispute the identity of the bomber and his motivation, although Steunenberg assassin Harry Orchard took credit for the crime.
19. Edward W. Carmack (1858–1908) was a former Nashville attorney and journalist who was elected to the US House of Representatives as a Democrat in 1896. In 1900 he was tapped by the Tennessee legislature for the United States Senate, in which he served a single six-year term. He was refused a second term and returned to practice law in Nashville in 1907. In November 1908, just four days after his 50th birthday, Carmack was assassinated in the streets of Nashville by political rival Duncan Brown Cooper, also a Tennessee Democratic politician.
20. Weldon B. Heyburn (1852–1912) was a two-term Republican member of the US

Senate from Idaho. Heyburn was a conservative attorney with investments in the mining industry, and he was an opponent of various proposals for conservation and economic reform.

21. Robert M. LaFollette, Sr. (1855–1925) was a progressive Republican who served a five-year stint as governor of Wisconsin before being selected for the United States Senate in 1906. LaFollette would remain in the Senate for the rest of his life, where he was a champion of the labor movement throughout the progressive era. An anti-militarist, LaFollette was a leading opponent of the US entry into World War I, conscription, and the Espionage Act. In 1924 the aging LaFollette made an independent run for president of the United States, which was directly endorsed by the attenuated Socialist Party of America—a race in which he won 16.6 percent of the vote. LaFollette was publisher of *LaFollette's Magazine,* later renamed *The Progressive,* a social democratic monthly, which has survived into the twenty-first century.
22. George Dewey (1837–1917) was an American commodore who became a national hero when he obliterated or captured the entire Spanish Pacific fleet while suffering minimal losses in the 1898 Battle of Manilla Bay. Following this pivotal triumph of the Spanish-American War, Dewey enjoyed a series of promotions, culminating in his elevation to the special rank of Admiral of the Navy in 1903.
23. Elihu Root (1845–1937), a Republican from New York, served as Secretary of War and Secretary of State under Theodore Roosevelt. He was elected to a term in the United States Senate in 1908. In June 1917 he was dispatched by Woodrow Wilson to Russia to head the so-called "Root Commission," which attempted to bolster the commitment of the new revolutionary regime to fight in World War I.
24. "Boss" William M. Tweed (1823–1878) was the legendary head of Tammany Hall, the nerve center of the Democratic Party's political machine in New York City. Tweed made use of patronage to preserve his political power and enriched himself massively through graft and corruption in city contracts. Tweed was ultimately tried and convicted on corruption charges and served one year in jail.
25. Edward Henry Harriman (1848–1909) was a New York railroad speculator and executive who was president of both the Southern Pacific and Union Pacific railroads during the first decade of the twentieth century.
26. Harry Kendall Thaw (1871–1947) was the son of a millionaire Pittsburgh coal and railway tycoon. Thaw sensationally shot and killed renowned architect Stanford White on June 25, 1906 on the rooftop theater at Madison Square Garden in front of hundreds of witnesses. After a hung jury in a first trial, Thaw was found not guilty by reason of insanity in the second and was sentenced to a life term at Matteawan State Hospital for the Criminally Insane in Fishkill, New York.
27. Reference is to Edward Fitzsimmons Dunne (1853–1937), who served as mayor of Chicago from 1905 to 1907.
28. Governor Theodore Roosevelt had the final say in the scheduled March 20, 1899 execution of Martha Place at Sing Sing Prison in Ossining, New York. Roosevelt declined to intervene and the double-murderer Place became the first woman to die on the electric chair. The refusal of Roosevelt to commute the sentence of the

"wretched, insane woman" was condemned by Debs's personal hero Robert Ingersoll as "a disgrace to the state."

29. Theodore Roosevelt, *Ranch Life and the Hunting-Trail* (New York: The Century Co., 1899), 10.
30. George B. Cortelyou (1862-1940), former personal secretary to William McKinley, emerged as the chief of staff for new president Theodore Roosevelt after McKinley's assassination in 1901. In 1903 he was named the first secretary of the Department of Commerce and Labor, before becoming Postmaster General in 1905, and Secretary of the Treasury in 1907.
31. James Hazen Hyde (1876–1959) was the son of Henry B. Hyde, founder of the Equitable Life Assurance Society of the United States. He inherited majority control of the company in 1899 at the age of 23.
32. That is, the 1905 State of the Union address.
33. Matthew S. Quay (1833–1904) was a prominent Republican political boss from Pennsylvania.
34. See "Arouse, Ye Slaves!" March 10, 1906, this volume; and "Labor's Awakening," April 7, 1906, this volume.
35. See "A Few Words, Mr. President: An Open Letter to Theodore Roosevelt," April 15, 1906, this volume.
36. William Loeb, Jr. (1866–1937) was the longtime personal secretary and political advisor of Theodore Roosevelt. He was the father of William Loeb III, publisher of the right-wing *Manchester Union Leader.*
37. An early self-description by publisher Julius Augustus Wayland, emphasizing his folksy style of front page editorializing.
38. Davis H. Waite (1825–1901) was a lawyer and newspaper publisher from Aspen, Colorado. Waite was an organizer of the 1892 national convention of the People's Party in Omaha and the party's successful nominee for governor of Colorado in the election of November 1892. As governor, Waite was supportive of the strike efforts of the Western Federation of Miners and the American Railway Union. Waite was defeated in his bid for reelection in 1894.
39. Eugene D. Engley (1851–1910) was a Colorado attorney who was elected state attorney general in 1893 on the People's Party ticket. He served a single two-year term in office. Engley later moved to Cripple Creek, Colorado, where he was an active supporter of the Western Federation of Miners in the bitter strike of 1903–4, suffering forced deportation in August 1904, from which he bravely returned.
40. The Ruskin Colony was a utopian socialist community established in rural Tennessee. Wayland donated his newspaper and its press to the effort as its official organ.
41. A self-critical account of the failure of the Ruskin colony by a participant may be found in Isaac Broome, *The Last Days of the Ruskin Cooperative Association* (Chicago: Charles H. Kerr & Co., 1902).
42. Reference to a fictional island described in a Utopian novel by William Dean Howells, *A Traveler from Altruria* (1894). The story was first serialized in *The Cosmopolitan* magazine from November 1892 to October 1893.

43. The best known of these was A. S. Edwards, who went from editing *The Coming Nation* to future roles as editor of the *Social Democratic Herald, The Industrial Worker,* and *Industrial Union Bulletin.*
44. Active supporters of the *Appeal* who hustled subscriptions and ordered and distributed bundles of special editions were known as the "*Appeal* Army." This is a play on that term.
45. The 58-year-old J. A. Wayland committed suicide with a handgun on November 11, 1912. As Debs presciently predicts in this piece, an official history of his *Appeal to Reason* was published shortly after his death. See George Allan England, *The Story of the Appeal* (Girard, KS: Appeal to Reason, 1913). The newspaper continued through several name changes, finally terminating as *The American Freeman* in 1951 following the accidental death by drowning of his eventual successor, Emanuel Haldeman-Julius.
46. Mark Twain, *A Connecticut Yankee in King Arthur's Court* (New York: Charles L. Webster & Co., 1889), 157.
47. Jean Reynolds, daughter of Debs's friend and close political associate Stephen M. Reynolds, had fallen gravely ill in September 1906. It was not until about two weeks before this letter was written that news the girl had made a full recovery had been received; she was consequently very much in Debs's thoughts. See also Debs to Reynolds of April 12, 1907, in Constantine, ed., *Letters of Eugene V. Debs, Vol. 1,* 237.
48. Bartholemew W. B. "Bat" Masterson (1853–1921) was an Army scout, gunfighter, and renowned sheriff of Dodge City, Kansas. From 1902 he was a reporter and columnist in New York City on the staff of the *Morning Telegraph.* Masterson was a close friend of New York Governor Theodore Roosevelt.
49. Assuming that Masterson wrote chronologically, this refers to a strike in the summer of 1892 called over a reduction of wages and expansion of working hours. Gun battles between strikers and company security guards took place at several mines in the area, with two killed in the conflict. Martial law was declared and both National Guard and US Army troops inserted. About 600 strikers were rounded up and held without formal charges in miserable concentration camp conditions known as the "bullpen."
50. This refers to the Cripple Creek strike of 1894. Populist Davis H. Waite was a one-term governor of Colorado, serving from January 1893 to January 1895.
51. The editorial in question appeared in print on May 3, 1907. It declared that regardless of the guilt or innocence of Charles Moyer and Bill Haywood in their Idaho trials, "whether they are undesirable citizens is a closed question," as their only public status was as officials of the Western Federation of Miners—"a criminal organization, an organization of men who made a business, not merely of murder, but of massacre." See "Undesirable Citizens," *New York Times,* vol. 56, whole no. 17,996 (May 3, 1907), 6.
52. John Swinton (1829–1901) was an editorial writer for the *New York Times* during the decade of the 1860s and for the *New York Sun* from the second half of the 1870s. In 1883 he launched a labor paper in New York City, the eponymous *John Swinton's Paper,* which terminated for financial reasons in 1887. He would subsequently return

to the editorial staff of the *Sun* as well as write an early monograph on the Pullman strike, a project which provided the vehicle for his becoming personally acquainted with Debs. See John Swinton, *Striking for Life: Labor's Side of the Labor Question* (New York: Western W. Wilson, 1894), reissued as *A Momentous Question: The Respective Attitudes of Capital and Labor* (Philadelphia: Keller Publishing Co., 1895).

53. News of Roosevelt's first letter was dated April 22, 1907 and was written in response to a April 19 communication from Honoré Jackson (also spelled Jaxson) of Chicago, chair of the Cook County Moyer-Haywood Conference. Jackson had queried Roosevelt about his reference to Debs, Moyer, and Haywood as "undesirable citizens" in recently published October 1906 correspondence with E. H. Harriman. Roosevelt rebuked Jackson for having stated "death cannot, will not, and shall not claim our brothers," charging the language "shows you are not demanding a fair trial or working for a fair trial, but are announcing in advance that the verdict shall be one way and that you will not tolerate any other verdict." This, Roosevelt contended, was "flagrant in its impropriety and I join heartily in condemning it." Roosevelt went on to declare that "Messrs. Moyer, Haywood, and Debs stand as representatives . . . who have done much to discredit the labor movement as the worst speculative financiers or most unscrupulous employers and debauchers of legislators have done to discredit honest purposes and fair-dealing men." Roosevelt charged that such labor leaders "habitually appear as guilty of incitement to or apology for bloodshed and violence." See: *New York Times,* vol. 56, whole no. 17,987 (April 24, 1907), 1.

54. Roosevelt's second letter, sent to the Moyer-Haywood-Pettibone committee of the Central Federated Union of New York, was dated May 2, 1907 and was written as a formal response to a visit of the committee to him in Washington, DC. In it Roosevelt extensively quoted a March 25 letter sent to Attorney General Charles Bonaparte, in which he said "there must be no condonation of lawlessness on our part, even if the lawlessness takes the form of an effort to avenge the lawlessness of others." Roosevelt further declared that "the intemperate violence with which the socialistic or labor papers, like that of Debs, and I am sorry to say some labor organizations, have insisted without any knowledge of the facts upon treating these men as martyrs to the cause of labor," which "has unquestionably resulted in tremendous pressure being brought to bear upon the authorities of Idaho to discharge or acquit them, whether guilty or innocent." Roosevelt quoted the writing of Debs on the case and characterized it as "murderous and treasonable" and an effort "to obstruct the course of justice." See: *New York Times,* vol. 56, whole no. 17,999 (May 6, 1907), 1.

55. Brigadier General Sherman M. Bell (1867–1942) commanded the Colorado National Guard during the labor wars that swept the state in 1903 and 1904. The former Rough Rider Bell has been described by one historian as "an arrogant megalomaniac who thought that all labor problems involving the [Western Federation of Miners] were susceptible to a military solution." See George G. Suggs, Jr., *Colorado's War on Militant Unionism* (Detroit: Wayne State University Press, 1972), 81.

56. On April 12, 1904, Captain Bulkley Wells and Adjutant General Sherman M. Bell of the Colorado National Guard were declared in contempt of court by district judge Theron Stevens for failing to comply with a writ of habeas corpus calling for Western Federation of Miners President Charles Moyer to be brought to court from confinement in Telluride. Declaring that "if there is to be a reign of military despotism in this state and civil authority is to have no jurisdiction, the latter might as well go out of business," Judge Stevens ordered that Moyer be released from custody, fined Wells and Bell $500 each, and ordered their arrest. Bell responded belligerently, declaring that he would be arrested only "over the dead bodies of all the soldiers under my command in this county," and that he would take orders to release Moyer only from Governor James H. Peabody. See: *New York Times,* vol. 53, whole no. 16,933 (April 12, 1904), 1. Wells, an 1892 graduate of Harvard University, was himself appointed Adjutant General of the Colorado National Guard in April 1905, succeeding Bell. He narrowly survived an assassination attempt in March 1908 in which his home was blown up with dynamite. In 1921 he was named president of the Comstock Mining Company.
57. Allusion to "A Psalm of Life" (1838) by Henry Wadsworth Longfellow (1807–1882).
58. George III (1738–1820) became heir-apparent to the British throne in 1751 following the premature death of his father and was coronated in October 1760, at the age of 22, following the death of his grandfather. He pursued an unwavering hard line against American colonial independence and the fledgling United States of America throughout his 60-year reign.
59. Harry A. Buchtel (1847–1924), a Republican, was elected in November 1906 to succeed the retiring Jesse McDonald as governor of Colorado. An ordained Methodist minister, Buchtel served a single two-year term as governor. He was chancellor of the University of Denver for more than two decades, a period spanning his brief time in the state house.
60. Apparently an allusion to John D. Rockefeller of Standard Oil.
61. Osawatomie, Kansas was a small anti-slavery town from whence abolitionist guerrilla leader John Brown hailed. In August 1910 Theodore Roosevelt would himself visit the town at the dedication of the John Brown battleground and there deliver his famous "New Nationalism" speech.
62. The phrase is that of US Senator William H. Seward of New York, who in a widely published speech delivered in Rochester on October 25, 1858 declared that the collision of the free and slave systems of economy through expanded railway transportation had generated "an irrepressible conflict between opposing and enduring forces" so that "the United States must and will, sooner or later, become either entirely a slaveholding nation, or entirely a free-labor nation." See: *The Liberator* [Boston], vol. 28, no. 45 (November 5, 1858), 1.
63. Ralph Waldo Emerson (1803–1882) was a philosopher and poet and is recognized as a founder of the transcendentalist movement, based upon individualism, freedom, and appreciation of the natural world. An ordained Protestant minister, Emerson was a staunch supporter of the controversial abolitionist movement and was personally

acquainted with anti-slavery insurrectionist leader John Brown.

64. The exact words of Emerson, uttered as part of his lecture "Courage," delivered on November 8, 1859 at Tremont Temple in Boston, called John Brown "The Saint, whose fate yet hangs in suspense, but whose martyrdom, if it shall be perfected, will make the gallows as glorious as the cross." The large crowd assembled is said to have responded in a "most enthusiastic manner." See *The Liberator* [Boston], vol. 29, no. 45, whole no. 1506 (November 11, 1859), 2.
65. Long-lasting floral arrangements, frequently made of evergreens.
66. This comment by Russian Tsar Nikolai II has not been located, although it was also briefly mentioned, before being stricken by objection, by Haywood defense attorney E. F. Richardson during jury questioning on May 24, 1907.
67. The Idaho legislature approved two funding measures totaling more than $100,000 to pay for the costs of prosecuting the Western Federation of Miners leaders, thereby transferring the legal expense from the county to the state government.
68. This is an excerpt of one of five Chautauqua lectures delivered in the summer of 1907. All were contracted months in advance, prior to Debs joining the staff of the *Appeal to Reason,* and he took a short leave to fulfill these speaking contracts. The full speech was two hours long and was delivered under a big-top tent to a crowd estimated between 1,000 and 2,000 people.
69. The suggestion of a nomination of Big Bill Haywood for president by the Socialist Party was first made in "The Coming Climax in the Irrepressible Struggle for Emancipation," *Appeal to Reason,* May 18, 1907, reprinted in this volume.
70. The reference is to the Haymarket affair.
71. The *Industrial Union Bulletin* was the official organ of the majority faction of the Industrial Workers of the World. Editor A. S. Edwards inserts the following argumentative footnote here: "The writer should also have said, in behalf of historical accuracy, that the movement for industrial unionism, i.e. the Industrial Workers of the World, has met with bitter opposition from Socialist Party leaders, who, for the sake of winning votes, flirt with those who now uphold 'the lower primal forms of trade unionism.'"
72. The Mollie Maguires were an Irish secret society which became active in the anthracite coal mines of Pennsylvania after the economic panic of 1873. In December 1874 coal operators announced a 20 percent wage reduction, which triggered an extended period of strikes and violence, including assassinations and killings on both sides. Franklin Gowen, head of the Philadelphia & Reading Railroad, hired the Pinkerton Detective Agency to help suppress the organization, which was successfully infiltrated. Testimony of Pinkerton undercover operative James McParland led to the conviction and execution of 10 alleged members of the organization in June 1877.
73. Franklin B. Gowen (1836–1889), chief counsel of the Reading Railroad, was named president of the line in 1869. Already deeply involved in coal hauling, the aggressive Gowen was instrumental in vertically integrating the railroad into its own mining operations—a decision which brought him into direct conflict with mine workers in future strike actions. Also conveniently serving as district attorney, Gowen hired

the Pinkerton Detective Agency to help crush the incipient effort of mine worker organization, with James McParland (later of Haywood-Moyer-Pettibone fame) the Pinkerton operative who successfully infiltrated the secret union, leading to its violent repression for culpability in strike-related murders. The Reading Railroad ran into deep financial problems in 1880, culminating in a bankruptcy, with Gowen remaining in charge until his ouster in a November 1886 reorganization. Thereafter he returned to the practice of law. Gowen died in December 1889 of a self-inflicted gunshot wound.

74. The failed 1888 strike of locomotive engineers and firemen against the Chicago, Burlington & Quincy Railroad (also known as the "Burlington" and the "Q") was a seminal event in the intellectual development of Gene Debs. The defeat of the isolated and undermined enginemen in this lengthy and bitter conflict led him away from craft insularity and to the idea of federating multiple brotherhoods of the railroad running trades in 1889 under the banner of the Supreme Council of the United Orders of Railway Employees. The failure of this latter organization due to jurisdictional infighting led Debs in 1893 to make a bid at industrial unionism of all railroad workers regardless of craft in the American Railway Union. See *Selected Works of Eugene V. Debs,* volumes I and II, *passim.*
75. Reference is to the railroad switchmen's strike of 1892.
76. Reference is to the Pullman strike of 1894.
77. From "A Plea for Captain John Brown" (1859), by Henry David Thoreau (1817–1862). Thoreau delivered several lectures in Massachusetts in late October and early November on "The Character and Actions of Captain John Brown," attempting to rally public support for his case.
78. On December 2, 1859, believing John Brown had received a last-minute reprieve from execution, French novelist Victor Hugo wrote a letter to the *London News* extolling the condemned anti-slavery militant. In it, Hugo held up George Washington as "a majestic form" which "rises before the imagination" and condemned the prospective killing in "the land of Washington" as an "irreparable fault" that would "penetrate the Union with a gaping fissure which would lead in its end to its entire disruption." He concluded his appeal for clemency with the words "there is something more terrible than Cain slaying Abel: It is Washington slaying Spartacus." It is unclear whether or where Hugo ever used the words attributed to him by Debs. Brown was in fact executed on the day Hugo wrote his letter.

1908

For Joint Action in 1908: Letter to Frank Bohn, National Secretary Socialist Labor Party of America†

January 9, 1908

Terre Haute, Indiana, January 9, 1908

Mr. Frank Bohn
National Secretary, SLP
New York, NY

Dear Comrade:—

I have just received a copy of the *Daily People* of the 7th inst. [January 7, 1908] containing the resolutions adopted by the Executive Committee of the SLP [Socialist Labor Party] on the unity question, and I drop you this line to extend congratulations to your board and to say that the resolutions, in spirit and purport, have my hearty concurrence.[1] No matter what differences there may be, they are not of sufficient account to prevent joint nominations and political unity all along the line in the national, state, and local campaigns this fall.

I shall do all I can to have the Socialist Party accept the resolutions of the Socialist Labor Party in the spirit in which they are offered. I am writing National Secretary Barnes and sending an article to the *Appeal to Reason,* urging favorable action.[2]

Earnestly hoping for the successful outcome of this move and for a united and vigorous campaign against the common enemy, I remain,

Yours Fraternally,
E. V. Debs

† Published in *Daily People,* vol. 8, no. 21 (January 28, 1908), undetermined page. Reprinted in *Weekly People,* vol. 17, no. 45 (February 1, 1908), 6.

Samuel Gompers in Politics†

January 18, 1908

The press reports advise us that Samuel Gompers, president of the American Federation of Labor, and other leaders, local, state, and national, are going to take a hand in politics. With a flourish of trumpets the announcement is made that their opposition is to be concentrated upon William H. Taft, Republican candidate for the presidency of the United States.

After the results attending the political crusade of the same leaders in the recent reelection of Joseph Cannon as a member of Congress, and later as speaker of the House of Representatives,[3] saying nothing of the similar fiasco attending a similar campaign against Congressman Littlefield, of Maine,[4] it would seem in order to suggest that any further political announcement from that source would be treated as a huge joke.

Whenever and wherever Gompers and his lieutenants concentrate their attack upon a capitalist politician, it is for the sole purpose of electing some other capitalist politician and if this kind of politics has any effect at all it is to strengthen rather than weaken the candidate's chances and make his election, if at all doubtful, a foregone conclusion. In the case of "Uncle Joe" Cannon, the declaration of Gompers that he proposed to fight him had but little effect and that little was to rally Cannon's supporters and make his election unanimous.

Now we have always been in favor of labor going into politics, and not only this, but we have always been and are now in favor of labor running the government. But our position differs very decidedly from that of Mr. Gompers, and since we are now approaching a national election of the greatest importance, we take this occasion to address a few words to the workingmen of the United States, especially those who are organized in trade unions and affiliated with the American Federation of Labor.

We are going to speak as we feel, in perfect kindness and frankness. Our lot has long been cast with labor and all our hopes center in its triumph. We therefore have the right to invite the attention of workingmen and to have a heart-to-heart talk with them.

† Published as "Labor in Politics" in *Appeal to Reason,* whole no. 633 (January 18, 1908), 4.

First, President Gompers believes that the interests of labor and capital are identical or mutual. We do not. He believes these interests can be harmonized and justice done to both. We do not. We believe labor is entitled to all it produces and that labor must organize politically as well as economically to abolish the existing order, put itself in possession of the means of production, employ itself, and take all it produces.

Second, Mr. Gompers does not believe in independent political action. We do. Mr. Gompers and his lieutenants have been trying for many years to procure legislation in favor of labor. They have failed miserably, utterly, and we may say, contemptibly, and they always will. Mr. Gompers and his staff are divided between the Republican and the Democratic parties, both capitalist parties, the one more corrupt than the other, and between these two parties they have shifted back and forth, back and forth, alternating the amusement by being used as a football by both until they have become objects of contempt among politicians and the laughingstock of the people.

Third, we are agreed with Mr. Gompers upon just one point. We do not want the unions as such to become political bodies or to be used to promote political ends. We believe in the thorough organization of the working class upon the economic field and we also believe in the thorough organization of the working class upon the political field. Each of these has its own functions, and if wisely directed these will harmonize perfectly in the waging of the class struggle for industrial emancipation.

Fourth, we have said and wish to repeat that Mr. Gompers and his sub-leaders have secured practically nothing through legislation and never will. The reason is self-evident. Republican and Democratic congressmen are representatives of capitalism. Their respective platforms prove it. It is scarcely less than idiocy for labor leaders to expect these tools of capitalism to legislate in the interest of labor. It would be quite as reasonable to expect a cow to bray or a mule to bark. A capitalist congress can no more change its nature than a leopard can change its spots. Mr. Gompers and his crown use their influence to elect a capitalist congress; what right have they to object to capitalist legislation? If they want labor legislation, let them turn their efforts to the election of a labor congress, as socialists have long since done, and then they will get it and not before.

Mr. Gompers' eight-hour and injunction bills have been shoved into the wastebasket for so many years that it might be supposed that even Mr. Gompers himself would at last take a tumble. The legislatures of the several states have made monkeys of labor committees, while courts, high, low, jack and the game, have handed down one decision after another landing between the eyes of organized labor, and yet Mr. Gompers and his followers still persist in attempting to stop the thundering political engine of the capitalist class by laying pins on the tracks of capitalism.

We are not with Mr. Gompers in his fight on William H. Taft, or any other particular capitalist politician. We are against the whole bunch, whether labeled Republicans or Democrats, for they stand essentially for the same system and that system is the private ownership of the means of life and the slavery of the working class. And that is precisely what President Gompers stands for and we challenge him to disprove it.

Why, let us ask Mr. Gompers, does he propose a political crusade against Taft? Is it to beat Taft? Or is it to lead the labor vote on a wild goose chase to keep it divided and prevent it from organizing independent political action of its own to defeat not only Taft but to wipe out the whole brood of political tricksters who for years have trafficked in the ignorance and stupidity of labor, largely through the instrumentality of just such blind leaders of the blind of which Samuel Gompers, president of the American Federation of Labor, is the undisputed leader?

Again, if Mr. Gompers opposes Taft for president, whom does he favor for that office? The only candidate who will truly represent labor will be the Socialist, and Mr. Gompers will oppose him as he always has done. Then whom will he support? Why, some other capitalist candidate, of course; that is, some candidate who has not yet made his record on eight-hour laws and injunction decisions.

The only earthly difference between Taft and the other fellow whom Gompers will favor is that Taft has a record, a consistent capitalist record, while the other fellow has his still to make.

Gompers has learned nothing in his 25 years of labor leadership. He is still hanging on to the old method of supporting good candidates before election to be kicked by them after election and lining up his deluded followers to invite and receive the contempt of wily politicians who have no use for workingmen except as they can be used to further their political ends.

The political program of President Gompers is a farce. It is worse than this, it is a fraud without one redeeming feature.

Think of it a moment! Gompers has been "after Cannon"—a thousand miles or so after him. Now he is "after Taft"—so far after him that he seems very diminutive in the distance. It would be very laughable if it were not at the price of labor. Gompers will not suffer but the wage-slaves must foot the entire bill.

We appeal to such of our readers as belong to labor unions to think this matter over for themselves. We are not attempting to establish any leadership in opposition to that of Mr. Gompers or anyone else. We are wanting workingmen and women to open their eyes and see for themselves; to use their brains and think for themselves, and above all, to stop blindly following in the footsteps of some supposed leader who has been leading them by the nose, through ignorance or design, for lo! these many years, straight into the camp of the enemy.

If Mr. Gompers has planned a campaign to elect some capitalist president of the United States who is personally agreeable to him, let him elect that gentleman with the support of capitalist votes. Workingmen have no more interest in electing the pet capitalist candidate of Mr. Gompers than they have in defeating William Taft for the same purpose. All capitalist candidates look alike to us. We are for labor. We are opposed to the Tafts and Roots, the Hearsts and the Tillmans, and the whole raft of capitalist representatives who are for labor only when they want its vote and after they are inducted into office, by the help of Mr. Gompers and his followers, issue injunctions and send out soldiers in evidence of their capitalist gratitude for the working class votes which elected them.

We appeal to the working class to quit capitalist parties of whatever name and join the Socialist Party, the only party of the working class in the United States. We appeal to every sturdy son of toil in this presidential year to cast his lot with his class and with his class strike out bravely, resolutely, unflinchingly for freedom.

Progress by Prohibition [excerpt]†

March 1, 1908

Some well-meaning but deluded people think that all wickedness can be overcome and the millennium ushered in by prohibition. Anything they do not happen to like is bad, according to their ethics, and forthwith is put upon their prohibition list. These people strain at gnats and swallow camels. They throw a fit over a man taking a drink at 11:30 [a.m.] or playing a game of cards, but

† Published in *Terre Haute Tribune* (March 1, 1908). Reprinted in *St. Louis Labor*, vol. 6, whole no. 372 (March 21, 1908), 7.

they are not concerned about wage-slavery, or child-sweating, which have a thousand victims where the saloon has one.

These people are not satisfied to be permitted to spend their Sundays as they choose, but they must see to it that others spend their Sundays in the same way. According to these fanatics, practically everything in town is to be closed Sunday except the churches. This means that Terre Haute is to be converted into a Sabbatarian penitentiary. The gospel of gloom will then be triumphant and the spirit of bigotry and intolerance will seek other fields to conquer.

Thirty days of this kind of punishment would be a good thing for Terre Haute. A 60 days' sentence would be still better. It would cure the community of its puritanic affliction, as it has others, for many years.

There are some of us who prefer the theaters to the church; who would rather be entertained at a play than to listen to a stupid sermon. We do not in the least object to people going to church; it is their right and purely their own affair. We simply insist upon the same right to go to the theater, or to the ball park, or wherever we choose, so long as we do not interfere with the equal right of our neighbors.

It is wonderful how tamely people will submit to this spirit of intolerance, this mean and narrow fanaticism. I know that many are opposed to it and yet such is their economic dependence that they dare not speak out for fear they may lose some "trade," or some "practice," or some "prestige," or something else upon which they depend as a means of livelihood.

It is quite the thing in this crusade to pounce upon the saloonkeeper and hold him up as a monster of iniquity. I have no brief to speak for him, but as long as the saloon is licensed by the government it is just as lawful as any other business in the profit-mongering system, and the saloonkeeper is entitled to the same consideration as any other citizen. The saloonkeeper is no more responsible for the saloon than the preacher is for the church, and the saloonkeeper is not necessarily a bad man, nor the preacher necessarily a good one. Speaking for myself, if I were hungry and friendless today I would rather take my chances with the average saloonkeeper than with the average preacher.

It seems not a little strange that this gospel of puritanism, born of the same spirit which hanged witches and tortured Quakers, should be preached in the name of Jesus Christ. There is not a word in all he ever uttered to justify it, and if he happened to enter Terre Haute today as he entered Jerusalem, presenting the same appearance, having the same mission, and being followed by the same crowd, these solemn bigots would be the first to call him a hobo and demand that he be sent to the rock pile for profaning the Sabbath.

Shall Warren Be Railroaded?†

March 28, 1908

There have been many curious turns in the federal prosecution instituted against Fred D. Warren, editor of the *Appeal,* since the indictment was first brought against him and he was placed under arrest a trifle less than a year ago.[5] Since then he has been constantly under bail, has had two hearings and repeated consultations with his lawyers, but the case is as uncertain as ever as to its final outcome. The only thing known for certain is that the law provides that Warren may be fined $5,000 and sentenced to the penitentiary at hard labor for five years. It is not pleasant to have such a sentence hanging over one's head for so long a time, and in some respects is worse, in fact, than the sentence itself, but Warren has never once complained, and although the uncertainty of his fate has somewhat hampered him in his plans for the future, he has gone on with his work as undaunted as if no case against him were pending.

On his own personal account he is not concerned about the outcome, but the probable effect upon the paper, and by reflex upon the movement, in case of an adverse verdict, has been seriously considered, and as a result it has been concluded to resist the indictment as far as legal ability can successfully do so, and to this end Clarence S. Darrow has been employed to re-enforce General Boyle, Judge Doster, and L. H. Phillips, counsel for the defense.

Mr. Darrow will make the principal address to the jury, and this feature of the trial and the forensic effort he will feel inspired to make on behalf of a free press will create widespread interest.

Whatever may be our opinion of the courts under capitalism, there is a vital principle involved in this case, and the outcome may have an important bearing upon the socialist press and free speech in the United States. I have always believed this to be a case of critical importance although pivoted upon what seems a very trivial incident.

Of course, no one who has followed the case supposes for an instant that the prosecution was inspired by a sense of outraged justice on behalf of ex-Governor Taylor of Kentucky, the only person who could have been wronged in the remotest by the publication which provoked the indictment. The whole

† Published in *Appeal to Reason,* whole no. 643 (March 28, 1908), 1.

case rests upon the offer of the reward for the fugitive Taylor and sending it through the mails, a mere repetition in a small way of what the authorities of Kentucky had been doing on a large scale. It was a trifling incident. Taylor did not complain. Why should anyone else?

The reason is obvious. Here was an opening, so long looked for, to strike the *Appeal* a deadly blow. It was not to defend Taylor—they care nothing about him—but to destroy the *Appeal* that the proceeding was instituted.

It was not to preserve the purity of the mails, for every day hundreds of similar rewards offered by sheriffs are sent through the mails, and no one has ever dreamed of filing a complaint.

No, it is not to vindicate Taylor, nor to send Warren to the penitentiary, but to intimidate the *Appeal*'s policy, bankrupt its treasury, and compass its ruin. That is the object and the hope of the prosecution, and whether it succeeds or fails is a matter of far less consequence to Fred Warren, even if he is put in stripes, than it is to the socialist and labor press, and to the working people of the United States.

There is not the slightest doubt that Inspector Chance told the truth when he said that the order had come from the department at Washington to "reopen the case" and push it to a successful termination. Assistant District Attorney West virtually confirmed this when in the course of his heated argument at Fort Scott [Kansas] he said he had received a letter from the department at Washington saying that the offense with which Warren was charged came within purview of the law, and that he could, and should, be convicted. Further evidence is found in the following paragraph taken from a special dispatch from Washington to the *Dallas News* of March 13th in regard to the defeat of the Penrose bill:

> The Penrose bill makes eight printed lines, but, like dynamite, it was potential in small quantities. It proposed to vest the postmaster general with an absolute power of censorship.

Of course, it wasn't intended that this absolute power should be used in an absolute way. The introduction of the bill was occasioned by the lurid utterances of a socialist organ in a western state, and while it was to be a general law it was intended only for particular application.

The staff correspondent of the *News* who sent this dispatch to his paper was on the ground and knew whereof he spoke. The Penrose bill was intended, not to have general application, but to suppress the *Appeal*, and that is precisely what was predicted by the prosecuting attorney at the time of the Warren hearing—that is, the next session of Congress a bill would be introduced that would "fix the *Appeal*."[6]

The *Kansas City Journal* regretted that there was not already a Penrose bill on the statute books when it said editorially: "It is unfortunate that a technicality has to be invoked in order to make a case against the *Appeal*." In the same editorial the *Journal* stated that the prosecution had been directed from Washington by no less a person than President Roosevelt himself, and that the suppression of the "viperous sheet known as the *Appeal to Reason*" would have the hearty support of the national administration.

It is therefore seen at a glance that it is not Warren, but the *Appeal*, that is on trial, and in fact the socialist press, for if the *Appeal* can be loaded down with court costs, and its editor put in stripes, so can the *Chicago Socialist*,[7] the *New York Worker*,[8] and other revolutionary papers, and the most trifling incident will be sufficient to serve as justification for the assault.

Ever since the Haywood trial, the *Appeal* has been under the ban. But for the socialist press the conspiracy would have succeeded. The baffled conspirators swore vengeance. Since then they have made repeated attempts to have the *Appeal* excluded from the mails. The suit against Warren was one attack; the Penrose bill another. There were others made by stealth, of which no report can now be made. Enough to say that the postmaster at Girard has be superseded in office because he was reported as "too friendly to the *Appeal*." The truth is that he treated the *Appeal* honestly and would not be a party to the machinations to oust it from the mails, and it is now predicted that previous attempts which failed on his account will now be renewed.

The trial which opens May 4th in Fort Scott[9] will be the trial of the radical press of the United States. It is not the *Appeal* alone that is to be silence but the whole revolutionary press that is to be suppressed, and if the attempt is successful and a paper escapes, it will be because it is not of sufficient consequence to menace the ruling class.

Of course the charge is falsely made that the *Appeal* is a violent and anarchistic sheet, and ought to be suppressed in the interest of peace and order. That is mere subterfuge. Every journal that scourges capitalism and exposes its crimes and iniquities is a "nest of vipers to be exterminated," in the lurid phrase of a capitalist paper recently applied to the *Appeal*.

The attack on Warren was conceived in revenge. It is an attack on labor and the reason for it is plain enough. Moyer, Haywood, and Pettibone escaped the gallows. That was a bitter pill for the kidnappers. The *Appeal* helped to administer it and Warren was in editorial control of the *Appeal* and responsible for its policy.

ᘓ

In the fight for the lives of the federation leaders, Warren led repeated charges that staggered the conspirators. From the very first he plunged into the conflict; he was ever at the front, and in the thickest; he never wavered. His courage was heroic and his example an inspiration. He staked all and asked no favors. Hundreds of his readers warned, pleaded, and threatened. They were sure he was too radical and that the *Appeal* would be ruined; that it was simply another Haymarket and that radical and inflammatory speech would but intensify the public prejudice and seal the fate of the kidnapped comrades.

To all such entreaties and protests Warren was deaf. He had taken his stand and there could be no retreat. He relied wholly upon arousing the militant spirit of the working class, and upon the socialist press as the chief means to that end, and more than any other, Fred Warren contributed by his daring, his resourcefulness, and his unflinching tenacity to that magnificent national demonstration of working class solidarity which palsied the kidnappers and snatched their intended victims from their nerveless grasp and saved them from the bloody executioner.

Had the battle been lost, Warren would have been condemned, ruined, and disgraced. But the battle was won. Warren was happy and modestly resumed his usual round. But he was marked. The black hand now pointed in his direction. The prey had escaped and he was chiefly to blame.

Moyer, Haywood, and Pettibone could not be hanged, but Warren could be put into chains, and the *Appeal* out of business. And so happened the discovery that Warren had circulated "scurrilous, defamatory, and threatening matter" through the mails and that the majesty of the outraged law must be vindicated.

Had Warren been the editor of a capitalist paper, or of a labor paper without circulation, and had mailed precisely the same matter, the charge would never have been dreamed of. The Democratic papers of Kentucky had spread vastly more threatening matter about Taylor and had offered all kinds of rewards for his return, but they were capitalist papers—they were not the "vile anarchistic Kansas sheet" which had so much to do with stirring up the working class and liberating the "federation criminals."

Now, what was the specific charge against Warren? What was his crime? Why, he is charged with putting in the mails a reward of $1,000 for the capture of a fugitive capitalist politician under indictment for murder, a thing done by sheriffs and other persons every day, and all over the country. But it was not this of itself that served as the subterfuge for the arrest and prosecution. It was the effect it had. It was a strategic move and proved a master stroke. It drew the capitalist lightning. No single incident equaled it. It lighted up the scene and stripped the conspiracy naked. Its effect was instantaneous. The Associated Press was opened by this charge of dynamite. It vomited abuse. The enemy was hit. The St. Louis papers had a full page sensationally illustrated.

It was the dramatic element in the episode which appealed to the public. It was bold and daring, and this excited interest, tense and thrilling.

In a crisis the mass is deaf to calm reason, dead to mere logic. Warren knew this; he exploded a bomb and created a sensation. This gave him the crowd. Pointing to Moyer, Haywood, and Pettibone in the shadow of the gibbet, he said: "There are three honest workingmen kidnapped by a conspiracy of two governors, and a lot of rich mine owners; the president has pronounced them guilty and the Supreme Court has legalized their kidnapping." Then turning to Taylor he said: "There is a governor, indicted for murder, a fugitive from justice; the president pronounces him innocent, and the courts will not allow him to be arrested."

The effect it had was to arouse resentment; to fan the militant fire into a conflagration. It was not intended to kidnap Taylor, nor to "defame" or "threaten" him; but simply to point out an object lesson and it served the purpose.

It was the socialist and labor press and an aroused working class which saved the federation leaders, and the same forces should rally to the support of Warren. It is for fighting the same battles of the working class that he has been marked and is now to be sentenced. It is a continuation of the same determination on the part of the mine owners and other capitalists to punish labor's champions, gag its press, crush its unions, silence its mutterings, and perpetuate its slaver.

It is Warren's turn today—whose will it be tomorrow, and the next day?

Haywood and Pettibone were tried in the state court by a judge elected by the people. Warren will be tried in a United States court by a judge appointed for life by President Roosevelt. The jury will consist wholly of political opponents, more or less prejudiced against socialism, and the prosecutor will doubtless make an impassioned plea to crush "the viper of anarchy and assassination."

The case has dragged on within a few days of a year. The expense already foots up $4,000, and the trial has not yet actually begun. How many more thousands will be levied can only be conjectured. The average socialist or labor paper would already be bankrupt, but if the *Appeal* only had an average circulation, it would not be in the toils.

There is method in the court's delay. The longer the trial, the greater the costs, and socialist papers are not noted for their swollen bank accounts.

ᔕ

At the preliminary hearing in November last, Judge Pollock, apparently, all but dismissed the case. Everyone was surprised. His implications were too clear and direct to be misinterpreted. At the close of the session Warren's lawyers and friends gathered around him and tendered their congratulations. The case was as good as dismissed.

In chambers, a few weeks later and without a word of comment, [Judge Pollock] denied the motion to quash the indictment and set May 4th as the date for trial.

In a few days more the trial will begin. How long it will last or what the outcome will be, no one can tell. From all appearances the case will be hotly contested and no effort will be spared to secure a conviction.

It is the duty of the socialist and labor press to stand by Warren as he stood by Moyer, Haywood, and Pettibone, and I am confident such will be its attitude. To once more arouse the working class and to have it understand what this trial means to it is now the task, and this, and this alone, will save Warren from prison as it saved our western comrades from the gallows.

This is election year, and this fact can be turned to advantage. If the workers of the nation show their determination to stand by Warren, as is their duty, he will never be convicted, and another crushing defeat will be administered to the enemy and another splendid victory achieved for the working class.

When Warren faces trial I shall be with him, regretting only that I cannot share the penalty if he is sentenced. It is not merely on his own personal account, or on account of his wife and children that I sympathize with him and shall give him all the aid in my power, but because he has fought the good fight unflinchingly and deserves the loyal and enthusiastic support of the whole working class of the nation.

The Federal Court and Union Labor: The Buck Stove and Range Case†

April 11, 1908

The recent decisions of the Supreme Court of the United States leave no doubt as to the attitude of that tribunal toward organized labor. These decisions, so far as they are vital, are uniformly and emphatically hostile to labor unionism. The decision outlawing the boycott and holding a union and its members liable for damages sustained by a boycotted employer practically disarms the union and places its members at the mercy of their employers.

The strike and the boycott are now both virtually outlawed and this leaves labor without any lawful means of defense under the present system.

The decision of the federal court at Washington in the injunction proceedings instituted by Buck Stove and Range Company against the American Federation of Labor and its national officers not only makes the boycott unlawful but goes so far as to prohibit the officers and members of a labor union, "either by printed or written word, or orally," from calling their employers by name or making any allusion to their unfairness to labor.[10]

To even whisper of an employer's hostility is to be in contempt of court. It must be borne in reverential silence. Thou shalt not call the name of the employer, thy master, in vain!

When this injunction was made permanent by Judge Gould, of the district federal court at Washington, and Mr. Gompers, president of the American Federation of Labor, was enjoined from publishing the usual "unfair list" in his official organ,[11] it was intimated in the press dispatches that he would refuse to obey the order of the court. In an editorial in a succeeding issue, he said: "With all due respect to the court it is impossible for us to see how we can comply with all the terms of this injunction." Nevertheless, Mr. Gompers did comply with it insofar as the "unfair list" was concerned, and it has not since appeared. In issuing his appeal for financial aid in defense of a free press and free speech, Mr. Gompers said: "The injunction invades the liberty of the press, the liberty of speech." And yet Mr. Gompers, as the official leader of organized labor, abjectly obeys it.

† Published as "The Federal Court and Union Labor" in *Appeal to Reason,* whole no. 645 (April 11, 1908), 1.

Wendell Phillips once said that real men trample down unjust laws and defy those who enact them. This decision, or order, of the federal court enjoining the working class from publishing, writing, or speaking the names of its enemies is not even a law. It is simply the *ipse dixit*[12] of a corporation lawyer who happens to be a federal judge.

That is all.

Most of the laws which now fetter labor unionists, restrict its operations within harmless bounds, and stifle its speech are made in that way. The constitution of the United States never conferred any such power upon the Supreme Court and federal judges. They have simply usurped it, helped themselves, and the people have submitted.

There are times when forbearance is a disgrace and submission a crime.

The labor movement should call a halt. To appeal to Congress, composed of the representatives of the trusts and corporations for fresh laws to be declared unconstitutional, is the climax of folly and sycophancy. The Supreme Court is supreme and will be so long as the people tamely submit to its usurpation of power, and so long as its despotic and outrageous decisions remain unchallenged.

The working class is supreme when it wills.

I have been asked what I should have done in the place of Mr. Gompers. I should have expressed myself as Mr. Gompers did, only more so, and then I should have done what he did not do. Upon that issue I should rather have been in jail than not to have been in contempt.

I should have ignored the injunction, continued the "unfair list," and compelled the court to rescind its order or enforce it. Moreover, I should have advised all labor papers not carrying the list to incorporate it in their columns. And they would have done it, and in so doing would have been backed up by 3 million union men. Then let the Supreme Court of the trusts and corporations put the American labor movement in jail for contempt!

It is just such spineless submission which invites such judicial contempt. The labor decisions, or rather anti-labor decisions, of the federal court are a travesty upon justice and an insult to the intelligence of labor, if it has any, and if once treated accordingly the court would in that hour purge itself of contempt for the working class.

The organized workingmen and women of this country should not hesitate to express their contempt for any court when it is deserved. In this war of the classes in capitalist society, labor has the undoubted right of refusing its patronage to its enemies and of calling them by name. If it has not that right, it has no right at all and is in abject slavery; and any order which denies that primal right ought to be ignored and the court that issues it treated with contempt.

The organized workers of the United States would undoubtedly support an attitude of defiance to such an outrageous invasion of their fundamental rights as human beings.

Labor's Fight for Freedom†

April 11, 1908

The trade union movement of the present day has enemies within and without, and upon all sides, some attacking it openly and others insidiously, but all bent either upon destroying it or reducing it to impotency.

The enemies of unionism, while differing in method, are united solidly upon one point, and that is in the effort to misrepresent and discredit the men who, scorning and defying the capitalist exploiters and their minions, point steadily the straight and uncompromising course the movement must take if it is to accomplish its allotted task and safely reach the destined port.

These men, though frequently regarded as enemies, are the true friends of trade unionism and in good time are certain to be vindicated.

The more or less open enemies have inaugurated some startling innovations during the past few years. The private armies the corporations used some years ago, such as Pinkerton mercenaries, coal and iron police, deputy marshals, etc., have been relegated to second place as out of date, or they are wholly out of commission. It has been found after related experiments that courts are far more deadly to trade unions, and that they operate noiselessly and with unerring precision.

Step by step the writ of injunction has invaded the domain of trade unionism, limiting its jurisdiction, curtailing its powers, sapping its strength, and undermining its foundations.

Injunctions have been issued restraining the trade unions and their members from striking, from boycotting, from voting funds to strikers, from

† Published in *Appeal to Reason,* whole no. 645 (April 11, 1908), 3.

levying assessments to support their members, from walking on the public highways, from asking non-union men not to take their places, from meeting to oppose wage reductions, from expelling a spy from membership, from holding conversations with those who had been taken or were about to take their jobs from congregating in public places, from holding meetings, from doing anything and everything—directly, indirectly, or any other way—to interfere with the employing class in their unalienable right to operate their plants as their own interests may dictate and to run things generally to suit themselves.

The courts have found it in line with judicial procedure to strike every weapon from labor's economic hand and leave it defenseless at the mercy of its exploiter; and now that the courts have gone to the last extremity in this nefarious plot of subjugation, labor, at last, is waking up to the fact that it has not been using its political arm in the struggle at all; that the ballot which it can wield is strong enough not only to disarm the enemy, but to drive that enemy entirely from the field.

The courts, so notoriously in control of capital, and so shamelessly perverted to its base and sordid purposes, are, therefore, exercising a wholesome effect upon trade unionism by compelling the members to note the class character of our capitalist government and driving them to the inevitable conclusion that the labor question is also a political question and that the working class must organize their political power that they may wrest the government from capitalist control and put an end to class rule forever.

Trade unionists for the most part learn slowly, but they learn surely, and fresh object lessons are prepared for them every day.

They have seen a Democratic president of the United States send the federal troops into a sovereign state of the union in violation of the constitution, and in defiance of the governor and the people, to crush a body of peaceable workingmen at the behest of a combination of railroads bent on destroying their union and reducing them to vassalage.[13]

They have seen a Republican president refuse to interpose his executive authority when militarism, in the name of the capitalist class, seized another sovereign state by the throat and strangled its civil administration to death while it committed the most dastardly crimes upon defenseless workingmen in the annals of capitalist brutality and military despotism.

They have seen a composite Republican-Democratic Congress, the legislative tool of the exploiting class, pass a military bill which makes every citizen a soldier and the president a military dictator.

They have seen this same Congress, session after session, making false promises to deluded labor committees pretending to be the friends of workingmen and anxious to be of service to them, while at the same time in league with the capitalist lobby and pledged to defeat every measure that would afford even the slightest promise of relief to the working class. The anti-injunction bill and the eight-hour measure, pigeonholed and rejected again and again in the face of repeated promises that they should pass, tell their own story of duplicity and treachery to labor of the highest legislative body of the land.

They have seen Republican governors and Democratic governors order out the militia repeatedly to shoot down workingmen at the command of their capitalist masters.

They have seen these same governors construct military prisons and "bull-pens," seize unoffending workingmen without warrant of law, and thrust them into these vile quarters for no other reason than to break up their unions and leave them helpless at the feet of corporate rapacity.

They have seen the Supreme Court of the nation turn labor out without a hearing, while the corporation lawyers, who compose this august body, and who hold their commissions in virtue of the "well done" of their capitalist retainers, solemnly descant upon the immaculate purity of our judicial institutions.

They have seen state legislatures, both Republican and Democratic, with never an exception, controlled bodily by the capitalist class, turn the committees of labor unions empty-handed from their doors.

They have seen the state supreme courts declare as unconstitutional the last vestige of law upon the statute books that could by any possibility be construed as affording any shelter or relief to the labor union or its members.

They have seen these and many other things and will doubtless see many more before their eyes are opened as a class; but we are thankful for them all, painful though they be to us in having to bear witness to the suffering of our benighted brethren. In this way only can they be made to see, to think, to act, and every wrong they suffer brings them nearer to their liberation.

The "pure and simple" trade union of the past does not answer the requirements of today, and they who insist that it does are blind to the changes going on about them and out of harmony with the progressive forces of the age. The attempt to preserve the "autonomy" of each trade and segregate it within its own independent jurisdiction, while the lines which once separated them are being obliterated, and the trades are being interwoven and interlocked in the process of industrial evolution, is as futile as to declare and attempt to enforce the independence of waves of the sea.

A modern industrial plant has a hundred trades and parts of trades represented in its working force. To have these workers parceled out to a hundred unions is to divide and not to organize them, to give them over to factions and petty leadership and leave them an easy prey to the machinations of the enemy. The dominant craft should control the plant or, rather, the union, and it should embrace the entire working force. This is the industrial plan, the modern method applied to modern conditions, and it will in time prevail.

The trade autonomy can be expressed within the general union, so far as that is necessary or desirable, and there need be no conflict on account of it. The attempt of each trade to maintain its own independence separately and apart from others results in increasing jurisdictional entanglements, fruitful of dissension, strife, and ultimate disruption.

The work of organizing has little, if any, permanent value unless the work of education, the right kind of education, goes hand in hand with it. There is no cohesiveness in ignorance.

The members of a trade union should be taught the true import, the whole object of the labor movement and understand its entire program. They should know that the labor movement means more, infinitely more, than a paltry increase in wages and the strike necessary to secure it; that while it engages to do all that possibly can be done to better the working conditions of its members, its higher object is to overthrow the capitalist system of private ownership of the tools of labor, abolish wage-slavery, and achieve the freedom of the whole working class and, in fact, of all mankind.

I Would Prefer to Give My Tongue a Rest: Letter to Ben Hanford in Chicago [excerpt]†

May 4, 1908

[Terre Haute, May 4, 1908]

* * *

As to my throat and general health, I have improved considerably since I have had a chance to lead something like a regular life and get a reasonable amount of rest.[14] I visited a specialist again a few months ago, and he assured me that my throat was greatly improved. At present I feel no ill effects. My general health is about all that could be desired. So far as strength is concerned, I never had more to my credit, if as much. In the coming campaign, however, I would prefer, if I had my choice, to see what I could do with my pen and give my tongue a rest. I feel as if I can write a campaign and make some of the enemy take notice that there are socialists in the field.

Now, I will tell you candidly just how I feel. I have never refused to do, so far as I could, anything the party commanded me to do, and never shall. I have taken the nomination under protest, but I have no desire to run for office and a positive prejudice against the very thought of holding office. To obey the commands of the Socialist Party, I violated a vow made years ago that I would never again be a candidate for political office. My whole ambition—and I have a goodly stock of it—is to make myself as big and as useful as I can, as much opposed to the enemy and as much loved by our comrades as any other private in the ranks.

You need have no fear that I shall shirk my part in the coming campaign. I shall be in condition and I hope there will be no good ground for complaint when the fight is over.

Very sincerely,
Eugene V. Debs

† As read by Ben Hanford into the record of the 1908 Socialist Party convention. Published in John M. Work, ed., *National Convention of the Socialist Party Held at Chicago, Illinois, May 10 to 17, 1908: Stenographic Report* (Chicago: Socialist Party, 1908), 151–2.

I Had Hoped That My Name Would Not Be Mentioned: Telegram to Seymour Stedman†

May 14, 1908

[Girard, Kansas, May 14, 1908]

Seymour Stedman
Chicago, Illinois

My Dear Steddy:—

Telegram sent by yourself, Williams, and Berger has been received this moment. I am sorry to be unable to comply with your request.[15] The *Appeal* has undertaken certain special work of some importance on the strength of my being here, and I cannot well abandon it at this time.[16] I should be happy, of course, to attend the convention and to meet the comrades if the situation were such that I could do so.

I see that my friends have again been very kind to me in this matter of nomination. I had hoped that my name would not be mentioned in that connection this year and have done what I could to discourage it; the reasons for this, purely from the party standpoint, seem quite apparent to me. As for myself personally, I never had any ambition along that line. If I do anything worthy of keeping my name alive, I prefer that it shall be done as a private in the ranks and not by having my name associated with some public office.

With loving regards, etc., I am yours in the same old way,
Eugene V. Debs

† Published in John M. Work (ed.), *National Convention of the Socialist Party Held at Chicago, Illinois, May 10 to 17, 1908*, 149.

Telegram Accepting the 1908 Nomination for President of the United States†

May 15, 1908

Girard [Kansas], May 15 [1908]

Fred Heath
Secretary, Socialist Party[17]
Chicago, Illinois

My Dear Comrades:—

Deeply touched by the incomparable honor you have for the third time conferred upon me. I accept the nomination for the presidency, returning to each of you, to the convention as a whole, and the party at large my sincere thanks.[18] The hearty unanimity with which the nomination is made and the magnificent spirit in which it is tendered fill me and thrill me with inexpressible emotions and arouse within me all the latent energy and enthusiasm to serve the Socialist Party and the great cause it represents, with all the mental, moral, and physical strength of my being.

Personally I had earnestly hoped the convention would choose otherwise,[19] but as individual desire is subordinate to the party will, I can only wish myself greater strength and fitness to bear the revolutionary banner of the working class you have placed in my hands. Permit me to congratulate you upon the nomination of Comrade Hanford and to express my personal gratification in having a comrade so loyal to share in upholding the proletarian standard.

At a later date I shall make a formal answer to your notification. The campaign is now fairly opened and the command to advance must be issued to all the hosts of socialism and emancipation.

The working class of the United States must be aroused this year and made to feel the quickening pulse, the throbbing hope, and the stern resolve of the social revolution.

The greatest opportunity in the history of the socialist movement spreads out before us like a field of glory.

† Published as "Debs' Telegram of Acceptance" as part of the article "Echoes of the Convention" in *Appeal to Reason*, whole no. 652 (May 30, 1908), 2.

The principles of the Socialist Party are resplendent with the truths which crown them; its very name is prophetic, and its spirit is literal fulfillment. In this auspicious hour, supreme with opportunity, duty to the cause transcends all else, and touching elbows and hearts keeping time to the quicksteps of the revolution, we march beneath the banner of "No Compromise" to certain victory.

My love and greeting to you all, my comrades. My heart is full and overflowing. With every drop of my blood and every fiber of my being, I render obedience to your command and offer myself, body and soul, to the Socialist Party, the working class, and the revolution.

Eugene V. Debs

The Issue: Speech at Courthouse Park, Girard, Kansas†

May 16, 1908

Ladies and Gentlemen:—

When I made some inquiry a few moments ago as to the cause for this assembling, I was told that it was the beginning of another street fair. I am quite surprised, and agreeably so, to find myself the central attraction.[20] Allow me in the very beginning to express my heartiest appreciation of the more than kind and generous words which have been spoken here for me this afternoon. There are times when words—mere words—no matter how fitly chosen or tenderly expressed are almost meaningless. As the rosebud under the influence of sunshine and shower opens, so does my heart receive your benedictions this afternoon.

I am a new resident of Girard; have been here but a comparatively short time, and yet I feel myself as completely at home among you, most of whom disagree with me upon very vital questions, as I do in the town in which I was born and reared and have lived all the days of my life. Since the day I first came

† Published as "Citizens of Girard Unite in Expression of Good Will for 'Gene Debs" in *Appeal to Reason,* whole no. 651 (May 23, 1908), 1, 4. Reprinted as "The Issue" in *Debs: His Life, Writings, and Speeches* (Girard, KS: Appeal to Reason, 1908), 473–91, and as a pamphlet published in Chicago by Charles H. Kerr & Co.

here, I have been treated with uniform kindness. I could not have been treated more hospitably anywhere. I have met practically all of your people and all of them have taken me by the hand and treated me as cordially as if I had been neighbor and friend with them, and to say that I appreciate this is to express myself in hackneyed and very unsatisfactory manner.

As to the Presidency

The honor to which reference has been made has come to me through no fault of my own.[21] It has been said that some men are born great, some achieve greatness, and some have greatness thrust upon them.[22] It is even so with what are called honors. Some men have honors thrust upon them. I find myself in that class. I did what little I could to prevent myself from being nominated by the convention now in session at Chicago, but the nomination sought me out, and in spite of myself I stand in your presence this afternoon the nominee of the Socialist Party for the presidency of the United States. Long, long ago I made up my mind never again to be a candidate for any political office within the gift of the people.[23] I was constrained to violate that vow because when I joined the Socialist Party I was taught that the desire of the individual was subordinate to the party will, and that when the party commanded it was my duty to obey.

There was a time in my life when I had the vanities of youth, when I sought that bubble called fame. I have outlived it. I have reached that point when I am capable of placing an estimate upon my own relative insignificance. I have come to realize that there is no honor in any real sense of that term to any man unless he is capable of freely consecrating himself to the service of his fellow men. To the extent that I am able to help those who are unable to help themselves, to that extent and to that extent alone, do I honor myself and the party to which I belong. So far as the presidency of the United States is concerned, I would spurn it were it not that it conferred the power to serve the working class; and he who enters that office with any other conception prostitutes and does not honor that office.

The Bounty of Nature

Now, my friends, I am opposed to the system of society in which we live today, not because I lack the natural equipment to do for myself, but because I am not satisfied to make myself comfortable knowing that there are thousands upon thousands of my fellow men who suffer for the barest necessities of life.

We were taught under the old ethic that man's business upon earth was to look out for himself. That was the ethic of the jungle, the ethic of the wild beast. Take care of yourself, no matter what may become of your fellow man. Thousands of years ago the question was asked: "Am I my brother's keeper?"[24] That question has never yet been answered in a way that is satisfactory to civilized society. Yes, I am my brother's keeper. I am under a moral obligation to him that is inspired, not by any maudlin sentimentality, but by the higher duty I owe to myself. What would you think of me if I were capable of seating myself at a table and gorging myself with food and saw about me the children of my fellow beings starving to death?

Allow me to say to you, my fellow men, that Nature has spread a great table bounteously for all of the children of men. There is room for all, and there is a plate and a place and food for all, and any system of society that denies a single one the right and the opportunity to freely help himself to Nature's bounties is an unjust and iniquitous system that ought to be abolished in the interest of a higher humanity and a civilization worthy of the name. And here let me observe, my fellow men, that while the general impression is that human society is stationary—a finality as it were—it is not so for a single instant. Underlying society there are great material forces that are in operation all of the circling hours of the day and night, and at certain points in the social development these forces outgrow the forms that hold them, and these forms spring apart and then a new social system comes into existence and a new era dawns for the human race.

The great majority of mankind have always been in darkness. The overwhelming majority of the children of men have always been their own worst enemies. In every age of this world's history, the kings and emperors and tsars and the potentates, in alliance with the priests, have sought by all the means at their command to keep the people in darkness, that they might perpetuate the power in which they riot and revel in luxury while the great masses are in a state of slavery and degeneration, and he who has spoken out courageously against the existing order, he who has dared to voice the protest of the oppressed and downtrodden, has had to pay the penalty, all the way from Jesus Christ of Galilee to Fred Warren of Girard.

Coronations and Crucifixions

Do you know, my friends, it is so easy to agree with the ignorant majority. It is so easy to make the people applaud an empty platitude. It takes some courage to face that beast called the Majority, and tell him the truth to his teeth! Some men do so and accept the consequences of their acts as becomes men, and they live in history—every one of them. I have said so often, and I wish to repeat it on this occasion, that mankind have always crowned their oppressors, and they have as uniformly crucified their saviors, and this has been true all along the highway of the centuries. It is true today. It will not always be so. When the great majority have become enlightened; when the great mass know the truth, they will treat an honest man decently while he lives and not crucify him, and then a thousand years afterward rear a monument above the dust of the hero they put to death.

I am in revolt against capitalism (and that doesn't mean to say, my friends, that I am hating you—not in the slightest). I am opposed to capitalism because I love my fellow men, and if I am opposing you, I am opposing you for what I believe to be your good, and though you spat upon me with contempt I would still oppose you to the extent of my power.

New System Needed

I don't hate the workingman because he has turned against me. I know the poor fellow is too ignorant to understand his self-interest, and I know that as a rule the workingman is the friend of his enemy, and the enemy of his friend. He votes for men who represent a system in which labor is simply merchandise; in which the man who works the hardest and the longest has the least to show for it. If there is a man on earth who is entitled to all the comforts and luxuries of this life in abundance, it is the man whose labor produces them. If he is not, who is? Does he get them in the present system?

And, mark you, I am not speaking in a partisan sense this afternoon. I appreciate the fact that you have come here as Republicans and Democrats as well as Socialists to do me a personal honor, and I would be ungrateful, indeed, if I took advantage of such an occasion to speak to you in an offensive and partisan sense. I wish to say in the broadest possible way that I am opposing the system under which we live today because I believe it is subversive of the best interests of the people. I am not satisfied with things as they are, and I know that no matter what administration is in power, even were it a Socialist administration, I know that there will be no material change in the condition of the people until we have a new social system based upon the mutual economic interest of the people. Not until you and I and all of us collectively own those things that we collectively need and use.

That is a basic economic proposition. As long as a relatively few men own the railroads, the telegraph, the telephone; own the oil fields and the gas fields and the steel mills and the sugar refineries and the leather tanneries—own, in short, the sources and means of life—they will corrupt our politics, they will enslave the working class, they will impoverish and debase society, they will do all things that are needful to perpetuate their power as the economic masters and the political rulers of the people. Not until these great agencies are owned and operated by the people can the people hope for any material improvement in their social condition. Is the condition fair today, and satisfactory to the thinking man?

The Unemployed

According to the most reliable reports at our command, there are at least 4 million workingmen vainly searching for employment. Have you ever found yourself in that unspeakably sad predicament? Have you ever had to go up the street, begging for work, in a great city thronged with surging humanity—and, by the way, my friends, people are never quite so strange to each other as when they are forced into artificial, crowded, and stifled relationship.

I would rather be friendless out on the American desert than to be friendless in New York or Chicago. Have you ever walked up one side of the street and come back on the other side, while your wife, Mary, was waiting at home with three or four children for you to report that you had found work? Quite fortunately for me I had an experience of somewhat similar nature to this quite early in life.[25] Quite fortunately because, had I not known from my own experience just what it is to have to beg for work, just what it is to be shown the door as if I were a very offensive intruder, had I not known what it is to suffer for want of food, had I not seen every door closed and barred in my face, had I not found myself friendless and alone in the city as a boy looking for work, and in vain, perhaps I would not be here this afternoon. I might have grown up, as some others have, who have been, as they regard themselves, fortunate. I might have waved aside my fellow men and said: "Do as I have done. If you are without work it is your own fault. Look at me; I am self-made. No man is under the necessity of looking for work if he is willing to work."

Nothing is more humiliating than to have to beg for work, and a system in which any man has to beg for work stands condemned. No man can defend it. Now, the rights of one are just as sacred as the rights of a million. Suppose you happen to be the individual one who has no work. This republic is a failure so far as you are concerned.

Every man has the inalienable right to work.

Evolution of Industry

Here I stand, just as I was created. I have two hands that represent my labor-power. I have some bone and muscle and sinew and some energy. I want to exchange it for food and clothing and shelter. Between my right to apply my labor to the tools with which work is done there stands a man artificially created. He says, "No, no!" Why not? "Because you cannot first make a profit for me."

Now, there has been a revolution in industry during the last 50 years, but the trouble with most people is that they haven't kept pace with it. They don't know anything about it and they are especially innocent in regard to it in the small western cities and states, where the same old conditions of a century ago prevail. Your grandfather could help himself anywhere. All he needed was some very cheap, simple, primitive tools and he could then apply his labor to the resources of Nature with his individual tools and produce what he needed. That era in our history produced our greatest men. Lincoln himself sprang from this primitive state of society. People have said: "Why, he had no chance. See how great he became." Yes, but Lincoln had for his comrades great, green-plumed forest monarchs. He could put his arms about them and hear their heartthrobs, as they said: "Go on, Abe, a great destiny awaits you." He was in partnership with Nature. He associated with flowers and he was in the fields and he heard the rippling music of the laughing brooks and streams. Nature took him to her bosom. Nature nourished him and from his unpolluted heart there sprang his noble aspirations.

Had Lincoln been born in a sweatshop, he would never have been heard of.

How is it with the babe that is born in Mott Street, or in the lower Bowery, or in the East Side of New York City? That is where thousands, tens of thousands, and hundreds of thousands of babes are born who are to constitute our future generations. I have seen children 10 years of age in New York City who had never seen a live chicken. They don't know what it is to put their tiny feet on a blade of grass. It is the most densely populated spot on earth.

You have seen your beehive—just fancy a human beehive of which yours is the miniature and you have the industrial hive under capitalism. If you have never seen this condition you are excusable for not being a socialist. Come to New York, Chicago, San Francisco with me; remain with me just 24 hours, and then look into my face as I shall look into yours when I ask: "What about socialism now?" These children by hundreds and thousands are born in sub-cellars where a whole grown family is crowded together in one room, where modesty between the sexes is absolutely impossible. They are surrounded by filth and vermin. From their birth they see nothing but immorality and vice and crime. They are tainted in the cradle. They are inoculated by their surroundings and they are doomed from the beginning. This system takes their lives just as certainly as if a dagger were thrust into their quivering little hearts, and let me say to you that it were better for many thousands of them if they had never seen the light of day.

Now I submit, my friends, that such a condition as this is indefensible in the twentieth century. Time was when everything had to be done in a very primitive way, and most men had to work all their days, all their lives, to feed themselves and shelter themselves. They had no time, they had no opportunity for a higher development, and so they were what the world calls "illiterate." They had little chance. It took all their time and energy to feed the animal; but how is it today? Upon the average 20 men can today, with the aid of modern machinery, produce as much wealth as a thousand did a half century ago. Can you think of a single thing that enters into our daily existence that cannot be easily produced in abundance for all? If you can, I wish you would do me the kindness to name it.

Why Suffer Amid Abundance?

I don't know it all. I am simply a student of this great question, and I am serving as best I can and I know my eyes are ready for the light, and I thank that man, no matter what he be, who can add to the flame of the torch that I bear in my hand. If there is a single thing that you can think of that cannot be produced in abundance, name it. Bread, clothing, fuel—everything is here.

Nature's storehouse is full to the surface of the earth. All of the raw materials are deposited here in abundance. We have the most marvelous machinery the world has ever known. Man has long since become master of the natural forces and made them work for him. Now he has but to touch a button and the wheels begin to spin and the machinery begins to whirr, and wealth is produced on every hand in increasing abundance. Why should any man, woman, or child suffer for food, clothing, or shelter? Why? The question cannot be answered. Don't tell me that some men are too lazy to work. Suppose they are too lazy to work, what do you think of a social system that produces men too lazy to work? If a man is too lazy to work, don't treat him with contempt. Don't look down upon him with scorn as if you were a superior being. If there is a man who is too lazy to work, there is something the matter with him. He wasn't born right or he was perverted in this system. You could not, if you tried, keep a normal man inactive, and if you did, he would go stark mad! You go to any penitentiary and you will find the men there begging for the privilege of doing work.

I know by very close study of the question exactly how men become idle. I don't repel them when I meet them. I have never yet seen the tramp I was not able to receive with open arms. He is a little less fortunate than I am. He is made the same as I am made. He is the child of the same Father. Had I been born in his environment, had I been subjected to the same things to which he was, I would have been where he is.

Tools and Tramps

Can you tell me why there wasn't a tramp in the United States in 1860? In that day, if someone had said "tramp," no one would have known what was meant by it. If human nature is innately depraved and men would rather ride on brake-beams and sleep in holes and caves instead of comfortable beds, if they would do that from pure choice and from natural depravity, why were they not built that way 50 years ago? Fifty years ago capitalism was in its earlier stages. Fifty years ago work was still mainly done by hand, and every boy could learn a trade and every boy could master the tools and go to work. That is why there were no tramps. In 50 years that simple tool has become a mammoth machine. It is larger and larger all the time. It has crowded the hand tool out of production.

With the machine came the capitalist. There were no capitalists nor was there such a thing as capital before the beginning of the present system. Capitalists came with machinery. Up to the time that machinery supplanted the hand tool, the little employer was himself a working man. No matter what the shop or factory, you would find the employer sitting side by side with his men. He was a superior workman who got more orders than he could fill and employed some men to help him, but he had to pay them the equivalent of what they produced because if he did not, they would pack up their tools and go into business for themselves.

Now, the individual tool has become the mammoth machine. It has multiplied production by hundreds. The old tool was individually owned and used. The modern tool, in the form of a great machine, is social in every conception of it. Look at one of these giant machines. Come to the *Appeal* office and look at the press in operation. Here the progressive conception of the ages is crystalized. What individual shall put his hand on this social machine and say, "This is mine! He would apply labor here must first pay tribute to me."

The hand tool has been very largely supplanted by this machine. Not many tools are left. You are still producing in a very small way here in Girard, but your production is flickering out gradually. It is but a question of time until it will expire entirely. In spite of all that can be said or done to the contrary, production is organizing upon a larger and larger scale and becoming entirely cooperative. This has crowded out the smaller competitor and gradually opened the way for a new social order.

Will Make Home Possible

Your material interest and mine in the society of the future will be the same. Instead of having to fight each other like animals, as we do today, and seeking to glorify the brute struggle for existence—of which every civilized human being ought to be ashamed—instead of this, our material interests are going to be mutual. We are going to jointly own these mammoth machines, and we are going to operate them as joint partners, and we are going to divide all the products among ourselves.

We are not going to send our surplus to the Jim Hills, Goulds, and Vanderbilts of New York. We are not going to pile up a billion dollars in John D. Rockefeller's hands—a vast pyramid from the height of which he can look down with scorn and contempt upon the "common herd." John D. Rockefeller's great fortune is built upon your ignorance. When you know enough to know what your interest is, you will support the great party that is organized upon the principle of collective ownership of the means of life. This party will sweep into power upon the issue of emancipation just as Republicanism swept into power upon the abolition question half a century ago.

In the meantime, don't have any fear of us socialists. We don't mean any harm! Many of you have been taught to look upon us as very dangerous people. It is amazing to what extent this prejudice has struck root. The capitalist press will tell you of a good many evil things that we socialists are going to do that we never intend to do. They will tell you we are going to break up the home. Great heavens! What about the homes of the 4 million tramps that are looking for work today? How about the thousands and thousands of miserable shacks in New York and every great city where humanity festers? It would be a good thing if they were torn down and obliterated completely, for they are not fit for human habitation. No, we are not going to destroy the home, but we are going to make the home possible for the first time in history.

Progress Born of Agitation

You may think you are very comfortable. Let me make you a little comparison. You may not agree with me. I don't expect you to and I don't ask you to. I am going to ask you to remember what I say this afternoon and perhaps before I am elected president of the United States you will believe what I say is true. Now there are those of you who are fairly comfortable under the present standard. Isn't it amazing to you how little the average man is satisfied with? You go out here to the edge of town and you find a small farmer who has a small cabin with just room enough to keep himself and wife, and two or three children, which has a mortgage on it, and he works early and late and gets just enough in net returns to keep him in working order, and he will deliver a lecture about the wonderful prosperity of the country.

He is satisfied, and that is his calamity.

Now, the majority of you would say that is his good fortune. "It is a blessing that he is satisfied." I want to see if I can show you that it is a curse to him and to society that he is satisfied. If it had not been for the discontent of a few fellows who have not been satisfied with their condition, you would still be living in caves. You never would have emerged from the jungle. Intelligent discontent is the mainspring of civilization.

Progress is born of agitation. It is agitation or stagnation. I have taken my choice.

This farmer works all day long, works hard enough to produce enough to live the life of a man—not of an animal, but of a man. Now there is an essential difference between a man and an animal. I admire a magnificent animal in any form except the human form. Suppose you had everything that you could possibly desire, so far as your physical wants are concerned. Suppose you had a million to your credit in the bank, a palatial home, and relations to suit yourself, but no soul capacity for real enjoyment. If you were denied knowing what sorrow is, what real joy is, what music is, and literature and sculpture; and all of those subtle influences that touch the heart and quicken the pulses and fire the senses, and so lift and ennoble a man that he can feel his head among the stars and in communion with God himself—if you are denied these, no matter how sleek or fat or contented you may be, you are still as base and as corrupt and as repulsive a being as walks God's green earth.

The Farmer's Need

You may have plenty of money. The poorest people on this earth are those who have the most money. A man is said to be poor who has none, but he is a pauper who has nothing else. Now this farmer, what does he know about literature? After his hard day's work is done, here he sits in his little shack. He is fed, and his animal wants are satisfied. It is at this time that a man begins to live. It is not while you work and slave that you live. It is when you have done your work honestly, when you have contributed your share to the common fund, that you begin to live. Then, as Whitman said, you take out your soul; you can commune with yourself; you can take a comrade by the hand and you can look into his eyes and down into his soul, and in that communion you live. And if you don't know what that is, or if you are not at least on the edge of it, it is denied you to even look into the promised land.

Now this farmer knows nothing about the literature of the world. All its libraries are sealed to him. So far as he is concerned, Homer and Dante and Dickens might as well not have lived; Beethoven, Liszt, and Wagner, and all those musicians whose art makes the common atmosphere blossom with harmony [has] never been for this farmer. He knows nothing about literature or art. Never rises above the animal plane upon which he is living. Within 15 minutes after he has ceased to live he is forgotten; the next generation doesn't know his name, and the world doesn't know he ever lived. This is life under the present standard.

You tell me this is all the farmer is fit for? What do I propose to do for that farmer? Nothing. I want to awaken the farmer to the fact that he is robbed every day of the week, and if I can awaken him to the fact that he is robbed under the capitalist system, he will fall into line with the socialist movement, and will march to the polls on election day; and, instead of casting his vote to fasten the shackles upon his limbs more firmly, he will cast a vote for his emancipation. All I have to do is to show that farmer, that day laborer, that tramp, that they are victims of this system; that their interests are identical, that they constitute the millions and that the millions have the votes. The Rockefellers have the dollars, but we have the votes; and when we have sense enough to know how to use the votes, we will have not only the votes but the dollars for all the children of men.

Who Will Save Us From Congress?

This seems quite visionary to some of you, and especially to those of you who know absolutely nothing about economics. I could not begin to tell you the story of social evolution this afternoon; of how these things are doing day by day, of how the world is being pushed into socialism, and how it is bound to arrive, no matter whether you are for it or against it. It is the next inevitable phase of civilization. It isn't a scheme, it isn't a contrivance. It isn't anything that is made to order. The day is coming when you will be pushed into it by unseen hands whether you will it or not. Nothing can be introduced until the people want it, and when the majority want it they will know how to get it.

I venture the prophesy that within the next five years you will be completely dispossessed. You are howling against the trusts, and the trusts are laughing at you. You keep on voting in the same old way, and the trusts will keep on getting what you produce. You say Congress will give you some relief. Good heavens! Who will save us from Congress? Don't you know that Congress is made up almost wholly of trust lawyers and corporation attorneys? I don't happen to have the roll of this one, but with a few exceptions they are all lawyers. Now, in the competitive system the lawyer sells himself to the highest bidder, the same as the workingman does. Who is the highest bidder? The corporation, of course. So the trust buys the best lawyer and the common herd gets the poor one.

Politics Reflex of Economics

Now it is a fact that politics is simply the reflex of economics. The material foundation of society determines the character of all social institutions—political, educational, ethical, and spiritual. In exact proportion as the economic foundation of society changes, the character of all social institutions changes to correspond to that basis. Half of this country was in favor of chattel slavery, and half was opposed to it, geographically speaking. Why was the church of the South in favor of chattel slavery? Why was the church of the North opposed to chattel slavery? The northern capitalist wasn't a bit more opposed to chattel slavery *from any moral sense* than was the Southern plantation owner. The South produced cotton for the market by the hand labor of Negro slaves. On the other hand, the North wasn't dependent upon cotton—could raise no cotton. In the North it was the small capitalist at the beginning of capitalism, who, with the machine, had begun to manufacture, and wanted cheap labor; and the sharper the competition, the cheaper he could buy his labor. Now, chattel slavery of the Southern plantation owner was the source of his wealth. He had to have slaves, and what the plantation owner had to have in economics, the preacher had to justify in religion. As long as chattel slavery was necessary to the Southern plantation owner, as long as that stage of the economic condition lasted, the preachers stood up in the pulpits of the South and said it was ordained by God and proved it by the Bible. I don't know of any crime that the oppressors and their hirelings have not proven by the Bible.

Analogies from History

Then, competition between workers began as machines took the place of hand labor. Manufacturers wanted larger and larger bodies of labor and that competition spread out here to Kansas, and I have always felt when in Kansas that I stood on sacred soil. When I hear the name of Kansas I doff my hat in reverence. The Free Soilers came here, despised, hated, and persecuted. They were the enemies of the human race. Why? Because they had hearts throbbing in their breasts. Because they looked with pity and compassion upon the Negro slave who received his wages in lashes applied to his naked back, who saw his crying wife torn from him and his children, pleading, snatched from his side and sold into slavery, while the great mass looked on just as the great mass is looking on today, and the preachers stood up in their pulpits and said: "It is all right. It is God-ordained." And whenever an abolitionist raised his head, he was persecuted and hounded as if he had been a wild beast.

I heard this story from Wendell Phillips one evening. I never can forget it. How I wish he were here today. We sat together and he said: "Debs, the world will never know with what bitter and relentless persecution the early abolitionists had to contend." Wendell Phillips was the most perfect aristocrat in everything I have ever seen; who came nearest to being a perfect man; who, when he stood erect, instantly challenged respect and admiration—almost veneration. Wendell Phillips was treated as if he had been the worst felon on earth. They went to his house one night to mob him, and why? Because he protested against sending a young Negro girl and a Negro man back into slavery. They came to take them back, and the whole Commonwealth of Massachusetts said: "Take them back! Obey the law!" That is what they are everlastingly saying to us—"Obey the law!" Just above the door of the statehouse there was an inscription: "God Bless the Commonwealth of Massachusetts." Wendell Phillips said: "If Massachusetts has become a slave hunter, if Massachusetts is in alliance with the slave catchers of the South, that inscription over the portal of the doors should be changed, and in place of 'God Bless the Commonwealth of Massachusetts,' it should be 'God Damn the Commonwealth of Massachusetts!'" God smiled in that same instant.

Growth of Socialism

All of the slave catchers and holders, all of the oppressors of man, all of the enemies of the human race, all of the rulers of Siberia, where a large part of this earth's surface has been transformed into a hell—all have spoken in the name of the Great God and in the name of the Holy Bible.

There will be a change one of these days. The world is just beginning to awaken, and is soon to sing its first anthem of freedom. All the signs of the times are cheering. Twenty-five years ago there was but a handful of socialists; today there are a half million. When the polls are closed next fall you will be astounded. The socialist movement is in alliance with the forces of progress. We are today where the abolitionists were in 1858. They had a million and a quarter of votes. There was dissension in the Whig, Republican, and Free Soil parties, but the time had come for a great change, and the Republican Party was formed in spite of the bickerings and contentions of men. Lincoln made the great speech in that year that gave him the nomination and afterward made him President of the United States.

If you had to say to the people in 1858, "In two years from now the Republican Party is going to sweep the country and seat the President," you would have been laughed to scorn. The Socialist Party stands today where the Republican Party stood 50 years ago. It is in alliance with the forces of evolution; the one party that has a clear-cut, overmastering, overshadowing issue; the party that stands for all the people and the only party that stands for all the people. In this system we have one set who are called capitalists, and another set who are called workers; and they are at war with each other over the division of the product.

Will Establish Private Property

Now, we socialists propose that society in its collective capacity shall produce, not for profit, but in abundance to satisfy human wants; that every man shall have the inalienable right to work and receive the full equivalent of all he produces; that every man may stand fearlessly erect in the pride and majesty of his own manhood. Every man and every woman can be economically free. They can, without let or hindrance, apply their labor, with the best machinery that can be devised, to all the natural resources, do the work of society and produce for all; and then receive in exchange a certificate of value equivalent to that of their production. Then society will improve its institutions in exact proportion to the progress of invention.

Whether you work in the city or on a farm, all things productive will be carried forward on a gigantic scale. All industry will be completely organized. Society for the first time will have a scientific foundation. Every man, by being economically free, will have some time for himself. He can then take a full and perfect breath. He can go to his wife and children because then he will have a home.

We are not going to destroy private property. We are going to introduce and establish private property—all private property that is necessary to house man, keep him in comfort, and satisfy all his physical wants. Eighty percent of the people in the United States have no property of any kind today. A few have got it all. They have dispossessed the people, and when we get into power we will dispossess them. We will reduce the workday and give every man a chance. We will go to the parks, and we will have music, and we will have music because we will have time to play music and inclination to hear it. Is it not sad to think that not one in a thousand know what music is? Is it not pitiable to see the poor, ignorant, dumb human, utterly impervious to the divine influence of music? If humanity could only respond to the higher influences! And it would if it had time.

Release the animal, throw off his burden; give him a chance; and he rises, as if by magic, to the plane of a man. Man has all of these divine attributes. They are in a latent state. They are not yet developed. It does not pay to love music. Keep your eye on the almighty dollar and your fellow man. Get the dollar and keep him down. Make him produce for you. You are not your brother's keeper in this system. Suppose he is poor! Suppose his wife is force into prostitution! Suppose his child is deformed! And suppose he shuffles off by destroying himself! What is that to you? But you ought to be ashamed. Take the standard home and look it in the face. If you know what that standard means, and you are a success, God help the failure!

Our conduct is determined by our economic relations. If you and I must fight each other to exist, we will not love each other very hard. We can go to the same church and hear the same minister tell us in good conscience that we ought to love each other, and the next day we approach the edge of some business transaction. Do we remember what the minister told us? No, it is gone, until next Sunday. Six days in the week we are following the Golden Rule reversed. Now, when we approach the edges of a business transaction in competition, what is more natural than that we should try to get the better of the transaction? Get the better of our fellow man? Cheat him if we can.

And if you succeed that fixes you as a successful businessman. You have all the necessary qualifications. Don't let you conscience disturb you—that would interfere with business.

Humanity and the Future

Competition was natural enough once, but do you think you are competing today? Many of you think you are competing. Against whom? Against Rockefeller? About as I would if I had a wheelbarrow and competed with the Santa Fe from here to Kansas City. That is about the way you are competing, but your boys will not have even that chance—if capitalism lives that long. You hear of the "late" panic. It is very late. It is going to be very late. This panic will be with us five years from now, and will continue from now till then.

I am not a prophet. I can no more penetrate the future than you can. I do study the forces that underlie society and the trend of evolution. I can tell by what we have passed through about what we will have in the future; and I know that capitalism can be beaten, and the people put ultimately in possession. Now, then, when we have taken possession, and we jointly own the sources and means of production, we will no longer have to fight each other to live; our interests, instead of being competitive, will be cooperative. We will work side by side. Your interest shall be mine, and mine will be yours. That is the economic condition from which will spring the humane social relation.

When we are in partnership and have stopped clutching each other's throats, when we have stopped enslaving each other, then we will stand together, hands clasped, and we will be friends. We will be comrades, we will be brothers, and we will begin the march to the grandest civilization that the human race has ever known.

I did not mean to keep you so long this afternoon. I am sure I appreciate the patience with which you have listened to me. From the very depths of my heart I thank you, each of you—every man, woman, and child, for this splendid testimonial, for this beautiful tribute which I shall remember with gratitude and love until memory empties its urn into forgetfulness.

An Evening in Girard: An Informal Speech among Friends†

May 21, 1908

Comrades and Friends:—

After all that has been said here this evening, and so well said, I think, indeed I feel sure, that I could well afford to remain silent.[26] There are times when words are mere beggarly sounds; when they express seemingly less than nothing. I am quite sure that no words of mine could begin to adequately express the feeling which possesses me at this hour. I have been in Girard but a little while, and yet I feel as if I had been here many years, and if there were to be held here a meeting of the old settlers I should feel slighted if I were not invited to a seat on the platform!

Girard, in some respects, epitomizes the history of the entire nation. When Comrade Wayland first located here, the sentiment was such that it could truthfully have been said that he was a resident in a hostile community. The majority of the citizens looked upon him as an intruder. He had the misfortune to be in advance of his time. Since then he has grown into the affections of the people, and were he to give his consent he could easily be the mayor of Girard today. There has been a very decided change of sentiment. The people who were once hostile have become perfectly friendly. The change has been entirely on their part. They now understand the man, his principles, and his mission. Fifty years ago when a man whose soul revolted against the crime of property in human flesh came within the borders of Kansas, he was looked upon as a monster of iniquity. The Free Soiler[27] was put to death and he was buried head first, and upon the soles of his protruding boots there was written the inscription "Mark the fate of the Free Soiler!" The people applauded such monstrous crimes. It is different today. There has been some progress. Kansas, the world, is nearer civilized.

A little while ago a socialist was looked upon as the enemy of the human race, but socialists have become very numerous; they have become correspondingly respectable. I have always been proud of being a socialist and never more

† Published as part of the pamphlet *An Evening in Girard: Just an Informal Incident Following the Return of Delegates from the Chicago Socialist Convention: Camaraderie and Fellowship on Tap: Responses by Visiting and Resident Comrades, Including "Our" Gene* (Girard, KS: [Appeal to Reason], 1908), 29–34.

proud than I am this evening. Looking into your faces and catching your spirit, I feel myself rising to exaltation. Socialism to us is something more than a mere conviction. It courses in our veins; it throbs in our hearts; it fires and sanctifies our souls; and it consecrates us to the service of humanity.

The convention just closed at Chicago was in my judgment the greatest and most important convocation of men and women in all the history of this nation. Its significance is not yet understood by the people. Fifty years must elapse and it must have its perspective, and then it will have its true proportion. In all that body of thoroughly honest, earnest, and conscientious men and women, there was not a single one who was in any sense a self-seeker, not one who had any personal ambition to gratify. All of them were there for the one splendid purpose of perfecting the political party whose historic mission it is to emancipate the working class from the thralldom of slavery. The Socialist Party has a mission different from that of any party that ever existed. It is different—far different—from any other party in organization. Its mission is not to reform the present system, but to absolutely abolish it; to wipe out wage-slavery, to emancipate not only the working class, but the capitalist class; to abolish class rule so that, unfettered, the children of men may begin the march to what may be called real civilization. Competition, the controlling principle of capitalism, vanishes with the adoption of cooperative society. Not that we socialists are less selfish, but that our selfishness is enlightened selfishness. We shall still compete with each other in socialist society, not for a material advantage, however, but to excel in good works.

How fully, how perfectly, how beautifully the spirit of socialism has been expressed at this festal board this evening! You have all joined in literally loading me with honors that I so illy deserve. I am simply a bit more fortunate than you. Of my own account I amount to so little. It is my good fortune that I have you as my comrades, and because of this fact I have been praised and I have been given credit to which I feel and know I am not justly entitled.

Here we have in miniature the society of the future. How perfectly fine it is! How it touches! How it thrills! How it inspires and how it ennobles all human beings! There is only one cause in all the world, as Comrade Hogan[28] has so well said, that is worth living for, worth doing battle for, and, if need be, worth dying for, and that is socialism, and it is coming just as certain as the sun rises. Scattered all over this country there are the thousands and the hundreds of thousands who are keeping step to the inspired music of the new emancipation, and for the first time in human history there is an international movement and it is spreading all over the civilized and uncivilized world. It is all-embracing. No single human anywhere is excluded from fellowship. We may not live to see the full fruition of our work, nor does it matter; so insidiously can a man feel socialism, so completely consecrated can he be to the cause of socialism that he lives within the realization of it, even now.

I don't wish to make myself subject to the criticism of the gentleman who was invited to say a few words on a certain occasion, and took a long while in saying them, and after adjournment one of the guest remarked that the gentleman could make the best 15-minute speech in three hours that he ever heard!

I am very happy to be here to take the visiting comrades by the hand. It has been a long while since I have seen Comrade [W. P.] Metcalf. I met him down in Arizona. I remember how eager I was to press his hand. He is a pioneer down in that section, and every time I think of New Mexico I can see him, stalwart, erect, and magnificent. He used to stand alone, but he has all that country peopled with socialists. They are almost as numerous as the leaves of the forest. Here is another, at my right, Comrade Dan Hogan, who has been battling valiantly down in Arkansas. I wondered about Dan up in Chicago, in that great madhouse that I escaped from. I had some doubt about my own sanity after I got away from there. The only time in all my experience in Chicago that I felt myself really in a peaceful, quiet state was when they had me locked up.[29] I found more real fellowship among the so-called "criminals" than I did among the whole body of desirable citizens on the outside. The good people in Chicago they lock up; those that ought to be locked up walk the streets, free. There are 2 million people and they are packed together, heaps of them; they are total strangers to each other, and they have good reasons for being. They are strangers, not because they don't know each other, but because they do. I don't know what we will do with Chicago when we come into possession of it.

I am more than glad to see all these comrades here this evening. It has been a great pleasure to me to take them by the hand, look into their eyes, and hear their words of cheer and encouragement. I feel we are just barely making our beginning. The campaign just opening is certainly going to be an historical one. Four years ago they were still ridiculing the socialist movement. If it excited any comment at all it was as to its insignificance. In one breath they said we were bloodthirsty cranks and in the next harmless dreamers, but they have now concluded that the socialist movement has merit enough to be reckoned with. The *Globe-Democrat*, of St. Louis, had an editorial the other day that was more than surprising. The statement was frankly made that the Socialist Party was the coming party in the United States. A number of other capitalist papers have made similar statements. Socialism has grown so rapidly that it is now regarded as a menace to capitalism. They are beginning to pay some attention to us. It is becoming so influential that they can no longer write about it as they used to.

I don't quite feel at liberty to invite you to the White House, but when the invitation can be extended, if I happen to be there, you will all be desirable citizens, I can assure you!

I just want to say a word about my quiet colleague over here. Comrade Fred Warren is entitled to a great share of the credit for the work that is being done here in Girard. He and Wayland were providentially joined, I think. They fit each other exactly; they are necessary to each other. I don't know of a stronger combination. Men of glorious intellect, firm heart, moral courage without question, their chief failing is their extreme modesty. They don't allow their pictures to be taken. I had to have myself photographed often enough to serve the whole combination. Our toastmaster [Eli W. Richardson] does the honors on all such popular little occasions as this, and he does them very gracefully, as I am sure you will all bear willing testimony. We have a picture here for memory's wall. We will never all be together again. When we meet somebody will be missing, but we can remember this picture and cherish it, and I am sure that we shall. I wish you all long life and strength and health and inspiration, and for the cause, victory. In the campaign that is now opening you are all going to do your duty, I know. All of you are going to give an account of yourselves and I feel quite safe in predicting that when the polls close on the first Tuesday in November, the returns will be such as to surprise Girard and Kansas, the nation and the world. In this great work we all have our places and we all have our duties. We have the small satisfaction of knowing that we are not working for a personal advantage, but that we are working for the common interests of our common humanity.

> He's true to God who's true to man; wherever wrong is done,
> To the humblest and the weakest, 'neath the all-beholding sun,
> That wrong is also done to us; and they are slaves most base,
> Whose love of right is for themselves, and not for all their race.[30]

We Will Have 5,000 Open Air Speakers: Statement to the Press†

June 1, 1908

I will begin my campaign in Chicago on the first of September and after a tour through the different cities will wind it up in Chicago two days before election. Every indication points to a large Socialist vote this year. Of course, I do not expect to be elected, but the result of the election will show that in spite of all obstacles the socialist idea is growing and will continue to grow.

We will have five thousand open air speakers when the campaign opens and the Countess of Warwick[31] is coming here in the fall and will take an active part in it. The five thousand speakers will speak from trucks or soapboxes wherever there is a chance. I shall speak in New York probably twice at least during the campaign.

It will be noticed in the platform of principles adopted by the party this year that the immediate demands on the government are more comprehensive than in any other declaration of the kind. Before socialism takes the place of capitalism, the way will have to be paved for it by gradual reforms.

There is not the slightest doubt in my mind that the Socialist vote this year will be larger than it ever was before in this country. One reason is the large number of people out of work. There are 400,000 railroad people alone who are out of work. I was in Chicago a day or two ago and was shown a line a mile long of mogul locomotive engines which were standing idle. This in itself to my mind is a good argument for socialism.

The Republican Party has thrown its traditions to the one side, and whether the Republican national convention nominates Taft or is stampeded for Roosevelt, it is not the solid, homogeneous party it once was. The Democratic Party will probably be united to some extent by Bryan, but the ranks of neither party are so solid as they were four years ago.

Asked what he thought the effect of the organization of the Christian Socialist Fellowship and the Ministers Socialist Conference would be,[32] *Debs said:*

---

† Published as "Debs Discusses Campaign Before Leaving for West" in *New York Call,* vol. 1, no. 3 (June 2, 1908), 4. A short snippet including a few of these remarks also appeared in the *New York Times* of the same date.

I believe the effects will be the spreading of socialist propaganda in new channels which the regular socialist propagandists do not reach. It will also help to do away with a good deal of the prejudice which has existed in many quarters against socialism among people who without taking the pains to study the matter thought socialism was bad and dangerous. The ministers who are trying to spread socialism are doing so because they sincerely believe, as I do, that socialism is the best condition and are acting as their consciences dictate.

I have the utmost respect for the opinions of those who honestly differ with me. I believe in being tolerant of other people's beliefs and I believe in socialism and am a socialist by conviction because I believe, whether the time is long or short, it is bound to become the system of the future and that matters are tending surely that way.

Debs said that as the South was the weakest as far as socialism was concerned, organizers would be sent to the Southern states before the campaign. He would make a tour through Oklahoma and Texas in July and August, he said.

Vigorous War on the Socialist Press Forthcoming†

June 5, 1908

Washington, DC, June 5 [1908]

The active warfare against the socialist press by the capitalist authorities is to begin July 1. On that day the amendment to the postal law (somewhat shorn of its teeth, as reported last week) takes effect, and it is believed here that strenuous efforts will be made to deny the stronger of the socialist papers the mails, or so handicap with restrictions as to practically prohibit their publication. All this is done under the pretense of combating the abuse of a free press and suppressing anarchists.

When the Penrose bill in the Senate was exposed by the *Appeal*, a storm of indignation swept the country and the bill was hastily withdrawn. Now,

† Published in *Appeal to Reason*, whole no. 654 (June 13, 1908), 1.

however, the substance of the Penrose bill, which was aimed at the socialist press in general, and the *Appeal* in particular, has been surreptitiously put through Congress as a rider to the appropriation bill and is now a law, becoming effective July 1st. This is the smooth way capitalist congressmen have of slipping through special legislation offensive to the people; it is first introduced and "tried out" as a bill on its own merits, and if it fails the substance of it is put in form of an amendment to the appropriation bill, and goes through slick as an eel without the people being wiser until the courts begin to tighten around the intended victims.

The Penrose bill, in spite of the storm of opposition, is now a law under the head of "appropriation," and is certainly in both object and method eminently appropriate capitalist legislation. To be properly classified it should be entitled the "Sneak Thief Act." The original law provided against the admission of indecent matter to the mails. The amendment just passed reads as follows: "And the term 'indecent' within the intendment of this section shall include matter of a character tending to incite arson, murder, or assassination."

The postmaster general being empowered to interpret the law and decide what is indecent, that functionary is now a dictator, and may upon his own motive choke off the mail privilege and suppress any publication. It may as well be understood that these capitalist hounds are on the trail of the socialists.

A committee clerk has given me the information that the socialist papers, especially the *Appeal*, were the theme of heated discussion in the committee room. The fact that the *Appeal* has been sent to each senator, congressman, judge, cabinet minister, and other federal officials during the session just closed has had its effect. Speaking to a congressman this morning, he raised the lid of his desk, and taking out a copy of the *Appeal* said: "They all hate the damned sheet, but they read it just the same."

One of the bitterest enemies of the *Appeal*, I am told, is Senator Aldrich,[33] the Standard Oil statesman, who declared with emphasis when the amendment was under discussion that some way must be found to put that "treasonable and anarchistic sheet" out of business.

Let me warn all socialist papers to keep a sharp lookout between now and July 1st, when the amendment takes effect. I have it upon good authority that a corps of secret operatives has been employed to scan the columns of all socialist papers, translate the foreign ones, and make due report of everything that may be construed as "indecent" and warrant the revocation of the second class privilege. In addition to this, an army of secret inspectors is to be employed to examine each issue of each socialist paper for the purpose of discovering anything that can be construed as a violation of the amended postal law.

The friends of the *Appeal* here think the *Appeal* is in grave danger, and freely express their opinion that it will be crushed in the midst of the presidential campaign. The amendment, it will be noted, was made to take effect about the time the campaign opens, allowing a few weeks for the government detectives and spotters to furnish the evidence upon which to base the intended action.

There is a conspiracy to destroy the socialist press at a time when it is most needed. The postmaster general now has the absolute power, and it is only a question as to whether, when the time comes, he will dare to exercise it. My idea is to keep within the law as in the past, defy the conspirators, and if they attack the socialist press, fight to the last ditch.

The Socialist Conflagration†

June 27, 1908

The most glowing reports which could be put in words would fail to do justice to the socialist situation in the middle and eastern states through which I recently traveled. I was astonished and delighted at every point. Four years ago the sentiment was weak and sporadic. This year it is spontaneous, widespread, and so intense that it cannot be described. Within the past few months there has been a marvelous change in the entire status of the socialist movement in the United States. In places where up till now it had existed in only a lambent state, it has burst forth like a conflagration.[34]

In New York, where I have often been before, I have never seen or felt such burning and consuming enthusiasm. It has a vital and thrilling spirit which hitherto had been lacking. It held one fast in its grip from the moment one came within its influence. What was equally gratifying was the spirit of comradeship among the leaders, some of whom had heretofore been the heads of belligerent factions. The harmony which now prevails in New York and in

† Published as "Socialism Rampant" in *Appeal to Reason,* whole no. 653 (June 27, 1908), 1.

the East generally is the consummation the socialists in that section have been looking forward to these many years.

The battles of the past have always been fought under disadvantages for the reason that the militant strength was largely dissipated in factional warfare. This year it will be entirely different. Not only are these factions united, but the very differences which formerly arrayed them against each other seem now to impart an element of strength which would not be possible had there always been smooth sailing. It was a scene good to look upon to see the old warriors in the movement all united and filled with the one desire to marshal all the forces against the common enemy.

The launching of the *Evening Call* in New York was an event of great importance in the movement, and marks a new era in the propaganda, which is already sowing the most excellent results.

The visit at national headquarters in Chicago could not have been more gratifying. The subcommittee delegated with authority to make the preliminary arrangements for the campaign was perfectly united and all aglow with the spirit of enthusiasm. The outlook was considered infinitely more promising than ever before, from every possible point of view. The work before the committee was disposed of with dispatch, and the general campaign outlined in a comprehensive canvas of the entire country.

The national headquarters is a veritable hive of activity. Housed with the *Daily Socialist*, almost the entire building is now required and all the vast floors are closely crowded with busy workers who are all vying with each other to do most for the advancement of the party's interests.

In all places covered in my journey to New York, Washington, Chicago, and other points, there is but one opinion among socialists, and that is that for the first time the Socialist Party is fairly and squarely launched as a national party and will figure as a decisive factor in the national campaign. It is wonderful to what extent this has become a conviction in the minds of socialists, and this conviction has given them fresh zeal and an air of confidence in the triumphant march of socialism which they have never had before.

In the campaign of 1900 the Socialist Party was a relatively insignificant factor.[35] In the campaign of 1904, the party attracted considerably more attention, and when the returns were announced a sobering expression was noticeable upon the features of capitalist politicians. Since then, the industrial collapse and the widespread discontent consequent thereupon have intensified the opposition to the existing order and the ranks of socialism have been recruited at a correspondingly rapid pace. The outlook is therefore all that even the most pessimistic could desire. The entire general situation is this year for the first time wholly in our favor. The movement has a strength and virility it has never known before. The very thought of it is an inspiration and as we look with eager, happy eyes upon the rapid spread of our conquering movement, we begin to feel the first joyous thrills of the realization of our ideals.

No Negro Question Outside the Class Question: Open Letter to J. Milton Waldron†

June 30, 1908

Girard, Kansas, June 30, 1908

Reverend J. Milton Waldron[36]
Washington, DC

My Dear Mr. Waldron:—

I have received and carefully read your communication of the 25th instant and beg to say in reply that I am in hearty sympathy with you insofar as your organization seeks the political and economic freedom of the Negro race. The people of your race are entitled to all the rights and opportunities that other races are entitled to, but they have never had them, nor will they have them under the administration of either the Republican or Democratic Party.

Let me say to you candidly that in the individual matter of defeating William H. Taft as the candidate of the Republican Party, we cannot join you. We Socialists attach no importance to mere individuals in political campaigns, and have no sympathy with any movement designed to inflict punishment on individual candidates for real or fancied wrongs. We are organized to overthrow the capitalist system which is maintained politically by both the Republican and Democratic parties, and to establish the socialist republic in which all men and

† Published as "Not Racial But Class Distinction Last Analysis of Negro Problem—Debs" in *New York Call*, vol. 1, no. 77 (August 27, 1908), 1, 3.

all women, regardless of race, nationality, or creed, may enjoy equal freedom. To accomplish this we are not making war upon individuals, but upon a social and industrial system in which individuals, especially those prominent in political life, do practically as they must to obtain their ends.

The Brownsville affair,[37] we admit, was disgraceful and indefensible; but it cannot be said that it was due to race discrimination. At least the outrage cannot be supported upon that theory. The officials of the Western Federation of Miners were not Negroes, but white men, and yet they were kidnapped by conspiracy of the Republican governors and by sanction of President Roosevelt at the behest of the Mine Owners' Association. It is not a question of race, but a question of class. The white workingman is no higher in the present social scale than is the Negro, and although the prejudice of the one against the other is assiduously cultivated by the ruling class, that class has no more real regard for a wage-slave of one color than of another. Here we have the crux of this question.

I agree perfectly to what you say about President Roosevelt. He is in truth a tsar, but whether he is or is not makes but little difference, after all, in this capitalist system. The president of our so-called republic has equal power, to say the least, with the emperor of Germany or the king of England, and, as a matter of fact, he makes use of power which neither of these monarchs would dare exercise over his subjects.

This country is ruled today by the president and the Supreme Court, and this resolves itself practically into the president alone, since Supreme Court judges are the creatures of his appointment. Whether this president happens to be Mr. Roosevelt, Mr. Taft, or Mr. Bryan makes no difference so far as the working class is concerned. The fact remains that under the present system, government is controlled absolutely in the interest of the capitalist class and its chief function is to keep the working class in subjection.

I have not now time to go into this matter, nor is it necessary for the purpose of this communication. The point I wish to make is that the capitalist system is a class system and that we live today under class rule, whether the administration is Republican or Democratic, and that the president and Supreme Court and Congress—the executive, judicial, and legislative branches of the government—are simply the functionaries of the ruling class and could not, even were they so disposed, materially change conditions resulting from the class ownership of the means of production, that is to say, the means of life.

In this system, class rules class and while the system lasts, and this, as I have already indicated, is not a race question, but a class question, and when the Negroes, the great mass of whom are wage workers, develop sufficient intelligence to understand their true economic and political interests, they will join and support the Socialist Party, the only political party in the world today whose declared purpose it is to abolish class rule and establish a republic whose fundamental principle is the equal rights and freedom of all.

Ever since the close of the Civil War, the Republican Party has used the Negro as a political asset. The Republican Party cares not one whit more for the Negro than does the Democratic Party, its protestation to the contrary notwithstanding. The boasted love of the Republican politicians for the Negro is sheer buncombe. The Northern Republican manufacturer places precisely the same estimate upon the Negro as the Southern cotton-grower. He esteems him for the use he can make of him and the surplus value he can extract from his labor-power. When it comes to the capitalist politician, he simply speaks for the ruling class, and if for a brief period preceding the election he develops a passion of friendship for the Negro, it is to get that Negro to cast his vote to perpetuate the rule of his master and his own political degradation and economic slavery.

Even Senator Foraker himself,[38] who is now almost a demigod in the eyes of many Negroes, does not differ from President Roosevelt or from any of the rest of the politicians in the matter regarding Negroes, and white men as well, who work for wages as unfit, as a class, to rise above the dead level of wage-slavery. Senator Foraker, like President Roosevelt, is a political representative of the capitalist class, serves that class in every speech he makes and every vote he casts in the Senate, and upon this proposition I challenge his record and defy successful contradiction.

Senator Foraker, like President Roosevelt, believes in the capitalist system and is, in fact, a capitalist himself; supports the private ownership of the means of production, and believes that the great mass of workers, who produce all wealth and support all government and all civilization, should be dependent upon the capitalists for the opportunity to work, and therefore doomed to live and die in wage-slavery.

There is no Negro question outside of the class question. Abolish capitalism, the private ownership by the few of the means whereby the great mass live, give Negroes economic freedom so that they may have the right to work and to receive and enjoy all they produce, and the race question, as it menaces capitalist class society, will be no more. As it is now, the wage working Negro, like the wage working white, is simply merchandise, bought and sold in the "labor market." The Republican Party does not intend that he shall ever be anything else, and as for the Democratic Party, which is even now depriving Negro wage-slaves of their political franchise in the South, it is not necessary to even raise the question as to where it stands.

Between the two capitalist parties there is no economic difference so far as the great mass of the people is concerned. They are both committed to capitalist ownership, class rule, and wage-slavery.

To awaken the Negro, the same as the white man, who works for a living, to open his eyes and to educate him along true lines is now the great problem to which the Socialist Party is giving itself with all the means at its command. It already has several Negro organizers in the field and expects to have more in the near future.

Here let me say that the Socialist Party is not seeking to get the votes of Negroes except upon the one condition that the Negroes who give it their support do so not only of their own will, but have intelligence enough to know what they are voting for and what a vote for socialism means to them. If the Socialist Party could by the trickery and fraud employed by the Republican and Democratic parties obtain the entire vote of the 600,000 Negroes for whom you speak, it would scorn to stoop to that level.

The Socialist Party knows that the great mass of Negroes are ignorant and it is the only party that refuses to traffic in that ignorance, to build upon and exploit that ignorance, that a few may riot in luxury and some others hold fat offices as the fruit of their part in robbing and degrading their unfortunate fellow beings.

The Socialist Party wants every Negro vote it can get, provided it represents the intelligence, dignity, and honesty of the man who casts it. The Socialist Party does not invest in whiskey and cigars as a means of influencing the votes of Negroes or others, nor does it spend a single cent to influence any man's vote except as that vote can be influenced in an educational way. The Republican and Democratic parties, on the contrary, rely upon the ignorance of their supporters, use their means to corrupt them and their power to keep them in ignorance, that they may continue to be exploited by the class which supports and is supported by these parties.

I read with much satisfaction of the part taken by yourself and co-workers in the late Republican convention[39] and of the vigorous protest made by you against the subservient attitudes of that party toward the trusts and its cowardly attitude toward your race. The spirit which animated you is splendid, and I congratulate you upon having the courage to freely stand up in defense of your convictions. This to me is the signal that henceforth the Republican Party is no longer to confidently and coolly base its certainty of success upon its title deed to the Negro voting population of the United States. The influences back of you, while not yet clear and conscious in their aim, are yet right and full of promise of better, far better things in the near future.

I should be only too glad to meet you and your people, and but for the fact that I am having to leave here to fill a series of speaking engagements, I should seek a personal interview with you and your colleagues at the earliest opportunity. As you are near New York let me suggest that you arrange to meet the representatives of our movement located there. You will find the headquarters at 6 Park Place, where the official papers, daily and weekly, of the Socialist Party are also published.[40] You will find there a number of representative socialists who will be glad to meet you and your associates and talk over this entire matter with you. Let me further suggest that you get in touch with the national office of the party, which is located at Chicago, the national secretary being J. Mahlon Barnes, whose address is 180 East Washington Street. Mr. Barnes will be glad to give you any information you may desire in regard to the party and furnish you with such printed matter as may be of interest to you in the consideration of this question.

At a later day I may have the pleasure of meeting with you in person, and meantime I wish you all success in your very commendable undertaking.
Believe me

Very sincerely yours,
Eugene V. Debs

Independence and Liberty: A Fourth of July Message†

July 3, 1908

From the earliest dawn of history, the soul of man has aspired to independence and liberty. The desire was not born with the sires of '76, nor first expressed in the Declaration of Independence, since ages before the poets had sung of the sweet flower of liberty, and brave men had given their lives to secure independence from tyrant and king. Leonidas[41] dying at Thermopylae, Judas

† Published as "Independence and Liberty" in *Chicago Daily Socialist,* vol. 2, no. 213 (July 3, 1908), 1.

Maccabeus[42] marshaling the Jews against the encroachments of the Romans, Charles Martel[43] hammering the invading Saracens from Europe, Joan of Arc[44] battling for her native king, Huguenots[45] and Puritans[46] fleeing to America from the restrictions that surrounded them—all had visions of independence and liberty, as they saw them, that glorified to them the future and transfigured them before the eyes of men.

But, after all, it was only a partial vision that these men and women had. They were hampered, as we are, by environment; their aims were not full, their work was not perfect. The Grecian who was ready to repel a Persian tyrant would accept an Alexander;[47] the Maid of Orleans,[48] chafing for freedom from foreign domination, saw in her sweet virgin visions nothing better than the rulership of a French king in France; the Puritan who sought on the shores of New England "freedom to worship God" was ready to drive a Roger Williams[49] or Anne Hutchinson[50] from his community; and even the signers of the Declaration of Independence suppressed the paragraph which demanded liberty for the Negro.

Their very expressions, the very words they used, to voice the aspiration that burned within them, were circumscribed and inadequate. For countless centuries the world looked forward to liberty and independence as the acme of its hopes, and both were inadequate, because they failed to take into consideration the great social life which is at the base of all advancement.

The man who would be independent cannot be social. He must go to the wilderness and live and die unto himself, building his own house, tilling his own field, making his own clothing, providing his own amusements. If he should specialize his effort, and if he should look toward his fellow man, he ceases to be independent; for upon one he becomes dependent for his shoes, another for the cloth in his coat, another for the salt that seasons his food, and upon an army of men and women for the articles that supply him with comfort and variety.

If he would have liberty he must not be restrained. The civil law restricting him in the use of land, the unwritten social law prescribing what is fit and decent, and the moral law suggesting that he restrain certain propensities he may have, are all limits to his liberty. It is only as he abrogates all of these, throws aside the claims of society and the suggestions of sentiment and humanity, doing only as his whim or notion may dictate, that he can have perfect liberty.

But of late years there has grown up a higher conception of things, a more clear seeing idealism, which demands neither the independence of the pioneer and ascetic, or the liberty of the anarchist or voluptuary. Instead of independence it speaks of interdependence; instead of liberty it seeks for freedom.

Interdependence is the order of organization, the law of society and commerce. It is not servile, but it serves. While independence limits one to his own talent and capacity, interdependence brings to his touch the talents and capacity of all men, the wide world over. Whether in iron machinery or in social life, interdependence assembles parts and uses them in beautiful harmony, to the accomplishment of grand results. Independence clothed the world in skins; interdependence has robed it in silks and fabrics of textures and tints that delight the eye. Independence at meat burned on coals and bread made from cracked corn; interdependence searches the world for delicious and wholesome foods and serves them temptingly in every home. Independence lived in the cave, the hollow tree, the wigwam, or the tent; interdependence builds the modern cottage and the palace of glass.

Then, liberty has grown into a higher feeling for freedom. There is liberty in the wood, far from society; but there is freedom of motion in well-regulated association. The perfect machine, moving in rhythm, is so jointed and attached, part to part, that there is no liberty for any; yet with what splendid freedom it moves, frictionless and logically, working out its marvelous design!

This is the highest destiny of man, the perfection of evolution from the solitary life of Eden to the higher society of the Kingdom of Heaven.

Mastery of the Machine: Campaign Speech in Oklahoma City [excerpt]†

July 5, 1908

Ladies and Gentlemen, Comrades and Fellow Workers:—

I need hardly say that I appreciate this cordial reception. It is more than a passing pleasure to me to stand in this inspiring presence.

† Published in *Appeal to Reason,* whole no. 660 (July 25, 1908), 3. Probably a reprint from the Oklahoma City press, source undetermined.

Yesterday, 132 years ago, the Declaration of Independence was issued. Crowns and scepters sunk together, and for the first time in human history man stood forth the political sovereign.

When great changes have occurred in human history, when great principles have been involved, as a rule the majority have been wrong, the minority right. In the march of time, the minority, in alliance with the forces of evolution, become the majority; their principles are enrolled and then all the world applauds. Living, these men are reviled, they are treated as the enemies of human society; dead, they are almost deified and monuments are erected where they sleep.

But, my friends, we are not yet free. It is true that we are living in a so-called republic, but no man is truly free unless he is master of the means that sustain his life. The revolutionary patriots proved to the world that politically they were capable of self-government. It now remains to prove to the world that we are also capable of industrial self-government.

A political party expresses the material interest of its supporters provided they have intelligence enough to understand their material interests. When your grandfathers and great-grandfathers lived, they worked with their own tools. They were the masters of their product and they were reasonably free. It was about that time that the simple tool was transformed; it became the machine, and industrial revolution had a beginning. Up to this time the employer was also a workingman and had to pay them substantially what they produced as they could quit his service and provide themselves with the simple tools required and work for themselves. But the tool became the machine and we have today one class who are the tool-owners, called capitalists, and on the other hand, that great class who are tool users and who are known to us as the wage earners. These two have different interests and are continually pitted against each other, and we have a constant succession of strikes and lockouts, sometimes accompanied by bloodshed. This, my friends, is the class struggle. The capitalist seeks to obscure this fact that his position and possession may be perpetuated, but the socialist points it out that we may put an end to it, that we may work side by side and begin to march to the noblest civilization that the human race has ever known.

In this system, in which the capitalist owns the machine that he does not use and the workingman uses the machine that he does not own, we have a fundamental contradiction—social labor, social production upon every hand

and individual appropriation of the social product. Eighty-five percent of the wealth is produced by the machine of today. When it was produced by hand, the man who produced it furnished a market for it. But the machine does not furnish a market for what it produces. The capitalist produces for the whole world in competition with the capitalists of the world. In order to hold his market he must produce more cheaply than his competitor. To produce more cheaply, he must have a more effective machine, and in exact proportion as machinery replaces labor the market is restricted and destroyed. This accounts for the fact that every few years we are afflicted with what is called overproduction, and we suffer all these ills because we have machinery with which we can produce in such overwhelming abundance.

Upon the average you can produce 20 times as much wealth as your grandfathers did. Why should you that are willing to work suffer for the want of it? And have you ever thought about it long enough to satisfy yourself that every system of society first appears immature, then matured, and then passes away to make room for one more in harmony with the onward march of civilization? Capitalism is only about 175 years old. We have passed through all the early stages of it. Competition has been and is being constantly eliminated. Going forward we shall soon have industry organized upon a cooperative basis, all workers working together cooperatively in every department of activity, and thus laying the foundation gradually for a new social order and for a higher civilization than mankind has ever known.

How fares the master in this system? We are taught that he is its beneficiary and that he has solved the problem of success. But take the average capitalist, subject him to ordinary examination, and you will find that he is wonderfully deficient in all those qualities that dignify and glorify manhood. I am not referring to the smaller capitalists, but to those that are full-grown. Most of you have just started your pinfeathers. Most of you are opposed to socialism. Most of you are not ready for a king. You have but little and that little not for long. We are not going to take from you what you have. Your larger competitor will tend to that and when he gets through with you, you will be ready for us. But take the full-grown capitalist. He has an abnormal brain development. He is not wise but cunning. He can see an opening for profit; he knows how to take advantage of his fellow men; he can beat you in a trade; he is very unscrupulous. But ask him a few simple questions about the history of his own country and you will find that he doesn't know as much as a schoolboy ought to know; ask him about evolution and he has never heard of it; ask him about the science of economics, or again of literature, and he knows nothing about it, nor of art nor of the sciences. He simply knows how to gouge profit out of the working class. He knows nothing about the higher enjoyments; though he lives in a palace and fares sumptuously and has a private yacht, he does not enjoy the ecstasy of the handclap of comradeship; loves no one and is loved by no one.

John Boyle O'Reilly[51] says [the capitalist] lives apart from the common heart of humanity; does not know the meaning of human brotherhood. Take him out into the woods, and if your ears are attuned you can hear the trills of birds making the woods vocal with their melodies, and he looks at the great monarch of the forest that towers aloft—I never see one but I want to put my arms around it and hear its heartthrobs—and when the capitalist looks at it he can tell you to a nicety how many feet of lumber it contains and how much profit this will bring in the market. He is filled with fear and dread; he knows about the pitfalls of trade, is suspicious of his fellow men, and when he appears in the streets, he tries to hide his identity.

ശ

The Republican Party held its convention a few days ago. I would do them no injustice, but I would ask you as workingmen what they did for you. Now your father may have been a Republican, and may have had good reasons for being a Republican. The trouble with you is that you do not think for yourself. You do not know that parties are subject to the laws of evolution and that parties that serve a good purpose today may be out of date tomorrow. Many of you workingmen vote the Republican ticket because your fathers and grandfathers did. You imagine that you are respecting their memories. As a matter of fact you are disgracing them. There is only one way in which you can respect their memories, and that is by being true to yourselves. Did it ever occur to you that you have a brain and that you should use it in your interest instead of being satisfied to use your arms in the interest of your master? A beast can fight—it takes a man to think. It is his highest and noblest characteristic.

Shakespeare said there is no darkness, but ignorance;[52] and there is no slavery but ignorance. The great majority of mankind have always been ignorant, and this is why they have always crowned their oppressors and crucified their saviors. There is no longer any excuse for ignorance or poverty, and but for ignorance there would be no poverty. Nothing is so easily produced as wealth. All the earth consists of raw material—in every sunbeam, in every waterfall—which properly applied transmute these raw values into wealth. If there is a human being upon earth who cannot secure life's necessities, it is not due to Nature, it cannot be charged upon the Almighty—it is due to man.

ര

The right kind of an education is the great need of this time. Are the capitalists trying to educate you workingmen? Are they not doing what they can through the politicians to perpetuate the power by which you are enslaved? You are satisfied with too little. The average worker with a wage that will keep body and soul together is content, and he is told that he is blessed to be content. I am doing what little I can to incite him to discontent. Intelligent discontent is the torchbearer of civilization. Jefferson, Payne, Otis,[53] Franklin, Adams—all of the revolutionists whose memories you revere, yesterday were agitators. It is a choice between agitation and stagnation. The majority said: "Let well enough alone or you'll bring trouble upon the country." They did bring trouble upon the country and it resulted in American independence, and if it had not been for their agitation, you would still be British subjects. Many are proud to call themselves the children of the revolution, but talk to them of the revolution coming and they have chills and fever. Being now on top, they want to suspend the law of evolution, and the revolution that is coming is condemned. Why, do you suppose that we have had our last revolution? Do you suppose that the laws of evolution can be suspended by any class until at last mankind in the aggregate is released from the degrading thralldom of the ages?

The workingman has had to struggle through all the phases of his development. He was the abject slave of ancient masters; he was the serf of feudal barons; after which he is the exploited wage worker of modern capitalists. He is to become the free man in socialism, the next stage of our advancing civilization.

There will be this difference between the impending social revolution and all others which have preceded it since the dawn of history: Hitherto in every revolution the ruling class has been overthrown by another lower, but middle, class—which then became the ruling class; but the working class can only emancipate themselves by emancipating all humanity.

As I speak here this evening, about one-fifth, 20 percent, of the working class is in a state of enforced idleness. There are about 30 million of these and there are about 6 million out of work. Take the coal miners in this vicinity. Many of the mines have been shut down four long months, and the miners are in a state verging on starvation. I have just been in the coal fields. I have seen the victims of this insane system. I know of what I speak. Now what do you think—and bear in mind that this condition prevails under Republican and Democratic administrations? In the past 24 years we have had 8 years under the latter and 16 under the former, and panics with enforced idleness under them both. Don't talk to me about tariff or about the currency when thousands are starving for the opportunity to work.

From ten thousand rostrums, the Declaration of Independence was read, that all men are created equal, that they have certain inalienable rights—life, liberty, and the pursuit of happiness. No man has the inalienable right to life unless he also has the inalienable right to work. Whatever stands between him and work must be removed. Now why don't the thousands of miners work? Is it because they are not willing to work? No, because they are denied it. I have already stated it. There is no demand for their labor-power. They themselves are in a state of degeneracy. They will become tramps and criminals. It is in this way that criminals are created—all the way from petty larceny to homicide.

How are you workingmen going to make it possible for you to have the inalienable right to work? In just one way. First of all, you must recognize your interests—you must unite. The very hour you unite, there is nothing between this earth and the starry heavens that can stand between you and emancipation; but as long as you divide upon election day, as long as you vote for the capitalist ticket, you will be responsible and you must accept the consequences. It is you who must change this. It will not be changed until you do change it. You have a part in this great struggle—every workingman who has a conception of the duties he owes himself, his country, and his family, and everyone who sympathizes with the workingman and his class, and there are many of them and I pay to them the humble tribute of my respect. They are only a few, but they are so highly organized, spiritually and intellectually, that they espouse this cause, this cause that is ultimately the cause of humanity.

I was in New York last month and attended a meeting there of seven hundred people, called together by 210 ministers of the gospel, representing all of the various denominations, and in that meeting these ministers, who are the true followers of the Nazarene, the carpenter, these ministers appealed to their people to vote the Socialist ticket this fall.[54] There never was such an awakening in all the history of the United States.

We are just beginning to understand the true meaning of civilization. We are just beginning the first anthem of real freedom. Many here, men and women, are joining this conquering movement. Many of understanding are rallying to the standard of emancipation. Don't think the Socialist Party wants your property. Disabuse your mind of that vagary. You cling to a grain of sand and you become an insect and you are afraid you will lose it . . .

ೞ

Now the Socialist Party is differently organized than any other party in the field. It has no corruption fund. It has never bought a vote and never will. If it could buy the vote of Oklahoma with a five-cent piece and sweep into power this fall, it would scorn to do so. Socialists know that socialism can't come until the people are ready for it, and the people will be ready for it as soon as they know what it is. Most of you have everything to gain and nothing to lose, and from a true rational point of view, you have everything to gain and nothing to lose. No one has any reason to fear it.

The two old parties organize just before election. They represent the predatory interests, and they both get their campaign funds from the same interests. Even Mr. Bryan's party got $15,000 from Thomas Ryan,[55] the notorious traction manipulator in New York. Mr. Bryan says he knew nothing about it, but his party not only accepted it, but sent a committee to New York to get it. That is the party I am discussing and not the individual. Do they rely upon the intelligence of the people? Don't they do all they can to keep the people ignorant? Don't they make campaign funds just as large as they can for the purpose of debauching the people? The corruption funds flow out like lava. If the Democratic Party is the [more] scrupulous, it is because it can't raise the same amount. As a rule the big capitalists belong to the Republican Party and the little ones to the Democratic Party. The little ones would be big; they stand for the same principle and I defy anyone to show me the slightest difference so far as the workers are concerned.

The middle class is being ground to atoms in the mill of capitalism, and the Democratic Party that is the expression of the middle class is in a state of disintegration. What is "Democratic" is the great question. A few days ago Mr. Parker offered a resolution before the Democratic convention. At once there was an uproar. It was charged that in glorifying Mr. Cleveland he was outraging Mr. Bryan.[56]

In due time the big capitalists will find their way into the Republican Party, and the little ones finally into the Socialist Party. We will have but one party representing the capitalist class and the Socialist representing the working class. They will have the dollars and we will have the votes.

ഗ

In the last session of Congress, Senator LaFollette named one hundred capitalists who absolutely control our industrial and political life. No man is appointed to the courts unless his record is perfect—not only his ability, but his willingness to obey; and every time the decisions are in favor of the capitalist class and against the working class.

A striking case was that in which William Howard Taft issued one of the first injunctions that paralyzed organized labor. This same gentleman appears on an anti-injunction platform appealing to workingmen for support. Can you think of anything more grotesque? And but for the injunctions he issued, I would not be the candidate for the presidency on the Socialist ticket. A certain engineer refused to haul certain cars, preferring rather to quit work. This man was arrested and sent to jail. Bear in mind that he was a free-born American citizen and he simply exercised the right to quit work. The Brotherhood of Locomotive Engineers appealed his case to the Supreme Court. The Supreme Court affirmed this decision—that a workingman hasn't the right to quit work unless his employer is willing.

In another case, where a workingman had been discharged for belonging to a union, he took the case to the lower court, and then to the Supreme Court and the Supreme Court decided that the company had a right to discharge him and place his name upon the "blacklist" so that he cannot again obtain employment and must become a hunted vagabond until he commits suicide.

ശ

We have 30 million wage-slaves—about 7 million of these are women and about 2 million of them are children. The capitalist system wants the cheapest kind of labor. Women and children can operate the machinery and they receive just enough to keep them in working order. They say we are going to destroy the home. What kind of a home can a woman have on $3.20 a week? Go there, if you have time to spare in this savage competitive system, go to any of the great industrial centers with their red light and slum districts. What kind of homes are these? In this miserable system the laboring man must exchange his labor-power for just enough to keep him in working order and after a while he loses even this. He has his two hands and sinew to exchange for those things that are needed for himself and wife and three or four children; but the mills are closed down, so he leaves the home, their very humble home, where there is no paper nor pictures on the wall, and starts looking for employment that can't be found. He doesn't ride on a Pullman, but on the trucks—if he is not found—and renews his search for work. He can live only by permission. He has no tools; they are privately owned though socially used. He becomes a mendicant; his clothes become seedy; nobody knows him but the policeman. He reaches a point three or four hundred miles from home; he is a stranger in a city of thousands of human beings, famished in heart. He takes a backward look at the little cottage; he is heart-sick; he recognizes that on all of God's earth there is no one to call him to the banquet board of nature. He is a tramp. It is but a stop from this condition into crime.

That is why we are having great and growing armies of tramps—why all our penitentiaries are filled to overflowing; why the insane asylums must be more numerous; why crime is rampant. In all the centers of population these are the fruits of capitalism, which has outgrown its usefulness, and ought to be abolished, not only in the interest of the working class, but in the higher interest of all mankind. It is this which constitutes the issue in this election, and on this issue we make our appeal to you. There are mill hands, factory hands, farm hands—all hands and no head. They want you to run to hand. You remember Lincoln said that if God Almighty had meant for some men to do all the eating and others all the working, he would have produced some all mouth and others all hands.[57] They don't want you to think. When they think, they think in their interest, and when you think it will be against their interest. I mean their so-called interest. Ultimately it will be in their interest.

Their grandchildren will rear monuments to where you sleep. You are in the majority, but you do as others do. They tell you that socialism would destroy your individuality. That would be miraculous—that would be a miracle! Because you have none. No man has any individuality who has got to bet for permission to live. They charge us with destroying what doesn't exist. That is true of the charge of destroying the home. The great majority have no homes.

Socialism is going to make them masters of the machinery they work with so that they will have the inalienable right to work. Then work will be as elevating as it is now degrading. It is well enough for you in an office to talk about the dignity of labor, but let me put you in a sawmill or mine and then ask you what you think about the dignity of labor—under a boss who treats you as a menial and then ask you what you think about your individuality. If you marry a nice girl, you have got to reduce her to your level if she is not already there. The wage-slave feels his insecurity. It is bad enough to be a single man when you are out of work; it is infinitely worse if you are married. Every man ought to have a family and taste the sweets of home where the noblest aspirations are induced.

These things don't exist and never will under capitalism. Every charge capitalism makes against us it is guilty of itself. It is claimed that socialism is a dream, that it is impossible; and so long as you think it is impossible, it will be; but when you think that you can make a machine and then own it, we will have socialism. Your grandfather owned the tools he worked with. You don't though you produce twenty times as much as your grandfather could. Every man ought to have abundance, and every man would have abundance if the tools that are socially used are socially owned. That is the issue that divides the socialists from the capitalists.

How are you going to effect this change? It is so easy that a child can grasp it. You have a majority of the votes. Read the Socialist platform. That party is the only party that declares that when it succeeds to power it will transfer the machinery of production to the people. It can be done legally and peacefully if the capitalists will submit to the majority, and if they don't, it will come anyway. Now when the Socialist Party succeeds to power, it can legally relieve Rockefeller and Vanderbilt of their burdens. They will not have to relieve themselves. We will have to do that for them. Their great-grandchildren will thank us. We can afford to wait.

∽

What can we promise you? Ostracism and persecution. We can promise you more. We promise you victory in the interest of the human race. I want to see the time come when every human being on this earth is free. I want to see the time when human society is reconstructed—not by destroying private property, but by establishing private property, making it possible for every human being who works to possess the fruits of his labor, making it possible for him to live a complete life. We don't propose a public ownership of pictures and musical instruments. These are privately used. We propose the common ownership of the things collectively used. When industry has culminated in the private monopoly, such as the oil monopoly, we will socialize it.

Now can we run it? It is running itself now. When Rockefeller was put on the witness stand, he testified that he had nothing to do with the oil business for seven years. He might just as well live upon another planet. Here's a full-fledged capitalist. We propose to deprive him of his taxing power. Socialism will transfer this social enterprise to the people. It is already cooperative and self-operative, since competition is eliminated. Society will take these enterprises and operate them for the benefit of all. First the firm, then the corporation, then the trust—next the people. Society is to succeed the trust. As soon as we have socialized these trusts, we will give work to all. Then the working day need not be more than four or five hours long. What it will be, will be determined by society. Society could not be given a perfected machine now, but they are being educated and when evolution has completed its work, revolution will come as the climax. There need not be a drop of bloodshed.

No Prospects for Hearst's Independence Party†

July 31, 1908

Terre Haute, Indiana, July 31 [1908]

The Independence Party is not likely to be an appreciable factor in the present campaign. It seems perfectly clear that the Independence Party was brought into existence from motives of pique and revenge, and not of principle. Had Bryan supported Hearst for the nomination for the presidency four year ago, there would not now be an Independence Party in the field.

Mr. Hearst supported Bryan heartily eight years ago, in spite of the reasons he now urges against him. Every objection Hearst makes to Bryan now could have been made with equal reason eight years ago, so there must be some other cause for the formation of a new party to defeat Mr. Bryan.

As the Independence Party has no prospects, not even the remotest, of electing anybody, it is not probable that the patriots will flock to its standard in overwhelming numbers.

And yet, here in Indiana, where the election may be close, the Independence Party may have some influence in determining results. To what extent this may prove [the case] is purely problematical.

The truly radical and progressive Democrats who have become disgusted with the Bryan-Murphy-Connors-"Train Robber" Sullivan-"Bath House John"-"Hinky Dink" aggregation of reformers are now heading straight for socialism and will not be halted by Mr. Hearst and his personal "Independence" Party.

---

† Published in *New York World,* circa August 1, 1908, unspecified page. Reprinted as "There Is No Room for Hearst's Party" in *St. Louis Labor,* vol. 6, whole no. 393 (August 15, 1908), 2.

Women Needed in Campaign[†]

August 1908

As this campaign develops, the need for every available comrade to serve in the ranks will press upon us, and one of the greatest will be for women on the rostrum and in the field as speakers and propagandists. There are certain advantages which women have over men which give their work special influence of a character which is sorely needed at this time. The appeal of women for socialism comes, too, with peculiar force, and it fills a place in our propaganda which must otherwise remain vacant. My observation is that our movement is strongest where women's influence is felt most, and since our movement is a human movement, and since our party is the only party which recognizes woman as a human being, the way should be paved as much as possible for all women who have the time and capacity to enter the arena and give voice and influence to the one cause in which success means emancipation.

Not long ago I saw and heard one of our socialist women in action. She was addressing a crowd on the street. Her eyes sparkled, her cheeks glowed, and her voice was vibrant with enthusiasm. She held the crowd close to her while she drove home her telling points.

The crowd always listens to a woman with respectful attention, and when she is animated by socialist principles and ideals she at once becomes a power in molding thought and in starting the crowd on the right track. Most earnestly do I hope to see every woman who understands socialism, and is in position to speak about it, out on the hustings when the campaign opens. My only regret is that we have not twice as many to serve, and our committees everywhere should make it as easy as possible, by those who are available, to join in the greatest political battle ever waged for freedom by the working class of the United States.

† Published in *The Socialist Woman* [Girard, KS], vol. 2, whole no. 15 (August 1908), 4.

The Democratic Injunction Plank†

August 8, 1908

In reply to numerous inquiries as to what I think of the alleged anti-injunction plank of the Democratic Party, I have to say that it is a delusion and a snare, a fraud and a false pretense, without the shadow of an element to redeem it from condemnation.[58]

It was incorporated as a political bait to catch labor suckers and for no other purpose. Democratic politicians are not one whit more friendly to organized labor than are Republican politicians, and their party record in Congress and in state legislatures proves it.

The so-called injunction plank adopted at Denver, when analyzed, is found to mean nothing, and it is not improved in the least by Mr. Gompers's puerile elucidation.[59]

During my official connection with organized labor, I had injunctions issued against me by the courts from the Atlantic to the Pacific—more than has ever been issued against any labor union official before or since—and I may, therefore, I hope, without presumption, claim attention when that subject is under discussion.

The injunction is one of the most effective weapons the capitalist class has in keeping the working class in subjection, and it has no more intention of surrendering the rapid-fire instrument, or suffering it to be turned into a flintlock, than it has of surrendering the profit it gouges out of its enslaved and enjoined victims.

The labor injunction is one of the tentacles of capitalism and will never be destroyed until capitalism itself is destroyed; and the Democratic plank purporting to defend organized labor against it is a rank counterfeit, an unadulterated sham, an unmitigated fraud.

From free silver in 1896, the Democratic Party has turned to gold bricks in 1908, and that is the only change it has undergone.

For a quarter of a century Gompers, of the American Federation of Labor, shrieked "no politics" as the slogan of union labor. The logic of events, and the socialist movement, have at last driven him from his reactionary position,

† Published in *Appeal to Reason,* whole no. 662 (August 8, 1908), 1.

and now his banner is no longer inscribed "No Politics," but instead "Into the Democratic Party." No wonder Belmont[60] and Carnegie regard him as a safe leader of the working class.

Let every union man consider well the spectacle of Gompers, whose whole official career has been one of mad opposition to the political activity of union labor, now attempting to steer the trade union movement into the shambles of the Democratic Party.

Gompers does not dare to stand on any public platform in my presence and defend his Democratic gold brick injunction plank, nor show in what respect the Democratic Party is less a capitalist party or more a labor party than the Republican Party.

Organized Labor's New Turn to Politics[†]

August 9, 1908

Girard, Kansas, August 9 [1908]

In their platform declarations and campaign methods the dominant political parties concede the tremendous political power of organized labor. But this power is latent and has never yet produced any really important result for the benefit of workingmen as a class; much less has it been effective in shaping any of our great principles or policies of government. There is a very good reason for this noneffectiveness of the so-called labor vote. And there is also a good reason, one that is rooted deep in the salient facts of our wonderful industrial development, why the power of organized labor to produce political results for its own benefit must be reckoned with from this time forth.

That the economic interests of labor and capital are identical is an argument that has controlled the political course of labor for many years. In this belief the workingman has voted for the political party favored by his employer on the theory that what was good for his employer must necessarily be good for him also.

---

† Published as "Debs Says Labor Has Been Forced Into Politics" in *New York World*, August 10, 1908, unspecified page. Reprinted as "Debs Says Organized Labor Must Enter Politics to Protect Itself" in *New York Call*, vol. 1, no. 62 (August 10, 1908), 1.

Recent developments in the industrial world have cast doubt upon the correctness of this theory and cause workingmen to become somewhat suspicious of it.

Since the campaign of 1876, the vote of organized labor has been pretty evenly divided between the Republican and Democratic parties, except that four, eight, and twelve years ago the railroad employees most generally voted the Republican ticket, because that was the course dictated by their employers and they believed their economic interests lay in that direction. This year will mark a decided change. Through the activity of such organizations as the Manufacturers' Association and the zealous and unremitting war of such leaders as Van Cleave, Parry, and Post upon the fundamental principles of labor unionism, a vast number of workingmen have perceived the hollow mockery of the plea that the interests of labor and capital are identical. They know that their interest lies in organization, and if the interest of capital lies in destroying their unions, then the two interests cannot well be identical.

Why Labor Takes a New View

They know, too, that courts have declared their unions criminal conspiracies; they know that an attempt to boycott an unfair employer of labor has been declared illegal by the highest court in the land, and they know further that this same high court has declared that Congress has not even power to pass a law forbidding an employer of labor to boycott and blacklist a workingman simply because of his membership in a labor union. These results have been hailed with shouts of satisfaction by the capitalists, which joyful attitude on the part of their employers workingmen cannot reconcile with the theory that the interests of labor and capital are identical.

Also, when the representatives of organized labor, smarting under the injuries inflicted upon their unions by the decisions of the courts, have appealed to Congress for some measure of relief through legislation, they have found themselves opposed by a vigorous and successful capitalist lobby and their pleas for justice treated with contempt. Again this attitude cannot be made to fit in with the theory that the interests of labor and capital are identical.

Therefore workingmen have been forced to develop what our strenuous president denominates "that evil thing which is called class consciousness." Finding themselves shut out from those methods of economic relief with which they are familiar, they naturally turn to politics. They feel the necessity of controlling the government and the lawmaking power, just as the capitalists now do, in order that their interests may be protected.

Labor Forced to Act

Never before in the entire history of trade unionism has a leader representing the whole field of organized labor, as does Mr. Gompers, boldly and publicly advised workingmen to vote for a particular political party. Such advice is contrary to one of the most sacred traditions of organized labor, namely, "we must keep politics out of the unions." This is an important and highly significant phase in the development of that "class consciousness" which Mr. Roosevelt contemplates with such holy horror, and of which the *Washington Post* says editorially, "It would be difficult to conceive a greater calamity that could overtake labor than its entry into the field of politics as a class." What these superficial observers fail to perceive is that labor can do nothing else. Labor did not create the issue. It has been forced upon workingmen by industrial development, and they must accept it willy-nilly.

What is to be the effect of Mr. Gompers's pronouncement? First and foremost it will bend to the political solidarity of the working class. It cannot be expected that the vote of organized labor will be delivered solidly to the Democratic Party simply because Mr. Gompers favors that party and publicly announces his preference. Indeed, it may well be doubted that his attitude will have any appreciable effect on the general result. Nevertheless, it marks an epoch in the labor movement.

Naturally this change in the attitude of organized labor will be productive of some political surprises when the votes are counted next November. The truth is, politicians are at sea. No one at this time can estimate the effect of the labor vote on the general result this fall. What is practically certain is that a large number of labor votes will be cast for the Independence Party and a surprisingly large number will be cast for the Socialist Party.

Unity and Victory: Speech to the Kansas State Convention of the American Federation of Labor†

August 12, 1908

Mr. Chairman, Delegates, and Fellow Workers:—

It is with pleasure, I assure you, that I embrace this opportunity to exchange greetings with you in the councils of labor. I have prepared no formal address, nor is any necessary at this time. You have met here as the representatives of organized labor, and if I can do anything to assist you in the work you have been delegated to do, I shall render that assistance with great pleasure.

To serve the working class is to me always a duty of love. Thirty-three years ago I first became a member of a trade union.[61] I can remember quite well under what difficulties meetings were held and with what contempt organized labor was treated at that time. There has been a decided change. The small and insignificant trade union has expanded to the proportions of a great national organization. The few hundreds now number millions, and organized labor has become a recognized factor in the economics and politics of the nation.

There has been a great evolution during that time, and while the power of the organized workers has increased, there has been an industrial development which makes that power more necessary than ever before in all the history of the working class movement.

This is an age of organization. The small employer of a quarter of a century ago has practically disappeared. The workingman of today is confronted by the great corporation which has its ironclad rules and regulations, and if they don't suit he can quit.

In the presence of this great power, workingmen are compelled to organize or be ground to atoms. They have organized. They have the numbers. They have had some bitter experience. They have suffered beyond the power

---

† Stenographic report by Frankie Cox, probably first published in *Proceedings of the Second Annual Convention of the Kansas State Federation of Labor,* source unavailable. Stenogram revised by Debs and published as the pamphlet *Unity and Victory: Speech of Eugene V. Debs Before the State Convention of the American Federation of Labor, at Pittsburg, Kansas, August 12, 1908* (Chicago: Charles H. Kerr & Co., February 15, 1910).

of language to describe, but they have not yet developed their latent power to a degree that they can cope successfully with the great power that exploits and oppresses them. Upon this question of organization, my brothers, you and I may differ widely, but as we are reasonable men, we can discuss these differences candidly until we find common ground upon which we can stand side by side in the true spirit of solidarity—and work together for the emancipation of our class.

Until quite recently the average trade unionist was opposed to having politics even mentioned in the meeting of his union. The reason for this is self-evident. Workingmen have not until now keenly felt the necessity for independent working class political action. They have been divided between the two capitalist parties, and the very suggestion that the union was to be used in the interest of the one or the other was in itself sufficient to sow the seed of disruption. So it isn't strange that the average trade unionist guarded carefully against the introduction of political questions in his union. But within the past two or three years there have been such changes that workingmen have been compelled to take notice of the fact that the labor question is essentially a political question, and that if they would protect themselves against the greed and rapacity of the capitalist class, they must develop their political power as well as their economic power and use both in their own interest.

Workingmen have developed sufficient intelligence to understand the necessity for unity upon the economic field. All now recognize the need for thorough organization. But organization of numbers of itself is not sufficient. You might have all the workers of the country embraced in some vast organization and yet they would be very weak if they were not organized upon correct principles; if they did not understand, and understand clearly what they were organized for, and what their organization expected to accomplish.

I am of those who believe that an organization of workingmen, to be efficient, to meet the demands of this hour, must be organized upon a revolutionary basis; must have for its definite object not only the betterment of the condition of workingmen in the wage system, but the absolute overthrow of wage-slavery that the workingman may be emancipated and stand forth clothed with the dignity and all other attributes of true manhood.

Now let me briefly discuss the existing condition. We have been organizing all these years, and there are now approximately 3 million American workingmen who wear union badges, who keep step to union progress. At this very time, and in spite of all that organized labor can do to the contrary, there is a condition that prevails all over this country that is well calculated to challenge the serious consideration of every workingman. To begin with, according to the reports furnished us, 20 percent of the workingmen of this country are now out of employment. I have here a copy of the *New York World* containing a report of the labor commissioner of the state of New York who shows that during the quarter ending June 30 there were in that state an army of union men out of employment approximating 35 percent of the entire number; that is to say, in the state of New York today, out of every one hundred union men (these reports are received from the unions themselves, verified by their own officers, so there can be no question in regard to them), out of every one hundred union men in New York, 35 are out of employment. The percentage may not be so large in these western states where the industrial development has not reached the same point, but go where you may, East or West, North or South, you will find men, union men, who are begging for the opportunity to work for just enough to keep their suffering souls within their famished bodies. A system in which such a condition as this is possible has justified its mission, stands condemned, and ought to be abolished.

According to the Declaration of Independence, man has the inalienable right to life. If that be true, it follows that he has also the inalienable right to work. If you have no right to work, you have no right to life because you can only live by work. And if you live in a system that deprives you of the right to work, that system denies you the right to live.

Now man has a right to life because he is here. That is sufficient proof, and if he has the right to life, it follows that he has the right to all the means that sustain life. But how is it in this outgrown capitalist system? A workingman can only work on condition that he finds somebody who will give him permission to work for just enough of what his labor produces to keep him in working order.

No matter whether you have studied this economic question or not, you cannot have failed to observe that during the past half century society has been sharply divided into classes—into a capitalist class upon the one hand, into a working class upon the other hand. I shall not take the time to trace this evolution. I shall simply call your attention to the fact that half a century ago, all a man needed was a trade and having this he could supply himself with the simple tools then used, produce what he needed and enjoy the fruit of his labor. But this has been completely changed. The simple tool has disappeared and the great machine has taken its place. The little shop is gone and the great factory has come in its stead. The worker can no longer work by and for himself. He has been recruited into regiments, battalions, and armies, and work has been subdivided and specialized; and now hundreds and thousands and tens of thousands of workingmen work together cooperatively and produce in great abundance, not for themselves, however, for they no longer own the tools they work with. What they produce belongs to the capitalist class who own the tools with which they work. A man 50 years ago who made a shoe owned it. Today it is possible for that same worker, if still alive, to make a hundred times as many shoes, but he doesn't own them now. He works today with modern machinery which is the property of some capitalist who lives perhaps a thousand miles from where the factory is located and who owns all the product because he owns the machinery.

I have stated that society has been divided into two warring classes. The capitalist owns the tool in modern industry, but he has nothing to do with its operation. By virtue of such ownership he has the economic power to appropriate to himself the wealth produced by the use of that tool. This accounts for the fact that the capitalist becomes rich. But how about the working class? In the first place they have to compete with each other for the privilege of operating the capitalist's tool of production. The bigger the tool and the more generally it is applied, the more it produces, the sharper competition grows between the workers for the privilege of using it, and the more are thrown out of employment. Every few years, no matter what party is in power, no matter what our domestic policy is, how high the tariff, or what the money standard, every few years the cry goes up about "overproduction" and the working class is discharged by the thousands and thousands, and are idle, just as the miners have been in this field for many weary months.

No work, no food, and after a while, no credit, and all this in the shadow of the abundance these very workers have created.

Don't you agree with me, my brothers, that this condition is an intolerable and indefensible one, and that whatever may be said of the past, this system no longer answers the demands of this time? Why should any workingman need to beg for work? Why forced to surrender to anybody any part of what his labor produces?

Now, I ask this question, and it applies to the whole field of industry: If a hundred men work in a mine and produce a hundred tons of coal, how much of that coal are they entitled to? Are they not entitled to all of it? And if not, who is entitled to any part of it? If the man who produces wealth is not entitled to it, who is? You say the capitalist is necessary and I deny it. The capitalist has become a profit-taking parasite. Industry is now concentrated and operated on a very large scale; it is co-operative and therefore self-operative. The capitalists hire superintendents, managers, and workingmen to operate their plants and produce wealth. The capitalists are absolutely unnecessary; they have no part in the process of production—not the slightest.

Now I insist that it is the workingman's duty to so organize economically and politically as to put an end to this system; so as to take possession in his collective capacity of the machinery of production and operate it, not to create millionaires and multimillionaires, but to produce wealth in plenty for all. That is why the labor question is also a political question. It makes no difference what you do on the economic field to better your condition, so long as the tools of production are privately owned, so long as they are operated for the private profit of the capitalist, the working class will be exploited, they will be in enforced idleness, thousands of them will be reduced to want, some of them to vagabonds and criminals, and this condition will prevail in spite of anything that organized labor can do to the contrary.

The most important thing for the workingman to recognize is the class struggle. Every capitalist, every capitalist newspaper, every capitalist attorney and retainer will insist that we have no classes in this country and that there is no class struggle. President Roosevelt himself has declared that class-consciousness is a foul and evil thing. Now, what is class-consciousness? It is simply a recognition of the fact on the part of the workingman that his interest is identical with the interest of every other workingman. Class-consciousness points out the necessity for working-class action, economic and political.

What is it that keeps the working class in subjection? What is it that is responsible for their exploitation and for all of the ills they suffer? Just one thing—it can be stated in a single word. It is ignorance. The working class have not yet learned how to unite and act together. There are relatively but few capitalists in this country; there are perhaps 20 million wage workers, but the capitalists and their retainers have contrived during all these years to keep the working class divided, and as long as the working class is divided it will be helpless. It is only when the working class learn—and they are learning daily and by very bitter experience—to unite and to act together, especially on election day, that there is any hope for emancipation.

The workingmen you represent, my brothers, are in an overwhelming majority in every township, county, and state of this nation. You declare you are in favor of united action, but still you don't unite. You unite under certain conditions within your union, you get together upon the economic field to a limited extent, but you have yet to learn that before you can really accomplish anything, you have got to unite in fact as well as in name. The time is coming when workingmen will be forced into one general organization. The time is coming when they will be compelled to organize on the basis of industrial unionism.

At this very hour there is a strike on the Canadian Pacific. Eight thousand workingmen who are more or less organized and who have been wronged in many ways, have finally gone out on strike. There are other thousands remaining at their posts and non-union men flowing in there will be hauled to their destination by union men, and union men will continue to work until their eight thousand brothers have lost their jobs and many of them have become tramps. That is called organization, but it is not so in fact. It is at best organization of a very weak and defective character. Now, the right kind of organization on the Canadian Pacific would embrace all the workers. They should all be included within the same organization and then have one general working agreement with the company so that if there was a violation of it, it would concern every man in the service. But how is it at present? The engineers, conductors, trainmen, and switchmen are in separate unions and after they have been signed up, the company can treat the rest just as they please, for they know that if they strike and the others remain in their service, as they are bound to do under their agreement, they can very easily supplant them and remain in perfect control of the system. We have had enough of that kind of experience and we ought to profit by it. We ought to realize that there is but one form of organization that answers completely, one in which all subscribe to the same rules and act together in all things, and you will have to organize upon that basis or see your unions become practically worthless.

Now let us consider another line briefly for the benefit of those who have opposed political action. We are all aware of the trend of the decisions recently rendered by the United States Supreme Court. Three decisions have been rendered in rapid succession which strike down the rights of labor and virtually strip organized labor of its power. Under these decisions organized labor has been outlawed, and while upon this question I want to suggest that this body at the proper time in its deliberations put the following questions to the candidates for the United States Senate and House of Representatives in the state of Kansas and request them to answer:

In view of the fact that the United States Supreme Court has rendered a number of decisions placing the working class at a tremendous disadvantage in its struggle with the employing class for better conditions, we respectfully submit to the candidates for the United States Senate and House of Representatives the following questions:

1. Are you in favor of issuing injunctions against trade union members because they refuse to patronize a non-union employer and advise their friends to do likewise?

2. Will you introduce and vote for a measure setting aside the decision of the supreme court of the District of Columbia in the case of Buck Stove and Range Company against officers of the American Federation of Labor, making it a criminal act for a labor union to place an employer on its unfair list?

3. Are you in favor of classifying trade unions as "trusts in restraint of trade" as was done by the Supreme Court in the case of *Loewe vs. Lawler*,[62] and will you introduce a measure, should you be elected, providing for the exemption of trade unions from the operation of the anti-trust law under this court decision?

4. Do you endorse the Supreme Court decision making it lawful for a corporation to discharge a man because of his membership in a labor union? If you do not, will you introduce and vote for a bill setting aside this decision of the Supreme Court and making it unlawful for a corporation to discharge a man because he is a member of a trade union?

Here are these candidates in the state of Kansas for the United States Senate and House of Representatives, and if they are elected they will have the power to control legislation, and it is perfectly proper that you, as the representatives of the workers, should put these questions squarely to these candidates and demand that they answer them. They are very simple questions. The United States Court has rendered a decision to the effect that a trade union is a trust and that if it exercises its ultimate powers, it is a criminal conspiracy in restraint of trade. That decision of the court Congress has the power to set aside, and if a man stands as a candidate for Congress in the upper or lower branch and appeals to you for your vote—and bear in mind he can only be elected by your vote—it is right and proper that you should know if he is in favor of the decision or opposed to it. And if he is in favor of this decision, he is your enemy.

Now, these candidates are trying to carry water on both shoulders. They declare they will give both labor and capital a square deal, and I want to say that is impossible. No man can be for labor without being against capital. No man can be for capital without being against labor.

Here is the capitalist; here are the workers. Here is the capitalist who owns the mines; here are the miners who work in the mines. There is so much coal produced. There is a quarrel between them over a division of the product. Each wants all he can get. Here we have the class struggle. Now, is it possible to be for the capitalist without being against the worker? Are their interests not diametrically opposite?

If you increase the share of the capitalist, don't you decrease the share of the workers? Can a door be both open and shut at the same time? Can you increase both the workers' and the capitalist's share at the same time? There is just so much produced, and in the present system it has to be divided between the capitalists and the workers, and both sides are fighting for all they can get, and this is the historic class struggle.

We have now no revolutionary organization of the workers along the lines of this class struggle, and that is the demand of this time. The pure and simple trade union will no longer answer. I would not take from it the least credit that belongs to it. I have fought under its banner for 30 years. I have followed it through victory and defeat, generally defeat. I realize today more than ever before in my life the necessity for thorough economic organization. It must be made complete. Organization, like everything else, is subject to the laws of evolution. Everything changes, my brothers. The tool you worked with 25 years ago will no longer do. It would do then; it will not do now. The capitalists are combined against you. They are reducing wages. They have control of the courts. They are doing everything they can to destroy your power. You have got to follow their example. You have got to unify your forces. You have got to stand together shoulder to shoulder on the economic and political fields and then you will make substantial progress toward emancipation.

I am not here, my brothers, to ask you, as an economic organization, to go into politics. Not at all. If I could have you pass a resolution to go into politics, I would not do it. If you were inclined to go into active politics as an organization, I would prevent such action if I could. You represent the economic organization of the working class, and this organization has its own clearly defined functions. Your economic organization can never become a political machine, but your economic organization must recognize and proclaim the necessity for a united political party. You ought to pass a resolution recognizing the class struggle declaring your opposition to the capitalist system of private ownership of the means of production, and urging upon the working class the necessity for working class political action. That is as far as the economic organization need to go. If you were to use your economic organization for political purposes, you would disrupt it, you would wreck it. But I would not have you renounce politics, nor be afraid to discuss anything. Who is it that is so fearful you will discuss politics? It is the ward-heeling politician, and isn't it because he knows very well that if you ever get into politics in the right way he will be out of a job? He is afraid you will get your eyes open.

Why should a union man be afraid to discuss politics? He belongs to a certain party; his father belonged to that party and his grandfather belonged to that party, and perhaps his great-grandfather belonged to the same party, and that is probably the only reason he can give for belonging to that party. He doesn't want anybody to suggest to him the possibility of being lifted out of that party and into some other.

Parties change. The party that was good 40 years ago is completely outgrown and corrupt and has now no purpose but the promotion of graft and other vicious practices.

Workingmen in their organized capacity must recognize the necessity for both economic and political action. I would not have you declare in favor of any particular political party. That would be another mistake which would have disastrous results. If I could have you pass a resolution to support the Socialist Party I would not do it. You can't make socialists by passing resolutions. Men have to become socialists by study and experience, and they are getting the experience every day.

There is one fact, and a very important one, that I would impress upon you, and that is the necessity for revolutionary working class political action.

No one will attempt to dispute the fact that our interests as workers are identical. If our interests are identical, then we ought to unite. We ought to unite within the same organization, and if there is a strike we should all strike, and if there is a boycott all of us ought to engage in it. If our interests are identical, it follows that we ought to belong to the same party as well as to the same economic organization. What is politics? It is simply the reflex of economics. What is a party? It is the expression politically of certain material class interests. You belong to that party that you believe will promote your material welfare. Is not that a fact? If you find yourself in a party that attacks your pocket, do you not quit that party?

Now, if you are in a party that opposes your interests, it is because you don't have intelligence enough to understand your interests. That is where the capitalists have the better of you. As a rule, they are intelligent and shrewd. They understand their material interests and how to protect them. You find the capitalists as a rule belonging only to capitalist parties. They don't join a working class party and they don't vote the Socialist ticket. They know enough to know that socialism is opposed to their economic interests. Now, both Republican and Democratic parties are capitalist parties. There is not the slightest doubt about it. It can be proved in a hundred different ways. You know how the Republican Party treated the demands of labor in its recent national convention. You know, or ought to know, what has taken place under the present administration. You know, or ought to know, something about the Democratic Party, national, state and municipal. If there are those who say that the Democratic Party is more favorable to labor than the Republican Party, it is only necessary to point you to the Southern states where it has ruled for a century. In no other part of the nation are workingmen in so wretched a condition. In no other part are working people so miserably housed, so wretchedly treated as they are in the Southern states where the Democratic Party rules supreme.

At this very hour miners in Alabama are on strike under a Democratic administration. I know the condition there, for I have been in the mines. I know many of those men personally. I know under what conditions they have had to work. I have been in the shacks in which they live and have seen their unhappy wives and ill-fed children. I know whereof I speak. Only in the last extremity have those men gone out on strike. They bore all these cruel wrongs for years and were finally forced out on strike. And then what happened? The very first thing the Democratic governor did was to send the soldiers to scab the mines. It doesn't make any difference to you, if workingmen are starved and shot down, which party is in power. It occurs under both Republican and Democratic administrations. There will be no change as long as you continue to support the prevailing capitalist system, based upon the private ownership of the tools with which workingmen work and without which they are doomed to slavery and starvation.

Now, I repeat that this body should declare against this system of private ownership and in favor of the collective ownership by the workers of the tools of production. This will give you a clear aim and definite object. This will make your movement revolutionary in its ultimate purpose, as it ought to be, and as for immediate concessions in the way of legislation by capitalist representatives and more favorable working conditions, you workingmen have only to poll 2 million Socialist votes this fall, and you will get those concessions freely and you will not get them in any other way. You will not frighten, you will not move the great corporations by dividing your votes between the Republican and Democratic parties. It doesn't make any difference which of these two parties wins, you lose! They are both capitalist parties and I don't ask you to take my mere word for it. I simply ask, my brothers, that you read and study the platforms for yourself. I beg of you not to have an ignorant, superstitious reverence for any political party. It is your misfortune if you are the blind follower of any political leader, or any other leader. It is your duty as a workingman, your duty to yourself, your family, to quit a party the very instant you find that that party no longer serves you; and if you continue to adhere to a party that antagonizes your interests, if you continue to support a system in which you are degraded, then you have no right to complain. You must submit to what comes, for you yourself are responsible.

Let me impress this fact upon your minds: the labor question, which is really the question of all humanity, will never be solved until it is solved by the working class. It will never be solved for you by the capitalists. It will never be solved for you by the politicians. It will remain unsolved until you yourselves solve it. As long as you can stand and are willing to stand these conditions, these conditions will remain; but when you unite all over the land, when you present a solid class-conscious phalanx, economically and politically, there is no power on this earth that can stand between you and complete emancipation.

As individuals you are helpless, but united you represent an irresistible power.

Is there any doubt in the mind of any thinking workingman that we are in the midst of a class struggle? Is there any doubt that the workingman ought to own the tool he works with? You will never own the tool you work with under the present system. This whole system is based upon the private ownership by the capitalist of the tools and the wage-slavery of the working class, and as long as the tools are privately owned by the capitalists, the great mass of workers will be wage-slaves.

You may, at times, temporarily better your condition within certain limitations, but you will still remain wage-slaves, and why wage-slaves? For just one reason and no other—you have got to work. To work you have got to have tools, and if you have no tools you have to beg for work, and if you have got to beg for work the man who owns the tools you use will determine the conditions under which you shall work. As long as he owns your tools he owns your job, and if he owns your job he is the master of your fate. You are in no sense a free man. You are subject to his interest and to his will. He decides whether you shall work or not. Therefore, he decides whether you shall live or die. And in that humiliating position anyone who tries to persuade you that you are a free man is guilty of insulting your intelligence. You will never be free, you will never stand erect in your own manly self-reliance until you are the master of the tools you work with, and when you are you can freely work without the consent of any master, and when you do work you will get all your labor produces.

As it is now the lion's share goes to the capitalist for which he does nothing, while you get a small fraction to feed, clothe, and shelter yourself, and reproduce yourself in the form of labor-power.

That is all you get out of it and all you ever will get in the capitalist system.

Oh, my brothers, can you be satisfied with your lot? Will you insist that life shall continue a mere struggle for existence and one prolonged misery to which death comes as a blessed relief?

How is it with the average workingman today? I am not referring to the few who have been favored and who have fared better than the great mass, but I am asking how it is with the average workingman in this system. Admit that he has a job. What assurance has he that it is his in 24 hours? I have a letter from an expert glass worker saying that the new glass machine which has recently been tested has proven conclusively that bottles can be made without a glass blower. Five or six boys with these machines can make as many bottles as 10 expert blowers could make. Machinery is conquering every department of activity. It is displacing more and more workingmen and making the lot of those who have employment more and more insecure. Admit that a man has a job. What assurance has he that he is going to keep it? A machine may be invented. He may offend the boss. He may engage in a little agitation in the interest of his class. He is marked as an agitator, he is discharged, and then what is his status?

The minute he is discharged he has to hunt for a new buyer for his labor-power. He owns no tools; the tools are great machines. He can't compete against them with his bare hands. He has got to work. There is only one condition under which he can work and that is when he sells his labor-power, his energy, his very life currents, and thus disposes of himself in daily installments. He is not sold from the block, as was the chattel slave. He sells 10 hours of himself every day in exchange for just enough to keep himself in that same slavish condition.

The machine he works with has to be oiled, and he has to be fed, and the oil sustains the same relation to the machine that food does to him. If he could work without food, his wage would be reduced to the vanishing point. That is the status of the workingman today.

What can the present economic organization do to improve the condition of the workingman? Very little, if anything. If you have a wife and two or three children, and you take the possibilities into consideration, this question ought to give you grave concern. You know that it is the sons of workingmen who become vagabonds and tramps, and who are sent to jail, and it is the daughters of workingmen who are forced into houses of shame.

You are a workingman, you live in capitalism, and you have nothing but your labor-power, and you don't know whether you are going to find a buyer or not. But even if you do find a master, if you have a job, can you boast of being a man among men?

No man can rightly claim to be a man unless he is free. There is something God-like about manhood. Manhood doesn't admit of ownership. Manhood scorns to be regarded as property.

Do you know whether you have a job or not? Do you know how long you are going to have one? And when you are out of a job, what can your union do for you? I was down at Coalgate, Oklahoma, on the Fourth of July last, where six hundred miners have been out of work for four long months. They are all organized. There are the mines and machinery, and the miners are eager to work. But not a tap of work is being done, and the miners and their families are suffering, and most of them live in houses that are unfit for habitation. This awful condition is never going to be changed in capitalism. There is one way only and that is to wipe out capitalism, and to do that we have to get together, and when we do that we will find the way to emancipation.

You may not agree with me now, but make note of what I am saying. The time is near when you will be forced into economic and political solidarity.

The Republican and Democratic parties are alike capitalist parties. Some of you may think that Mr. Bryan, if elected, will do great things for the workers. Conditions will remain substantially the same. We will still be under capitalism. It will not matter how you may tinker with the tariff or the currency. The tools are still the property of the capitalists and you are still at their mercy.

Now let me show you that Mr. Bryan is no more your friend than is Mr. Taft. You remember when the officials of the Western Federation of Miners were kidnapped in Colorado, and when it was said they should never leave Idaho alive. It was the determination of the Mine Owners' Association that these brave and loyal union leaders should be foully murdered. When these brothers of ours were brutally kidnaped by the collusion of the capitalist governors of two states, every true friend of the working class cried out in protest. Did Mr. Bryan utter a word? Mr. Bryan was the recognized champion of the working class. He was in a position to be heard. A protest from him would have tremendous weight with the American people. But his labor friends could not unlock his lips. Not one word would he speak. Not one.

Organized labor, however, throughout the length and breadth of the land, took the matter in hand promptly and registered its protest in a way that made the nation quake. The Mine Owners' Association took to the tall timber. Our brother unionists were acquitted, vindicated, and stood forth without a blemish upon their honor, and after they were free once more, Mr. Bryan said, "I felt all the time that they were not guilty."

Now if your faithful leaders are kidnapped and threatened to be hanged, and you call upon a man who claims to be your friend to come to the rescue and he refuses to say a word, to give the least help, do you still think he is your friend? Mr. Bryan had his chance to prove his friendship at a time when labor sorely needed friends, when organized labor cried out in agony and distress. But not a word escaped his lips.

Why did not Mr. Bryan speak? He did not dare. Mr. Bryan knew very well that the kidnappers of those men were his personal friends, the association of rich mine owners, who had largely furnished his campaign funds. For Mr. Bryan personally I have always had a high regard. I am not attacking him in any personal sense at all.

But the extremity to which a man is driven who tries to serve both capital and labor! It can't be done. Mr. Bryan did not dare to speak for labor because if he had, he would have turned the mine owning capitalists against him. He is afraid to speak out very loudly for capitalists for fear the workers will get after him. He has compromised all around for the sake of being president.

You have heard him denounce Roger Sullivan.[63] Mr. Bryan, four years ago, in denouncing this corruptionist, at the time of the nomination of Alton B. Parker, said he was totally destitute of honor and compared him to a train robber. Notwithstanding this fact, Mr. Bryan recently invited Sullivan to his home in Lincoln, took him by the hand and introduced him to his family. Mr. Bryan also invited Charley Murphy,[64] the inexpressibly rotten Tammany heeler of New York. Mr. Bryan had him come to Lincoln so as to conciliate Tammany, and they were photographed together shaking hands.

No man can serve both capital and labor at the same time.

You don't admit the capitalists to your union. They organize their union to fight you. You organize your union to fight them. Their union consists wholly of capitalists; your union consists wholly of workingmen. It is along the same line that you have got to organize politically. You don't unite with capitalists on the economic field; why should you politically?

You have got to extend your class line. You can declare yourselves in this convention and make your position clear to the world. You can give hope and inspire confidence throughout the state.

And now in closing, I wish to thank you, each of you, from my heart, for your kindness. I appreciate the opportunity you have given me to address you and whether you agree with me or not, I leave you wishing you success in your deliberations and hoping for the early triumph of the labor movement.

The Greatest Optimists in the World†

August 19, 1908

The socialist never sees anything but victory ahead. Even where the vote is small, and outward indications might, to the average beholder, carry but little hope, the socialist sees nothing but ultimate triumph. The socialist is the greatest optimist the world has ever produced. No one but he has ever planned for a world free from want, and no one but he has steadfastly believed that his ideals would be wrought into a fact so glorious as to excel all the utopias of which man has dreamed.

And yet the socialist is not a visionary. He believes in the future just as much as the inventor believes in the machine which as yet exists only in his brain, because he has figured it out on scientific principles and knows that it will work. He is sure socialism will come, because he has caught the scientific meaning of history and realizes that the next step after capitalism must be socialism.

Socialism Logical Development

The truth of his position is seen in the development of the worldwide socialist movement within the past 30 years and in the recognition of the power of socialism by thoughtful men everywhere. But the socialist is neither surprised nor unduly elated. It is precisely what Marx predicted nearly 50 years ago, and is merely the logical development of events and industry that is believed in rather than hoped for.

Non-socialists are not expected to see this. But they do begin to recognize the way events are shaping themselves. Even in 1900 the astute Mr. [Mark] Hanna predicted that the fight of the future in the United States would be between republicanism and socialism. Mr. Roosevelt, the executive of the capitalist class, has for several years lost no opportunity to attack socialism, and the fact that he has repeatedly referred to it as a menace is proof that he recognizes its growing power.

† Published as "Socialism to Overthrow Republicanism" in *New York Evening World*, vol. 49, whole no. 17,165 (August 19, 1908), 5. Garbled lines corrected in accord with the reprint "Democracy to Dissolve; Debs" in *Chicago Daily Socialist*, vol. 2, no. 258 (August 27, 1908), 1–2.

But it was not until this campaign that socialism was mentioned in the platform of a dominant party.[65] That it should be given a large place in the Republican platform this year shows that the battle lines forecasted by Mr. Hanna are already being drawn.

The fact is that the contest, even this year, is between the Republican Party and the Socialist Party. The Republican Party stands definitely for the capitalist class. It refused to grant the working class even so much as an injunction plank. But the Democratic Party is without policy and without principle. It pleads for the votes of all, without giving either class any assurance that will warrant its support.

The Democratic Party lives in the past and imagines that the middle class of small capitalists and independent farmers which existed in the days of Thomas Jefferson and Andrew Jackson is dominant today and can elevate a party to power. It has failed of power these many years because its class was disappearing, and in appealing to conflicting classes it presents a ridiculous straddle which condemns it with all.

Republican Party's Strength

But the Republican Party, frankly representing the capitalist class from the time this class overpowered the slave-owning class until now, when it has half the voters of the country working for it and depending on it for a job, and half the farmers either tenants or borrowers from it, has grown in power because it has represented something definite, even though bad, and has stood for a class that was growing instead of decadent.

The present campaign is the last political stand of the middle class, and after it is over the Democratic Party, which has been disintegrating for the past dozen years, will rapidly reach dissolution, while the Socialist Party will remain as the logical and living opponent of Republicanism. And why should the two be pitted against each other? Because Republicanism represents the wage system and has reduced a majority of the people of America to dependence on it for a job, while the Socialist Party is the avowed enemy of wages and profits and the exponent of every man owning himself by virtue of owning his job.

Many suppose that the present capitalist system has been dominant through all time. The fact is that it has been dominant for only the last 50 years, or during the life of the Republican Party. It is true that there was a mild commercialism before that and some worked for wages. But, as a system, it was not a controlling force.

The frontier enabled the wage worker to escape from his position and to become what was then not inappropriately called an independent farmer. Slavery was more of a dominating force in politics and industry at that time than was the wage working system, for the factory system has been mainly built up since 1860. The invention of machinery was the real force that wrought this change. The machine did so much more than the individual could accomplish that manufacturing was done by the machine, and, as the machine grew, it naturally passed into the hands of the rich or the corporation. We have reached the present state of dependence on the few rich owners of railroads and manufacturing plants because these men have come to own the machine and exact their tribute by virtue of that ownership.

Socialism Workman's Champion

Socialism arises as the champion of the growing working class. Even the farmer is becoming a wage worker to a large extent, as the machinery of the farm is growing and making it impossible for a man of small capital to work as extensively and as efficiently as can the wealthy farmer. It will, in future days, become more and more so, and as the people begin to recognize this fact, or to become, as the socialist puts it, class conscious, the capitalist system will be overpowered at the polls and the dominance of the system will be at an end.

Socialism will restore to the worker the tools of production, which will enable him to be master of his own job and to retain his full product, instead of paying tribute of profit to the owner of the machine. It will not subjugate him in the least, but, on the contrary, will make him master of his own life and earnings. So far from telling men what it will do with them and for them, it tells them that it will merely establish an industrial democracy and enable them to work out their own salvation under perfect freedom.

To this issue must things come ere long. Even now there are outward and visible signs that it is nearer than many think. The fact that the dues-paying members of the Socialist Party—those who pay the campaign and agitation expenses—are more than twice as numerous as ever before, argues, within itself, a vote for this year far above a million.[66] Another very hopeful sign is the fact that Socialist speakers all over the country report a far larger attendance than ever before with an enthusiasm that is plainly absent at the old party gatherings; and as more than five times as many speeches are being made as in any previous campaign, this is most significant. Plenty of Socialists predict a Socialist vote this year of from 1,500,000 to 2,000,000, and the election of Socialist congressmen.

Ballots Not Furnished

Letters received from the *Appeal to Reason* from the recent primary election held in Oklahoma reveal a surprising condition. Some 50 precincts report that the old parties sent to the various precincts only enough ballots to supply the Socialist voters from the last election, and there were calls for ballots from two hundred to eight hundred percent greater than the supply furnished. In many cases the Socialists wrote their ballots out and voted them. In other places, where the judges refused to accept such ballots, they contented themselves with canvassing the community for subscribers for socialist papers, and with success.

So the socialist outlook is encouraging—tremendously encouraging. Even from the standpoint of immediate results, it is cheering. But from the larger viewpoint, it is sure and undeniable. It is going to capture America, and, more than that, it is going to capture the world.

Yet, if it was merely the triumph of a party, the encouragement and glory of it all would be but small indeed. It is only when we reflect that it means the freeing of all men and women from economic want and the lifting of the world to a higher and juster plane, the giving of equal opportunity to every child, and the laying of a sound economic foundation that shall give basis for a grander idealism than ever prevailed in this weary world, that the outlook for socialism is transfigured and glorified by the outlook of a regenerated earth.

What a Million Votes for the Socialist Party Will Mean†

September 1908

It is predicted that at least a million votes will be cast for the Socialist Party next November. To obtain a clear idea of what such a vote will mean, it is necessary to consider the nature of the Socialist Party and take note of what it stands for.

† Published in Joseph Medill Patterson, ed., *Socialist Campaign Book* (Chicago: National Headquarters, Socialist Party, October 1908), 5–10.

The Socialist Party is an uncompromising working class political organization. It is fighting the battle of the wage workers of the world and stands for their welfare without qualification or evasion. Its demand is that all the means and instruments of production and distribution shall be used for the benefit of the actual producers of wealth, and that government shall be controlled by the workers and administered in their interest. Its platform is an honest and direct expression of working class demands, with a clear statement of the means proposed for their accomplishment.

Unlike the platforms of the Republican and Democratic parties, the Socialist Party platform is a plain and simple declaration of principles and policies which all may understand. It was not framed merely with a view to winning votes. Its utterances are straightforward and to the point. There is no ambiguity; no evasion of vital issues; no possibility of double construction.

There is no attempt to compromise with capitalism; no effort to throw a sop to the enemies of labor; no adherence to the miserable fiction that the interests of labor and capital are identical. The Socialist Party, in short, proposes to place the workers in possession of all the wealth they produce and to insure to every individual full and free opportunity to labor. The elector who casts his vote for its candidates may do so with the positive assurance that whenever the opportunity arises, every pledge of the party platform will be carried out to the letter.

The Socialist Party does not disguise the fact that its ultimate aim is the entire abolition of rent, interest, and profit and the collective ownership and operation of all the monopolized industries of the nation. A million votes for its candidates will, therefore, be an unmistakable challenge from the working class to capitalism. A million votes for the Socialist Party will be a notice served on capitalism that the workers are at last united and alive to their class interests. It will mean that the working class intends to use its political power, through the machinery of popular government and free elections, to force compliance with its demands by peaceful, legal, and constitutional methods, to the end that wage-slavery may be entirely abolished. The issue thus made up and clearly expressed is one that the leaders of capitalism cannot ignore. But they will be unable to meet the issue in the ordinary way and must adopt new tactics in dealing with working class demands.

As long as the votes of workingmen are divided between the Republican and Democratic parties, capitalism has nothing to fear, as both these parties are its equally subservient tools. Whichever of these parties is in power, capitalism has nothing to fear. As a matter of fact, there is no real difference between the

Republican and Democratic parties. Both are supporters of the existing competitive industrial system, and it is now impossible to tell a Republican from a Democrat by any policy that he favors or opposes.

This condition is so obvious that it is admitted even by the capitalists themselves. The capitalist press has already said, "it is not going to make a vital difference to the country whether the Republicans or the Democrats win this year." Capitalism must have a party in its service that can be used as a foil to the demands of socialism, and as the usefulness of the Democratic party in that direction has departed, a million votes for the Socialist Party is bound to force a new political alignment and bring a new party, of middle class radical tendencies, into the field.

When the People's Party counted a million popular votes for Weaver[67] and Field[68] in 1892, capitalism became alarmed, and to guard against the possibility that the reforms demanded by the Omaha platform[69] might be inaugurated, a conspiracy was at once set on foot to destroy the party. This conspiracy was completely successful, and in the election of 1896 the People's Party lost its autonomy through fusion with the Democrats. A conspiracy of this nature directed against the Socialist Party cannot succeed. There will be no such thing as fusion, with any middle class reform party, as the Socialist Party is class conscious. It accepts the gage of battle thrown down by President Roosevelt in his message of April 27. It is striving "to arouse this feeling of class consciousness in our working people" and seeks, not to reform the existing wage system, but to destroy it.

The only argument that has weight with capitalism is the argument of power. When the workers demonstrate that they have strength to compel, capitalism will concede. Nowhere in the world have the interests of labor ever been recognized except as the result of a display of power by the workers which the ruling class dared not ignore. This is emphatically true of Germany and England, in both of which countries socialism is a virile political force. Notwithstanding the severe repressive measures that were directed against the socialists of Germany in 1879, their inefficacy was well recognized. The German emperor himself said that repressive laws were not sufficient to check the growth of socialism, and that it was necessary also to do something to cure the evil from which the working classes were suffering. With the emperor's approval, Bismarck inaugurated a comprehensive plan of remedial legislation; hence the compensation, liability insurance, and pension laws which measurably lighten the horrors of wage-slavery for the German workingman. Similar laws in England give expression to the fear of the ruling class, engendered by the remarkable show of strength which English socialists have manifested in recent years.

That high priest of capitalism, Theodore Roosevelt, with greater political insight than other leaders of his class, has urged his so-called reform program for the express purpose of checking the spread of socialism. He has pointed out that "a class grievance left too long without remedy breeds class consciousness, and, therefore, class resentment," and has plainly stated that in the measures he advocates he is "trying to steer a safe middle course, which alone can save us from a plutocratic class government on the one hand, or a socialistic class government on the other." "We are trying," said he, "to avoid alike the evils which flow from government ownership of the public utilities by which interstate commerce is chiefly carried on, and the evils which flow from the riot and chaos of unrestricted individualism." The fear to which Roosevelt gives expression is latent in the capitalist class, and a million votes for the Socialist Party will at once fan it into burning activity. The immediate effect of such a vote would probably be a demand for the enactment of repressive laws to check the growth of socialism, and it is probable that a number of idiotic and entirely futile measures of that character would be placed on the statute books. But the large and permanent result will be the enactment of remedial laws in the interest of wage workers, laws for the enactment of which the trade union representatives of the country have been vainly pleading for many years.

A million votes for the Socialist Party will mean the speedy enactment of an anti-injunction law, no matter whether the Republicans or the Democrats win the election. It will also mean a law exempting labor unions from the penalties of the Sherman anti-trust law, as well as measures for the relief of the unemployed, municipal, state, and national. Eight-hour laws, compensation and liability acts, and measures for the prevention of child labor and the supervision of mines and factories will be forthcoming; and all such laws will be upheld by court decisions declaring them valid and binding whenever they are put to the test. The judicial point of view respecting the constitutionality of labor legislation will undergo a sudden and remarkable change. Even the august Supreme Court of the United States may suddenly discover that Congress can enact laws forbidding railroad companies to discharge and blacklist their employees for belonging to labor unions without interference with the fundamental principles of this government. The effect of a million working class votes upon Congress, state legislatures, municipal councils, the courts from the highest to the lowest, as well as upon all the executive and administrative offices of government, will be immediate, and will be felt and registered in all their acts relating to organized labor and the working class. The mere announcement of such a vote will accomplish more for labor in the way of concessions than could be obtained from the ruling class by 10 years of striking and pleading for justice.

Nowhere else in the world are the workers exploited so shamelessly as they are in the United States. Nowhere else in the world are the lives of wage workers so brutally sacrificed and their rights so little regarded. In no other civilized country on earth is the workingman so little protected by statute law, and nowhere else in the world are the laws designed to benefit labor so contemptuously ignored by the ruling class. Speaking of industrial conditions in the United States as he observed them during his visit to this country a few years ago, John Burns,[70] the English labor leader, said:

> America, so far as the toiler is concerned, is hell with the lid off—hell with just sufficient daylight to see that there is a way out of it. ... Sooner or later every trade in America will come to realize that the same fight for existence awaits them. Unless a check is put upon them, these bloodsuckers who go on forming trusts will dominate the souls as well as the bodies of the American workingmen.

Recent events have awakened the leaders of the trade union movement to the truth of what Burns observed. They have come to realize that the capitalist class already dominates the souls as well as the bodies of American workingmen. In pleading for the passage of anti-injunction and other labor laws before the judiciary committee of the House of Representatives at the last session of Congress, Samuel Gompers, President of the American Federation of Labor, said:

> I know that when we attempted to make some effort along political lines to secure even the election of one man or the defeat of another, we were lampooned as if we were committing some unholy act. The mere fact that we believed in and expressed a preference for one man over another at election, and exercised our rights as American citizens to appeal to our fellows that they might assist us at the polls in the advancement of the things for the interest that we feel to be ours and in jeopardy, met with this result. Well, if to take action at the polls is improper, if it is unjust and we ought not to do it, if the strike and the boycott are made unlawful and criminal, if the very agreements that we have with our employers, brought about peaceably, brought about by mutual consent and desire, are taken as proof of the success of our conspiracy and held against us, then, I ask you, what are the American workingmen to do?

At this same meeting Mr. Gompers took occasion to threaten members of Congress with the opposition of labor at the polls. He said:

> I think we are going to be heard of in the next campaign, or this impending campaign. I do not think that you, gentlemen, are going to have it all your own way. I think you will hear from us, and perhaps you may again tell us that we have got Congressmen on the unfair list.

But neither arguments nor threats had the slightest effect upon Congress. As always in the past, the demand of labor for remedial legislation was contemptuously ignored.

Why this attitude? Simply because it makes little difference to capitalism which one of its henchmen is elected to office. As long as labor confines its political activity voting for the candidates of capitalist parties, capitalism is safe, and the mere fact that one candidate may be defeated and another one elected makes no difference in the general result. The working class will obtain no relief through defeating Republicans simply to elect Democrats or independents in their stead. Yet this is the only sort of political action that has been proposed by the trade union leaders, and workingmen have been treated to the humiliating spectacle of Mr. Gompers, as the representative of labor, fresh from his decisive defeat before Congress, knocking at the doors of both the Republican and Democratic conventions and imploring first one and then the other to place in its platform an insincere promise to do what Congress has absolutely refused to do for 14 years past, although the request has been continuously before it during all that time, and always supported by just such arguments and threats as those presented by Mr. Gompers at the last session of Congress.

Is it any wonder that capitalism treats labor with contempt and ignores its demands for relief?

A million votes for the Socialist Party will change this attitude of indifference and contempt to one of respect and consideration. Such a vote will mean that the capitalists no longer own the franchise of their wage-slaves, and the edict will at once go forth that concessions must be made to labor in order that the menace of Socialism may be removed. The trade unionist who is really anxious to perform a service for labor will cast his vote for the Socialist Party. Such a vote will not be wasted; on the contrary, the Socialist Party vote next November is the only vote that will bring results, and the larger it is the more it will accomplish. The million votes that will surely be counted will force the demands of labor into prominence and compel their recognition, and just to the extent that the million is increased will emphasis be added to the determination of the working class to emancipate itself from the thralldom of wage-slavery.

Future contests between the capitalist class and the working class will be waged upon the political as well as the industrial field. To a far greater extent than in the past will the battle be fought at the polls than through the medium of strikes, lockouts, and boycotts, and every accession to the Socialist Party vote, demonstrating increased unity and power in the working class, will be followed by concessions from capitalism. It is a fight to the death between the two classes as to which shall dominate and control the functions and administration of government.

A million votes for the Socialist Party will indicate that the working class has arrived at such a stage of progress in its campaign for political power that all of the fake issues of capitalism must be abandoned, and a united front made against the one and only dominating and supreme issue that threatens the very existence of the capitalist system itself—*socialism*. The different warring wings of the capitalist political parties will get together and harmonize their differences. The conservatives and radicals will separate into different parties, but both will stand opposed to the bid for power. The contest on the political field will therefore be between *socialism and capital.*

A million votes for the Socialist Party will bring hope and joy to socialists throughout the world. It will nerve the arms of our comrades in the United States and give them courage and renewed strength to go forth and labor in the crusade for working class emancipation. It will solidify the movement and render it strong to resist oppression as well as aggressive to extend the bounds of its activity. It will mean the rise of Socialism as the dominant political force in the United States and the beginning of the end of capitalist rule. It will mean joy to the friends of labor; consternation and dismay to the enemies of the working class. A million votes for the Socialist Party will be a sure indication that the reign of capitalism is nearing its end and that an era of justice, freedom, and brotherly love is soon to dawn upon the world.

Samuel Gompers a Cowardly Falsifier: Statement to the Press†

September 4, 1908

On the Red Special, en route to Denver, September 4 [1908]

A few weeks ago I ventured the opinion that the so-called anti-injunction plank of the Democratic Party was a false pretense to catch the votes of the ignorant, and in effect meaningless. This seems to have given a fit to Mr. Gompers, president of the American Federation of Labor. In the September [1908] issue of his personal organ, *The American Federationist,* he has covered several pages with a tirade of misrepresentations and falsehoods.[71] I have but little time to waste on Mr. Gompers, but what I have to say will be to the point.

After 25 years of his brilliant leadership, the trade union movement is stripped of its power, by court decisions and otherwise, and is practically paralyzed and helpless.

In the state of Alabama six thousand miners, who have been helping to pay his salary, have just been crushed by the iron heel of the Democratic administration, to which he has pledged his support in the present campaign. In all his official career, Mr. Gompers has not only never won a victory, but has never been in a fight worth mentioning except at a safe distance from the battlefield.

During all this time he has been violently opposed to any political activity on the part of the trade unions, and when he was finally forced from his attitude of "pure and simple" unionism, it was to negotiate with capitalist parties for the support of his benighted followers. In other words, when he was at last driven into politics he used all his influence to steer union men into the shambles of a capitalistic party. It was only a short time after August Belmont, the agent of the Rothschilds, had crushed the strike of subway employees in New York, with the aid of Farley and his army of strikebreakers, that Belmont and Gompers sat together as boon companions at the same sumptuous festal board.

† Wire service report, as published as "Debs Raps Gompers" in *The Daily Republican* [Cherryvale, Kansas], vol. 11, no. 50 (September 5, 1908), 1.

Every essential statement respecting me in his tirade is either a flagrant misrepresentation or an unqualified falsehood, and Gompers, the labor leader, who has always led backward, knows it.

To test his sincerity I challenge him to meet me before his own followers and the general public anywhere in the United States—Washington, the headquarters of the federation, preferred. I know the gentleman's record. He has charged me with being a failure, but I will venture the opinion that if he will meet me—which he will not, for he will have to "catch a train"—he will agree that I am not a failure at exposing a cowardly falsifier and in making his own deluded followers repudiate him with indignation and contempt.

Mr. Gompers stood before his last convention and told how he had spurned a bribe offered him by wicked capitalists, and was frantically cheered by his followers for what was a blot upon his honor and insult to their intelligence.

This statement is not made by me as a Socialist candidate and the Socialist Party is in no wise responsible for it. The attack of Gompers was upon my labor record, for which I am alone responsible.

Eugene V. Debs

Theodore Roosevelt and the Socialist Movement [excerpt][†]

September 5, 1908

When the press announced recently that "the difference between the square deal and socialism" was the text of a "characteristic" speech by President Roosevelt at the unveiling of the Underhill monument at Matinecock, Long Island,[72] socialists knew what to expect and when they read the speech and beheld in fancy the Don Quixote of the White House assaulting another windmill, they smiled with mingled amusement and contempt.

President Roosevelt is known as an exceedingly "characteristic" gentleman, and he is never quite so "characteristic" as when dealing with socialists and the socialist

† Published in *Appeal to Reason,* whole no. 666 (September 5, 1908), 1.

movement, and the reason for this is that they, of all others, can see through him and his bourgeois "square deal" policy without the aid of cathode rays.

Capitalist President

Being a capitalist in both the economic and the ethical sense and inflated by his egotistical idealism, it is quite natural that he should oppose democratic tendencies and set his face against equal freedom as a social ideal, but he has gone farther than this, and in his "characteristic" and unbridled individualism, which brooks no opposition, has conceived a violent hatred for socialists which defies all restraints and violates all proprieties, as when he publicly denounced workingmen about to be tried for their lives as "undesirable citizens," an astounding violation of official dignity without a precedent, and which shocked the moral sense of the entire nation. Thousands of other men were under arrest but not noticed by the president—they were not socialists.

On every possible occasion Mr. Roosevelt vents his spleen against socialists and like the true capitalist functionary he is, warns his countrymen against their pernicious philosophy. He has the distinction of being the first president to write socialism in his message to Congress, as he also has the distinction, such as it is, of naming his own successor and also writing socialism in his political platform.

Anthracite Commission

When President Roosevelt some years ago interposed his authority as president in the anthracite coal strike and appointed a commission which ultimately settled the strike in the interest of the coal barons, he explained to Congress in his next ensuing message that he was prompted to such action by the conviction that it was the only way to head off socialism, showing that he was faithful to his trust and that he guarded sedulously the private ownership of the anthracite mines, even though the miners and their families were verging upon starvation.

Rate Legislation

When he recommended his railroad rate legislation to Congress, in which he yielded point after point to the railroads until there was nothing left but the echo of the ignorant multitude who were applauding his supposed bravery in bearding the railroad lion in his den, the burden of his plea was "the socialists'll get you if you don't watch out."[73]

So socialism must come in for some credit, even among its implacable foes, for if the settlement of the anthracite strike was a great achievement and Roosevelt's railroad policy is an inestimable boon, as they vociferously claim, it is due entirely, according to the president himself, to socialism, or, rather, the fear of socialism.

President's Latest Outbreak

The president's latest outbreak occurred at the commemoration of the death of an Indian fighter named Underhill, who died some two hundred years ago.[74] What he had to do with socialism there was no attempt to explain, but it would have seemed grotesque, to say the least, if anyone, save Roosevelt alone, had led a furious attack on modern socialism in dedicating a monument to a dead Indian fighter, especially one of the Middle Ages.[75]

* * *

Yet in spite of all Mr. Roosevelt and his party of grafting individualists have done "to keep the avenues of occupation open"—and they have been in absolute power for years—millions of workingmen are in compulsory idleness and suffering the pangs of starvation, and when in their agony and despair they turn to Roosevelt and his individualistic regime and implore for escape from the pitiless lash of the hunger-whip; when they ask in the name of mercy what is to become of them, they are complacently told that "God knows!" and that while they voted for Roosevelt they must look to God for means of rescue from their unhappy fate.

"God Knows"

Mr. Roosevelt feels inexpressibly outraged because socialists are not satisfied with the way he and his capitalist party have kept "the avenues of occupation open," but if instead of being the well-groomed president of the ruling parasites, pampered like a prince, he had to tramp through weary months in vain search of a job to finally find his place in the bowery midnight breadline, he could, perhaps, understand that his is not the only point of view and that the millions who are exploited and without mercy and abandoned to "God knows" what fate are finally driven to do something for themselves; and that this is the genesis of the socialist movement and explains its phenomenal growth and why it is class conscious and revolutionary and must finally conquer, though every capitalist were a Rockefeller and every politician a Roosevelt.

Does President Roosevelt believe that the present condition of things under the capitalist rule of the Republican Party is the best that "it is humanely possible to achieve" and that industrial evolution has exhausted itself in producing capitalism? Or does he omit the working class entirely in calculating the possibilities of human achievement?

If capitalism can do no better in the way of providing "equal opportunity for each man to show the stuff that is in him" than it has already done, it has proved a stupendous failure, for not only have millions no opportunity at all, but other millions are slain in their babyhood, while still other millions are denied proper sustenance from their infancy, cheated out of their growth, robbed of their vitality, and exploited of all the means that enable the human being to rise above the deadline of defeat, despair, and degradation.

Armies of Idle

The commissioner of labor of the state of New York reported recently that 35 percent of the organized workers of that state, as shown by the reports of their unions, were out of employment. President Yoakum,[76] of the Rock Island system, has made the statement within a few days that 400,000 railroad employees—25 percent of the entire number employed on the railroads of the United States—were idle since the "panic" set in last October.

It is estimated that almost if not quite 6 million, or 20 percent of all wage workers in the country, are out of work. This number may or may not be approximately correct and there is no way to verify it, for the United States government, although it squanders millions of dollars in supporting information and statistical bureaus of all descriptions so as to retain an army of ward-heeling politicians in office, very discreetly refrains from furnishing any statistics upon the vital question of the unemployed. It is worthy of note in this connection that Mr. Taft's voluminous letter of acceptance contains no hint that there is a grand army of men and women begging for work in the United States, with no hope in finding it.

The census bureau has recently issued a report which shows that in certain industries, the weekly earnings of children is $1.84, of women $2.26, and of men $5.23. These figures will be found under the heading of "the earnings of wage earners" and are secured from "123,703 establishments throughout the country, some 63 percent of all manufacturing concerns having employees."

Is It Worthwhile?

Does Mr. Roosevelt maintain that these hapless victims of industrial servitude have "equal opportunity for each man to show the stuff that is in him?" Is it worthwhile to argue with him that these children are having all the "stuff" ground out of them for the benefit of the capitalist class and that there is nothing left of them when they are grown except the empty shell, if they survive at all?

What has Mr. Roosevelt to say of a system based upon such brutal exploitation in which even babes, millions of them, are fed alive to Mammon? Is it because socialists protest that this brutality and crime is an impeachment of capitalism and a rebuke to civilization that Roosevelt so furiously denounces them? And is it because they propose a reorganization of society upon a basis of cooperative labor freely performed by free men, thus putting an end to Big Stick rule, and its countless iniquities, that he has branded socialists as "undesirable citizens?"

If Mr. Roosevelt, instead of spending his time in spectacular self-exploitation, will look about him, he will see enough of all that is corrupt and menacing to society, for which his administration is responsible, without going out of his way to denounce the socialists.

It was not a socialist who, as governor of New York, signed the bill which made possible the gigantic railroad robbery known as the "Alton deal;" it was not a socialist who was elected president by the hugest political corruption fund, put up by the trusts and corporations, in the history of American politics; it was not a socialist president who invited one he afterward denounced as a thieving magnate to come around to the White House in the dark of the moon to help him write his message.

Not the socialists are they who maintain lobbies to debauch legislation, who steal franchises, rob the people, subvert the public will, and conspire in every conceivable manner to rob honest labor and keep the common people in subjection.

Reward of Toil

Mr. Roosevelt talks glibly about "reward" as if the idle capitalist class honestly earned its colossal private fortunes. Not satisfied with insulting socialists by imputing to them certain theories they do not hold, he resorts to downright mendacity when he says:

> There can be no grosser example of privilege than that set before us as an ideal by certain socialistic writers—the ideal that every man shall put into the common fund what he can, which would mean what he chose; and should take out what he wanted.

There is not a word of truth in this charge. It is pure fabrication and is inspired by cold-blooded malice. Who are the "socialistic writers" engaged in exploiting this ideal? Mr. Roosevelt cannot name a single one who is recognized as an authority on socialism. The Socialist Party in the United States has recently adopted a platform and a program in which its principles, policies, and purposes are clearly set forth. Let this authoritative statement of the party as to its attitude and intent be examined, and it will be found that there is not the slightest justification for the president's deliberate misrepresentation.

If President Roosevelt deems it necessary to resort to such undignified, to say nothing of indecent, methods of combating the socialist movement and obstructing its rapid progress, he must be hard pressed and his intelligent readers among non-socialists who may be temporarily deceived will not be slow to rebuke his presumption upon their credulity when they learn the truth.

"If the service is equal, let the reward be equal," proceeds the president as if he were saying something that anyone, let along socialists, had ever disputed. It is precisely because the reward is not equal for equal service rendered that socialists are opposed to capitalism. The figures above quoted prove conclusively that they who do the actual work in the present system, the work that is useful, are treated as menials and starved into inanity and premature graves. Millions of these victims, though dumb, and resigned, cry to heaven against the cruel injustice of the present system which dooms them to bitter poverty and finally to death by slow torture.

Panic and Paralysis

In contemplating the present situation and its countless horrors confronting one upon every hand under President Roosevelt's administration, I recall the "panic" of 1893, which the Republican platform adopted in 1896 charged upon the incompetency, dishonesty, and unfitness of the Democratic Party. If the Democratic Party was responsible for the "panic" of 1893, and there is no doubt about it, then the Republican Party is responsible for the "panic" of 1908. There is absolutely no escape. It was when the Republican Party came into power and increased the tariff to its highest levels and adopted the gold standard that the promise was made and the assurance given that prosperity would henceforth be perpetual in the United States. The "full dinner pail" campaign of 1904 is still remembered.

In 1900 the Republican slogan was "Let well enough alone;" in 1904, "Stand pat." But in spite of it all "prosperity" has suddenly vanished; there is a larger number of idle workers in the country than ever before in all its history. The Republican Party is and has been in absolute control and what is its answer? "God knows!"—and that is why the president froths at the mouth in denunciation of the socialists and exhibits his impotent rage because they propose to put an end to this outworn and rotten system and reorganize society upon a rational basis and in harmony with the forces underlying it and determining the course of its development.

Rule of Beak and Claw

Mr. Roosevelt, like every other self-sufficient individualist, believes in the supremacy of beak and claw, of fang and hoof. The very thought of a time coming when these will rule no more is abhorrent to him and arouses him to furious denunciation. This is as far as Mr. Roosevelt has risen in the scale of civilization, and that is why he is the beau ideal of the ignorant masses under the domination of capitalism.

It would be horrible, according to Mr. Roosevelt, if a time ever came when a giant could not have the whole feast and the dwarf only the crumbs. The giant's strength is to be forever rewarded and the dwarf's weakness to be everlastingly punished. The president would set a beautiful example at his own table if he made practical application there of the ideals (?) he expresses in his violent diatribe against socialism.

What would Mr. Roosevelt say if men today proceeded to make distribution of rewards upon the basis of physical strength and muscular equipment? Would he not be the first to say they ought to be shot and order out the soldiers for that purpose? What better moral justification can he plead for the distribution of rewards on the basis of superior mental capacity? The time will come when the human being will rise somewhat higher than the beast in this regard, but it will never be under the sway of capitalism which Mr. Roosevelt is so eager to buttress against the assaults of socialism that he is driven to the most flagrant misrepresentation.

Let it not be inferred that I am now assuming to define the attitude of the Socialist Party in respect to the rewards of labor or the distribution of wealth. The Socialist platform is clear enough upon this point, and there is no excuse for misunderstanding. Each worker is to receive his socially due share of the product, the entire product, and when the time comes the workers themselves will establish a basis of reward and remuneration to suit themselves. To presume to say what that basis will be, or rather what it will not be, and then condemn it is nothing less than vulgar impertinence, quite characteristic of the present occupant of the White House.

Equality of Reward

When Mr. Roosevelt charges socialism with demanding "equality of reward," he is as wide of the mark as he is of every other vital proposition he discusses in his memorial tirade. There is absolutely nothing in the Socialist platform or its program that warrants the assumption that it stands for "equality of reward." Personally there are socialists who take that position and it is eminently to their credit, seeing that they are men of exceptional capacity and who, in the grab-all game, could, if they would, rake in the spoils, but who are too decent to do it. This, of course, Mr. Roosevelt is wholly incapable of understanding.

But with all this, socialism as a movement has nothing to do and will have nothing to do until it comes into power and as the people themselves will then rule in the purest and completest democracy yet evolved it is entirely probable, Mr. Roosevelt to the contrary notwithstanding, that they will distribute the wealth equitably among those who produce it.

Clipping the Claws of Individualism

But blindly and venomously as Mr. Roosevelt is opposed to socialism, he is yet driven to the extremity of making some concession to it. He would not have done this a year or two ago, but he is compelled to do it now, and in a year or two more he will be compelled to make still further concessions, galling as it may be to him. In his closing paragraph he says: "In the interest of true individualism, the collective and common power of the community must be exercised to control and regulate for the common good this business use of vast wealth," etc.

Precisely! It will not do to admit, even for the sake of "individualism," that the trust pirates shall have absolute sway. Mr. Roosevelt is too adroit a politician to take such a position. He must in some manner placate the people who are being eaten up and so he invokes the "collective power" to curb the individual will.

But when he curbs individualism, it is no longer individualism and such curbing means the application of another and an entirely different principle to personal rights and social relations.

It is only quite recently that Mr. Roosevelt and others like him have begun to talk about "curbing individualism" and about exercise of the collective power for the collective good. It is distinctively a socialistic principle that Mr. Roosevelt would apply and a socialistic power that he would invoke to protect society against the ravages and barbarities of the very individualism of which he has been and is yet such a strenuous advocate.

Periodical Tirades

As the industrial and social development proceed, Mr. Roosevelt's complications will increase and his entanglements multiply. He has lost none of his vindictiveness for those who disagree with him and especially for socialists, who know him, but he is at last compelled to turn to the "collective power" to extricate him from the meshes of the brutal individualism of decadent capitalism.

The answer of socialists to Mr. Roosevelt is that his periodical tirades are the most convincing proof of the progress of their movement. Each attack of the president is another certificate of approval and another voice of encouragement.

Socialists are not visionaries, nor are they dupes and blind followers. They are students and investigators and they understand from a scientific interpretation of history the laws underlying society and the trend of its development. They not only hope for socialism and believe in it, but they know it is coming. With them it is not a matter of speculation, but a certainty.

Capitalism is hurrying to its doom. The capitalists cannot save it. They cannot even manage it, nor prevent it from breaking down and exposing its corruption and decay; its impotence and other symptoms of advancing dissolution.

"Collective Power"

The "collective power" to which Mr. Roosevelt himself must at last turn will have to be invoked more and more to prop up collapsing capitalism, but this can at best prolong it, for it is as certainly doomed, having fulfilled its mission, as the feudalism which preceded it and from which it sprang.

Yes, capitalism and its merciless votaries and mercenary menials has about run its course, and every sane mortal on earth ought to join in heartfelt gratitude. In a hundred years hence its history will be an extension of the period of barbarism and its ideals, if such they may be called, reflected in the slavery and suffering, the sorrow and despair, the blood and fears of its countless victims, sparing neither babyhood nor old age, will be regarded with unspeakable abhorrence by civilized human beings.

Lewis H. Morgan foreshadows in his *Ancient Society* the coming civilization:

> Since the advent of civilization the outgrowth of property has been so immense, its forms so diversified, its uses so expanding, and its management so intelligent in the interests of its owners, that it has become, on the part of the people, an unmanageable power. . . . The time will come . . . when human intelligence will rise to the mastery over property, and define the relations of the state to the property it protects as well as the obligations and the limits of the rights of its owners. The interests of society are paramount to individual interests, and the two must be brought into just and harmonious relations . . . . Democracy in government, brotherhood in society, equality in rights and privileges, and universal education, foreshadow the next higher plane of society to which experience, intelligence, and knowledge are steadily tending.[77]

This is socialism, and it is going to triumph in the United States of America and all the world.

A Million Votes or More: Statement to the Press in Missoula, Montana [excerpt][†]

September 17, 1908

* * *

What do I think of the chances for the Socialist Party's success this year? Listen! The Socialist ticket will get over one million votes at the November election. I am even inclined to believe that half a million more may be added to the estimate. This is the working man's year. The man who works is beginning to wake up.

† Published in *The Missoulan,* vol. 35, no. 136 (September 18, 1908), 8.

This is the first time in almost three weeks of unceasing travel that we have been more than a minute behind our schedule at any stop.[78] It is a great disappointment to me that the "Red Special" could not get into Missoula this afternoon on its regular time. We have been subject to most disgusting delays since leaving Wallace, where I spoke 35 minutes to a tremendous crowd.[79] Gravel trains, freight trains, cattle trains, and construction trains seemed to have right-of-way over us today, and we have spent half the time on sidetracks this afternoon.[80]

I am also very sorry that this passenger train had to cut me off from my audience.[81] The trip has been very successful. Everywhere the crowds have been much larger than four years ago. It is on this that I base my high estimate of the vote to be polled by the Socialist ticket.

Answering Gompers's Charge: Statement to the Press[†]

October 3, 1908

Gompers dare not meet me and make this statement.[82] His statement is an unqualified falsehood. If you will have Gompers come here, I will come across the continent to meet him and prove him a vulgar falsifier.

He said I betrayed the locomotive firemen, but I have an invitation to their convention. When I resigned they gave me $2,000. I refused to take it. Has Gompers ever refused anything? When I was at the head of the American Railway Union, Gompers was doing all he could to break the strike.

If he ever dare face me, I will prove to his face that he is a coward and a liar. Gompers this year is for the Democratic Party, but he does not dare go to Alabama to make speeches. All the atrocities of the Middle Ages are perpetrated in the South. Gompers has harped about keeping out of politics, but now he is trying to bring the workingmen to be sheared at the Democratic shambles in the South.

† Published in *Chicago Tribune,* vol. 67, no. 40 (October 4, 1908), 5.

The New Emancipation: Campaign Speech at the Hippodrome, New York City†

October 4, 1908

How deeply I am touched by the kind and gracious and appreciative words which have been spoken by the comrade who has preceded me, and how fully I appreciate this very cordial reception and this splendid demonstration of good will, I shall not now attempt to say. There is nothing that is grander or more inspiring than the awakening of the working class.

We have a truly magnificent demonstration of it here this afternoon. This audience is so vast, this assemblage is so great that it is bewildering and overwhelming, and it seems almost like audacity to stand in its presence. But it is the same everywhere—the spirit of socialism is abroad in the land and rousing the people from their slumber. Two weeks ago we were on the Pacific coast and the outpourings there were so vast that the largest auditoriums had not half capacity to hold them.

A Marvelous Age

It is our good fortune, whatever our lot may be, to live in the most marvelous age known to history. The discovery of the power of steam and electricity and the application of this power to industry has revolutionized the modern world. The material achievements of the past century outrival those of all preceding ages, and now for the first time in history it is possible to produce wealth in abundance for all. It is possible to abolish poverty and ignorance, to really civilize the human race.

The capitalist system, in which these gigantic productive powers have been developed and in which these mighty changes have taken place, has about run its historic course, and now the very forces which brought it into existence are operating to overthrow it. This system has broken down. Another period of industrial depression has set in. It is now writing its record in failures, in poverty and misery that defy the power of all language to properly describe.

† Published as "Unparalleled Socialist Greeting to Eugene Debs Astounds New York" in *New York Call,* vol. 1, no. 110 (October 4, 1908), 1, 5.

Two Panics

The last panic, so-called, occurred under a Democratic administration in 1893. The Republicans were swift to exclaim, "Behold, the fruit of Democratic misrule!" They charged this panic upon the Democratic Party, and if you will read the Republican platform for 1896, you will find this charge made in specific terms.

Up to this time the working class had not yet learned to any great extent to think or to act for themselves. They were still responsive to the plea of the capitalist demagogue. Hundreds of thousands of them swept from the Democratic Party into the Republican Party, and that party went into power upon that issue.

In the meantime the panic had run its course, industry was in some measure revived, and the Republican Party took full credit for it and again exclaimed, "Behold, when the Republican Party goes into power, prosperity comes to the country!" In 1900 the slogan of that party, coined by its chief prophet, was "Let well enough alone;" in 1904, "Stand pat." In 1908 it is, "God knows."

There are at this very hour more idle and despairing men in the United States than ever before in all its history, and when this great army of the unemployed, which stretches from the Atlantic to the Pacific and from the Lakes to the Gulf, turned to the chief standard-bearer of the Republican Party and asked him what they are to do when they are suffering, when their wives are in want and their children are about to be put upon the street, he meekly referred them to Jehovah—but he is completely willing to accept their votes by proxy.

Think of this just for a moment. Mr. Taft very frankly confesses that when large bodies of workingmen are in enforced idleness and when they are tormented by hunger pangs, he does not know what can be done for them; and yet he has the audacity to ask these same men to elect him president of the United States. Whatever may be said of Mr. Taft, there is nothing the matter with his nerve.

Theodore Roosevelt

What has the Republican Party ever done for the working class? What has it not done for the capitalist class? If you are a workingman and you are in that party, you are as sadly out of place as John D. Rockefeller would be in the Socialist Party. You have been looking up to President Roosevelt as your friend, and you have in your ignorance been waiting for him to do something for you. As a matter of fact, President Roosevelt is the archenemy of the working class, and his record proves it. And when he graduates from the White House to the jungles of Africa, where he properly belongs, if he remains there he will have rendered his first distinctive service to the working class of the United States.

It is he who preaches political homilies, moralizes the people, spends his time talking about civic righteousness and political purity, [who was himself] elected by the aid of the biggest debauching fund in the history of American politics.

A Debauching Fund

It was the Standard Oil Company that dropped $100,000 into his campaign fund when he wasn't looking. He said not a word about it until the discovery was made public, and then, as is his habit, he exploded in virtuous indignation. He said, "It's got to go back"—but up to this date it hasn't gone back.[83]

When that $100,000 was contributed to his corruption fund, it came so easily that Bliss[84] touched Rogers,[85] or tried to, for $200,000 more. Rogers objected, and then President Roosevelt took his pen in hand and wrote "My dear Mr. Harriman, come around to the White House in the dark of the moon. Help me write my message to Congress."

He said nothing about Harriman raising $200,000 for him, or about $240,000 more being stolen from the stockholders of the insurance companies, until the fact was made public, and then he turned on his boon companion, his political ally Edward Harriman, and denounced him as a liar and a scoundrel. He has a happy habit of kicking a man when he's down, but if he has any act of bravery, if he has any brave act to his credit besides shooting a Spaniard in the back, I have never heard of it.

Explaining Records

The workingmen of this country are just beginning to find him out. He's been given credit for settling the anthracite strike. He did, when it was practically won by the miners, and then he appointed a commission that turned the victory over to the anthracite coal companies.

He has nominated his own political successor, a gentleman who has won his distinction by issuing injunctions which have paralyzed labor organizations. Mr. Taft never deigned to make any explanation of these until he became a candidate for president, and now he declares that the reason he issued injunctions was because of his interest in and love for the working class. But he never attempted to prove his love for the capitalists in the same way. He never enjoined them, nor did he ever send one of them to jail. And the reason for this is so simple and so self-evident that it suggests itself.

How can any workingman with ordinary intelligence, with all the facts before him, think of casting a vote for William Howard Taft? All I have to say is that if you are a workingman and familiar with his record—and there is no excuse for your not being—and still vote to make him president, you stand in need of a political guardian.

Old Parties Alike

There is absolutely no difference between the Republican and the Democratic parties so far as the working class is concerned. They are exactly alike. They are both committed to the capitalist system. They are both committed to wage-slavery, and whether the one or the other wins, you workingmen always lose. Your condition remains the same.

You have tried these two capitalist parties over and over again, with the same inevitable result. The politicians who used you to vote to perpetuate the system in which you are slaves have no respect for you. They treat you with contempt. When the Republican convention met in Chicago, there were no workingmen there.[86] The voice of labor was not heard in its councils. This convention consisted of plutocrats, office-holders, politicians, and parasites. The Democratic convention consisted of the same element.[87]

The Socialist convention consisted of representatives of the working class, adopted a working class platform, and made its appeal to the working class of the United States.

A Cause for Shame

It's about this season of the year, or a little later, that the capitalist politician comes before you workingmen to tell you how delighted he is to have the opportunity of looking into your manly faces and telling you what bright and intelligent fellows you are. This is the politician who calls you the "horny-handed sons of toil," and would have you proud of your misshapen hands, when as a matter of fact you ought to be ashamed of them. You ought to blush to look you hand in the face, and if you do, you find written in unmistakable characters an impeachment of your intelligence, an indictment of your manhood. If you would use your brains in your own interest, you would not have to deform your hands in the interest of your masters.

"Oh, but," you say, "I have grown wise his year, I am going over to the Democratic Party, over to Bryan and Haskell[88] and Gompers this time. That's a fine combination, isn't it?" That's worse still, if possible.

In the "Solid South"

The Democratic Party—all I have to do in answer is point toward the "Solid South," where the Democratic Party has reigned supreme for a century. Nowhere are wages lower, nowhere are industrial conditions more wretched, nowhere is the percentage of illiteracy so large; and the Solid South, ruled by the Democratic Party, has a system that makes men and angels weep.

In that part of the land, where men are out of work and wander hungry, and beg for bread, they are arrested and jailed as vagrants, and then they are farmed out to heartless bloodsuckers; they are manacled together, and, as I have seen again and again, they are beaten and lashed into insensibility. All of the atrocities and all the barbarities of the Middle Ages are reenacted in the Solid South, ruled by the Democratic Party.

Only a little while ago the seventeen thousand miners in the Birmingham district went out on strike. Their wages were but 47 cents a ton, the lowest scale in the United States. These mines are owned by the Steel trust, which has been piling up hundreds of millions of dollars wrung from the sweat and blood of the working class, but these pirates were not yet satisfied.

A Democratic Governor

They knew that these miners were at their mercy. They ordered a final reduction that reduced the miners to a pittance that did not suffice to keep their souls within their ragged bodies. Seventeen thousand of them went out on strike, and when they did, Governor B. B. Comer,[89] the Democrat, the millionaire who has made all of his money grinding the faces of children, this savage, ordered out the militia, turned them on these famishing miners, and dispersed them.

They went to the fields that had been leased for them by their union. They had been provided with tents to shelter their wives and children from the elements, and this angered the Democratic governor, the political ally of William Jennings Bryan. He sent soldiers into those fields. Part of them took out their knives and cut those tents to shreds; the rest of them stood by with shotted guns, ready to murder these starving miners if they objected to having their wives and children exposed to the elements.

This is how the Democratic Party proves its friendship for the working class.

Mr. Bryan's Lost Opportunity

But you tell me that Mr. Bryan, the standard bearer, is the champion of the common people; he's the friend of the workingmen. And I deny it. Two years and a half ago Mr. Bryan had the supreme chance of his life. You remember when the officials of the Western Federation of Miners were seized and deported and thrown into the penitentiary. You remember this famous outrage that shocked the nation.

In this extremity the workers who had followed Mr. Bryan through two campaigns loyally and enthusiastically turned to him and said: "Mr. Bryan, speak for our leaders; save them from murder." But he turned a deaf ear to the working class. His lips were sealed. He was as silent as the Sphinx.

William Jennings Bryan couldn't speak without attacking the mine owners who had financed his campaign. After these men were tried and acquitted, then his lips were unsealed for the first time and he said he believed all the time that they were innocent. If he believed they were innocent, why did he not say so? In this hour Mr. Bryan forfeited forever the right to appeal to the working class.

Mr. Bryan's Friends

It was four years ago, if you remember, that Mr. Bryan denounced Alton B. Parker[90] as the tool of Wall Street and said that no self-respecting Democrat could vote for him. The Democratic convention nominated Mr. Parker and then Mr. Bryan went out among the American people and used all the powers of his eloquence to make this "tool of Wall Street" president of the United States.

Four years ago Mr. Bryan denounced Roger Sullivan, the Illinois corruptionist, as one who has secured his election as delegate by methods that would disgrace a train robber. Where is that train robber today? He is side by side with Mr. Bryan, one of his chief supporters. And only a few weeks ago this train robber was at Fairview, Nebraska, Mr. Bryan's home, by his invitation, and by him was introduced to his family.

Four years ago Mr. Bryan denounced Tammany. This year he is hand in glove with Tammany, and here let me say, and I know it's true, that Tammany is the vilest and corruptest political organization on the American continent. Tammany is a political leper. Tammany pollutes everything it touches. Tammany levies tribute upon your tenderloin [tavern district]. Tammany extorts from fallen women the proceeds of their shame. That is Tammany. And Mr. Bryan has compromised with Tammany and had Murphy at his Fairview home in order that he might carry New York and become president. I wouldn't object to being elected president; but, upon my honor, I would never pay that price for that or any other office on this earth.

There's nothing for you in these two corrupt and decadent parties. They have fulfilled their mission. They belong to the past. The Socialist Party is the party of the present and the future. Waste your time and your energy and your substance no longer. The Socialist Party is the only party that has a claim upon you, the only party in which you can stand in your true proportions, in which you can stand erect as becomes a man, in which you can do your work and in doing write your name in the deeds that live forever.

Woman Under Capitalism

I am indeed glad to see so many women in this audience, and here let me say that the Socialist Party is the only party that recognizes woman as a human being. It's the only party that recognizes woman at all. In capitalist society you women have to obey the laws, but have no voice in enacting them, and if you are the daughters of workingmen you are economic menials, you are political nonentities. Under the present regime you are taught to look upon your husbands as your lords and your masters, and I want to say to some of you "lords," how my heart does go out to the women!

In this system 8 million of your sex are in wage-slavery, 8 million of them whose life is a continuous struggle all the year, from youth to old age, economic bondage, the victims of capitalism, in which private profit is vastly more important than human life.

What prospect is there for these women? None. All the doors are barred against them. Upon their heads society pours its garbage. They are social inferiors. They belong to the working class, and upon the brow of labor there is still the band of inferiority.

It is at this season of the year that you are called sovereign by the politicians, the politicians who insult your intelligence (if you have any) by flattering your ignorance. They tell you that you are intelligent to keep you ignorant; Socialists tell you very frankly how ignorant you are, that you may become intelligent.

The Abject Class

The workingmen produce all wealth. How much have you to show for it? You working men support all government. You working men create and conserve all civilization. Without you society would perish. Without you the whole fabric of our so-called civilization would collapse. And yet you are the lower class. You have always been the lower class—in the ancient world for thousands of years abject slaves, and then the serfs of the Middle Ages, and now the wage workers of modern society. Society has always been organized, and is today, upon the basis of exploitation and the degradation of those who toil.

In this country we have 30 million wage workers, 18 million of them men, 8 million women, 4 million children, who have no tools of their own to work, and never will have under the administration of either the Republican or Democratic parties. No matter which of these is in power, no matter if the tariff be high or low, if we have the gold standard or free silver, or what our domestic policy may be; since these 30 million workers have no tools of their own with which to work, they will be in a state of slavery and their lives will be broken. They will die wretched failures. If now and then there is one who escapes, it is simply the exception which serves to prove the rule.

Merely "Hands"

What is the status of the workingman in this system? The truth is that he is not a man at all, and the terminology of capitalism proves it. When the capitalist wants him he calls for a "hand"—a factory hand, a mill hand, a shop hand, a farm hand. Hand, hand, hand. That's what you are in capitalism—simply a hand. You have been putting a boycott on your brain, you have been putting a boycott on your head.

Nor has anyone been doing it, putting it there for you; you do it yourself. There's nothing I can do for you. There's nothing you can't do for yourselves. You have an overwhelming majority of the votes. Surely it should require but little intelligence to teach you workingmen that you have got to unite economically and politically; act together. From the hour you do this, this earth is yours.

When you workingmen stand forth in solid, class-conscious array, there's nothing between this earth and the stars that can stand between you and emancipation. You have but to develop your economic and your political power.

Where Did He Get It?

Your interests are diametrically opposed to the interests of the capitalists who exploit you of what you produce. Let me give you just one concrete illustration. It applies to every department of industrial activity. A few weeks ago, John D. Rockefeller, who is a fully developed capitalist, who is ripe and therefore a profit-taker and a parasite—for no ripe capitalist has any function that is useful to society—he was on the witness stand in a federal court at Chicago in the trial of that $29 million joke,[91] and he was asked certain questions about the Standard Oil Company.

His answer was that he knew nothing about the Standard Oil Company because he had had no connection with it for seven years. And yet during these seven years he received from the Standard Oil Company in the way of dividends, profits, an average of $5 million a month, $60 million a year, $420 million in all. According to his own confession he had absolutely nothing to do with the production of this wealth, and yet he took it all. And that is what you vote for every time you vote the Republican ticket or the Democratic ticket.

How did Rockefeller come into possession of this vast amount of wealth produced by the working class? By the mere fact of his privately owning the great storehouses of nature, the sources from which the raw materials are drawn, and the social machinery with which these raw materials are transmuted into the finished product called wealth.

He produces no oil. Carnegie produces no steel. Havemeyer and Spreckels[92] produce no sugar. The working class do all of this—produce all the wealth—but the capitalists, who own the resources from which the raw materials are drawn, and the machinery, come into possession of it all.

Capitalism's Ending

The 30 million wage-slaves can't work without tools. The tools belong to the capitalists. The 30 million wage-slaves have to sell their labor-power to the capitalists, and when they have done it, the wealth that is produced by that labor-power belongs to the capitalists and not to themselves. And every few years they have produced so much more than can be consumed, the markets are glutted, the mills are closed, industry comes to a standstill, hundreds of thousands of workers are idle and suffer in the presence of the very abundance their labor has created.

This simply proves that capitalism has fulfilled its mission, that the capitalist class can no longer control the productive forces, that the capitalist class can no longer manage industry, can no longer give employment to the workers. And so the historic mission of this movement is to abolish the capitalist system based upon private ownership, and recognize society upon a basis of collective ownership of the means of production and distribution.

And this change is coming just as certainly as I stand in your presence this afternoon. It will come as soon as you are ready for it, and you will be ready for it just as soon as you understand what socialism means. The trouble with most of you is that you know but little about it and that little is not true. You have read that in capitalist newspapers and they tell you that in socialism you will be reduced to a dead level of degradation.

You are there now.

Individuality

I was in the bread line in New York last winter. They don't tell you anything about that. They tell you that socialism will destroy your individuality. You haven't got any. The wage-slave as no individuality.

What is individuality? It is the expression unhampered of the individual's mental and moral and spiritual qualities. It is the human being in full bloom. But the 30 million wage workers who are dependent upon the capitalist are walking apologies, most of them. They have hinges in their knees, they doff their hats in the presence of a two-by-four boss. They may be discharged. They are repressed and cramped and their aspirations are stifled, because they have got to beg for work and therefore they have got to beg to live, and they have no individuality.

Untrue Charges Against Socialism

Then they tell you that in socialism you will have no incentive to work. You are exploited of nearly all you produce today and you are supposed to have great incentive to work, but if—as in socialism—you will get all you produce, then you will throw down your tools and starve to death. They won't do that to you, that will happen under socialism.

And then they tell you that socialism is going to break up the family, and that would be too bad. There are only eighty thousand divorces a year in capitalism. The family? Why, capitalism destroys the family all over the country in all the circling hours of the day and night.

How about the families of the 5 million who have no work—who have got to leave their families and their huts or their hovels or their lairs in a vain search somewhere else for other masters? After they reach a point four or five hundred miles away from their home and their last penny is gone and their clothes are seedy, they receive a letter from home. Observe them closely as they read it; you will find the tears coursing down their cheeks. The wife reports that the rent is due and she is about to be put upon the street. The children are hungry. These men become tramps. Their lives are destroyed, their homes are wrecked, and the happiness of all these people is wrecked.

All of these charges against socialism are untrue. Every one of these things is true of capitalism.

The Fruits of Capitalism

In this system that has run its course, one-sixth of the entire productive capacity of the nation is paralyzed. One out of every six workers is idle. There are over a million human degenerates called tramps. Over 800,000 thieves, burglars, and convicts. About 600,000 fallen women.

Prostitution is a fixed, permanent, increasing factor in capitalist society. In every so-called civilized community, there is a red-light district, and this is recruited from the working class. The daughters of the rich may be immoral, but they don't have to go to the slums.

All of our jails are packed, and all of our penitentiaries crowded, and all of our insane asylums overflowing, and suicide is increasing at a startling rate. Every issue of every capitalist newspaper is a chronicle of vice and immorality and crime. Pick up any New York newspaper tomorrow morning and then blue-pencil the graft and the corruption and the thieves and the hold-ups and the revelations of all descriptions and the hunger and the rape and the vice and the murders. Eliminate these and there's hardly anything left. This is capitalism.

Nothing is certain in this system except uncertainty. You may have $50,000 and die in an almshouse and sleep your last sleep in a potter's field.

Destroying the Girls

If you are a workingman and you have a little girl of eight or ten and your wage is small or you are out of a job at the vey age when this child ought to be under the care of a loving mother and have a comfortable home and be out in the sunlight and have wholesome food—and nothing is so easily produced—this child is under the hunger-whip of capitalism, and at eight or ten she has got to go to the mill or factory and she stands beside the machine all day long.

She feeds the machine. The machine starves her. She gets but a pittance. The air is foul, the environment is unsanitary, she inhales lint and filth and her lungs are diseased. Her blood is impoverished. She remains here until she is 18 or 19. She approaches the marriage state. She assumes the functions of motherhood. She is unfit for them. Her nerves are worn out. Her tissue is exhausted, her vitality is spent. She has been fed, literally, to capitalism. Her offspring are born tired. That's why there are so many failures in capitalist society.

And here is another little girl of the same age and she is scourged by poverty and she has got to go to a department store and she gets $3 a week. She has got to be neat and tidy and attractive, and in her infancy she is subjected to a hundred temptations a day, and in an unguarded moment she takes her first misstep. It is fatal. She is then swept into that ever-broadening, ever-deepening stream that empties into the gulf of disgrace and despair and death.

This is capitalism. And if it be written in the book of fate that that blue-eyed child of yours that you love far more than you do your own life, if it be written in the book of fate that she shall perish in a brothel hell, I want you to know that you are responsible for it if you vote to perpetuate the capitalist system.

The Glorious Few

Upon this great issue, my friends and comrades, we are going to conquer, we are going to sweep into power. I appeal to you, workingmen, to come to the front in this campaign. Toe the mark of duty squarely. it is too late to any longer halt or hesitate. The call goes directly to you, and it is your duty to yourself, to your wife, to your child, to your class, to humanity—it is your duty to respond. Never mind what others may say or think or do; be true to yourself. You may be called an "undesirable citizen," and this will be your glory.

Let me say that in every age of this world's history the pioneers of progress, the pathfinders in the wilderness, the evangelists of civilization, the heralds of the dawn, have all been undesirable citizens.

One hundred and fifty years ago it was Jefferson who was a rebel, Adams an incendiary, Patrick Henry a traitor. You are teaching your children to revere the memories of these undesirable citizens, while all of the respectable majority sleep in oblivion.

So it was with the abolition movement. The respectable majority murdered Lovejoy, mobbed Garrison, persecuted Phillips, and hanged John Brown, the greatest liberator this county has produced. All of them were undesirable citizens. They all had the courage of their convictions. They all did their duty and placed their names where they will remain forever.

When great changes have occurred in history, when great principles have been involved, the majority have always been ignorant, reactionary, cowardly. The few have gone to the front, the few have paved the way to better conditions for the human race.

You and I who are on earth today are under great obligation to the splendid men, the magnificent women who made sacrifices that we might enjoy some degree of liberty, some degree of civilization. We can only discharge that obligation by doing or trying to do something in the interest of those who are to come after us. It ought to be the high mission of every man to do something to make it possible for some child to come to his grave and place a flower where he sleeps and say, "This world is better for me because of his having been here."

A Worldwide Crusade

Another mighty crusade is organizing. It is spreading over the face of the whole earth. Already the millions that are to be found in all of the zones that belt this globe are keeping step to the inspiring music of the new emancipation. This is the call that goes out to you, and if you are true to yourself you will respond, you will take your place in the ranks, and then for the first time you will rise to your full stature, you will feel your heart throb to the first forward march, you will expand to your true proportions, you will feel the thrill of a newborn aspiration. If on account of this you are persecuted, all the better for you, because your latent powers will be developed, you will become stronger than you dream, and you will write your name in the deeds that live forever

The Horrors of War

When this great party sweeps into power here in New York, in the United States, in all other nations, war between nation and nation will be ended forever. Why should the working class of one country murder the working class of another country in the interest of the capitalist class that exploits the working class of all countries? Civilized nations would not murder one another.

I remember not long ago reading the description of a battlefield in the Russian-Japanese War, of the 20,000 who lay dead on a single field, men mutilated and gasping. If you have but a bit of imagination you can see them. You can see that some of them are writing in their death agonies, heart-rending, as the last despairing sigh is wrung from them. You can see far, far away, the loved ones. Yes, and you can see the silver-haired mother bowed in her last great sorrow when she hears that the boy she loved is killed.

When I think of a cold steel bayonet being pushed into the white, soft, and quivering flesh of a human being, I recoil with horror. The socialist movement is doing what lies in its power to hasten the coming of that day when war shall curse this earth no more. With the end of industrial and commercial competition comes the end of war, and with the beginning of worldwide cooperation comes the inauguration of the reign of peace on earth and goodwill toward all men.

So that when this movement sweeps into power and establishes an industrial democracy, every man will have the inalienable right to work, will receive what he produces, may stand forth a free man, enjoy the fruit of his labor, have a comfortable home, a happy wife, his children at play or in school; in that hour the badge of labor will be the only badge of honor.

Then another proclamation of emancipation will be issued. We will fill this land with wealth. We will abolish poverty as it now scourges the ace, and all of its brood of concomitant ills. And then we shall reduce the workday in proportion to the products of invention, until every man may have leisure so that he may cultivate his mind and give his heart a chance so that he may enjoy the comradeship of his fellow men.

Then our economic interests will be mutual, and instead of clutching at each other's throats we can work together side by side in the true spirit of humanity. Remember that until then you have a duty.

It was Lowell who said:

> He's true to God who's true to man; wherever wrong is done,
> To the humblest and the weakest, 'neath the all-beholding sun,
> That wrong is also done to us; and they are slaves most base,
> Whose love of right is for themselves, and not for all the race.[93]

Message to Yale Students†

October 8, 1908

The world is ruled by ideas.[94] Colleges and universities propagate and disseminate ideas. The college men of America therefore have an extraordinary opportunity to take part in the solution of the great problem presented to labor—a problem that after waiting centuries for adjustment is about to be solved. But the college men of America will utterly fail to live up to their great opportunities if they do not bring to their task correct ideas on economics and governmental subjects. Wrong ideas can rule for a while, but they cannot rule always. And no college education is really worthwhile that does not teach men to do right.

This, American colleges do not do. It is not right that in a land of plenty, most men should be poor and that the poor should be those whose labor makes plenty. Thoughtful men have in the last 75 years invented and perfected machinery with which can be produced more than can be consumed. You students know that this ample product is not now satisfying the needs of anyone. You can see in any street evidence of misery, faces that show the constant fear of want [for some] and [for others] the harassing cares of trying to keep more than he can use. So we have those two things, abundance for all and misery for the want of the very things that can be produced so readily. This is the problem to be solved.

You can take a useful part in the solution of the problems before us. Justice, working through the Socialist Party, needs you. This party proposes to organize the working classes and take possession of government here and in every other nation. It proposes to operate all industry for the benefit of all and not for profit. We offer you greater opportunities than you will find when you graduate and go out to look for a job.

Commercial life, the profession of law, medicine, engineering, especially journalism, and all other lines of effort are tainted by the profit system. You will go out into life with high ideals, but they cannot be realized through activity in trade, industry, or the professions as operated or conducted today. There are exceptions, but they only prove the rule.

† Published as "Debs to Students" in *New Haven Morning Journal-Courier,* vol. 63, no. 243 (October 9, 1908), 2.

I have said that this system satisfies no one. The so-called successful men are not happy. They see about them misery and complete happiness is not possible when there is one hungry child in the world. Most of you will become members of the working class, using your fine minds for wages. You may think you are economically different from the bricklayer, trainman, and others, but you will not be different. We want you to go to the library and study socialism. If you do, you will be one of us and certainly be of conspicuous use to your fellow man.

Diaz's Plot to Murder Our Mexican Comrades Must Be Foiled†

October 10, 1908

There is no longer the least doubt, if there ever was any, that the United States government, through its present administration, has entered into a conspiracy with the bloody and barbarous government to foully murder the revolutionary leaders of the Mexican people. The visit of Secretary of State [Elihu] Root to the Mexican capital, the pomp and display with which he was received, and the continuous ovation that was tendered him, are well remembered, as is also the fact, by socialists at least, that the object of that love feast was to pave the way for the exploitation of this undeveloped country by American and Mexican capitalists. The *entente cordiale* was established between the House of Roosevelt and the House of Díaz,[95] and since then there has been perfect understanding and harmonious cooperation in carrying out the international program.

When the Mexican revolutionists established their junta at St. Louis and were followed by the bloodhounds of Díaz, the latter were reinforced by Furlong's detectives and the junta was finally destroyed by the joint persecution of the minions of the American and Mexican governments.

The Mexican revolutionists, whose only crime was their opposition to Díaz, the bloody butcher of the so-called Mexican Republic, are men of heart

† Published as "This Plot Must Be Foiled: Conspiracy to Murder Mexican Comrades Now Imprisoned in This Country by Order of Diaz" in *Appeal to Reason,* whole no. 671 (October 10, 1908), 2.

and brain and conscience who could not endure witnessing the atrocities perpetrated upon the ignorant masses; they were animated by the same passion for freedom as were the American revolutionists a century and a half ago and with far greater justification for resisting tyranny and oppression.

Gruesome and Revolting

Driven from their own country by the relentless pursuit of the Díaz bloodhounds, they crossed the Rio Grande in the vain hope of finding shelter and security in the great American Republic. But alas! Roosevelt and Díaz are the best of friends, and from the standpoint of real freedom there is but little difference between the "republic" in which labor leaders are kidnapped and deported by the authorities and the "republic" where they are hunted down and shot without trial.

From the moment the Mexican revolutionists, the leaders of labor and friends of the people, crossed the international boundary line, they were hunted and pursued and finally lured into ambush and seized by the joint secret agents and detectives of the United States and Mexico, operating under the sanction and with the backing and support of both governments.

It is here seen that under Roosevelt's capitalist administration, Uncle Sam is willing to act as a bloodhound of Díaz, to hunt down the noble souls who aspire to see their countrymen free, in consideration of favors to be granted to American capitalists.

It is a gruesome and revolting picture!

Buried Alive in Dungeon!

In a recent issue of the *St. Louis Post-Dispatch* there is an illustrated article covering a full page on the situation in Mexico and the fate of its brave revolutionary leaders. The article is entitled "Buried Alive in a Loathsome Dungeon." It has reference to Juan Sarabia,[96] vice president of the St. Louis Mexican Junta. Sarabia is one of the grandest of men and the most heroic of liberators, but he is rotting alive in a frightful hole as the price of his martyrdom. This brave comrade of ours was lured across the line by a ruse of American and Mexican detectives, seized, and then disappeared. Neither his family nor his friends knew what had become of him until finally it was disclosed that he was in the horrible military prison at San Juan de Ulua, known as "The Purgatory."

Sarabia is in a five-foot cell far below the surface, where water seeps in, where all light is excluded, and where he is literally devoured alive by vermin.

The horror of his fate defies description. The very thought of it fires the blood and flushes the cheek with flame. What cowards we are, all of us, to see a noble patriot, a great and tender soul, consigned to such a hellish fate!

Loaded with chains and reduced to a skeleton, this comrade is made to realize what it costs to serve humanity in this twentieth century of Christian civilization. At the top of the foul hole in which he is chained like a leprous beast are seated the Mexican guards with shotguns in their hands, waiting for the last spark of life to flicker out and fearful that even this may escape and light the smoldering fires of revolution.

The account says:

> Juan Sarabia is dying in the military prison at San Juan de Ulúa. He lies helpless in "The Purgatory." More than two or three months he cannot live, possibly not more than a few weeks. He is facing a slow death in the most terrible dungeon on the American continent.

Begged Permission to See Son

The devoted mother of this comrade, his ministering angel, 80 years of age, found her way to "The Purgatory" and begged to be permitted to see but once more her loved and loving boy. She was refused and fell in a faint and was dragged away.

Such unspeakable cruelty is enough to make even the hearts of stones throb with revolution.

I again quote from the account:

> The old woman begged on her bended knees to be allowed to go down to see her son, that he might be brought to the door and mother and son pass greetings even at that distance. She told the keeper that she would never see her boy again; that at her age death was only a little way ahead, that in Juan's state of health he could not be expected to live long in that dungeon. But the man was obdurate. At last she asked that Juan might be permitted to write her a note, and finally that he be allowed to write his name—nothing more, if they feared a plot. But no. And the old woman fainted at the mouth of the passageway leading down to "The Purgatory."
>
> "So much for the mother of a breed of scorpions," said the keeper as she was carried away.

Who can contemplate this inexpressible cruelty and crime without feelings of horror and revolt!

Woe to you, Díaz, you bloody demon, and your mercenary minions at the day of retribution! The storm of wrath is now gathering and every atrocity perpetrated by your bloody regime will be wiped out in the blood of inhuman tyrants and human devils!

A Marked Family

Quoting again from the *Post-Dispatch* account we read as follows:

> The Sarabias are a marked family in Mexico. Juan is most hated, but even young Manuel, his cousin, now in jail in Los Angeles—little more than a boy—was thought sufficiently important that Mexican emissaries bribed American officials to allow them to take him from an American jail, hurry him, gagged and blindfolded, into a swift automobile and across the border and turn him over to Mexican *rurales* in uniform—showing the actual connivance of the Mexican government. He was carried away down on the west coast to Hermosillo, in the heart of the Yanqui country, and there thrown into jail until the American press forced the American government to make diplomatic representations to Mexico and secure his return to the soil of the United States.

Liberty? Protection for political exile? Traditions? The flag of the free? Bah! Such an act committed by Spain on a member of the Cuban junta, by Russians on an expatriated Pole, by England on the famous Irish, Number One of the Phoenix Park affair, who found asylum in this country, would have meant war—nothing less.

A Shame and a Disgrace

The Mexican comrades, Magón,[97] Villarreal,[98] and Rivera,[99] like Juan Sarabia, are charged with political offenses and are held prisoners in Los Angeles at the behest of the Mexican government and with the connivance of the government of the United States.

It is a burning shame and a disgrace to us all.

These comrades have been engaged in a peaceful agitation on behalf of their wretched and suffering countrymen. Forced into exile by the ruling class, they came to the United States, but they soon found that their dream of security was a delusion and a snare. They were arrested first upon one charge and then another, and since then every effort has been made to extradite them that they may be shot dead by the bloody Díaz for daring to dream of freedom and resolving to achieve it. They should never have been arrested at all, for there is no charge against them that will bear the light an instant.

But the Roosevelt administration has been doing the bidding abjectly of the Díaz government. Attorney General [Charles] Bonaparte has taken personal charge and is bound that our comrades shall be sent back to Mexico and there foully murdered, even as Moyer, Haywood, and Pettibone were to meet the same fate if the designs of the conspirators had not been thwarted by an aroused working class.

Struggling for Freedom

Ricardo Flores Magón, Antonio I. Villarreal, Librado Rivera, and L. Gutiérrez de Lara[100] are our comrades in the social revolution! They have been doing in Mexico what we are doing in the United States and by practically the same means. If they ought to be shot, so ought we. The truth is that they are four reformers in the highest sense of that term, highly educated, cultured, pure in mind, exalted in thought, noble of nature, and lofty of aspiration. They are victims of a foul conspiracy between two capitalist governments to put them to death. They are traitors to Mexico, even as Franklin, Paine, Jefferson, and Patrick Henry were traitors to Great Britain. They are leaders in a mighty cause and every hour they serve in an American dungeon is an outrage upon justice and a burning disgrace to the government of the United States.

This case has not had a fraction of the attention it deserves. It is true that our comrades in California have done what they could with the means at their command and are entitled to full credit for their fealty to their Mexican comrades, but the case is of more than local interest; it has national and international significance and gravity, and it is time the working class of the United States were aroused to that fact.

The very least we can do is to appeal to the workers of America to go to the rescue of these comrades. The most vital and far-reaching principle is involved. It is nothing less than a dastardly international conspiracy of capitalists to murder labor leaders who cannot be silenced in any other way.

Murder Must Not Be Permitted

Comrades and fellow workers, this foul and atrocious murder of our comrades must not be permitted. They are the truest of men, the most loyal of comrades, and the most valiant of warriors. They are serving their countrymen under the most desperate conceivable circumstances. But for the fact that they are heroes of the noblest type, they would not now be where they are, nor would two capitalist governments be in conspiracy to have them shot to death. They are charged with treason only because they are true to the people and seeking to overthrow their oppressors and despoilers. It is for this that they have risked their lives, it is for this that they have been hunted down as if they had been wild beasts, and it is for this that they have been for two years locked up in dungeons with the certainty of death staring them in the face if the Mexican bandits in control of that government can get them in their clutches.

Arouse ye workingmen and women, everywhere, and shake the nation with your protest against this satanic international conspiracy!

The Socialist Party's Appeal for 1908[†][101]

October 15, 1908

At a public meeting in New York City some months ago, the present presidential candidate of the Republic Party was asked this question: "What is a man to do who is out of work in a financial panic and is starving?"

This is an intensely human as well as a very practical question. It epitomizes the problem of the unemployed and places it in bold relief. It is not too much to say that the future welfare and progress of our country—aye, the fate of civilization itself—depends upon a correct solution of this problem. In view of the supreme importance of the question, it might naturally be expected that the Republican Party would offer some practical and well-defined method of dealing with it, and one might suppose that the party's standard-bearer would be in a position clearly to expound that method in making reply to his interrogator. But how pitifully inadequate was the answer! It is at least creditable to Mr. Taft's honesty that he frankly replied, "God knows!"

---

† Published as "The Socialist Party's Appeal" in *The Independent* [New York], vol. 65, whole no. 3124 (October 15, 1908), 875–80.

When Mr. Kern,[102] the vice-presidential candidate of the Democratic Party, was asked recently what his party proposed to do for the relief of the unemployed, he is reported to have answered, "Nothing directly, nothing socialistic. We hope that carrying out the general ideas in our platform will so restore confidence that industry will start up again. But that's about all. In fact, that's enough."

These answers are not cited for any partisan purpose, but because they serve admirably to illustrate the really essential difference between the Socialist Party and its most formidable political rivals. The Socialist Party does not refer this important problem to the Deity for solution. It recognizes the fact that it is of human creation and must be solved by human effort. It proposes to do something "directly," something "socialistic," for the relief of the unemployed. The Socialist Party recognizes the serious nature of the unemployed problem and aims to solve it in the only way it can be solved, namely, by removing its cause. As a means of temporary relief, applicable during the period of transition to a collective system of industry, the party proposes "immediate government relief for the unemployed workers by building schools, by reforesting of cut-over and waste lands, by reclamation of arid tracts and the building of canals, and by extending all other useful public works." Both from the standpoint of effectiveness and that of practicability, this program may be offered without comment in lieu of Mr. Taft's "God knows!" and Mr. Kern's "hope" of restored confidence.

As a matter of fact, it is an entire impossibility for either the Republican or the Democratic Party to offer any practicable solution for our industrial ills, because those ills are the inevitable and perfectly natural outgrowth of the wage system of industry, which system both parties are alike pledged to support and defend. That the economic policy of the Republican Party is impotent to stay the periodic recurrence of industrial and financial crises is proved by the existing depression, and as the party's platform utterance in relation to labor pledges it to a continuance of what is denominated "the same wise policy," there is certainly no hope of relief from that quarter. With regard to the Democratic Party, the country already has had sufficient experience with its methods of dealing with important economic problems to justify the suspicion that Mr. Kern's "hope" may prove somewhat elusive.

The Socialist Party of the United States is part of a great international movement which far overshadows any other movement recorded in history. Its basic idea is the complete and permanent emancipation of labor all over the world. To quote from a recent article by George Allan England:[103]

> First of all, the fact should be made quite clear that the Socialist Party is far and away the largest political unit not only of today but of any time. To the uninformed who conceive of socialists as a rather obscure and fantastic sect of utopians—of "dreamers"—the discovery must come as something of a shock that the world's socialist vote now stands between 8 million and 9 million, representing about 30 million adult socialists. This latter number includes, of course, women and disfranchised persons, who in the socialist concept of government, in the "state within a state" which socialism is building up, enjoy equal rights with present voters. There is something peculiarly disconcerting to the present governments of, by, and for plutocracy in those 30 million "dreamers," all so active in propaganda, all so terribly in earnest—in that ever widening acceptance of the visionary axiom that "without rights there shall be no duties; without duties, no rights.

In the second place, it should be definitely understood that the movement is already breaking into legislative bodies all over the civilized world, to an extent hardly realized by the casual critic. The United States is practically the only large country of modern type in which the party has no national representatives—a state of affairs, be it said in passing, which will soon be remedied.

* * *

Prophecy is dangerous, but 1908 should for many reasons hold in store a great surprise for the old party politicians. From now on there is "a new Richmond in the field."[104]

The Socialist Party is the political expression of what is known as the "class struggle." This struggle is an economic fact as old as history itself, but it is only within the past generation that it has become a thoroughly conscious and well-organized political fact. As long as this struggle was confined to its economic aspect, the ruling classes had nothing to fear, as, being in control of all the means and agencies of government, they were always able to use their power effectively to suppress uprisings either of chattel slaves, feudal serfs, or free-born and politically equal capitalist wage workers. But now that the struggle has definitely entered the political field, it assumes for the present ruling class a new and sinister aspect. With the whole power of the state—the army, the navy, the courts, the police—in possession of the working class by virtue of its victory at the polls, the death knell of capitalist private property and wage-slavery is sounded.

This does not mean, however, that the workers will wrest control of government from the capitalist class simply for the purpose of continuing the class struggle on a new plane, as has been the case in all previous political revolutions when one class has superseded another in the control of government. It does not mean that the workers and capitalists will merely change places, as many poorly informed persons undoubtedly still believe. It means the inauguration of an entirely new system of industry, in which the exploitation of man by man will have no place. It means the establishment of a new economic motive for production and distribution. Instead of profit being the ruling motive of industry, as at present, all production and distribution will be for use. As a consequence, the class struggle and economic class antagonisms as we now know them will entirely disappear.

Did the Socialist Party have no higher political ideal than the victory of one class over another, it would not be worthy of a moment's support from any right-thinking individual. It would, indeed, be impossible for the party to gain any considerable strength or prestige. It is the great moral worth of its ideals that attracts adherents to the socialist movement even from the ranks of the capitalist class, and holds them to their allegiance with an enthusiasm that suggests a close parallel with the early days of Christianity; and it is the mathematical certainty with which its conclusions are stated that enables the Socialist Party to expand and advance with irresistible force the goal it has in view, in spite of the appalling opposition it has had to encounter. It is this certainty, and the moral worth of its ideals, which moved Mommsen,[105] the venerable German historian, to say that "this is the only great party which has a claim to political respect."

The capitalist was originally a socially useful individual, but the evolution of our industrial system has rendered him a parasite, an entirely useless functionary that must be eliminated if civilization is to endure. It is a leading thought in modern philosophy that in its process of development each institution tends to cancel itself. Born out of social necessity, its progress is determined by repulsions and attractions arising in society, which produce effects tending to negate its original function. Now, that is what has happened to the capitalist. He is no longer useful. He is merely a clog to social progress and must be abolished, just as the feudal lord and chattel slaveholder have been abolished.

The capitalist was originally a manager who worked hard at his business and received what economists call the "wages of superintendence." So long as he occupied that position, the capitalist might be restrained and controlled in various ways, but he could not be got rid of. He performed real functions, and as society was not yet prepared to take those functions upon itself, it could not afford to discharge him. But now the capitalist proper has become absolutely useless. Finding it easier to combine with others of his class in a large undertaking, he has abdicated his position of overseer and has put in a salaried manager to act for him. This salaried manager now performs the only social function of the capitalist, while the capitalist himself has become a mere rent or interest receiver. The rent or interest he receives is paid for the use of a monopoly which not he, but a vast multitude of people created by their joint efforts.

This differentiation between manager and capitalist is a necessary part of the process of capitalistic evolution due to machine industry. As competition led to waste in production, so it also led to the cutting of profits among capitalists. To prevent this, the concentration of capital was necessary, by which the large capitalist could undersell his small rivals in the marketing of good produced by machinery and distributed by agencies initially too costly for any individual competitor to purchase or set on foot. For such massive capitals the contributions of several capitalists are necessary. Hence the joint stock company, the corporation, and finally the trust. Through the medium of such agencies, a person in the United States can own stock in an enterprise in Africa or South America which he has never visited and never intends to visit, and which, therefore, he cannot "superintend" in any way. He and the other stockholders put in a manager with injunctions to be economical. The manager's business is to earn the largest possible dividends for his employers. If he does not do so he is dismissed. To secure high dividends the manager will lower wages. If that is resisted there will probably be either a strike or a lockout. Cheap labor will be imported by the manager, and if the workers resist by intimidation or organizing boycotting, the forces of the state will be used against them, and in the end they must submit. The old personal relation between the workers and the employer is gone.

From the point of view of the corporation owners, the workers are simply an extension of the machine of profit production. The workers are not regarded as having human attributes. Their labor is trafficked in as a commodity, like iron and steel, and the only interest the capitalist retains in production is in his interest as an idle dividend receiver. Society can get along without the capitalist; it refuses longer to support him in idleness and luxury.

The process of industrial evolution that has rendered the capitalist a useless functionary has at the same time evolved an organization, cooperative in character, whereby industry may be carried on without friction for the benefit of the whole people instead of for the profit of the individual capitalist. The conduct of industry will be entrusted to men who are technically familiar with its processes, precisely as it is now entrusted to managers by the stockholders of a corporation; in short, the whole of industry will represent a giant corporation in which all citizens are stockholders, and the state will represent a board of directors acting for the whole people. Details of organization and performance may well be left to the experts to whose direction the matter will be given when the time comes. It is not the mission of the Socialist Party to speculate concerning the manner in which the workers will conduct their affairs when they have come into possession of their inheritance which the ages have prepared for them. Standards of right and justice under the new regime, however, may well be indicated.

"Without rights there shall be no duties; without duties no rights." What will be the practical interpretation of this socialist axiom? Obviously, social parasitism must cease; every man must be a producer, or perform some socially useful function, in order to procure title to any share in the product of the collective industry. The only citizenship held honorable will be economic citizenship, or comradeship in production and in the sharing of product.

The spectacle of strong men walking the streets idle and hungry, vainly begging for a chance to work for the pittance that will suffice to ward off starvation from themselves and their loved ones, will be no more. The cruelty of children of tender years being forced hungry to school in a great city like New York will disappear. No longer will there be a problem of the unemployed, and the capitalist will be elevated from his present condition of parasitism to that of a worker and producer of wealth. The class struggle must necessarily cease, for there will be no classes. Each individual will be his own economic master, and all will be servants of the collectivity. Human brotherhood, as taught by Christ 19 centuries ago, will for the first time begin to be realized.

The struggle for working class emancipation, which finds its expression through the Socialist Party, must continue, and will increase in intensity until either the ruling class completely subjugates the working class, or until the working class entirely absorbs the capitalist class. There is no middle ground possible, and it is this fact that makes ludicrous those sporadic reform movements typified by the Populist [People's] and Independence parties.

But the subjugation of the working class is out of the question. Intelligence has gone too far for that; it is the capitalist class that is doomed. Hence the only possible outcome of the present struggle is victory for the working class and the absorption by that class of all other classes.

When the present Socialist Party has accomplished its mission of uniting the workers of the world into a solid political phalanx, the end of capitalist domination is at hand, and the era of industrial peace so long wished for by philanthropists and seers will dawn upon the world.

Throwing Away Their Votes†

October 26, 1908

It is eminently fitting that workingmen, and especially organized workingmen, should examine their position in the existing wage system and consider remedies for the political and industrial ills that afflict them. This is particularly true at the present juncture when we are engaged in a political contest that will decide which party shall control the agencies of government for another term of four years.

A man's vote is an expression of his right to impress his will upon the machinery of government so as to make it operate in the manner he desires. His vote expresses his right to alter or repeal existing laws and to make new laws, or to inaugurate new policies or systems of government if he wishes to do so. Naturally men have no desire to throw away their votes. They want them to count as fully as possible in the accomplishment of the results they are seeking to attain.

ࠩ

It may be assumed without argument that workingmen vote to improve their condition. They seek to impress their will upon the machinery of government so as to make it operate for their benefit. In short, they seek by their votes to accomplish the best results for themselves. If it shall appear that with all their voting, workingmen have failed to improve their condition; that, on the contrary, their condition has actually grown worse; that they have been robbed of their constitutional guarantees to life, liberty, and the pursuit of happiness, both through the law and in defiance of it; that their economic condition today is virtually one of slavery, as irksome and infinitely more brutal than the chattel

† Published in *Chicago Daily Socialist,* vol. 2, no. 304 (October 26, 1908), 6.

slavery that has been abolished, then it must be evident that they have been throwing away their votes all these years.

The political spellbinder's stock of eloquent platitudes when fishing for the votes of workingmen have been marshaled around such meaningless phrases as "pauper labor," "protection to American labor," "the full dinner pail," "European conditions," "American standard of living," and others of like import, though fully as meaningless.

Workingmen have been told and will be told again in the impending campaign by Republican and Democratic orators that the very life of our glorious republic depends upon maintaining "our present high American standard of living." They have been taught that this alone is the real foundation of all our greatness and glory as a nation; that this it is which enables us to stand forth as the one successful experiment in nation building in the history of the world; that this it is which has truly made America the land of the free and the home of the brave; and they have been, and will again be, implored, for God's sake and the sake of their wives and children; for the sake of their homes, their families, and their glorious country; for the benefit of posterity and their common humanity, by the memory of Washington, Jefferson, Jackson, and all the other saints in our political pantheon, to walk up to the polls and save this country from degradation by casting the ballot of a free and enlightened American citizenship for the candidates of the Republican or Democratic parties, both of which have the interests of the dear workingmen at heart and would never consent to have them reduced to the "pauper level of European conditions." Above all, they have been warned, as they will be again, not to "throw away their votes" by giving them to the Socialist Party.

ᔕ

Should we look for results to correspond with the professions of the old party politicians, we might naturally expect to find workingmen generally enjoying an exceptionally high standard of living. Indeed, we might look for them all to be in affluent circumstances. But it is not so. On the contrary, the American standard of living has been steadily lowered, until it now practically conforms to European conditions.

During more than a generation past, there has not been a legislative measure advocated or enacted that has not been supported by the plea of benefit to the workingmen. Distinctly and repeatedly have American workingmen been told that the main purpose of all legislation was to uphold their wages and improve their condition—all for the good of the country, of course—and after all this legislation, founded upon burning anxiety for the welfare of the free and independent American wage earners, what are the results?

While money wages in a few selected trades have increased to some extent, actual wages in all trades and callings, as compared with the cost of living, have enormously declined. By the indisputable evidence of official reports from capitalist sources themselves, workingmen are now receiving a far smaller portion of the product of their labor than ever before. Millions of them are on the verge of want even when employed, and when deprived of work from any cause are at once thrown into pauperism and slow starvation. By the enactment of laws and the judicial interpretation of laws already enacted, their most sacred constitutional rights have been trampled upon and ignored. Their unions have been declared criminal conspiracies, and a law enacted to protect them from discharge and blacklist by their employers, simply because of their membership in a union of their craft, has been declared unconstitutional by the highest court of the land.

They have been forbidden by law to boycott unfair employers of labor in the effort to maintain union conditions of employment, and have even been denied the right to strike except in a manner that will work no inconvenience or loss to the business of their employers; and in addition to the criminal penalties for disobedience to this mandate, they are subject to threefold damages for any injury to the business of their employers which may be sustained by reason of a strike or boycott. In short, workingmen have been deprived of every vestige of protection afforded them by their unions, and are turned over, bound hand and foot, to the tender mercies of the most heartless oligarchy of wealth that ever existed in any age of the world.

ශ

In this country men are theoretically equal. John Smith and John Rockefeller are assumed to have precisely equal rights and powers in the government. It is the cant of capitalism that we have no classes, and John Smith has been urged to support, and has supported, the same political party as John Rockefeller, on the fallacious assumption that the interests of labor and capital are identical. Smith is not to be blamed for this, as, sad to relate, the leaders of his union, whom he has looked to for advice and instruction in economic matters, have vied with the capitalist spellbinders in dinning this untruth into his ears, and have pictured to him in somber colors the dire results that would follow the introduction of politics in his union. Even now these same leaders, although forced by the inexorable logic of events to abandon their cry of "no politics in the unions," are endeavoring to steer the votes of workingmen into the Democratic Party, which is equally responsible with the Republican Party for the deplorable conditions of the unions. They still insist that the interests of labor and capital are identical, and seek to prevent workingmen from voting for the only party which accurately represents their class interests on the plea that such action would be equivalent to throwing away their votes!

Workingmen necessarily throw away their votes when they cast them for any capitalist party, as the relation between capitalist and laborer is one of thorough antagonism, and as long as a capitalist party, no matter by what name it is called, remains in control of the government, the laws will favor capitalism and the workers will be robbed. It is only by placing themselves in control of government, through a political party representing their own class interests as opposed to capitalism, that workingmen will obtain their rights, and they should remember that no vote to this end is a vote thrown away.

Every vote cast for the Socialist Party increases the strength of labor's protest and adds to the fear of capitalism. A united labor vote demanding justice for workingmen is the one thing that capitalism dreads, and every effort will be made to prevent voters from supporting the Socialist Party, as capitalism truly recognizes that party is the only one which is uncompromisingly opposed to its rule. It is only by demonstrating its power that labor can command respect, and even from the standpoint of palliative legislation workingmen should unhesitatingly support the Socialist Party.

As the strength of socialism increases and is registered through the party vote, the economic condition of workingmen is improved by ameliorative legislation forced from capitalism through fear. This is true of all countries where socialism has become an organized political force, and it will be true here.

ഗ

Remember that the Socialist Party proposes not to reform the capitalist system, but to abolish it. By the magic of private property the capitalist has acquired ownership of the tools and materials of wealth production. He has obtained possession of the instruments which the laborer must use in order to obtain the means of life. By reason of this ownership, the capitalist draws to himself wholly, without labor and by the mere right of ownership as it is legally recognized, the whole product of the workingman's industry, save barely enough to support his existence, which is returned to him in the name of wages.

Under this system the whole product of industry belongs to the capitalist; all that the laborer can claim are his wages, which are determined by laws of competition over which he has no control, and which, according to economic statement and the demonstration of actual facts, always tend to the minimum that will support existence at the worker's accustomed standard of living.

Under capitalism the worker builds a palace and lives in a hovel; weaves the finest fabrics and clothes himself in shoddy or in rags; makes fine shoes and wears the coarsest brogans; produces elegant silk hats and wears a fustian cap; builds luxurious carriages and breeds fine horses to draw them and then walks; extracts fuel from the earth, where a beneficent creator has placed it for the use of all his children, and freezes for the lack of it; in short, he produces everything and enjoys nothing. The entire produce of his ingenuity and his industry flows into the possession of the capitalist class as the price of permission to labor for a bare existence.

ᔓ

In former days the slave was compelled to labor for the benefit of others by virtue of brute force exerted by the strong arm of his master, reinforced by law. In these days the slave is called a free man and is compelled to labor for the benefit of others by virtue of his master's law-enforced ownership of the tools of production and his own necessity to live.

Give to one man the right to own and control the means of another's existence and he is as truly that other's master as though he stood over him with whip and gun and hunted him with bloodhounds if he attempted to escape, although the other may be called as free as his master. It is the result of the exercise of the power of man over man that constitutes the essence of slavery, not the manner in which the power may be exercised, and the laborer of today is as truly a slave as was his prototype in ancient and feudal times.

Capitalism is the latest, best, and most perfected form of mastership. The capitalist has merely stepped into the shoes of the ancient slaveholder and feudal baron.

This is the condition that is frankly recognized by the Socialist Party, and which it proposes to correct by abolishing the competitive wage system and placing the worker in possession of the entire product of his industry through the collective ownership and operation of the means and instruments of production. Actually, as well as theoretically, it will give John Smith and John Rockefeller precisely equal rights and powers in the government.

A vote for socialism is never thrown away.

Socialist Ideals†

November 1908

While socialism is a political movement with an industrial purpose, and, because it pays chief attention to the bread-and-butter problem, has been called materialistic, it is really the most idealistic movement of the centuries. So idealistic is it in its aims that, while having no specific religious tendency or purpose, it partakes somewhat of the nature of a religious movement and awakens something of a religious enthusiasm among its adherents.

Of course there are misconceptions of socialism. These neither agitate nor surprise the socialist, because they are to be expected. Without referring to any of them categorically, believe me when I say that socialism is not so much a cut-and-dried program as it is a method by which industry is to be operated. It does not say what it will do or what you shall do, but only that the people, the workers and producers, shall be master of themselves and do with industry and the proceeds of their toil what they may think best. It is a continuation of the old fight against monarchy and in favor of democracy, which was begun in 1776 and which has since been growing into an enlarged world-demand.

Then the ideal was for the overthrow of the political autocracy that prevailed and the establishment of political democracy in its stead. After our forefathers won in that revolution of blood, the ideal inspired France to a glorious but unintelligent struggle for popular rule, and it has been growing and spreading ever since, until now it is only here and there, in isolated places, that political autocracy prevails; for even though England may have a king and Germany an emperor, they both have constitutions and parliaments elected by the people. Democracy has been so successful that it is safe to say that the people will never permit a return to absolute kingly rule.

Socialism is merely an extension of the ideal of democracy into the economic field. At present, industry is ruled by the owners of the machines of production and distribution, who have literally the power of life and death over the subjects. There are now, in round numbers, 17.5 million people in America who are wage workers and dependents on others for means of life. There are at least 30 million more who are dependents on the wage workers for a livelihood.

† Published in *The Arena,* vol. 40, whole no. 227 (November 1908), 432–4.

But these are not the only people who are affected by the monarchy that prevails in industry. In many lines the prices of necessary articles of consumption are fixed arbitrarily, and in all cases a tribute of profit is exacted on all things bought and all things sold.

Through these means the entire people are constrained and made helpless before the system. Under political absolutism the emperor did not kill unless there was at least the semblance of crime, but under industrial absolutism the masters of the machine may cut off the means of life at their will and without charge or trial, so that the innocent, the helpless, are left without means whereby they may live. Socialism proposes to put industry in control of the people so that they may no longer be dependents on others for a job, so that they may be freed from the tribute of profit, and so that they may manage industry in their own way, as seems best to them.

It is evident that our forefathers who established political democracy in America could not have known all the uses to which democracy would be put through the years; they only believed that the people would fare better if they were permitted to manage the government for themselves than if a few private individuals should manage it for private good, and on these principles were ready to risk the future. Few there are today who will deny that their judgement was sound. Today the socialist does not pretend to forecast what measures the people will take under popular rule of industry. He only believes in the people, that it will be better and safer for them to manage industry in their interest, than it will be to longer permit the owners of the machine to dominate industry in their private interest.

It is not entirely a new and untried principle, but only an extension of the principle for which our forefathers struggled in 1776. We do not need, like them, to resort to arms, but may use the democracy they bestowed on us as a means for obtaining further democracy; in the sense that political democracy is to be used as a means for the obtaining of industrial democracy is socialism a political movement, and in no other sense. It will necessarily differ largely from political democracy in its application, and it is believed, will be the completion of the system begun so long ago that will make it automatic and simple in operation and successful in the solution of the problems that have hitherto baffled the ages. We know not what the people will do when they control the means by which they make their living, but we believe they will use them in their own interest and with a reasonable degree of intelligence. If they do, they can accomplish these results:

They can make it so no one who wants to do productive labor can be deprived of the opportunity of doing it, at any time.

They can make it possible to banish want from the face of the earth.

They can make it possible for every family to have a home and to be immune from the fear of want for themselves and their children.

They can make it possible for every child to have a good education, to be able to see the world, and to make its way without the least danger of losing out economically.

They can make it possible for every man to marry and support a family in comfort and security.

They can make it possible for every woman to be free economically, so that she may get along whether she marries or not.

These are part of the ideals that the socialist cherishes. They are not mere visions, but are things that may be wrought into concrete form, whenever men shall have free access to the means with which things are produced and distributed. They have been impossible of attainment in the past, only because the earth and its fullness was held from the people by either political or industrial masters. In brief, socialism holds as its great ideal that freedom of action which shall make the making of a living a simple, easy thing, possible to all; and beyond this lies the greater hope of being able to live, to really live.

Hitherto we have been engaged in a struggle for bread. We have been so busy seeking to make a living that we have not been able to make a life. So there have been no real men and no noble women in the world, in the high sense which they may be when men and women are free. If socialism meant the solution of the bread-and-butter problem alone, then it would be the most wonderful idea ever given to earth, for with all our philosophy and with all our machinery we have not yet accomplished this. If it meant the solution of the bread-and-butter problem only, even then it would surpass all other movements the world has seen, because it would mean an end of the slum and the sweatshop, of child slavery and white slavery, of the worry that kills and the anxiety that ages and destroys both temper and joy.

But it will mean infinitely more than this. When the bread-and-butter problem is settled and all men and women and children, the world around, are rendered secure from dread of war and fear of want, then the mind and soul will be free to develop as they never were before. We shall have a literature and an art such as the troubled heart and brain of man never before conceived. We shall have beautiful houses and happy homes such as want could never foster or drudgery secure. We shall have beautiful thoughts and sentiments, and a divinity in religion, such as man weighted down by the machine could never have imagined.

Think the best you can of good and beauty now, and it is only a rude and grotesque conception of that which will be possible when man is really free by virtue of being master of his own life and free from the mastery of the devils of want and worry.

Religion in its primaries is a great conception, a masterful longing, a transfiguring ideal. To Israel emerging from Egypt it took the form of aspiration for a land flowing with milk and honey, where every man might sit under his own vine and fig tree. This was as materialistic a conception as that which actuates the socialist. But beyond that was the individual desire to make of his own life the best and happiest thing he possibly could. The socialist wants the same thing. His vision of a free world is auxiliary to his ideal of making his own life better and sweeter. And when freedom comes, when the vision enlarges because of the horizon lifting with the higher plane man takes, then the ideal will expand beyond what is beheld now, until it reaches a grandeur such as eye hath not seen, nor ear heard, nor it hath entered into the heart of man to conceive.[106]

We Make Our Appeal to the Working Class: Speech at Terre Haute Coliseum [excerpt][†]

November 2, 1908[107]

The Socialist Party is the political expression of the socialist movement, and the historic mission of the socialist movement is the emancipation of the working class from wage-slavery. The capitalist system in which we live has about run its historic course, fulfilled its mission; and upon every hand we behold the unerring signs of change. The capitalists can no longer manage industry in the

† Published as "Debs Stirs Home Folk" in *Terre Haute Star,* vol. 58, no. 308 (November 3, 1908), 10.

present system. They can no longer employ the working class. This system has again broken down. Another period of industrial depression has set in. It has just begun to write its record of bankruptcy and failure, of idleness and distress, of despair and death.

The last panic, so-called, came in 1893. Industry was paralyzed, and hundreds of thousands of workingmen were thrown out of employment. The Republican Party in its platform, adopted in the campaign of 1896, charged the panic of 1893 upon the Democratic Party. They declared that the panic was due to the incompetency, the dishonesty, and unfitness of the Democratic Party to rule. Then, by their own logic, the Republican Party is convicted of responsibility for the panic of 1908.

In the campaign of 1900 the slogan of the Republican Party, coined by Mark Hanna, was "Let well enough alone." In 1904 the slogan was "Stand pat." In 1908 it is "God knows."

ꕥ

We must at least give Mr. Taft, the Republican candidate, credit for perfect candor. Millions of you are out of work; 20 percent of the American people are without money; and when they turn to Mr. Taft and ask what they are to do, he conveniently and complacently refers them to Jehovah. But he is perfectly willing to accept their votes by proxy. Whatever else there may be the matter with Mr. Taft, there is certainly nothing the matter with his nerve.

In the light of the experience of the working class during the last 10 years, why should they any longer cast their votes for either the Democratic or Republican Party? They are both capitalist parties; their principles are essentially the same. They are both committed to the existing social order. The Republican Party is in favor of the system as it is. The Democratic Party is in favor of the same system as it was.

The Republican Party is dominated by the big capitalists, who are relatively few in number. The Democratic Party is dominated by a large number of small capitalists. But they are all capitalists. As workingmen it does not matter to you in the least if you are exploited of what you produce by a single big capitalist or by a hundred small ones. What does it matter if you are swallowed by an alligator or devoured by a swarm of mosquitoes?

The fact is, none of you have a job which you can call your own. The Republican Party frankly tells you that nothing can be done for you. The Democratic Party promises to guarantee you only your bank deposits. How many of you workingmen are lying awake at night worrying over your bank deposits?

You are looking for a master; looking for a job. The politicians call you sovereign citizens, but think of a sovereign looking for a job. The Socialist Party is the only party that will guarantee you a job.

ᔓ

Both the old parties get their campaign funds from the same source. Mr. Upham[108] and Mr. Peabody[109] own the great coal trust of Chicago, which freezes people to death in the winter by charging extortionate prices for coal. Mr. Upham is a Republican, and Mr. Peabody is a Democrat. Mr. Upham is collecting campaign funds for Mr. Taft, and Mr. Peabody is collecting campaign funds for Mr. Bryan. Both campaign funds come from the same source; both are used for the same purpose—to keep the working class in ignorance.

It is about this season of the year when the politician comes before you, and tells you how proud he is to stand in your presence. He tells you how intelligent you are; and you applaud him as if it were true. He calls you the horny-handed sons of toil. What he thinks is that you are the horny-headed sons of toil. He tells you that the beads of sweat that glisten on your manly brows are more precious to him than the jewels that flash in the diadem of a queen. But he doesn't decorate himself with that kind of jewelry. That is one of the things of which you workingmen have a complete monopoly. He insults your intelligence by flattering your ignorance. He tells you you are intelligent to keep you ignorant. The Socialist tells you you are ignorant in order that you may become intelligent.

We are making our appeal to the working class. We are not seeking the votes of the capitalists. We know that we should be foolish if we did. They know enough to know how to vote. And that is the reason they are in power. They are class conscious, and it is because the working people are not class conscious that they are in subjection.

ᔓ

It has been charged that the workingmen have no brains, and it is painful to have to admit that there is some truth in the indictment. If they have brains, then they have been making very poor use of them. The workingman, however, pays strict attention to the cultivation of his hands. In this system he is no longer a man. He is a hand, and in thousands of cases he has been reduced to a handout. When the capitalist wants you, he advertises for a hand; he doesn't want heads. He uses his own head and your hands. If you did not put a boycott upon your brains, you would not have to deform your hands in order to make a wretched living. Many of you ought to be ashamed to look your hands in the face.

There are over 30 million workers in this country who have no tools of their own with which to work. Man is a tool-using animal. And if he cannot get access to the tools of production, he must starve. In this system the capitalist owns the tools, although he has nothing to do with the work of production. And the man who owns your tools, who owns your job, owns you. That is what you vote for every time you vote the Democratic and Republican ticket. If this arrangement suits you, then I think that by strict economy the capitalists will manage to get along.

ဢ

There are two distinct economic classes; and classes, if they are intelligent, give expression to their economic interests through political parties. A workingman in one of the old political parties is as much out of place as John D. Rockefeller in the Socialist Party. If you are a Republican it is probably because your father was. But in your father's time the Republican Party had a mission. It has now outlived its usefulness and is the property of the plutocracy. Perhaps you say that now you are a Democrat. That will be because your grandfather was. But everything has changed since your grandfather's day, except his grandson. The Democratic Party has degenerated considerably since the days of Jefferson and Jackson down to Roger Sullivan,[110] Charles Murphy,[111] Bath House John,[112] and Hinky Dink.[113]

Whatever notoriety Mr. Taft has achieved has been as the judge who let loose the judicial lightening which paralyzed the trade unions. He put labor leaders in jail; and yet he has the audacity to ask workingmen for their votes. He is pledged to carry out the policies of Mr. Roosevelt, although nobody has ever yet been able to find out what those polices are. Wall Street is supposed to be deadly opposed to Mr. Roosevelt, but Mr. Taft, who is the nominee of Mr. Roosevelt, is quite acceptable to Wall Street. The people of this country are beginning to find Mr. Roosevelt out. They know now that while Mr. Roosevelt was giving forth daily homilies on purity in politics, he was himself elected to the presidency by the biggest debauching fund in the history of this country. The Socialist campaign has put the old parties in such a fright, socialist sentiment has spread in such an astounding manner, that they will have to bestir themselves, or the workers will in the very near future take the government into their own hands. The old parties are full of domestic trouble at the present moment. Each charges the other with being corrupt to the core. And they are both right.

ဢ

As for Mr. Bryan, he is one of the most pathetic figures in the world today. Once a wholehearted and virile advocate of justice, he now finds himself affiliated with all the corruption that distinguishes politics. He is suffering just what any man must suffer who compromises with capitalism. He appears to be on the brink of a mental and physical breakdown, and his plight is pitiable.

Mr. Bryan posed as the champion of labor. When the officials of the Western Federation of Miners were kidnapped, and were in danger of judicial lynching, Mr. Bryan had the supreme moment of his lifetime to demonstrate his loyalty to the working class. He was appealed to on behalf of these men, but never a word passed his lips. He was as silent as the Sphinx. He knew that if he said anything in favor of Haywood, Moyer, and Pettibone, he would sacrifice the support of the Mine Owners' Association, without whose contribution his chance of becoming president would vanish forever. But after these men had been acquitted, and stood before the world without a blemish on their character, Mr. Bryan spoke for the first time. He said that he had known all the time they were innocent. Is that the way to show friendship for the working class?

ɕɔ

Four years ago Mr. Bryan denounced Alton B. Parker as a tool of Wall Street. And when Parker was nominated for president, Mr. Bryan used all the powers of his matchless eloquence to get this tool of Wall Street elected. Four years ago Mr. Bryan said that Roger Sullivan, the notorious corporation corruptionist of Illinois, had secured his election as a delegate to the convention by methods that would disgrace a train robber. A few weeks ago that train robber was the honored guest of Mr. Bryan at Fairview.[114] Another honored guest recently at the home of Mr. Bryan was Charles Murphy, the prophet of Tammany. Tammany, the most corrupt political organization on this continent. Tammany, which levies tribute upon the tenderloin. Tammany, which extorts from fallen women the proceeds of their shame. Bryan was himself photographed hand in hand with Murphy. I would not mind being president of the United States, but, upon my word, I would not have the presidency at that price.

To those who think that this time they will vote the Democratic ticket in the hope that something will be done for labor, I need only point to the "Solid South," where the Democratic Party has ruled for a century, and where the conditions of labor are more degrading than in any other country; where the Democratic governor of Alabama has smashed upon the mine workers' union, ripped up the tents of the starving strikers, and dispersed their wives and families by training Gatling guns upon them.

I cannot do anything for you. There is nothing you cannot do for yourself. At present you build all the palaces and live in rented hovels. You build all the automobiles, and walk. Except on election day, when you ride to the polls to vote, you walk the other 364 days of the year. You must become class conscious. The Republican Party swept into power upon the issue of chattel slavery. The Socialist Party is going to sweep into power upon the issue of wage-slavery.

The End of a Magnificent Campaign†

November 3, 1908

Terre Haute, Indiana, November 3, 1908

The campaign is ended and my very first thought is of the kindness shown me and the loyal support given me in every part of the country. While at times the exactions were trying, I was sustained every hour by the loving care and unflagging support of comrades. To me this was the most beautiful and satisfying feature of the campaign. It expressed the true spirit of socialist comradeship, which is the making of our movement and which will sustain it through every ordeal till it is finally triumphant.

The one incident we all deeply regretted was the illness of Comrade Ben Hanford.[115] With all his heart he yearned to be where he always has been, in the thick of battle, but he had given himself too freely all his life, utterly forgetful of self, until at last his physical powers succumbed and he was compelled to see others on the firing line while he was reserved for less strenuous service that he might have some chance for physical recuperation. His very illness bears testimony to his many years of service in the past when it required courage and sacrifice to be a socialist, and all of us join most fervently in the hope that he may recuperate his impaired powers and again take his wonted place in the activities of the movement.

Truly this has been a magnificent campaign for the Socialist Party. Our meetings from coast to coast have been the marvel of all, and such enthusiasm has never been displayed in any political campaign.

---

† Published as "To Our Comrades" in *New York Call,* vol. 1, no. 136 (November 4, 1908), 6.

The hundreds of young, forceful, and effective orators, both men and women, who have taken part in this battle have been developed mainly since the last national contest, and their magnificent work contributed tremendously to the success of the campaign. The socialist papers all did their best and are entitled to the largest measure of credit. Through our papers we were able to checkmate every attempt on the part of the capitalist press to deceive the workers, and no such attempts were made along that line as were made in previous campaigns.

The national office in all its departments was most efficiently organized, and under its supervision the most effective work was done in promoting a uniform and vigorous educational propaganda throughout the country.

As for the Red Special, I prefer that its work shall speak for itself. I only wish to say that I feel deeply indebted to each and every member of it for the faithful service and personal devotion of which I was the recipient from the first to the last hour of its journey. Each member of the crew discharged his duty faithfully and to each and all I owe a debt of personal gratitude I shall never be able to repay.

The Red Special Band was an invaluable accessory of the Red Special tour and a decided factor in its success. At many points it was just what was needed to kindle enthusiasm and round out the meeting and give it the power needed to stir the crowd into action.

If it were possible to keep a Red Special moving constantly, it would hasten by many months the development of the movement and the overthrow of capitalist misrule. Since this cannot be at present, perhaps steps might be taken to have a socialist car built and kept moving over the country the year around, making its stop at each point long enough to thoroughly stir up the community and sow the seeds of socialist though and activity.

At this time I have no idea of what our vote is, but I have no doubt it will be equal to all reasonable expectations. The country knew this year for the first time that the Socialist Party was a factor to be reckoned with in the campaign. We have every reason to congratulate ourselves upon the success of the campaign and to face the future with renewed assurance that the day of victory is drawing near.

Comrades, one and all everywhere, again I thank you and salute you!

You have fought a magnificent battle and now you are to prepare without loss of time for the next. Let the campaign of 1912 be opened all along the lien. There is no reason why it should halt. The capitalist enemy may now for a brief time riot in its spoils, but for us the struggle must be continuous until that enemy is driven from the field and a triumphant working class proclaims the socialist commonwealth.

Yours for the next battle,
Eugene V. Debs

Big Interests Are the Power That Rules: Letter to the Editor of the *Terre Haute Star*†

circa November 30, 1908

Editor, *Star,* Terre Haute:—

In your editorial on "Aspects of Popular Government" in yesterday's issue, which I read with much interest, the following paragraph appealed for comment:

> In the recent election two champions of the square deal were beaten—Roosevelt and Beveridge. They were marked for slaughter by Big Business and the people stood idly by in indifference or in hostility to their champions. In New York the alliance between Wall Street and Tammany Hall was obvious. In Indiana the desires of Big Business were executed by the brewery trust.

It all depends, Mr. Editor, on what is meant by "the square deal." In the campaign of 1904 Big Interests contributed about $6 million to the Roosevelt campaign fund, solicited, in part, by Mr. Roosevelt himself, while the Pennsylvania Railroad system alone furnished him with more than $100,000 worth of palatial free transportation.

In the late election Mr. Roosevelt ventured to make the charge you now repeat, namely, that "in New York the alliance between Wall Street and Tammany Hall was obvious." Immediately following this charge, Judge Alton B. Parker, Democratic candidate for president in 1904, made a speech at Plattsburg, New

---

† Published in *Terre Haute Star,* unspecified date. Reprinted as "Debs Answers the *Terre Haute Star*" in *Chicago Daily Socialist,* vol. 5, no. 32 (December 2, 1908), 6.

York, in which he said the alliance charged by Mr. Roosevelt was really between the Republican Party and Wall Street. He then produced a circular issued by the Republican leaders appealing to Big Interests for funds and proceeded to read the names of the contributors to Mr. Roosevelt's New York campaign fund, among which were Cornelius Vanderbilt, Ogden Mills,[116] Cornelius Bliss, and other representatives of Big Interests, owners of corporations, and directors of trusts and other financial institutions.

Judge Parker succeeded in showing that at least half the Big Interests represented in Wall Street were financing Mr. Roosevelt's Republican campaign, admitting candidly that the other half were financing Tammany and the Democratic campaign.

And still Mr. Roosevelt stands for the square deal!

When the Mine and Smelter Trust kidnapped three labor leaders and attempted to hang them, and they appealed to the Supreme Court, Mr. Roosevelt, then president, invited the members of that tribunal to the White House and read to them a letter he had written in which he denounced the said labor leaders as "undesirable citizens." The Supreme Court ignored their constitutional rights, denied their appeal, and turned them over to the executioner of Big Interests.

All the Big Interests in the land applauded this exhibition of the square deal. But a little later when the federal court, which Mr. Roosevelt had always maintained must be treated as an almost sacred and infallible institution, decided against him in his suit growing out of the Panama Canal scandal, he denounced Judge Anderson[117] of the federal bench at Indianapolis, according to Harry New,[118] as "a damned jackass and crook."

All of which simply shows that the square deal is entirely a matter of point of view. The wolf devouring a lamb undoubtedly stands for the square deal—from his point of view.

The kind of a square deal Mr. Roosevelt and Mr. Beveridge[119] stand for is not the kind that will be of any good to the common people. One of Senator Beveridge's staunchest supporters in the late campaign was David M. Parry, millionaire manufacturer, ex-president of the Manufacturer's Association, and one of the bitterest and most implacable enemies of organized labor in the United States.

Mr. Parry, too, is a vaunted champion of the square deal, and yet he would, if he had the power, destroy every labor union and reduce the working class to a state of unresisting vassalage.

In Senator Beveridge Mr. Parry clearly sees a true champion of the square deal.

If the brewery interests financed Kern and the Democratic Party in Indiana, it is quite as certain that the commercial and manufacturing interests financed Beveridge and the Republican Party.

They are alike, Mr. Editor—only more so.

The Republican and Democratic parties are financed from the same source and maintained for the same purpose, and that is to serve Big Interests, and if the Democratic Party secures complete control of Congress, it will be just as subservient to Big Interests as the Republican Party has been under the administrations of Presidents Roosevelt and Taft.

Here in Terre Haute, Big Interests rule with autocratic sway, and this is all the same whether the Republicans or the Democrats have a majority in council. The power that rules is the power that owns, and this is and will be Big Interests until triumphant socialism dispossesses Big Interests and supplants the present economic despotism with an industrial and social democracy.

More and more of the American people, opening their eyes to the real situation confronting them, and looking first over the record of the Republican Party and then that of the Democratic Party, exclaim: "A plague on both your houses," and turn toward the rising revolutionary movement that is to usher in the era of the square deal for all mankind.

Eugene V. Debs

Notes

1. The National Executive Committee of the Socialist Labor Party met for its semi-annual meeting on January 5–7, 1908 at party headquarters in New York City. It passed a resolution on the second day in which it acknowledged the 1904 and 1907 resolutions of the Second International urging its adherents to unite as a single party in each country, and it elected a unity committee of seven members for this purpose. These were to meet a like number of delegates of the rival Socialist Party of America in March "in order to consider whether unity of the two parties of socialism in America is possible, and on what special basis." See "Resolution on Unity Question," *Weekly People,* January 11, 1908, 6. This Socialist Labor Party proposal was received in Chicago by National Secretary Mahlon Barnes and passed on to the governing National Committee of the Socialist Party of America for decision through the weekly bulletin. Debs pointedly stood aloof from daily party politics and thus had no realistic opportunity to steer this debate. Instead, the Socialist Labor Party's proposal drew an antagonistic comment and a hostile motion from Victor Berger of Milwaukee, an arch-foe of labor party editor Daniel DeLeon and his organization. Berger's counterproposal invited members of the SLP to "join our party individually or in sections, and make their applications to our respective locals," upon the pledge "to accept our platform and our tactics." Berger's proposal, effectively a call for the SLP's total surrender, passed by a margin of 36 to 20, with 8 abstentions, effectively killing the short-lived 1908 unification effort. See Motion No. 11, *Socialist Party Official Bulletin,* February 1908, 3.
2. No such article seems to have been published, nor did Debs take the logical step which might have actually yielded practical results, personally lobbying the 64 members of the National Committee of the Socialist Party of America.
3. Joseph G. Cannon (1836–1926), a Republican from Illinois, served 46 years in the US House of Representatives, including a stint of nearly eight years as speaker. As speaker, Cannon exerted a powerful influence, controlling the fate and shape of all bills brought to the floor. In 1906, Cannon was targeted for defeat by the American Federation of Labor, which deeply resented his stymying an eight-hour bill, anti-injunction legislation, and legislation providing for employer liability in industrial accidents.
4. Charles E. Littlefield (1851–1915) was a Republican congressional representative from Maine. In the summer of 1906 Samuel Gompers became actively involved in the effort to defeat Littlefield in a September Maine election due to Littlefield's vocal opposition to anti-injunction legislation. Gompers made a dozen speeches in Littlefield's district for his Democratic opponent during the campaign in what was effectively a test of American Federation of Labor strength in breaking Republican stonewalling of pro-labor legislation. Although his plurality was reduced in the 1906 vote, Littlefield was nevertheless reelected.
5. Fred D. Warren, editor of the *Appeal to Reason,* was indicted by a grand jury early in May 1907, accused of misuse of the US mail. Warren was specifically charged with having violated section 498 of postal regulations, forbidding the mailing of "scurrilous or defamatory matter" on the outside of an envelope by printing offers

of a $1,000 reward for anyone who would kidnap ex-governor William S. Taylor (1853–1928) of Kentucky, a Republican, and return him to that state for trial as an alleged accessory in the assassination of his Democratic rival in the contested election of 1899, William J. Goebel (1856–1900). Taylor escaped prosecution by fleeing to Indiana, which refused to extradite him. He was pardoned by the Republican governor of Kentucky in 1909.

6. The Penrose bill, introduced by Republican Senator Boies Penrose (1860–1921) of Pennsylvania, proposed that "when any issue of any periodical has been declared non-mailable by the post office department the periodical may be excluded from second-class mail privileges at the discretion of the postmaster general." Although clearly designed as a tool to eviscerate the rapidly growing *Appeal to Reason,* newspapers of all political stripes raised their voices in objection to the "tyrannical" power of censorship which would be thereby assigned to a single unelected bureaucrat, and the measure was defeated. The same principle of one-man censorship based upon "unmailability" triggering the withholding of subsidized postage rates would be later used to decimate the anti-militarist radical press during the period of American participation in World War I.
7. The *Chicago Socialist,* launched as the *Workers' Call* in 1899, moved to a daily frequency in June 1906, thereby becoming the first daily newspaper in the United States affiliated with the Socialist Party of America. It was terminated in 1912 for financial reasons. The paper was initially edited by A. M. Simons (1870–1950).
8. *The New York Worker,* launched in 1899 by the anti-DeLeon faction of the Socialist Labor Party as a dissident version of *The People,* evolved into the daily *New York Call* in May 1908. Making used of local deliveries, it managed to survive World War I despite harassment of the post office department. Briefly changing its name to the *New York Leader* in 1923, the paper expired soon afterward. It was succeeded by another publication, known as *The New Leader.*
9. Fort Scott is the county seat of Bourbon County, Kansas, located directly north of Crawford County, the seat of which is Girard.
10. Labor conflict with Buck Stove and Range Company began in August 1906 with a strike of unionized workers against the firm in a battle for retention of a nine-hour day. The company was placed on the American Federation of Labor's "unfair" list and its name published in *The American Federationist,* which sent the company to court in August 1907 for an injunction against such a listing. The case made its way to the Supreme Court in 1911 as *Gompers v. Buck's Stove and Range Co.* The court rejected the American Federation of Labor's argument of protection under the first amendment to the United States Constitution but overturned jail terms imposed on Gompers and other federation leaders by a lower court on the basis that they had imposed sentences for criminal contempt in a civil suit and failed to allow for protection of the accused against self-incrimination. As the reversal was made without prejudice, a second contempt trial was held in 1912, which again found Gompers, Mitchell, and Morrison guilty of contempt, but this again appealed to the Supreme Court and was overturned in 1914 on the basis that the new proceedings

had not been begun within the three-year statute of limitations for such cases.

11. The official organ of the American Federation of Labor was the monthly magazine *The American Federationist,* with Samuel Gompers listed as the nominal editor of the publication.
12. Assertion without proof.
13. Reference is to the Pullman strike of 1894. See Eugene V. Debs, *Selected Works: Volume 2: The Rise and Fall of the American Railroad Union, 1892–1896* (Chicago: Haymarket Books, 2019), *passim.*
14. There is no indication that Debs delivered a single public speech during the five and a half month interval between a November 12, 1907 lecture on "Emancipation" at Union Hall in Girard, Kansas, and the writing of this reply to a Ben Hanford letter of May 2, 1908. For the text of Hanford's earlier communication as well as his May 6 reply to this missive, see Constantine (ed.), *Letters of Eugene V. Debs: Volume 1, 1874–1912,* 263–4 and 266–7.
15. Stedman, attuned to the fact that Debs was still on the mend from throat surgery and did not desire the 1908 nomination for president, had requested that Debs appear at the Chicago convention to dissuade delegates from making the nomination. He read this telegram into the record as part of his speech nominating A. M. Simons as the Socialist Party's 1908 presidential nominee.
16. Note that Debs's previous explanation for his non-attendance of the 1908 convention, "sickness in the family," has been forgotten.
17. Frederick Heath, editor of Victor L. Berger's *Social Democratic Herald,* was the secretary of the nominating convention of the Socialist Party, held in Chicago May 10–15, 1908.
18. Debs was elected one of the four delegates of the Socialist Party of Indiana and was scheduled to join Morris Hillquit, May Wood Simons, and Joshua Wanhope as a speaker at a mass meeting preceding the opening of the quadrennial convention in Chicago on May 10. Continuing what was by now a highly predictable pattern of behavior, Debs once again skipped the convention, however, recycling the excuse of "family illness" as the reason for his inability to attend. An alternate delegate was seated in his stead. Debs remained in Girard, Kansas during the week, hundreds of miles from his home in Terre Haute.
19. For many months Debs had been boosting the candidacy of William D. Haywood as the Socialist Party's nominee for 1908, including attendance of a January meeting with him along with top officials of the Socialist and Socialist Labor parties in the New York City office of Morris Hillquit to explore the idea of a joint SP–SLP ticket in the fall campaign.
20. In a letter written the next day to his brother Theodore, Gene Debs emphasized that the Girard assemblage was "a *complete* surprise." Debs was introduced by Eli W. Richardson, a socialist businessman from Girard, and a tribute was paid by Mayor William H. Ryan, a Democrat. See Eugene V. Debs to Theodore Debs, May 17, 1908, in Constantine (ed.), *Letters of Eugene V. Debs, vol. 1,* 268–9.
21. Reference is to Debs's nomination for president by the national convention of the Socialist Party of America, held in Chicago from May 10 to 17, 1908.

22. From William Shakespeare, *Twelfth Night* (c. 1601), Act 2, Scene 5.
23. Debs had previously been elected as a Democrat to two terms as city clerk in Terre Haute (1879, 1881) and to a two-year term as a member of the Indiana House of Representatives (1884). See *The Selected Works of Eugene V. Debs: Volume 1: Building Solidarity on the Tracks, 1877–1892* (Chicago: Haymarket Books, 2019), *passim.*
24. Allusion to Genesis 4:9.
25. A reference to a brief period of unemployment in the fall of 1874 when as a fledgling locomotive fireman Debs was unable to find a permanent job in the St. Louis area. The 18-year-old Debs soon returned home to the parental nest in Terre Haute.
26. Debs spoke at a gathering held to welcome home delegates and visitors to the 1908 National Convention of the Socialist Party of America, which was held in Chicago from May 10 to 17. E. N. Richardson served as master of ceremonies and a number of short speeches were given by local and regional luminaries, including J. A. Wayland, Fred D. Warren, J. E. Snyder, and Dan Hogan.
27. The Free Soil Party was a short-lived anti-slavery political party of the late 1840s and early 1850s that was a forerunner of the Republican Party. The party experienced some electoral success, sending two senators and 14 representatives to Congress as a result of the election of 1848.
28. Dan Hogan (1871–1935) was a leading figure in the Socialist Party of Arkansas. A lawyer and political journalist, Hogan was active in the People's Party during the 1890s, entering the socialist movement around the turn of the century. Hogan launched his first socialist newspaper, *The Southern Worker,* in 1901. He was the state secretary of the Socialist Party of Arkansas from 1906 to 1910. Hogan was a member of the committee on war and militarism at the 1917 Emergency Convention of the Socialist Party of America and served on the party's National Executive Committee from 1918 to 1920. He was a close political associate of Oscar Ameringer and published a newspaper jointly with him in Oklahoma City at the time of his death.
29. This is hyperbole. Debs had a short and unpleasant stay at the overcrowded Cook County jail in January 1895 prior to being transferred at the request of the American Railway Union's attorneys to the McHenry County jail at Woodstock, Illinois. It was there that he served a six-month term for contempt of court.
30. Stanza from "On the Capture of Fugitive Slaves Near Washington" (1845) by James Russell Lowell (1819–1891).
31. Frances Evelyn "Daisy" Greville (1861–1938) was the London-born wife of Francis Greville, eldest son and heir of George Greville, the fourth earl of Warwick. She was won to socialism by Robert Blatchford and became a member of the Social Democratic Federation in 1904. She was active in socialist causes and philanthropic work. In 1923 she ran for the House of Commons on the Independent Labour Party ticket.
32. On May 31, Debs was a keynote speaker at the third national conference of the Christian Socialist Fellowship, held at Carnegie Hall in New York. Secretary of the organization was John Dietrich Long of the independent Parkside Church, Brooklyn.
33. Nelson W. Aldrich (1841–1915) was a Republican politician from Rhode Island. First elected to the US Senate in 1881, Aldrich would serve continuously in that

body for three decades, gaining considerable decision-making authority over time.

34. After a hiatus of more than 10 months, Debs returned to public speaking at the end of May 1908. Despite the intimation here, he did not participate in another tightly booked speaking tour at this time, but rather traveled to New York to deliver speeches at a gathering in celebration of the launch of the *New York Evening Call* on May 30 as well as an address the following evening to the National Conference of Christian Socialists at Carnegie Hall. Taking a year off from the Chautauqua circuit, Debs would also speak that summer at special events in front of 2,500 people at Oklahoma City on July 5 and as keynote speaker at a grand Social Democratic Party picnic in Milwaukee on July 12. His all-consuming tour aboard the Red Special would begin at the end of August.
35. The 1900 campaign was actually conducted by an uneasy alliance of two rival political organizations, each calling itself the Social Democratic Party of America. See *Eugene V. Debs Selected Works,* vol. 3.
36. J. Milton Waldron (1863–1931), born in Richmond, Virginia, was an ordained Baptist minister who spent nearly two decades at the Bethel Baptist Church of Jacksonville, Florida, where he became known for his outspoken opposition to lynch law. He later assumed the pastorate at the Shiloh Baptist Church of Washington, DC, where he served for a time as treasurer of the Niagara Movement, a civil rights organization launched in 1905 by historian W. E. B. Du Bois and journalist William Monroe Trotter. He was later president of the Washington, DC chapter of the National Association for the Advancement of Colored People. Waldron's National Negro American Political League was a short-lived attempt to exert political influence on behalf of the African-American community within the Republican Party; the group changed its name to the National Independent Political League in 1912 and moved close to Woodrow Wilson's Democratic administration. Waldron supported American participation in World War I through an organization called the Committee of One Hundred.
37. The Brownsville Affair revolved around the August 13, 1906, shooting of a white bartender and wounding of a white police officer—acts for which the black soldiers of the segregated 25th Infantry Battalion were duplicitously implicated. Following an investigation by the Army's Inspector General, President Theodore Roosevelt issued dishonorable discharge orders for 167 men, ostensibly for having participated in a "conspiracy of silence" as to the identity of the shooter or shooters. The military affairs committee of the US Senate conducted an investigation of its own in 1907 and 1908, with a majority ultimately supporting Roosevelt's decision in their March 1908 report. A new investigation by the Army in 1972 found the soldiers innocent and posthumous honorable discharges were granted, with the sole living participant awarded a $25,000 cash award and tax-free pension by Congress.
38. Joseph B. Foraker (1846–1917) was a corporation attorney from Ohio elected as the Republican candidate for governor of Ohio in 1885. In 1896 Foraker was elected to the first of two terms in the United States Senate. Foraker was a leading exponent for public scrutiny and fairness toward the 167 black soldiers of the 25th Infantry Battalion embroiled in the 1906 Brownsville Affair. He filed a minority report

proclaiming the innocence of the soldiers in the Senate military affairs committee's investigation of the incident.

39. The 1908 Republican national convention was held June 16–19 in Chicago. It nominated Judge William Howard Taft and Representative James S. Sherman to head its ticket in the fall general election.
40. There was no party-owned press in New York City at this time; Debs refers here to the privately owned daily *New York Call* and the weekly *New York Socialist* (formerly *The Worker*), both of which were close to the Social Democratic Party of New York but neither of which was technically official. The German-language daily *New Yorker Volkszeitung* and Yiddish-language daily *Forverts,* also privately held socialist broadsheets, were published at other locations in the city.
41. Leonidas I (c. 540 BC–480 BC) was a king of Sparta who commanded the combined forces of Greece against the Persian invasion led by Xerxes I (519 BC–465 BC). In August 480 BC, Leonidas led an army of 7,000 men against massively superior forces to defend a narrow pass at Thermopylae. After two days of fighting, during which more than 10,000 Persians were killed by the defenders, Leonidas sent the bulk of his forces to the safety of retreat, remaining to fight to heroic death in battle with a rump force of just over 2,000 men.
42. Judas Maccabeus (d. 160 BC) was a Jewish priest who led an armed revolt against the Hellenic Seleucid Empire to defend recently banned religious practices, a struggle that lasted from 167 to 160 BC. Although he was killed in March 160 BC at the Battle of Elasa, the struggle was carried on by his brothers, who ultimately defeated the Seleucids and established an independent kingdom in Judea.
43. Charles Martel (c. 688–741) was a Frankish king who has been commonly attributed to have led a victorious campaign over Arab Muslim invaders, the so-called Saracens, in 732. Martel was the grandfather of Charlemagne (742–814), who became emperor of the Romans in 800.
44. Joan of Arc (c. 1412–1431) was a military leader for the uncrowned King Charles VII of France. She distinguished herself helping to breaking the English siege of Orléans in 1429, an incident in the Hundred Years War. She was captured in 1430 and after a trial for religious heresy was burned at the stake in May 1431.
45. The Huguenots were Protestant religious dissidents associated with the Reformed Church of France, a Calvinist sect. They were heavily persecuted by the Catholic French state, especially during the eighteenth century.
46. Puritans was a broad term applied to seventeenth-century English Protestant religious dissidents who sought reform of the Church of England.
47. Alexander III of Macedon (356 BC–323 BC) assumed the throne in 336 BC following the death of his father. He spent the next decade in an unrelenting military campaign of conquest, building a massive empire that stretched as far as India.
48. Reference is to Joan of Arc.
49. Roger Williams (c. 1603–1683) was a Puritan theologian in the Massachusetts Bay Colony who was tried for "dangerous opinions" in 1635 and ordered to be banished. After his expulsion he established the settlement of Providence in what became the new

colony of Rhode Island, attracting an array of religious dissidents to the enterprise.

50. Anne Marbury Hutchinson (1591–1643) was a Puritan lay religious leader who espoused free grace theology—an insistence that salvation depended upon belief in the divinity of a savior rather than upright behavior, personal development, and good works—an idea regarded as heretical by religious leaders of the Massachusetts Bay Colony. She was tried for the doctrine she advocated in 1637 and was sentenced to banishment, relocating to the new, less doctrinaire colony of Rhode Island.
51. John Boyle O'Reilly (1844–1890) was an Irish-born American poet, journalist, and writer who as a youth was active in the Irish Republican Brotherhood, the so-called Fenians. As a result of his activity in the Irish revolutionary movement, he was sentenced by the British to 20 years of penal deportation to Australia, from which he escaped to America.
52. Allusion to William Shakespeare, *Twelfth Night* (c. 1601), Act 4, Scene 2.
53. James Otis, Jr. (1725–1783) was a Massachusetts lawyer, pamphleteer, and politician. A friend of Thomas Paine, Otis was active in the political movement against the Stamp Act and penned the famous slogan "Taxation without representation is tyranny."
54. Debs spoke to the National Conference of Christian Socialists on May 31, 1908, at Carnegie Hall in New York City. Others delivering addresses to the gathering included Edmond Kelly, former counsel to the American legation at Paris; E. E. Carr, editor of *The Christian Socialist;* and former Socialist Party national organizer Charles H. Vail.
55. Thomas F. Ryan (1851–1928) was one of the wealthiest people in America, a multimillionaire who founded his financial empire in public transportation. Ryan established the forerunner of the Metropolitan Traction Company in 1883, soon dominating street railroad service in New York City. He was also a founder of the American Tobacco Company and further expanded his vast holdings with the 1905 purchase of the Equitable Life Assurance Society, one of the three biggest insurance companies in America.
56. Former President Grover Cleveland was associated with the Democratic Party's conservative "Bourbon" wing, William Jennings Bryan with its progressive faction.
57. Allusion to a speech made by Lincoln in Cincinnati on September 17, 1859. Lincoln's exact words were reported as "I hold that if the Almighty had ever made a set of men that should do all of the eating and none of the work, He would have made them *with mouths only,* and no hands; and if He had ever made another class that He intended should do all the work, and none of the eating. He would have made them *without mouths,* and with *all hands!*"
58. The 1908 Democratic platform reaffirmed a commitment to anti-injunction legislation passed by the US Senate in 1896 providing for trial by jury in cases of indirect contempt associated with injunctions. It also declared that "the parties to all judicial proceeding should be treated with rigid impartiality, and that injunctions should not be issued in any cases in which injunctions would not issue if no industrial dispute were involved." It further promised to defend the right of workers to "organize for the protection of wages and the improvement of labor conditions" and that such activity "should not be regarded as illegal combinations in restraint of trade."
59. In advocating for the adoption of an anti-injunction plank by the Democratic Party

at its July 1908 national convention in Denver, American Federation of Labor President Samuel Gompers stated: "We do not ask for special privileges, but merely for justice and equality. We insist that the injunction not be made an instrument of oppression." Adopted over the objection of the Democratic Party's conservative wing, headed by the party's 1904 presidential nominee, Judge Alton B. Parker, the plank was a clear bid to win the support of organized labor for the 1908 Democratic ticket headed by William Jennings Bryan.

60. August Belmont, Jr. (1853–1924) was a wealthy financier and Democratic Party kingpin best known as head of the Interborough Rapid Transit Company and financier of construction of the New York City subway system.

61. Debs was a founding member of the Vigo Lodge No. 16 of the Brotherhood of Locomotive Firemen in February 1875. The organization favored individual betterment and opposed strikes and was more akin to a fraternal benefit society than a modern trade union. See *Selected Works of Eugene V. Debs: Volume 1, Building Solidarity on the Tracks, 1877–1892, passim.*

62. *Loewe v. Lawler,* commonly known as the Danbury Hatters's case, was a 1908 Supreme Court decision, which ruled that a boycott by the United Hatters of North America against the open shop D. E. Loewe & Co. represented a violation of the Sherman Anti-Trust Act of 1890 and overturned the dismissal of the suit by a lower court. A new trial in 1909 found against the union to the tune of $74,000 in damages, tripled to $222,000 under terms of the Sherman Act. This result was upheld by the Supreme Court in 1914 with the union ultimately paying out $234,000 in 1917.

63. Roger C. Sullivan (1861–1920) was a Democratic Party powerbroker from Chicago and was a leading figure in the Cook County Democratic Party. A long-time nemesis of William Jennings Bryan, Sullivan was influential in tipping the Democratic nomination to Woodrow Wilson at the 1912 Democratic convention, stymying Bryan's effort to deadlock the convention and gain nomination as an alternative unity candidate.

64. "Boss" Charles F. Murphy (1858–1924), a former teamster and saloon owner, was the head of New York City's corrupt Tammany Hall Democratic Party establishment from 1902 until the time of his death. Murphy was the kingmaker back of New York Mayor George B. McClellan, Jr., who defeated a challenge by William Randolph Hearst and his Municipal Ownership League in 1905, thereby assuring continued private ownership of the city's subway system—operated by a firm with financial ties to Murphy.

65. A lengthy paragraph of the Republican platform of 1908 declared that "present tendencies of the two parties are even more marked by inherent differences. The trend of [the Democratic Party] is toward socialism, while the Republican Party stands for a wise and regulated individualism. . . . In line with this tendency the Democratic Party of today believes in government ownership, while the Republican Party believes in government regulation." The Socialist Party is not mentioned in the document.

66. Socialist Party membership grew to a monthly average of 41,751 in 1908—an increase of 42.6 percent over the 1907 monthly average tally of 29,270. It was thus factually incorrect for Debs to assert that the total was "more than twice as numerous as ever before." The Debs-Hanford ticket would ultimately receive just under

421,000 votes in November 1908 (2.83 percent of votes cast).

67. James Baird Weaver (1833–1912) was an anti-slavery Republican newspaper publisher who joined the Greenback Labor Party after the Panic of 1873. He was first elected to Congress in 1878 on a Greenback-Democratic fusion ticket and returned again for the first of two more terms in 1884. In 1892 Weaver was the nominee of the People's Party for president of the United States, collecting more than a million votes and 22 electoral votes in the November election.
68. James G. Field (1826–1901) lost a leg fighting for the Confederate States of America in the Civil War. He later served five years as attorney general of Virginia. He came out of a decade of political retirement to run for vice-president of the United States on the People's Party ticket in 1892.
69. The Omaha platform was adopted at the foundation convention of the People's Party on July 4, 1892. It called for the unity of labor forces, the free and unlimited coinage of silver, adoption of a graduated income tax, government ownership of the telegraph and telephone systems, reclamation of unused land deeded to railroads, abolition of the Pinkerton system, adoption of the initiative and referendum, and opposition to corporate subsidies for any purpose, among other things.
70. John Burns (1858–1943) was a venerable British labor leader, active in the Social Democratic Federation beginning in 1881. He was active in the London Dock Strike in the summer of 1889 and was first elected to Parliament as a Liberal in 1892. Although socialistically inclined, he never joined the Independent Labour Party, remaining affiliated with the Liberals. He became more conservative in his declining years.
71. The polemical editorial by Gompers, entitled "Debs, the Apostle of Failure," appears in Stuart B. Kaufman, Peter J. Albert, and Grace Palladino, eds., *The Samuel Gompers Papers: Volume 7, The American Federation of Labor Under Siege, 1906–9* (Urbana: University of Illinois Press, 1999), 401–405. Gompers invites his readers to "compare anything Debs may say with the most virulent attacks upon Labor by the [David M.] Parry/[Charles W.] Post/[James W.] Van Cleave gang" and to "note the remarkable similarity about them—then it becomes easy to guess as to where Debs gets his inspiration, and possibly even his financial backing." Gompers charges Debs with attempting to "disorganize the workers, lead them astray from the vital issues," and to "corral their votes" in de facto "assistance to the Republican Party."
72. President Theodore Roosevelt traveled to Matinecock, Long Island, New York on July 11, 1908 to deliver a speech at the dedication of a monument to Captain John Underhill (1597–1672), a leader of the militia of the Massachusetts Bay Colony.
73. Allusion to the refrain "An' the Gobble-uns'll git you ef you don't watch out!" from the poem "Little Orphant Annie" (1885) by James Whitcomb Riley (1849–1916).
74. Underhill achieved his fame leading the Massachusetts Bay Colony's militia alongside their Native American allies, the Mohegan people, against the Pequot people in the 11-month Pequot War of 1636–37. About 700 Pequots were killed or captured and enslaved in the conflict and the tribe's hegemony in the region was smashed, paving the way for European colonization.
75. Roosevelt used the occasion of the Underhill monument dedication to hold up the

Underhill family as a model of rugged individualism and to slam "certain socialistic writers" who had put forward "the ideal that every man shall put into the common fund what he can, which would mean what he chose, and could take out whatever he wanted.." Thus, said Roosevelt, "the man who is vicious, foolish, a drag on the whole community . . . should take out what is not his, what he has not earned; that he shall rob his neighbor of what that neighbor has earned. This particular socialistic ideal would be to enthrone privilege in one of its grossest, crudest, most dishonest, most harmful, and most unjust forms." See "President on Reward," *Washington Post,* whole no. 11,721 (July 12, 1908), 2.

76. Benjamin Franklin Yoakum (1859–1929) was a railroad executive that as chairman of the Chicago, Rock Island & Pacific Railroad attempted to build a massive unified system running from the Midwest to Mexico. Briefly, the largest system under unified individual control, the so-called Yoakum Line came to grief in the early 1910s because of financial problems; Yoakum's partner the St. Louis-San Francisco Railway filed for bankruptcy in 1913.
77. Lewis H. Morgan, *Ancient Society, or, Researches in the Lines of Human Progress from Savagery through Barbarism to Civilization* [1877] (Chicago: Charles H. Kerr & Co., n.d. [1907]), 561–2.
78. Debs had been slated to arrive in Missoula at 3:20 p.m., but his train had rolled in more than five hours late, at 8:30 p.m. He gave an impromptu long speech to a vast crowd that assembled at the Northern Pacific rail yard. His regularly scheduled evening hall meeting in the mining town of Butte was cancelled. Three hundred people waited all night to hear Debs speak for 20 minutes in Butte the next morning.
79. Debs had been slated to arrive in Wallace, Idaho at 8:30 a.m. and to remain at the station there for half an hour.
80. The Lewiston socialist weekly *Montana News* later charged that Debs's Montana tour had been deliberately sabotaged by Northern Pacific railway officials with a goal of shutting down the Butte meeting. See "Red Special Ditched in Montana," *Montana News,* September 24, 1908, 1.
81. Immediately after beginning his speech to the great crowd in the Missoula rail yard, an arriving train had arrived on parallel tracks, effectively splitting the audience in half. A 20-minute delay ensued, during which Debs gave this brief statement to a reporter from the local press.
82. Debs was called out by the editor of a Syracuse labor paper to answer charges levied against him by American Federation of Labor President Samuel Gompers in his high-profile September 1908 *American Federationist* editorial, "Debs, the Apostle of Failure." Gompers asserted that as president of the American Railway Union, Debs had "hoped and worked and plotted for the destruction" of the Brotherhood of Locomotive Firemen, "the organization of which he was a responsible official." This inflammatory reply by Debs was made from the rostrum in Syracuse and was subsequently picked up by national news wire services. See Samuel Gompers, "Debs, the Apostle of Failure," 403.
83. Reference is to a financial scandal of the 1904 presidential campaign, during which a six-figure donation by the Standard Oil Trust to the Republican Party became public

knowledge.

84. Cornelius N. Bliss (1833–1911) was a millionaire businessman and New York Republican Party stalwart. Bliss was secretary of the interior during the William McKinley administration and treasurer of the Republican National Committee during the election of 1904.
85. Henry Huddleston Rogers (1840–1909) was a financier who was a top decision-maker in the Standard Oil Company from the 1870s. He was the conduit for financial contributions by the Standard Oil Trust to the Republican Party during the 1904 general election campaign.
86. The 1908 Republican National Convention assembled at the 11,000 seat Chicago Coliseum, located on Wabash Avenue between 14th and 16th Streets June 16–19.
87. The 1908 Democratic National Convention was held July 7–10 in Denver, Colorado. It was the first major party presidential nominating convention held west of the Mississippi River.
88. Charles N. Haskell (1860–1933) was an oilman who was elected the first governor of the new state of Oklahoma in 1907. Haskell was the treasurer of the Democratic National Committee during the election of 1908.
89. Braxton Bragg Comer (1848–1927) was a plantation owner with investments in cotton mills and his brother's mining operation near Birmingham. He was elected governor of Alabama in 1906. In July 1908, District 20 of the United Mine Workers of America went out on strike throughout the Birmingham district, a bitter conflict in which black and white miners acted in concert against mine owners; one black striker was lynched in the town of Brighton. Comer ordered out the national guard in August, which wiped out the strikers' tent colony and hastened the end of the two-month strike.
90. Alton B. Parker (1852–1926) was the conservative judge nominated by the Democratic Party for president in 1904. His nomination over the semi-populist William Jennings Bryan was instrumental in the Socialist Party's comparatively strong showing in that campaign.
91. Reference to the 1908 court decision by Judge Kennesaw Mountain Landis fining Standard Oil Company of Indiana $29.24 million for violating anti-trust law through its shutting down of the Chicago & Alton Railroad to its competitors. Regarded as a sensationally large fine at the time, the award was overturned on appeal.
92. Henry Osborne Havemeyer (1847–1907) and Claus Spreckels (1828–1908) were rival magnates in the heavily trustified sugar industry.
93. From "On the Capture of Fugitive Slaves Near Washington" (1845) by James Russell Lowell (1819–1891).
94. This is the response to a question about the influence of politics on the students of Yale College asked at Debs's New Haven campaign appearance.
95. Porfirio Díaz (1830–1915) was a Mexican general who first came to power as President of Mexico in 1876. With the exception of a four-year stint during which one of his close associates held the reins of power, Díaz exerted de facto dictatorial control of the country for more than a quarter century. He was forced to resign in 1911 as part of the first phase of the Mexican Revolution and emigrated to Spain days after.

96. Juan Sarabia Díaz de León (1882–1920) was a Mexican journalist and founder and leader of the Mexican Liberal Party. Sarabia went into exile in the United States in 1904 and participated there in a junta which sought the overthrow of the dictatorship of General Porfirio Díaz. Sarabia was jailed in Mexico in 1907 and remained incarcerated until the fall of the Díaz regime in 1911. After his relelase Sarabia was active in the politics of San Luis Potosí, serving another brief stint in prison when Victoriano Huerta disolved the legislative assembly in 1913. He was elected a Senator of San Luis Potosí in 1920, dying later that same year.
97. Cipriano Ricardo Gerónimo Flores Magón (1873–1922), known as Ricardo Flores Magón, was a Mexican journalist and anarchist leader. An activist in the radical political movement against General Porfirio Díaz, Magón was arrested and forced into exile in the United States in 1904. There he was a member of the junta of the Mexican Liberal Party, established at a convention held in St. Louis, Missouri, in 1905 and he remained active in the effort to overthrow Mexico's right wing dictatorship. During World War I Magón ran afoul of the United States government, which accused him of sabotaging the war effort, and he was sentenced to 21 years in prison. He died in 1922 from an illness contracted in prison.
98. José Antonio Villarreal González (1879–1944), known as Antonio I. Villarreal, was active in the radical movement which sought the overthrow of General Porfirio Díaz, serving as secretary of the Liberal Club in San Luis Potosí. He was a founder of the Mexican Liberal Party in American exile in 1905 and 1906 editor of the periodical *Regeneración,* published in Los Angeles.
99. Librado Rivera (1864–1932) was a Mexican teacher, journalist, and political activist who was a leading figure in the organization of the Mexican radical movement through the Liberal Clubs from 1900. He was a friend of Ricardo Flores Magón and was arrested for the first time in 1902, ultimately being forced into American exile. He was a founding member of the Junta Organizadora in 1905 and of the Mexican Liberal Party in St. Louis, Missouri in 1906. Rivera was arrested in 1918 as part of the American government's wartime crackdown on the radical press and was imprisoned at Leavenworth Federal Penitentiary until 1923. Following his release he returned to Mexico, where he remained active in the anarchist movement.
100. Lázaro Gutiérrez de Lara (1870–1918) was a Mexican attorney hailing from a wealthy family in Mexico City who worked for the Secretary of Foreign Relations and served as a judge. After meeting Ricardo Flores Magón, Gutiérrez de Lara joined the Mexican Liberal Party. He was arrested in 1906 in Sonora for speaking on behalf of striking copper miners but was freed through the intercession of his family and forced into emigration in Los Angeles. There he became a member of the party's governing junta and editor of the party's official newspaper. Gutiérrez de Lara was the friend and translator of American socialist John Kenneth Turner and traveled undercover with him to research a muckraking series of magazine articles detailing the repressive regime of Mexican strongman Porfirio Díaz, collected into the book *Barbarous Mexico* (1910). In 1909 Gutiérrez de Lara was arrested as an alleged "anarchist" by the US government on behalf of the Díaz regime. He returned to Mexico in 1912 where he continued his

socialist activism. In January 1918 he was arrested in conjunction with a miners' strike in Cananea and was summarily executed.

101. Part of a quadrennial series in which the presidential nominees of major and minor parties were allowed free access to the pages of the national public affairs weekly, *The Independent,* to state their official party "appeal" to the voters.
102. John Worth Kern (1849–1917) was a lawyer from Kokomo, Indiana elected to the Indiana state senate in 1893. Kern was tapped as the running mate for William Jennings Bryan in his third run for the presidency in 1908. In 1910 Kern was elected to the US Senate, in which he would serve a single term, retiring in 1917 due to poor health and dying shortly thereafter.
103. George Allan England (1877–1936) was a Harvard-educated author who would run for governor of Maine on the Socialist Party ticket in 1912. In addition to prominence as a writer for popular magazines, England gained a degree of fame for his socialist-tinged fiction, authoring more than a dozen novels between 1910 and 1926.
104. George Allan England, "International Socialism as a Political Force," *American Review of Reviews,* vol. 37, no. 5 (May 1908), 580–1.
105. Christian Matthias Theodor Mommsen (1817–1903) was a professor of Roman history at the University of Berlin from 1861 to 1887. He was awarded the 1902 Nobel Prize for literature for his magnum opus, the three-volume *Römische Geschichte* (1854–1856), the landmark of an extensive career as a historical writer. He is one of the only individuals to have won the Nobel for literature for a work of nonfiction.
106. An allusion to 1 Corinthians 2:9, which reads, "But as it is written, Eye hath not seen, nor ear heard, neither have entered into the heart of man, the things which God hath prepared for them that love him."
107. After being on the road for the entire months of September and October 1908, Debs returned to Terre Haute in the evening of November 2 where he was met by jubilant crowds awaiting speeches by him at two large venues. This was the essence of his address at the second of these gatherings delivered to a crowd of more than 1,500 people, the final speech of the 1908 presidential campaign. Debs was introduced by Industrial Workers of the World leader Bill Haywood and was greeted by a full minute of uninterrupted cheering when he stepped to the rostrum.
108. Frederick Wiliam Upham (1861–1925) was president of the Illinois Manufacturers' Association and briefly served as a Chicago city alderman in 1898. He was president of the Fred W. Upham Lumber Company and a vice president of the Peabody Coal Company. Upham was chair of the convention committee of the 1908 Republican National Convention.
109. Francis Stuyvesant Peabody (1859–1922), the son of a prominent Chicago attorney, was the founder of Peabody Coal Company, becoming a millionaire as a coal supplier to consumers. He was active in the Democratic Party and was on the list of those considered for Vice President of the United States in 1912. Peabody's company survives today as Peabody Energy, a Fortune 500 firm.
110. Roger Charles Sullivan (1861–1920) was for two decades a boss of the Cook County Democratic Party. Sullivan became a millionaire through an unsavory combination

of business investments and Chicago city franchises. He was a long-time political opponent of reform Democrat William Jennings Bryan and was one of the primary political string-pullers that enabled Woodrow Wilson to garner the Democratic nomination at the deadlocked convention of 1912.

111. Charles Francis Murphy (1858–1924) was a Democratic political boss fromNew York City. Murphy sat as head of Tammany Hall from 1902 to 1924 and as such was a kingmaker in New York politics. Murphy parlayed an appointment as Commissioner of Docks in 1897 to establishment of the New York Trucking and Docking Company, making money through city contracts expedited by friends.
112. "Bath House John" Coughlin (1860–1938) was a corrupt Chicago alderman and leading boss of the Cook County Democratic Party. Coughlin worked hand-in-glove with his associate Michael "Hinky Dink" Kenna collecting kickbacks for the award of city franchises and protection money from the gambling and prostitution industries.
113. Michael "Hinky Dink" Kenna (1857–1946) was a Chicago alderman from 1893 and top Democratic Party boss in the Cook County Democratic Party. A successful saloon owner, Kenna made a great deal of money taking kickbacks for protection from law enforcement from businesses engaged in gambling and prostitution.
114. Fairview was the Victorian mansion home of William Jennings Bryan, built in Lincoln in 1901–02 at a cost of $17,000. It and surrounding land was donated by Bryan to the Nebraska Conference of the United Methodist Church for establishment of a hospital in 1922. The building was declared a National Historic Landmark in 1963 and restored to its original appearance in 1994.
115. Stricken with cancer, 1904 and 1908 Socialist Party vice-presidential nominee Ben Hanford would survive for more than a year, dying in New York City on January 24, 1910.
116. Darius Ogden Mills (1825–1910) was a multimillionaire financier with investments in railroads and banking.
117. Albert Barnes Anderson (1857–1938) was first appointed to the federal bench by Theodore Roosevelt in December 1902. He would be promoted from district court to the US Court of Appeals in 1925, remaining in that capacity until the time of his death.
118. Harry S. New (1858–1937) was a prominent journalist and political activist. New was elected as a Republican to the US Senate from Indiana in November 1916. He later served as postmaster general during the Harding and Coolidge administrations.
119. Albert J. Beveridge (1862–1927) was a progressive Republican ally of Theodore Roosevelt from Indiana. He was elected to the first of two terms to the US Senate in November 1898 before falling to defeat in a bid for a third term in 1910. He turned to the writing of history in his later years, winning a Pulitzer Prize in 1920 for his four-volume biography of Supreme Court Justice John Marshall.

1909

The Gompers Jail Sentence [excerpt]†

January 2, 1909

Justice Wright of the supreme court of the District of Columbia,[1] hitherto unknown, has suddenly achieved national distinction, enviable or otherwise, according to the point of view, by deciding Samuel Gompers, John Mitchell, and Frank Morrison guilty of contempt of court in the case of the Buck Stove and Range Co. and sentencing them to jail for one year, nine months, and six months, respectively.[2]

It is worthy of note that coincident with the decision of the supreme court of the District of Columbia sentencing the federation leaders to jail, the Supreme Court of the United States rendered its decision absolving Edward Harriman, the railroad king, from answering the questions of the Interstate Commerce Committee[3] in reference to certain stock jugglery and other shady manipulations.

The Gompers contempt case began in August 1907 and grew out of the boycott placed upon the company by the American Federation of Labor and the publication of the company's name in the "unfair list," and it is for the alleged violation of this injunction that Justice Wright now sentences Gompers, Mitchell, and Morrison to jail.

Justice Wright's review of the case, his argument and summing up are without flaw, his decision absolutely correct and his sentence reasonable and just, from the capitalist point of view. From the labor point of view it is the precise opposite and is nothing less than an exhibition of supreme judicial despotism, which outrages every workingman who has intelligence and self-respect enough to know when he is outraged.

The capitalist class character of the federal court, especially in its supreme branches, is well established among the few who see and think for themselves, and this decision of Justice Wright will do much to open the eyes of the unthinking and idolatrous many who still look upon courts in open-mouthed wonder and awe as sacred and infallible institutions.

† Published in *Appeal to Reason*, whole no. 683 (January 2, 1909), 4.

All through the decision "handed down" by Justice Wright, labor is treated as a commodity and in this the court is entirely logical, and so far as those who regard labor as a commodity are concerned and treat it accordingly, there is no valid reason for objection and no good ground for complaint.

But labor is not a commodity but life, human life, with a soul in it, and as sacred as the God who created it, and that is why Justice Wright's decision is heartless and infamous; and if Gompers, Mitchell, and Morrison are in contempt of his capitalist court—and if they are not they ought to be—his court is in an infinitely larger degree in contempt of enlightened human conscience.

I have nothing to say here about Gompers, Mitchell, and Morrison as labor leaders. Their official attitude, views, and policies I have no sympathy with, not the slightest, but this is not the time nor the place for such discussion, nor for the exploitation of any other differences or disagreements. In this fight, forgetting all else, I am with them, not half-heartedly, but as thoroughly in earnest as if they were my socialist comrades, and I shall gladly give them all the support in my power.

This jail sentence which has been imposed upon them is an attack not nearly so much upon them as it is upon organized labor and the working class and as such it ought to be resented with indignation by all the workers of the country.

When Moyer, Haywood, and Pettibone were kidnapped, the *Appeal to Reason* and other socialist papers took the lead in the fight to rescue them because they had been attacked for serving labor, and the same is true in this instance of Gompers, Mitchell, and Morrison, and every socialist and labor paper and every socialist, trade unionist, and workingman, and every sympathizer with labor, should make this fight his own and raise such a storm of protest that even capitalist courts will be given to understand that labor is not a commodity to be treated as hair, hides, and tallow, and that it will no longer stand for outrageous court decisions jailing its officials for the meek and humble offenses of serving notice that it will not patronize its enemies.

* * *

Gompers, Mitchell, and Morrison have not been tried by a jury of their peers, but have been sentenced to jail by the arbitrary will of a judge before whom, in the very nature of things, they were foredoomed to conviction. If in this case they are guilty of anything to their discredit, it is not for openly defying the insolent and despotic order of the court in the first instance.

The same federal court refused to take cognizance of the kidnapping and deportation of labor leaders in flagrant violation of the Constitution of the

United States, and it also legalized the blacklisting of workingmen, and now it caps the climax by ordering union officials sent to jail for simply calling by name the enemies of organized labor.

Federal judges are extremely jealous of the sacred rights of capitalist "property," but supremely indifferent to working class life. The boycott of labor is punished with a jail sentence, but the blacklist by capital, under which a workingman is driven to suicide and his wife and children to starvation, is no infraction of law or equity, as administered by corporation judges, and no capitalist has ever been as much as fined, saying nothing to being sent to prison, for that infamous crime.

It is only in these latter days since corporations and trusts have become supreme that courts proceed to such extremities in subjugating labor, and if labor submits without protest it will soon be shorn of the last semblance of its dignity and the last vestige of its rights.

Whether this decision of Justice Wright is allowed to stand and Gompers, Mitchell, and Morrison go to jail depends entirely upon the working class. Upon this issue they can all unite—radical and conservative, organized and unorganized—in such widespread, emphatic, and determined protest as will not only rebuke the court and prevent the sentence from being carried into execution, but absolutely secure them against any such despotic decision in the future.

The *Appeal*, in this fight, is for the federation officials and against the federal court. Every labor union and every socialist local should rise in protest. The measure of labor's slavery and degradation is the measure of its supine submission when it is wronged. It can at least protect and give evidence of its consciousness that it is wronged and of its determination to draw the line at some point and maintain some degree of its self-respect.

Let but the workers make this case their own—for such it is—and a storm of protest will sweep over the nation and never again will such a decision be rendered in the United States.

Gompers and Capitalism†

January 23, 1909

Whichever way he turns, President Gompers of the American Federation of Labor finds himself face to face with difficulties which are the outgrowth of his own reactionary policy. In the recent campaign he used such influence as he had with his followers in support of the capitalist system, and within a few weeks after the election he and his colleagues were sentenced to jail by one of the capitalist courts to which he had given his support at the polls. His conviction, outrageous though it be, is entirely consistent with his political attitude and the fact is self-evident that he got what he worked and voted for.

It is significant that his friend, William J. Bryan, was discreetly silent when he was sentenced, making the politician's excuse that it was not his custom to criticize the courts. It remained for the Socialists, whom Gompers had repeatedly charged with being the enemies of organized labor, to denounce the courts and pledge him their loyal support in defeating the outrageous decision which sent him to jail.

In his annual report to the recent Denver convention, Mr. Gompers said, in discussing the courts:

> I can see no remedy for these outrageous proceedings, unless there shall be a quickening of the conscience of our judges or the relief which the Congress of our country can and should afford.[4]

Mr. Gompers appears very naive here, childlike and bland. He hopes there will be a "quickening of the conscience of our judges or the relief which the Congress of our country can and should afford." He hopes in vain. Judges are placed where they are not because they have consciences to move them but because they are known to be trustworthy servants of the ruling class. If Mr. Gompers does not know this, he has learned but little in his many years of service in organized labor, and if nothing short of a jail sentence will teach him this simple lesson, even this will prove to be a blessing.

The leading Democratic politicians with whom Mr. Gompers consorted during the campaign are all silent. The Socialists he traduced by charging that

† Published in *Appeal to Reason*, whole no. 686 (January 23, 1909), 2.

their "Red Special" had been financed by the Republican Party are all active on his behalf. They realize that a principle is involved of fundamental interest to organized labor and under this test his Democratic political associates turn their backs upon him while the despised Socialists rally as one to his support.

It seems strange that Mr. Gompers has not yet learned that we live under a capitalist government; that we are engaged in a class struggle and that the interests of labor and capital are not identical. For many years Mr. Gompers has been meekly begging Congress for an anti-injunction law and an eight-hour law which, if enacted, would be of questionable value to labor. But even this handout has been denied him and he has been turned away with contempt session after session until one would conclude that even he must be satisfied that labor will get nothing from a capitalist Congress until it develops and asserts its own political power as proposed by the Socialists alone. But the papers announce that Mr. Gompers is to go before Congress again to renew his plea, which suggests that up to this time his jail sentence has had no appreciable effect in opening his eyes to what he is actually up against.

The increasing vexations and contradictions in which Mr. Gompers finds himself enmeshed are the fruit of his own economic unwisdom and inconsistency. He believes in the brotherhood of capital and labor, and this is the starting point of his troubles. He has dined with Carnegie, Belmont, and other labor exploiters and union wreckers so often that he feels a sense of kinship with them, but labor and capital are deadly enemies just the same, and the class struggle is a fact which will assert itself in spite of all the Civic Federation banquets and other machinations and sophistications designed to conceal it.

The lesson to be learned by the rank and file is that the working class must develop its economic and political power along uncompromising class lines. They must unite within one great industrial organization of class-conscious workers and the same workers must act together in the Socialist Party on the political field and then they will secure material relief, and in time industrial emancipation.

Had the trade unionists under the lead of Gompers and his colleagues, instead of being divided between the Republican and Democratic parties, joined with the Socialists and polled 2 million clear-cut working class votes, the decision of Judge Wright would never have been rendered, Gompers would not have been sentenced, and Congress would have responded with alacrity to the demand for anti-injunction and eight-hour laws.

Enfranchisement of Womanhood[†]

March 1909

Karl Marx declared that the emancipation of the working class must be achieved by the working class itself. The same is true of the enfranchisement of womanhood. The disabilities imposed upon and accepted by woman in the past on account of her sex can be removed only by herself.

The socialist movement is the first to recognize and proclaim the injustice of sex distinction in reference to the rights, privileges, and opportunities of civic and social life, and the Socialist Party is the first to pledge itself unqualifiedly to abrogate that relic of barbarism and place woman where she ought to be—on an equal plane with man.

There is no need to argue here the question of "woman's sphere" in bourgeois society, it being well understood to be limited by woman's meek submission to the will of her lord and master and by the conventional rules and regulations imposed upon her without her consent.

If she be rich she is ordained to be a doll, a plaything, a coquette, spending her time in vain and frivolous, if not harmful and immoral, indulgences, wasting her life, dissipating her energies, and ending her useless existence in mental childhood, leaving no trace of service to society, and no memory of duties nobly fulfilled to preserve her name.

If she be poor, she is doomed to drudgery and is all but a social outcast.

But rich or poor, woman has been and still is treated as the inferior of man in all that is essential to her mental and moral development. She is denied the freedom and opportunity, without which she can no more develop the latent qualities of her nature than a flower can bloom without the vitalizing influence of the atmosphere and sunlight.

This is particularly true of the working class woman, who even in her bondage is made to feel the added weight of her sex inferiority and to bear all the odium of being an economic menial, a political nonentity, and a social exile.

But happily the days of woman's sex servitude are almost ended. No longer does she tamely acquiesce in her inferiority and degradation. At last she realizes

---

† Published in *The Progressive Woman* [Girard, KS], vol. 2, whole no. 32 (March 1909), 5.

that she has been victimized, that she has been shut out of life's golden opportunities under the hypocritical pretense that she is the "weaker vessel;" and with the growing consciousness of her rightful place in the family, in the state and in society, she is making her influence felt, and in a corresponding degree the horizon of her sphere is expanding.

But even among socialists there are traces—sadly out of place—of the miserable Middle Age superstition that woman is but the shadow of man, that she should maintain the deferential attitude of being the beneficiary of a privilege granted, instead of a right conceded, and that her voice should be seldom heard in the party councils, or not at all.

It is true that this sentiment prevails to no great extent in the Socialist Party, and yet such is the perversity of ancient prejudice that while equality in the abstract is recognized, the true spirit of it is denied in unconscious discrimination.

Here, as elsewhere, the remedy lies with woman herself. She may not in justice to herself or the party acquiesce in any restriction whatsoever, least of all when dictated by a custom born of ignorance and hoary with age. She must insist upon the recognition due her as a human being in the socialist movement, not merely in the perfunctory sense declared in the law, but in the spirit and essence of its emancipating philosophy.

There are too few women in the Socialist Party organization, in proportion to its male members, and far too few who are active in the management and direction of its affairs.

There is no reason why there should not be as many women as men in our locals and in our municipal, state, and national conventions. Nor is there any valid reason why they should not be equally represented in the field as lecturers and organizers, and on our tickets as candidates. All that stands in the way is custom, the ignorance implied in the childlike observance of conventional "properties," and this should be battered down with the ruthless iconoclasm the revolutionary spirit has for hoary shams.

Woman loses not one whit of her innate modesty in braving the frowns of fossils, whatever their standing or sex.

In proportion to her numbers, woman has a remarkable work to her credit in the socialist movement. Without her influence and activity, the Socialist Party would scarcely have an existence. All her zeal and enthusiasm are brought into play, all her patience, persistence, and unconquerable fortitude are developed in the struggle for freedom, and she has already proved herself to be a powerful propagandist in the revolutionary movement.

If the socialist women would realize their ambition to be free and fulfill their manifest destiny, they must take their proper places in the movement and demand in all things the consideration due them as equal factors with men in the struggle for emancipation.

Arise, Ye Hosts of Liberty!†

March 6, 1909

The advance of capitalism to plutocracy has shorn the common people of their liberties until but few remain. The national Congress and state legislatures, reinforced by federal, state, and county judges, have, by statute and decree, so buttressed capital upon the one hand and so enjoined and restricted labor upon the other that a situation confronts the people which must alarm them if they are not dead to every sentiment of manhood and deaf to every appeal of their vanishing freedom.

Not only are these forces of oppression working within national boundary lines, but they have spread over all other nations, and now operate on an international scale. This is one of the results of capitalist development. American capitalists have over a billion dollars invested in Mexican railroads, mines, smelters, and other industries: they have multiplied millions invested in Russian bonds and in the bonds of other despotisms and monarchies of the Old World. Likewise, the capitalists of Russia. England, Mexico, and other nations are the owners of millions of acres of land and billions of invested wealth in the United States.

This is the secret of the diplomatic intrigues between the United States and Russia and the United States and Mexico for the capture and return of political refugees.

They used to be patriots and lionized; under the American flag, now they are criminals and hounded to death.

† Published in *Appeal to Reason*, whole no. 692 (March 6, 1909), 1. Unsigned editorial at front of the special "Liberty Edition" edited by Debs.

And the American people have remained quiescent under these monstrous perversions of the fundamental principles upon which their republic was founded!

Is it not time to awaken from this hideous nightmare? Has not the plutocracy gone far enough? Is it not about time to rise in our might and shake off the vampire? Is there any possible excuse for the present slavish conditions except our own craven cowardice? Are we to remain as inert as clams until the last drop of blood has been drained and the last spark of liberty extinguished?

Behold Antonio Araujo, Ricardo Flores Magón, Antonio Villarreal, Librado Rivera, and Manuel Sarabia, the Mexican patriots, who, for more than 15 months have been festering in the Bastilles of our boasted republic for the heinous crime of having attempted to emancipate their countrymen from the filth and squalor of peon slavery.

Behold Samuel Gompers, John Mitchell, and Frank Morrison, leaders of the American Federation of Labor, sentenced to jail for the atrocious crime of having in cold blood mentioned the name of a capitalist!

Behold Jan Pouren, the Russian refugee hunted down and thrown into an American prison by the American police, under orders from the Russian tsar for the monstrous crime of having objected to the starvation, exile, torture, and assassination of men, women, and children in his native land.

Behold M. R. Preston and Joseph Smith, labor unionists, in felon's stripes, in the penitentiary at Carson City, Nevada, for the shocking crime of having protected a friendless working girl and slaying, in self defense, the employer who had wronged her.[5]

Behold Fred D. Warren under heavy bail for the outrageous crime of having offered a reward for a fugitive from justice charged with murder.

Of the men here named who are in jail or penitentiary, or out temporarily under bail, five are Mexican patriots, cultured, educated gentlemen. battling bravely to ameliorate the awful conditions of their robbed and enslaved fellow beings; one is a Russian peasant, honest to the core, who protested against the butcheries of the tsar and fled to an asylum to find a dungeon; five are labor leaders of prominence, who, had they been capitalists, would have been extolled in florid phrase for the acts which have brought them to prison doors, and the remaining one is a socialist editor who has fearlessly denounced the crimes of the plutocracy and loyally served the cause of right and justice.

These 11 men should and shall be set free. The only crime with which their names are associated is their conviction.

The cause of these men and a number of others of lesser prominence who are in jails all over the country, and who are equally innocent, is the cause of the people.

It is your cause and my cause and the sentence of these men is your disgrace and my disgrace. But for our cowardice the capitalist courts would never have dared to convict them. It is therefore your conviction and my conviction. The brand of shame is upon you and me and there is but one way to remove it, and that is by rising as men all over this country and issuing our united protest in terms that will shake plutocratic courts to their foundations.

Let the names of these 11 men be committed to memory by every unionist, by every wage worker, and by every man, woman, and child who would preserve the little liberty there remains in the United States before the last spark of it has been totally extinguished.

Let the courts which have convicted and Imprisoned these men be denounced in the name of that liberty which the founders of this republic fought and died for, and handed down to their children.

Let us unite all our forces, whatever differences there may be, until these men are liberated.

Let us hold a thousand indignation meetings and in swelling numbers vow we shall not retreat—until these libertarians are free.

Let us rally this very day, a million strong, resolved to do our duty and blot out our disgrace; to arouse the sleeping hosts and stir the nation from center to circumference with our protest of indignation and our demand for liberation.

Liberty for the Imprisoned Refugees: The Right of Asylum Shall Be Preserved Inviolate![†]

March 6, 1909

The cases of the Mexican patriots in United States prisons is at this hour the most important that confronts the American people. Its significance grows out of its relation to the life and death struggle between the capitalist exploiters and the exploited workers of the United States and Mexico. The case in its present aspect resolves itself into an international conspiracy. Mexico is to be exploited with peon labor to the profit of American capitalists. Díaz is to keep the hordes of peons in subjection. Fabulous fortunes are to be amassed and the booty divided among the brigands. Patriots who protest are to be imprisoned or shot, and if any escape to the United States the federal authorities are to "take care" of them. Peon slavery is to be maintained in Mexico at all hazards, and the working class of the United States is to be reduced in due time to that foul and beastly state.

Magón, Villarreal, Sarabia, Rivera, and Araujo are five of the leading patriots in revolt against this infernal conspiracy. Díaz, the despot from whom they escaped, is bending all his energies to get them into his cruel clutches. If he succeeds, the closing chapter in their heroic struggle will be written in their own blood.

The authorities of the United States are in criminal collusion with the Díaz administration. The great exploiting capitalists control both governments, and both are bent upon the suppression of revolt against the hellish peonage of the Mexican masses.

Of the five patriot-refugees above named, one, Araujo, is already sentence and is serving his term in the United States military prison at Fort Leavenworth, Kansas. Another, Sarabia, is out under bail pending trial, while the three others, Magón, Villarreal, and Rivera, are held "incommunicado," having been refused bail, at Los Angeles. When they are to be tried, no one knows. They have already been in prison over a year and the administration at Washington has lent all its powers to prevent their release.

---

† Published in *Appeal to Reason*, whole no. 692 (March 6, 1909), 1. Unsigned article at front of the special "Liberty Edition" edited by Debs.

We shall not at this time repeat the long list of outrages which these staunch patriots and many others like them have suffered. These have already been graphically set forth in all their harrowing details by the *Appeal's* own special correspondent, after thorough personal investigation.[6] We are here concerned only with the duty—stern, imperious, uncompromising—which confronts us, the duty of rescuing these patriots from the clutches of their persecutors and would-be murderers. These men are heroes and humanitarians in the loftiest sense. For this very reason the price of the despot they defied is upon their heads. They are one with Patrick Henry: "Give me Liberty or give me Death."

These brave revolutionists, the hope of their crushed and despairing people, have sought asylum beneath the American flag, and here they are entitled to the protection of American law. They came as hosts of other refugees have come to seek refuge from the tyrant's avenging wrath, and every liberty-loving citizen should welcome them with open arms. Instead of this we see them pursued by Mexican spies and cutthroats and conniving with them, to our shame, the very authorities whose duty it is to protect them, hounding them to prison cells, cutting off their communication with the outer world, and secretly plotting to deliver them to their savage and bloodthirsty executioner.

The blood of every American not dead to the sentiment of liberty must burn with shame and indignation. These patriots are our sacred charge and their release our solemn responsibility.

Let the workers of the nation and the patriots of the Republic arise in protest all over the land! Let it not pass into history that these infamous outrages chronicle the eternal cowardice and shame of the present generation.

Not only must the sentiment of revolt spread like fire, but it must be organized and take definite form to accomplish its end. Happily this is now underway. A permanent organization has already been instituted. John Murray, specially commissioned by the Mexican patriots to represent them and given full authority, is at its head. He is the incarnation of the hour, the very man for the place, and has established himself at the Socialist national headquarters, 180 E. Washington Street, Chicago, Illinois. Miss Jane Adams, the famous reformer and humanitarian, has been chosen treasurer of the movement and all defense contributions should be directed to her at Hull House, Chicago.

The Socialist Party, through its National Committee, has pledged its unqualified support to the movement; the American Federation of Labor, in its annual convention, has taken the same action, and President Gompers recently filed with President Roosevelt the Federation's petition and protest, embracing a comprehensive and masterly review of the cases and demanding the release of the prisoners.

The burning issue of the hour is the liberation of these Mexican revolutionists imprisoned in American jails. There is not a shadow of justification for their outrageous persecution under the American flag. It is the infamy of international capitalism and its aim is the international slavery of the working class. If the hidden forces operating at the mainspring of this damnable treachery were visible to the American people, indignation would flame forth as white heat, and the whole nation would seethe with revolt. Oh, the atrocious crime, the burning shame, of hounding humanitarians, punishing patriots, and imprisoning liberators in the great American republic!

There is but one way to deal with this case, and that is to demand and insist upon immediate and unconditional release of the prisoners. Let that constitute the issue and let it be made so hot that the United States confederates of Díaz, the Mexican Nero, who draw salaries for serving the American people, will not dare to carry out their treasonable complicity.

Magón, Villarreal, and Rivera, like Moyer, Haywood, and Pettibone, are refused trial. The reason is the same. Were they guilty of crime they would long ago have been convicted. The fact that the government does not dare to try them, but is waiting for a favorable opportunity to smuggle them over the line to Díaz, is itself *prima facia* evidence of their innocence.

Let us put it up to the federal authorities squarely and with such emphasis as to jar them loose from their official dignity and cold-blooded indifference.

When are these men to be tried? We, the people, want to know. We have a right to know. We do not propose to see patriots who have sacrificed all but life and are ready to sacrifice that in the cause of liberty, rot in American bastilles to further a criminal conspiracy of American and Mexican capitalists to crush labor with an iron heel and reduce the whole working class to the filth and rags of Mexican peonage.

Hundreds of refugee liberation leagues should be organized and set in motion the machinery of agitation. Thousands of agitators should leap from the ranks in public places and tell the story of Mexico's crimes and America's dishonor. Thousands of dollars should be contributed to the legal defense fund.

The issue involved is as much American as it is Mexican, so far as the outcome is concerned. Defeat would mean disaster here as well as there, while victory will not only vitalize the drooping spirits of the Mexican people, but will animate with fresh zeal the hosts of labor who are fighting the battles for emancipation from plutocracy in the United States.

Does God or the Church Change?[†]

March 6, 1909

Those who make private property of the gifts of God pretend in vain to be innocent; for, in thus retaining the subsistence of the poor, they are the murderers of those who die every day for want of it.

Whom do you suppose brought this drastic indictment against the private ownership of land—the most essential gift of God? Some wild-eyed socialist? Not so. It was none other than Gregory the Great,[7] the first Pope of Rome of that name, and who has been canonized. If that was good Catholicism in days gone by, what is the matter with it today?

St. Gregory saw that by the few owning the earth, they could and did levy tribute upon the poor for the use of the land, and he called them murderers.

Are there any high churchmen today denouncing the private ownership of God's gifts? You do not hear of them, do you? On the other hand, they are defending the private ownership of the earth and everything that is in it or on it, under it, or above it.

The rich have captured the church and use it to oppress the poor. I suppose some will denounce the *Appeal* for calling attention to this, or they may claim that God has changed since St. Gregory was the head of the church. Read it over and see how it harmonizes with the teachings of the church today.

† Unsigned article published in *Appeal to Reason*, whole no. 692 (March 6, 1909), 4. Part of the special "Liberty Edition" edited by Debs, attributed to Debs by style.

Secret Agents at Work†

March 6, 1909

In every age since there has been a ruling class, spies and secret agents have been employed to prevent successful revolt of the class in subjection. By this means the secret plans of subjects have been betrayed, their leaders arrested, and their attempts frustrated.

In Russia the tsar relies mainly upon the efficiency of his spying system which spreads over the vast domain like a tarantula. In Mexico Díaz the dictator has his secret agents in every party and every organization to keep him informed of every move that is made and every whisper that is uttered in reference to his administration.

Similarly, in the United States the capitalist class has its spies in every party and every union of the working class. Some of the most enthusiastic supporters of radical measures and consequently least suspected are secret agents in the service of the capitalist class.

It was by such vicious means that the early organization of the coal miners in the anthracite regions of Pennsylvania was destroyed and the leaders hanged as "Molly Maguires." The truth about that base betrayal and the tragedy which followed has yet to be written. All that has so far been written has been by the capitalist class through the prostituted scribes in its service.

The Western Federation of Miners has had a corporation spy in every local union, as was shown in the trial of Moyer, Haywood, and Pettibone, and is not yet free from their baleful and pernicious influence. All other labor unions have secret agents of the capitalist class enrolled as members, whose business it is to have the unions run in the interest of their masters.

Two articles pregnant with the most damning facts in reference to the spying system have recently appeared in the *Saturday Evening Post*, entitled "The Long Arm of the Secret Police,"[8] from which we quote briefly as follows:

> The secret agent finds another line of employment in the espionage to which trade unions and similar associations of employees are submitted by the great employers of labor. Many of the great railways and manufac-

† Unsigned article published in *Appeal to Reason*, whole no. 692 (March 6, 1909), 4. Part of the special "Liberty Edition" edited by Debs, attributed to Debs by style.

> turing concerns of the country maintain regularly-organized secret intelligence systems, by means of which they are kept constantly informed of all that goes on in their shops and at the meetings of the unions to which their employees belong. These agents are instructed to have themselves elected to office and appointed on important committees in the unions, the employers thus being able to obtain advance notice of strikes, boycotts, or proposals of arbitration. It is by means of these same agents that the employers are enabled to direct the thoughts of their employees into the "right channels," which means, when translated, opposition to socialism, the evils of certain forms of trade unionism, and the like.[9]

This statement is absolutely correct. There is food in it for every socialist and every union man. We have here the reason why so many unions are "conservative" and why so many cheap skates[10] and ward-heeling politicians function as labor leaders. It is well for every union and every party of the working class to be on the alert for these deadly vipers.

War Is Murder in Uniform†

March 27, 1909

Douglas Jerrold once said that "war is murder in uniform."[11] That it should survive to the nineteenth century would be an inexplicable mystery, if it were not for the knowledge that it is a mere adjunct to wholesale and persistent robbery committed under the organization falsely called civilization. There has never been a war, save wars of rebellion and revolution, that had not robbery for its motive.

In the olden days the warrior was frankly a freebooter, and his victim was the man of wealth, the merchant and capitalist. But since capitalism has come into dominance, the victim is not the merchant, unless he is a foreigner, but the farmer and factory worker, who produced the wealth that was taken.

In the old days the conquered was deprived of all and reduced to open slavery. Of late years the victim is despoiled of hope in life and of freedom, just

† Published in *Oakland World*, March 27, 1909, unspecified page.

as of old, only now he is mad to believe that he is free and is flattered with the hope that someday he himself may become a robber.

In olden days they slaughtered with sword and battle-axe, in contests which involved some risk, but now they kill at a distance, and bribe the worker at $13 a month to murder his brother worker.

In olden days war was a matter of battles and sudden spoliation, but now they not only slaughter with the finest machinery that human ingenuity can devise, but after the battle is over, they tie both the victim and the conquering worker to other machines that evermore squeeze money from their bodies.

Oh, the horrors and terrors of war! When Sherman, who knew of it from having burned a road 60 miles wide through a prosperous region, was asked what war is, he faltered for a word to describe it and then answered, "It is hell." It is hell, and the profit-mongers for whom it exists and for whose aid armies and navies are maintained are devilish.

I never look on brook or river, stealing through fertile lands, but that I fancy they do not run with wholesome water, but with blood and sweat and tears. I never look on a great city, that wonder-picture of man's creative power, but that I see its wall masoned with human bones. When I would express my horror of war, my hatred of war, I am silent, because words cannot tell it. But I wonder how long the workers will continue to march up to the yoke, how long they will let the masters inflame them with hatred toward each other, how long they will go out to red slaughter for the glory of others and their own enslavement.

Are we not all brothers? Then why should some ride others, and why should some have all and others naught?

Are we not of one blood? Then why should we kill each other, making wives widows and children orphans, that we may enable the rulers of men to feast the more?

Oh, unspeakable barbarism! Oh, needless suffering and foolish burden-bearing! Awake, men of the world, brothers of the world, from the old madness, and stand with the light of a better day glorifying the foreheads that have learned to think and kindling the hearts that have at last learned to love in deed and in truth, and then war shall be no more; for if the workers shall cease to kill each other for others' gain, the monstrosity of war will pass away like a horror of the troubled night.

Property and Public Welfare†

May 1909

Socialists are the real conservators of true property rights. It is just because socialism insists that the individual is entitled to the fruits of his toil and shall be permitted free and unrestricted enjoyment thereof that it demands the collective ownership of capital together with the abolition of the economic categories of rent, interest, and profit.

Property is a conventional arrangement, pure and simple. Its laws are of human—not divine—origin, sanction, and regulation. Society has created those laws; society may destroy them. No man enjoys a right of property except by the consent of society. These are truisms that have only to be stated to be understood. The object of property is the social good. Society attaches a right of property to certain things with a view to promote the general welfare and insure the stability of government. This right is constantly changing in obedience to paramount social demands. Within the memory of thousands of men yet living, society sanctioned the right of property in human beings. It does so no longer.

With regard to the vast wealth which Mr. Rockefeller has accumulated under existing property arrangements, socialists are indifferent. He may retain possession of his wealth if he so wills; he may leave it to his son when he dies. What socialists contend for is not a redistribution of present wealth, but the abolition of those conventional property arrangements which have enabled Mr. Rockefeller to accumulate a fortune of $500 million within the brief period of 40 years.

In what does the property of Mr. Rockefeller consist? Is it mines and factories, railroads, steamships, pipelines, stocks and bonds, houses and lands? No, it is none of these things. His right to property is the right which constitutes the essential nature of legally recognized ownership—the right to reap the fruits of the productive exploitation of natural opportunities, or material wealth of any description without exercising the functions of use and possession; the right,

† Published as "Property Exists for the Benefit of the Many, Not for the Profit of a Few" as part of the symposium "Whose Is It?" in *The Circle* [New York], vol. 5, no. 5 (May 1909), 268, 319. Reprinted as "Property and Public Welfare" in the *New York Call*, June 5, 1909.

in short, which enables him to enjoy the fruit of the labor of others without in any manner contributing to the result of such labor. The proprietor merely receives tribute from those who labor for not exercising toward them his legally recognized right of exclusion.

His tribute—rent, interest, and profit—expresses his right of limitation on the production and consumption of wealth which the law has endowed him with, and is pure robbery. This right to enjoy without exercising the functions of use and possession constitutes the essential nature of property. It is really all there is to the right of property as now recognized. It is this right which socialism would abolish in the interest of the common good.

Under the existing system the primary motive leading to the production and exchange of all wealth is profit, not use. Clothing is not made because people want to wear it. Wheat is not grown and animals are not slaughtered because society needs bread and meat to preserve its members from starvation. All the things which are vitally necessary to the life of mankind, together with those which contribute merely to man's comfort or convenience, are produced and distributed primarily for the reason that producers and trades are able to realize profit therefrom. The use function of these things is purely a secondary consideration.

When profit ceases, industry comes to a standstill, notwithstanding that numberless social units must suffer the pangs of cold and starvation because of such stoppage. Thus the profit of the individual is given precedence over the common social good. Socialism contends that the primary industrial motive should be use; that bread, meat, and clothing are profitable to [but] a few of the individual members of society.

When Mr. Rockefeller was questioned recently about the actual details of the business of the Standard Oil Company, he admitted his ignorance. He retired from active participation in the affairs of the company some years ago. Its operations are now conducted by other persons, yet Mr. Rockefeller still receives the lion's share of the profits. Mr. Carnegie no longer has anything to do with the actual operations of the Steel Trust. He no more contributes his labor and talent to the production of steel than Mr. Rockefeller does to the production of oil, yet his profits from the steel business are still very considerable. Mr. Harriman knows very little about the actual operating details of his railroads. He is busy with financial schemes to make his railroads produce dividends. Their actual operation is conducted by other men.

As a matter of self-preservation, society must finally decree the collective ownership of all these great industries, must extinguish the individual right of property therein and so the individual's right to receive tribute therefrom. In that event Mr. Rockefeller may be left with his $500 million, Mr. Carnegie with his $300 million, and Mr. Harriman with his $100 million. They will no longer be able to reinvest their vast accumulations so as to exact tribute from industry, and their wealth will represent merely a power of consumption. The accumulations must constantly decrease, being no longer augmented by dividends and interest, to finally disappear altogether. Society can well afford to permit them and their children to remain idle, seeing that they will no longer have the power to decree idleness to thousands of helpless human beings at will.

Why must society abolish the right of private property in capital as a matter of self-preservation? Because it is an impossible right, founded upon a destructive principle, that of interest. Had one cent been loaned at 6 percent interest, compounded semiannually, AD 1 and been left to accumulate all the years until 1900, it would amount to a sum so vast that many millions of globes, each as large as our earth and all of solid gold, would be required to equal it. A solid chain of $20 gold pieces, reaching from the earth to the most distant planet in our solar system and back to earth again, would scarcely be missed from the thoroughly unrealized accumulation that would result.[12] The fact is that it is utterly impossible to so manipulate capital as to make it yield sufficient increase to satisfy the accumulated demands of interest after setting aside sufficient wealth to support the population (even though many of the people are always half-starved and a good percentage of them wholly so) and there must come periodic breakdowns in which the property titles of the smaller holders become extinguished.

Now, take a look at the obverse of this interest problem: If a man were able, by the labor of his hands or brain, to satisfy all his needs and lay aside $1 every day in the year, he would be in an enviable position, would he not? Let us suppose, then, that a man had begun working and saving on January 1, 1 AD, and that his life had been miraculously preserved through all these years until January 1, 1909, he continuing to add $1 to his store at the end of every day, how much would he be worth, barring interest? He would be worth $596,420, but little more than half a million. Hardly enough to give him a single flyer on the stock exchange!

Fred D. Warren Convicted by a Packed Jury[†]

May 15, 1909

It was the common remark of the spectators at the trial of Fred D. Warren, managing editor of the *Appeal to Reason*, which opened before Judge Pollock of the federal court at Ft. Scott, Kansas, on May 4th [1909], that he would be tried by a packed jury. The evidence of this was so apparent and striking as to make it self-evident. Not by socialists alone was this said, but by others who personally knew the jurors, their politics, and their prejudices.

Under the federal law the United States Marshal for the district impanels the jury. He can choose whomsoever he pleases. In the panel from which the Warren jury was chosen, there was not one who was not known to be an opponent of socialism, if not a hater of the *Appeal to Reason*. It was a jury of Republicans. It was impaneled to convict and so began at last the Warren trial.

For over two years this case has been hanging fire. Four separate times the government asked for a postponement. Contrary to the expectations of the prosecution, the interest did not die out, but increased. Only in one respect were the government's expectations realized and that was in the enormous expenses to which the *Appeal* has been subjected and which it was hoped would be the means of putting it out of business.

Of course, the prosecuting attorney, Bone,[13] knew that he could secure a conviction, for he knew that his friend the United States marshal would furnish the material for the right kind of jury. But the court feared the effect of a conviction and at a previous trial the judge took occasion to say that it might result in increasing the power of the publication aimed at, instead of abating the nuisance.

All the government wanted was a conviction, and Warren's lawyers were given to understand that if they would enter a plea of guilty the defendant would be released on a small fine. This was refused. The prosecution then declared that if they were compelled to fight, they would fight to win and the defendant would get the limit. To this Warren answered that he would a thousand times rather accept the limit than to be so cowardly as to surrender to the enemy to his own personal benefit.

† Published as "Warren Convicted by a Packed Jury" in *Appeal to Reason*, whole no. 702 (May 15, 1909), 1.

The chief witness of the prosecution proved to be ex-Governor Taylor, of Kentucky. The case of Mr. Taylor need not be discussed here. For several years he was a fugitive from justice, making his residence in Indiana and not venturing to return to Kentucky, where he was under indictment and where a large reward was offered for his return. The Republican governor recently elected in Kentucky issued a pardon to ex-Governor Taylor, and it has been strongly intimated that the Warren trial was held in abeyance until this pardon was granted so that he might appear at the trial without an indictment hanging over him. Be this as it may, it is at least an interesting coincidence that the Warren trial has been postponed for over two years and that it was called just after the governor of Kentucky granted a pardon to ex-Governor Taylor so that he might testify against the defendant.

Ex-Governor Taylor was placed upon the stand, but his examination was very brief. He was simply identified as the ex-Governor for whose return Editor Warren had offered a reward of $1,000.

Post Office Inspector Chance was placed on the witness stand and testified that Warren had told him that he had destroyed the mailing list and that he could not, therefore, say whether or not the letter containing the offer of the reward for the return of Taylor had been sent to the person named in the indictment. In making this statement, Chance told a deliberate lie. Warren never said any such thing. The postmaster of Girard, who was present during the conversation, testified against Chance upon this point.

This falsehood was uttered to convict Warren in the minds of the jury of having destroyed the evidence against him. As a matter of fact, the mailing list was not destroyed, nor did Warren say it was, nor did anyone think such a thing until Chance invented the lie to serve his malign purpose.

The evidence was soon in. The fact is the prosecution had no evidence at all, or anything worthy to be called by that name. It was the flimsiest case ever tried outside of a mock court. The spectators smiled audibly at the farce that was being enacted in a so-called temple of justice.

The defense put Comrade George D. Brewer,[14] former manager of the mailing department, on the witness stand and he testified that so far as he knew no letter offering the reward complained of had been sent to the person, one Pierson, named in the indictment. Brewer testified that the mailing lists had been carefully examined and that they contained no such name and that so far as he knew nothing had been sent to that person from the *Appeal* office. When it is taken into account that Brewer had complete charge of the mailing department at the time, his evidence is conclusive upon that point.

The letter upon which the indictment was based and out of which the whole case grew was alleged to have been sent to a person named Pierson in California, and this was the letter filed in evidence against the *Appeal.* But, strange to say, Pierson, who is responsible for the prosecution, has not been heard of and no one knows if he be dead or alive or even if there be such a person. In his argument to the jury, Attorney Darrow did not hesitate to say that Chance, the post office inspector, very likely had a confederate and that Pierson was the fictitious person to whom this matter was sent as the basis of his prosecution of the *Appeal.* It would have been very easy for anyone to do this very trick and it would not be at all surprising if there was no such person as Pierson and that a letter was directed to him by some post office sleuth as a means of indicting and prosecuting the *Appeal.*

The little courtroom at Fort Scott was packed with interested spectators. So large was the crowd that the judge had to issue an order placing guards at the doors to keep the throng out. Notwithstanding this, they packed the hall to the stairways and 9 out of every 10 were in hearty sympathy with the defendant.

Warren was attended by Wayland, Debs, and the whole *Appeal* staff, besides a number of comrades who went up from Girard. The comrades of Fort Scott and vicinity were on hand early and remained without even going to their meals until the verdict was rendered.

At 4 o'clock in the afternoon. on the second day of the trial, the case went to the jury after being ably argued by the counsel for the defense and after receiving the instructions from the court which, it must be said in justice to the judge, were perfectly fair and free from reasonable objection. The jury at once retired and remained in session 22 hours. Notwithstanding the fact that the jury was packed, there were three of its members who had consciences which would not permit them to be a party to such an unwarranted and outrageous prosecution. Their better natures revolted and they refused to lend a hand to such persecution and it was only after a siege of 22 hours that they were finally overruled by their brethren and persuaded to abide by the verdict of the majority.

The verdict of guilty was not a surprise. It was expected. It would have been a surprise only if it had been otherwise.

Immediately the verdict was rendered, the lawyers for the defense entered a motion for a new trial. This motion will be argued in 10 days from the time it was entered. In the meantime, sentence is suspended.

The maximum penalty is five years in the penitentiary at hard labor and a fine of $5,000. It is this that has been hanging over Warren's head during the past two years. Ordinarily the suspense would be great, but in this case the defendant has been serene, feeling in his heart that he had committed no wrong but that he was being persecuted for no other reason than that he was the editor of a powerful socialist paper which the plutocratic administration had determined to put out of existence.

Whether Warren is finally sentenced or not, there is a mighty issue involved in his case. No one in his sane mind supposes for an instant that Warren is being prosecuted for violating the postal laws. Thousands of similar publications have been made all over the country, but no one has ever dreamed of prosecuting a person offering a reward for a fugitive from justice. Had Warren been a Republican or a Democrat, this case would never have been heard of.

But he is a Socialist and the editor of a powerful socialist paper which is a thorn in the flesh of the grafters now in control of the government, and for years they have had their sleuths on his trail and have been watching for some chance to strike the blow and to cripple if not destroy the paper of which he is the editor.

The prosecution may take advantage of the power they have to fine and imprison Warren, but they would better beware of the day to come. Nothing would so thoroughly arouse the people of this country as the conviction of Warren upon this flimsy charge. It would be a monstrous outrage which fair and honest people, regardless of politics, would condemn and it would be certain to react powerfully upon those responsible for it.

Moreover, this prosecution, based upon an envelope quite likely made to order, must be regarded as an attack upon a free press. If the editor of the *Appeal* can be sent to the penitentiary simply because he is a socialist, some other man, or any other man, can be convicted for being something else, and in that case the freedom of the press is destroyed and a censorship is established as odious and infamous as that which prevails in Russia and Mexico.

Principle Features of the Fred D. Warren Trial†

May 22, 1909

Liberty of the press is the issue involved in the case of Fred D. Warren, editor of the *Appeal to Reason*, which has been pending in the United States court since the indictment found at Fort Scott, Kansas, May 7, 1907, over two years ago.

This is of course denied by the prosecution, the contention being that an individual offense has been committed and that the punishment of an individual is all that is contemplated. It will be remembered that precisely the same contention was made in the cases of Moyer, Haywood, and Pettibone when it was insisted by the prosecuting officials and the mine owners who were backing them that these were but plain murder cases and that no other issue was involved. It developed during the trials and is now clearly understood that the real issue was capital vs. labor and the right of the Western Federation of Miners to maintain its existence and defend the interests of its members against the aggressions of the Mine Owners' Association.

Similarly in the present case, the issue involves far more than the punishment of an individual for the alleged violation of a federal law. If this were all, the case would have been settled long ago and would have excited but little interest.

But readers of the *Appeal* are too well informed and have been following the trend of events too closely to be misled by any such specious plea on the part of those who are far more interested in suppressing the *Appeal* than they are in punishing its editor for an alleged individual offense.

Let us briefly review the main features of this now celebrated case which has extended over so long a period and has had so many curious turns and windings that there is no other like it in all the history of American jurisprudence.

First.— The indictment charges Warren with having sent, or caused to be sent, to one Pierson in California an envelope bearing [advertisement for] a reward for the return of ex-Governor Taylor to the state of Kentucky, from whence he was a fugitive and where he was under indictment for murder. This envelope fell into the hands of a post office inspector and the indictment followed. Pierson himself, to whom the envelope was directed, made no

† Published as "The Trial and Conviction of Fred D. Warren" in *Appeal to Reason*, whole no. 703 (May 22, 1909), 1.

complaint. For some reason as yet unexplained, he did not even receive it. How it came to be directed to him no one knows. His name is not on the *Appeal*'s lists. Neither Warren nor the *Appeal* had ever heard of him, nor has he even been heard from since the trial began. Who Pierson is, or if there is such a person, no one knows. For all that the evidence shows he is simply a dummy who has been made to serve in what seems to have been a plot to indict the Appeal, a thing which had been long before and repeatedly threatened.

Second.— Warren was arrested, placed under bail the day following his indictment, and asked for immediate trial. This was denied and the case went over until the November term of court. Since then there have been four distinct postponements, all on motion of the government, every effort of the defendant to have the trial proceed proving unavailing until the case was finally called at the May term of court, 1909, two years after the indictment.

Third.— The specific charge in the indictment was that Warren had violated the federal statute prohibiting the mailing of "scurrilous, defamatory, and threatening matter." By no stretch of the imagination can the matter complained of be construed as having any such meaning. Ex-Governor Taylor did not complain. In truth he had nothing to complain about. The state of Kentucky had offered a $100,000 reward for his return to that state and spread it broadcast. The *Appeal* had offered but $1,000. Taylor himself, so far as anyone knows, did not feel aggrieved. If anyone was injured it was he, and if he was not injured no one could have been, for he was the only one mentioned. No one denies that Taylor was under indictment, that he was a fugitive, and that a reward had been offered for his return by the legislature of Kentucky. All these facts are well known, and Warren simply took advantage of them to ascertain if a capitalist politician as well as a workingman could be legally kidnapped. He found out. He at least compelled the federal government to show its hand. When Moyer, Haywood, and Pettibone were kidnapped, the Supreme Court decided that it could take no cognizance of that fact in the consideration of their appeal, in effect legalizing the kidnapping of workingmen. Associate Justice McKenna dissented from the court in a ringing opinion in which he declared that the state officials of Colorado and Idaho were the real criminals and should be dealt with accordingly. Warren's offer of the reward for Taylor, although it has subjected him and the *Appeal* to thousands of dollars of expense and it may yet result in his imprisonment, has demonstrated at least one fact of no mean importance and that is that while under the present capitalist government, workingmen can be kidnapped and forcibly deported by sanction of the Supreme Court and denounced in advance of trial by the president, a representative of the capitalist class is protected by all the powers of government and the mere suggestion that he be kidnapped, even if a fugitive with a reward upon his head, is promptly followed by indictment and prosecution of the offender.

Fourth.— At the preliminary hearing Deputy Prosecuting Attorney West stated, in an impassioned plea for the prosecution of the defendant, that orders had been received from the Department of Justice at Washington to prosecute the case against Warren, the assurance being given that the indictment was good, that the law had been violated, and that a conviction could be secured. If the case involved but an individual offense, as contended by the prosecution, is it probable that the Department of Justice at Washington would have been so vitally interested in securing a conviction? Would the president of the United States have been so eager to direct the prosecution from the White House as announced by the press dispatches and commented upon editorially by such a powerful capitalist daily as the *Kansas City Journal*? Is it customary for the president and attorney general to direct the prosecution of individual offenders in cases of minor importance? But one answer is possible and that is that the administration was interested in the case, not because of Fred Warren, the individual offender, but because of Fred Warren, the editor of the *Appeal to Reason*, the most widely circulated socialist paper and the most formidable opponent of capitalism in the United States.

Fifth.— A significant remark made by a gentleman of high official standing, whose name we cannot disclose without betraying the source of our information, throws a clear side light on the animus of the prosecution and also explains the cause of this long-drawn trial and its repeated postponement. The remark was to the effect that if the *Appeal* could be reached in no other way, it could be kept in court indefinitely and loaded with fees and costs until "the damned reptile was bled to death." This view was inadvertently corroborated by Prosecuting Attorney Bone in his speech to the jury in which the said, "the name of this sheet, the *Appeal to Reason*, should be changed to the *Appeal to Treason*." And yet Mr. Bone in his opening statement declared that it was simply a case of trying the defendant for depositing a letter in the mail which was not mailable under the law. If this was true, what had the mailing of this letter to do with the *Appeal to Reason*, and why did he deem it necessary to denounce the *Appeal* as a treasonable sheet? It was here that he gave his entire case away and revealed too clearly to admit of doubt that it was the *Appeal to Reason* as a socialist paper he was after and not Warren as an individual offender.

Sixth.— Judge Pollock in interrogating the deputy prosecuting attorney at the preliminary hearing shook his head significantly in denial of the latter's contention that the mailing of rewards for fugitives from justice was in violation of the federal statute, and then sounded the precautionary note in words too plain to be misunderstood that such a prosecution directed against an editor would be construed as an attack upon the liberty of the press and would probably have an effect opposite that intended. It was at the close of this hearing that the attorneys for the defense expressed the opinion that there was nothing in the case and that it had been postponed so that it might die out and be stricken from the docket. It was about this time that the Department of Justice at Washington was heard from, the purport of its order being that if there was "not a case against the *Appeal* to make one!" Then followed the announcement that if Warren did not plead guilty, thereby fastening the odium of having committed a crime upon himself as editor of the *Appeal to Reason*, he would be prosecuted to the limit of the law.

Seventh.— Rewards for criminals and fugitives from justice are mailed daily in all parts of the country by sheriffs, mayors, detectives, bankers, and private individuals, but no one has ever before thought of charging them with violating postal laws. The claim that in the case of Warren he offered his reward to kidnap a fugitive and therefore commit a crime will not hold, seeing that the United States Supreme Court has legalized kidnapping by refusing to take cognizance of the kidnapping of Moyer, Haywood, and Pettibone when they appealed to that august tribunal. If it is not a crime to kidnap a workingman who has not been indicted, then it cannot be a crime to kidnap a capitalist politician who has been indicted. That is the point at issue. The Supreme Court of the United States is welcome to either horn of the dilemma. The case may not be clothed here in the legal terminology designed to mystify the issue and convey doubtful meanings, but in substance and effect it is clearly stated.

Eighth.— When the case was finally called for a trial, a jury had to be chosen from a panel which had been prepared by the United States marshal. The panel was carefully selected and no mistake was made, and as a result the jury was a packed jury. There was no socialist or socialist sympathizer upon that jury. There was not a Democrat or a Populist. It consisted of rock-ribbed Republicans, who regard the *Appeal to Reason* as a treasonable sheet and its editor as a criminal. While the jury was being chosen, Judge Pollock took occasion to state that the matter of politics was not to be considered in the trial. In the light of the plain facts in this case, this must be considered a joke although the judge looked too solemn to have intended it. If there was no politics in the case, how did it happen that there was not a socialist on the panel or on the jury and that Warren had to be tried by a jury consisting wholly of his political enemies?

Ninth.— Even then it required the jury 22 hours to decide upon a verdict of guilty. Three of the members, notwithstanding their political hostility, were opposed to a conviction upon such a flimsy charge and held out until they were finally overcome by the large majority against them. When the verdict was announced, the judge suspended sentence, the attorneys for the defendant making a motion for a new trial. The judge stated that he would hear argument upon the motion in 10 days or two weeks from the date. Following adjournment, however, the judge postponed the entire matter, including the passing of sentence, until the November term of court—and here the case rests. Why the judge hesitated to pronounce the sentence in accordance with the verdict found in his court and postponed the case for another six months is left wholly to conjecture. It is quite evident that notwithstanding the insistence of the prosecution, and the power behind the prosecution, upon a conviction, there is still some reluctance to execute the law and enforce the penalty imposed by the court.

∽

We have here reviewed the principal features of this remarkable case. Our readers may arrive at their own conclusion as to whether it is merely the prosecution of an individual or an attack upon the socialist press in particular and the liberty of the press in general. Without the *Appeal to Reason*, this case would never have been heard of. Warren might have deposited the same envelope in the post office every day to the end of his life and no grand jury would ever have dreamed of indicting him.

The *Appeal to Reason* recognizes the issue and faces the attack without fear of the ultimate outcome. Its managing editor has violated no law, but has been indicted in the orderly discharge of his duties for no other reason than that he is the editor of a paper which is opposed to the present capitalist regime and which has influence enough among the people to make itself felt in the struggle of the masses to abolish capitalist misrule and emancipate themselves from wage-slavery.

The *Appeal to Reason* is fortunate in having the support of as loyal a body of men and women as ever consecrated themselves to any cause, and with these to back it up it is ready to face any attack which may be made upon it, and if its colors are ever lowered it will only be when it is overwhelmed by superior numbers.

You Are of One Class: Speech to Pressed Steel Car Company Strikers, McKees Rocks, Pennsylvania [excerpt]†

August 24, 1909

There are 15 nationalities represented here this morning, but you are of one class.[15] You are workingmen, united in a single cause. You are wage-slaves in the eyes of the corporation.[16] Though I cannot understand your language, I can read your hearts and can make myself understood to you.

I, too, have suffered. I have been on strike and have become involved in riots. I know what it is to face a heartless power.

This desperate fight must be continued. The eyes of the civilized world and the eyes of all the laborers of the world are upon you. It is the greatest labor fight in all history. The laboring men in Pittsburgh particularly should stand by their fellow workers in this fight.

I want to warn you of traitors. Beware of spies. They circulate among you and talk your language. They pretend to suffer with you when in reality they are employees of the Pressed Steel Car Company. They are employed by parasites who are lounging in their summer retreats while you are suffering and starving. You make the money which the degenerate sons of these parasites squander on champagne.

They hold that the cheapest thing in the world is human flesh. Your blood means nothing to them. Because you have walked away from your work, you are to be shot.

You are not responsible for the horrors that have occurred. It was precipitated through a minion of the corporation who was hired to assassinate workingmen. I have seen the wage envelopes of some of the workingmen since I came to Pittsburgh,[17] and the situation seems very similar to that of the Pullman Company, which likewise deducted the rent for the house and other charges from the pay of the men until there was nothing left.

† Published as "Debs Flays the Car Corporation" in *Pittsburgh Press*, August 25, 1910, 1–2.

This is a time for somber thought, for serious thought. It is not a time for violence. Be true to yourself. You were born in poverty. You have no opportunity. You have been reared in privation. You have had no opportunity to develop minds with which to cope with the subtle methods which has wrested this enormous wealth from you. Your masters hold you in contempt, they take away your production for their own selfish use.

They do not go to your hovels and see how you live.[18] They compel you to live in shanties which they would not use as kennels for their dogs, yet your children are reared among just such surroundings.

A wage worker who for the sake of employment sacrifices his wife is despicable. What infamy!

Statement to the Press on the McKees Rocks Strike†

September 1, 1909

There is a situation at McKees Rocks unlike any other strike situation in American history.[19] The great plant employing 5,000 workingmen is a vast stockade—more properly, a slave pen. The company owns not only the works, but the stores, houses, and all other things, including private jails in which they incarcerate their employees at will.

Years ago the plant sent its agents abroad to scour the countries of the Old World for the cheapest kind of labor, with the result that 16 separate nationalities are represented among the employees, the least of which is the United States. But a very few of the number can speak the English language, a great mass of them are illiterate and are practically the peons of the corporation.

The most striking feature of this great strike is that there is not a union man in the entire body. They were brought to this country for the purpose of destroying unionism and lowering the standard of living to abject slavery. It cannot therefore be charged that the strike is due to mischievous agitation on the part of any labor leader.

† Published as "Debs Views Steel Strike" in Ardmore [OK] *Morning Democrat*, vol. 4, no. 70 (September 2, 1909), 1.

It is this that is remarkable about the McKees Rocks strike. It is not the result of unionism, or of any concerted action on the part of employees to raise wages or better their condition but a spontaneous revolt of 6,000 wage serfs whose terrible condition was no longer tolerable even to themselves.

The entire public sympathy is with the strikers, and some of the most powerful papers in Pittsburgh are openly pleading the cause of the employees. But in spite of all this, the corporation with its $25 million of capital and its fabulous resources is holding the entire community in contempt.

Such a situation is bound to open the eyes of the people to the tremendous and irresponsible power concentrated in the hands of a few industrial despots and is certain in the end to be fruitful of good results to the people.

Flag of Freedom†

October 16, 1909

The capitalist press takes advantage of every opening to squirt its venom at the "red flag of treason and anarchy." It is a historic fact that the battle of Bunker Hill and other battles of the American revolution were fought under the "red flag of treason and anarchy."

The red flag was the symbol of the revolutionary spirit that gave us the republic.

All the fruit of the revolution is eagerly sought and claimed by the "sons and daughters of the revolution," but the red flag under which the ragged continentals fought the Tory power of Great Britain is repudiated with scorn and hate as a vile and loathsome thing.

And why?

Because it is still the sign of progress and symbol of revolution; and the corn-fed, ham-fat bourgeoisie want no more revolution.

The revolution that put the bourgeoisie in power was great and its red flag was glorious; the revolution now under way, whose historic mission it is to drive the bourgeoisie out of power, is infamous and its red flag is treason.

† Published in *Appeal to Reason*, whole no. 724 (October 16, 1909), 7.

In other words, the bourgeoisie, the capitalist class, glorify all the revolutions of the past and shake their fat fists at all the revolutions of the future. The capitalist class has been put in power by past revolutions; therefore, they are glorious. The capitalists yearn to remain in perpetual power; therefore, there must be no more revolutions.

The earth must come to a halt; evolution to a standstill; progress to a dead stop.

The capitalist class, Joshua-like,[20] has spoken and its command is as inexorable as the fiat of Jehovah. Revolution shall be no more! Haul down the red flag of revolt, the scarlet emblem of treason, the hated rag of the rabble!

Another bit of red flag history is recalled by the great demonstration that occurred in Rome a few days ago, of which the press dispatches give full account. September 27th was the 37th anniversary of the occupation of Rome by Italian troops[21] and the fall of the temporal power of the papacy.[22] A tremendous celebration of the event took place and the red flag was everywhere in evidence. The Associated Press report from Rome says:

> Armed men in the service of the pope have been on guard all day long at the entrances of the Apostolic palace, and the Vatican has been under the special protection of a detachment of royal troops, but there has been no active outbreak of anti-clerical sentiment.

* * *

There were two big parades this afternoon through the streets of the city, and the *red shirts* of the Garibaldian veterans were conspicuous in the throng. The first parade was official, and composed of the members of 50 local associations. . . . The other parade was popular and unofficial. It marched past the capitol, carrying banners inscribed with anti-clerical sentiments. *Returning, the crowd raised a red flag over the equestrian statue of Marcus Aurelius.*

During the day the police seized a number of anti-monarchist proclamations, and the walls of the city were placarded with appeals of the people to "complete the anti-clerical victory at the coming municipal elections."

The events of 37 years ago are celebrated in Italy every year, but this time there were indications that the populace would take advantage of the demonstrations to indulge the anti-clerical sentiments that of recent months have cause the Vatican authorities considerable anxiety.

The day was celebrated throughout the peninsula as well as in Rome. When Garibaldi and his followers fought their historic battles for Italian independence and separation of the state from papal authority 40 years ago, they carried red flags and wore red shirts as the emblems of revolt against the insufferable despotism of state and church. All over the world, Garibaldi and his soldiers were cheered and urged on in their struggle for Italian independence and for freedom from the grasp of the church, and in no country were they more enthusiastically applauded than in the United States of America.

Garibaldi and his patriot followers were fighting tyranny and oppression, and they were fighting it as freedom-loving patriots have always fought it, under the red banner of revolt, and but for the spirit this hated standard symbolizes, the human race the world over would still be in abject slavery, cowering like whipped beasts beneath the lashes of their masters.

The red flag has always been hated by every tyrant ruler, every titled parasite, and every privileged robber of honest toil.

Forty years ago American editors whose veins still tingled with the blood of their own revolutionary sires cheered the red flag and the red shirts of Garibaldi and his revolutionary followers. They were not then the servile scribes of Standard Oil, the beef trust, the railroads, and other corporations as they are today. They had some manhood, some self-respect, and dared to salute the red flag of revolution which now, in their base and vulgar subserviency, "that thrift may follow fawning,"[23] they renounce with all the venom of their craven apostasy.

"I remember distinctly," writes Henry L. Drake, an old warrior of the cause, "the revolution in Italy; the red flag and the red-shirted Garibaldians, and the unstinted praise given them by the New York press and the Albany press, notably the *New York Tribune,* under Horace Greeley;[24] the *Albany Journal*, under Thurlow Weed,[25] and the *Detroit Free Press*, under Wilbur F. Storey.[26] These and many others, the principal papers of the country, freely applauded the red flag and the red shirts as emblems of liberty in that great struggle."

There has been no change in the red flag or in its character as a signal of protest and a harbinger of freedom. The change has been wholly in the vassal editors, so-called, more properly subsidized scribblers, who now affect to detest the principles their fathers avowed and the flag they felt proud to honor.

One of the old-time New York editors, who achieved fame because of his rugged honesty, expressed intense disgust in his latter days because of the degeneracy of the American press. He was then connected with one of the New York dailies, known as an "independent" paper. Accosted by a friend one day who inquired if the paper was really independent, he answered sharply: "Independent, hell! It's simply an intellectual house of assignation."

And that describes the general character of the plutocratic press, the capitalist cacklers against the red flag and the social revolution whose mission is the overthrow of wage-slavery. But the red flag will continue to wave and the revolution will continue its march to victory.

Statement of Protest over the Jailing of Lázaro Gutiérrez de Lara[†]

October 23, 1909

[Conneaut, Ohio, October 23, 1909]

When Lázaro Gutiérrez de Lara cried aloud in protest against the intolerable conditions in Mexico, Diaz ordered him shot. He escaped to the United States as other liberators, such as Kossuth,[27] had done before him and were received with open arms. But, alas! times have changed and the United States, instead of being a haven of refuge for the oppressed, is the bloodhound of despots and turnkey of assassins.

But the people are awakening and one of these days, ye plutocrats, you will reap the whirlwind you are sowing. The arrest of Gutiérrez de Lara, the Mexican patriot, by order of the dictator Díaz, his imprisonment incommunicado is an atrocity second only to the court-martialed assassination of Ferrer in Spain.

The United States is rapidly being Russianized and Mexicanized. Díaz, the monster, may now reach over here and imprison patriots, have them deported to Mexico, and assassinated in cold blood.

Mexico under Díaz is an inquisition of horrors. Hell is a paradise in comparison. Eighteen million peons' lives are ground under the iron heel of that monster. Mexico is no more a republic than a brothel is a saints' community.

Díaz rules, and by assassination. Thirty thousand atrocious murders lie at his door. This is the bloody monster Taft embraced in the name of the American people.

---

† Telegram to the United Press. Published as "'We Are Being Russianized' Says Agitator Debs" in *Buffalo Courier*, October 24, 1909, 33.

The Wall Street plutocrats have a billion dollars invested in American railways, mines, smelters, steel and cotton mills there. Mexico furnishes them with peon labor, and they divide the bloody booty with Díaz.

Three Mexican heroes are rotting in our federal dungeon at Florence, Arizona, and the federal prison at Leavenworth, Kansas, holds two more. Braver men than these have never sacrificed their freedom in the cause of humanity, and yet they are chained in the prison cells of our asylum for the oppressed upon the request of Díaz.

On the day Taft was in San Antonio, a number of socialists were thrown into jail without warrant or hearing upon the order of his secret service satraps. Gutiérrez de Lara, the latest victim, is of wealthy family and a graduate of the University of Mexico. He was a judge upon the bench and a member of the diplomatic corps of Mexico, but because he cried aloud in protest against the acts of Díaz, he incurred his enmity and is now being persecuted.

Woman—Comrade and Equal[†]

November 1909

The London *Saturday Review* in a recent issue brutally said: "Man's superiority is shown by his ability to keep woman in subjection."[28] Such a sentiment is enough to kindle the wrath of every man who loves his wife or reveres his mother. It is the voice of the wilderness, the snarl of the primitive. Measured by that standard, every tyrant has been a hero, and brutality is at once the acme of perfection and the glory of man.

But it is a lie and a libel. The author of it is an unnatural son striking his mother, a brutal husband glorying because he is able to fell his faithful wife to the earth, a beastly father beating his daughter with his fists and gloating as she falls because he is stronger than she.

Yet the sentiment is not confined to a moral degenerate who writes lies for pay, or to sycophants who sell their souls for the crumbs that arrogant wealth

---

† Excerpt first published in *Appeal to Reason*, whole no. 566 (October 6, 1906), 3. Published in full in *The Progressive Woman*, vol. 3, whole no. 30 (November 1909), 2. Reprinted as a leaflet by the National Women's Committee of the Socialist Party.

doles out to its vassals. It is embodied and embedded in the cruel system under which we live, the criminal system which grinds children to profits in the mills, which in the sweatshops saps women of their power to mother a race of decent men, which traps the innocent and true-hearted, making them worse than slaves in worse than all that has been said of hell. It finds expression in premiers hiding from petticoated agitators, in presidents ignoring the pleading of mothers of men, in the clubbing and jailing of suffragettes, in Wall Street gamblers and brigands cackling from their piles of loot at the demands of justice. It is expressed in laws which rank mothers and daughters as idiots and criminals. It writes, beside the declaration that men should rebel against taxation without representation, that women must submit to taxation without representation. It makes property the god that men worship, and says that women shall have no property rights. Instead of that, she herself is counted as property, living by sufferance of the man who doles out the pittance that she uses.

Woman is made the slave of a slave, and is reckoned fit only for companionship in lust. The hands and breasts that nursed all men to life, as scorned as the forgetful brute proclaims his superior strength and plumes himself that he can subjugate the one who made him what he is, and would have him better had his customs and institutions permitted.

How differently is woman regarded by the truly wise and the really great! Poala Lombroso, one of the deepest students of mind that time has ripened, says of her:

> The most simple, most frivolous and thoughtless woman hides at the bottom of her soul a spark of heroism, which neither she herself nor anybody else suspects, which she never shows if her life runs a normal course, but which springs into evidence and manifests itself by actions of devotion and self-sacrifice if fate strikes her or those who she loves. Then she does not wince, she does not complain, nor give way to useless despair, but rushes into the breach. The woman who hesitates to put her feet into cold, placid water throws herself into the perils of the roaring, surging maelstrom.[29]

Sardou,[30] the analytical novelist, declares:

> I consider women superior to men in almost everything. They possess intuitive faculty to an extraordinary degree, and may almost always be trusted to do the right thing in the right place. They are full of noble instincts, and, though heavily handicapped by Fate, come well out of every ordeal. You have only to turn to history to learn the truth of what I say.[31]

Lester F. Ward,[32] the economist, the subtle student of affairs, gives this testimony:

> We have no conception of the real amount of talent or genius possessed by woman. It is probably not greatly inferior to that of men even now, and a few generations of enlightened opinion on the subject, if shared by both sexes, would perhaps show that the difference is qualitative only.[33]

I am glad to align myself with a party that declares for absolute equality between the sexes. Anything less than this is too narrow for twentieth century civilization, and too small for a man who has a right conception of manhood. I declare my faith that man, like water, cannot rise higher than his source. I am no greater than my mother. I have no rights or powers that do not belong to my sisters everywhere.

Let us grant that woman has not reached the full height which she might attain—when I think of her devotion to duty, her tender ministries, her gentle spirit that in the class and struggle of passion has made her the savior of the world, the thought, so far from making me decry womanhood, gives me the vision of a race so superior as to cause me to wonder at its glory and beauty ineffable.

Man has not reached his best. He never will reach his best until he walks the upward way side by side with woman. Plato was right in his fancy that man and woman are merely halves of humanity, each requiring the qualities of the other in order to attain the highest character. Shakespeare understood it, when he made his noblest women strong as men, and his best men tender as women.

Under our brutal forms of existence, beating womanhood to the dust, we have raged in passion for the individual woman, for use only. Someday we shall develop the social passion for womanhood, and then the gross will disappear in service and companionship. Then we shall lift woman from the mire where our fists have struck her, and set her by our side as our comrade and equal and that will be love indeed.

Man's superiority will be shown, not in the fact that he has enslaved his wife, but in that he has made her free.

Notes

1. Daniel Thew Wright (1864–1943), a former prosecutor from Hamilton County, Ohio, was nominated to a seat on the bench of the supreme court of the District of Columbia by President Theodore Roosevelt in November 1903. He resigned in October 1914, in the face of a forthcoming inquiry by the House Judiciary Committee over allegations that Wright illegally accepted legal fees, wrongfully appropriated money, falsified records, and engaged in acts of judicial misconduct while on the federal bench.
2. On December 23, 1908, Samuel Gompers, John Mitchell, and Frank Morrison, executive officers of the American Federation of Labor, were issued jail terms ranging from six months to a year for contempt of court for the continuing boycott of the Buck Stove and Range Company. The three were released on bail totaling $12,000 pending appeal and a protracted legal battle followed in which the AF of L leaders lost at every turn. The case went to the US Supreme Court in January 1911. In May of that year, several months after the AF of L and Buck Stove and Range had settled their legal dispute, the high court set aside the sentences against the three labor leaders as wrongful, ruling that the case against them was civil rather than criminal and that only fines could be imposed by judicial fiat, not jail terms.
3. That is, the Interstate Commerce Commission, established in 1887 by the Interstate Commerce Act. The commission was abolished in 1995.
4. Gompers made this statement to the Denver convention of the American Federation of Labor in his opening address on November 9, 1908. The words here are out of context. In his speech, Gompers advocated a novel strategy, that rather than bankrupting itself on legal fees, the organized labor movement should provoke a legislative denouement by having its indicted leaders make a personal appeal to the mercy of the court. Gompers declared: "If it is the intention of those who are hostile to the interests of the toilers of our country to take advantage of the trend of court decisions for the usurpation of the toiler's rights by the injunctions, let them proceed as they will without our assuming to do the impossible; that is, to be represented by competent legal counsel. If the situation is to become so acute, let us personally, as best we can, defend our rights before the courts, taking whatever consequences may ensue. For one, I can see no remedy for these outrageous proceedings, unless there shall be a quickening of the conscience of our judges or the relief which the Congress of our country can and should afford." See "President Gompers's Report," *Report of Proceedings of the Twenty-Eighth Annual Convention of the American Federation of Labor, Held at Denver, Colorado, November 9 to 21 Inclusive, 1908* (Washington, DC: National Tribune, 1908), 27. Whether this radical and risky idea of Gompers, expressed to the delegates as a personal view rather than formal policy recommendation, was serious or rhetorical remains questionable.
5. On March 10, 1907, Goldfield, Nevada restaurant owner John Silva was killed by two walking delegates of the Industrial Workers of the World, M. R. Preston and Joseph W. Smith. The pair had been picketing Silva's establishment as "unfair to labor" over an incident involving back pay for a waitress who had left Silva's

employment. In the dispute which resulted, Silva brandished a gun toward Preston, who fired and fatally wounded the restauranteur, later claiming that he had acted in self-defense. On May 27, Preston was convicted of second degree murder and sentenced to 25 years in state prison for shooting Preston; Smith received a term of 10 years for involuntary manslaughter for his role as an accessory to the crime. The Socialist Labor Party briefly nominated Preston as its candidate for president of the United States in 1908 before replacing him with another candidate.

6. The *Appeal to Reason* published a series of articles written by journalist John Kenneth Turner (1879–1948), who traveled twice to Mexico undercover with his wife Ethel Duffy Turner to investigate corruption and miserable working conditions and interview opponents of the Porfirio Díaz regime. Turner's work was published in book form as *Barbarous Mexico* (Chicago: Charles H. Kerr & Co., 1910).
7. Pope Gregory I (c. 540–604) was born to a wealthy Roman family with a long connection to the Christian church. He was well-educated and followed his father as prefect of Rome, the city-state's highest civil office, at the age of 33. He later converted the family villa into a monastery and took a vow of poverty. Selected as pope in 590, Pope Gregory oversaw numerous reforms of liturgical practice; he is the namesake of the Gregorian chant. Upon his death he was canonized by acclamation and is regarded as a saint by both the Roman Catholic and Eastern Orthodox churches.
8. E. Alexander Powell, "The Long Arm of the Secret Police," *Saturday Evening Post,* vol. 181, no. 28 (January 9, 1909), 3–4, 21–4; no. 29 (January 16, 1909), 19–20.
9. Powell, "The Long Arm of the Secret Police," no. 29, 20.
10. According to the *Shorter Oxford English Dictionary,* a skate is a "mean, contemptible, or dishonest person." The slang expression "cheap skate," which originated in the 1890s, has evolved into a common synonym for "miserly" in contemporary usage.
11. Adapted from "The Folly of the Sword" (1843) by Douglas William Jerrold (1803–1857). The original quote: "What a fine-looking thing is war! Yet, dress it as we may, dress and feather it, daub it with gold, huzza it, and sing swaggering songs about it— what it is, nine times out of ten, but murder in uniform? Cain, taking the sergeant's shilling?"
12. As bizarre as this assertion sounds—that a chain of approximately 252 trillion $20 gold pieces could be painlessly subtracted from the nominal value of a penny invested at 6 percent annual interest, compounded semiannually, 1900 years later—Debs's claim does appear to be substantially correct.
13. Harry J. Bone (1862–1918), prosecutor in the Fred Warren case, was an 1885 graduate of Cumberland University law school of Lebanon, Tennessee. He was several times a Republican candidate for the Kansas legislature during the 1890s, winning a seat in 1894, working as an assistant US district attorney after leaving office. Bone ran unsuccessfully for attorney general of Kansas in 1902 but was named private secretary to Kansas Governor Willis J. Bailey following his defeat. Bone again became an assistant prosecutor in the fall of 1904 and made use of his connections in the Republican establishment to win appointment to the position of US attorney for Kansas in the fall of 1905.

14. George D. Brewer (1877?–1967) was born on a farm near Marion, Kansas, on which he worked until the age of 17. He left farming to become a railroad brakeman, interrupting this career to join the army during the Spanish–American War. Stricken by typhus during military training in Tennessee, Brewer never saw action in the war. He mustered out at the end of the conflict and returned to working as a brakeman until suffering a permanent injury to his left foot and ankle in a car-coupling accident. An ardent Populist in the 1890s, Brewer turned to socialism after reading a radical newspaper in a public library in 1900. He enrolled in Ruskin College of Trenton, Missouri, in 1901, remaining there until going to work on the editorial staff of the *Appeal to Reason* in 1903. Brewer, a Socialist national committee member, was the author the book *The Fighting Editor; or, Warren and the Appeal* (Chicago: Charles H. Kerr & Co., 1910) and was the focus of two major political campaigns, losing as a Socialist candidate for Congress in the Kansas 3rd congressional district in 1912 and winning election to the Kansas legislature in the 20th district in 1914. Brewer later left the Socialist Party and moved to the upper Midwest, where he was active in the Non-Partisan League.
15. Defying threats of arrest or possible violence, Debs traveled by car to the Indian Mound at McKees Rocks, Pennsylvania, where he addressed an estimated 2,000 striking workers for about 20 minutes.
16. In July 1910, 40 riveters for the Pressed Steel Car Company of McKees Rocks, a suburb of Pittsburgh, walked off the job over a corrupt system of pooled payments and excessive rents for ramshackle company dwellings. When they attempted to return to work three days later, they were promptly fired. A massive strike of 5,000 workers at Pressed Steel Car, the second largest producer of railroad cars in the nation, followed in protest over these terminations. As was the case with the Homestead strike of 1892, the company attempted to import strikebreakers to its manufacturing facility by riverboat, which similarly came under gunfire and was forced to retreat. Deputy sheriffs and the Pennsylvania state constabulary was called in to maintain order. Strikers were forcibly evicted from company dwellings, with further inflamed the situation. On Sunday, August 22, just two days before Debs's arrival, rioting erupted, resulting in the death of about 11 people, including several state troopers. Martial law was imposed in the aftermath. The strike was ultimately terminated on September 8, with the adoption of an improved wage scale, the termination of strikebreakers, and the rehiring of striking workers.
17. Debs made a planned detour to Pittsburgh en route from a scheduled August 22 speaking engagement at a grand labor festival in Boston and a return to speaking at various socialist encampments in Oklahoma later that week.
18. Accompanied by socialist activist John W. Slayton, Debs had toured so-called "Hunkytown," the impoverished district occupied by striking immigrant workers, earlier that same day.
19. Debs arrived in Ardmore, Oklahoma to address a socialist encampment near that city at Lorena Park. He spoke briefly prior to departing for that meeting with a journalist from the *Ardmore Morning Democrat.*

20. Joshua was said to have been the top assistant of Moses, who according to the Bible became the supreme leader of the Israelite tribes following the death of Moses.
21. The papal city-state of Rome was occupied in September 1870, so 1909 would have marked the 39th anniversary of the event. Its October 2, 1870, annexation by Italy is regarded as the final event in the process of national unification.
22. Giuseppe Garibaldi (1807–1882) was an anti-papal Italian nationalist military leader who championed the cause of Italian unification.
23. From William Shakespeare, *The Tragedy of Hamlet, Prince of Denmark,* Act 3, Scene 2.
24. Horace Greeley (1811–1872) was one of the preeminent journalists of the nineteenth century, best known as the founder and editor of the *New York Tribune,* to which Karl Marx was an occasional contributor from 1852 to 1861. Greeley was a candidate for president of the United States in November 1872, heading the ticket of the Liberal Republican Party, winning six of 37 states in a loss to Republican incumbent Ulysses S. Grant.
25. Thurlow Weed (1797–1892) was a newspaper publisher from Albany, New York. Weed helped establish the Whig Party in the United States, in which he was one of the top leaders in New York State. Following the implosion of that party, he cast his lot with the anti-slavery Republican Party in 1856.
26. Wilbur F. Storey (1819–1884) was an American newspaper editor who purchased his initial stake in the *Detroit Free Press* in 1853. He purchased the *Chicago Times* in 1861. A supporter of Stephen Douglas against Abraham Lincoln in the election of 1860, during the American Civil War he pursued a defeatist "Copperhead" political line, which led to the paper being shut down for several days in 1863.
27. Lajos Kossuth (1802–1894) was a Hungarian lawyer and politician who is regarded as the father of Hungarian liberal democracy. He was a leader of the 1848 revolution of the Hungarian people against the Austrian empire and served as Regent-President of Hungary until the democratic regime was overthrown through the efforts of Tsar Nikolai I. He was forced into emigration in Turkey late in 1849 before making his way to England in 1851 and visited the United States at the end of that year, where he was entertained by President Millard Fillmore. In his later years he lived in Italy.
28. From *The Saturday Review of Politics, Literature, Science and Art.* Original article has not been located.
29. Probably from Poala Lombroso, *Children of the Italian Poor* (New York: Tucker Publishing Co., 1900).
30. Victorien Sardou (1831–1908) was a French playwright who staged dozens of dramas over the course of a fifty-year career, many of which were later adapted into films. His best-known works include *Divorçons!* (1880), *Fédora* (1882), and *La Tosca* (1887).
31. Quoted in "How Sardou Wrote His Plays," *Strand Magazine* [London], vol. 37, whole no 217 (January 1909), 93.
32. Lester F. Ward (1841–1913) was an American natural scientist and sociologist. A fierce critic of the survival of the fittest theories popularized by Herbert Spencer, Ward was elected as the first president of the American Sociological Association in 1906.
33. Lester F. Ward, *Applied Sociology* (Boston: Ginn & Co., 1906), 232.

1910

A Working Man Has No Chance in Federal Court: Speech at Orchestra Hall, Chicago† [excerpt][1]

January 13, 1910

One of the commanding figures in this great struggle is Fred D. Warren, managing editor of the *Appeal to Reason* [*applause*]—recently sentenced by Judge John C. Pollock [*hisses*], a notorious corporate hireling, to serve a sentence of six months in jail and pay a fine of $1,500.

What is his crime? He is the champion of the working class! [*Applause.*] He can be neither bought nor bribed nor intimidated. [*A voice: "That is true."*] He is a man with all the integrity of nature. He is the incarnation of class struggle. Were he sordid and grasping as so many are in these days, were he inclined to traffic in his magnificent intellect, he could long since have been the managing editor of a great metropolitan newspaper in New York City and drawing a salary of $25,000 a year, having social standing, being recognized as an eminently respectable citizen of the republic, and at his death a great monument would be erected to his memory, covered with lies. [*Applause.*]

He is one of those who, because of his fidelity to his convictions, has incurred the ill will of the ruling class; one of those who has been pictured as a mischievous agitator and malcontent. Every possible effort has been made to destroy his influence. I have been in very close touch with him during the past few weeks. I know him very well, and let me say to you this evening that so far as his moral character is concerned, there is neither scar nor blemish upon it. [*Applause.*]

But he is a man of capacity, he is a man of great sympathy with the working class, a man of unquestioned integrity. How came he to be so hated by the minions of power? Let me repeat a little ancient history. The Warren case, as it is now known, is of vital interest to the whole American people. They ought to know the truth about it.

---

† Published as "Jail for Grosscup, Declares Debs, If Justice Were Done," *Chicago Daily Socialist*, vol. 4, no. 69 (January 15, 1910), 1, 3. Expanded edition published as "Debs Flays Grosscup in Chicago," *Appeal to Reason*, whole no. 739 (January 29, 1910), 3. Although structured slightly differently by the editors of these papers, these two accounts appear to derive from the same original stenographic report. The most logical sequence of argument has been reconstructed here.

The Warren Case

This case is the sequel to the kidnapping of Moyer, Haywood, and Pettibone, which occurred almost four years ago. In 1899, through the influence of the working class, the legislature of the state of Colorado enacted an eight-hour law for the benefit of the workers who were employed in and around the smelters and mines and engaged in occupations exceedingly injurious to their health. Because of the poisoned fumes, hundreds of men were dying in their very prime. Because of this the eight-hour law was enacted.

Soon after it was placed upon the statute book, this law was declared unconstitutional by the supreme court of the state of Colorado, which belonged bodily to the Mine Owners' Association. The working men then proceeded to have an amendment submitted to the people of that state in the election of 1903. Every political party in that election was pledged to enact that law if the amendment was adopted by a majority of the people. Every candidate was pledged to vote for that same law. That amendment was carried by a majority of 46,500 votes.

The legislature convened. It is of record that its members were openly bought by the Mine Owners' Association and that that legislature adjourned in defiance of the mandate of the people without enacting an eight-hour law.

That was the beginning of all the trouble in the state of Colorado. After the mine owners had succeeded in defeating the eight-hour law in spite of the majority of almost 50,000 votes, they proceeded to destroy the Western Federation of Miners by discriminating against its members and discharging them from employment. Then came a strike. The mine owners promptly engaged the services of a number of thieves, thugs, gunmen of all descriptions, and there occurred that long line of atrocities which were charged upon the Western Federation of Miners. Among these there was the explosion at Independence, the blowing up of the railroad station, in which the lives of 13 non-union men were destroyed. It was proved beyond the question of a doubt that this crime was perpetrated by the mine owners themselves to discredit the Western Federation of Miners.

The Matter of Kidnapping

These outrages culminated finally in the assassination of ex-Governor Steunenberg in December 1905. Shortly afterwards, in February, Moyer, Haywood, and Pettibone, the tried and trusted leaders of the Western Federation of Miners, were kidnapped by a conspiracy of the mine owners in collusion with the governors of two states, the state of Idaho and the state of Colorado.

In the dead of night these three workingmen were seized and thrown in jail. A little later they were placed aboard a special train and rushed away from their homes—across the country a thousand miles without being given a chance to communicate with their families, to consult counsel, to be heard in their own defense. And when they were finally delivered in the penitentiary, the statement was made in the spirit of exultation that they never should leave that state alive. President Roosevelt complacently declared that they were "undesirable citizens" [*laughter*], to make certain that they should not escape the gallows.

A little later, in the election that followed, William Howard Taft—now president of the United States, at that time a member of the president's cabinet—went to Idaho and in a series of speeches there appealed to the people to reelect and vindicate Governor Frank Gooding, one of the two governors in collusion with the mine owners to murder the leaders of the Western Federation or make certain they should not escape the gallows. The capitalist press promptly denounced these three labor leaders as criminals. The truth was they had been absolutely true to the working class, and for this they must be murdered, and to this end a kidnapping conspiracy was concocted. It would have been carried out but for the fact that the working class were to a large extent organized. They had a press of their own, they had some means of reaching and arousing the people.

Warren Exposes WFM Conspiracy

It was at this time that Fred D. Warren, managing editor of the *Appeal*, turned the flashlight of his paper upon the hideous conspiracy [*applause*], exposed it, aroused the people to its true significance—and from that hour he was a marked man. The statement was made that he would dearly pay for it. At once an inspector was transferred into the district in which the *Appeal to Reason* is published, for the purpose of finding some pretext upon which to base an indictment of Fred D. Warren, that he might be imprisoned and the paper suppressed.

You remember that it was about this time or a little later that the state of Kentucky offered a reward of $100,000 for the apprehension and return of the murderer of Governor-elect Goebel. The leaders of the Western Federation had appealed to the Supreme Court of the country for the protection of these citizens; they sought by this end to assert their constitutional rights, but the Supreme Court turned a deaf ear to their plea, virtually sanctioning the crime of kidnapping. Had Moyer, Haywood, and Pettibone been three capitalists instead of three working men, the Supreme Court of the United States would have promptly come to the rescue—would have sought out and summarily punished the criminal.

It occurred to Fred D. Warren to test the consistency of this high tribunal, and so he published a reward, offering a thousand dollars for the apprehension and return of ex-Governor [William S.] Taylor, who was under indictment for murder and who was a fugitive from Kentucky. Before mailing this offer he presented it to the postmaster at Girard and asked him if there was anything that made it unmailable. The postmaster promptly answered that there was not; that such postal cards were daily mailed and that he could deposit it in the mails with perfect safety. He did so. It was this that furnished the pretext upon which an indictment was based, and in due course of time he was arrested and tried, and after repeated postponements he was finally found guilty by a packed jury. Three of the jurymen, as was proved, had declared in advance of the trial that Warren ought to be run out of the country, and that the *Appeal* ought to be suppressed. It so happened that all 12 of the jurymen were good Republicans, not a single exception among them. [*Laughter.*]

Condemned Before Trial

Because of this Warren was fore-condemned to conviction. The trial was a farce. When the time came Judge Pollock, who was placed upon the bench through the influence of railroad corporations, pronounced sentence. The case was appealed. It is now up for hearing before the circuit court of appeals. What the decision will be is not difficult to imagine. [*Laughter.*] We are quite sure that the circuit court will affirm the decision of the lower court and that Fred D. Warren will go to jail, but if he goes there it will not be with his head bowed in shame and humiliation—he will go there with the accusation of no wrong festering in his conscience, but with his head erect, his soul unfettered. And I would a thousand times rather be Fred Warren in jail than to be the infamous and corrupt judge who sent him there. [*Continued applause.*]

Here let me say that Fred D. Warren will live in history, and his memory will be honored long after Judge Pollock has been dumped into the alley of oblivion. [*Laughter and applause.*]

Warren himself understands that his trial and his conviction is but an incident in this great struggle. He himself, in the closing words of his masterly address before the judge when he was asked if there was any reason why sentence should not be pronounced upon him, said:

> This case is but an incident in the mighty struggle of the working class for emancipation. Slowly, painfully, proceeds the struggle of man against the power of Mammon. The past is written in blood and tears, the future is

> dim and unknown, but the outcome of this worldwide struggle is not in doubt. Freedom will conquer slavery; truth will prevail over everything; the light will vanquish the darkness and humanity, disenthralled, will rise resplendent in a glory of universal brotherhood. [*Applause.*]

Refers to the Pullman Strike

In discussing this Warren trial, I am inclined, with your indulgence, to recall a similar trial that occurred here in Chicago about 15 years ago. [*Applause.*] I had a personal interest in that trial. [*Applause.*] That trial grew out of what is known as the Pullman strike—a strike that was completely victorious. [*Cries of "hear, hear"; applause.*] Some of the old warriors are here tonight [*Cries of "You bet!" Laughter and applause.*] And they know that the railroad corporations were defeated at every point. But the victory must be wrested from the working class, and one day, 4,200 thugs and ex-convicts were sworn in by the railroad corporations, and if you would know the character of these man, you have but to read the official report made at the time by Mr. Brennan, the chief of police, to the city council. He said: "They are thieves and thugs and ex-convicts, the very worst that were ever turned loose upon any community." [*Laughter.*]

That night some cars began to burn and trouble broke out generally, and the next day a number of those thugs called at the office of the American Railway Union, took possession of the books, papers, and unanswered letters—took complete charge of it, because it had been declared that we were engaged in a conspiracy to uproot and overthrow this peaceable community. The corporations have tremendous power. All of the organized forces of society, all of the powers of government, are at their disposal. They had to have a series of injunctions as preliminary measures; to secure these there had to be trouble. To instigate this trouble the 4,200 thugs and thieves and ex-convicts had to be sworn in and the trouble began, and at once the report flashed over all the wires that Chicago was in the grasp of a bloodthirsty mob. [*Laughter and applause.*] The papers did their full share to create this impression in the minds of the American people. It was then that the injunctions were issued restraining us from doing what we had no intention of doing—promptly, sir, followed by my arrest. At once a grand jury of those who were known to hate labor unions was impaneled, and we were indicted; and then came the trial and the conviction. I have a very vivid recollection of it. [*Laughter and applause.*]

I remember that while I was serving a sentence of six months at Woodstock, I was brought to the city of Chicago daily in charge of two officers of the law, because I was regarded as a very dangerous character, and returned there in the evening, and the people of Woodstock even protested against having such a disreputable character in their jail. [*Laughter and applause.*]

One of the judges who tried me was Peter S. Grosscup. [*Hisses.*] If justice were done him, instead of wearing the judicial ermine, he himself would be in stripes. [*Long continued applause.*] And yet he has all the qualifications essential to a federal judgeship. As a tried and trusted friend of the corporations, he is eminently qualified to kiss the Bible and swear to serve the people. The trial began, and we would have been convicted had it not been for an incident that proved to be of great significance. We discovered that the general managers had held a secret meeting with the managers of the Pullman corporation; that they had jointly conspired to crush the employees in the Pullman service and to destroy the American Railway Union.

Now the crime we were really guilty of was sympathizing with the wage-slaves at Pullman. At that time women were sewing carpets all day long for 42 cents a day. After the rents and other little expenses were deducted, not a penny remained. Hundreds of them were in a state of destitution. Their condition was such that it defies the power of language to describe. It was for sympathizing with these unfortunates that we were indicted and placed upon trial, precisely as was the crime of Fred Warren for having sympathized with the men who were kidnapped, and who were about to be executed because of their loyalty and devotion to the working class.

Pullman Conspiracy Exposed

During the course of the trial, when the discovery was made that this joint meeting had taken place, we called for the official proceedings of this meeting. It developed that each manager and member of the association had a single copy in his strong box. This demand could not be refused by the court, because a similar demand had been made upon the American Railway Union, and we had been compelled to introduce in court all of the proceedings of our meetings.

That noon court adjourned. Judge Grosscup was very sorely troubled. After the lunch hour had passed and court was reconvened, the judge gravely announced that a juryman had been suddenly taken ill; that the trial could not continue. [*Laughter.*] I have never learned the price of the illness. [*Laughter and applause.*] And so the case was postponed from day to day and from week to week until the interest in the case gradually died out, and at last, after months had passed, a very small, obscure press dispatch announced that the case had been stricken from the docket.

Had the trial proceeded to its close, a verdict of not guilty would have been rendered, and we would have been vindicated, and this would not do, since we were already serving time in jail on a charge involving practically the same offense.

A Worker Has No Chance

A workingman has no fair chance before a federal court. All of the 131 members of the federal court are appointed through the influence and power of corporate wealth. All nine members of the United States Supreme Court are corporation attorneys—every one of them, there isn't an exception to the rule. They are not elected by the people. They are not responsible to the people. They are not in touch with the people. All of their official lives they have served the trusts and the corporations, and when there is an issue that arises between the corporations and the people they universally decide in the interests of the corporation. The Supreme Court has virtually sanctioned the kidnapping of working men. It has outlawed the boycott, and practically the strike, so that it has stripped organized labor of practically all of its power and left it helpless at the feet of corporate power.

The workingmen are just beginning to understand the issue that is involved in this great struggle. Many of them are beginning to ask why it is that they must press their rags still closer lest they jostle against the silken garments that their finders have finished.

Why is it that they must offend their hunger by the odor of banquets they have spread but may not touch? Why is it that they must walk, weary and shelterless, in the shadow of palaces they have erected but may not enter? They are beginning to think; they will soon begin to act. They will not much longer beg for their rights, but they will take them. [*Applause.*]

They are developing their power upon the economic field and upon the political field, and in spite of all the forces that are in operation against them, they are steadily increasing their power, and in due course of time they will achieve the victory. For the first time in history a universal movement has been organized. It is spreading over the face of the world. It is a movement primarily of the working class, and the working class has had to struggle through all the various phases of its development. From slaves they became serfs; from serfs they became wage workers—to become free men in socialism, the next inevitable phase in our advancing civilization. [*Applause.*]

Here in Chicago we have a fully developed capitalist metropolis. Upon one hand the fortunes mount skyward and upon the other there is unspeakable misery and want and woe. Is it possible for any human being with a good heart in his breast to be satisfied with conditions as they are? Go up any of these crowded thoroughfares and no matter how violently you may be opposed to socialism, you will see multiplied thousands in whose pink faces there is traced an indictment of capitalism and our much vaunted Christian civilization.

The Flower Dies

Man to a very large extent is a product of his environment. Under the influence of sunshine the flower bursts into bloom, in all its beauty. It does so only because soil and climate is adapted to its growth. Transfer this flower from the sunlight to a cellar filled with noxious gasses and it withers and it dies. The same law applies to physical human beings. All life has a physical basis. The industrial soil and the social climate must be adapted to the development of men and women, and then we will cease producing the many thousands whose very appearance is a rebuke to this system.

No, it is not possible for anyone whose heart throbs with sympathy for his fellow men to be satisfied with conditions as they are. The workers are united for the purpose of overthrowing this system, and taking possession of the tools of industry and to have industry for the purpose of producing wealth that all may have who are willing to do their share of useful social work. In this system the wealth of the country is gradually gravitating into the hands of a few. A billionaire has been produced, and from my point of view he serves us as a warning, not as an example. [*Laughter.*] It is said that a man is poor who has no money, but is much poorer if he has only money. [*Laughter.*] From my point of view John D. Rockefeller, the chief product of capitalism, is an abject pauper. He has a billion dollars and not a single friend. [*Laughter and applause.*] If there is a human being who loves him for his own sake, I have not heard of him.

Vote Together

And now just a word to the working class. I appeal to you in closing to unite—unite your forces upon the economic field. Disregard the advice of those leaders who may be keeping you separated; unite upon the principles of industrial unionism. [*Applause.*] You are in control of industry now, if you just knew it, and you can build up the socialist commonwealth within capitalism itself. Join the same organization, acting together all along the line.

You have had to learn to do a great many things together in this system; to work together, to be locked out together, to look for work together, to be enjoined together. [*Laughter.*] And to go to jail together. [*Laughter and applause.*]

You still have to learn to do a very important thing together, and that is to vote together on election day. And in due course of time the change will come, for the triumph is certain.

The Loss of Ben Hanford: Telegram to the *New York Call*†

January 25, 1910

[Omaha, Nebraska]

[January 25, 1910]

The death of Comrade Ben Hanford removes from the socialist movement one of its most gifted writers, eloquent speakers, and loyal supporters. For many years he served with pen and tongue with all the ability and energy at his command. He never wearied in the struggle, never uttered a disheartening word, and never lowered his colors.

Ben Hanford was a perfect type of the proletarian revolutionist. He had the clear head of a philosopher and the brave soul of a warrior. His personality was virile and magnetic, his character unique and commanding. His enthusiasm, notwithstanding his frail body, was contagious. Wherever he went, he was respected and loved and wherever he was heard he won converts to the cause.

During the past few years, he did his work under the extremest difficulties. Almost any other would have yielded to pain and torture and given up in

† Published as "Debs on Hanford's Death" in *New York Call*, vol. 3, no. 26 (January 26, 1910), 1.

despair. But Ben Hanford had sprung from the loins of the working class and knew no such word as surrender. Many an agony was wrung from his emaciated body, but he never halted in his march and never wavered in his devotion to duty and his fidelity to the movement.

He had patience, fortitude, serenity, and unconquerable heroism. He did as much as any other and under circumstances more than any other, to make the socialist movement in the United States what it is today, and his life of splendid service is an example and his unflagging devotion to principle an inspiration to us all.

The death of this brave comrade is a distinct loss to the socialist movement. Personally, I keenly feel his taking off, and my deepest sympathy goes to his widowed comrade.

There is consolation in knowing that Hanford's unselfish services will preserve his memory and that his heroic soul is in the great movement he lived and died to serve.

The More I Think of It, the Hotter My Blood Becomes: Letter to Fred D. Warren†

February 5, 1910

Hamilton, Ohio, February 5th, 1910

My Dear Fred:—

Enclosed I hand you the letter just received from [Ricardo Flores] Magón.[2] The more I think of this case, the hotter my blood becomes. I can hardly restrain myself. It is the most important case before the American continent. The more I think of it, the more convinced I am that this is the case for the *Appeal* to open its batteries on as soon as it can clear its decks. If you can win this fight,

† Typed letter, signed, with handwritten postscript. Copy in *Papers of Eugene V. Debs* microfilm edition, reel 1, frames 728–9. Not included in Constantine (ed.), Letters of Eugene V. Debs: Volume 1, 1874–1912.

your own is won in advance and you can fight a thousand times better for others than you can fight for yourself.

The outrages already perpetrated against these noble souls staggers belief. If there is a drop of fighting blood in a man's carcass, this case puts him on the warpath. Just think of these grand heroes being already three years shut up in dungeons and tied up in convicts' stripes! Compared to this, a mere jail sentence is a May Day excursion. If the *Appeal* can tell this story in bold, striking, sensational style, we can start a conflagration of protest that will make hell pop about the ears of the American plutocracy, and we can at least prevent the re-arrest of these comrades when they are released. I am ready to unsheathe my sword and take my stand at the head of the army in this fight. I am willing to stake all I have and lose all I have upon this issue.

The terms expire July 31st. The country must be aroused before that time. The grandest opportunity in the history of the *Appeal* is now looming before it in the Mexican cases. This fight will not detract from your fight but will be the making of it and ensure victory for both.[3]

Yours always,
Debs

[P.S.] Mailing you paper from Ashland, Ohio—they gave us great sendoff.

First Speaking Tour of 1910: A Short Report[†]

February 24, 1910

Terre Haute, Indiana, February 24th [1910][4]

The speaking tour of six weeks, which closed in Philadelphia last night [February 23], was in all regards the most successful in my experience. Beginning at

† Published as "Debs' Own Report of the Meetings" in *Appeal to Reason*, whole no. 744 (March 5, 1910), 2.

Chicago on January 13th, the entire tour was in the nature of a vast demonstration. The country was covered between Nebraska and Pennsylvania. The attendance, without a single exception, was large, and the real fire was everywhere in evidence. In some cases large numbers were turned away for want of room.

The beginning of the wonderful trip, at Chicago, was most unfortunate for me. A magnificent audience, exceptionally keen, had gathered in the teeth of a fierce and blinding snow storm, and everything had been arranged for a masterly address. But the principle speaker, unfortunately myself, had the grippe,[5] and fell down flatly, to his inexpressible chagrin and mortification. The only plea I have is that, with all the strength I had to stand on my feet I did my best, and nothing outside of a socialist meeting would have been sufficient to induce me to leave my bed that day.[6] Fortunately, the never failing Jim Brower[7] officiated as chairman and so stirred and swayed the audience that he saved the day, for which I shall always remember him with gratitude.

So keenly did I feel this failure on my part that by sheer force of will, I determined to throw off the sickness, and from that time till the close of the tour the grippe let me severely alone.

Fifty thousand subscribers were added to the *Appeal* list during the six weeks we were out by our meetings alone, an average of over a thousand a day.[8] Enough literature was disposed of to stock a good-sized establishment. At each point we left the comrades full of enthusiasm and resolved to work with renewed energy for the movement. At several places where there was local dissension we succeeded in restoring harmony, giving the local a fresh start and a clear field.

The Warren case, the exposure of the federal judiciary, and the *Appeal*'s fight for a free press, free speech, and free assemblage are among the livest [sic] issues now before the American people. The keen interest of the masses in these issues accounts largely for the tremendous gatherings which greeted us all over the country. Every mention of Warren was cheered to the echo, and every reference to the *Appeal* evoked a significant demonstration.

We are indebted to comrades along the line for kindnesses too numerous to mention. The glad greetings everywhere revive and refresh a weary comrade, and send him on his way, rejoicing that he has lived long enough to know the meaning of socialism and the comradeship it inspires.

It is merely justice to Comrade [George D.] Brewer to say that he has made himself indispensable. He cannot be beaten. He knows just what to do and always does it. He is never caught napping. His 15-minute introductory speeches never fail to put the audience in the happiest mood, making it easy for the speaker who follows him. The people everywhere were impressed by Brewer's earnestness, his clearness, and his frankness, relieved by flashes of wit. Whenever he has occasion to address the people at length, as he doubtless will have in the future, he will be greeted by large and appreciative audiences. Brewer is one of the rising young comrades, and high honors await him on the platform of the socialist movement.

We are not going to rest until the *Appeal* has a half a million subscribers and until every corrupt federal judge has packed his grip for Egypt or some other clime.

Fight to the Last! Speech at Philadelphia Labor Lyceum†

March 19, 1910

This is a meeting of the working class, and I feel, therefore, very much at home. You are waging a class fight, and I am not here today to theorize or philosophize. I am here to fight. There is no reason why this strike should not be won absolutely.[9]

There has been a great deal of talk about arbitration. No workingman should use the word "arbitration" in strikes; he should not use it in this strike. There is nothing to concede and there is nothing to arbitrate. I appeal to you workers to stand absolutely for the whole program. Your demand is such a very modest one that if you concede anything, you lose everything.

Why are there any workers at work in Philadelphia at this time? Why are they not out today on strike? You are fighting their fight, and they ought to know it. But they are held in restraint by the sanctity of a contract. In a word, a contract with a capitalist is more important than their lives and the lives of their wives and babes. If I had the power, I would destroy every such contract in the United States. I have no respect for any contract that is made at the expense of the working class.

† Published as a leaflet. Philadelphia printers' union bug, no publisher or date indicated (probably March 1910). Copy in *Papers of Eugene V. Debs* microfilm edition, reel 7.

Conscienceless Piracy

If there was a time when the working class should be united in one solid phalanx, it is right here and now in Philadelphia. For years you have been dominated by as conscienceless a crew of pirates as ever robbed a municipality anywhere.

I am going to speak very deliberately today, and I stand absolutely responsible for every word I utter. I was told, on my way here, that perhaps I might not be allowed to speak at all, but if any steps had been taken to silence me I would not have turned back like a sheep. When the time comes that I cannot stand erect like a man and exercise my right to speak for my class, I will die right there!

I am not here in the capacity of a leader, nor as an orator, but simply as a workingman. I have earned my right to a place in the working class, and there is where I belong; there is where I am, and when there is a fight of the working class, here or anywhere, I recognized that it is my fight. I discharge my duty as I understand it. I have said, and I repeat, that you can, if you will, win the strike. Not, however, by showing the white feather; not by being cowards and poltroons but by being men; by standing erect and presenting a solid front, making your demand, and standing by it. Don't be afraid to sacrifice, because if you lose you may lose everything; you sacrifice a great deal more in defeat than you do in fighting manfully for your rights.

What are you asking for? Just a pittance of what you are entitled to. You are the Philadelphia Traction Company. Without you there is no such enterprise. You operate it in every essential department, and you are asking for just enough to enable you and your wives and your little ones to live; just enough to provide yourself and them with coarse food, scant clothing, and shelter enough so that you may recuperate sufficiently to enable you to return to your work the next day and perform your dreary round. And so on, day after day, you grind away your life as a wage-slave, until at last, in old age, death comes to the rescue and still the aching heart, lulling the victim of capitalism to sleep.

Demands Too Modest

You are asking for a very small and modest part of what you are entitled to. Stand up for that and concede nothing. If you cannot win on that basis, you cannot win at all.

In the Philadelphia press this morning, Mahon[10] is quoted as saying that he is perfectly willing to leave the entire matter of settlement with George H. Earle, Jr.,[11] but I do not believe that he made any such statement, because if any leader would make such a statement, why not place the matter in the hands of the traction company? You would say that Earle is the city's representative, but the traction company is the city. Your City Hall is simply a robber's roost.

It is time for the people of Philadelphia to arouse themselves from their lethargy, their indifference. They have submitted all too long to the indignities of these pirates, these robbers. All these outrages are being perpetrated in the name of the law. And right here let me say that every great crime committed by these pirates is done within the law. Compare this with what happens to a workingman, who, driven by hunger, enters a railroad yard and steals enough scrap iron to buy himself a ham sandwich. He is arrested, thrown into jail, fined, and then you are told that the majesty of the law has been vindicated! These pirates steal a whole railway system and they are eminently respectable citizens. And then they have the nerve to tell you workingmen that you ought to be perfectly peaceable and law-abiding.

This is your opening, this is your chance, this is your supreme opportunity. I am appealing to you to take advantage of it. Cease to crawl, to beg; stand erect and see how long a shadow you can cast in the sunlight!

Two Kinds of Law

You know that there are just two kinds of rule today. There is a professor at Harvard University who had the moral courage to say so. The economic dependence of the professor in our educational institutions acts as a curb on their tongues; they have to hold onto their jobs. If these professors have courage enough to speak their honest convictions, and these convictions happen to conflict with the interests of the ruling class, the professors profess no longer. They retire to private life. But this professor had the courage to say that there are but two kinds of rule, one being thief rule and the other mob rule. The professor said that of the two he preferred mob rule, and that expresses my sentiments.

There are times when to obey the law is a crime. The revolutionary patriots of the 13 colonies had no respect for the laws of King George. They were called law-breakers and traitors and were regarded as undesirables. Yet today you are teaching your children to honor their memory. If it had not been for the courage of these law-breakers in doing this, you and I would still be British subjects instead of American citizens. There is something splendid about the man who has the qualities that enable him to hold his head erect, who faces the world unafraid and alone. It makes no difference what others may say or what others may think, he is invincible in his own mental and moral resources. He takes his stand upon what he conceives to be right, and there he stands, and if he falls he falls standing there; and in due time humanity comes and stands where he stood and erects there a monument in gratitude to his manhood and nobility of nature.

It does not take an educated man, nor a college-bred man, to have that simple quality that will permit you to see whether or not this is a righteous fight. You must say to yourself: "This is my fight; I am not going to play the part of a sneak or a scab; I am going to be true to myself and my conviction of right; I will do my duty no matter what the consequence are." Then you will hear the siren's voice, and if you trace it to its source, you will find that it comes from City Hall, where the brigands are in conference. When they meet it is a conference; when you meet it is a mob. They are the makers of the laws. You are the lawless. This is because you, in your ignorance, used your votes to place them where they are. I do not want to use any harsh language. Nothing would suit me better than to tell them face to face what I am saying to you now. But if they were treated as they should be treated before the law upon their merits and in accordance with justice, every one of them would be in a felon's cell today.

Settlement or Paralyzed Industry

I remember the streetcar strikes—there were two of them—in Terre Haute, the city where I live. I happened to be away when the first occurred. They telegraphed to me to hasten home. I broke all my engagements and responded to the call.[12] At that time the company was owned by local capitalists. We gave them just so much time in which to settle everything with us and gave them notice that if they didn't we would paralyze every industry in town. The strike was a success.

A year or so later there was another strike.[13] Again I happened to be away from the city. They again wired me to return. I found that the men were absolutely right in their demands, which were very modest. I said to them: "Stand where you are, we will issue a call and next Saturday we will have a demonstration of the working class along the entire length of Main Street, and show the respectable citizens what this beast, the working class, is. You are such inferior beings, you live in the hovels and the caves on the outskirts of the city. They do not come in touch with you; they cannot suffer themselves to be in the same section or vicinity with you. We will now show them the character of this working class beast." We issued a call to all the workers in the city. Promptly the newspapers sent reporters to see me and said that if there was any bloodshed, it would be on my head. I said that I could stand it. In the meantime the cars were being run by the scabs.

On Saturday morning, the day set for the demonstration, the workers began to pour in from all directions. Among others there were 6,000 miners. They came in their working and fighting clothes. They fell in line, the procession extending from the river to the city limit. The working class was out in full force, and when the working class is out in full force it is the people. They ran the cars into the barns and sent for me. They asked me upon what terms we would settle, and I said we demanded absolute surrender. They called me into the office and said that they were in a "peculiar position," that they were perfectly willing to do the fair thing, but they wanted to be let down decently. I told them that we had no desire to humiliate the company before the public, and asked them what they would suggest. They said let us arbitrate and we will appoint you the fifth member of the board. The company appointed two men, the strikers appointed two men, then they chose me as the fifth. I okayed the grievances of the men and the strike was settled. We arbitrated that strike by giving the men everything they asked. The only fault I found with the men was that they didn't ask for one-half of what they were entitled to.

It is so often the case that the men who become successful as labor leaders serve the capitalist class. You don't hear them glorifying me in these parts, although I have been three times candidate for president on the Socialist ticket. You don't find my name in the capitalist papers. This is as it should be; my name doesn't belong there. But I want to serve notice upon you that I'm going to put it there before I'm through.

A Typical Union Man

Now I'm going to tell you about a typical union man who figured in this strike in Terre Haute. He had been born into capitalism poor, never had a chance to get any schooling, but he had the true dignity of a man: quiet, unobtrusive, firm—absolutely to his convictions. He was the chairman of the committee. When the strike broke out, I formulated the grievances to be presented to the company, gave them to him, and told him to take them to the office of the management, and told him to be firm. He didn't say a word, but took the papers and went on his errand.

As I told you, the strike was won completely, but after it was all over the manager of the company said: "Debs, the strike is over and I am very glad that it is. I have no fault to find with the terms of the settlement, but I have a personal grievance that I want to lay before you. The chairman of your strike committee at the beginning of the strike came to me. In my office were present three or four members of the board of directors. Your chairman rushed in without knocking. Keeping his hat upon his head, he thrust out his hand and said: 'Repatore, put your "Hancock" on this document.' I said to him, 'Please excuse me for a moment, I am busy.' 'Come now, no monkey business—put your hand to that.' Now do you think this was fair treatment?"

"I can hardly believe," I said to the manager, "that he would subject you to such harsh treatment. I'll send for him and see what he has to say." I sent for him and said: "Did you say so and so to Repatore?" He said: "Yes, don't you remember, you told me to be firm?" "What do you understand by being firm?" I asked him. "Why, to give him hell from the word jump!"

There's a true type of the working class leader. He had no frills, no furbelows, but he had all the true attributes of manhood. He stood pat; he won out, and if we had more of that type, there would be no trouble in winning out everywhere.

If you don't win out here in Philadelphia, it is your own fault. Fight without quitting. And the first thing I would do would be to serve notice upon the rapid transit company that it is a fight to the finish. We have given you all this time, you have spurned us with contempt. We have conceded practically everything. You have granted nothing. In the interest of peace we have all but given our cause away and from this hour forward there is to be a change of deal, there is to be a new program. We withdraw our proposal to arbitrate anything. We serve notice upon you that we are going to fight you along the economic line as well as along the political.

Banking on Your Meekness

I want to tell you men that J. Pierpont Morgan could settle this strike here in Philadelphia in just five seconds. All he would have to do would be to press a button in his office. If you want to settle you have got to fight for it. They are banking entirely upon your meekness, your submissiveness; upon your cowardice. They know that if they wait long enough, your case becomes hopeless.

I can read their papers between the lines. I can tell you that in reading one of Earle's interviews I could see what was written between the lines and I want to tell you that if you allow yourselves to be deceived by all this talk of peace and arbitration, you will go down in defeat. And the result will be the blacklist for your bravest men and the destruction of your organization. What in the name of sense are you workingmen of Philadelphia waiting for? If you don't fight now, when do you expect to? Every loyal workingman in this city ought to throw down his tools on Monday and not do another tap of work until this is settled.

If you allow the streetcar men to be defeated, your time will come next. Let these men go down in defeat and let their organization be destroyed, let these men who fought most bravely be placed on the blacklist and hounded out of Philadelphia, from city to city, until some seek escape through the back door of suicide; allow all this to be done through your treachery, your cowardice, and you will suffer the penalties which you cannot hope to escape. If I could only, by some magic power, talk in my one voice to all the workers in Philadelphia, I would paralyze your plutocratic administration.

No Concession or Compromise

The working people of Philadelphia are being held back by mere threads. They are in a peculiar restraint. They are timid and afraid; they do not know what to do. What they need is to stand erect upon a vigorous and absolutely true policy, and not upon one of concession and compromise. This uncertainty is disastrous. The men don't know where they stand or what tomorrow will bring forth.

A very important industrial battle is being fought. Why do you allow yourselves to be destroyed in detachments, regiment by regiment? Why do you not present the solid front of the entire industrial army? If the workers of Philadelphia would come out in one general strike, it would be won in two hours' time. Then you would not have to go down on your knees and beg for arbitration that you might gain a few more crumbs of stale bread for your children. You have the power; you only need to exercise it. If you fail, it is your own fault and you are responsible for the consequences and you will not escape the penalties.

I appeal to each one of you to go out from here as an emissary of the working class. Go out among the workers, make your appeal to them to be true to the working class in this fight. Suppose you do lose your jobs—it is better than losing your manhood. The man who thinks more of his job than he does of his manhood loses both.

Traction Officials and City Officials Are One

I have read some of the interviews of the officials of the traction company in the city of Philadelphia. You needed to discriminate between a city official and a traction official. The official is the official of both. Let us say traction official and we have said all. The Philadelphia city authorities are the clerks of the traction company. You must realize that the traction magnates are few compared to you. You are in the overwhelming majority. If you united for one minute, you would not need to fight them. The victory would come without the strike, without the fight.

I have seen some of their interviews, and I can see that they hold you in contempt and don't hesitate to say so. And when I come to think seriously of it, I can hardly blame them. They don't like the socialists, but I can tell you that in their heart of hearts they respect them. You don't find us around City Hall down on our knees with our hats in our hands begging for crumbs. They know that we represent a revolutionary movement; that we are not begging, but that we are going to take what we want in due time. They tell us that if we are only law-abiding everything will come our way. Just be quiet and meek while you starve and there will be no trouble. Just starve to death like good law-abiding slaves and they will have no fault to find with you. But do they obey their own laws? Bear in mind that they enact all of them. They don't consult you any more than if you were sheep or hogs.

Government, so called, is simply a combination of clerks in the service of the capitalists. The government belongs to the capitalists in every department. I know who pulls Reyburn's[14] strings, and all the rest of them. These officials are all alike; they are all the tools of corporate power, that is why they have been placed where they are. They could not serve you if they would. They have been placed where they are because they are subservient to the ruling economic masters. Don't you know that the economic master is always the ruler? In feudal society and in modern society it is the masters who make the laws and the workers who have to obey the laws. But those capitalists do not obey their own laws when the laws interfere with their conspiracies to plunder the public.

Sovereigns Seeking Jobs

Let me give you just one concrete illustration. When they demand that you shall obey the law, when they tell you not to touch the man who takes your job, there is one thing that is impressed upon you, and that is that you do not own a job. When a man takes your job, it is because it is not your job. You have no right to defend your job because you have none. Do not let the logic of this proposition escape you in this strike. They tell you that you are sovereigns. Ask them how you can be a sovereign when you don't even own a job. Just think of a sovereign looking for a job!

When you attempt to speak to the man who is about to take your job from you, you violate the law. The courts have so declared. The laws always serve as fetters for the workers and as instruments in the hands of the ruling class to gain their ends. In this way they have legalized the kidnapping of workingmen. That is what the Supreme Court decided in the case of Moyer, Haywood, and Pettibone. It is because of this that Pettibone lies today in his grave.[15] If it had not been for the uprising of the working class all over the land, Moyer, Haywood, and Pettibone would have been hanged.

The traction magnates have all this power, although they are few in number. They have only to press a button and Reyburn comes, like a jumping jack, and performs with alacrity just like a monkey in a circus. Then they press another button connected with the judicial department; then one connected with the councils and the department of justice. Under capitalism all our judicial nets are so adjusted as to catch the minnows and let the whales slip through. Then they press another button and the department of public safety responds. Did you ever hear of such sarcasm as a department of public safety in the City of Brotherly Love?

Public safety! When innocent children are shot dead in their tracks for being in a thoroughfare. And women, and others, who happen to be in the line of the bullets because, perhaps, they happen to be in sympathy with the striking workingmen.

Socialists Want No Compromise

They talk about the department of justice, about the department of safety. It is this organized crime behind which are entrenched the capitalist pirates that the socialists are organized to destroy. We know them, and they know us; and they know that we are not asking for any kind of a compromise. We, however, know them better than they know us. They think they have defeated us when we are crushed beneath the iron heel of their power. That is where they are mistaken, for every time they crush us we rise with power renewed and increased. When they think they defeat us, they simply screw down the safety valve; they increase the pressure, and when they have screwed down that safety valve far enough, and create a pressure strong enough, there is going to be an explosion.

They keep telling you that you must not do any overt act. All the capitalists and all their pliant tools tell you to observe the peace. Of course this is a battle and in a battle they would have you use nothing stronger than eau de cologne and attar of roses.

Don't strike a blow. Don't object to having your job taken away from you. Don't mind such a small thing as seeing your wife starving or your children hungry and perhaps homeless, about to be evicted because the rent cannot be paid. Just remember that you ought to be a law-abiding citizen and allow them to die.

Now let us analyze the solicitude of the capitalist for the observance of the law. Let me show you the hypocrisy of it, which I hope will not offend the tender sensibilities of these traction magnates, who, by the way, are headed by a Wolf,[16] fangs and all. He is very properly named. Now when you sheep fight a wolf don't use your teeth, they tell you. Just allow him to shear you and be submissive.

Traction Wolves Tenderhearted

You know this wolf and he is only one of a type. I have no quarrel with him or with any individual. If it were not for his official capacity, I would probably never have heard of him. Now you know this wolf and the other wolves are heartbroken when they hear of a scab being hit with a brick. But it does not disturb them in the least to know that children are ground up in the mills of Mammon into rich man's gold. They are born into tragedy; they start on the downward road, and if you trace them a little while along that track, you will find them behind the red curtains of a house of shame. All this does not disturb the wolves. But if you dare touch a scab, then they cry out that you are breaking the law.

Let me show you how they obey the law when it interferes with their purposes. I am going to repeat a bit of history, but first listen to the inspiring battle cry of one of the greatest of our poets, Shelley:

> Men of Labor, heirs of Glory,
> Heroes of unwritten story.[17]

Let this inspiring battle cry be your shibboleth during the remainder of this fight, and keep it up until your cause is crowned with victory.

Courts Set Aside People's Will

Let me show you how they obey the law, and when they talk to you about the law, fling this into their teeth. In Colorado in 1899 the miners and smelter men were partly organized, and through their efforts the state legislature enacted an eight-hour law. This was because of the fact that men were dying because they were compelled to inhale the deadly fumes of the ores in the reducing processes. They were working 10, 12, and 14 hours a day, and the people said their workday must be shortened. The legislature responded to the public sentiment and enacted the eight-hour law. Follow this carefully, and when they talk to you about the law, tell them this story. Just after this law was placed upon the statute books, the Supreme Court, which consists of judges who are lickspittles and tools of the Guggenheims,[18] and belong body and soul to the Smelter Trust, declared that law unconstitutional.

Now the working class didn't get excited; they didn't go out on strike, but simply said that if that law is unconstitutional they would present an amendment to the Constitution. And, in 1902, they had that amendment submitted to the people, and by a majority of 47,600 it was adopted. All of the 100 candidates, both Republican and Democratic, for the legislature stood upon a platform which committed them to vote for the eight-hour law. The majority had ordered their servants, the legislature, to reenact that law. They themselves had just made it constitutional. But the legislature was bought, just as Armour buys mutton, and the legislature refused to enact that law. I said then, I say now, and will always say, that the workers of Colorado should have instituted an insurrection, there and then.[19]

They had appealed to the law and they had been turned away. The people had been insulted and outraged. The capitalists do not only not obey their own laws, but they trample upon them with impunity.

At the head of the Western Federation of Miners stood Moyer, Haywood, and Pettibone. I don't believe in anything like hero worship, but it is appropriate that you applaud the names of these men for the way in which they fought the Mine and Smelter Trust. The Smelter Trust did not have money enough to buy Moyer, Haywood, and Pettibone. They didn't have power enough to intimidate them. In spite of all their force and all their threats, these men stood true as steel to their class.

The Smelter Trust owned everything in Colorado—the legislature, the courts, newspapers, also the judges and the pulpiteers. At the order of the Smelter Trust, Moyer, Haywood, and Pettibone were kidnapped in the dead of night and carried a thousand miles and lodged in jail in Idaho. It was [detective James] McParland who declared that they would never leave Idaho alive. There sits on this platform one of the ablest fighters in that battle for the lives of these three workingmen—Comrade Luella Twining.[20] She was one of those who aroused the workers all over the country, until from coast to coast the slogan "If Moyer, Haywood, and Pettibone die, 20 million workers will know the reason why." It didn't take them long to let go. The capitalist papers had said that these men were red-handed murderers, and that they would be hanged, and they would have been hanged if it were not for the fact that we had something of a press of our own. It was the working people of this country that saved Moyer, Haywood, and Pettibone, and what you did for them you can do for yourselves.

This is an example which shows how the capitalists themselves obey the law. Did the Smelter Trust obey the law in Colorado when, after a majority of the people ordered them to reenact the eight-hour law, they refused to do so?

Merciless as Hawks to Doves

They have no respect for the people. They never have had. They talk about laws and democracy. There never has been any democracy. There has never been a time when the people ruled themselves.

After this country freed itself from England, it established itself as a republic, where the people were going to rule. Alexander Hamilton had no respect for the people, he held them in contempt. He tried to have the president elected for a life term. He said, just change the name of King to President and tell the people that they are free and they will believe you. He wanted the president to exercise absolute veto power to enable him to repeal entirely and cancel any law that might be initiated by the people. He tried four times to get this clause put into the Constitution, and every time it was put up, it was defeated by an overwhelming majority.

Notwithstanding this fact our Supreme Court, which is composed of corporation judges, is steadily increasing its own power until its power is now supreme and final. And a dove might as well appeal to a hawk for protection as a workingman to this capitalist judiciary despotism. I don't take off my hat to any judge that ever walked unless he takes off his hat to me. I don't see any halo around the head of a corporation lawyer after he gets on the bench. After they get on the bench, their heads become like chipmunks and their pockets like balloons.

Socialists on the Job

Law-abiding sheep should become law-defying men when that law stands between them and their right. It is the same power you are fighting today, and the socialists are with you to the finish. We are not only preaching the class struggle, but we are with you in your fight. I am with you, I will march with you in the front ranks, and if there are any heads to be clubbed, I'll volunteer mine. If you have any red blood in your veins, now is the time to show it. I appeal to every socialist here to fight with the carmen. You are not true to the movement unless you do. It is not sufficient to talk socialism, now is the time to show your colors. Come victory or defeat, come jail or the gallows, come what will, you will show your colors, you will prove yourself true, you will inspire the weak, you will strengthen the rank and the file, will develop the moral and physical fiber of the working class, you will bear the revolutionary banner of victory in the city of Philadelphia.

The hour has struck, this is your time: allow it to pass and you will never cease to regret it. This is your opening, this is your chance, this is your supreme opportunity. I appeal to you to take advantage of it. Cease to crawl, to beg, stand erect and see how long a shadow you can cast in the sunlight. Go out side by side, let your shoulders touch, let your hearts throb to the forward marches of the drum in this great battle. Don't turn your faces backward, but press forward, step by step, increasing your powers, developing your strength, until the enemy before you quake in their stolen boots. Keep this up day by day and then within the next three or four days there will be a transformation. Weakness and uncertainty spell disaster.

In closing I appeal to you, to each one of you. I look into your faces, I catch your spirit, and I feel myself expanding in your presence; I am simply the tongue of the working class making this appeal from the working class to the working class. I appeal to every man, woman, and child that is present, and right here let me say that I am very glad that the women are here, for they have the true revolutionary spirit. If you want to win your fight, take your wife by the hand and bring her to the meeting. Bring your wife, bring your mother, bring your sister. Let them all go into the streets, one hundred thousand of them with you, and then let them stop you if they dare.

Dressed-Up Degeneracy

I spoke here a short time ago, and there was a minister over in New Jersey—I guess you read what he had to say about my address in this hall—he said that I was guilty of high treason; that I ought to be hanged, and that he would be very glad to officiate on the other end of the rope. This comes from a meek and lowly follower of the humble Nazarene, who preached the doctrine that you must love your enemy; that if he smites you on the one cheek, turn the other; if you are asked for your coat, give your whole suit; if you are asked to walk a furlong, walk a mile. No doubt this minister got an increase to his mess of pottage.

The ruling class have always had their retainers, their pulpiteers, their lick-spittles. They have them in all our educational institutions. No degeneracy is more repugnant than that which is dressed up. These servers of the ruling class are simply whited sepulchers. They appear to be men, but they are such in appearance only. They serve the ruling class and feather their own nests; they fawn at the feet of the corporate . . . Oh, give me the workingman in his overalls and brogans, who is despised because he has a robust manhood that refuses to be bought. I take off my hat to such a man, he is the hope of the world. Looking into his face, I feel myself inspired, I see in him an ally and a comrade. I clasp hands with him; I double my own strength. There are many such in Philadelphia and they are the hope of the situation. Come into the line and the revolutionary spirit will thrill and inspire you; and there will be a solidarity that will be economic, and in due course of time it will be political. Then, for the first time, you will be respected, and you will find that you are moving toward emancipation.

Do your part in this struggle: this is your chance. I cannot do it for you—you must do it for yourselves. If you are defeated, you will have to bear all the penalties of defeat. Let me tell you that just as certain as you unite your forces; just as certain as you sound the uncompromising slogan, you will win a victory in Philadelphia, the effect of which will inspire the whole working class, and the report of which will sound around the world.

Prostitution of Religion†

April 23, 1910

It may be set down as a rule that the gentry who constitute the self-appointed protectorate over the domain of religion and who charge socialists with being infidels and socialism with attacking religion are themselves hypocrites who are profiting by the ignorance and superstitions of the people and who use the cloak of religion to conceal their evil practices. Their pretended solicitude for socialism is a sham. What they really fear is not that religion will be destroyed, but that hypocrisy and false pretense will be discovered.

---

† Published in *Appeal to Reason*, whole no. 751 (April 23, 1910), 2.

Those pious misfits who do not know what real religion is are one in raising the cry against socialism in the name of religion. Most of them have never read a chapter of socialist economics and are utterly ignorant of what socialism really means, or else, knowing what it means, deliberately misrepresent it to receive the "well done" and the stipend from their masters.

It is so much safer for the average clergyman to speak against socialism than for it, so far as his charge is concerned, his income and his position in society. Some of them are by reflex so imbued with the hostility for socialism of the capitalists who pay their salaries that they deem it their special duty to denounce socialism as an attack upon the church and a conspiracy against religion. Of course they speak in the name of religion, the religion of Jesus Christ, the homeless wanderer who sympathized and associated with the poor and lowly, and whose ministrations were among the despised sinners and outcasts.

These pious pickets of capitalism prostitute religion in the service of Mammon. Of all men on earth, they are the least fit to speak in the name of religion. They have no religion or they would not serve in such a degenerate role.

They are full of cant and glibly parrot their creed, but of real religion, the spiritual influence which exalts man and consecrates him to the loving service of his fellow man, they are as destitute as the arctic region is of sunflowers. Christ knew them perfectly and denounced them as hypocrites.

It is false and slanderous to charge that socialism aims to destroy religion. The truth is that socialism proposes to destroy the conditions which make religion impossible. It is the veriest sarcasm to talk about religion in the cannibalism of the present system in which men devour each other like hyenas and in which the millions who are robbed of what they produce sink into hopeless poverty while their sons are driven to crime and their daughters to prostitution.

Never until this brute struggle for existence is ended and our industrial life is organized on a basis of democratic mutualism will religion come to abide with men, not the religion of creeds written in books, but of deeds written in the hearts of men whose brethren are all mankind.

Industrial Unionism and the Philadelphia Streetcar Strike [excerpt]†

circa May 1, 1910

Certain battles are memorable and certain battlefields become historic. The recent struggle of the carmen at Philadelphia will be among these when the history of the war for industrial freedom is written.[21]

I never saw a more magnificent body of fighting industrialists.[22] They were aroused as few similar bodies have been to a true consciousness of the situation, and had it not been the temporizing in dealing with the brutal corporation and its myriad murderous hirelings, and some other tactical errors, they would have scored a complete triumph. The fighting spirit of the rank and file was above question and their solidarity under fire was perfectly admirable. Besides this, public sentiment was overwhelmingly with them and if they had persisted in all their demands, conceded nothing, and stood their ground, they could not have failed. They were driven to fight, and fight it should have been to the finish. When they began to concede they began to weaken, and the many fruitless conferences, parleyings, and palaverings but served to sap their waning strength.

The weakness of the strike—the essential weakness of every craft union strike—lay in the fact that it was concerned wholly with securing nominal concessions under the wage system, instead of being also directed against the system itself. Any strike which lacks the conscious aim to overthrow the wage system, however bravely it may be fought, or however favorable may seem the outcome, is certain in the long run to prove more or less barren of substantial results.

A body of blind strikers, blind as to the ultimate aim of what they are striking for, never really won a victory, even though victory be conceded. A body of class-conscious strikers who fight for temporary advantages only as a means of strengthening their position in the struggle for freedom never encounter a defeat, even if their strike is lost.

The former lose when they win, and the latter win when they lose.

† Published as "Historic Labor Battle" as part of the pamphlet *Unionism, Industrial and Political: The Philadelphia Street Car Strike and General Strike* (Philadelphia: Socialist Party of Philadelphia, 1910), 3–6. Reprinted as "Debs Tells Where Craft Unions Fail" in *New York Call*, vol. 3, no. 158 (June 7, 1910), 1, 3.

The object of every strike must be the undermining and ultimate overthrow of wage-slavery, and if it lacks this vital element, it is but a blind revolt and has to be fought over and over again until the eyes of the slaves are finally opened to what they are up against, and to the imperative necessity of training and drilling, fitting and equipping themselves to take possession and control of the industrial masters.

The utter weakness and hopelessness of craft unionism was so glaringly manifest, so palpably and painfully in evidence in Philadelphia, that its blindest devotees were compelled to admit it. Left entirely to themselves, the carmen would have been beaten from the start, and the strike would hardly have created a ripple on the surface; but the strong and irresistible class instinct of the workers prevailed and they rushed headlong into the fray, in defiance of their leaders and without regard to consequences to themselves, and this was the commanding feature of the strike, fanned into a roaring conflagration, in the light of which the class struggle loomed in bold relief, and gave to this industrial conflict historic value and significance.

Scathing as a rebuke to craft unionism was the magnificent act of the Baldwin Locomotive Works, who marched out in a body in sympathy with the strikers, although not organized at all, and not only gave to the strike its chief element of support, but struck horror to the hearts of the capitalist all over the eastern states. The inference follows logically that if all the workers of Philadelphia had been free to follow their class instinct, instead of being bound up in craft agreements, they would have all gone out on strike in sympathy with the carmen, as did the unorganized Baldwin employees, and won the strike in an hour.

The obvious lesson of the Philadelphia strike is industrial unionism and united political action along strictly class lines. It is the working class against the capitalist class, and industrial freedom against wage-slavery!

The strikers at Philadelphia fought a splendid fight, but they can fight a far better one—and they will. They at least showed, a majority of them, that they can think and act for themselves, and that it is not the part of wisdom for intelligent workingmen to blindly follow their leaders, instead of scrutinizing their every act and giving them loyalty and support only when they deserve it.

Let them now strengthen their position and prepare for the future by pushing out into industrial unionism, the only unionism which can cope successfully against the master class, and let them also carry their unionism into politics by joining the Socialist Party, the only party which stands unequivocally for the working class on the political field.

To organize a so-called labor party will be to profit but meagerly by recent experience. Such a party is at best but a makeshift and provides the scheming labor politician with a further opportunity to ply his political prostitution at the expense of his misguided followers.

If the workers at Philadelphia are not class conscious, if they are blind to the class struggle, if they accept wage-slavery as a finality, a labor party can do them no possible good; if they are class conscious and their eyes are open to the class struggle, and their conscious purpose is to abolish wage-slavery, they will join the Socialist Party.

As a closing word I wish to say that I am proud of the attitude and actions of the socialists of Philadelphia during the strike. They were the first to espouse it and the last to leave the field; they never flinched under fire, never wavered in their loyalty, and the strikers know it and admit it with full appreciation.

Let socialists everywhere follow this splendid example and not only preach the class struggle, but incarnate it and serve in it in every skirmish and every battle of the workers everywhere in the War for Emancipation.

An Unsocialistic Immigration Proposal: Open Letter to George D. Brewer[†23]

circa May 19, 1910

My Dear Brewer:—

Have just read the majority report of the Committee on Immigration.[24] It is utterly unsocialistic, reactionary, and in truth outrageous, and I hope you will oppose it with all your power. The plea that certain races are to be excluded because of tactical expediency would be entirely consistent in a bourgeois convention of self-seekers, but should have no place in a proletarian gathering under the auspices of an international movement that is calling on the oppressed and exploited workers of all the world to unite for their emancipation . . . [25]

† Published in *International Socialist Review*, vol. 11, no. 1 (July 1910), 16–17.

Away with the "tactics" which require the exclusion of the oppressed and suffering slaves who seek these shores with the hope of bettering their wretched condition and are driven back under the cruel lash of expediency by those who call themselves socialists in the name of a movement whose proud boast it is that it stands uncompromisingly for the oppressed and downtrodden of all the earth. These poor slaves have just as good a right to enter here as even the authors of this report who now seek to exclude them. The only difference is that the latter had the advantage of a little education and had not been so cruelly ground and oppressed, but in point of principle there is no difference, the motive of all being precisely the same, and if the convention which meets in the name of socialism should discriminate at all it should be in favor of the miserable races who have borne the heaviest burdens and are most nearly crushed to the earth.

Upon this vital proposition I would take my stand against the world and no specious argument of subtle and sophisticated defenders of the Civic Federation unionism, who do not hesitate to sacrifice principle for numbers and jeopardize ultimate success for immediate gain, could move me to turn my back upon the oppressed, brutalized, and despairing victims of the old world, who are lured to these shores by some faint glimmer of hope that here their crushing burdens may be lightened, and some star of promise rise in their darkened skies.

The alleged advantages that would come to the socialist movement because of such heartless exclusion would all be swept away a thousand times by the sacrifice of a cardinal principle of the international socialist movement, for well might the good faith of such a movement be questioned by intelligent workers if it placed itself upon record as barring its doors against the very races most in need of relief, and extinguishing their hope, and leaving them in dark despair at the very time their ears were first attuned to the international call and their hearts were beginning to throb responsive to the solidarity of the oppressed of all lands and all climes beneath the skies.

In this attitude there is nothing of maudlin sentimentality, but simply a rigid adherence to the fundamental principles of the international proletarian movement. If socialism, international revolutionary socialism, does not stand staunchly, unflinchingly, and uncompromisingly for the working class and for the exploited and oppressed masses of all lands, then it stands for none and its claim is a false pretense and its profession a delusion and a snare.

Let those desert us who will because we refuse to shut the international door in the faces of their own brethren; we will be none the weaker but all the stronger for their going, for they evidently have no clear conception of the international solidarity, are wholly lacking in the revolutionary spirit, and have no proper place in the socialist movement while they entertain such aristocratic notions of their own assumed superiority.

Let us stand squarely on our revolutionary, working class principles and make our fight openly and uncompromisingly against all enemies, adopting no cowardly tactics and holding out no false hopes, and our movement will then inspire the faith, arouse the spirit, and develop the fiber that will prevail against the world.

Yours without compromise,
Eugene V. Debs

Building the Industrial Union: Open Letter to Tom Mann†

circa June 1910

Your communication of the 19th ult. [May 19, 1910] has been received and has been noted with special interest and appreciation. Of course I know you and have known you for a number of years by your excellent work. I followed you to Australia and read a number of your articles from there but did not know until your letter came that you had returned to England.[26]

Let me thank you most warmly for your kind words in reference to myself personally and to say in answer that I have the same high regard, the same strong attachment for you as a fellow worker and revolutionist.

Touching the matter of industrial unionism to which you refer, we have had, as you are aware, some peculiar and distressing experiences on this side. But we are not in the least discouraged, nor any less ardent in our advocacy of the principles of industrial unionism, while we have profited somewhat, I trust, by that experience.

† Published in *International Socialist Review*, vol. 11, no. 2 (August 1910), 90–1.

By evening mail I am sending you a few booklets in which you will find my views upon the essentials set forth pretty fully, if not as clearly as I would wish to present them. In answer to your direct inquiry I have to say that I too am opposed, like yourself, to undertaking to destroy the old unions. Such a policy can be fruitful only of mischief to industrial unionism, as we have reason to know on this side. It is true that the old unions are for the most part thoroughly outgrown, reactionary, and utterly hostile to revolutionary agitation and activity, and that their leaders are of the same character, if they are not corrupt besides, and yet to attempt to destroy them is to make them more impregnable as strongholds of capitalism, strengthen their leaders in the estimation of the rank and file, and give them a new lease of prestige and power.

I do believe that an industrial union should be organized and it should carry forward a most vigorous and comprehensive propaganda. There are millions of unorganized to whom it can make its appeal, as well as to those who are organized and lean toward industrial unionism. It should be distinctly understood that to smash the existing unions and establish industrial unions by force is not its mission, but that on the contrary, it has come as the most intelligent and effective expression of labor unionism, that its purpose is to build and not to destroy, to help and not to hinder, thus inspiring the confidence of the workers, whether organized or unorganized, and recruiting its ranks from the most intelligent and experienced in every department of industrial activity.

The taunts and sneers of the "pure and simple" leaders who have nothing to lose but their jobs, and whose leadership depends upon their keeping the workers segregated in craft unions, may well be ignored, instead of allowing ourselves to be goaded into attacking them, thereby giving warrant to these leaders in charging us, which they are only too eager to do, with seeking to destroy their unions. The effect of this is invariably to fortify these unions more strongly in their reactionary attitude, and their so-called leaders in their corrupt and degrading domination.

It is far wiser, as our experience has demonstrated, to devote our time, means and energy to advocating the principles of industrial unionism, building up our organization and vitalizing our propaganda by an appeal to the intelligence and integrity of the workers, bearing with them patiently and perseveringly, while at the same time aiding and encouraging them in all their struggles for better conditions, than to waste time in denouncing, or seeking to destroy, these reactionary old unions and their leaders.

Industrial unionism, as organized and applied, to find favor with the workers, must give proof of its sympathy with them in all their struggles, rejoice with them when they win, and when they lose cheer them up and point the way to victory.

It matters not what union it is that happens to be engaged in a fight with the master class, or what its attitude may be toward industrial unionism, the invariable policy of the industrial union should be to back up the contestants and help them win their struggle by all the means at its command. This policy will do more, infinitely more to inspire the faith of the workers in industrial unionism and draw them to its standard than any possible amount of denunciation or attempted destruction of the old unions.

Nor do I believe in organizing dual unions in any case where the old union substantially holds the field. Where an old union is disintegrating, it is of course different. Here there is need of organization, or rather reorganization, and hence a legitimate field for industrial unionism.

Industrial evolution has made industrial unionism possible and revolutionary education and agitation must now make it inevitable. To this end we should bore from within and without, the industrial unionists within the old unions working together in perfect harmony with the industrial unionists upon the outside engaged in laying the foundation and erecting the superstructure of the new revolutionary economic organization, the embryonic industrial democracy.

The difficulties we have encountered on this side since organizing the Industrial Workers have largely been overcome, and I believe the time is near at hand when all industrial unionists will work together to build up the needed organization and when industrial unionism will receive such impetus as will force it to the front irresistibly in response to the crying need of the enslaved and despoiled workers in their struggle for emancipation.

The economic organization of the working class is as essential to the revolutionary movement as the sun is to light and the workers are coming more and more to realize it, and the triumph of industrial unionism over craft unionism is but a question of time, and this can be materially shortened if we but deal wisely and sanely with the situation.

Believe me in the bonds of industrial unionism and socialism,

Your comrade and fellow worker,
Eugene V. Debs

Roosevelt and Prizefighting†

July 30, 1910

A few days ago, according to reports, three men of national prominence in the East were discussing Roosevelt. All three concluded that he was insane, a madman. Whether they are right or wrong is not for us to say, but the evidences are certainly multiplying that the Sage of Sagamore is in a bad way. For instance, in the last issue of *The Outlook*, of which he is the reputed associate editor, Lyman J. Abbott,[27] reformed preacher, being the editor-in-chief, discusses prizefighting over his own name.[28] This epistle is certainly self-contradictory enough to be regarded as the effusion of a disordered mind. Admitting that he has been a patron of the ring, that he has attended a number of prizefights and enjoyed them, that it is a "manly" sport, that he numbers some professional pugs among his personal friends, he concludes by advocating the suppression of the game and forbidding even the pictures of these "manly" exhibitions.

Can anyone conceive of Lincoln sending a telegram of congratulation to a prizefighter after he had beaten his opponent into pulp and matted gore? That is what Roosevelt did to Bob Fitzsimmons[29] while he occupied the executive seat of the nation.

How is that for a "moral example" by the president of the United States? And what have the preachers and purists to say about it? And what would they not have to say about it had Roosevelt been a Socialist instead of a Republican?

Socialists have been accused by Roosevelt of having low morals, but there is not one among them all whose morals are so low that he would not blush for shame to have Roosevelt's record, public and private, on the subject of prizefighting.

The many thousands who crowd about a prize ring to see two brutes maul and mangle each other into bloody, insensible wreckage, most of them plug-hatted and patent leather-shoed, with the president of the United States as a guest of honor, are all opposed to socialism on the ground that socialism is a menace to public morals.

Socialists are not patrons of brutal, degrading prize rings and are not the personal friends and associates of prizefighters. Socialists are at their humble

† Published in *Appeal to Reason*, whole no. 765 (July 30, 1910), 3.

cottages with their families, reading sound literature, studying the science of society, and yielding the distinctions of bloody prize ring and its disgraceful associations to Roosevelt and the bourgeoisie of whom he is the idol and patron saint.

Unionism Is the Flower of the Past Century: A Labor Day Message[30] [excerpt][†]

September 3, 1910

The wage earners of the world today are poor as a rule and ignorant as a class, but they constitute the overwhelming majority. In other words, they have the power but are not conscious of it. The supreme demand of the day is to make them conscious of the power they possess by reason of their vast numbers.

Labor Day celebrations in the United States are advancing numerically, but in the enlightenment of the wage earner, in the awakening of him to the realization of his power, they are accomplishing nothing. Labor Day will see vast assemblages of men in parade. With banners and floats, uniforms and bands, they will march through the city, listen to some suave speaker, enjoy the fellowship of their kind, point out the great showing they make in their numbers, and the next day they will be back in the factories and the mills, toiling and sweating and not one particle better off for their celebration.

The working class alone does the world's work, creates its capital, digs its wealth from out of the ground, builds its factories, its mills, its railroads, conquers the rivers and the mountains, manufactures the things that support the people, feeds and clothes the multitude, and rears the majestic palaces that shelter the parasites.

The working class alone increases the knowledge and adds to the wealth of society. It is the only class that is essential to society and, therefore, the only class that can survive in the worldwide struggle for freedom.

† Published as "Debs Pronounces Unionism Flower of Last Century" in *Terre Haute Tribune*, September 4, 1910, undetermined page. Copy in *Papers of Eugene V. Debs* microfilm edition, reel 7.

A century ago the trade union movement started to develop into the tremendous power it is in the land today. Unionism, as applied to labor in the modern sense, is the fruit and flower of the last century. It has come to us for the impetus of our day in pursuit of its worldwide mission of emancipation. It is the manifestation of the desire and the need of the great majority that constitutes the working class to unite in order that they may rule as the sovereigns they are told they are but are not.

Wendell Phillips, in 1872, said: "I hail the labor movement for the reason that it is my only hope for democracy."[31] Unless there is power in your movement, industrially and politically, the last knell of democratic liberty in this Union is struck.

In the wage-earning army of this country lies the power to rule righteously and honestly. The immense numbers of laborers is the manifestation of that power. All that is needed is the awakening. That the laboring man does not realize his right and his power to rule is not all his fault. Deprived of education by the necessity of earning bread, spending his waking hours in endless toil, returning to his modest home at night with his energies spent in laboring for another's profit, he has little time to study, to learn, to think of the power he should exercise, and always there are those who would confuse him, minions hired to boss him, shrewd lieutenants of the rich paid to lead him astray, to falsely inform him, to prevent him from realizing his strength and so hold him in bondage.

But there is ground upon which to be optimistic. There is reason to rejoice at the growth of trade unionism. Wage-earners are awakening to the fact that the important thing to impress upon the mind of the trade unionist is that it is his duty to cultivate the habit of doing his own thinking.

The moment he realizes this, he is beyond the power of the scheming politician, the emissary of the exploiter, in or out of the labor movement. And you may quote me as saying that the laboring men of Terre Haute are today in the grasp of men who would and do exploit them for their own gains. "No politics in the union" is the cry of these men. By it they hope to keep the wage-earner from exercising that right of franchise by which the laboring class, the great majority, could rule for itself. By dividing the votes between the two great political parties, they hope to maintain for the men who boss them the power to rule the multitude.

To them this Labor Day demonstration is a credit. They are exhibiting their stock. They are showing the big bosses the vast army they lead. They are impressing their followers with their strength while all the time they are carefully guiding that strength to suit their own purposes by keeping the union out of politics.

In Terre Haute's Labor Day celebration, one man I know has awakened and will take part. He is one of the great army that toils in a mill. He has not had the advantages of a good education. But in his modest little home there are all the standard works on economics and in his idle moments you will find him studying them. Place this man before a workingman's audience and he would route Senator Beveridge with his oratory. He has learned the lesson of doing his own thinking. He knows why the wage-earner should rule and he knows the wage-earner does not rule.

It is in men like him that the future of this country rests. His kind will set this overwhelming majority of toiling workmen to thinking for themselves, acting for themselves, voting for themselves, and then Labor Day, with all its pomp and parade and music, will have a new significance. Then, and not until then, will labor exercise its power and right to rule the world.

Working Class Politics: Speech at Riverfront Park, Chicago[32] [excerpt][†]

September 18, 1910

We live in the capitalist system, so-called because it is dominated by the capitalist class. In this system the capitalists are the rulers and the workers the subjects. The capitalists are in a decided minority and yet they rule because of the ignorance of the working class.

So long as the workers are divided, economically and politically, they will remain in subjection, exploited of what they produce and treated with contempt by the parasites who live out of their labor.

The economic unity of the workers must first be effected before there can be any progress toward emancipation. The interests of the millions of wage

† Published in *International Socialist Review*, vol. 11, no. 5 (November 1910), 257–61.

workers are identical, regardless of nationality, creed, or sex, and if they will only open their eyes to this simple, self-evident fact, the greatest obstacle will have been overcome and the day of victory will draw near.

The primary need of the workers is industrial unity, and by this I mean their organization in the industries in which they are employed as a whole instead of being separated into more or less impotent unions according to their crafts. Industrial unionism is the only effective means of economic organization, and the quicker the workers realize this and unite within one compact body for the good of all, the sooner will they cease to be the victims of ward-heeling labor politicians and accomplish something of actual benefit to themselves and those dependent upon them. In Chicago where the labor grafters, posing as union leaders, have so long been permitted to thrive in their iniquity, there is especially urgent need of industrial unionism, and when this is fairly under way it will express itself politically in a class conscious vote of and for the working class.

So long as the workers are content with conditions as they are, so long as they are satisfied to belong to a craft union under the leadership of those who are far more interested in drawing their own salaries and feathering their own nests with graft than in the welfare of their followers, so long, in a word, as the workers are meek and submissive followers, mere sheep, they will be fleeced, and no one will hold them in greater contempt than the very grafters and parasites who fatten out of their misery.

It is not Gompers, who banquets with Belmont and Carnegie, and Mitchell, who is paid and pampered by the plutocrats, who are going to unite the workers in their struggle for emancipation. The Civic Federation, which was organized by the master class and consists of plutocrats, politicians, and priests, in connivance with so-called labor leaders, who are used as decoys to give that body the outward appearance of representing both capital and labor, is the staunch supporter of trade unions and the implacable foe of industrial unionism and socialism, and this in itself should be sufficient to convince every intelligent worker that the trade union under its present leadership and, as now used, is more beneficial to the capitalist class than it is to the workers, seeing that it is the means of keeping them disunited and pitted against each other, and as an inevitable result, in wage-slavery.

The workers themselves must take the initiative in uniting their forces for effective economic and political action; the leaders will never do it for them. They must no longer suffer themselves to be deceived by the specious arguments of their betrayers, who blatantly boast of their unionism that they may traffic in it and sell out the dupes who blindly follow them. I have very little use for labor leaders in general and none at all for the kind who feel their self-importance and are so impressed by their own wisdom that where they lead, their dupes are expected to blindly follow without a question. Such "leaders" lead their victims to the shambles and deliver them over for a consideration, and this is possible only among craft-divided wage-slaves who are kept apart for the very purpose that they may feel their economic helplessness and rely upon some "leader" to do something for them.

Economic unity will be speedily followed by political unity. The workers once united in one great industrial union will vote a united working class ticket. Not only this, but only when they are so united can they fit themselves to take control of industry when the change comes from wage-slavery to economic freedom. It is precisely because it is the mission of industrial unionism to unite the workers in harmonious cooperation in the industries in which they are employed, and by their enlightened interdependence and self-imposed discipline prepare them for industrial mastery and self-control when the hour strikes, thereby backing up with their economic power the verdict they render at the ballot box, it is precisely because of this fact that every Socialist, every class-conscious worker should be an industrial unionist and strive by all the means at his command to unify the workers in the all-embracing bonds of industrial unionism.

The Socialist Party is the party of the workers, organized to express in political terms their determination to break their fetters and rise to the dignity of free men. In this party the workers must unite and develop their political power to conquer and abolish the capitalist political state and clear the way for industrial and social democracy.

But the new order can never be established by mere votes alone. This must be the result of industrial development and intelligent economic and political organization, necessitating both the industrial union and the political party of the workers to achieve their emancipation.

In this work, to be successfully accomplished, woman must have an equal part with man. If the revolutionary movement of the workers stands for anything, it stands for the absolute equality of the sexes, and when this fact is fully realized and the working woman takes her place side by side with the working man all along the battlefront, the great struggle will soon be crowned with victory.

My First Job†

October 1, 1910

It was at Terre Haute, Indiana, on May 23, 1870, that I first went to work. I was 14. Although 40 years have passed since then, I still have the most vivid recollection of that, to me, eventful day. It was my first job, and as I reported for duty, clad in my first suit of overalls, I felt as if I had all at once become a man.

A short time previously I had quit school to make my own living. P. A. Solomon, foreman of the paint shops of the TH&I Railroad Co.,[33] now part of the Pennsylvania system, was a personal friend of our family and through his influence I secured my first job in said shops. I was the only "cub." While Mr. Solomon was the only "boss" listed on the payroll of the company, as a matter of fact all of the master painters, about 15 in number, were my bosses, and I soon learned (and many a time since I have felt thankful for it) what it is to serve an apprenticeship in an industrial trade.

My first work consisted of removing grease from the trucks of passenger coaches, with the aid of potash, preparing them for the painters, and putting in my odd time grinding paint with an old fashioned mill and responding to the calls of my numerous bosses.

It was sometimes very cold work and the potash gnawed the nails from my fingers, but I was satisfied withal, for was I not learning a trade and making my own living? It is true that my wage was only 50 cents a day, but that seemed a considerable amount at that time, and when on June 1st, I received my first pay envelope containing $4.00 for eight days' work, I felt myself quite the richest and perhaps the proudest boy in town. It was but a few swift steps from the shop door to my home that evening and I can still see the glow of pride that lighted up the face of my dear mother as I handed her the unopened envelope containing the first money I had ever earned.

After I had been at the shop for a time, I was permitted to handle the brush at some of the coarser work and later on I was taught how to letter freight cars and still later I was given a chance to try my hand on passenger coaches. In this way I served a year and a half, mastering a good deal of the trade and very

† Published in *Appeal to Reason*, whole no. 774 (October 1, 1910), 3.

well satisfied with the progress I was making, except that the work, most of it confining, did not agree with my health.

One day an extra fireman was needed on a yard engine and I was pressed into service. I had never before been aboard of a locomotive, and I remember distinctly that the engineer told me, by way of encouragement perhaps, that I was the greenest fireman he had ever seen. But it was this job that at once appealed to me, for reasons that every boy who has ever fired a locomotive will readily understand. From that time forward I was a locomotive fireman, and I do not know what my career might have been had not my good mother, who was in constant fear that I might be killed or maimed, finally prevailed upon me to quit the railroad service.

I am glad indeed to have had the experience I had as an apprentice and as a workingman. It has been the means of enlisting the interests and energies of my maturer life on behalf of the boys and girls who have to go out in the world and make their own living, especially those who are not as fortunate as I was in having the loving aid and unceasing care of good parents to give me my start in life.

There have been many changes since then in the course of our industrial evolution, and the day is coming when we shall have a social system in which every boy and every girl will be given full time and ample opportunity for physical development and mental and moral training before being required to go out into the world to make their own living.

Capitalist Class Rule: Executive, Legislative, Judicial†

October 8, 1910

The capitalist class is in power; the working class is in slavery. This is the situation in all lands, including the United States.

President Taft is a capitalist executive; Congress is a capitalist legislative body, and the Supreme Court a capitalist judicial instrument. These several

† Published as "Throttling Organized Labor" in *The Coming Nation*, October 8, 1910, unspecified page. Copy on *Papers of Eugene V. Debs* microfilm edition, reel 7.

governmental powers originate in the capitalist Constitution of the United States. There was not a working man in the convention which framed the Constitution; there has never been a working man in the presidential chair; there is no working man in the Supreme Court, and there is not a representative of the working class in the Congress of the United States.

In the present system the capitalists are the rulers, rich and defiant; the workers are the subjects, poor and submissive. The Republican and Democratic parties stand for the rulers; the Socialist Party for the subjects. Choose ye between them!

But this is only preliminary to the specific matter to be discussed in this article, the purpose of which is to show how organized labor is throttled by the powers of capitalist government.

The state of New York enacted a law through a recent legislature providing for reasonable hours and sanitary conditions in the bake shops of that state.[34] The capitalist bakers promptly appealed to the courts; the state courts at first, consisting of judges elected by the people. The trial judge held the law constitutional. The capitalist masters then appealed to the appellate division and that court affirmed the decision of the trial judge. The case was next carried to the state court of appeals and again the law was declared constitutional.

The final move was to appeal the case to the Supreme Court of the United States, consisting not of judges elected by the people, but of corporate attorneys appointed by a capitalist president and holding office for life. Of course the capitalist Supreme Court decided the case in the interest of the capitalists owning the bake shops and against the slaves who toil in them. The law was declared to be unconstitutional and by a stroke of the pen wiped from the statute books.

The people of New York demanded the law; the Supreme Court at Washington denied it. If this is not despotism, pure and simple, what is it? Has the tsar of Russian more absolute power than this?

The organized workers of New York to a man pleaded for this law; the people of the state recognizing it to be in the interest of public health favored it, but the capitalist proprietors of the bread factories, whose profit would have been reduced, were opposed to it, and their court annulled it. If this is not a clear case of capitalist class rule and a perfect demonstration of capitalist class government what, then, may it be called?

The infamy, the heartlessness, the utter moral depravity of this decision, entirely apart from its class nature, defies characterization. Profit is safely guarded; health and life wantonly destroyed.

Now for another case.

In 1890 Congress enacted what is known as the Sherman Anti-Trust law. Its object was, as stated by its author and supporters at the time, to prevent capitalist monopolies in restraint of trade. It was explicitly understood that it was not to prevent workingmen and farmers from combining to advance their interests.

This law was on the statute books totally inoperative, a dead letter, for four years. In 1894 the Pullman strike occurred. Like a flash the Sherman Anti-Trust law appeared. Its real purpose was not to interfere with capitalists—that was a mere blind—but to throttle organized labor and crush any rebellion of the slaves. Under this law the strike was broken up, the leaders jailed, and the railroad corporations came out with flying colors.

Another case of capitalist class rule and capitalist class government; another demonstration of capitalist class supremacy and working class slavery. Republican and Democratic votes are for this very sort of thing. The capitalist bake shop owners of New York all vote the Republican and Democratic tickets, and so do the capitalist owners of the railroad corporations. In the name of common sense, why should the wage-slaves vote with these capitalists to drive the nails into their own coffins instead of giving their votes to the Socialist Party which proposes that the workers themselves shall rule the land and control its institutions?

Now for the climax.

The last Congress voted $485,000 to the secret service as an incentive to "detect crime," and $200,000 more "to detect and prosecute infringements of the Sherman Anti-Trust law. When this measure was pending, an amendment was offered providing that no part of this $200,000 appropriation should be used for the prosecution of organized labor. Here the line was clearly drawn and the issue sharply defined between capitalist corporations and labor unions. President Taft at once leaped into the breach, condemned this amendment as "class legislation," and used all his power as executive to defeat the amendment—and succeeded. As a result, organized labor, whenever and wherever it develops sufficient power to menace capitalist class rule, will promptly be crushed by a capitalist court, backed by a capitalist army, under the direction of a capitalist executive, for all of which a capitalist Congress has made an annual appropriation of $200,000, every dollar of which is wrung from the very wage-slaves who are to be crushed by it.

One can easily fancy the capitalists and their Republican and Democratic puppets softly crooning: What jackasses these workers be!

Gould Turns Democrat†

(October 8, 1910)

George J. Gould,[35] railroad magnate, son of the immortal Jay and director of the Gould millions, has returned from Europe and on landing announced that he had quit the Republican Party and would vote and support the Democratic ticket this year. In this George simply follows in the footsteps of his father, who said: "In a Republican state I am a Republican, in a Democratic state I am a Democrat, but everywhere I am for Jay Gould."

The announcement of George Gould is worth considering. What does it mean? Simply that a capitalist has no politics except his class interests. There is no moral principle involved, any more than there is a moral difference between the Republican Party of Depew of New York and the Democratic Party of Clark of Montana.[36]

George Gould realizes that the rule of the Republican Party has become so rank and rotten that it is time to switch over to the Democratic Party for a fresh lease of power. The capitalists need the Democratic Party for that very business, or it would long since have ceased to exist.

The election returns from Maine show which way the political wind blows this year.[37] George Gould and his capitalist allies are putting their money on the Democratic hoss in this heat, and don't you forget it, and the spavined old critter will be allowed to win this time so as to give the fool people a chance to shout and forget while the Republican nag is being groomed for the next race.

This is an off year and the game will work like a charm. The fool people can be depended on to do their part to play into the hands of the plutes.

Say, Mr. Workingman, why do you suppose George Gould is a Democrat this year? Because the Democratic Party is the workingman's party? He knows what he is about, and if you only knew half as well you would go into the Socialist Party for the same reason that he goes into the Democratic Party.

In the light of the record of the Democratic Party and of the facts clear as the noonday sun, the man who says that the Democratic Party is a workingman's party is either a shrewd capitalist, a scheming politician, an arrant knave, or else his head is painfully in need of a surgical operation.

† Published in *Appeal to Reason*, whole no. 775 (October 8, 1910), 4.

The *Los Angeles Times* Bombing—Who Committed That Crime?†

October 15, 1910

The blowing up of the *Los Angeles Times* and the snuffing out of 20 human lives is another of the atrocious crimes committed in the heat and passion of the class war.[38] Who committed that crime? Harrison Gray Otis,[39] proprietor of the *Times*, and the capitalist press of the Pacific coast in general, charge it directly and specifically upon organized labor. The shock of the explosion was followed by the charge that union labor was guilty of the crime as swiftly as the capitalist press could telegraph the indictment to the country.

It appears well settled in Mr. Otis's statement and the *Times's* account that the *Times* building was blown up by dynamite, and equally well settled that the crime was committed by labor unionists. As one who knows the *Los Angeles Times* by personal experience with that vicious, lying, and criminal sheet, I want to express it as my deliberate opinion that the *Times* and its crowd of union-haters are themselves the instigators, if not the actual perpetrators, of that crime and the murderers of the 20 human beings who perished as its victims.

First of all, let me relate my own experience with General Harrison Gray Otis and the *Los Angeles Times*. At the time of the railroad strike of 1894, the *Los Angeles Times* lied about me outrageously, charged me with every conceivable crime, editorially stated that I deserved the gallows, and did all in its power to send me there. Shortly after the strike I went to Los Angeles after filling my immediate engagements to make answer to this outrageous indictment; and here let me say that any man who would make such false and fiendish charges against another to glut his insane hatred of organized labor would commit any other crime to serve the same base end.

A few days later I returned to Los Angeles to find the old Hazard's Pavilion packed to the doors, every inch of standing room occupied, and thousands turned away, to hear my answer to Otis and the *Times*.[40] It so happened that I had in my grip the documentary evidence, including government reports, to prove my innocence of the most vicious of these charges. In one hand I held up

† Published as "The *Los Angeles Times*—Who Committed That Crime" in *Appeal to Reason*, whole no. 776 (October 15, 1910), 1.

the *Los Angeles Times* and in the other the positive proof of its criminal mendacity. I went through the 13 charges seriatim and literally tore them to tatters. I had not proceeded far until someone in the audience shouted, "Otis is in the house," and this proved to be true. I at once challenged General Otis to come forward and face me, whom he had so outrageously maligned, before his own people. It is needless to say that, although the crowd yelled "Otis, Otis, Otis," he did not dare to come and he would gladly have disappeared if the packed and jammed condition of the hall had not barred his escape.

But from that day to this, although the monstrous lies have long since found them out, General Otis and his leprous sheet have never uttered one word of retraction, and it is not their fault that I was not lynched or hanged for crimes of which I was as innocent as are the union men of Los Angeles upon whom General Otis is now seeking to fasten his atrocious calamities as he did upon me and my fellow unionists 15 years ago.

Now let us examine some of the facts in regard to the blowing up of the *Times* and some of the circumstantial evidence, and let us see if it is not impossible to escape at least the inference, if not the positive conclusion, that Otis and his gang are themselves the conspirators and criminals.

The theory that he who is benefited by a crime is most apt to have a hand in its commission is peculiarly applicable to this case. Financially and morally, Otis and the *Times* have everything to gain as certainly as organized labor has everything to lose in bearing the crushing odium of the crime. Let it be remembered that General Otis was perfectly certain that the outrage, almost before it was committed, was the dastardly act of union labor. He personally was at a safe distance, and all the victims were wage-slaves, and what do Otis and his crowd of exploiting plutocrats care about the lives of slaves? Now for a few of the facts:

First, the class war on the Pacific coast had reached its acutest stage and was rapidly approaching a grave crisis at the time of the explosion. It was in striking analogy to the blowing up of the Independence platform in the class war in Colorado five years ago, and we now know beyond the shadow of a doubt what side committed that revolting crime and what was its object.[41]

Second, the tide of organized labor in California was steadily rising, the Socialist campaign was in full swing, and there was to be a culminating demonstration of labor forces at Los Angeles but a few days after the *Times* was blown up. The demonstration was promptly called off by the leaders of the unions, a grievous blunder on their part, which places them in a defensive and apologetic attitude utterly unwarranted by the circumstances of the situation. Instead of pleading not guilty to the criminal charge preferred against the workers without a scintilla of proof, they should have immediately accused Otis and his gang of union-haters and called upon them to prove that their own hands were not red with the crime.

Third, the *Los Angeles Times* is the most venomous foe of organized labor in the United States, and its own record proves that there is no crime too abhorrent for it to commit to wreak its vengeance on the labor movement.

Fourth, the statement is made by the *Times* itself and confirmed by press dispatches from Chicago that General Otis, "having anticipated such an eventuality," had a duplicate printing plant and a duplicate working force in reserve, all in readiness to leap into the breach and rescue the paper when the expected bomb exploded. This admission proves too much. It is fatal to Otis and the *Times*. What cause had Otis to anticipate the explosion and prepare for it? Suppose a labor unionist had made such an admission, or even intimated that he knew the explosion would occur, would he not promptly be arrested on suspicion and lodged in jail?

Yes, we are only too ready to believe that Otis and his pals expected the explosion and were entirely prepared for it when it came.

Fifth, the united league of newspapers, which embraces a chain of daily papers scattered over the country, and friendly in their attitude toward organized labor, recently sent a special correspondent to California to investigate conditions growing out of the war between labor and capital on the Pacific coast, and his series of articles is now running in those papers. These articles describe a situation and a desperation on the part of the capitalists that has a fitting climax in the blowing up of the *Times*, as the same war had in the blowing up of the Independence platform in Colorado.

In the second article of this series—and let it be remembered that these are capitalist papers and not labor papers—the capitalists composing the Manufacturers' Association are described as in a state bordering on frenzy in their determination to utterly annihilate "at any cost and at all hazards" organized labor on the Pacific coast. The chairman is personally quoted as saying to the correspondent representing these capitalist newspapers: "We will never cease until the last vestige of union labor has been wiped off the Pacific coast."

This vehement and bloodthirsty declaration was made only a short time before the *Times* was blown up and the united workers, a few days later, were to have their mammoth demonstration.

Sixth, the discovery of the bombs is the one farcical feature of this gruesome tragedy, which every human being not utterly void of feeling must deplore with all his heart. To prove that it was the fiendish plot of the unionists, other bombs, accessories to the crime, and pointing to the identity of its perpetrators, must be located and unearthed. Of course it was known instantaneously where to look for the bombs, and of course they were all found according to specifications. In each case they were located at the palatial homes of the proprietors and managers of the *Times* and the Manufacturers' Association, but in no case did one of these bombs explode.

The bomb that did explode bled up the wage-slaves of the *Times* only; the bombs that did not explode did not blow up any of the aristocratic owners and managers. There is a peculiar bomb-consciousness in evidence here that clearly draws the line between capitalists and wage workers.

In Chicago following the Haymarket riot, a regular crop of bombs was harvested in plutocratic reservations until finally the thing was overworked by the army of detectives who were discovering bombs and holding up the plutocrats at so much per bomb, and then the pay was stopped and no more bombs were discovered.

It is not a little strange, to put it very mildly, that of all the bombs located upon the premises of the owners and managers of the *Times* and other aristocrats, not one did its deadly work? That all of them proved to be flat failures? And that all of them were discovered just in the nick of time?

According to the *Times*, one of the bombs was in a suitcase. Upon its discovery a policeman was sent for. The "cop" took out his knife, cut a hole in the grip, smoke issued from the orifice, whereupon he picked up the grip and threw it from him to see it blown into atoms when it struck the ground. If it is excusable to jest at all in connection with such a shocking affair, it may be in order to suggest that this suitcase episode is peculiarly fitted for the sleuth series of dime novels and that on the vaudeville platform it would evoke roars of merriment.

And suppose it is not a bomb that blew up the *Times*. Evidence seems to be that gas, which was carelessly permitted to escape for days preceding the explosion, may have caused the disaster, in which case Otis and the *Times* would be responsible for it. Yet, with the offer of $10,000 or more for the conviction of any person of the crime, there is a bribe for conscienceless detectives to railroad some worker to the gallows, though innocent, by manufacturing evidence against him.

There are other circumstantial evidences and more or less corroborative details that might be added, but enough has been given to warrant the conclusion that the finger of guilt points steadily in the direction of General Harrison Gray Otis and his union-destroying allies and confederates.

What do they and their kind care for the loss of a few thousand dollars, or the sacrifice of a score of working class lives? Absolutely nothing. The lives of thousands of wage-slaves and their wives and babes are wantonly sacrificed every day of the year on the alter of Mammon to satisfy the insatiate greed, the mercenary rapacity of these pirates and freebooters, who know no law, human or divine, except the law of survival of beak and fang, hoof and claw, in the subjugation, exploitation, and degradation of the toiling millions.

Berger Victory Heralds New Political Era†

November 10, 1910

The election of Victor L. Berger, of Wisconsin, and the near election of five other Socialists to Congress and 35 representatives to state legislatures means the dawn of a new era in American politics.[42] For the first time the working class will have a representative in the American Congress, elected on the working class platform of a working class party pledged to working class emancipation. From now on in every succeeding election, the Socialist Party, the political expression of the rising working class, will increase the number of representatives in Congress and in all state legislatures until it has a majority, and then it will wrest the powers of government from the capitalist class and establish an industrial democracy. All the forces that are now playing upon society are operating to this inevitable end.

In proportion as the capitalist system is outgrown and breaking down, the political parties representing that system are breaking up. The Republican and Democratic parties are both torn into warring factions and never can be harmonized again on any progressive national basis. More and more will their impotency to deal with the great new vital issue of the day become manifest to the people, while upon the other hand the rising Socialist Party, born of the travail of capitalism and steadily developing the vigor and virility of a new-born movement, historically destined to grapple with the wage-slave power

† Published as "Debs Sees Dawn in New Election" in *Terre Haute Tribune*, November 10, 1910, unspecified page. Copy on *Papers of Eugene V. Debs* microfilm edition, reel 7.

as the Republican Party grappled with the chattel slave power half a century ago, will in due time sweep into power and reorganize society upon a basis of collective ownership of the social utilities and the means of life and usher in a higher civilization than mankind has yet known.

Danger Ahead†

written December 1910

The large increase in the Socialist vote in the late national and state elections is quite naturally hailed with elation and rejoicing by party members, but I feel prompted to remark, in the light of some personal observations during the campaign, that it is not entirely a matter for jubilation. I am not given to pessimism, or captious criticism, and yet I cannot but feel that some of the votes placed to our credit this year were obtained by methods not consistent with the principles of a revolutionary party, and in the long run will do more harm than good.

I yield to no one in my desire to see the party grow and the vote increase, but in my zeal I do not lose sight of the fact that healthy growth and a substantial vote depend upon efficient organization, the self-education and self-discipline of the membership, and that where these are lacking, an inflated vote secured by compromising methods can only be hurtful to the movement.

The danger I see ahead is that the Socialist Party at this stage, and under existing conditions, is apt to attract elements which it cannot assimilate, and that it may be either weighted down, or torn asunder with internal strife, or that it may become permeated and corrupted with the spirit of bourgeois reform to an extent that will practically destroy its virility and efficiency as a revolutionary organization.

To my mind the working class character and the revolutionary integrity of the Socialist Party are of first importance. All the votes of the people would do us no good if our party ceased to be a revolutionary party, or only incidentally so, while yielding more and more to the pressure to modify the principles and

† Published in *International Socialist Review*, vol. 11, no. 6 (January 1911), 413–15.

program of the party for the sake of swelling the vote and hastening the day of its expected triumph.

It is precisely this policy and the alluring promise it holds out to new members with more zeal than knowledge of working class economics that constitutes the danger we should guard against in preparing for the next campaign. The truth is that we have not a few members who regard vote-getting as of supreme importance, no matter by what method the votes may be secured, and this leads them to hold out inducements and make representations which are not at all compatible with the stern and uncompromising principles of a revolutionary party. They seek to make the socialist propaganda so attractive—eliminating whatever may give offense to bourgeois sensibilities—that it serves as a bait for voters rather than as a means of education, and votes thus secured do not properly belong to us and do injustice to our party as well as to those who cast them.

These votes do not express socialism and in the next ensuing election are quite as apt to be turned against us, and it is better that they be not cast for the Socialist Party, registering a degree of progress the party is not entitled to and indicating a political position the party is unable to sustain.

Socialism is a matter of growth, of evolution, which can be advanced by wise methods, but never by obtaining for it a fictitious vote. We should seek only to register the actual vote of socialism, no more and no less. In our propaganda we should state our principles clearly, speak the truth fearlessly, seeking neither to flatter nor to offend, but only to convince those who should be with us and win them to our cause through an intelligent understanding of its mission.

There is also a disposition on the part of some to join hands with reactionary trade unionists in local emergencies and in certain temporary situations to effect some specific purpose, which may or may not be in harmony with our revolutionary program. No possible good can come from any kind of a political alliance, express or implied, with trade unions or the leaders of trade unions who are opposed to socialism and only turn to it for use in some extremity, the fruit of their own reactionary policy.

Of course we want the support of trade unionists, but only of those who believe in socialism and are ready to vote and work with us for the overthrow of capitalism.

The American Federation of Labor, as an organization, with its Civic Federation to determine its attitude and control its course, is deadly hostile to the Socialist Party and to any and every revolutionary movement of the working class. To kowtow to this organization and to join hands with its leaders to secure political favors can only result in compromising our principles and bringing disaster to the party.

Not for all the vote of the American Federation of Labor and its labor-dividing and corruption-breeding craft unions should we compromise one jot of our revolutionary principles; and if we do we shall be visited with the contempt we deserve by all real socialists, who will scorn to remain in a party professing to disreputable methods of ward-heeling by a revolutionary party of the working class while employing the crooked and politicians to attain their ends.

Of far greater importance than increasing the vote of the Socialist Party is the economic organization of the working class. To the extent, and only to the extent, that the workers are organized and disciplined in their respective industries can the socialist movement advance and the Socialist Party hold what is registered by the ballot. The election of legislative and administrative officers, here and there, while the party is still in a crude state and the members economically unprepared and politically unfit to assume the responsibilities thrust upon them as the result of popular discontent, will inevitably bring trouble and set the party back, instead of advancing it, and while this is to be expected and is to an extent unavoidable, we should court no more of that kind of experience than is necessary to avoid a repetition of it. The Socialist Party has already achieved some victories of this kind which proved to be defeats, crushing and humiliating, and from which the party has not even now, after many years, entirely recovered.

We have just so much socialism that is stable and dependable, because securely grounded in economics, in discipline, and all else that expresses class conscious solidarity, and this must be augmented steadily through economic and political organization, but no amount of mere votes can accomplish this in even the slightest degree.

Voting for socialism is not socialism any more than a menu is a meal.

Socialism must be organized, drilled, equipped, and the place to begin is in the industries where the workers are employed. Their economic power has got to be developed through efficient organization, or their political power, even if it could be developed, would but react upon them, thwart their plans, blast their hopes, and all but destroy them.

Such organization to be effective must be expressed in terms of industrial unionism. Each industry must be organized in its entirety, embracing all the workers, and all working together in the interest of all, in the true spirit of solidarity, thus laying the foundation and developing the superstructure of the new system within the old, from which it is evolving, and systematically fitting the workers, step by step, to assume entire control of the productive forces when the hour strikes for the impending organic change.

Without each economic organization and the economic power with which it is clothed, and without the industrial cooperative training, discipline, and efficiency which are its corollaries, the fruit of any political victories the workers may achieve will turn to ashes on their lips.

Now that the capitalist system is so palpably breaking down, and in consequence its political parties breaking up, the disintegrating elements with vague reform ideas and radical bourgeois tendencies will head in increasing numbers toward the Socialist Party, especially since the greatly enlarged vote of this year has been announced and the party is looming up as a possible dispenser of the spoils of office. There is danger, I believe, that the party may be swamped by such an exodus and the best possible means, and in fact the only effectual means of securing the party against such a fatality, is the economic power of the industrially organized workers.

The votes will come rapidly enough from now on without seeking them, and we should make it clear that the Socialist Party wants the votes only of those who want socialism, and that, above all, as a revolutionary party of the working class, it discountenances vote-seeking for the sake of votes and holds in contempt office-seeking for the sake of office. These belong entirely to capitalist parties and their bosses and their boodle and have no place in a party whose shibboleth is emancipation.

With the workers efficiently organized industrially, bound together by the common tie of their enlightened self-interest, they will just as naturally and inevitably express their economic solidarity in political terms and cast a united vote for the party of their class as the forces of nature express obedience to the laws of gravitation.

A Word About Mexico, Mr. President†

December 10, 1910

President Taft, I mean. Isn't it time for you to take another trip to the Rio Grande? Things are looking very squally for your friend Díaz. You, and Roosevelt before you, did everything possible on this side to keep the bloody clutches of your friend Díaz at the throats of the 10 million peons worked in Mexico and owned and robbed on Wall Street. You had your secret service thugs and assassins turned into the bloodhounds of Díaz, and you had every patriotic Mexican soul who was fighting for his countrymen, and sought refuge here, thrown into United States dungeons, buried alive, and devoured by vermin, to entrench and prolong the reign of the decorated cannibal who masquerades as the president of Mexico, and whose bloody claws you grasped in fell and hearty fellowship as you assured him of your profound respect and the absolute confidence of your mutual masters on Wall Street.

Do you remember this occasion, Mr. President, when your own people were shut out and one of your most ardent admirers was murdered by a guard in his eagerness to witness the ceremony?[43] Do you remember the soldiers that surrounded you, with shotted guns in their hands, and pressed in closely upon you to guard you against your own chosen people while you, with ashen, cowardly lips, delivered the message of your masters?

Lest you have forgotten your speech on that occasion, I will here quote from it as it appeared in the newspapers at that time:

> it gives me the greatest pleasure and I esteem it a special honor to assure your excellency that the American people regard you with the highest respect as an illustrious ruler who has always been profoundly concerned in the prosperity of his country and the happiness of his people, and the beneficiaries of whose reign will be recorded in the pages of history.[44]

Oh, what a lie! What a wicked, ghastly, damnable lie! That lie should have stuck in your throat and strangled you until you were as black in the face as the administration you were glorifying. No wonder you and your Archibald Butt[45]

† Published as "Just a Word, Mr. President" in *Appeal to Reason*, whole no. 784 (December 10, 1910), 1.

had to shut out the people and have yourselves walled in with mailed murderers as the only fit witnesses to such an immoral and debasing exhibition.

There are two occasions in your life, Mr. President, that you ought not to forget: the one when you embraced the tsar of Russia, and the other when you grasped the hand of the tsar of Mexico. The countess ghosts of the victims of these bloody monsters do not envy you the presidency of the United States at the price you paid for it.

The Mexican people are not rising against the people of the United States; they are rising against Díaz and his Wall Street administration of assassination in Mexico, and they are going to overthrow the bloody despotism, based upon the robbery of the people and maintained by force and murder, in spite of the aid and comfort and connivance of your administration in the United States.

Oscar Lawler[46] may be in official clover and Flores Magón may rot in an American prison cell, but the eternal forces that unmake kings and tyrants, destroy thrones, crush iniquity, and triumphantly vindicate the right are at work, and when the hour strikes the revolution in Mexico will drive out its dictator and your friend Díaz will be lucky if he escapes with the head on his shoulders.

A Personal Note[†]

December 31, 1910

To Our Friends and Comrades:—

Fred D. Warren having been relieved of his official duties by Judge Pollock, by authority of the power in him vested by the "rich malefactors," under whose beneficent rule the *Appeal* has become the object of special solicitude, I have come to Girard to take his place (not to fill it—he alone can do that).[47] With a very efficient staff of writers and a most faithful corps of workers in every department of the paper, my task will be as easy as it is agreeable.

† Published as "Personal" in *Appeal to Reason*, whole no. 787 (December 31, 1910), 4. Reprinted as "Debs on Warren," *St. Louis Labor*, January 7, 1911.

Comrade Warren, it is due him to say, demurs to what is being printed in the *Appeal* in reference to himself, but as he has been judicially shorn of his editorial authority, it is to be understood that he is in no wise responsible for what now appears in these columns. I shall be wholly to blame for what is printed during the next six months, and I shall be entirely satisfied if at the expiration of that time Warren and I again exchange places.

Earnestly entreating all our friends to unite with us in the undertaking to hand the *Appeal* back to Comrade Warren with a million subscribers to hail his return to Girard,[48] I remain

Faithfully your servant,
Eugene V. Debs

Military Murderers[†]

December 31, 1910

Soldiers under capitalism are workers hired by capitalists to murder their fellow workers for a pittance that would put a scab to shame. And this the capitalists, for very good reasons to themselves, pronounce "patriotism" and hail as military glory; and the gruesome game has worked like a charm these many years.

But at last these hireling soldiers are catching on. And no wonder. At army posts and in camps, the officers are strutting tsars and the common soldiers cur dogs. The brutal treatment they are subjected to by the snobs and upstarts who lord it over them as their "superiors" I have heard from their own lips and it is revolting to the last degree.

Only a fool, a stupid, besotted fool, would submit to such brutality for such a pittance unless indeed he were a pervert and halfwit and gloried in his own degeneracy.

"Military glory" under capitalism has had its day. Its sun is setting. The suckers have about quit biting.

---

† Published in *Appeal to Reason*, whole no. 787 (December 31, 1910), 4.

Special orders have just been issued by the war department at Washington to all the recruiting stations to increase the pressure and offer all possible inducements to secure recruits. The most glittering and highly colored pictured, displaying the dazzling and attractive beauties of camp life, cover the billboards wherever a recruiting station is located. On these pictures soldiers are in clover as deep as they are in hell in the real thing.

Lolling back in easy chairs, smoking fragrant cigars, and surveying with field-glasses the surrounding landscape of ravishing beauty, a soldier's life at $13 a month is made to appear a symphony of rapture that would excite the envy of the gods, but when he has enlisted and is securely harpooned the illusion vanishes. He sups on embalmed jackass and moldy beans, and a two-by-four "superior" spits on him for dessert. And to desert this dessert is a crime punishable by imprisonment.

Last year, according to the official report of the adjutant general, there were over 4,000 desertions from the army of the United States. The total number of desertions for the ten years ending with the report just issued is not quite 50,000, an average of a trifle less than 5,000 a year.

Think of the supreme significance of 5,000 desertions from the United States army every year! Over 400 a month or about 15 a day for every day of the week.

How is this for an exhibition of patriotism and military glory by the soldiers of the United States Army?

A soldier has just told me that these unparalleled desertions are superinduced mainly by the teachings of socialism and the influence of the socialist movement. Thousands of soldiers have studied and understand more or less clearly the economics of militarism, and they appreciate keenly the position they occupy and the moral degradation it entails, as well as the sickening service they are required to render as their "patriotic duty," and there will be no unnecessary delay on their part in transferring their allegiance from murderous militarism to revolutionary socialism.

Woodrow Wilson[†]

December 31, 1910

The Democratic governor-elect of New Jersey, the ex-president of Princeton College, Woodrow Wilson, is being groomed by the big interests of the East for the presidential nomination in the next campaign. Woodrow was a particularly intimate friend of the late Grover Cleveland.[49] They entertained substantially the same principles and had the same views of what constitutes democracy. If Woodrow is ever elected president and there is a great labor strike, he will make the same use of the federal troops to crush it as did his friend Cleveland.

Mr. Wilson is out in an interview declaring defiance to the Democratic machine of his state and declaring that he will not be controlled by it. This sounds superfine to the people and will add greatly to his popularity and political prospects. But why, pray why, Mr. Wilson, did you wait until after the election before shaking your fist at the machine instead of doing so after your nomination? You can safely thump the machine now. It will help you doubtless and will not in the least hurt the machine. You may find it to your advantage to publicly repudiate the machine (after you have been elected by it), but you are quite evidently no novice when it comes to making personal use of its methods.

† Unsigned article published in *Appeal to Reason*, whole no. 787 (December 31, 1910), 4, an issue edited by Debs. Attributed to Debs.

Notes

1. This speech, the first of a six-week tour sponsored by the *Appeal to Reason,* was delivered before a crowd of about 4,000.
2. Debs had recently received a handwritten letter from the US Territorial Prison at Florence, Arizona from jailed Mexican radical political dissident Richard Flores Magón. In it Magón predicted that pressure of the brutal Porfirio Díaz regime in Mexico would lead to the immediate arrest of himself and his comrades upon the completion of their sentence for violation of the Neutrality Act later in 1910. Reminding Debs that he had already spent three years in prison, Magón pleaded: "I am asking you and comrades Wayland and Warren to reopen the fight in the *Appeal* before it may be too late." See Magón to Eugene V. Debs, January 13, 1910, in Constantine (ed.), *Letters of Eugene V. Debs: Vol. 1,* 327–9. Magón would ultimately die in federal custody at Leavenworth prison in 1922 at the age of 48, a victim of the Espionage Act of 1917.
3. For a short note by Debs indicating that Warren received this suggestion from Debs positively, see Eugene V. Debs to Warren, February 8, 1910 in Constantine, ed., *Letters of Eugene V. Debs: Vol. 1,* 341.
4. Sent by telegram to the *Appeal to Reason* on February 25, 1910.
5. An archaic term for influenza.
6. A postscript by Fred Warren notes that Debs was "really too ill to speak" in Chicago but that reports had been received that Debs had made a "magnificent effort" that had "thrilled" the audience and fueled a mass demonstration at what was actually a successful event.
7. James H. Brower was the Socialist candidate for lieutenant–governor of Illinois in 1904 and for governor in 1908.
8. The January–February 1910 tour was sponsored by the *Appeal to Reason,* for whom Debs worked as a paid contributor. According to Debs, J. E. Snyder of the *Appeal* handled logistics for the tour.
9. Debs appeared in Philadelphia during a strike of streetcar workers against the Philadelphia Traction Company, with Clarence O. Pratt, head of the Philadelphia carmen's association, in the chair. The appearance was part of a regularly scheduled tour by Debs of the East, with scheduled appearances in Maryland, the District of Columbia, New Jersey, and New York. The hall in which Debs spoke was packed to the rafters and the doors ordered closed by the police. Thousands who were unable to gain admission congregated in the streets outside.
10. William D. Mahon (1861–1949) of Detroit was the national president of the Amalgamated Association of Street Railway Employees of America. Mahon headed the union for 52 years, finally retiring in June 1946. A strong advocate of arbitration throughout his career, Mahon was close associate of Samuel Gompers and remained a vice-president of the American Federation of Labor until the time of his death.
11. George H. Earle, Jr. (1856–1928) was a conservative Philadelphia lawyer and financier deeply involved in the railroad industry. He would become the Republican candidate for mayor of Philadelphia in 1911, narrowly losing to his Democratic opponent.

12. The first of these strikes began on the morning of October 9, 1900, when employees of the Terre Haute Electric Railway Company walked off the job under the banner of the Central Labor Union. Debs was at that time in the middle of the 1900 presidential campaign tour, however, and his only day home in Terre Haute in October was on the 7th, an open date following his October 6 speech in Indianapolis—that is, *before* the strike actually began. He delivered well-documented speeches at campaign meetings in Illinois, Missouri, Kansas, Nebraska, Iowa, and points further east every evening for the rest of the month, with his only open date falling on the 15th. Whether Debs's memory fails him here or he consciously fabricates a heroic legend to inspire Philadelphia streetcar strikers, he certainly did not "break all engagements to hasten home." The 1900 Terre Haute strike was ultimately settled by a three-member arbitration committee, with the strikers choosing President Van Horn of the state miners' union as their representative.
13. The second Terre Haute street car strike took place in January 1902. Although details of his ongoing speaking trip are unclear, Debs was reportedly in Michigan earlier in the month before he appeared in town suddenly on January 20 to address a mass meeting of workers on strike against the Terre Haute Electric Railway Company in a stoppage called by the Central Labor Union. The situation had been tense, with damage inflicted to cars attempting to break the strike, resulting in many arrests.
14. John E. Reyburn (1845–1914), a former Republican member of Congress, served as mayor of Philadelphia from 1907 to 1911.
15. George A. Pettibone of the Western Federation of Miners was first diagnosed with cancer during his sensational trial. After his acquittal he returned to Denver where he underwent surgery for stomach cancer on August 1, 1908; he died two days later at the age of 46.
16. Clarence Wolf (1860–1937), a banker, was vice president of the Philadelphia Rapid Transit Company and was regarded by strikers as the source of the company's intransigence in contract negotiations. Wolf was elected as a Republican to the Pennsylvania state senate in November 1908, serving two two-year terms.
17. Adapted from a couplet in "The Masque of Anarchy" (1819) by Percy Bysshe Shelley (1792–1822). The original stanza reads: "Men of England, heirs of Glory / Heroes of unwritten story, / Nurslings of one mighty Mother, / Hopes of her, and one another; // Rise like Lions after slumber / In unvanquishable number, / Shake your chains to earth like dew / Which in sleep had fallen on you— / Ye are many—They are few."
18. Meyer Guggenheim (1828–1905) was the patriarch of one of the richest families in the world. Born in Switzerland, Guggenheim emigrated to the United States in the 1840s and made his vast fortune in Colorado silver mining and smelting. He was the father of art collector Solomon Guggenheim, for whom the Guggenheim Museum in New York is named.
19. There is no record of Debs ever having actually issued a public call for insurrection over this issue.
20. Luella Twining was a Socialist Party activist who had run for superintendent of public instruction in Colorado in 1904 and a delegate at the founding of the Industrial

Workers of the World. She worked as a special correspondent for the *Appeal to Reason* and helped to publicize the arrest of Moyer, Haywood, and Pettibone and the trials that followed. She spoke to a number of labor groups at the time on behalf of the Western Federation of Miners, helping to raise funds and consciousness about the affair.

21. The Philadelphia General Strike began in January 1910 when the Philadelphia Rapid Transit Company, which had previously rejected worker demands for a 25-cent per hour wage increase, unilaterally implemented a mandatory withhold for pension and other benefits while terminating 173 members of the Amalgamated Association of Street and Electric Railway Employees of America. The retaliatory strike of 6,000 streetcar workers began on January 18. Thousands of strikebreakers were brought in by the company in an effort to maintain operations; strikers began to sabotage cars and lines to keep them inoperable. On March 5, the city's Central Federated Union called for a general strike in solidarity with the striking streetcar workers, which began with the support of more than 60,000 workers and grew to idle an estimated 140,000 before its termination on March 27. Rapid Transit workers remained on strike until April 19, when the company finally agreed to a wage hike, the rehiring of strikers over a three-month period, and mediation for the 173 union members previously terminated. More than 10 people died in strike-related violence.
22. Debs delivered a speech in Philadelphia on March 19, 1910—a wild gathering in the middle of a great strike with an overflow of approximately 10,000 people who could not gain admission.
23. "This letter was written to Comrade [George] Brewer of Kansas while the Socialist Congress was in session [Chicago, May 15–21, 1910]. It would have been read to the congress but for the fact that the writer's permission was received too late. Fortunately the committee's majority report was rejected." (Charles H. Kerr in *International Socialist Review*).
24. The Committee on Immigration presented its majority and minority resolutions to the National Congress of the Socialist Party on the morning of May 17, 1910. Ernest Untermann of California delivered a lengthy report on behalf of the majority of the committee in favor of prohibiting Asiatic immigration to the United States, with committee member Victor L. Berger of Milwaukee providing support in the floor debate. The minority report, which favored allowing Asian immigration, was carried by John Spargo. Morris Hillquit of New York presented compromise language calling for a prohibition of importation of strikebreakers or contract labor, regardless of race or nationality—a position that was ultimately endorsed after long debate by a vote of 55–50, with 4 delegates absent.
25. Ellipses in original.
26. Tom Mann (1856–1941) was an English socialist and trade union activist, a member of the Amalgamated Society of Engineers and the Social Democratic Federation, later the British Socialist Party. Mann emigrated to Australia in 1902 and became active in the workers movement there, returning to Great Britain in May 1910. Mann was a leader of the 1911 Liverpool transit strike and an outspoken opponent of British entry into World War I. Mann was a foundation member of the Communist Party

of Great Britain in 1920 and was later active in the Comintern's UK trade union appendage, the National Minority Movement.

27. Lyman J. Abbott (1835–1922) was a Congregationalist minister from Massachusetts who assumed editorship of *The Christian Union* in 1881 and transformed it in 1893 into *The Outlook,* which became one of the leading news weeklies of the progressive era. His son Lawrence Fraser Abbott (1859–1933) was a personal friend of Theodore Roosevelt.
28. Theodore Roosevelt, "The Recent Prize Fight," *The Outlook,* vol. 95 (July 16, 1910), 550–1. In this article Roosevelt reaffirmed his support for the sport of boxing but noted that large cash prizes inevitably generated crooked results, served as a nexus for gambling, and created an atmosphere which contributed to race antagonism. He found the new trend toward motion pictures of prizefights adding another layer of exploitation and social demoralization to the unsavory industry and advocated their prohibition. Roosevelt had previously assumed the role of associate editor of *The Outlook* on March 5, 1909.
29. Bob Fitzsimmons (1863–1917) was a British boxer who made history as the first fighter to hold world titles in three weight classes when he won a 20-round light heavyweight match against George Gardiner in November 1903.
30. Excerpt of a 90-minute interview granted to the *Terre Haute Tribune,* held at Debs's home in that city.
31. Wendell Phillips, "Address to the Knights of St. Crispin," April 1872.
32. This is a short excerpt of the two-hour speech to an estimated 12,000 people at Chicago's Riverfront Park, which launched the 1910 election campaign of Local Cook County of the Socialist Party of Illinois.
33. The Terre Haute & Indianapolis Railroad was originally chartered as the Terre Haute & Richmond Railroad in 1847. The section from Terre Haute to Indianapolis was completed in 1851, and the first train ran there in January of the following year. The railroad was later sold and incorporated as the Vandalia Railroad.
34. In 1900, following two years of lobbying by the Journeymen Bakers' and Confectioners' Union, a law was passed by the New York Assembly restricting the hours of labor of bakery workers to 10 per day and 60 per week. This regulation was challenged by the New York State Association of Master Bakers, which litigated the matter for several years, the New York Court of Appeals finally ruling the law constitutional early in 1904. Upon final appeal the law was overturned by a narrow 5–4 decision of the US Supreme Court on April 17, 1905, with Justice Rufus R. Peckham delivering the opinion of the majority. Citing the 14th Amendment, Peckham declared "there is no reasonable ground for interfering with the liberty of persons or the right of free contract by determining the hours of labor in the occupation of a baker."
35. George J. Gould (1864–1923) was the inheritor of the Jay Gould fortune upon his father's death in 1892. He headed the Denver & Rio Grand Western Railroad and the Western Pacific Railroad, among other enterprises, and was instrumental in establishing the mainline route of the Western Pacific to San Francisco.
36. William A. Clark, Sr. (1839–1925) was a multimillionaire mine owner and railroad magnate. He served one partial term in the United States Senate from 1899 to

1900 before being elected to a full term as a Democrat in the general election of November 1900.

37. The nation was stunned by the September 13, 1910, election in staunchly Republican Maine, in which two of four congressional representatives, the governorship, and control of the state legislature (and thus one US Senate seat) turned over to the Democratic Party. The result was taken as a repudiation of the policies of the Taft administration and the Republican Party's corruption and corporatist orientation.
38. Just after 1:00 a.m. on the morning of October 1, 1910, a bomb detonated outside the printing plant of the anti-union *Los Angeles Times,* destroying much of the structure and igniting a massive blaze that killed 20 people. Secretary-Treasurer of the International Association of Bridge and Structural Iron Workers Union John J. McNamara and his brother James B. McNamara were implicated in the crime. After initially denying responsibility and going to trial, the pair pled guilty to avoid the death penalty in 1911, with James McNamara receiving a life sentence for placing the timer-detonated bomb and John McNamara sentenced to 15 years in prison for conspiracy.
39. Harrison Gray Otis (1837–1917) was the president of the Times-Mirror Company, publisher of the *Los Angeles Times,* assuming that position in 1882. Otis was a conservative big business Republican and outspoken opponent of the trade union movement. A Civil War veteran, Otis was appointed brigadier general during the Spanish-American War, serving in the Philippines.
40. Debs delivered his Hazard's Pavilion speech on March 31, 1896.
41. On the evening of June 6, 1904, a railroad platform at Independence, Colorado occupied by strikebreaking miners returning home from a day at work in the mines was destroyed by a bomb. The blast killed 13 and wounded 6. The Western Federation of Miners was immediately blamed for the crime. The blast was used as a pretext for raids on miners union headquarters and mass arrests and deportation of striking miners who refused to denounce their union. Responsibility for the bombing was later claimed in the Haywood-Moyer trial by Harry Orchard, who asserted that the terrorism was conducted by order of the Western Federation of Miners. No definitive proof of responsibility was ever made. For Debs's perspective at the time, see "The Independence Depot Bombing: A Case of Capitalist Infernalism," *Selected Works of Eugene V. Debs,* vol. 3, 604–8.
42. Debs's former close political associate Victor L. Berger, estranged since the formation of the Industrial Workers of the World in 1905, was elected to Congress from the 5th district of Wisconsin on November 8, 1910. Victory was not declared until 3:00 a.m. on the following day, with Berger emerging victorious with a narrow plurality of about 2,800 votes. It is unclear which five other Socialist congressional candidates were involved in races that could be accurately characterized as "near election."
43. The *El Paso Times* reported that during the morning of Saturday, October 16, 1909, there was a stabbing of 15-year-old Lawrence Wimber, an El Paso boy who had come to see President Taft by a member of the crowd gathered at San Jacinto Square. Noel Morgan, a 14-year-old classmate apprehended while fleeing the scene, was charged for the crime, reportedly the result of a petty dispute over an American flag. Morgan

was tried as an adult and acquitted by a six-member jury on May 17, 1910. Debs's assertion that a Taft bodyguard was responsible appears to be deeply misinformed.

44. William Howard Taft and Mexican ruler Porfirio Díaz met in El Paso, Texas and Ciudad Juárez, Mexico on October 16, 1909. The pair first met one-on-one for 20 minutes at the chamber of commerce building in El Paso with no interpreters or other officials present. The precise subject of this conversation by the two bilingual leaders was never revealed. A somewhat longer conversation followed later in the day at the Mexican customshouse at Ciudad Juárez, followed in the evening by an opulent banquet. The exact quotation cited here by Debs has not been successfully located in the contemporary press.
45. Captain Archibald Butt (1865–1912) was a military advisor to President William Taft who traveled with him to the October 1909 summit meeting with Mexican strongman Porfirio Díaz. Butt would later be among the victims of the April 1912 sinking of the RMS *Titanic.*
46. Oscar Lawler was a United States district attorney who handled prosecutions of the Magonistas.
47. Announcement was made in the issue of December 17, 1910 that Debs would be returning to Girard shortly from a few weeks' rest in Terre Haute to assume editorship of the *Appeal to Reason* during the jailing of editor Fred D. Warren. The issue dated December 31, 1910, seems to have been the first issue edited by Debs.
48. The December 31, 1910 issue of the *Appeal* listed a total of 464,115 subscribers for the week. Thus, Debs was calling for a doubling of the *Appeal's* subscriber count over the next six months.
49. Debs's political nemesis, former president of the United States and American Railway Union strikebreaker Grover Cleveland, died of cancer on June 24, 1908.

Appendix

Invitation to a Secret Conference to Plan a New Industrial Labor Union†[1]

November 29, 1904

Chicago, Illinois, November 29, 1904

Dear Brother[2]:—

Developments of the past year have convinced us that craft division and political ignorance are doomed to speedily end.

Asserting our confidence in the ability of the working class, if correctly organized, on both industrial and political lines, to take possession of and operate successfully for their own interests the industries of the country;

Believing that working class political expression, through the socialist ballot, in order to be sound, must have its economic counterpart in a labor organization built as the structure of socialist society, embracing within itself the working class in approximately the same groups and departments and industries that the workers would assume in the working class administration of the Cooperative Commonwealth;

Realizing that to wisely inaugurate such a movement will require the putting aside of every selfish consideration by those who undertake the tremendous task;

We invite you to meet with us in Chicago, Monday, January 2, 1905, in secret conference, to discuss ways and means of uniting the working people of America on correct revolutionary principles, regardless of any general labor organization of past or present, and only restricted by such basic principles as will insure its integrity as a real protector of the interests of the workers.

You are to notify the committee, through the secretary, W. L. Hall, No. 3 Haymarket Building, Chicago, of your compliance with this invitation.

Names on enclosed list are of those invited to participate in the conference.

Fraternally yours,
William E. Trautmann (Editor, Brewers' Journal***)***

---

† Published in W. E. Trautmann (ed.), *Proceedings of the First Convention of the Industrial Workers of the World: Founded at Chicago, June 27-July 8, 1905*, W. E. McDermut, stenographer (New York: New York Labor News Co., 1905), 82–3.

George Estes
W. L. Hall
Eugene V. Debs
Clarence Smith
Charles O. Sherman

Resolution for Postponement of the IWW National Convention, by Terre Haute Local Union No. 9[†]

Late April 1906

Whereas, the Moyer-Haywood affair is of absorbing interest to the Industrial Workers of the World and should have precedence over all others, and

Whereas, the annual convention of the Industrial Workers of the World is to be held about the time that the trial of our brethren will take place, and

Whereas, many of our Western unions could not be represented under existing circumstances, and the convention would cost a large amount of money which would better be used in this crisis for the defense of our persecuted brothers, therefore be it

Resolved, that the annual convention for this year be postponed until after the trial above referred to has been closed, subject to be called at such time thereafter as may be determined by the General Executive Board; [and be it further]

Resolved, that the foregoing proceeding had by Terre Haute Local Union No. 9, of the Industrial Workers of the World, be submitted to a referendum vote of the membership for decision.

P. K. Reinbold, *Chairman*
Theodore Debs

† Published as "Resolution for Postponement" in *The Industrial Worker,* vol. 1, no. 5 (May 1906), 6.

Eugene V. Debs
Committee

What the Matter Is in America and What to Do About It: An Interview with Debs by Lincoln Steffens†

July 12, 1908

All radicals have programs. They differ radically among themselves. They cannot, therefore, all have "the" program of God and man which each one thinks his is. Not one of them may be sound, reasonable, desirable, or right. They may all be impossible. But, at least, they are programs, not merely platforms. Therefore they concern us.

For we want to know what the causes are of our American corruption and the cure.

We have asked the leaders of the two old parties, and, excepting LaFollette, they said, or they showed, that they didn't really know. Socialists, with other radicals, are sure they do know. So we will let them tell us what they think the matter is and what they think we ought to do about it.

The President, Taft, and John Johnson[3] don't believe there is any "it;" they set aside the suggestion that most of our greater evils are traceable to a few fundamental, removable causes. There's the money question and the tariff issue; the regulation of railroads, trusts, and criminals. They recognize seriously, though separately, these problems of business and money. Not so the problems of men and women: labor, poverty, crime. As the old political parties of Europe did so long, ours deny or ignore the social problem. The socialists (whence the name) not only recognize, they offer a solution for it. Therefore socialism grows.

For there is a social problem, and men find it out. The schools don't teach it; the churches don't preach it; the press won't mention it; and, brought up, as we are, to mind our own business, we become too absorbed in that to pay

---

† Published in *Everybody's Magazine,* vol. 19, no. 4 (October 1908), 455–69.

much attention to our public business. But when the railroad magnate discovers that, to make his property pay, he must corrupt politics, and that, having done so, he is first honored, then disgraced, he learns that there is something wrong somewhere. And when the willing worker out of work sees the market glutted with goods he and his family need but cannot buy, he, also, realizes that there are problems of humanity, as well as of money, in a money panic. The "bum," who is often an ex-child laborer, and the shop-girl who ekes out a living by taking a "gentleman friend" — they feel it vaguely. And I, going about from city to city and from state to state, and finding everywhere much the same conditions, due to essentially the same forces, operated by all sorts of men using similar methods for one everlasting purpose and to one identical end, I, slowly, reluctantly, am convinced that we all are facing some one great common problem.

And we are. There is some relation between the unhappy capitalist facing the prison bars and the miserable workman staring into the shop window. There is some causal connection between the man and the money that are out of employment. And the trust, the railroad rebate, the bribed legislator, the red-light dive, and the working girl gone wrong form a living chain that can, and shall, be broken.

This is the problem of society as a whole, and as men find it out in fear and doubt, they look first to their old leaders, not for a final solution; all they ask is some recognition of it, some word of interest, comfort, hope. But when, seeing Congress passing an emergency currency bill to help money in distress, the unemployed assemble to exhibit their needs and "are given the stick;" when, watching Capital forming trusts and combines, Labor organizes unions and, asking relief from a power the courts have abused, gets an ambiguous anti-injunction plank; when, asking where they can find work, men hear that "God knows;" then, slowly, reluctantly, but naturally, they turn to the agitator on the street comer. He says he knows, and he makes it all plain; too plain, perhaps; but at least he understands the troubles of all those that are weary and heavy-laden, and he says he will give them rest. Is it any wonder they go to him, as they do?

The Socialists more than double their number every four years in the United States, and in Europe they did so till now they have in every parliament a strong, disciplined, uncompromising minority which seeks reform, not office; the socialist leaders that have accepted seats in cabinets have been read out of their party. No, this remarkable international organization stands there compact and keen, demanding, amending, debating, and reporting back to the people. And that counts. The Socialist Party is dictating policies to all the first-class governments abroad. Holding up its own menacing program in one hand and pointing with the other at its ever-growing vote, it is compelling the old parties to attempt social, not only financial and political, reforms.

"We had to take up social reforms," said the prime minister of England, Sir Henry Campbell-Bannerman,[4] just before he died, to an American friend of mine. "Germany was driven to them long ago; France, Italy, Austria, Holland, Belgium, and, finally, we English, all had to follow. And you, in the States, you cannot continue to ignore the demand. It becomes more and more pressing all the time, you know, and the radicals take advantage of every denial of it."

Of course they do. The radicals are themselves evidences of the growing consciousness of a common, as well as an individual, problem of civilized living; and, as between the leadership that denies and that which acknowledges it, the majority of men (with the suffrage, now, remember) are bound either to sink into animal contentment or to follow radicals, like the socialists, who not only recognize, but rejoice in, the work to be done; and, burning with their faith, offer not only hope, but something for every man to do; and not only a way out, but—a heaven on earth. Absurd? Maybe it is, but don't I illustrate my own point? I'm looking for light, and I don't care where I get it. If I don't find it in one place, I'll try another; if the Republicans and the Democrats shed only gloom, I'll apply to the Socialists; if my old leaders say there is no light—why, then, I'll have to ask Debs.

Yes, Eugene V. Debs is the keeper of the socialist heaven. Locomotive fireman, labor agitator, strike leader—he was jailed once and the Socialists, who take advantage of the misery of men to win them over, converted Debs in his cell at Woodstock. And now he is the leader of the Socialist Party. I must confess that I didn't want to take my socialism from Debs. Having use only for the truth, not the excesses and fallacies, of socialism, I desired to get the best possible view of it, so I had picked out another man to interview, a hard-headed, intellectual student. But if the Socialists preferred Debs, the "undesirable citizen," "the incendiary," who wrote: "Arouse, Ye Slaves!" and called for a mob to follow him to Idaho,[5] why, I felt that in a sense it was their party, not mine. And so, when they nominated him (the third time) for president of the United States, I saw Debs.

I don't know how to give you my impression of this man; I suppose I can't; I can hardly credit it myself, and I wouldn't, I guess, if I hadn't discovered so often before that the world (in the French phrase, "all the world") hates a lover of the world. And that's what Gene Debs is: the kindest, foolishest, most courageous lover of man in the world. Nor am I the only one that thinks so. Horace Traubel[6] says:

> Debs has ten hopes to your one hope. He has ten loves to your one love. You think he is a preacher of hate. He is only a preacher of men. When Debs speaks a harsh word, it is wet with tears.

And there's James Whitcomb Riley, the Hoosier poet, who says:

And there's 'Gene Debs—a man 'at stands
And jest holds out in his two hands
As warm a heart as ever beat
Betwixt here and the Jedgment Seat.

That's a true, and an essential, description. I met Debs at a Milwaukee socialist picnic (25,000 paid admissions)[7] where he was to speak,[8] and, as he came toward me with his two hands out, I felt, through all my prejudice, that those hands held as warm a heart as ever beat. Warm for me, you understand, a stranger; and not alone for me: those two warm hands went out to all in the same way: the workers, their wives, their children; especially the children, who spring at sight right into Debs's arms. It's wonderful, really. And when, piloted, plucked at, through the jammed mass of waiting humanity, he went upon the platform to speak, he held out his handfuls of affection to the crowd. He scolded them. "Men are beginning to have minds," he said; "some of you don't know it." There was nothing demagogic about that speech. It was impassioned, but orderly; radical, but (granting the premises) logically reasoned. It was an analysis of the platforms and performances of the two old parties to show that they would do for Business as much as they dared and for Labor as little; and the conclusion was an appeal to the workers—not to vote for Debs.

"I don't ask that," he said, and sincerely, too. "All I ask is that you think, organize, and go into politics for yourselves."

Delivered from a crouching attitude, with reaching hands and the sweat dripping from head and face, the speech fairly flew, smooth, correct, and truly eloquent. Debs is an orator.

"If Debs were a priest," wrote Eugene Field, "the world would listen to his eloquence, and that gentle, musical voice and sad, sweet smile of his would soften the hardest heart."

Half the world does listen to Debs, and his eloquence does soften its heart. But it wasn't art that kept that Milwaukee crowd steaming out there in the sun and, at the close, drew it crushing down upon the orator. And it wasn't what he said, either; too much of the gratitude was expressed in foreign tongues. It was the feeling he conveys that he feels for his fellow men; as he does, desperately.

Debs is dangerous; it is instinct that makes one half of the world hate him; but don't. He loves mankind too much to be hurt of men; and that's the power in him; and that's the danger. The trouble with Debs is that he puts the happiness of the race above everything else: business, prosperity, property. Remarking this to him, I said lightly that he was, therefore, unfit to be president.

"Yes," he answered seriously, "I am not fitted either by temperament or by taste for the office, and if there were any chance of my election I wouldn't run. The party wouldn't let me. We Socialists don't consider individuals, you know; only the good of all. But we aren't playing to win; not yet. We want a majority of Socialists, not of votes. There would be no use getting into power with a people that did not understand; with a lot of office-holders undisciplined by service in the party; unpurged, by personal sacrifice, of the selfish spirit of the present system. We shall be a minority party first, and the cooperative commonwealth can come only when the people know enough to want to work together, and when, by working together to win, they have developed a common sense of common service, and a drilled-in capacity for mutual living and cooperative labor. I am running for president to serve a very humble purpose: to teach social consciousness and to ask men to sacrifice the present for the future, to 'throw away their votes' to mark the rising tide of protest and build up a party that will represent them. When socialism is on the verge of success, the party will nominate an able executive and a clear-headed administrator; not—not Debs."

It may be deemed expedient to hang Debs some day, and that wouldn't be so bad; but don't try to hurt him. In the first place, it's no use. Nature has provided for him, as she provides for other sensitive things, a guard; she has surrounded Debs with a circle of friends who go everywhere with him, shielding, caring for, adoring him. They sat all through my interview, ready to accept what I might reject. So he gets back the affection he gives, and no strange hate can hurt him. It can hurt only the haters. And as for the hanging, he half expects that.

"How could you," I asked, "thinking as you do that Socialists must learn by party service and personal sacrifice to deserve power, how could you have put out that call for a mob to rescue Moyer, Haywood, and Pettibone?"

"Oh, that," he answered. "The 'Arouse, Ye Slaves!'? Why, my God, man, that was only a cry. That was pain. You know Colorado—"

Yes, I know Colorado. I know that there was, that there is now, and that it is planned that there shall be, no justice in that state; know it, too, from the unjust themselves. "But," I urged, "the folly of mob force."

"True," said Debs, hanging his head. " It was folly, but," he added, looking up as if frightened, "do you know, I sometimes think I am destined to do some wild and foolish, useless thing like that and—so go."

Debs has written much about John Brown. Socialists see the repetitions of history, they read it in parallels, and they have found in it heroes of their own. Debs's hero is John Brown.

"The most picturesque character, the bravest man, the most self-sacrificing soul in American history was hanged at Charlestown, Virginia, December 2, 1859." Thus Debs begins an article which fairly worships John Brown's "moral courage and single-hearted devotion to an ideal for all men and for all ages. He resolved," says Debs, "to lay his life on Freedom's altar and to face the world alone. How perfectly sublime!"

That's Debs, I suspect. His adoration of John Brown is a view into himself. It gives us the ideal and the dread; the use and the danger; the strength and the weakness of the man. One must allow for personality in an interview, and in this case we should not forget for one moment that we are dealing with a man who speaks and acts from his heart, not his head; who honestly believes that there is something wrong in the world—some one big, removable "it," which meanwhile works terrible injustice to his kind of people, and who, therefore, feels that he may do "some wild and foolish, useless thing like"—John Brown.

I had a foil for Debs, however. The interview proper was at the house of Victor L. Berger, "the bear"—leader of the Wisconsin Socialist Party,[9] which has forceful minorities in the state legislature and the Milwaukee city council. Berger is the man that made a socialist of Debs,[10] and the teacher, a most aggressive personality, took a most aggressive part in his pupil's interview, which was fortunate. For Socialism seems to be a science. It is an interpretation of history; a theory of the evolution of society; no mere, man-dreamed Utopia, as I have thought, but a faith, a calculation that, since the economic forces which have brought man from savagery up to the present state of civilization are continuous, we can foresee the next inevitable step. But it takes no little study of economics and much reading in the mass of socialist literature to speak with authority on the subject, and Berger—with a library coveted by the University of Wisconsin[11]—is an acknowledged authority.

"We believe," said Debs (for example), "that socialism would come without the socialists."

"Ach," said Berger, with his strong German roll, "we know it. Can't we see it?"

"Yes," said Debs. "The trusts are wiping out the competitive system. They are a stage in the process of evolution: the individual; the firm; the corporation; the trust; and so, finally, the commonwealth. By killing competition and training men to work together, trusts are preparing for the cooperative stage of industry: socialism."

"Then you would keep the trusts we have and welcome others?" I asked.

"Of course," he answered, and Berger nodded approval.

"They do harm now," I suggested.

"Yes," said Debs, but Berger boomed: "No; not the trusts. Private owners of the trusts do harm, yes; but not the trusts."

"Well, but how would you deal with the harm?"

"Remove 'em," snapped Berger, and Debs explained: "We would have the government take the trusts and remove the men who own or control them: the Morgans and Rockefellers, who exploit; and the stockholders who draw unearned dividends from them."

"Would you pay for or just take them?"

Berger seemed to have anticipated this question. He was on his feet, and he uttered a warning for Debs—in vain.

"Take them," Debs answered.

"No," cried Berger, and, running around to Debs, he stood menacingly over him. "No, you wouldn't," he declared. "Not if I was there. And you shall not say it for the party. It is my party as much as it is your party, and I answer that we would offer to pay."

It was a tense but an illuminating moment. The difference is typical and temperamental; and not only as between these two opposite individualities, but among socialists generally. Debs, the revolutionist, argued gently that, since the system under which private monopolies had grown up was unjust, there should be no compromise with it. Berger, the evolutionist, replied angrily that it was not alone a matter of justice, but of "tactic;" and that tactics were settled by authority of the party.

"We (socialists) are the inheritors of a civilization," he proclaimed, "and all that is good in it—art, music, institutions, buildings, public works, character, the sense of right and wrong—not one of these shall be lost. And violence, like that, would lose us much." Berger cited the Civil War: "All men can see now that it was coming years before 1861. Some tried to avert it then by proposing to pay for the slaves. The fanatics on both sides refused. We all know the result: slavery was abolished. But how?

Instead of a peaceful evolution and an outlay of, say, a billion, it was abolished by a war which cost us nearly 10 billion dollars and a million lives.[12] We ought to learn from history, so I say we will offer compensation; because it seems just to present-day thought and will prove the easiest, cheapest way in the end.

And anyhow," he concluded, "and besides, the party, it has decided that we shall offer to pay."

And Berger was orthodox.

Looking up the point afterward, I found that the "authorities" are on his side; the party will offer compensation for property taken by eminent domain.

"Debs?" said Berger. "Debs, with the soft heart—Debs is the orator." And he meant "only" an orator. Berger loves his pupil's "soft heart," but he loves socialism more, and so during the interview, while Debs was trying to convert me, "the bear" was intent upon the orthodoxy of my report; and while Debs's other friends sat close up around him, under the light of the lamp, to protect the man, Berger hovered about in the shadow, anxious, on guard, to protect—"the cause."[13]

"To begin with," said Debs, without waiting for questions, "we socialists know what the matter is: it's capitalism; and we know what the cure is: it's socialism."

"Words," I muttered.

"No," said he, drawing near and reaching out his hands. "Capitalism is a thing, a system; it's the organization of society under which we all live. And it's wrong, fundamentally wrong. It is a system of competition for wealth, for the necessities of human life, and a survival of the old struggle of the jungle, it forces the individual to be selfish, and rewards him for beating and abusing his fellow man. Profit is made the aim of all human effort, not use, not service. The competitive system sets man against man, class against class; it puts a premium upon hate; and love—the love of a man for his neighbor—is abnormal and all but impossible. The system crucifies the prophets and servants of mankind. It pays greed the most, honors highest the ruthless, and advances swiftest the unscrupulous. These are the fit to survive."

Debs seized my arm. "It's wrong, isn't it? It's inherently unjust, inhuman, unintelligent, and—it cannot last. The particular evils you write about, graft and corruption,[14] and the others about which I speak, the poverty, crime, and cruelty, they are evidences of its weakness and failure; the signs that it is breaking down."

"Why not wait, then, for it to break down?"

Debs drew back, rebuffed. "Because we have minds," he said. "Man can understand, and he can ride, the economic forces which now toss him so helplessly about, as well as he can the sea. And, having intelligence, he should. For human intelligence also is a force of nature. It could assist the process of evolution by searching diligently for the root of all evils as they arise."

"Panics and graft?" I suggested. "War, child labor, crime, poverty?"

"All," he declared, "all are traceable to one cause. Take the panic, for example. Men lie about it, cover it up. Why not look it in the face? It's the proof that capitalists cannot handle industry, business, no, nor even money. And how can they when they are thinking, not of perfecting the machinery of life, but only of making profits out of it! So they don't understand the panic. We socialists do. The capitalists attribute it to a variety of causes, all but the right one: capitalism, profits.

"No, wait," said Debs, waving me back. "They produce more than they want themselves, don't they? Of course. They make goods to sell; not for use, primarily, but to make a profit. That's their god; and that's the devil, really. For see: Reduce our 80 millions to one hundred and our great continent to an island. The hundred all are workers at first. Each produces all that he wants. That's a low order of society. By and by they improve the tools, specialize their labor, and produce more. Steam, for example, applied to big, invented tools, does the work of a hundred small tools. Each man multiplies his productive capacity a thousand times. Should not the hundred on the island have all that they need?"

"Unless the population has increased."

"The more men, the more they producc. Every worker that can get at a machine can produce more than he needs himself. No, the hundred and the children of the hundred should have all that they want. But they don't. And one reason is that some have much more than they need: in profits; capital; new capital, upon which, you understand, labor must earn interest and a profit, for profits come first under capitalism, and necessarily, or capital vanishes. But let's go on.

"Ten of the hundred own all the big new machines; 20 struggle along with the little old tools; and 70 have no tools at all of their own. The biggest, best tools are the trusts, and the 10 who have them are the trust magnates, full-fledged capitalists. The 20 are beaten, but they don't understand that yet; they are crying out against the trusts just as Labor used to mob machinery. Bryan represents them; he wants to return to the competitive system with its anarchy, waste, and wars. Taft represents the trust magnates, opposing only their necessary crimes. We socialists represent the 70, who are the bulk of the population and the key to the situation. Consumers, as well as producers, they are the market, and when 'too much' is produced they must buy the surplus. But they can't. Having no tools of their own, and prevented from organizing effectively, they compete for the chance to get at the tools and sell their labor. That puts wages down. Receiving only a pittance of what they produce, they can buy back only a pittance. The surplus grows, a load on the market, till the crash comes, production halts, men are discharged, prices fall, and—there's your panic."

"And the need of foreign markets," I suggested. "Why wouldn't the other islands meet the need?"

"They would, temporarily," said Debs. "If there were enough islands, capitalism and wage-slavery might go on forever. But there aren't enough and—the other islands have the same system."

"And the same panics," Berger grunted, "thank God."

Debs winced, and I, thinking (also, I guess) of the misery, exclaimed: "Why thank God?"

Debs answered: "Berger sees there the chance for a higher civilization."

"Where?" I asked.

What Causes Panics?

"Oh, don't you see?" Debs pleaded. "The limitations of the world's market and the panics will force us some day to unite and solve our problem. And what is it? It's the problem of distribution. That of production is in the way of solution already. With machinery constantly increasing the productive power of the worker, and the trusts cutting out the waste and disorder of duplicated plants, man can produce enough. The capitalists themselves say so when they ascribe their panic to 'overproduction.' They are wrong there, of course. The panic is due, not to overproduction, but to underconsumption. No, the supply is there and so is the demand. The masses haven't all they need, and yet there's an abundance, a surplus. The hitch is in distribution. The capitalist, producing, not to supply the demand, but to get his profit, seeks to make the Hindu buy shoes he doesn't want, while the American at home goes about ill-shod because, don't you see, his wages, fixed by competition, won't enable him and his kind to buy all they need. Profits, not losses, make panics: and panics make losses. The losses drive more small capitalists into the trusts or back to labor, and the suffering of all opens people's eyes, spreads discontent, and stimulates action. Panics compel progress."

"And panics," said Berger, from somewhere in the dark, "panics are periodic."

"Businessmen are becoming more intelligent," I observed. "They are forming associations, combines, pools, and, as you've said, trusts. They may govern production and distribution, too."

"They can't govern themselves," said Berger. "They can't control prices, because they can't control their own human nature, which, bred under the sordid profit system, gets too strong for them. If they had one absolute trust, they might limit the output, but—"

The Problem of Distribution

"But why," cried Debs, seizing my coat sleeve, "why limit production while men are in need?"

"Well, then, they can raise wages."

"Ah," said Debs, "that would postpone the panic, and the crisis, for a while, if it were feasible. But it isn't feasible. In the first place, no one employer can raise wages. He must act with his competitors, and the meanest sets the pace. That's why organized labor must raise its own wages. Capital can't do it.

"And there, by the way, you have the cause of child labor. Many a well-meaning manufacturer would like to spare the children, but he can't. If one glass manufacturer employs boys and girls, the others must do the same. Capitalists, too, are victims of the competitive system."

"But a trust?"

"A monopoly," Debs answered, "has potential competition to look out for. If it were too generous with wages, new competitors would seize the chance, by paying a living wage, to undersell the trust and buy it out. The system is ruthless, you see. The conflict between wages and profits is absolutely unavoidable. Capital and Labor cannot get together for long. For assume now that there is one universal trust, privately run for profit, and no possibility of competition; even then Capital couldn't raise wages high enough to make possible complete consumption of the surplus, without wiping out what Capital calls 'legitimate profits.' And the moment Capital does that, it abdicates."

"How would socialism do it?"

"By abolishing profits," said Debs. "Socialism will be an entirely different system. It will produce for use, not profit; and production for use is practically unlimited. Socialist society could produce ten times as much as we do now, because a cultured civilization would have ten times as many wants as we have. But if we found we were making more of one kind of goods than people could use, we would decrease the attractiveness of labor in that branch and increase it in another; and with workers schooled as we would school them (and as Germany is training them now), Labor would go much more easily from one machine to another."

"You think that is possible?"

"Why," said Debs, "we've just seen that capitalism does it in its brutal way. It drives men from one place to another by the blind force of panics and starvation. Under socialism, all industry would be intelligently managed as a trust manages it now on a small scale. And, freed from the brutalizing temptation of profits, it would apply civilized remedies in a civilized spirit."

The Root of the Evil

"Then it's profits you want to abolish."

"That's it," said Debs. "We want the producers to get all they produce."

"Who are producers?"

"All who labor in any productive way, mentally or physically. We would get rid only of the capitalists, stockholders, and financiers, who rake off fortunes for themselves and leave property in machinery and wage-slaves to keep their children in idleness, folly, or vice, a curse to themselves and a burden on the race for ever and ever and ever."

"Who would stand the losses?"

"Those who stand them finally now, the masses. For capitalists may rise and capitalists may fail, but capital grows on forever."

"But if you took away the chance of profits, wouldn't you take away all incentive—"

Berger sprang up, groaning, and just as Debs answered "No," the bear said: "Yes." We looked at Berger. "Yes, I say," he thundered. " We take away all incentive to steal and graft and finance and overproduce and shut up the shop sudden. But—" and he came around and stood over me, "you," he said, "you wouldn't write except to get paid? And you wouldn't come here and talk with us, except for profit? I get wages, good wages, but no more. Won't I run my paper except for profit, and help in politics except for graft? Bah! I love my work."

As to Incentives

"Berger's right," said Debs. "We all would do our work, as most of us do it now, without the incentive of a fortune in prospect. Wage workers haven't that. John Wanamaker,[15] with all his millions, was proud to accept a job at $8,000 to run the post office. Jefferson didn't write the Declaration of Independence for pay. Wouldn't a fireman save a child's life if he didn't get $60 a month? And Harriman — wouldn't he operate railroads for a salary? Of course he would."

"But," said Berger, "he wouldn't finance 'em except for the incentive of millions of profit."

"Ah, no," said Debs, pleading, "men are better than you think; they are nobler now, and less selfish than your 'economic man.' We have heroes of altruism under the present system."

"True," I said, "but we haven't enough of them to build a society on. Self-interest is safer than altruism."

"Socialists don't propose to substitute altruism for self-interest."

"But you'd level men down and destroy individuality."

"Haven't I got individuality," called Berger, "and Debs?"

"Yes," I laughed, "too much, and so have most socialists; but you all are products of the capitalist system."

"But the capitalist system," Berger retorted, "doesn't it level most men down now? Yes, it takes all the individuality, all the courage, self-respect, liberty, and beauty out of the great mass of men to produce a few—"

"And look at those few," said Debs. "I'll leave your civilization to that test alone, the test of its most successful men: Harriman, Rockefeller, Morgan. They are the flowers of the system; not the roots, remember. No, the monstrous specimens we produce today of individual greed, cruelty, selfishness, arrogance, and charity—not love, and not justice, but degrading, corrupting, organized charity—these are one of the results of the struggle for life and riches, and the other is that beast—the mob."

Debs paused; then, more quietly: "There would be emulation after competition is abolished. Men would vie in skill and service, and that would produce individuality and character, though of a different sort. A society where all men were safe would produce more such real men and women as you find in the well-to-do class now. We would level up, not down. We would let human nature develop naturally. And—this you must believe—if we took away the fear of starvation on the one hand and on the other the tremendous rewards for crookedness and exploitation; removed all incentives to base self-seeking, and arranged things so that the good of the individual ran, not counter to, as at present, but parallel with, the good of society, why, then, at last, human nature would stand erect, manlike, frank, free, affectionate, and happy."

"But we are off on the cure," I said. "Let's get back to what the matter is."

"It's this," said Debs. "Some men live off other men."

"But how does that account for war, for example, and graft; political corruption, ignorance, child labor, crime, and poverty?"

Wage-Slaves

"We've accounted for poverty," said Debs. "We see the mass of men working for the few. That's what we call wage-slavery, and it is slavery. You say they might quit work; that the boss will let them go. But I tell you the fear of starvation is the boss's slave-driver. They don't dare quit. You can't leave a trust and get back, and maybe the trust controls the work in your trade. And then there's the blacklist. Well, the wage-slaves work in competition, and they produce goods that they need but haven't enough money to buy. That's poverty. And the measure thereof is the riches of the exploiters of labor, industry, and finance, and of their children till vice exhausts the family and returns the grafted wealth through the dives and divorce courts back to society. And there's one cause of capitalistic vice accounted for, as well as of poverty. And the other cause of poverty is the waste of competition and the artificial halt of production—to keep up prices and profits."

"And crime?"

"Petty and professional crime," said Debs, "are a result of poverty; high crime springs from wealth-seeking."

"But vice, intemperance?"

"Frances Willard began her career telling working people that they wouldn't be so poor if they weren't so intemperate. She closed saying that the poor weren't poor because they drank; they drank because they were poor."

"But the rich drink," I protested.

"Idly," said Debs. "What else have they to do? Among busy businessmen, intemperance is rare, and when it occurs is inherited or due to the abnormal tension of the gamble which much business is now; an abnormal vice itself.

The Cruelty of Capitalism

"Child labor we have touched on before," Debs continued. "It is simply the meanest form of the exploitation of human beings by human beings, and, as I showed, is due, not to any inherent cruelty in the employer, but to the system of which he also is a victim—the capitalistic system which puts profits first and children—"

"How does your theory account for political corruption?" I asked.

"Why," said Debs, "you know about that. That's the capitalist class corrupting government to maintain them and their system of labor exploitation."

"I don't know that at all," I objected. "Not all business men take part in the corruption of politics. Only those do that have privileges from the government, franchises, and the like."

"Oh," said Debs, "you are thinking only of the big businesses, the railroads, public utilities, and so forth, which attend to the corruption of politics directly. But they do it for the rest of their class."

"No, they don't," I contradicted. "They do it for themselves. They don't know they belong to a class."

"I don't charge all of them with class consciousness," Debs answered. "Some of them do understand, but, whether they are intelligent or not, in that way they do make the government represent the business class. And, as for the smaller business men, they get the benefit. They contribute to campaign funds, and that's the big source of corruption, or, at any rate, they vote for one or the other of the two parties which the big fellows have corrupted and control, both of them."

"For privileges," I insisted. "Why isn't that the root of the evil?"

Debs shook his head, and, taking my arm in both his hands, he said: "No, it's deeper than that. It's profits. The big fellows corrupt and rob railroads, insurance companies, banks; they finance and exploit the corporations and trusts. What governmental privilege is there in these businesses to explain the corruption of them?"

I'll have to let the single-taxers answer that. I can't. It's crucial, but I was stumped, and Debs went on:

"Privilege won't account for it all. Profit, gain, private property, in land and natural resources, machinery, and all means of production, that is at the bottom of it. And if you call these privileges, why, very well, I'll go along with you. For I believe myself that wage-slavery, the power to exploit labor and live off one's fellow men, is a privilege; the greatest privilege left since chattel slavery."

"How do profits account for war?" I said.

"We saw the cause of wars," he answered, "when we looked around for foreign markets."

"And bad workmanship," I proceeded, "one of the worst evils of the day?"

Profits and Bad Work

"We remarked," said Debs, "that captains of industry were turned from productive effort to finance. Capitalism will take a man who is a natural born operator, say, of a railroad, make him president, and pay him salary enough to make him want more profits. He gambles. He is taken into Wall Street; he sees how easy it is to exploit and finance. He is fascinated; he neglects operation; the railroad suffers; people are killed. Bad work that—for profits, for fascinating unearned profits.

"So with the worker," Debs added. "Do you teach him, by example and precept, to love to turn a piece of wood to fit a place? No. He doesn't know where the piece is to go. He works without interest, to live; he must; he works for wages. He sees the exploiters making their money easily; he hears industrial leaders, dishonest and self-indulgent themselves, insisting upon his honesty and industry. He understands; if he does more and better work his employer gets the benefit, not he. He rebels; he catches the capitalistic spirit. His boss robs him and the public; so he loafs, skimps, and robs the boss. All he is after is all the boss is after—money. That's the system."

"Now for your remedy: socialism," I said. "What is it?"

What Is Socialism?

"You know the old stock definition," Debs answered. "'The cooperative control and the democratic management of the means of production.' I'll try another: Socialism is the next natural stage in the evolution of human society; an organization of all men into an ordered, cooperative commonwealth in which they work together, consciously, for a common purpose: the good of all, not of the few, not of the majority, but of all."

"How would that induce the worker to do good work?"

"Well, if there were no inspiration in the idea of a common good, there would be the assurance of a full return for the product of his labor."

"But how could such a complicated system give any such assurance?"

"By abolishing capitalists and all non-producers."

"But managers—organizers?"

"They would be well paid. Men would be paid according to their social use; skill and ability would count, but so would the disagreeableness of a job; to get it done, society would have to make it attractive somehow—with short hours or big pay. For men would be free, you understand; much freer than now, and not only industrially, but politically, intellectually, religiously—in every way. We would have no churches that didn't dare preach Christianity. But the point is that nobody would get such pay as Rockefeller gets now."

"Not even if he corrupted business and government and churches and colleges and men," said Berger.

"But Rockefeller did a service, you say yourselves," I retorted, "when he socialized the oil industry."

"Yes," said Debs, "but hasn't he been paid enough? A billion, they say. That's too much; but let him have it. All we socialists say is that he should not be allowed to buy up railroads and mines and natural resources, and neither should oil consumers go on paying his children fortunes for generations. No, we must get rid of the Rockefellers, and keep only the organization they build up."

"But," I challenged, "if you took away Rockefeller's trust, wouldn't the other trust builders stop work?"

"Men don't organize trusts because they want to," said Debs, "but because they must. Competition drives them to it, that and their instinct for organization. Trust building can't be stopped; you might as well try to stop an ocean current."

Would Men Work Under Socialism?

"But how would socialism secure the services of eminent talent like that of the great organizers, instinctive operators, and natural managers?"

"The words you use to describe them—'instinctive,' 'natural'—show that you think of them as born to a kind of work," said Debs. "They would want to do that kind of work. They couldn't help falling into it, and socialism would offer such men greater incentives and more opportunities than they have now: pay according to service, public appreciation, and the chance they yearn for: to do good work unfretted (and uncorrupted) by grafting high financiers who are keen, not for excellence (look at our railroads), but for profits. We would release the art instinct of the race."

"Geniuses might respond," I said, "but how about ordinary men?"

"All able-bodied persons of age would have to work," said Debs, "but they want to. I've heard convicts beg to be allowed to break stone. Man must be active, and a society that produced for use and not for profits would have plenty of work to have done, and all would have to help do it, excepting only the incapable. For them society must provide, as it does now, only better; more regularly, with justice, not charity. The first thing the socialists abroad went after was the old-age pension, which gives worn-out workers the right to draw on society for sustenance. We want to remove from the earth the fear of starvation."

"How, then, will you deal with loafers and vicious persons?"

"They are abnormal," said Debs, "and, by removing the cause, poverty and riches, we should soon have no more of them. The idle children of the present rich would be without their graft, but they would foresee their predicament, and the best of them would go to work. Some of them seem to inherit from their parents talents which capitalistic society now gives them every incentive to neglect. Under socialism—an inspiration, you realize, as well as an organization—they would probably exercise their abilities for the common good and their own greater satisfaction."

"Good," I said; "but the idle poor?"

"They are made what they are just as the idle rich are," said Debs. "Take a willing worker, overwork and underpay him, keep him on the verge, and then when he and his kind cannot consume what they produce, discharge him. He leaves his family to hunt a job, and, finding none, tramps or commits a crime. His children suffer, go young to work; they learn that their father is a bum or a crook. They are discouraged. The father drinks; they drink. Their children are, the best of them, perhaps, criminals, and the others, vagrants. This you see, and you ask me what socialism will do with them? I'll tell you: we will treat, with physicians, as sick, the children that have inherited weak or wicked tendencies from parents and grandparents who lived under capitalism." Debs paused to restrain himself, then he concluded: "And we will stop making more by abolishing the cause—poverty and riches."

Socialism and Art

"If there is no rich, leisure class, what will become of art and culture and manners?"

"They will become common," said Berger, and Debs said: "All men will have some leisure. They will come strong and well paid from their work, ready to enjoy healthily all the good things of the earth. There will be no ignorance. Education will be free, not only in the money sense, but intellectually. The schools will teach liberty and the trades, justice and democracy and work, beauty, truth, and the glory of labor, efficient and honorable. The arts will thrive, as they always have thriven, in a free, cultivated democracy."

"Who will do the dirty work?"

"Machines," said Berger, "which clean my house now."

"Yes," said Debs; "only machines that increase profits are introduced now. Apparatus of great utility exists, but is suppressed by capital because human strength is cheaper, and improvements reduce profits. You doubt that? Ask the telephone and telegraph monopolies about the patents they own and don't use. But let me answer the question fully. There always will be some work less attractive than other kinds, and we should have to offer more pay or shorter hours to induce men to do it; men who want time to do unproductive things."

"If some men would get more pay than others," I asked, "why, then, couldn't they accumulate property?"

Socialism for Private Property

"They could," he answered. "Socialism does not abolish private property, except in the means of production. We want all men to have all they produce, all; we are for private property; it is Capitalism that is against it. Under Capitalism only the few can have property. And so with the home; and love. Capitalism is against homes. It makes it inexpedient for young workers to marry; that makes for prostitution, which is against the home. And so is the tenement system of housing, which is good for profits and rents, but bad for homes—and love. And so is marriage for money against love."

"But, Debs, you must admit that you socialists preach class war, and that engenders hate."

"No, no," he answered, rising all his great height over me, "we do not preach hate; we preach love. We do not teach classes; we are opposed to classes. That is capitalism again. There are classes now, and we say so. Why not? It's true, terribly true. But it's exactly that we are trying to beat. The struggle of the best men now is to rise from the working into the exploiting class. We teach the worker not to strive to rise out of his class; not to want to be an employer, but to stay with his fellow workers, and by striving all together, industrially, financially, politically, learn to cooperate for the common good of the working class to the end that some day we may abolish classes and have only workers—all kinds of workers, but all producers. Then we should have no class at all, should we? Only men and women and children."

"How are you socialists going to get all this?"

"We socialists aren't going to get it," said Debs. "It's coming out of the natural evolution of society, and the trusts are doing more toward it than we. Socialists are only preparing the minds of men for it, like the labor unions. They are taking the egotism out of men; subordinating the good of the individual to that of the union; and teaching self-sacrifice and service.

"So with us. The party is the thing. It is governed by its members, who must pay to belong to it, and all perform services besides. They work, write, speak—what they can. But it's theirs, our party is. They elect officers, and delegates; they nominate tickets; and they are taught to vote a straight party vote, no matter how hopeless the contest. That's often a sacrifice of the present for the future, of the individual for society. But isn't that good? That's discipline. It's an education in cooperation. Their reward will come when, by and by, we shall have everywhere, as we have here in Wisconsin now, a minority in office of representatives trained in that school, enlightened as to general economic and moral principles, and inspired with an ideal that is as fine as any religion in the world ever had—the good of all."

"That's slow," I said, "and you, Debs, are impatient."

Foundation Love of Man for Man

"Yes," he said, "I am in a hurry, but socialism isn't. Socialism is the most patient of reforms, but also it is the surest, and the truest. For we believe in man and in the possibility of the love of man for man. We know that economic conditions determine man's conduct toward man, and that so long as he must fight him for a job or a fortune, he cannot love his neighbor. Christianity is impossible under capitalism. Under socialism it will be natural. For a human being loves love and he loves to love. It is hate that is unnatural. Love is implanted deep in our hearts, and when things are rearranged so that I can help my fellow man best by helping myself, by developing all my skill and strength and character to the full, why, then, I shall love him more than ever; and if we compete, it will be as artists do, and all good men, in skill, productiveness, and good works."

Notes

1. This document was probably written by W. E. Trautmann. It was preserved as a quotation in a short historical paper written by committee member Clarence Smith. This was read into the stenographic minutes of the founding convention of the Industrial Workers of the World and published as part of that document.
2. According to Clarence Smith, this document was sent to about 30 prominent radical labor leaders and newspaper editors. Two of these rejected it outright and refused to attend the meeting—Victor L. Berger, publisher of the Milwaukee *Social Democratic Herald* and editor of *Die Wahrheit* (The Truth), and Max S. Hayes, editor of the *Cleveland Citizen.* Both objected to the new organization as a declaration of war against the American Federation of Labor, instead favoring continuation of the "boring from within" tactic, applying pressure for change from inside the organization.
3. Apparently a colloquial expression rather than a reference to John Albert Johnson (1861–1909), Democratic governor of Minnesota.
4. Henry Campbell-Bannerman (1836–1908), head of the Liberal Party, was prime minister of Great Britain from December 1905 to April 1908. During its brief tenure the Campbell-Bannerman government strengthened the trade union movement by indemnifying unions from being sued for damages by employers as a result of a strike and granting workers the right of compensation if injured in an on-the-job accident.
5. "Arouse, Ye Slaves!" was first published in the *Appeal to Reason,* March 10, 1906. See this volume.
6. Horace Traubel (1858–1919), well-known as a biographer of Walt Whitman, was the founder of the literary journal *The Conservator*. A committed socialist, Traubel was a regular contributor to the New York socialist weekly *The Worker* and its daily successor, the *New York Evening Call.*
7. Editor Fred Heath of the *Social Democratic Herald* pegged the number at "over 20,000." See "Eugene V. Debs a Milwaukee Picnic," *Social Democratic Herald,* vol. 11, no. 12, whole no. 520 (July 18, 1908), 3–4.
8. Debs spoke at the seventh annual picnic of the Social Democratic Party of Wisconsin, held at Pabst Park in Milwaukee during the afternoon of June 12, 1908, with those in attendance paying 10 cents for admission. Prominent muckraking journalist Lincoln Steffens (1866–1936) conducted this interview with Debs at Victor Berger's home following the conclusion of the event. Debs's appearance at the picnic marked his first speech in Milwaukee since November 4, 1904, a campaign event that was followed in April 1905 by a personal break with Berger over the matter of the Industrial Workers of the World. Debs's articles were no longer reprinted and his name only rarely mentioned in the pages of Berger's *Social Democratic Herald* during the months that followed this split, although the two prominent socialist leaders did not polemicize against one another in public and retained a degree of personal affection. This interview by Steffens underestimates the degree of political tension between the two.
9. The official name of the Wisconsin state affiliate of the Socialist Party of America was the Social Democratic Party of Wisconsin, retaining this historic name even after the

merger of the two rival Social Democratic parties in the summer of 1901. This was not unique; in New York the party was forced to appear on the ballot during this period as the Social Democratic Party of New York, while in Minnesota both the words "socialist" and "democratic" were forbidden by statute, being words already used by other parties, with the Socialist Party of America organization therefore relegated to calling itself the Public Ownership Party.

10. Although Debs himself originated this myth in a magazine article published in April 1902, this assertion remains highly debatable. Debs and his American Railway Union associates immediately constituted themselves a "cooperative commonwealth of Woodstock Jail" and read books by an array of socialist authors from the time of their first incarceration, with Debs a socialist in all but name for many months or even years prior to that. See *Selected Works of Eugene V. Debs: Volume 2, The Rise and Fall of the American Railway Union, 1892–1896,* passim. Debs's famous "How I Became a Socialist" article appears in the appendix to that volume.
11. Victor L. Berger's papers did indeed ultimately land with the University of Wisconsin–Madison, home of the State Historical Society of Wisconsin.
12. Historians have traditionally accepted a death toll of 620,000 through all causes in the American Civil War. Current scholarship pegs the number at approximately 750,000, compensating for an apparent undercount of Confederate losses.
13. Steffens completed the writing of this piece on July 31, 1908, and sent an advance copy to *Appeal to Reason* staff writer Debs for correction. This was also reviewed by *Appeal* editor Fred D. Warren. Berger's prominent appearance in the interview as a socialist authority was the source of great consternation on the part of Warren, a factional foe of the arrogant Berger, and he petulantly declared that as a result he would no longer promote the issue of *Everybody's Magazine* with the Debs interview to the hundreds of thousands of *Appeal* readers. Steffens took umbrage to Warren's factional temper tantrum, explaining to Debs: "I didn't mean at the time to report Berger did take part, as you know . . . but as I came to think over my material, I saw that the contrast between his bluff manner and your kindness, his views and yours, added not only to the attractiveness but likewise the clearness of the interview . . . . If Mr. Warren can't see that, his judgment is worthless as to the presentation of any matter." See Steffens to Eugene V. Debs, August 13, 1908, in Constantine, ed., *Letters of Eugene V. Debs,* vol. 1, 274–5. Debs intervened with Warren and rationality prevailed, the squabble was patched up, and the magazine with the Debs interview as its cover story was ultimately given an appropriate promotional push in the pages of the *Appeal.*
14. Steffens was well-known for his muckraking journalism and his book *The Shame of the Cities* (New York: McClure, Phillips & Co., 1904), which dealt with systemic corruption in civic government in New York, Chicago, Philadelphia, Pittsburgh, St. Louis, and Minneapolis. In it Steffens wrote that "politics is business" and "a politician is a businessman with a specialty."
15. John Wanamaker (1838–1922) was a department store magnate from Philadelphia. He served as postmaster general under President Benjamin Harrison from 1889 to 1893.

Index

Page references to illustrations are indicated in **bold**.

About the Editors

Tim Davenport is involved with several online radical history projects, including his Early American Marxism website, Marxists Internet Archive, and Wikipedia. He is a member of the Historians of American Communism, the Organization of American Historians, the Society for Historians of the Gilded Age and Progressive Era, and the Labor and Working-Class History Association. He is coeditor, with Paul LeBlanc, of *The "American Exceptionalism" of Jay Lovestone and His Comrades, 1929–1940* (Haymarket Books, 2018).

David Walters is a lifelong socialist and trade unionist. He was one of the founders of the Marxists Internet Archive and remains with the MIA as a volunteer, managing the site's Eugene V. Debs archive. He is the past director of the Holt Labor Library in San Francisco.

About Haymarket Books

Haymarket Books is a radical, independent, nonprofit book publisher based in Chicago. Our mission is to publish books that contribute to struggles for social and economic justice. We strive to make our books a vibrant and organic part of social movements and the education and development of a critical, engaged, international left.

We take inspiration and courage from our namesakes, the Haymarket martyrs, who gave their lives fighting for a better world. Their 1886 struggle for the eight-hour day—which gave us May Day, the international workers' holiday—reminds workers around the world that ordinary people can organize and struggle for their own liberation. These struggles continue today across the globe—struggles against oppression, exploitation, poverty, and war.

Since our founding in 2001, Haymarket Books has published more than five hundred titles. Radically independent, we seek to drive a wedge into the risk-averse world of corporate book publishing. Our authors include Noam Chomsky, Arundhati Roy, Rebecca Solnit, Angela Y. Davis, Howard Zinn, Amy Goodman, Wallace Shawn, Mike Davis, Winona LaDuke, Ilan Pappé, Richard Wolff, Dave Zirin, Keeanga-Yamahtta Taylor, Nick Turse, Dahr Jamail, David Barsamian, Elizabeth Laird, Amira Hass, Mark Steel, Avi Lewis, Naomi Klein, and Neil Davidson. We are also the trade publishers of the acclaimed Historical Materialism Book Series and of Dispatch Books.

Also available from Haymarket Books

The American Socialist Movement, 1897–1912
Ira Kipnis

The Bending Cross: A Biography of Eugene Victor Debs
Ray Ginger, introduction by Mike Davis

Lucy Parsons: An American Revolutionary
Carolyn Ashbaugh

The Labor Wars: From the Molly Maguires to the Sit Downs
Sidney Lens

A Short History of the U.S. Working Class: From Colonial Times to the Twenty-First Century (Revolutionary Studies)
Paul Le Blanc